PROPERTY RIGHTS

AND

LAND POLICIES

Property Rights
and
Land Policies

Edited by

Gregory K. Ingram and Yu-Hung Hong

LINCOLN INSTITUTE
OF LAND POLICY
CAMBRIDGE, MASSACHUSETTS

© 2009 by the Lincoln Institute of Land Policy

All rights reserved.

Library of Congress Cataloging-in-Publication Data
Property rights and land policies /
edited by Gregory K. Ingram and Yu-Hung Hong.
p. cm.
Includes index.
ISBN 978-1-55844-188-0
1. Land tenure. 2. Land use. 3. Real property. 4. Eminent domain.
I. Ingram, Gregory K. II. Hong, Yu-Hung. III. Lincoln Institute of Land Policy.
HD1251.P77 2008
333.3—dc22   2009002563

Designed by Vern Associates

Composed in Sabon by Achorn International in Bolton, Massachusetts.
Printed and bound by Puritan Press Inc., in Hollis, New Hampshire.
♻ The paper is Rolland Enviro100, an acid-free, 100 percent PCW recycled sheet.

MANUFACTURED IN THE UNITED STATES OF AMERICA

CONTENTS

ILLUSTRATIONS

Tables

Figures

PREFACE

Property rights are fundamental to the conceptualization and implementation of land policies. In the United States, the debate over public rights in private land was heightened by the Supreme Court's 2005 decision on the case of *Kelo v. City of New London*, 545 U.S. 469, affirming the legitimacy of government taking of private property for economic development. Not only did the ruling put the dispute on the front page of the newspapers, but it also motivated 39 states to pass laws restricting government exercise of eminent domain.[1] In developing countries, land titling has been viewed by some policy makers as a means to alleviate poverty. The idea, recently popularized by de Soto (2000), is that land tenure could unlock the entrepreneurship of poor people by allowing them to use their real estate assets as collateral to borrow investment capital.

To assess the impacts of these changing perceptions of private property on land use planning, property taxation, and urban development, the Lincoln Institute held a property rights workshop in February 2007 and a journalist conference in April to discuss the outlook of eminent domain in the United States. Building on these two events, the Institute's 2008 land policy conference brought together international scholars from different disciplines including economics, law, political science, and planning to exchange views and present papers on the relationships between property rights and land policies. The chapters and commentaries in this book summarize the conference participants' perspectives on the subject.

The essays discuss three issues. First, they explore the evolution of property rights institutions. A long-standing design principle for property rights institutions holds that unbundling the different elements of property rights and repackaging them according to varied circumstances allows property relations to be structured in many ways. In the implementation and enforcement of a design, rules are constantly challenged and revised by interested parties as new economic, political, and social situations unfold.

Second, several essays examine the delicate balance between public and private rights in land. In addition to analyzing eminent domain in Brazil, Colombia, Mexico, and the United States, the essays investigate issues related to regulatory takings in selected Western countries. The discussion reveals the importance of empirical research on the actual use of eminent domain and the influence that different judicial systems have on the effectiveness of this government power. Transferable development rights and the symmetry between public takings and givings are also introduced as potential means to mediate controversies involved in takings compensation.

---

1. See the Web site of National Conference of State Legislatures at www.ncsl.org/programs/natres/EMINDOMAIN.htm.

Third, applications of the property rights approaches to poverty alleviation, land conservation, and provision of affordable housing are reviewed. Current experiences of land titling in developing countries seem to have positive impacts on property investments, but inconclusive effects on credit access by the poor. The pros and cons of using conservation easements to conserve natural resources and a comparison of inclusionary housing policy and the voucher program are presented in detail.

The volume contains a wealth of innovative ideas and cross-border studies. The contributors' willingness to share their research and comments and their efforts in revising their papers have made the publication of the book possible. The planning and production of the land policy conference and this publication have been facilitated by many people. We thank Diana Brubaker for her assistance in identifying the speakers and discussants for the conference and Brooke Digges, Mary Hanley, and Rie Sugihara for their careful attention to the logistical details of the meeting. Finally, we are indebted to our editorial and design team, including Nancy Benjamin, Sybil Sosin, Emily McKeigue, and Vern Associates for their expertise and professional help.

Gregory K. Ingram
Yu-Hung Hong

REFERENCE

de Soto, Hernando. 2000. *The mystery of capital: Why capitalism triumphs in the West and fails everywhere else.* New York: Basic Books.

INTRODUCTION

1

Examining Land Policies from a Property Rights Perspective

Gregory K. Ingram and Yu-Hung Hong

A good understanding of how public and private property rights are conceptualized, applied, and balanced in different institutional environments is essential for making and analyzing sound land policy. To take stock of current research on this subject, the Lincoln Institute of Land Policy convened a group of international scholars in June to present and discuss their research on the nexus between property rights and land policies. Three themes emerged from the meeting. First, the linkages between the design principles for property rights institutions and the political and cultural history of a country were examined in China, Estonia, Russia, the United States, and Vietnam.[1] Second, participants discussed private property rights, the public interest, and compensation for eminent domain and regulatory takings in Brazil, Colombia, Mexico, the United States, and selected Western European countries. Third, participants debated the effectiveness and fairness of using varied property rights approaches to poverty reduction, environmental conservation, and the provision of affordable housing. Ideas exchanged at the conference are grouped within the three topics and presented in the chapters and commentaries in this book. This introductory chapter discusses the three themes. The next section highlights the connections between private property and institutions, which is the primary perspective of the book.[2]

---

1. *Institution* is defined as a set of rules that guides members of a society to select actions that are socially acceptable and that prohibits them from making undesirable decisions (North 1990).

2. See Eggertsson (1990) and Furubotn and Richter (2005) for detailed discussions of the literature on property rights institutions.

Each of the following three sections summarizes key messages of the chapters and commentaries related to each theme. The conclusion discusses ideas and findings drawn from these contributions.

Private Property Rights and Institutions

Private property is perceived as an essential institution for economic development and wealth generation in developed and developing economies. Private property rights guarantee an owner the exclusive right to use, develop, consume, sell, mortgage, transfer, and exchange possessions with other entities (Bentham 1978). This bundle of rights serves three key social and economic functions. First, private property prevents aggression. Clearly delineated and rigorously enforced private property rights protect owners from forced dispossession by the state or other parties (Blackstone 1979). Hence, they assure the individual liberty and security necessary to maintain peace within a community. Second, private property mediates the problem of intertemporal investment. It assures an investor that returns on today's investment in land or production can be retained in the future. Without the right to exclude others from reaping the potential rewards, there will be no incentive for a holder of resources to invest in long-term improvements. Third, private property facilitates division of labor. In a complex society where economic activities require coordination and cooperation among individuals with different talents and skills, private property allows wealth created by a person to be an exchangeable asset. Individuals can pool their assets and labor to take advantage of the efficiency gained from specialization, thereby generating greater riches than a single person could achieve alone (Smith 1776). With the assurance of peace on one hand and the promotion of mutual gains through voluntary exchanges on the other hand, private property has transformed primitive societies into highly sophisticated agricultural and industrial economies (North 1981, 1990; North and Thomas 1973).

These benefits of private property notwithstanding, the maintenance of this ownership system can be conflict-ridden. The key assumption of the above arguments for private ownership is that externalities generated from the individual ownership of property can be internalized at no cost. This assumption is often challenged in the case of land. Take a typical example of conflict associated with real property ownership. A factory owner wants to maximize profit by operating the facility at its full capacity. The increase in production will raise noise, congestion, and pollution levels, affecting neighboring property owners. If the factory owner can identify all appropriate negotiating parties, determine the amount of compensation, negotiate an agreement, and enforce the settlement at minimum transaction costs, the assignment of the responsibility to internalize the externality will have no welfare effect on the community (Coase 1960, 1988). For example, suppose the factory owner is liable for the damages and needs to compensate the residents for the harm that by-products of the manufacturing activity inflict on them. If negotiation costs are negligible, the parties will haggle until the total amount of compensation equals the welfare loss of the residents. Alternatively, the property owners can pay the factory owner to curtail production to the level at which the marginal revenue forgone is equal to the marginal benefit of having less pollution in the neighborhood. However, where the transaction costs of bargaining are high, both scenarios seldom actualize (Coase 1960; Wallis and North 1986).

When negotiation in property rights disputes is costly, the scope of the bundle of rights and duties of private ownership matter. The control over the varied rights by different entities will shape the bargaining outcomes, thereby creating distributional and efficiency effects on the economy that are likely to be suboptimal (Samuelson 1966). In the design of property rights allocation, there are some key questions:

- Which of the full bundle of rights does an owner need in order to secure private property rights?
- How does the assignment of property rights differ in varied institutional settings? Are there any design principles?
- What are the wealth effects of different allocations of property rights?
- After rights are assigned, how do the conceptualization and enforcement of the assigned rights evolve in varying circumstances?
- How can the allocation of property rights help government achieve economic and land policy goals?

Although theoretical and empirical contributions to these subjects are accumulating, they remain open questions.

The Design and Evolution of Property Rights Institutions

Initial theories of private property development suggested by economists are mainly based on cost-benefit analysis (Anderson and Hill 1975; Barzel 1989; Eggertsson 1990). In his classic explanation of the establishment of private land ownership in eastern Canada, Demsetz (1967) argues that increases in the value of beaver furs due to the opening of trade created the incentive for the Indians to establish exclusive rights to their territories. These private property rights prevented the overharvesting of beavers in an individual (or communal) territory and thus ensured the owners exclusive access to a continuous supply of furs. North and Thomas (1973) also apply a similar rationale to explain the changes in property rights institutions that led to the prehistoric shift from nomadic hunting to settled agriculture. As the size of the population increased, open access to natural resources led to diminishing returns from hunting. To alleviate problems associated with the tragedy of the commons (Hardin 1968), the benefits of settled agriculture with the exclusive right to cultivate land outweighed the enforcement costs of private or communal property.

This approach is adequate in explaining the evolution of private property rights and the emergence of rudimentary legal and political institutions. In today's economies, however, the influences of legal, social, and political institutions are paramount. In the United States, for example, when disagreements over public infringement on private property arise, courts play a critical role in deciding whether compensation should be paid. Because juridical decisions must be enforced to be effective, governance structure and bureaucratic capacity for upholding laws and orders are important. In other countries where the legal system plays a less prominent role in conflict resolution, social norms or reciprocity can be the key mechanisms for resolving property rights disputes. Hence many researchers have examined the roles of law, politics, and cooperation in designing institutions that support the functioning of varied property rights regimes (see Alston, Eggertsson, and North 1996; Buchanan 1984, 1991; Coase 1960; Commons 1934; Ellickson 1989, 1991; Libecap 1989; North 1990; Ostrom 1990, 2005, 2007; Williamson 1985).

Elinor Ostrom, one of the pioneers in developing the theory of property rights, challenged the then-conventional wisdom that common-pool resources will be overharvested if clearly delineated private property rights or state interventions do not exist. In her research Ostrom (1990) found that parties jointly using a common-pool resource often create workable formal and informal rules for resource allocation. A governance structure that is based on private property rights enforced by external authorities is not always necessary or optimal. Users are often capable of nurturing trust and reciprocity to solve their collective action problems.

How do involved parties design and implement robust self-organizing common-property institutions? In her 1990 study Ostrom proposed eight design principles (see chapter 2, table 2.1, for a list of these principles). In chapter 2 of this book, she examines the validity of the principles by reviewing their application to 33 empirical cases published in research papers written by other scholars. Three-quarters of these cases show strong or moderate support for the usefulness of Ostrom's design principles. Scholars who reviewed the applications of the design principles suggest more precise specifications for some principles. Some argue that the principle of delineating boundaries for commons should be divided into two parts, one for defining the boundaries of the resource, and the other for stipulating who should be included as authorized users. Also, the principle of balancing rights and responsibilities of appropriating a common-pool resource should be separated into three types: (1) harmony with the local ecology; (2) congruence with the local culture; and (3) equitable distribution of rewards to participants according to their contributions. Ostrom also translates all eight design principles into questions to assist in the diagnosis of institutional deficiencies. This approach, she argues, would enhance their application.

Ostrom's research highlights the importance of high transaction costs of defining resource boundaries and determining who is authorized to use the resource. Determining the size of future expenditures for sustaining the resource and assigning them to users in proportion to the benefits received is also costly. Minimizing these costs requires a set of carefully crafted institutions, including (1) a participatory decision-making process; (2) an effective monitoring system that provides inspectors with proper incentives; (3) gradual and adjustable sanctions according to the seriousness and circumstances of the offenses; (4) low-cost conflict resolution mechanisms at both regional and local levels; (5) recognition of the importance of self-governance by users and outsiders; and (6) a multiple-layer, polycentric governance structure to connect smaller subgroups nested in a larger commons. Ostrom's approach illustrates that the establishment and modification of property rights systems necessitate heavy and prudent long-term investment in institutional building.

In chapter 3 Harvey M. Jacobs examines the conceptualization of private property rights in U.S. history and argues that the current private property rights system is unique and is constantly evolving. Current legal and political interpretations of individual property rights vis-à-vis the government's ability to control these rights for the public good are shaped by specific historical and cultural experiences.

Starting in the colonial era, private land ownership was a major attraction to European migrants who tried to escape feudalism in Europe and sought freehold ownership in North America. Private property was viewed as a means to secure political and economic freedom. Therefore, private property symbolizes the political and ideological beliefs upon which the United States is founded, and strong constitutional protection of private property was deemed necessary.

When population, urbanization, and industrialization expanded in the twentieth century, the government began to limit individuals' right to use and develop their lands. Conflicts over public rights in private land emerged. The courts were called upon to define and reinterpret the takings clause of the Fifth Amendment to the Constitution. Several Supreme Court cases found that the government has the legal right to expropriate private property for "public purposes" with "just compensation." The courts also found that the government could constrain the use of private property without compensating the affected owners so long as its regulations did not amount to a taking. These legal decisions have been continuously challenged through political and social channels by private property rights advocates. As Jacobs asserts, disagreements over the meaning of private property rights allow the system to evolve and adapt to changing social, economic, and technological environments.

Given the unique process of private property evolution in the United States, to what extent is its experience transferable to other countries? Jacobs argues that the legal and social status of private property in the United States is converging with that in some Western European countries. Although the Western European countries started with a greater allocation of property rights to governments, recent changes in planning laws to accommodate a more market-oriented land management system and to uphold individual property rights have brought them closer to the U.S. system. As to the lessons for developing nations, Jacobs speculates that, like the United States, many countries may also experience ongoing challenges to and renegotiation of private property rights. The tension between the public right to manage scarce urban resources and individual entitlement to newly created wealth intensifies when the pace of urbanization and economic development accelerates.

Jacobs's suggestion provides good insight into the development of private property in China. As discussed by Dwight H. Perkins in chapter 4, the development of Chinese real estate markets has generated tensions between different segments of the population and between the government and private property owners. In some coastal cities where residential housing markets are well developed, affluent residents can purchase their homes in the private market. City dwellers whose incomes are low typically purchase apartments from their work units and receive large subsidies. According to Perkins, both groups have experienced significant improvements in living space from the recent housing reform. However, private property ownership is not available to rural-to-urban migrants who cannot register as city residents under the current household registration (or *hukou*) system and are not entitled to government services and subsidies. Perkins estimates that about 400 million people will migrate to cities over the next two decades, and their exclusion from home ownership needs to be addressed.

In addition, Perkins is concerned about the lack of legal and political support for enforcing private property rights in China. Although the Chinese legal system has been gradually professionalized, court decisions are still influenced by the Communist Party and the government. More importantly, court rulings must be enforced by the central and local governments. Given the heavy reliance of local public finance on land revenues, enforcement of private leasehold rights, such as paying adequate compensation to leaseholders when their land is taken for public use, might face strong bureaucratic resistance.

Echoing Perkins's concern, Scott Rozelle believes that weak enforcement of the Rural Land Contracting Law by local governments could be the main reason for insecure land tenure in rural China. Efforts to encourage farmers to register their leasehold rights are absent. This leads to reliance on informal arrangements for subleasing land when farmers leave their villages for urban employment. Rozelle argues that informal rental agreements are of short duration (one year) and are subject to considerable ambiguity. These institutional deficiencies hinder the pooling of smaller plots into a sizable farm for long-term investment, thereby creating inefficiency and slowing income growth in rural China.

Like China, Russia has attempted to develop property rights institutions to facilitate the development of private real estate markets since 1991. As of 2008 only one city (Veliky Novgorod) of 171 medium and large municipalities has adopted a fully integrated real estate registration system. Legal rules established for land reforms are unclear and incoherent. What explains Russia's failure to establish private land ownership? In chapter 5 Bertrand Renaud, Joseph K. Eckert, and R. Jerome Anderson argue that the absence of a tradition of secure private property in Russian history is paramount. The government has never been perceived as an impartial guarantor or protector of private property, and the concept of reciprocal obligation between ruler and citizens also did not exist. This legacy creates mistrust of the polity as an effective institution to enforce private property rights. Other, nonhistorical disabling factors include the lack of incentive for property owners to register their land, local fiscal dependency on land rents, an underdeveloped real estate financing system, and high property taxes.

Renaud, Eckert, and Anderson also compare the Russian experience with the process of private property reforms in Estonia. Unlike Russians, Estonians experienced a short period of private land ownership between the two world wars. The authors argue that this history, albeit brief, allowed Estonia to develop a coherent legal system for land privatization immediately after independence. Real estate market development was also carefully organized to support the larger strategy of enabling Estonia to achieve full independence from Russia, reenact a modern Estonian constitution, develop an open market economy, and become a member of the European Union. These linked objectives motivated the government to ensure the success of land privatization. The comparison of Russia and Estonia illustrates the importance of past institutions in shaping the development of new property rights regimes in transitional economies. This finding accords with the experiences of the United States and China. History matters in contriving property rights institutions.

In his commentary Robert M. Buckley proposes an additional explanation for Russia's slow land market reform: heavily subsidized utility prices. He argues that Russian housing stock is mostly energy inefficient. If utility costs were not set below market prices, there would have been strong incentive for owners to retrofit their houses or to shift to more energy-efficient homes. Both investments can, ceteris paribus, increase housing value and therefore raise the benefit of establishing private property rights. Thus, the lack of price reform in the energy sector might have thwarted land market development.

Vietnam is another case that has attracted much attention. In chapter 6 Stephen B. Butler discusses some institutional deficiencies of land market reform in Vietnam based on a survey conducted in 12 provinces. Six hundred sixty-five small and medium enterprises, 65 land market intermediaries, and 12 state land officials were interviewed for their opinions on land tenure security, land use planning effectiveness, ease of market transactions, and public administration capacity. Public officials and land market intermediaries believe the current land allocation method in Vietnam to be inefficient. To obtain land use rights for a development project, an investor must apply to local officials detailing the proposed land investment and technical plan for construction and provide evidence of sufficient capital to undertake the project. Upon the receipt of a license from the government, the developer can select a land site and sign a land contract with the government.

Butler asserts that this system has three problems. First, the procedure imposes tremendous burdens on local government capacity. In places where there is not enough staff or trained personnel to handle the applications, review standards become arbitrary. Second, the approval procedure distorts land prices and thus the supply of land. The survey reveals that inadequate land availability is the major complaint from business land users. Third, involving local governments in land rights allocation encourages rent-seeking behavior. The state confiscates land from holders with little compensation and leases the site to developers for high leasehold charges. This practice can lead to social conflict and jeopardize public confidence in the state as the protector of private property.

In her commentary Annette M. Kim agrees with Butler that the Vietnamese government ought to pay more attention to its method of assembling land, especially to issues related to compensation, but she disagrees about the role of the state in the assignment of land rights. While Butler sees government intervention in the land market as an impediment to its development, Kim thinks that the bureaucracy has been instrumental in mediating property rights disputes and administering land transactions during the transitional period. She suggests that since 77 percent of interviewed firms in Butler's survey have invested in land improvements, the government has given many landholders a sense of tenure security.

Public Compensations for Takings

The debate over government functions during the evolution of private property rights provides a nice transition to the second theme of this book: public compensations for takings. The right to use land is seldom absolute under any private property rights regime. Government, as a representative of the public, can control the type and intensity of land development through regulation. It can even confiscate private property with compensation to advance public purposes. The critical matter is to balance public and private rights in land. The determination of when public acts diminish private property rights to the extent that compensation should be paid to owners has generated contentious legal and political debates in many countries.

In chapter 7 Antonio Azuela examines the conditions under which eminent domain is used in São Paulo, Bogotá, and Mexico City. Brazil, Colombia, and Mexico all went through democratic transitions that changed the legal and political treatment of private property, and all three countries are experiencing increasing judicial activism. Despite these similarities, outcomes of the use of eminent domain differ. Azuela suggests four reasons for the diverse outcomes that shed important light on the design of eminent domain institutions.

First, the placement of eminent domain power at different levels of government matters. When local officials have the power of eminent domain, they are prone to utilize the legal authority to acquire private property for infrastructure development to satisfy the demands of the constituents who elect them. The experience of Bogotá seems to support this argument.

Second, the role of the judiciary in determining the validity of the use of eminent domain and the amount of compensation is important. In Brazil and Colombia, local governments must seek court approval before they can expropriate private property. Although judges in these two countries have typically

set compensation at high levels, they normally defer to the expertise and motives of local governments in exercising their eminent domain power. In Mexico,
although the constitution gives eminent domain power to the president and the
state governors, judges often grant affected owners injunctions to stop the process. They also modify the amount of compensation and scrutinize the motive
of an expropriation, which seems constitutionally dubious in Mexico. While
judges in Brazil and Colombia play enabling roles in the use of eminent domain,
the judiciary in Mexico complicates land expropriation.

Third, the fiscal implications of compensation also affect the use of eminent
domain in these countries. In all three cities examined by Azuela, exorbitant
compensations granted by the courts either have put local governments under
financial stress or have led to the abandonment of public projects. The determination of just compensation is the thorniest issue. Azuela suggests that better approaches to selecting and educating judges and to constraining them from
overstepping their constitutional duties are needed.

Stimulated by Azuela's study, Vicki Been proposes a research agenda that
focuses on identifying the actual users of eminent domain, the difference between
the total amount of compensation paid for expropriation and the total market
value of involved assets, the frequency of the actual use of eminent domain, and
the number of successful transfers of property under the threat of eminent domain. Been also emphasizes that knowing the distributional consequences of the
use of eminent domain under varying legal regimes is important.

In chapter 8 Jerold S. Kayden examines one of Been's questions: how often
do local governments in the United States exercise their eminent domain power
to condemn private property for economic development purposes? In view of
the controversy generated by the U.S. Supreme Court's decision on *Kelo v. City
of New London*, 545 U.S. 469 (2005), Kayden asked whether the public outcry
reflected a legitimate concern over government abuse of eminent domain power
or was simply a strategy used by private property rights advocates to challenge
planning. A survey of officials in 153 municipalities with population of greater
than 100,000 residents sought to determine the frequency of the actual use of
eminent domain for economic development purposes between January 2000 and
December 2004. Pending eminent domain cases and the threat of expropriation
were not counted in the survey. The measurement unit was the number of properties taken by local governments. The results showed that about one-quarter
of the cities in the sample reported takings during the study period. A total of
207 properties were taken, an average of less than two properties per city in five
years. Kayden concludes that state condemnation of private property for promoting economic growth is uncommon in the United States.

John Echeverria praises Kayden's effort in filling an important information
gap in the research on eminent domain. He thinks, however, that this survey
was limited by its focus on large cities and exclusion of cases where local officials threatened to exercise eminent domain power. He is also concerned about
reporting errors due to the sensitivity of the survey questions and the ambiguity

in defining "economic development purposes." Echeverria suggests a case study approach to investigating why some cities rely heavily on eminent domain to assemble land as a supplement to nationwide surveys.

Confiscation of an owner's property is not the only form of taking. If government regulations limit all viable uses of a property and cause a substantial decrease in its value, this in most cases is considered a taking, and the owner will need to be compensated for the financial loss. This is a controversial issue that strikes at the core of the debate over planning versus private property protection. In chapter 9 Vincent Renard describes the diversity in the ways Western European countries deal with this matter. Legislation in both Denmark and The Netherlands entitles property owners to be compensated for regulatory takings. There are no such legal provisions in France and Italy. Yet Renard cautions that practices do not always follow the legislation. For instance, French and Italian officials may negotiate with property owners about some form of compensation even though they are not legally required to do so. Although Denmark has explicit rules for compensation, they apply to very restrictive cases only. In general, compensation for economic damages caused by land use planning is rarely paid.

In extreme cases in which the burden of planning falls disproportionately on selected property owners or when land use planning eliminates all reasonable uses of an asset, compensation is required under the jurisprudence of the first protocol of the European Treaty on Human Rights. Renard proposes compensating affected owners with transferable development rights (TDRs). This approach requires redefining property rights and dividing the right to develop land into two types. One type is the development right that an owner paid at the time of purchase. The contents of this right are specified in the zoning law. The other type is the development right that goes beyond what the land use regulation allows. Because the original purchase price of the property did not reflect the owner's expectation of obtaining this extra development right, the owner needs to buy it from the government or from other owners who have surplus development rights for sale. The government will provide owners whose property is restricted by regulation with transferable rights as compensation for their loss of the first type of development right. The owners can then sell the development rights to another entity that needs them for high-density development.

Although this approach seems tenable in theory, Renard identifies several obstacles to its implementation. These include political and social resistance to redefining property rights, the complexity of valuing TDRs, and the possibility of disputes arising from identification of the "sending" and "receiving" zones of development rights across jurisdictions.

In his commentary, Barrie Needham disagrees with redefining property rights as a solution to compensation for regulatory takings. He thinks that TDRs have limited applications based on the British experience in nationalizing development rights in 1947. If one analyzes the compensation issue of regulatory takings from the perspective of government's equal treatment of citizens rather than private property protection, Needham asserts, it would be hard to argue against compensating owners who are disadvantaged by land use planning and not requesting payments from those who benefit.

Needham's argument raises a concern about the symmetry between takings and givings. Ideally, government could recoup the benefits of land use planning and redistribute them to those who bear the costs. In this case takings compensation is justified. Given the reciprocal nature of the matter, would it be sensible to argue against compensation for takings when there is no recapture of the benefits of givings? Abraham Bell analyzes this subject in chapter 10. He concludes that arguments for paying compensation for regulatory takings are compelling.

Bell first examines the economic justification for expropriation compensation to draw parallel lessons for the analysis of regulatory takings. Three arguments in favor of eminent domain compensation are (1) to keep government from underestimating the costs of takings; (2) to negate potential opposition from propertied interest groups; and (3) to minimize the risk of corruption. Bell claims that these arguments can also support paying compensation for regulatory takings.

Second, it is hard to argue against compensation for regulatory takings when there is consensus on the compensation requirement for eminent domain. For instance, if compensation were required for the use of eminent domain but not for regulatory takings, local governments would rely more on regulation than on property expropriation to manage land use, even when expropriation is more efficient. This fiscal incentive can generate distortions. In addition, when real estate owners are not charged for public givings, paying compensation to owners of condemned property but not to those whose assets lose significant economic value due to government regulation raises issues of unequal treatment.

Third, Bell suggests that property taxes can be treated as both a taking compensation and a giving charge if the effects of land use regulation are fully capitalized in property value. The positive effect of regulation (givings) will increase property value and thus result in higher tax payments (giving charge). Similarly, a taking reduces asset value, which in turn lowers property tax liability. Yet property taxes are generally a small percentage of asset value, and tax reductions compensate only a small percentage of takings. If capitalization is weak or absent, property taxes will become even less compensatory. Bell therefore argues that property taxation cannot provide a strong reason for not compensating owners for regulatory takings.

Perry Shapiro, the commentator for chapter 10, adds two points to Bell's discussion of the symmetry of takings and givings. First, even if there were effective charges for public givings, the transaction costs of determining compensation for regulatory takings would be high. Litigation might be the only way, and the potential legal and political costs could induce local governments to lower land use planning standards. Second, Shapiro questions giving special attention to compensating landowners because any government intervention unavoidably creates winners and losers. For example, if a government policy hampers the profitability and employment opportunities of an industry, should the affected manufacturers and workers demand compensation from the state for their losses?

Property Rights Approaches to Achieving Land Policy Goals ———

The use of property rights approaches to accomplish government goals has become increasingly popular. We focus on poverty reduction, air and land conservation, and affordable housing.

POVERTY REDUCTION

One common objective of establishing secure private property rights in land, particularly in developing countries, is to reduce poverty. The World Bank and other international aid agencies have provided tremendous resources to improve land registration systems in many developing countries. As suggested by de Soto (2000), secure land tenure reduces unproductive spending on protection of land rights and lowers the risks of expropriation by the government. Both factors encourage investment in land improvements, thereby increasing the net worth of the property. Property owners can use land as collateral for credit. Reliable information on ownership provided by the registration system reduces the risks of lending, thus expanding the scope of bank loans to facilitate property owners' entrepreneurial activities and create new wealth. In chapter 11 Klaus Deininger and Gershon Feder review the existing evidence on the validity of this logic.

The authors argue that strong tenure security appears to be connected with positive investment effects when other favorable conditions are also present. They cite such examples as the doubling of likelihood of soil conservation in Uganda, increased house renovations in urban Peru and Argentina, and higher investment in Ethiopia shortly after the issuance of land certifications. Land registration also seems to facilitate the development of land rental markets, although its impacts on off-farm employment remain uncertain. In Guatemala, for example, it is estimated that improving tenure security would increase total rental areas by 63 percent. In Vietnam, holders of registered long-term use rights have a higher tendency to rent their land to unrelated people than do land users who possess other tenure forms.

In terms of the impact on credit access, Deininger and Feder found that the expected benefits of increased tenure security are limited, especially among the poor. In Paraguay observable effects in the supply of credit were limited to medium and large landowners. Land registration in Peru increased the possibility of obtaining loans from state banks only. No effect of land registration on credit access was found in Buenos Aires.

Why did credit-related benefits of titling fail to live up to expectations? Deininger and Feder suggest deficient institutional designs for private property protection and credit markets as one reason. In some developing countries, government institutions for enforcing registered land rights are weak or even absent. Credible commitment from the state to desist from expropriation does not exist. Even if there is such commitment, it can be displaced overnight due to changes in political regime. Corruption and bad governance of the land registry also lead to asymmetric access to information, thus facilitating land grabs by elites and undermining the credibility of the entire system.

In terms of credit markets, imperfections and lack of liquidity are prevalent. In rural areas where farmers are subject to such risks as weather, flooding, and other natural phenomena, collateral does not protect lenders from default by many borrowers at once. Farmers mostly need short-term loans, which are often provided by informal credit markets in most developing countries. Because collateral is normally not required for short-term credit, the benefits of registration do not justify its costs. In some cases high registration costs due to inefficiency or inappropriate standards have led to the expansion of semiformal credit systems or reversion to informality. Risk rationing and fear of losing real assets also dampen the willingness of potential borrowers to use titles as collateral.

Commenting on the comprehensive review of research on land titling by Deininger and Feder, Alain Durand-Lasserve suggests that a social dimension should be added to the discussion, especially on conflicts associated with the programs. The assessment of the effectiveness of land registration reform in securing land tenure and diminishing poverty should be conducted by comparing the costs and benefits of land titling to the effectiveness of alternative options that could achieve the same objectives.

In chapter 12 Edésio Fernandes cites similar arguments about the effects of titling programs on credit access in Latin America. He argues that the designs of large-scale titling programs have been based on erroneous assumptions about the formation of informal settlements. This error, Fernandes argues, has created a legal environment that fosters informal land market development.

In addition to the reasons provided by Deininger and Feder for the disappointing titling effects on credit access, Fernandes believes that income and social networks are more prominent factors than formal titles for obtaining bank loans in Latin America. He asserts that establishing secure private property rights alone cannot solve the problem of poverty. The poor need to be integrated into the market economy. Public investments in infrastructure, affordable housing, and social services are required to upgrade urban living conditions. The key solution for informal land development is to understand factors that affect informality, including the definition of property rights, planning law, conditions of urban management, and the judicial system.

Fernandes also suggests an integrated approach for land regularization programs that contains both remedial and preventive policies. These include the promotion of socio-spatial integration and democratization of access to land and housing. He emphasizes that policy makers should pay special attention to different tenure arrangements for varied urban settlement settings, the objectives and scale of the plans, technical criteria for implementation, and institutional and financial capacity to support the projects.

Although Ernesto Schargrodsky, the commentator for chapter 12, agrees with Fernandes on the credit access impact of land registration, he disagrees that titling has no effect on poverty. Based on studies that he conducted with other scholars on a titling program in suburban areas of Buenos Aires, they found positive influences of secure property rights on investment in housing, children's education and health, and labor participation in the market economy. He hypothesizes that land titling helps eradicate poverty through increased physical and human capital investment, but not through access to formal credit markets.

ENVIRONMENTAL CONSERVATION

Property rights approaches are also employed to achieve environmental conservation. Two specific topics are examined here: tradable emission permits and conservation easements. The implementation of the tradable emission permits program (also referred to as the federal cap and trade program) for carbon dioxide (CO_2) departs from past U.S. environmental policy, which has devolved most regulatory powers over point sources to the states. The cap and trade program formalizes emission permission as a new form of property right. The federal government will assign a CO_2 emission budget to each state, and the state will allot the assigned permits to industries by public auction. The permits could then be bought and sold in a federally managed trading program. Dallas Burtraw and Rich Sweeney, the authors of chapter 13, estimate that the total value of the CO_2 program in the United States could amount to \$130–\$370 billion annually by 2015. Thus, the design of the system for allocating tradable emission permits will have significant distributional and efficiency effects on the U.S. economy.

The value created by the CO_2 program reflects the cost of reducing greenhouse gas emissions. This cost will eventually be passed along to consumers in the form of higher prices for direct and indirect energy consumption. Burtraw and Sweeney estimate the distributional impacts of these price increases and suggest that CO_2 policy could have heterogeneous effects across regions and populations in the United States. For example, low-income households spend a higher proportion of their income on energy consumption than do high-income households. The authors propose various options to mediate the regressive incidence of the policy, including transferring 65 percent of the revenue generated from auctioning the permits to households on a per capita basis, excluding some basic necessity industries such as the transportation sector from the CO_2 program, and providing free allocation to electricity consumers (retail utilities) based on consumption.

The authors also project the efficiency and distributional impacts of these options based on simulation models. Their estimates indicate that a nationwide auction program with revenue returned on a per capita basis would be one of the two most efficient approaches among the options reviewed. It will however impose a higher cost of electricity consumption on consumers in the Southeast and the Midwest, which have a relatively large number of coal-fire-generated electricity facilities. If the states allocate the permits to retail electricity consumers without charge, there are smaller deviations among the regions on their net CO_2 expenditures; but the estimated price for CO_2 increases by 17 percent (from \$41 to \$48 per $mtCO_2$), indicating an efficiency loss. Based on the results, Burtraw and Sweeney argue that the most likely scenario would be for the federal government to apportion emission allowances to the states with special consideration to the electricity sector. Each state would then auction the allowances and return a portion of the revenue to households.

In response to Burtraw and Sweeney's proposal, Wallace E. Oates agrees that the federal government ought to retain some control over the program, especially the aggregate number of tradable permits. He cites the experience of the European Union (EU) program that allowed individual countries to decide on the number of tradable permits to be allocated to industries. Because some countries set their cap too high, resulting in a large supply of permits in the EU trading system, the program was unable to achieve its environmental objective. Oates also proposes a price ceiling on permits and a banking system to allow unused emission allowances to be carried over to future periods.

Another commonly used property rights approach to conserving the environment is private conservation easements. In chapter 14 Gerald Korngold discusses the benefits of this policy and proposes methods to mediate some of his concerns about the program. In essence, a conservation easement gives a nonprofit entity or government a perpetual right to restrict changing the present use of the land. If the easement is donated to a nonprofit, the landowner receives tax benefits at the federal, state, and local levels.

Korngold argues that conservation easements have added tremendous value to land preservation in the United States. The method alleviates the government's need to spend scarce public resources on land conservation. It reduces the cost of acquiring land for conservation, because a nonprofit needs only to purchase the right to develop land, and the other attributes of the bundle of rights remain privately owned. An easement will not remove the property from the tax roll, thus allowing the municipality to collect taxes from the owner. The easement program is based on voluntary changes that could help government avoid controversy generated by land use regulation.

Despite the benefits of conservation easements, there are concerns. A tax subsidy is involved in donated conservation easements, and abuses of the tax code have been reported. According to Korngold, nonprofits do not always consider public benefits when they establish easements, making it hard to know whether forgoing the tax revenue is justified. Because the establishment of private conservation easements is based largely on the initiatives of landowners and nonprofits, the location of easements may not be in accord with the community-wide preservation plan. Although the creation of easements involves public subsidy and land use planning, nonprofits are not subject to special regulatory processes to ensure that their actions are in conformity with the public interest. Korngold notes that monitoring of easement stewardship by nonprofits is modest (and sometimes absent). Conservation easements are sometimes perceived as a program designed for high-income households, because large land sites owned by individuals are normally involved. Comprehensive data about the total number, location, ownership, and acreage of conservation easements are lacking. Finally, perpetual easements may add rigidity to land use. When economic and social conditions of a neighborhood change, more land may be needed for development. The control over the modification and termination of restriction on large tracts of land by nonprofits could create legal difficulty and uncertainty to land use planning.

Korngold suggests the following solutions. The tax code should be amended to allow federal tax deductions only if an easement has received prior federal, state, or local certification as having a significant public preservation benefit. States should legally require counties to establish separate records for conservation easements. To ensure the stewardship of nonprofits, a voluntary accreditation program can be established. Alternatively, state attorneys general could supervise the nonprofits. To increase the flexibility of conservation easements to adjust to future land use needs, legal changes are required, including clarifying nonprofit law, applying the rule that prohibits enforcement of covenants violating public policy to the case of conservation easement reversal, relying on a *cy pres* proceeding to permit easement modification and termination, and exercising the power of eminent domain to condemn easements.

Nancy A. McLaughlin disagrees with some of Korngold's concerns. She argues that conservation easements are essentially public land rights acquired by government or public nonprofit entities and enforced by state attorneys general and the Internal Revenue Service. Thus, the objectives of easements should not be in conflict with the public interest. Land trusts are more accountable to the public than is the government because their survival depends on public confidence and donations. Because most conservation easements have no improvements on land, they can easily be converted to other uses without removal of physical structures if a *cy pres* proceeding determines that the continuous protection of the land is no longer possible or practical. Because most jurisdictions do not engage in effective planning for land preservation, the argument that conservation easements do not conform to community-wide plans cannot be established. Moderate modifications of conservation easements are not difficult because many deeds contain an amendment provision that grants the holder the right to alter the restriction so long as changes are consistent with the purpose of the easement.

AFFORDABLE HOUSING

Increasingly, states are employing a property rights approach to confront exclusionary zoning at the local level. This approach relies on providing private developers with a density bonus or other zoning-related benefit as an incentive to challenge localities that do not comply with state mandates on affordable housing. Viewing this from a property rights perspective, extra development rights are transferred to private developers as payments for actions to enforce state housing objectives or actually build affordable units. In chapter 15 Keri-Nicole Dillman and Lynn M. Fisher call these systems "housing appeal regimes" and use a game theory framework to analyze the behaviors of developers and municipalities so as to understand the diverse bargaining outcomes of the programs.

From the developer's perspective, Dillman and Fisher suggest that the decision to challenge a noncompliant municipality depends on four preconditions: (1) a favorable market environment; (2) a high likelihood of winning the lawsuit; (3) a sufficient density bonus; and (4) a high possibility of recovering litigation costs. Based on their model, they predict three possible outcomes. If none of the four conditions is present, the developer does not confront the municipality, rendering the antiexclusionary zoning program ineffective. If the developer is uncertain about winning the lawsuit, she may be willing to accept the municipality's settlement offer of an impact-fee waiver or a permit that allows a higher-density development. If similar lawsuits have a sufficiently high success rate with adequate density bonuses to cover the costs of litigation and other inclusionary requirements, such as providing affordable housing units, the developer will not settle the case out of court.

How would these outcomes affect the behavior of the municipality? If enough lawsuits create a credible threat to local exclusionary planning practices, the municipality could either amend its land use plan or remain reactive to developers' legal challenges. The decision will depend largely on whether the expected benefits of changing zoning regulations are higher than the gains from bargaining with developers minus the costs of compliance. Developers can be seen as enforcers of state policy if their challenges alter the municipality's exclusionary zoning practice. They will be implementers if they adopt the role of providing affordable housing for low- and moderate-income households.

Alexander von Hoffman suggests that one way to enrich the model is to consider the differential bargaining power of large and small developers. In modeling the behavior of the municipality, he argues, other interest groups such as conservation and historical commissions, town engineers, the zoning board of appeals, and existing homeowners should be considered. The municipality's decision-making process is therefore more complex than the current model depicts. Without knowing interested parties' motives, strategies, and actions at local and state levels, assessing antiexclusionary zoning programs will be difficult.

While the authors of chapter 15 study the strategic interplay between developers and towns in making inclusionary housing decisions, in chapter 16 Robert C. Ellickson compares this affordable housing approach with the voucher program. He asserts that giving portable housing vouchers to needy households is superior to encouraging private mixed-income housing projects through the use of density bonuses or impact-fee waivers. Ellickson reviews several efficiency and equity arguments. Mixed-income housing units are less efficient because the transaction costs of applying for government subsidies increase production costs. Moreover, public subsidies reduce incentives for developers to be cost-effective. Mismatches between household preferences and housing units allotted emerge when units are assigned by lottery. The lock-in effect prevents tenants from modifying their housing consumption when economic and family conditions change. Lock-ins also lead to the deterioration of the landlord–tenant relationship. In terms of fairness, vouchers are more equitable than mixed-income projects because they target the most impoverished families. Ellickson states that many suburban mixed-income housing programs make some inclusionary units available to households with moderate incomes.

Ellickson also challenges the often-cited benefit of mixed-income housing projects, that is, the promotion of neighborhood social and economic integration. He argues that low-income households might not be able to fit in with neighbors of higher social and economic status. Vouchers are more discreet and allow holders to blend into the community. More fundamentally, he states that evidence on the benefits of social and economic integration is inconclusive. Given these doubts, the expected gains from mixed-income projects do not seem to offset the potential loss of efficiency and equity.

Ingrid Gould Ellen is more skeptical about the advantages of vouchers over mixed-income housing. She states that mixed-income housing projects could generate positive externalities for revitalizing economically depressed neighborhoods. Physical improvements and population growth due to increases in mixed-income housing projects may spur private investment, which in turn creates jobs and improves the fiscal condition of local governments.

Ellen also provides different interpretations of the evidence mentioned in Ellickson's chapter. For example, she argues that vouchers may increase rents for unsubsidized poor households. Roughly one-third of voucher holders were not able to use their vouchers in 2001 because of landlord discrimination, bureaucratic barriers to interjurisdictional transfer of vouchers, and lack of information about the availability of suitable rental units. As is the case with housing appeal regimes, additional systematic comparisons of the voucher program and mixed-income projects are deemed necessary.

Conclusions

Ideas discussed by the chapter authors and commentators contribute to three important areas of property rights research: (1) the design of property rights institutions; (2) property rights enforcement; and (3) policy applications. As illustrated, identifying a set of design principles for crafting property rights institutions is possible. Elements of the bundle of rights can be assigned to different parties depending on the purpose of delineating the private property rights. For instance, if the goal is to manage the use of a commons where the mobility of participants is low, the definition and allocation of the use right are most critical, and the right of alienation is secondary. By contrast, if the purpose is to encourage owners to invest in property improvements, the right to sell and transfer the asset must be included explicitly in the assignment, as indicated by the experiences of land titling. For conservation easements to exist, the right to develop land must be separated from land ownership. Different definitions and ownership of property rights may be required to meet varying needs and conditions. Building property rights institutions requires consistent and predictable outcomes.

Property rights security depends on enforcement. When the conceptualization of different claims to property is in flux, enforcing property rights arrangements is difficult and controversial. The ongoing debates over government authority to regulate private property and to set compensation for takings in Europe, Latin America, and the United States illustrate the legal and political intricacy involved in maintaining balance between the property rights of public and private entities. This constant renegotiation between the public and private landowners is the essence of the evolution of private property whose meaning is shaped by changing social, political, and economic conditions.

In countries where private ownership is emerging, credible commitment from government as the guarantor and protector of individual property rights is essential. History matters. If there is no track record of state protection of private property, it will take a long time for citizens to trust the judiciary system and the polity to safeguarding of assets. Current land reform experiences in China, Estonia, Russia, and Vietnam seem to support this argument.

Altering the assignment of property rights to accomplish policy objectives also seems feasible, if the approach is accompanied with the development of other supporting institutions. Land titling appears to have positive impacts on property investment, but its credit access effect remains inconclusive. Tradable emission permits systems and conservation easements require heavy investments in legal and administrative capacity to achieve their desired goals. More needs to be known about how the net benefit of these property rights approaches measures up with other options. The improved understanding of the institutional issues related to private property in general and property rights approaches as a policy tool in particular is invaluable to land policy making and research.

REFERENCES

Alston, Lee J., Thráinn Eggertsson, and Douglass C. North. 1996. *Empirical studies in institutional change*. New York: Cambridge University Press.

Anderson, Terry L., and Peter J. Hill. 1975. The evolution of property rights: A study of the American West. *Journal of Law and Economics* 8(1):163–179.

Barzel, Yoram. 1989. *Economic analysis of property rights*. New York: Cambridge University Press.

Bentham, Jeremy. 1978. Principles of the civil code. Reprinted partially in *Property: Mainstream and critical positions*, ed. C. B. Macpherson, 40–57. Oxford: Basil Blackwell.

Blackstone, William. 1979. *Commentaries on the laws of England: A facsimile of the first edition of 1765–1769*. Chicago: University of Chicago Press.

Buchanan, James M. 1984. The Coase theorem and the theory of the state. In *The theory of public choice*, ed. James M. Buchanan and Robert D. Tollison, 159–173. Ann Arbor: University of Michigan Press.

———. 1991. *The economics and the ethics of constitutional order*. Ann Arbor: University of Michigan Press.

Coase, Ronald H. 1960. The problem of social cost. *Journal of Law and Economics* 3(October):1–44.

———. 1988. *The firm, the market, and the law.* Chicago: University of Chicago Press.

Commons, John R. 1934 (1990). *Institutional economics: Its place in political economy.* Vol. 2. New Brunswick, NJ: Transaction Publishers.

Demsetz, Harold. 1967. Towards a theory of property rights. *American Economic Review* 57(2):347–359.

de Soto, Hernando. 2000. *The mystery of capital: Why capitalism triumphs in the West and fails everywhere else.* New York: Basic Books.

Eggertsson, Thráinn. 1990. *Economic behavior and institutions.* New York: Cambridge University Press.

Ellickson, Robert C. 1989. The case for Coase and against "Coaseanism." *Yale Law Journal* 99(3):611–630.

———. 1991. *Order without law: How neighbors settle disputes.* Cambridge, MA: Harvard University Press.

Furubotn, Eirik Grundtvig, and Rudolf Richter. 2005. *Institutions and economic theory: The contribution of the new institutional economics.* Ann Arbor: University of Michigan Press.

Hardin, Garrett. 1968. The tragedy of the commons. In *Managing the commons*, ed. Garrett Hardin and John Baden, 16–30. San Francisco: W. H. Freeman.

Libecap, Gary D. 1989. *Contracting for property rights.* New York: Cambridge University Press.

North, Douglass C. 1981. *Structure and changes in economic history.* New York: W. W. Norton.

———. 1990. *Institutions, institutional change and economic performance.* New York: Cambridge University Press.

North, Douglass C., and Robert P. Thomas. 1973. *The rise of the Western world.* Cambridge: Cambridge University Press.

Ostrom, Elinor. 1990. *Governing the commons: The evolution of institutions for collective action.* New York: Cambridge University Press.

———. 2005. *Understanding institutional diversity.* Princeton, NJ: Princeton University Press.

———. 2007. Collective action theory. In *The Oxford handbook of comparative politics*, ed. Carles Boix and Susan C. Stokes, 186–208. Oxford: Oxford University Press.

Samuelson, Paul A. 1966. Modern economic realities and individualism. In *The collected scientific papers of Paul A. Samuelson*. Vol. 2. Cambridge, MA: MIT Press.

Smith, Adam. 1776 (1979). *Inquiry into the nature and cause of the wealth of nations*, ed. R. H. Campbell and A. S. Skinner. Indianapolis: Liberty Classics.

Wallis, John J., and Douglass C. North. 1986. Measuring the transactions sector in the American economy. In *Long-term factors in American economic growth*, ed. S. Engerman and R. Gallman. Chicago: University of Chicago Press.

Williamson, Oliver E. 1985. *The economic institutions of capitalism: Firms, markets, and relational contracting.* New York: Free Press.

THE DESIGN AND EVOLUTION OF PROPERTY RIGHTS INSTITUTIONS

2

Design Principles of Robust Property Rights Institutions: What Have We Learned?

Elinor Ostrom

The Problem of Open Access

The problem of overuse of open-access resources was clearly articulated by Scott Gordon (1954) and Harold Demsetz (1967). Garrett Hardin (1968) speculated about the same problem, but stressed that the resource users themselves were trapped in tragic overuse and that solutions had to be imposed from the outside. Gordon, Demsetz, and Hardin ignited a general concern that when property rights related to a valuable resource did not exist, the resources would be overharvested.

Because of the existence of sufficient empirical examples of the problems facing users of land-based common-pool resources given the independence of actors in the absence of property rights, the empirical applicability of the theory was not challenged until the mid-1980s. For many observers, massive deforestation in tropical countries and the collapse of many ocean fisheries confirmed the worst predictions to be derived from this theory (Hutchings 2000; Jackson et al. 2001; Rudel 2005). Since harvesters are viewed as being trapped in these dilemmas, repeated demands that external authorities impose a different set of institutions on such settings have been made. Predictions of overharvesting have also been supported in the experimental laboratory when subjects made anonymous decisions and

Support from the National Science Foundation and from the Lincoln Institute of Land Policy is gratefully acknowledged. The research help of Michael Cox; the excellent comments by Yu-Hung Hong, Gregory K. Ingram, and Prakash Kashwan; and the outstanding help of Patty Lezotte are also greatly appreciated.

were not allowed to communicate with one another, but not when they were able to engage in face-to-face communication (Ostrom, Gardner, and Walker 1994).

Solving the Problem by Recommending Optimal Institutions ———

Many policy analysts have recommended a single optimal policy for solving the open-access problem. Some recommended private property as the most efficient form of ownership, as did Demsetz himself (Posner 1977; Raymond 2003). Others recommended government ownership and control (Lovejoy 2006; Terborgh 1999, 2000), even though it is difficult for a bureaucracy to make rational decisions given the high level of uncertainty involved in most resources (Whitford 2002). Grafton (2000) made a more nuanced argument for the state in governing resources, sometimes as the owner of a resource and sometimes providing good backup to those engaged in collective action. Theorists frequently implicitly assumed that regulators would act in the public interest and that they knew how ecological systems work and how to change institutions so as to induce socially optimal behavior (Feeny, Hanna, and McEvoy 1996, 195).

Unfortunately, many of the recommended optimal institutions are little more than stylized figures based on the underlying simple models that Gordon and Demsetz developed. Colin Clark (2006, 15) reflected on the power of these simple models to clearly illustrate the deep problems of overharvesting. The underlying "stick figures," however, are too simplistic for analysis that adequately captures the dynamics of all common-pool resources. Applying rules that bring the costs of harvesting up to the level that would induce sustainable yield is a simple solution when modeling, but not at all simple when faced with the complexity of field settings.

Self-Organized Development of Property Rights ————————

The possibility that the users of a resource would find ways to organize themselves was not considered in most economics, natural resource, and property rights literature until the last three decades. Organizing so as to create rules that specify rights and duties of participants creates a public good for those involved. Everyone included in the community of users benefits from this public good, whether they contribute or not. Getting "out of the trap" is itself a second-level social dilemma. Investing in diverse mechanisms to increase the likelihood that participants follow the rules they make also generates a public good. These investments represent a third-level social dilemma. Since the initial problem exists because the individuals are supposed to be stuck in a setting where they generate negative externalities on one another, it is not consistent with the conventional theory that they solve second- and third-level social dilemmas in order to address the first-level dilemma under analysis.

In the decades after Scott's, Demsetz's, and Hardin's famous articles, however, multiple empirical studies about common-pool resources have been undertaken (Berkes 1989, 2007; Dolšak and Ostrom 2003; McCay and Acheson 1987; National Research Council 1986, 2002). As a result of these studies, we now know that some (but not all) individuals who jointly use a common-pool resource will

- expend considerable time and energy trying to develop workable rules that they can use for governing and managing a resource;
- follow their own costly rules so long as they believe that most of the others affected also follow these rules;
- monitor each other's conformance with these rules; and
- impose sanctions on those who break rules at a cost to themselves.

Conventional economic theory would not lead to a prediction that anyone would undertake these four actions based on a model of maximization of short-term individual returns. Thus, to move our understanding ahead of earlier theories, it is necessary to dig into what we mean by property rights and how resource users may design their own property rights systems. Then, we need to examine an earlier effort to understand why some property rights systems were robust over long periods of time while others collapsed—the possibility that broad design principles underlay the successful efforts (Ostrom 1990). We then discuss a recent analysis of scholars' assessment of the usefulness of these design principles and conclude with an analysis of how the design principles should be revised in light of multiple studies and how we can use the design principles in practice without using them as blueprints.

What Are Property Rights?

One of the confusions related to the existence of property rights is that scholars have sometimes limited the concept of property rights to the existence of a right by one party (individual, family, organized group, or government) to sell all of the rights to some other party. Selling one's rights is frequently referred to as "alienation." Some scholars presumed that unless users had alienation rights, they did not have any property rights. Some of the early confusion about the capability of users to develop their own effective governance system related to the presumption that without the right of alienation, resource users had no property rights and were indeed trapped in overuse. After the first National Research Council report in 1986, we began collecting case studies written by historians, anthropologists, engineers, political scientists, economists, and other social scientists and started the challenging task of coding them systematically in the common-pool resources (CPR) database housed at the Workshop in Political Theory and Policy Analysis at Indiana University (for a description, see Ostrom, Gardner, and Walker 1994; Schlager 1990; and Tang 1992 for a general description of the effort, and Poteete and Ostrom 2008 for an overview of the challenge of doing a meta-analysis of the large number of relevant cases).

As we worked on this meta-analysis of governance systems related to common-pool resources, we kept finding established resource systems that had survived for long periods of time in which the users did not have the right to sell their holdings. This led Edella Schlager and me (1992) to draw on the earlier insights of Ciriacy-Wantrup and Bishop (1975) and Commons (1968) and to think of property rights systems in terms of bundles of rights rather than as a single right. We defined the following five rights that we found in empirical studies of operational resource systems in the field:

1. Access—a right to enter a defined physical property
2. Withdrawal—a right to harvest the products of a resource such as timber, water, and food for pastoral animals
3. Management—a right to regulate the use patterns of other harvesters and to transform a resource system by building improvements
4. Exclusion—a right to determine who will have the right of access to a resource and whether that right can be transferred
5. Alienation—a right to sell or lease any of the above rights

Schlager and Ostrom (1992) posed the possibility that one can relate the different ways that these bundles are combined to a set of positions that individuals hold in regard to operational settings. For many resources, one can define five types of positions held by people who have some type of property right and obligations that are related to that right. A person who has only access rights can be called an authorized viewer. When a person enters a national or state forest, for example, with a one-day (or one-season) permit, he has a property right as an authorized viewer. He may have had to pay a fee to obtain this right, and he has obligations to follow the rules established by the forest authority. Most state forests, for example, do not allow a person who has a one-day or monthly permit to harvest anything. The person can sit at picnic grounds and enjoy the forest, but he is not supposed to litter the forest. He may be authorized to camp overnight. He can do all sorts of viewing, but he is not supposed to harvest trees, mushrooms, or other plants.

A person who has access and withdrawal rights can be called an authorized user. In many pastoral systems and fisheries, users have evolved recognized rights to harvest. Frequently, those rights are matched with obligations in regard to the timing of harvest, the equipment that may be used in harvesting, and the purpose for which the harvested units may be used.

A person with access, withdrawal, and management rights is called a claimant. Many common-property institutions recognize the rights and obligations of a claimant to build fences around a jointly owned forest, to improve an irrigation system by lining the canals, or to make others of a wide diversity of improvements that relate to the management of the system. The obligations involved in these property rights enable the holders to achieve a longer-term perspective as a result of the investments they make in the long-term productivity and sustainability of the resource.

A person who has those three rights plus the right of exclusion is called a proprietor. A proprietor has substantial rights and obligations to regulate use, invest in the system, and determine who has access to the system.

Finally, the term *owner* identifies individuals who have all five rights and the obligations related to these rights. There are a variety of common-property institutions in which participants can sell any and all of their other bundles of rights to someone else. Sometimes they have to get permission from a council to do this, but they have that right subject to review. There are, however, many well-defined and operational common-property systems that have existed for a long time without the right of alienation (McKean 1982, 1992; Netting 1981).

Schlager (1994) analyzed the patterns of rights and outcomes for a set of inshore fishery cases that were well documented by the original case authors. She found that fishers from inshore fisheries who were claimants—who possessed the three rights of access, withdrawal, and management—had the capability to self-organize. Having the authority to exclude others (being proprietors) gave fishers even more capabilities to keep others from invading their inshore fishery and allowed still further investment in regulating use and investment. Schlager did not find that having the right of alienation was as essential as claimed in the literature.

In regard to irrigation systems, Tang (1994) found that having the rights of a proprietor made a substantial difference in regard to long-term management, but having the full rights of an owner was not crucial. In many common-property systems that have been sustained over long periods of time, none of the resource users has had the right to alienate their other rights. Thus, the right of alienation is not the key defining right for those who have been responsible for designing and adapting common-property systems in the field. Many users of common-pool resources do have property rights, even though these may not include the right of alienation.

Can Resource Users Create Their Own Property Rights?

While Hardin presumed that the users of a common-pool resource were hopelessly trapped in a system of overuse, the extensive research literature on common-property institutions provides strong evidence that the users are not always helpless (see overview in National Research Council 1986, 2002). In some legal systems—particularly those broadly based on Roman law traditions rather than English common law—the extent of autonomy to develop their own property rights systems granted to users of forests, irrigation systems, lakes, and inshore fisheries is restricted. Even in these systems, however, users of common-pool resource systems located in relatively remote settings have frequently (but not always) established some basic understanding of who was authorized to use the resource, how resource units should be harvested from the resource, and what the agreed-upon uses of these resources were.[1]

To create their own set of rules about boundaries and use practices, a group of users must solve a basic collective action problem—the second-level social dilemma referred to above (Leach, Mearns, and Scoones 1997; Mehta et al. 1999). They face a long-term problem that if they do not find a way of limiting use, they will destroy a resource that may be of high value to the users' personal and family economic well-being. Just facing such a problem is, however, not a sufficient condition for positing that users will engage in collective action. Many theorists have presumed, as Hardin did, that those involved in a collective action problem would not themselves solve it, since social dilemmas involve a conflict between individual rationality and optimal outcomes for a group (Alchian and Demsetz 1972; Coase 1960; Lichbach 1996; Schelling 1978). Even if some individuals cooperate, the others are predicted to free ride on them.

In formal models of social dilemmas, assumptions are made that (1) decisions about strategies are made independently and simultaneously; (2) participants have common knowledge of an exogenously fixed structure of the situation and of the payoffs to participants; and (3) no external authority is present to enforce agreements among participants. When these assumptions are made for a one-shot game, the theoretical prediction derived from classical, noncooperative game theory is unambiguous—zero cooperation.[2] In repeated situations, there are many solution concepts that vary all the way from zero to full cooperation (Abreau 1988).

Fortunately, collective action theory has now matured. Instead of predicting that participants will never engage in cooperation or that anything can happen, there is growing agreement on the attributes of the users and of the structure of the situation that combine to enable predictions regarding the likelihood of participants' engaging in collective action (see Ostrom 2007a for an overview; Gibson et al. 2005; Marshall 2005). Some of the variables considered in the collective action literature include the size and heterogeneity of the group involved and how individuals are potentially linked, the type of production functions users are facing, the type of transaction costs that a group faces, how easy it is to get good information about the results of past actions, and how

---

1. Since many policy analysts have assumed that property rights have to be established by an external authority—the state—self-organized common-property systems are frequently invisible to them. They presume that, unless they find legal documents creating a property system, it does not exist. As more conservation policies have been adopted in the last several decades, they have frequently imposed new centralized institutions on indigenous peoples, leading in some cases to increased destruction of delicate ecosystems rather than to increased protection of them.

2. In a very large number of one-shot public good experiments undertaken in diverse countries, however, subjects tend to contribute an average of between 40 and 60 percent of the optimal level of contributions (Davis and Holt 1993, 325; Sally 1995).

valuable solving the problem is to participants. Developing trust and reciprocity is crucial to building the social capital needed to create workable property rights (Ahn and Ostrom 2008; Ostrom 1998). This chapter does not delve into the variables that increase the probability that a group of resource appropriators engages in collective action to create a set of property rights, which has been covered in several past works (Ostrom 1990, 2001, 2005). Here, the point is that it is now well established that some users of common-pool resources in settings that are conducive to self-organization do create their own common-property institutions.

The Robustness of Self-Organized Common-Property Institutions

Not only have common-property scholars documented the possibility that resource users would themselves overcome dilemmas to create their own institutions, but many of these institutions have survived for multiple years—even centuries in some instances. In the late 1980s, after working with colleagues to amass, read, and code a large number of individual cases of long-lasting and of failed systems, I tried valiantly to find the specific rules that were associated with the systems that had survived for long periods of time using Kenneth Shepsle's (1989) definition of a robust institution as one that was long-lasting and had operational rules that had been devised and modified over time according to a set of higher-level rules (which institutional analysts would usually call collective choice rules). These higher-level rules might themselves be modified slowly over time. The contemporary definition of robustness in regard to complex systems focuses on adaptability to disturbances: "the maintenance of some desired system characteristics despite fluctuations in the behavior of its component parts or its environment" (Carlson and Doyle 2002, 2538; see also Anderies, Janssen, and Ostrom 2004; Janssen and Anderies 2007).

I spent weeks and weeks reading cases, writing them up, redoing statistical analyses, and thinking that I was a dope for not being able to identify regularities in the specific property rights of the successful cases. Finally, the idea dawned on me that I should stop trying to identify the specific rules that tended to generate success. Perhaps what I needed to do was move up a level or two in generality to try to understand more general institutional regularities among the systems that were sustained over long periods of time. I did not even know what I should call those regularities. The idea finally dawned on me that one way of talking about them would be as design principles.

I did not think that the irrigators, fishers, forest dwellers, and others who had invented and sustained successful common-property regimes over several centuries had these principles overtly in their minds. Not all artists have training in art and know the principles they use in painting outstanding works of art. So I thought of these regularities as underlying principles that one could draw out from the cases of long-sustained regimes. I compared the successes with the failures to assess whether the failures were characterized by the same principles. If they were, of course, the principles would not be a meaningful distinction between robust, long-surviving systems and systems that were not able to sustain themselves over time.

Thus, in *Governing the Commons* (Ostrom 1990), I laid out what I thought were eight key design principles related to long-term robustness of institutions crafted to govern common-pool resource systems. At the time, many colleagues read and commented on this effort and the cases used to derive and then illustrate the principles. I was uncertain that I had indeed identified the core set of principles, but I finally decided that I should share this analysis with other scholars so that they could challenge the findings, and we could develop a firmer foundation for better institutions in the future.

The Eight Design Principles Posited in 1990 ——————————

Since I described these principles in some detail in previous publications (Ostrom 1990, 2005), a brief overview will serve as a basis for further discussion (see table 2.1).

CLEARLY DEFINED BOUNDARIES

The first design principle is that the boundaries of a resource system, as well as the individuals or households with property rights, are clearly defined. The boundary rules related to who can enter, harvest, manage, and potentially exclude others affect a participant's presumption about the likely levels of trustworthiness and cooperation of the others involved. If the rules are not well defined, strangers who discover a valuable resource may start to use it. Because they are strangers, they may overuse it. When long-standing participants fear that others may start using a resource of value to them, creating well-defined boundary rules helps immensely in increasing the probability that a person who is cooperating in limiting harvests and providing maintenance is not being a sucker because others are overharvesting and not contributing to the maintenance.

Having a clear boundary for the resource itself is important for a different set of reasons. It clarifies what is meant by a particular resource system. Where may I go, and where may I not go? The free riding problem is addressed by systems that define their boundaries. If a group of users can determine its own membership—including those who agree to use the resource according to the agreed-upon rules and excluding those who do not agree—the group has made an important first step toward limiting access and developing greater trust and reciprocity. Using this principle enables participants to know who is in and who is out of a defined set of relationships and, thus, with whom to cooperate.

Just defining the boundaries may not be sufficient in and of itself, especially when the boundaries are drawn by external officials. The boundaries of the Maya Biosphere Reserve located in the capital city of Guatemala are well defined on

Table 2.1
Design Principles for Governing Sustainable Resources Derived from Long-Enduring Studies of Institutions

1. *Clearly Defined Boundaries*
   The boundaries of the resource system (e.g., irrigation system or fishery) and the individuals or households with rights to harvest resource units are clearly defined.

2. *Proportional Equivalence Between Benefits and Costs*
   Rules specifying the amount of resource products that a user is allocated are related to local conditions and to rules requiring labor, materials, and/or money inputs.

3. *Collective Choice Arrangements*
   Most individuals affected by harvesting and protection rules are included in the group that can modify these rules.

4. *Monitoring*
   Monitors, who actively audit biophysical conditions and user behavior, are at least partially accountable to the users and/or are the users themselves.

5. *Graduated Sanctions*
   Users who violate rules in use are likely to receive graduated sanctions (depending on the seriousness and context of the offense) from other users, from officials accountable to these users, or from both.

6. *Conflict Resolution Mechanisms*
   Users and their officials have rapid access to low-cost local arenas to resolve conflict among users or between users and officials.

7. *Minimal Recognition of Rights to Organize*
   The rights of users to devise their own institutions are not challenged by external governmental authorities, and users have long-term tenure rights to the resource.

For resources that are parts of larger systems:
8. *Nested Enterprises*
   Appropriation, provision, monitoring, enforcement, conflict resolution, and governance activities are organized in multiple layers of nested enterprises.

Source: Based on Ostrom (1990, 90).

many maps of the reserve, in the relevant national parks, and in many tourist brochures. In a survey of residents of an agricultural community in one of the buffer zones of the reserve, however, Sundberg (1998, 402) found that almost 80 percent of the farmers did not know anything about the reserve or its boundaries (see also the supporting online material for Dietz, Ostrom, and Stern 2003).

PROPORTIONAL EQUIVALENCE BETWEEN BENEFITS AND COSTS
The second design principle is that the rules in use allocate benefits proportional to inputs that are required. If users are going to harvest from a resource over the

long run, they must devise rules related to how much, when, and how different products are to be harvested. They also need to assess the costs on users of operating a system. The design principle related to proportionality of benefits and costs relates to the likelihood that participants will feel that the rules are equitable. If some people pay low costs but get high benefits over time, this inequity frustrates the other participants and may cause more and more to consider the rules unfair and refuse to abide by them. Thus, this design principle is directly related to the attitudes that are necessary to sustain a system over the long run. If some users get all the benefits and pay few of the costs, few of the others are willing to follow rules over time (Ensminger 2000, 2001).

COLLECTIVE CHOICE ARRANGEMENTS

The third design principle is that most of the individuals affected by a resource regime are authorized to participate in making and modifying the rules. Resource regimes that use this principle should be able to craft rules that fit local circumstances and that are considered fair by participants. As environments change over time, officials located far away do not know of the change, so being able to craft local rules is particularly important. Some local common-property institutions empower a local elite to make most of the collective choice decisions. In such cases, one can expect that the policies primarily benefit the elite and are not consistent with the second design principle (for example, see Ensminger 1990; Platteau 2003, 2004).

MONITORING

Few long-surviving resource regimes rely only on levels of trust and reciprocity among appropriators to keep rule-breaking levels down. Evidence of the importance of the fourth design principle—monitoring—has been presented by Gibson, Williams, and Ostrom (2005); Ostrom and Nagendra (2006); Hayes and Ostrom (2005); and Schweik (2000). A recent multivariate analysis by Coleman and Steed (2008) of 130 forests located in a dozen countries found that when local forest users were recognized as having a right of harvesting (having at least the position of authorized user), they were more likely to monitor patterns of harvesting by other appropriators. When this happened, the resource conditions were themselves better than when local users did not monitor each other.

Most institutional analysts have assumed that rules must be enforced in some manner to achieve robust governance, but have not always agreed on who should select the monitors. Most self-organized resource regimes select their own monitors. These monitors are accountable to authorized users and keep an eye on resource conditions as well as on harvesting activities. By creating official positions for local monitors, a resource regime does not rely only on the norms of local right holders to impose personal costs on those who break a rule. In some systems, everyone has a duty to be a monitor, and users rotate into the position. In others, the monitors are paid from funds collected from all authorized appropriators. With monitors appointed, those who want to cooperate with the rules so long as others also cooperate are assured that someone is generally checking on the conformance of others. No one likes being a sucker. Thus, participants can continue to cooperate without fearing that others are taking advantage of them.

GRADUATED SANCTIONS

The fifth design principle is the use of graduated sanctions. This finding puzzled me; my 15 years of empirical research on policing in metropolitan areas familiarized me with the literature on the economics of crime that stressed the importance of costly sanctions so that the expected value of breaking a law was higher than the benefit that could be obtained even when the probabilities of being caught were relatively low. In many self-organized systems, the first sanction imposed by a local monitor is so low as to have no impact on the expected benefit-cost ratio of breaking local rules (given the high payoffs that could be achieved by harvesting illegally, for example).

The initial sanction can be thought of more as information to the person who is caught as well as to others in the community. A user might break a rule in error or because of difficult problems. Letting an infraction pass unnoticed could generate a downward cascade of cooperation in a group that relies on conditional cooperation and has no capacity to sanction. When graduated punishments are used, a person who purposely or accidentally breaks a rule is notified that others have noticed the infraction (thereby increasing the individual's confidence that others would also be caught). Further, the individual learns that others basically continue to extend their trust and want only a small token to convey a recognition that the mishap occurred.

HOW DO THESE FIT TOGETHER?

The first five principles fit together to form a coherent theoretical explanation of why they may work together: when the users of a resource design their own rules (design principle 3) that are enforced "by local users or accountable to them (design principle 4) using graduated sanctions (design principle 5) that clearly define who has rights to withdraw from a well-defined resource (design principle 1) and that effectively assign costs proportionate to benefits (design principle 2), collective action and monitoring problems tend to be solved in a reinforcing manner" (Ostrom 2005, 267).

CONFLICT RESOLUTION MECHANISMS

The sixth principle is that there are rapid, low-cost, local arenas in which to resolve conflict among users or between users and officials. Rules have to be understood in order to be effective. Some participants may interpret a rule that they have jointly made in different ways. By devising simple local mechanisms to get conflicts aired immediately and resolutions that are generally known in the community, the number of conflicts that reduce trust can be reduced.

MINIMAL RECOGNITION OF RIGHTS TO ORGANIZE

Whether local users can develop more effective regimes over time is affected by whether a national or local government at least minimally recognizes the right to organize. Participants in resource regimes that are not recognized by external authorities have operated over long periods, but they have had to rely almost entirely on unanimity to change rules (Ghate 2000). Otherwise, disgruntled participants who voted against a rule change can call on the external authorities to threaten the resource regime. Changing rules using unanimity imposes high transaction costs and prevents a group from searching for better-matched rules at relatively lower costs. When external governmental officials presume that only they can make authoritative rules, sustaining a self-organized regime is difficult (Johnson and Libecap 1982).

NESTED ENTERPRISES

When common-pool resources that are being managed by a group are large, an eighth design principle may be present in robust systems. The nested enterprise principle is that governance activities are organized in multiple layers of nested enterprises. In addition to some small units, larger institutions exist to govern the interdependencies among smaller units. The rules allocating water among major branches of an irrigation system, for example, may differ from the rules used to allocate water among farmers along a single distribution channel (Yoder 1994). Consequently, among long-enduring self-governed regimes, smaller-scale organizations tend to be nested in ever-larger organizations.

A Current Evaluation of the Validity of the Design Principles ———

Michael Cox, a graduate student who is studying self-organized irrigation systems in New Mexico (the *acequias* established by migrants from Spain using many of the designs developed in their home country), has coded 33 research papers in which other scholars have evaluated whether the design principles hold up in their studies.[3] Each of the articles looked at one or more resources in some depth and examined which design principles were relevant and were positively related to the outcomes, negatively related, or did not make much difference.

Figure 2.1 presents the distribution across all cases coded with regard to their summary evaluations. It appears that 73 percent of the cases Cox has coded are either moderately or highly supportive of the usefulness of the design principles. Table 2.2 presents the distribution of cases across sectors and across design principles. In general, it looks like the principles are helpful for understanding why some common-property institutions are robust, and it seems that the design principles are themselves relatively robust (only 1 out of 33 studies strongly challenges them).

---

3. These articles are preceded by asterisks in the reference list.

Figure 2.1
Design Principles Evaluation

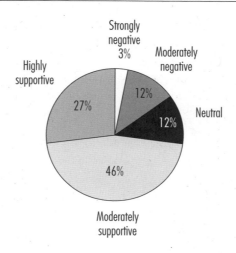

SOME GENERAL CONCERNS

While many of the articles were supportive, both general and specific concerns were raised. One had to do with the reliance on a modified rational choice approach. Several publications, including Cleaver (2000), Steins and Edwards (1999a, 1999b), and Young (2002), urged that the reliance on rational choice

Table 2.2
Evaluating the Design Principles

Sector	Forestry	Pastoral Systems	Irrigation Systems	Inshore Fishery	Multiple Resource Sectors	Total
Highly supportive	1		4	1	3	9
Moderately supportive	7	1	4		3	15
Neutral		1	2		1	4
Moderately negative	1	1		1	1	4
Strongly negative					1	1
Total	9	3	10	2	9	33

and collective action needed to be complemented (or perhaps substituted) by a constructivist approach. Steins, Röling, and Edwards (2000, 5), for example, criticized "the conventional scientific belief that reality can be divided into categories, and that its shaping mainly operates through cause-effect relations." I think it is useful to analyze the diverse components of the world we try to analyze. Sometimes those components can be examined using additive models, but I have stressed the importance of understanding how configurations of causal conditions affect incentives, behaviors, and outcomes (see Ostrom 2005, 2007b).

Another general concern was the omission of conditions that enhance the likelihood of crafting a working set of property rights. Scholars have urged the inclusion of such variables as small size, homogeneous groups, and active leadership (Baland and Platteau 1996); dependence on a resource (Gibson 2001); market integration (Tucker 1999; Tucker, Randolph, and Castellanos 2007); external government policies (Rodriguez 2007); and cross-scale linkages (Berkes 2002; Young 2002). All of these and others are important variables, and I used them and other variables in related work to explain the factors affecting the emergence of new institutions (Ostrom 2001). They are among the variables that affect whether resource users will organize to solve the collective action problem of self-organization in the first place. As such, they are causal variables of a process. The design principles, on the other hand, are an effort to understand why the results of this process are robust in some cases and fail in others.

CONCERNS REGARDING SPECIFIC PRINCIPLES

Clearly Defined Boundaries   Some scholars suggested dividing the principle of clearly defined boundaries into two parts, one focusing on the boundaries of those authorized to use a common-pool resource and the other related to the boundaries of the resource itself (Agrawal 2002). Specifying these as two principles may help in regard to another concern related to the rigidity of the boundary of a resource. Cleaver (2000) and Turner (1999) suggested that the boundaries of the resource can be fuzzier than the boundaries of who is authorized to use the resource. When two user groups work side by side, they may have backup arrangements that enable them to utilize each other's resource under commonly understood conditions.

One confusion about boundary rules is related to the difference between a careful definition of the boundaries of a resource (and potential of other related resources) and those boundaries being rigid and unchanging. For many pastoral resources, the boundaries of the physical resource may change depending on the season and patterns of rainfall. Most pastoral peoples' resources have several boundaries. One boundary relates to where they live most of the year. A second boundary relates to where they can pasture animals during normal seasons. A third—and possibly a fourth—boundary frequently exists for a backup region that may be available to a well-defined group in seasons when its home territory is facing dire scarcity. When rainfall is abundant, there are few questions about where to pasture animals. If the rainfall for that area has been scarce, other areas may have more adequate rainfall and forage availability. Most pastoral peoples have secondary and tertiary rights to pasture animals in the other regions depending on the season (Agrawal 1999). Quinn et al. described the problem as now compounded by the central designation of village boundaries:

> Physical boundaries on resources in Africa are often not clearly defined and there are two important facets as to why this is the case. The nature of semi-arid regions means that resource availability varies both spatially and temporally (Cousins 2000). . . . Imposed over this ecological variability in resource availability are the socio-political boundaries created by culture and political administration. For example, the political administration units created by villagisation in Tanzania do not necessarily relate to the underlying ecological boundaries. The tension between political and ecological boundaries creates a situation where the boundaries on resource users are often "fuzzy" as resource users are drawn from a wider community than just one village, and different social and ethnic groups use overlapping parts of the same resource. (2007, 105–106)

Thus, as we move to dividing the first principle into two parts, it is also important to clarify what is meant by clear boundaries. Even when scholars have used fuzzy set theory to define boundaries, the boundaries of each of the resources in a set of resources are relatively clearly defined. It is not reasonable to put up fences to clearly demark all boundaries in large pastoral or forest areas, but most such resources in the field do use some kind of stone or plant species to mark the boundaries on the various paths used frequently.

Niamir-Fuller focused extensively on this first principle from her own research experience on pastoral peoples in Africa. She also described the boundaries among different user groups as fuzzy and containing overlapping zones that "are jointly managed by the neighboring tribes" and buffer zones that "often did not come under strict management by any group, but access to them was negotiated between parties concerned on an ad hoc basis" (1998, 269). Niamir-Fuller pointed out that it is very important to understand that "although different people can use the same communal land, users are subject to regulations that determine their *priority* of use. Any group has priority of use within the boundary of its 'home territory,' but this land can also be used by others seasonally or infrequently" (1998, 272–273).

Morrow and Hull pointed out that many donor projects formally met the first design principle. Formal congruence with the first principle is not enough, however, to enable appropriators to defend their borders from free riders. They suggest rephrasing the first design principle as: "The resource itself and the users of the resources are clearly defined, and the appropriators are able to effectively defend the resource from outsiders" (1996, 1643). Given our own findings about the importance of defending boundaries, this rephrasing is a positive step forward (Gibson, Williams, and Ostrom 2005; Hayes and Ostrom 2005).

Congruence Between Appropriation and Provision and Local Conditions
The principle of congruence between appropriation and provision and local conditions should probably also be divided into subtypes: one related to the congruence with the local ecology, and a second related to the congruence between the
amount that a user is authorized to harvest and the user's responsibilities for contributing labor or other resources. Some scholars have also identified local conditions as involving the predominant culture, ideology, customs, and livelihood
strategies (Gautam and Shivakoti 2005; Hallum 2008; Morrow and Hull 1996;
Young 2002). Morrow and Hull restated it as "Appropriation and provision
rules are congruent with the resource and with the cultural norms and social
and economic patterns of interaction of the appropriators. The pace and scale of
the institution are congruent with traditional decision-making processes" (1996,
1643). Thus, this principle may need to have three subparts specifically dealing
with congruence with the local ecology, congruence with the local culture, and
congruence between benefits and costs.

Collective Choice Arrangements   The common choice arrangements principle
has been discussed extensively in the common-property literature. Platteau (2003,
2004), for example, indicated that the users of locally controlled resources do
not always have the opportunity to make their own rules. Some local resources
are dominated by an elite who decide to receive most of the benefits and pay
few of the costs. Where this happens, the collective choice arrangements are not
consistent with design principle 3.
     Several authors identified collective choice arrangements and related principles
as helping to explain outcomes achieved in different locations. Gautam and Shivakoti (2005), for example, examined the relevance of collective choice arrangements and other design principles for understanding the difference in outcomes
for two forest systems serving users with similar socioeconomic attributes located
in one ecological zone of Nepal. In Dhulikhel, the forest is legally a national government forest and formally administered by a local district forest office. Little
consensus exists among the users of the Dhulikhel Forest regarding harvesting
practices, and no mechanisms exist for the users to express their views about
the rules that should be used. In Jyalachitti, the forest was handed over to a
formally established forest user group (FUG) in 1992. Since then, the FUG has
developed its own rules based on local customs, livelihood strategies, and the
socioeconomic context. The rules have been designed to enhance the regrowth of
the Jyalachitti Forest, which was severely degraded in the 1960s when it was still
a national forest. Gautam and Shivakoti reported considerable regrowth in the
Jyalachitti Forest, but indicated that conditions were worsening in the Dhulikhel
Forest. The two forests also differed in regard to graduated sanctions and the
extent of conflict resolution mechanisms that, together with having their own
collective choice arrangements, have enabled the users of the Jyalachitti Forest to
achieve considerable improvement as contrasted to the Dhulikhel Forest.

Monitoring and Graduated Sanctions   In some cases, there was a little confusion between the process of monitoring and the process of sanctioning. Scholars, such as Wilson (2007), also pointed out the importance of environmental monitoring in complex ecological systems as well as monitoring the behavior of other users. Most of the studies coded in the spring of 2008 agreed with the importance of monitoring and graduated sanctions. Gautam and Shivakoti (2005, 169) recommended an addition to this principle that "there is no external pressure, which can effectively undermine local monitoring efforts" since they observed external processes that undermined effective monitoring and sanctioning in one of the forests they studied. Sarker and Itoh (2001) examined a set of long-enduring Japanese irrigation systems and found that while there were no official rules establishing monitoring arrangements and graduated sanctions, these principles implicitly characterized most of the irrigation systems they studied.

In the Guatemalan community that Hallum analyzed, she found that the users of the resource monitored compliance with harvesting rules using the maps and schedules they developed as they themselves used the forest. She pointed out that "in a close-knit rural community, it is very difficult for anyone to 'get away with' infractions" (2008, 17). If rules were broken, the sanctions tended to range from extra work assignments (in the community tree nursery or transplanting) to a reduction in access for obtaining firewood for infractions that were more serious. If even more serious rules were broken, a special meeting might be called at the local church and the church bell rung to call attendance and attention.

Trawick analyzed a community irrigation system in Peru where the farmers developed a contiguous pattern for irrigating one section of the system at a time before moving to other sections. This system was effective at conserving water, but it also made irrigation a public affair and monitoring much easier:

> Since everyone knows the rules that govern distribution, and thus the
> exact order in which they are supposed to receive water, and because
> the owners of adjoining parcels tend to irrigate on the same day, people
> are normally putting their fields in order, or simply waiting and watch-
> ing, while their neighbors finish their turns. This means that monitoring,
> an essential function in any irrigation system, is pervasive and routine,
> spread out among users throughout the system, rather than a special task
> put entirely in the hands of the water distributor. The vigilance helps the
> distributors in ensuring that traditional procedures are followed, and it
> has the vital effect of providing controls upon theft, favoritism on the part
> of water officials, and other forms of corruption. (2001, 15)

One of my own vivid recollections from doing fieldwork in the Middle Hills of Nepal during the 1990s was seeing an enclosed field with a domesticated cow in the center of a village. In response to my question about what was happening, my Nepali colleagues indicated that the enclosure was a kind of "cow jail." When three adult members of the local farmer-managed irrigation system agreed that a member had not followed water harvesting or maintenance rules after receiving a verbal warning, they were authorized to bring a cow from the errant farmer's fields to the village area. In an agricultural village, everyone knows who owns a cow. Thus, while the cow was grazing in the center of the village and producing milk for the village council to distribute, all the farmer's neighbors were learning about the farmer's nonperformance. Once the farmer had paid a modest fee for breaking the rules, the cow would be returned, so this second-stage sanction was not severe in the long run. Needless to say, most members of the irrigation system preferred to follow the rules rather than being embarrassed by this form of a graduated sanction.

Conflict Resolution Mechanisms   The need for relatively low-cost, speedy, and effective conflict resolution mechanisms had general support from the authors of the 33 studies. Gautam and Shivakoti described the provisions for conflict resolution in Jyalachitti—their successful case: "The forest users' committee usually resolves smaller internal conflicts, particularly related to the harvest and distribution of forest products. More complicated conflicts internal to the FUG are resolved in FUG assemblies, sometimes with facilitation by local forestry staff. The FUG seeks support from the DFO for resolving conflicts arising from external factors. Being a semiautonomous entity, the FUG has the right to go to court for more serious conflicts, but that has not yet happened" (2005, 165).

The problem of conflict resolution in their second, and less successful, case is more complicated given the substantial differences in views of how the forest should be managed and the fact that "traditional mechanisms for dealing with internal conflicts that worked for centuries have eroded in recent years due to strong political divisions among the users." They concluded that the "institutions governing the Dhulikhel forest system have also failed to provide low-cost, local arenas to resolve conflict" (Gautam and Shivakoti 2005, 165).

Minimal Recognition of the Rights to Organize   Considerable evidence exists in the case studies that violations of the principle of minimal recognition of the right to organize have been associated with less successful community-based resource management regimes. Sometimes NGOs that are created to help local groups, as well as government agencies, overlook the authority of locals. Morrow and Hull suggested the following wording: "The rights and ability of appropriators to devise their own institutions are not challenged by any other authorities, internal or external, that have the ability to undermine the institution" (1996, 1651). Gautam and Shivakoti (2005) made a similar recommendation.

Nested Enterprises   Scholars focusing on pastoral and irrigation systems stressed the importance of nesting smaller common-property systems in larger and still larger ones, given the high probability of their having cross-scale physical relationships (Lane and Scoones 1993; Niamir-Fuller 1998). Marshall (2008) described the challenge of applying this principle in designing more effective community-based environmental governance systems in Australia while agreeing with its importance. He stated that the "principle of subsidiarity" is helpful in understanding and applying the concept of nesting (see also McKean 2002). This principle implies "that any particular task should be decentralized to the lowest level of governance with the capacity to conduct it satisfactorily" (Marshall 2008, 80).

Armitage related the principle of nested enterprises to the concept of multilevel systems that is an essential attribute of natural systems analyzed by ecologists related to their resilience. He provided an overview of diverse experiences with linking governance and ecology across scales in Cambodia, Canada, India, Indonesia, and Sweden (2008, 12–13). As have others (myself included), Armitage warned against using design principles as a recipe in a top-down design process, pointing out that:

> Issues of power and control, the social construction of problems, knowledge valuation and the positioning of different groups suggest that adaptive, multi-level governance in specific places and at specific times is dependent on variables and events that require thoughtful deconstruction. . . . Deliberative processes which encourage reflection, observation and opportunities for communication and persuasion among social actors where uncertainties are high (see Stern 2005) will be important in helping to articulate the full range of principles, values, models and assumptions. (2008, 25–26)

Thus, the nesting principle is shown to be important, but without providing a simple formula that can be applied in a routine manner. Authors have stressed the importance of this principle and the multiple ways that it has been interpreted and applied in the field.

Where to from Here?

Scholars have looked critically at the relevance of the design principles and generally agree that they are capturing some important underlying elements in the wide diversity of institutional arrangements of groups that have sustainably used their resources over time. It appears that there are some advantages to rephrasing and expanding some of the design principles, and this will take place after additional articles have been analyzed and entered into the database. The major thrust of the revisions will likely be to clarify them and to add further related attributes.

Another task will be to address the question of whether meeting all the design principles is a necessary—or a necessary and sufficient—condition for robust and sustainable resources and long-lived institutions. Given the complexity of the resources that are included in the broad definition of common-pool resources, it is unlikely that any list of design principles could be both necessary and sufficient conditions for robustness. A group that designs a property rights system that meets most of the design principles has increased the probability of its surviving many disturbances over time and being robust. Further, if none of the design principles are present, relatively rapid failure can be predicted—as many empirical studies have shown.

Using the Design Principles

There is a danger that project planners searching for the right design will try to build a one-size-fits-all project based on the design principles (Campbell et al. 2006). It is important to match the rules of a system to the underlying biophysical world and type of human community involved. The question is often raised, however, of how the design principles can be used in practice in addition to their use in organizing continuing research.

Michael McGinnis (personal communication) has suggested drawing on the work of Herbert Simon (1972, 1981, 1995, 1999), who stressed the complexity of designing humanly engineered systems, whether they be computers, road networks, or institutional arrangements. My earlier work related to the impossibility of doing a complete analysis of a complex, adaptive system was strongly influenced by Simon's work. Simon pointed out that where one begins a search to improve the importance of a complex system can make a substantial difference in the quality and speed of the search process. Thus, in thinking about the practical implications of the design principles, one approach is to think of them as the starting point for conducting a search of appropriate means of solving problems. The principles can then be translated into a series of questions about improving the robustness of a common-pool resource system, such as this rough translation of the first six design principles:

1. How can we better define the boundaries of this resource and of the individuals who are authorized to use it so as to ensure clarity in who is authorized to harvest and where harvesting is authorized?
2. How can we improve the relationship between the benefits received and the contributions to the necessary costs of sustaining this system?
3. How can we enhance the participation of those involved in making key decisions about this system?
4. Who is monitoring this system, and do they face appropriate incentives given the challenge of monitoring?
5. What are the sanctions we are authorizing, and can they be adjusted so that someone who makes an error or a small rule infraction is warned sufficiently so as to ensure longer-term compliance without having to impose unrealistic sanctions?
6. What local and regional mechanisms exist to resolve conflicts arising over the use of a resource? (Ostrom 2005, 270–271)

Since the seventh and eighth principles relate to higher levels of governance, they could be translated as:

7. Are there functional and creative efforts by local appropriators to create effective stewardship mechanisms for local resources that should be recognized?
8. How do we create a multiple-layer, polycentric system that can be dynamic, adaptive, and effective over time?

Of course, these are not the only questions that local users and officials should ask in trying to implement an effective design process, but given the substantial evidence that the design principles do characterize successful systems, they can be thought of as a good beginning. We all face a long list of questions to be pursued in our future work.

REFERENCES

*Abernethy, Charles, and Sally M. Hilmy. 2000. Experiences of some government-sponsored organizations of irrigators in Niger and Burkina Faso, West Africa. *Journal of Applied Irrigation Studies* 35(2):177–205.

Abreau, Dilip. 1988. On the theory of infinitely repeated games with discounting. *Econometrica* 80(4):383–396.

*Adams, William M., Elizabeth E. Watson, and Samuel K. Mutiso. 1997. Water, rules and gender: Water rights in an indigenous irrigation system, Marakwet, Kenya. *Development and Change* 28(4):707–730.

*Agrawal, Arun. 1994. Rules, rule making, and rule breaking: Examining the fit between rule systems and resource use. In *Rules, games, and common-pool resources*, ed. Elinor Ostrom, Roy Gardner, and James Walker, 267–282. Ann Arbor: University of Michigan Press.

———. 1999. *Greener pastures: Politics, markets, and community among a migrant pastoral people.* Durham, NC: Duke University Press.

*———. 2002. Common resources and institutional sustainability. In *The drama of the commons*, ed. Elinor Ostrom, Thomas Dietz, Nives Dolšak, Paul Stern, Susan Stonich, and Elke Weber, 41–85. Washington, DC: National Academy Press.

*Agrawal, Arun, and Gautam N. Yadama. 1997. How do local institutions mediate market and population pressures on resources? Forest Panchayats in Kumaon, India. *Development and Change* 28:435–465.

Ahn, Toh-Kyeong, and Elinor Ostrom. 2008. Social capital and collective action. In *The handbook of social capital*, ed. Dario Castiglione, Jan van Deth, and Guglielmo Wolleb, 70–100. Oxford: Oxford University Press.

*Citations for papers that evaluated design principles developed in *Governing the Commons*.

Alchian, Armen A., and Harold Demsetz. 1972. Production, information costs, and economic organization. *American Economic Review* 62(5):777–795.

*Alcorn, Janis, and Victor Toledo. 1998. Resilient resource management in Mexico's forest ecosystems: The contribution of property rights. In *Linking social and ecological systems*, ed. Fikret Berkes and Carl Folke, 216–249. Cambridge: Cambridge University Press.

Anderies, J. Marty, Marco Janssen, and Elinor Ostrom. 2004. A framework to analyze the robustness of social-ecological systems from an institutional perspective. *Ecology and Society* 9(1):18.

Armitage, Derek. 2008. Governance and the commons in a multi-level world. *International Journal of the Commons* 2(1):7–32.

*Baland, Jean-Marie, and Jean-Philippe Platteau. 1996. *Halting degradation of natural resources: Is there a role for rural communities?* Oxford: Clarendon Press.

Berkes, Fikret, ed. 1989. *Common property resources: Ecology and community-based sustainable development*. London: Belhaven Press.

*———. 2002. Cross-scale institutional linkages: Perspectives from the bottom up. In *The drama of the commons*, ed. Elinor Ostrom, Thomas Dietz, Nives Dolšak, Paul Stern, Susan Stonich, and Elke Weber, 293–321. Washington, DC: National Academy Press.

———. 2007. Community-based conservation in a globalized world. *Proceedings of the National Academy of Sciences* 104(39):15188–15193.

Campbell, Bruce M., Iain J. Gordon, Marty K. Luckert, Lisa Petheram, and Susanne Vetter. 2006. In search of optimal stocking regimes in semi-arid grazing lands: One size does not fit all. *Ecological Economics* 60(1):75–85.

*Campbell, Bruce M., Alois Mandondo, Nontokozo Nemarundwe, Bevlyne Sithole, Wil de Jong, Marty Luckert, and Frank Matose. 2001. Challenges to proponents of common property resource systems: Despairing voices from the social forests of Zimbabwe. *World Development* 29(4):589–600.

Carlson, Jean M., and John Doyle. 2002. Complexity and robustness. *Proceedings of the National Academy of Sciences* 99 (suppl. 1; February 19):2499–2545.

Ciriacy-Wantrup, Siegfried V., and Richard C. Bishop. 1975. "Common property" as a concept in natural resource policy. *Natural Resources Journal* 15(4):713–727.

Clark, Colin. 2006. *The worldwide crisis in fisheries: Economic models and human behavior*. Cambridge: Cambridge University Press.

*Cleaver, Frances. 2000. Moral ecological rationality, institutions and the management of common property resources. *Development and Change* 31(2):361–383.

Coase, Ronald H. 1960. The problem of social cost. *Journal of Law and Economics* 3:1–44.

Coleman, Eric, and Brian Steed. 2008. Monitoring and sanctioning in the commons: An application to forestry. Working paper, Workshop in Political Theory and Policy Analysis, Indiana University, Bloomington.

Commons, John R. 1968 (1924). *Legal foundations of capitalism*. Madison: University of Wisconsin Press.

Cousins, Ben. 2000. Tenure and common property resources in Africa. In *Evolving land rights, policy and tenure in Africa*, ed. Camilla Toulmin and Julian F. Quan, 151–180. London: DFID/IIED/NRI.

Davis, Douglas D., and Charles A. Holt. 1993. *Experimental economics*. Princeton, NJ: Princeton University Press.

Demsetz, Harold. 1967. Toward a theory of property rights. *American Economic Review* 57:347–359.

Dietz, Thomas, Elinor Ostrom, and Paul Stern. 2003. The struggle to govern the commons. *Science* 302(5652):1907–1912.

Dolšak, Nives, and Elinor Ostrom, eds. 2003. *The commons in the new millennium: Challenges and adaptations*. Cambridge, MA: MIT Press.

Ensminger, Jean. 1990. Co-opting the elders: The political economy of state incorporation in Africa. *American Anthropologist* 92:662–675.

———. 2000. Experimental economics in the bush: Why institutions matter. In *Institutions, contracts and organizations*, ed. Claude Menard, 158–171. London: Edward Elgar.

———. 2001. Reputations, trust, and the principal agent problem. In *Trust in society*, ed. Karen S. Cook, 185–201. New York: Russell Sage Foundation.

Feeny, David, Susan Hanna, and Arthur F. McEvoy. 1996. Questioning the assumptions of the "tragedy of the commons" model of fisheries. *Land Economics* 72(2):187–205.

*Gautam, Ambika P., and Ganesh P. Shivakoti. 2005. Conditions for successful local collective action in forestry: Some evidence from the hills of Nepal. *Society and Natural Resources* 18:153–171.

Ghate, Rucha. 2000. The role of autonomy in self-organizing processes: A case study of local forest management in India. Paper presented at the Workshop in Political Theory and Policy Analysis Mini-Conference, Indiana University, Bloomington.

*Gibson, Clark. 2001. Forest resources: Institutions for local governance in Guatemala. In *Protecting the commons: A framework for resource management in the Americas*, ed. Joanna Burger, Elinor Ostrom, Richard B. Norgaard, David Policansky, and Bernard D. Goldstein, 71–89. Washington, DC: Island Press.

Gibson, Clark, Krister Andersson, Elinor Ostrom, and Sujai Shivakumar. 2005. *The Samaritan's dilemma: The political economy of development aid*. New York: Oxford University Press.

Gibson, Clark, John T. Williams, and Elinor Ostrom. 2005. Local enforcement and better forests. *World Development* 33(2):273–284.

Gordon, H. Scott. 1954. The economic theory of a common property resource: The fishery. *Journal of Political Economy* 62:124–142.

Grafton, R. Quinton. 2000. Governance of the commons: A role for the state. *Land Economics* 76(4):504–517.

*Guillet, David. 1992. *Covering ground: Communal water management and the state in the Peruvian highlands*. Ann Arbor: University of Michigan Press.

Hallum, Anne Motley. 2008. Finding common ground: Designing institutions for development and conservation in Central America. Paper presented at the colloquium at the Workshop in Political Theory and Policy Analysis, Indiana University, Bloomington.

Hardin, Garrett. 1968. The tragedy of the commons. *Science* 162:1243–1248.

Hayes, Tanya, and Elinor Ostrom. 2005. Conserving the world's forests: Are protected areas the only way? *Indiana Law Review* 37(3):595–617.

Hutchings, Jeffrey A. 2000. Collapse and recovery of marine fishes. *Nature* 406:882–885.

Jackson, Jeremy B. C., Michael Kirby, Wolfgang Berger, Karen Bjorndal, Louis Botsford, Bruce Bourque, Roger Bradbury, Richard Cooke, Jon Erlandson, James Estes,

Terence Hughes, Susan Kidwell, Carina Lange, Hunter Lenihan, John Pandolfi, Charles Peterson, Robert Steneck, Mia Tegner, and Robert Warner. 2001. Historical overfishing and the recent collapse of coastal ecosystems. *Science* 293:629–638.

Janssen, Marco A., and John M. Anderies. 2007. Robustness trade-offs in social-ecological systems. *International Journal of the Commons* 1(1):43–66.

Johnson, Ronald N., and Gary D. Libecap. 1982. Contracting problems and regulation: The case of the fishery. *American Economic Review* 72(5):1005–1023.

*Lam, Wai Fung. 1998. *Governing irrigation systems in Nepal: Institutions, infrastructure, and collective action.* Oakland, CA: ICS Press.

*Lane, Charles, and Ian Scoones. 1993. Barabaig natural resource management. In *The world's savannas*, ed. Michael D. Young and Otto T. Solbirg. Paris: UNESCO and Parthenon.

Leach, Melissa, Robin Mearns, and Ian Scoones. 1997. Challenges to community-based sustainable development: Dynamics, entitlements, institutions. *IDS Bulletin* 28(4):4–14.

Lichbach, Mark I. 1996. *The cooperator's dilemma.* Ann Arbor: University of Michigan Press.

Lovejoy, Thomas E. 2006. Protected areas: A prism for a changing world. *Trends in Ecology and Evolution* 21(6):329–333.

Marshall, Graham R. 2005. *Economics for collaborative environmental management: Renegotiating the commons.* London: Earthscan.

———. 2008. Nesting, subsidiarity, and community-based environmental governance at the local level. *International Journal of the Commons* 2(1):75–97.

McCay, Bonnie J., and James M. Acheson. 1987. *The question of the commons: The culture and ecology of communal resources.* Tucson: University of Arizona Press.

McKean, Margaret A. 1982. The Japanese experience with scarcity: Management of traditional common lands. *Environmental Review* 6:63–88.

*———. 1992. Success on the commons: A comparative examination of institutions for common property resource management. *Journal of Theoretical Politics* 4(3):247–282.

———. 2002. Nesting institutions for complex common-pool resource systems. In *Proceedings of the 2nd International Symposium on Landscape Futures, December 2001*, ed. Justine Graham, Ian R. Reeve, and David J. Brunckhorst. Armidale, Australia: Institute for Rural Futures, University of New England.

Mehta, Lyla, Melissa Leach, Peter Newell, Ian Scoones, Kartik Sivaramakrishnan, and Sally Way. 1999. Exploring understandings of institutions and uncertainty: New directions in natural resource management. IDS Discussion Paper no. 372. Brighton: University of Sussex.

*Morrow, Christopher E., and Rebecca Watts Hull. 1996. Donor-initiated common pool resource institutions: The case of the Yanesha Forestry Cooperative. *World Development* 24(10):1641–1657.

National Research Council (NRC). 1986. *Proceedings of the Conference on Common Property Resource Management.* Washington, DC: National Academy Press.

———. 2002. *The drama of the commons*, ed. Elinor Ostrom, Thomas Dietz, Nives Dolšak, Paul Stern, Susan Stonich, and Elke Weber. Washington, DC: National Academy Press.

Netting, Robert McC. 1981. *Balancing on an alp: Ecological change and continuity in a Swiss mountain community.* New York: Cambridge University Press.

*Niamir-Fuller, Maryam. 1998. The resilience of pastoral herding in Sahelian Africa. In *Linking social and ecological systems*, ed. Fikret Berkes and Carl Folke. Cambridge: Cambridge University Press.

Ostrom, Elinor. 1990. *Governing the commons: The evolution of institutions for collective action*. New York: Cambridge University Press.

———. 1998. A behavioral approach to the rational choice theory of collective action. *American Political Science Review* 92(1):1–22.

———. 2001. Reformulating the commons. In *Protecting the commons: A framework for resource management in the Americas*, ed. Joanna Burger, Elinor Ostrom, Richard B. Norgaard, David Policansky, and Bernard D. Goldstein, 17–41. Washington, DC: Island Press.

———. 2005. *Understanding institutional diversity*. Princeton, NJ: Princeton University Press.

———. 2007a. Collective action theory. In *The Oxford handbook of comparative politics*, ed. Carles Boix and Susan C. Stokes, 186–208. Oxford: Oxford University Press.

———. 2007b. A diagnostic approach for going beyond panaceas. *Proceedings of the National Academy of Sciences* 104(39):15181–15187.

Ostrom, Elinor, Roy Gardner, and James Walker. 1994. *Rules, games, and common-pool resources*. Ann Arbor: University of Michigan Press.

Ostrom, Elinor, and Harini Nagendra. 2006. Insights on linking forests, trees, and people from the air, on the ground, and in the laboratory. *Proceedings of the National Academy of Sciences* 103(51):19224–19231.

Platteau, Jean-Philippe. 2003. Community based development in the context of within group heterogeneity. Paper presented at the Annual Bank Conference on Development Economics, Bangalore, India.

———. 2004. Monitoring elite capture in community-driven development. *Development and Change* 35(2):223–246.

Posner, Richard. 1977. *Economic analysis of law*. Boston: Little, Brown.

Poteete, Amy, and Elinor Ostrom. 2008. Fifteen years of empirical research on collective action in natural resource management: Struggling to build large-N databases based on qualitative research. *World Development* 36(1):176–195.

*Quinn, Claire H., Meg Huby, Hilda Kiwasila, and Jon C. Lovett. 2007. Design principles and common pool resource management: An institutional approach to evaluating community management in semi-arid Tanzania. *Journal of Environmental Management* 84(1):100–113.

Raymond, L. 2003. *Private rights in public resources: Equity and property allocation in market-based environmental policy*. Washington, DC: Resources for the Future.

*Rodriguez, S. 2007. *Acequia: Water-sharing, sanctity, and place*. Santa Fe, NM: School for Advanced Research Press.

Rudel, Thomas K. 2005. *Tropical forests: Regional paths of destruction and regeneration in the late twentieth century*. New York: Columbia University Press.

Sally, David. 1995. Conversation and cooperation in social dilemmas: A meta-analysis of experiments from 1958 to 1992. *Rationality and Society* 7:58–92.

*Sarker, Ashutosh, and Tadao Itoh. 2001. Design principles in long-enduring institutions of Japanese irrigation common-pool resources. *Agricultural Water Management* 48(2):89–102.

Schelling, Thomas C. 1978. *Micromotives and macrobehavior*. New York: W. W. Norton.

Schlager, Edella. 1990. Model specification and policy analysis: The governance of coastal fisheries. Ph.D. diss., Indiana University, Bloomington.

———. 1994. Fishers' institutional responses to common-pool resource dilemmas. In *Rules, games, and common-pool resources*, ed. Elinor Ostrom, Roy Gardner, and James Walker, 247–265. Ann Arbor: University of Michigan Press.

Schlager, Edella, and Elinor Ostrom. 1992. Property-rights regimes and natural resources: A conceptual analysis. *Land Economics* 68(3):249–262.

Schweik, Charles. 2000. Optimal foraging, institutions, and forest change: A case from Nepal. In *People and forests: Communities, institutions, and governance*, ed. Clark Gibson, Margaret McKean, and Elinor Ostrom, 57–85. Cambridge, MA: MIT Press.

*Schweik, Charles, Keshav Adhikari, and Kala Nidhi Pandit. 1997. Land-cover change and forest institutions: A comparison of two sub-basins in the southern Siwalik Hills of Nepal. *Mountain Research and Development* 17(2):99–116.

Shepsle, Kenneth A. 1989. Studying institutions: Some lessons from the rational choice approach. *Journal of Theoretical Politics* 1(2):131–149.

Simon, Herbert A. 1972. Theories of bounded rationality. In *Decision and organization: A volume in honor of Jacob Marschak*, ed. C. B. McGuire and Roy Radner, 161–176. Amsterdam: North Holland.

———. 1981. *The sciences of the artificial*. 2nd ed. Cambridge, MA: MIT Press.

———. 1995. Near decomposability and complexity: How a mind resides in a brain. In *The mind, the brain, and complex adaptive systems*, ed. Harold J. Morowitz and Jerome L. Singer, 25–44. Reading, MA: Addison-Wesley.

———. 1999. The potlatch between political science and economics. In *Competition and cooperation: Conversations with Nobelists about economics and political science*, ed. James Alt, Margaret Levi, and Elinor Ostrom, 112–119. New York: Russell Sage Foundation.

*Singleton, Sara, and Michael Taylor. 1992. Common property, collective action and community. *Journal of Theoretical Politics* 4(3):309–324.

*Steins, Nathalie A., and Victoria M. Edwards. 1999a. Collective action on common pool resource management: The contribution of a social constructivist perspective to existing theory. *Society and Natural Resources* 12:539–557.

———. 1999b. Synthesis: Platforms for collective action in multiple-use common-pool resources. *Agriculture and Human Values* 16(3):309–315.

Steins, Nathalie A., Niels G. Röling, and Victoria M. Edwards. 2000. Re-"designing" the principles: An interactive perspective to CPR theory. Paper presented at the 8th conference of the International Association for the Study of Common Property, Bloomington, Indiana.

Stern, Paul. 2005. Deliberative methods for understanding environmental systems. *BioScience* 55(11):976–982.

Sundberg, Juanita. 1998. NGO landscapes in the Maya Biosphere Reserve, Guatemala. *Geographical Review* 88(3):388–412.

Tang, Shui Yan. 1992. *Institutions and collective action: Self-governance in irrigation*. San Francisco: ICS Press.

———. 1994. Institutions and performance in irrigation systems. In *Rules, games, and common-pool resources*, ed. Elinor Ostrom, Roy Gardner, and James Walker, 225–245. Ann Arbor: University of Michigan Press.

Terborgh, J. 1999. *Requiem for nature*. Washington, DC: Island Press.

————. 2000. The fate of tropical forests: A matter of stewardship. *Conservation Biology* 14(5):1358–1361.

*Trawick, Paul B. 2001. Successfully governing the commons: Principles of social organization in an Andean irrigation system. *Human Ecology* 29(1):1–25.

*Tucker, Catherine. 1999. Common property design principles and development in a Honduran community. *Praxis: The Fletcher Journal of Development Studies* 14:1–23.

*Tucker, Catherine, J. C. Randolph, and Edwin J. Castellanos. 2007. Institutions, biophysical factors and history: An integrative analysis of private and common property forests in Guatemala and Honduras. *Human Ecology* 35(3):259–274.

*Turner, Matthew D. 1999. Conflict, environmental change, and social institutions in dryland Africa: Limitations of the community resource management approach. *Society and Natural Resources* 12(7):643–658.

*Welch, John R. 1996. The dry and the drier. In *Canals and communities: Small-scale irrigation systems*, ed. Jonathan B. Mabry. Tucson: University of Arizona Press.

Whitford, Andy B. 2002. Threats, institutions and regulation in common pool resources. *Policy Sciences* 35(2):125–139.

Wilson, James. 2007. Scale and costs of fishery conservation. *International Journal of the Commons* 1(1):29–42.

*Wittayapak, Chusak, and Philip Dearden. 1999. Decision-making arrangements in community-based watershed management in northern Thailand. *Society and Natural Resources* 12(7):673–691.

*Yandle, Tracy. 2006. Sharing natural resource management responsibility: Examining the New Zealand Rock Lobster co-management experience. *Policy Sciences* 39:249–278.

*Yoder, Robert. 1994. *Locally managed irrigation systems*. Colombo, Sri Lanka: International Irrigation Management Institute.

*Young, Oran R. 2002. *The institutional dimensions of environmental change: Fit, interplay, and scale*. Cambridge, MA: MIT Press.

3

U.S. Private Property Rights in International Perspective

Harvey M. Jacobs

T his is a period of history in which there is intense focus upon and interest in private property rights and in the U.S. experience with these rights. This chapter first discusses briefly the nature of and reasons for this global interest, after which it turns to the U.S. experience with private property rights. In this discussion, both how and why the particular legal and social configurations of private property rights emerged in the United States are examined as well as the historical and contemporary tensions about these configurations. Finally, the chapter concludes with some thoughts on the transferability of the U.S. experience both to other developed countries (most particularly Western Europe) and to transition and developing countries.

The Global Interest in Private Property Rights —————————

Private property is a social and legal institution with a long history (Schlatter 1951). It has come into contemporary focus because of the changing nature of the global political economy.

With the fall of the Berlin Wall in the late 1980s and the dissolution of the Soviet Union in the early 1990s, some commentators believed that the grand social debates of the twentieth century were finished (Fukuyama 1989). Throughout the century, the debates had been structured by the relative merits of conflicting political economies: socialism versus capitalism and communism versus democracy. In the new era, it seemed that only one set of ideas would prevail: capitalism and democracy.[1] The new countries of Central and Eastern Europe and the former Soviet Union, which had had dependent relationships with the former Soviet Union, as well as other countries that were undergoing their own independent political changes (such as South Africa) began asking themselves and others how to become more integral to the global community. How does a country acquire the economic standing of the advanced developed countries? How does a country acquire the political legitimacy of the advanced developed countries? How does a country acquire capitalism and democracy? These became among the most pressing sets of questions of the late twentieth century.

An answer seemed to center on private property. Private property was the literal key to a market-based capitalist economy; likewise, private property was central to democratic political structures.

Over the last two decades, developing and transition countries around the world have, with the counsel of the multilateral and bilateral international aid agencies, moved to introduce the social and legal institutions of private property (Deininger 2003). This tendency has been further aided by advocacy suggesting that the creation of private property is the central variable to alleviation of poverty in developing countries (de Soto 2000).

In the last few years, the extent and substance of this trend has become clear. Two of the few remaining communist-led countries in the world have moved to embrace private property. In spring 2007 China made international news through its revision of national laws that established limited conditions for the ownership of private property in housing, and this spring Cuba introduced laws that would also allow the private ownership of houses (*New York Times* 2008).

All told, this has led to a global discussion of private property rights. Legal scholars are noting a "global debate over constitutional property" (Alexander 2006). Some suggest that the extent of private property rights serves as a reliable indicator of both economic strength and political freedom, leading to global rankings of private property rights robustness (Bethell 1998; Thallam 2008).

The U.S. Experience with Private Property Rights

As the global discussion about private property rights has accelerated, one focus has been the U.S. experience. The United States is commonly and broadly understood to be a strong private property nation and to have lengthy experience with private property rights as the bases for both its economic system and its political system (de Soto 2000; Thallam 2008).

---

1. Huntington's (1997) notion of a "clash of civilizations" is an alternate concept to the one advanced by Fukuyama (1989).

THE COLONIAL ERA

The role and place of private property rights was a subject of intense interest and debate among the country's founders. For a variety of reasons—philosophical, historical, and contemporary—there was a clear sense that the right to hold and control property rights was an important element of a democratic governmental structure (Ely 1992).

First there was the reality of the settlement process. Colonial America was settled by Europeans searching for religious and political freedom (the rights guaranteed in the First Amendment of the Bill of Rights of the U.S. Constitution) and for access to land (Ely 1992). In America's early years, European countries were still structured under the vestiges of feudalism. An elite owned most of the land, and the prospects for the ordinary person to obtain freehold (obligation-free) ownership were small. America offered an alternative. It was a place where any white male immigrant could get ownership of land and, with that land as capital, make a future for himself. America was, quite literally, the land of opportunity (Schleuning 1997; Scott 1977).

In America's colonial past, the existence of land converged nicely with the then-new political theories. In particular, drawing from the work of John Locke, ideas circulated about ownership and democracy. A person came to possess property through using it (which provided the justification for taking land from America's native inhabitants, who were not using it in the European sense of active agricultural and forest management), and freely constituted governments (democracies) existed for the protection of individual liberties, including the liberty to hold and control property.

The country's founders configured these ideas into a particular and specific relationship. Some argued that one of the principal functions of forming a government was protection of property. In the debate over the ratification of the proposed U.S. Constitution, James Madison wrote in *Federalist* 54 in 1788 that "government is instituted no less for the protection of property than of the persons of individuals" (Hamilton, Madison, and Jay 1961, 339). Others, including Alexander Hamilton and John Adams, concurred. Adams noted that "property must be secured or liberty cannot exist. The moment the idea is admitted into society that property is not as sacred as the laws of God, and that there is not a force of law and public justice to protect it, anarchy and tyranny commence" (1851 [1790], 280).

It was perhaps Thomas Jefferson who left modern Americans with their most enduring image of this perspective: that of the yeoman farmer. For Jefferson the idea of the yeoman farmer linked the individual's right to own and control property with the very existence and viability of democracy. According to Jefferson, because the yeoman farmer owned his own farm and could produce food and fuel for himself and his family, he was obligated to no one; he was literally free to exercise his political views as a democrat. For Jefferson the very act of ownership created the conditions that allowed democracy to exist (Scott 1977).

This view of the relationship of property to democracy, and the fact of asserting property's primacy, was not unchallenged. Also drawing from Locke, others saw the need for private property ownership to bow to social needs. As John Locke himself wrote, "For it would be a direct contradiction for any one to enter into society with others for the securing and regulating of property, and yet to suppose his land, whose property is to be regulated by the laws of society, should be exempt from the jurisdiction of that government to which he himself, and the property of the land, is subject" (1952 [1690], 68–69).

Echoing these sentiments were Thomas Jefferson (a founder whose opinions can be cited by all sides to this debate), Benjamin Franklin, and others. Benjamin Franklin was perhaps the most articulate proponent of a counter-position to the camp of Madison, Adams, Hamilton, and others. For example, in the debate over the ratification of the Pennsylvania state constitution, Franklin said: "Private property is a creature of society, and is subject to the calls of the society whenever its necessities require it, even to the last farthing" (1907 [1789], 59). In other words, Franklin did not see property rights as sacrosanct.[2] Instead he appeared to view as legitimate the public's right to create, re-create, take away, and regulate property as it best served public purposes.

Property—private property—was thus a confusing issue for the founders. How were these disparate positions resolved? With ambiguity. Even before the United States emerged as a new country, colonial governments had passed local laws that seem to be clear antecedents of modern land use and environmental regulations. For example, colonial Virginia regulated tobacco-related planting practices to require crop rotation and prevent overplanting; and colonial Boston, New York City, and Charleston all regulated the location of businesses such as bakeries and slaughterhouses, often to the point of excluding them from existing within city limits (Treanor 1995).

Thus in 1776 the Declaration of Independence promised each (free white male) American "life, liberty and the pursuit of happiness." What is telling about this phrase is that Thomas Jefferson, the Declaration's author, borrowed it from Locke. Locke's phrase was "life, liberty and property." That is what Jefferson wanted the Declaration to say, as a way of furthering his vision of a nation of yeoman farmers. Jefferson's ideas, however, did not hold sway (Scott 1977).

Eleven year later, in 1787, the U.S. Constitution was adopted as a replacement for the Articles of Confederation. What did it say about land-based private

---

2. These sentiments by Franklin were not isolated. As noted by Brands, "Franklin took a striking socialistic view of property." Brands provides these examples of Franklin's opinions: "All property . . . seem to me to be the creature of public convention." "All the property that is necessary to a man for the conservation of the individual and propagation of the species is his natural right, . . . but all property superfluous to such purposes is the property of the public, who by their laws, have created it, and who may therefore by other laws dispose of it whenever the welfare of the public shall demand such disposition" (2000, 623).

property? Nothing. It was not until 1791 and the adoption of the Bill of Rights that the now contentious "takings" (expropriation) phrase appeared as the closing clause to the Fifth Amendment to the Constitution: "nor shall private property be taken for public use, without just compensation."

With the adoption of this phrase, the Constitution formally recognized four concepts: the existence of private property, an action denoted as taken, a realm of activity that is public use, and a form of payment specified as just compensation. The interrelation of these concepts is that where private property exists, it may be taken (seized by the government over the landowner's objections), but only for a denoted public use and with the provision of just compensation. If any of these conditions is not met, a taking may not occur. But the clause does not say and colonial commentary does not clarify what constitutes private property, exactly when a taking has occurred, what a public use is, and what makes up just compensation.

In the colonial period and for a century afterward, disagreements about the place of private property in a democracy and the exact meaning of the takings clause were largely theoretical. There was little public infringement on private property rights. The new country had land in abundance, and the disposition of public land, not the acquisition or regulation of private land, dominated the public agenda (Gates 1968). Not until the twentieth century did this change.

THE TWENTIETH-CENTURY LEGAL FRAMEWORK

The twentieth century ushered in an entirely different period in the American experience relative to private property rights. The American frontier was settled: western acquisition and expansion had been completed (Gates 1968; Turner 1893). Public policy focus shifted from the disposition of America's public lands to the management of its land resources. With this shift, America experienced a significant reconfiguration of its demographic and spatial makeup. The 1920 U.S. Census officially recorded the shift from a rural to an urban nation (Scott 1969). The years 1880 to 1920 were a period of intensive immigration, industrialization, and urbanization. In response to these conditions, modern land policy and the modern relationship of the state to the individual via private property rights were born. Cities and states began to pass regulations to manage public health and safety. The impact of these regulations was to burden individual landowners, both private and corporate. Out of these new spatial and economic conditions arose a concern about the appropriate limits to government regulation.

In this context and throughout the century, the U.S. Supreme Court found itself called upon to interpret the meaning of the takings clause in conditions very different than those in which it had been written. There is a huge body of scholarship about how to understand and approach the jurisprudence of the Court (examples written for the nonspecialist audience include Bosselman, Callies, and Banta [1973] and Meltz, Merriam, and Frank [1999]). This discussion relies heavily on the analysis and interpretation of Kayden (2004).

A key case is *Pennsylvania Coal v. Mahon*, 260 U.S. 393 in 1922, in which the Court issued its famous dictum defining the twentieth-century concept of regulatory taking. The Court was asked to determine the validity of a state-based regulation that impacted the usability and integrity of mining-based private property rights. The justices had earlier validated a wide range of government regulations, some quite onerous, as long as the landowner was left with some property rights. In a decision that has echoed through the years, the Court said in *Penn Coal*: "The general rule . . . is, that while property may be regulated to a certain extent, if regulation *goes too far* it will be recognized as a taking" (415; emphasis added). In other words, a regulation can be equivalent to physical expropriation under the Fifth Amendment. If it is, however, compensation is required. But the Court did not exactly identify the location of the line that distinguishes a regulation that goes too far from a regulation that does not.

The second case of importance was the Court's ruling on the validity of zoning. New York City is credited with inventing zoning in 1916. Within a few years, zoning had spread across the country as a way for cities to manage growing populations, industrialization, and property values (Scott 1969). In 1926 the Court examined whether the idea of allowing a local government to regulate land use by designating land use zones that provided for different levels of development opportunities was acceptable (*Euclid v. Ambler Realty*, 272 U.S. 365). The Court decided that such an approach to the management of private property rights was acceptable.

As the Great Depression of the 1930s loomed, the Court said that regulation that goes too far is unacceptable, but that regulation of private property rights through zoning is acceptable. So where was "too far"? The Court did not define this in advance. In practice, this was not a problem, as most governmental bodies did not use their authority to impose onerous requirements upon landowners' private property rights.

After *Euclid*, the Court largely left the property rights arena for fifty years. During this quiescent period, however, there was one important case. In 1954, in the case of *Berman v. Parker* (348 U.S. 26), the Court took up the meaning of the "public use" phrase in the takings clause, ushering in the era of urban renewal. The question before the Court was the right of government to take private property, paying compensation, when the goal was to consolidate property for redevelopment, often by another profit-making owner, all under the justification of blight. The Court upheld government's right to do this.

In 1978 the Court again entered the property rights arena with renewed vigor by seeking to establish boundaries to governmental authority. In the nearly twenty-five years since *Berman*, things had changed: the composition of the Court, and America's attention to and involvement with private property rights. Since about 1970, the United States had experienced a literal explosion of laws, policies, and regulations at the national, state, and local levels that affected private property. The Clean Air Act, Clean Water Act, Coastal Zone Management

Act, and National Environmental Policy Act were all examples at the national level (see Moss [1977] for a contemporaneous chronicling of these). Among state governments, a so-called quiet revolution in land use control had occurred in which nearly a dozen states reasserted their constitutional authority to regulate private land use activities at the state level (Bosselman and Callies 1971). Local governments across the country were beginning what has become a decades-long experiment in public policy approaches to protecting and managing farm-lands, wetlands, open spaces, watersheds, threatened habitats, urban sprawl, and so on.[3]

Between 1978 and 1994, the Court heard a series of cases in which it began to redefine the rules of interaction between government and private property owners.[4] While the Court did not eviscerate the right of government to regulate private property, it did begin to more clearly say when the line of too far articulated in *Penn Coal* had been crossed. Of the cases decided in this period, *Lucas v. South Carolina Coastal Council*, 505 U.S. 1003 (1992), received a great deal of attention. Here the Court ruled that, when regulation had taken all economically viable use, it had gone too far, and compensation was owed the landowner. The outcome of these cases was ambiguous, however. As commonly understood by private property owners and their advocates and by government officials, regulation was still acceptable, but a regulating body needed to be precise in the formulation and administration of regulations.

The twentieth century ended and the twenty-first century began with two major cases decided by the Court, both of which seem to take a step back from the boundary-setting tone of the prior period. In the 2002 case of *Tahoe-Sierra Preservation Council v. Tahoe Regional Planning Agency* (535 U.S. 302), the Court took up the matter of a nearly three-year moratorium on development in light of some of its prior boundary-setting decisions. In a decision strongly in favor of government, the Court found that planning and regulation are normal and expected governmental functions and that the Court had no reason to interfere with regular planning activity (Kayden 2002).

Then, in June 2005, the Court issued its closely watched decision in the case of *Kelo v. City of New London*, 545 U.S. 469. Pressed by property rights advocates, the Court agreed to clarify its thinking about the "public use" phrase in the takings clause, revisiting what was for some its controversial 1954 decision in *Berman v. Parker*. In the *Kelo* case, there was not even an assertion of blight

---

3. Daniels and Bowers (1997) is an example of these approaches applied to farmland protection; Nelson and Dawkins (2004) is an example of these approaches applied to urban containment.

4. Some of the most prominent and discussed examples include *Penn Central Transport Co. v. New York City*, 438 U.S. 104 (1978); *First English Evangelical Lutheran Church v. County of Los Angeles*, 482 U.S. 304 (1987); *Nollan v. California Coastal Commission*, 483 U.S. 825 (1987); *Lucas v. South Carolina Coastal Council*, 505 U.S. 1003 (1992); and *Dolan v. City of Tigard*, 512 U.S. 374 (1994).

by the city. Instead, the city asserted its right to take private property, with compensation, when the public use was defined to be consolidation of the land for distribution to another private owner in order to facilitate and further economic development in the city through new jobs and increased property tax revenues. By a one-vote margin, the Court affirmed the city's right to do this.

THE PROPERTY RIGHTS MOVEMENT

These historical and legal themes come together in the formation and subsequent activism of the so-called private property rights movement. From the perspective of this movement, the intent of key American founders and the principles embodied in the founding documents make the protection of private property rights an essential element of the American political and social contract (Jacobs 1995, 1998b; Marzulla 1996). According to this view, one of the factors that makes the United States unique is the way the right to own property and the protection of that property provide a buffer to the power of the state (Ely 1992). Through ownership and control of property, the owner has material conditions that allow him to be literally free. Following from Jefferson's idea of the yeoman farmer, ownership provides the conditions upon which liberty and the exercise of democratic citizenship are based. Without the availability of property, liberty and democracy in the American configuration are not feasible. Thus, what is needed is a national state strongly committed to the ideal and the reality of private property, the protection of this property, and the integrity of this property.[5]

This framing of American history comes together with an alarmist view of twentieth-century public policy and law. From the position of the property rights movement, in the last 100 years the United States has appeared to move away from a view of property rights as integral and central to liberty and democracy. Instead, it appears that government has been allowed ever-increasing authority to intrude upon, reshape, and take away property without respecting the protections afforded by the Constitution. Despite the promise contained in *Penn Coal* that regulation that goes too far will be recognized as a taking, in practice legislatures and the Court seem to continuously affirm the right of government over the property rights of individuals (Bosselman, Callies, and Banta 1973; Salkin 2001). Even the Court's decisions of the late 1980s and early 1990s that appeared to hold promise for reining in governmental practices seem to have had little real impact on those practices at the local, regional, and national levels (Roddewig and Duerksen 1989). In the 2002 decision in *Tahoe-Sierra* and the 2005 decision in *Kelo*, activists concerned with the integrity of private property rights have found little promise and solace from the Court.

It was in part because of this that the political and social movement for private property rights protection was born (Gottlieb 1989; Miniter 1994). Although

---

5. Brick and Cawley (1996) and Yandle (1995) provide overviews of the property rights movement; Epstein (1985) is a foundational legal argument for their position.

the movement formally came into being in 1988, its intellectual and geographic antecedents originated at least with the rise of the modern environmental movement (for example, McClaughry 1975, 1976). What exists today is a national coalition targeting national, state, and local land use and environmental laws, policies, and programs, such as those on endangered species protection, smart growth, and farmland and wetland protection (Jacobs 1995; an early listing appears in Deal 1993). This coalition argues that such attempts at the management and restriction of private property are un-American, inefficient, and ultimately ineffective.

The property rights movement has pursued a multilevel strategy to achieve its objectives—judicial, legislative, policy, and public relations (Jacobs 1999b). While its proponents approach the judicial strategy skeptically (and the outcome of the *Tahoe-Sierra* and *Kelo* cases suggests their skepticism to be well founded), they will not forgo this option because they see the property rights issue as fundamentally constitutional. However, in conceptualizing an approach for engaging the issue, they decided early to not rely on legal decisions alone, supplementing a legal strategy with a policy and legislative strategy. In the early years, this strategy was focused at the national level, exploring what could be accomplished via executive orders issued by the president and through legislation proposed in the U.S. Congress (Folsom 1993; Pollot 1989). But much to proponents' frustration, there was little outcome from this activity. Quickly, therefore, the movement's strategy shifted toward state legislatures, where they found fertile ground for their arguments and ideas.

Since 1991 every U.S. state has considered state-based legislation in support of the policy position of the property rights movement, and 27 states have passed such legislation (Emerson and Wise 1997; Jacobs 1998a, 1999b). They include both "red" and "blue" states extending from Maine to Washington and the Dakotas to Texas, and 11 of them are east of the Mississippi River. But by the late 1990s, the property rights movement had come to a policy standstill. Its proponents had been effective in passing state-based laws and in promoting county-based laws, and they had garnered significant media attention, but they had been ineffective in changing the fundamental way government at the national, state, and local levels acted toward and upon property.

Why was there dissonance between legal change, public attention, and institutional behavior? Among the reasons are the fact that some of the laws adopted in states (such as Mississippi) and counties were purely symbolic; government activity has never required nor was ever expected to require invoking their provisions. In other states (such as Kansas) and counties, these laws were adopted over the objection of the executive branches, which had the responsibility of implementing them. Therefore, the executive branches developed implementation procedures that in effect diluted the intent and impact of the laws.[6] In addition,

---

6. These two state examples draw from research detailed in Jacobs (1999b).

while the property rights argument is initially appealing, individual landowners (including property rights advocates themselves) can be wary of a regulation-free land use environment. In effect, people trust themselves to be good land managers, but few trust their neighbors.

With the dawn of the twenty-first century, the movement had an opportunity to revise its strategy, largely as a result of the election of George W. Bush (Jacobs 2003). With a sympathizer occupying the president's office, the movement decided to try again for nationally based action through the president's office and through Congress. Initially, it appeared that the movement was going to have a great deal of influence. However, several factors—principally the systemic impact of the terrorist attacks of September 11 on administration priorities and congressional realignments—forced the movement back to a state-based strategy.

RECENT ACTIVITY

In fall 2006 the property rights movement had an opportunity to demonstrate the strength of its support among the American people. In 2004 it had achieved a substantial victory in Oregon with passage of a state law, Measure 37, intended to overturn a 30-year process of centralized state planning and regulation of private property rights (Jacobs 2007, 2008a). Another factor was the significant public outcry over the U.S. Supreme Court's 2005 decision in *Kelo*.[7]

So in 2006 the movement promoted a set of votes on property rights issues in six states. Using a provision of state law that exists in some, mostly western U.S. states, citizens petitioned to have a law passed. If such a petition is adopted by a majority of those voting in the election, the petition becomes law; legislators may not interfere with its implementation. Much to the surprise of the property rights movement—and to the delight of planning's supporters—the measure failed in five of the six states in which it was proposed, including some states with long-standing, well-known, strong property rights traditions (Hannah Jacobs 2007). The reasons for the failures were varied, reflecting the nuances of state politics and particular elections. But one theme that seems to tie the failures together was the way the initiatives were promoted. In several of the states, they appeared to be funded and coordinated by a single nonlocal, nonregional, antigovernmental think tank largely funded by one person, rather than by grassroots citizens' initiatives (Ring 2006). Opponents of the initiatives (environmental and planning supporters) thus described them as efforts "by outsiders to try and tell us what to do with our communities and our land." This fact was well publicized and was believed to be part of the backlash to the proposals.

Then in 2007 the citizens of Oregon, where the measure had passed, had the opportunity, under the same voting procedure described above, to reconsider their

---

7. Measure 37, the lawsuit leading to the *Kelo* decision, and the public outcry resulting from it had been engineered by the property rights movement, a fact proudly acknowledged by its proponents.

2004 vote. Again, much to the delight of planning's advocates, voters approved Measure 49, which was touted as turning back many of the more antiplanning, pro–property rights components of 2004's Measure 37, by a margin of nearly two-thirds.

Oregon's Measure 37 had been promoted as a law that would bring justice to small landowners relative to the oppressive nature of the original (and subsequently modified) 1973 statewide planning law. The 1973 law required, among other elements, the preparation of plans by all communities in the state, the coordination of that planning effort among adjoining communities, the designation of urban growth boundaries for urban areas, and explicit programs for the protection of farmland and infill of existing urban areas. It provided a cause of action for property owners who had continuously owned land since the time of its passage. Under Measure 37 government was required either to compensate owners for the impact of rules and regulations that restricted growth and land use or to revoke the impact of those rules and regulations upon affected owners. According to the media presentation by Measure 37's proponents, a few small landowners would benefit from Measure 37. But by fall 2007, over 7,700 claims had been filed, affecting nearly 800,000 acres and totaling over $19 billion.

Measure 49 sought to address this situation of extensive claims on large amounts of acreage for astronomical sums by denying claims for commercial or industrial development and providing three pathways for people who want to build homes. It allows landowners subject to the law to (1) develop as many as three homesites under a streamlined process; (2) build as many as ten homesites after proof by appraisal that regulations had devalued property; or (3) possibly proceed with even larger subdivisions if they can establish pre–Measure 49 vested rights.

What does all this mean? How does an observer make sense of what appears to be a pendulum swing of voter actions and opinions? Votes in 2006 and 2007 do not appear to mean that social conflict over private property rights is settled in the United States. Conflicting concepts about the rights of the individual and the right of government (as representative of the community) vis-à-vis property rights is a multi-century issue, the character of which changes with the social conditions of the times (Jacobs 1999a).

In the short term, the property rights movement has shown itself to be adept at learning from its experiences in the courts, in the legislatures, and with the media. Yet, it is a long-term project. While its proponents may be frustrated by short-term setbacks, they are impassioned by their perspective on property rights and their perceived need to restrain government power and reframe public discourse (Jacobs 2007).

Will there be an ultimate or final outcome of this debate? As I have argued elsewhere, I do not believe it will ever be settled (Jacobs 1999a). It may be that fighting over conflicting concepts of property rights is both central to and necessary for the American experience.

The Transferability of the U.S. Experience

The transferability of the U.S. experience has to be divided between the lessons for other developed countries and the lessons for developing and transition countries. With regard to the former, I concentrate my remarks on the transferability of the U.S. experiences to Europe, the current focus of my research (Jacobs 2006, 2008a, 2008b). While global attention has been focused largely on the efforts in transition and developing countries to invent and implement private property, a parallel effort has been occurring in Western Europe. Countries across Europe have been engaged in two significant and parallel activities: an effort to rewrite their national planning laws, and an effort to create a European constitution and parallel implementing institutions (Jacobs 2006). These efforts fit into a decades-long pattern of planning and implementation to create the structures for an integrated Europe. While the particular effort to create a European constitution stalled in summer 2005, the broader trend of European integration continues (Reid 2004).

In the area of land policy, Europeans (or at least European governments) appear to want to self-consciously move away from their twentieth-century structure of a strong state and a weaker set of rights in the relationship over private property (at least as compared to the U.S. model), and to move explicitly toward a U.S. model of strong private rights and a relatively weaker state (Jacobs 2006). Europeans are aware of and involved in both the contemporary debate about property's role in creating and re-creating democracies and market economies, and the American experience with trying to balance the rights of the individual and of the public in relation to individually owned environmental and land resources. As part of broader trans-European dialogue and policy initiatives, professionals, activists, and policy makers are actively reconstructing a half-century-old planning, management, and regulatory system strongly based on command and control into one more individual- and market-based.

Despite what is commonly depicted as essentially differing legal systems, I see a furtherance of what has become a global project (van Erp 2006). My research suggests a convergence of perspective with regard to the legal and social status of private property rights between the United States and Europe (Jacobs 2008a).

Examples are the situations in southern France and in Norway.[8] Under French law, government has authority to designate land in the peri-urban area for permanent nongrowth status. Once the land is designated, owners have little basis to claim compensation for the designation, even when there are significant impacts on the value of the land. In addition, French law gives government the right of first refusal for purchase. This right is so strong that if owners want to sell and

---

8. Both are discussed in Jacobs 2006; the French case is discussed in more depth in Jacobs 2008b.

government offers them a reasonable price (based on the land's designated status) but owners choose to refuse the price, the owners do not have the option of then selling the land in the open market. This authority has been extensively used with regard to productive agricultural land. It would appear to give French planners a strong set of tools to manage urban growth. Yet the situation in southern France (Montpellier, Nîmes) suggests that in practice this is not the case. For a complex set of reasons, owners of peri-urban agricultural land appear to be behaving analogously to American landowners in the same situation. They are pressuring political authorities to change land designations and increasingly asserting the primacy of their property rights over a regionally defined public good in order to capture potential nonagricultural land value.

The situation in Norway is similar. While Norway, like France, has a strong tradition of private property rights, it also has a strong tradition of governmental planning of land and natural resources, as well as a well-established set of social institutions for common access to rural and natural land. Yet, in 2006 interviewees spoke of tumultuous changes in Norwegian attitudes and policy toward private property and resulting changes in the relationship between the individual and the state over property. These changes are being pushed by the decline (and expected continued decline) of government support for agriculture and the relatively newly found wealth of Norwegian families. At the same time that there is a change in state policy toward agriculture, there is an increasing demand for rural land for recreational purposes by Norwegians and others. One way a Norwegian landowner can make money from a land resource is to sell it to urban Norwegians (and continental Europeans) who have the resources to acquire it.

The status of private property rights in Norway thus has to be understood on two levels. At the formal level, the state still has strong authority over property rights, and there is essentially no (or very limited) access to a claim for regulatory-based compensation as it is understood in the United States. However, at the informal level, bureaucrats, specialists, activists, and academics believe that a fundamental change is under way in Norway. While the change has not yet expressed itself in the Norwegian system of law and administration, those interviewed shared a sentiment that the property rights of individual owners were getting stronger relative to their position in the past. What direction this trend might take and how much the change would evolve is unclear. Some interviewees suggested that they would not be surprised to see the introduction of a form of U.S.-style regulatory takings in the not-too-distant future.

Will these social transformations lead to revision of European law to become more American in form? There is a great deal of debate about this. I believe the answer is that it will (Jacobs 2008a, 2009). The way European law functions and the social pressures that are being brought upon it will create a situation analogous to the way American law functions, despite the fact that the two legal systems are rooted in two different legal traditions (Jacobs 2008a). In addition, the way the European Court of Human Rights is beginning to engage Article 1, Protocol 1 of the European Convention on Human Rights (analogous to the takings clause of the U.S. Constitution) is providing individuals, such as in France and Norway, with a vehicle to challenge the provisions of national law and administration (Jacobs 2009). The net result is likely to be essentially the same functioning of both legal systems in terms of the rights of the individual, the rights of government, and the relationship between the two.

The U.S. experience is more complex for developing and transition countries, and the situation seems far removed from many of them. For example, the United States is a country with, inter alia, high levels of private land ownership; low levels of communal, tribal, and common land tenure; a system of law and law enforcement that is well developed and generally well respected by its citizens; relatively high levels of public sector administrative transparency; a robust private sector market system; high levels of income; a relatively high standard of living; and little explicit tribal or ethnic strife.

Yet, several key elements of the U.S. experience are worth noting, including the following:

- The role of government as an active manager of private property rights comes about because of increasing urbanization, increasing market activity, and increasing threats to public health, safety, and welfare. These conditions are now global in scope and partially explain why countries around the world look to the United States for lessons from its experience.
- The appropriate balance of private property rights and public activity (through, for example, regulation) is never fixed or settled; it is continually renegotiated as a function of changing social, economic, and technological conditions.
- Social conflict over private property rights is never over; it is a continuous process precisely because of the proxy role of private property rights in social dialogue.

I have been privileged to work in several transition and developing countries in the last two decades, among them Poland (1991), Albania (1994–1996, 2001), Kenya (1996), Zimbabwe (2001–2003), and South Africa (2001–2002), and of participating in ongoing training programs for mid-career, mid-level professionals and appointed and elected officials from transition and developing countries through the Land Tenure Center of the University of Wisconsin–Madison (1991–present), the International Center for Land Policy Studies and Training of Taiwan (1994–2008), and the Institute for Housing and Urban Development Studies, Erasmus University Rotterdam, The Netherlands (2006–2008). What seems clear to me from these experiences is the misunderstanding of the U.S. situation from the perspective of transition and developing countries.

First, there is often a belief that creation of social and legal institutions for private property rights will, by themselves, create conditions for functioning markets, robust economic development, and responsible and transparent democratic governance. Conversely, there is often limited understanding of how property rights are shaped by the particular historical and cultural experiences of the United States and how current conditions have evolved over more than two centuries. So, for example, in Albania it became clear to those of us associated with the Land Tenure Center that the creation of private property rights was woefully insufficient absent a parallel legal system in which lawyers and jurists had a shared understanding of the legal and social role of private property rights. Without this, property rights creation, transfer, and transformation could seem as arbitrary as it had under the prior communist regime.

Also, there is an often naive misunderstanding that private property is about rights but not about responsibilities. Throughout Central and Eastern Europe soon after the political transition of the early 1990s, new owners were clear about what they wanted to have, and equally clear about not wanting to have to think or function within a social and collective context (often as a reaction to the forced collective behavior of the prior decades). The advantages of private property were clear to all; the need to constrain their behavior with regard to that property was not at all evident. Similarly, reformers in South Africa expected a widespread distribution of property post-apartheid to address a wide range of social justice and economic development problems. But they have not appeared to have anticipated the push back from existing (white) owners of private property and the legacy of ethnic and tribal conflict that would make the distribution of property contentious. All in all, the experience of the post–Berlin Wall, post–Soviet Union world in this last decade and a half is that private property is not necessarily the singularly magical key that some thought it could be.

The developed, transition, or developing countries should not see the United States as a cowboy country with strong, unregulated private property, or as a country with strong social consensus about the balance of individual and social rights in property, or as a country with clearly resolved principles for how to manage this balance of rights. It is important to keep in mind that the United States has a strong cultural and historical tradition that promotes and respects private property, a relatively weak legacy of government intervention with private property rights, and a system of governmental planning and policy implementation oriented toward devolution and action by local government. While there is much to learn from the U.S. experience, the international community needs to understand the United States as a place where the social value of private property rights blunts public action and fuels substantial social conflict and public and administrative behavior (Fischel 2001; Molotch 1976), and that there is every reason to expect private property rights to continue to be influenced by these factors in the immediate future.

REFERENCES

Adams, John. 1851 (1790). Discourses on Davilia, A series of papers on political history. In *The works of John Adams*, vol. 6, ed. Charles Francis Adams. Boston: Little, Brown.

Alexander, Gregory S. 2006. *The global debate over constitutional property*. Chicago: University of Chicago Press.

Bethell, Tom. 1998. *The noblest triumph: Property and prosperity through the ages*. New York: St. Martin's Press.

Bosselman, Fred P., and David Callies. 1971. *The quiet revolution in land use control*. Washington, DC: U.S. Government Printing Office.

Bosselman, Fred, David Callies, and John Banta. 1973. *The taking issue: An analysis of the constitutional limits of land use control*. Washington, DC: U.S. Government Printing Office.

Brands, H. W. 2000. *The first American: The life and times of Benjamin Franklin*. New York: Anchor Books.

Brick, Philip D., and R. McGreggor Cawley, eds. 1996. *A wolf in the garden: The land rights movement and the new environmental debate*. Lanham, MD: Rowman and Littlefield.

Daniels, Tom, and Deborah Bowers. 1997. *Holding our ground: Protecting America's farms and farmland*. Covelo, CA: Island Press.

Deal, Carl. 1993. *The Greenpeace guide to anti-environmental organizations*. Berkeley, CA: Odonian Press.

Deininger, Klaus. 2003. *Land policies for growth and poverty reduction*. A World Bank Policy Research Report. Washington, DC: The World Bank and New York: Oxford University Press.

de Soto, Hernando. 2000. *The mystery of capital: Why capitalism triumphs in the West and fails everywhere else*. New York: Basic Books.

Ely, James W., Jr. 1992. *The guardian of every other right: A constitutional history of property rights*. New York: Oxford University Press.

Emerson, Kirk, and Charles R. Wise. 1997. Statutory approaches to regulatory takings: State property rights legislation issues and implications for public administration. *Public Administration Review* 57(5):411–422.

Epstein, Richard A. 1985. *Takings: Private property and the power of eminent domain*. Cambridge, MA: Harvard University Press.

Erp, Sjef van. 2006. European and national law: Osmosis or growing antagonism? Sixth Walter van Gerven Lecture. Leuven, Belgium: Leuven Centre for a Common Law of Europe. http://ssrn.com/abstract=995979.

Fischel, William A. 2001. *The homevoter hypothesis: How home values influence local government taxation, school finance, and land-use policies*. Cambridge, MA: Harvard University Press.

Folsom, Robin E. 1993. Executive order 12,630: A president's manipulation of the Fifth Amendment's just compensation clause to achieve control over executive agency regulatory decisionmaking. *Boston College Environmental Affairs Law Review* 20(4):639–697.

Franklin, Benjamin. 1907 (1789). Queries and remarks respecting alterations in the Constitution of Pennsylvania. In *The writings of Benjamin Franklin*, vol. 10, ed. Albert H. Smith. London: Macmillan.

Fukuyama, Francis. 1989. The end of history? *The National Interest* 16 (Summer):3–18.

Gates, Paul W. 1968. *History of public land law development*. Washington, DC: U.S. Government Printing Office.

Gottlieb, Alan M., ed. 1989. *The wise use agenda*. Bellevue, WA: The Free Enterprise Press.

Hamilton, Alexander, James Madison, and John Jay. 1961 (1788). *The Federalist papers.* New York: Mentor Books.

Huntington, Samuel P. 1997. *The clash of civilizations and the remaking of world order.* New York: Touchstone.

Jacobs, Hannah. 2007. Searching for balance in the aftermath of the 2006 takings initiatives. *Yale Law Journal* 116(7):1518–1566.

Jacobs, Harvey M. 1995. The anti-environmental, "wise use" movement in America. *Land Use Law and Zoning Digest* 47(2):3–8.

———. 1998a. The impact of state property rights laws: Those laws and my land. *Land Use Law and Zoning Digest* 50(3):3–8.

———. 1998b. The "wisdom," but uncertain future, of the wise use movement. In *Who owns America? Social conflict over property rights,* ed. Harvey M. Jacobs, 29–44. Madison: University of Wisconsin Press.

———. 1999a. Fighting over land: America's legacy . . . America's future? *Journal of the American Planning Association* 65(2):141–149.

———. 1999b. *State property rights laws: The impacts of those laws on my land.* Policy Focus Report. Cambridge, MA: Lincoln Institute for Land Policy.

———. 2003. The politics of property rights at the national level: Signals and trends. *Journal of the American Planning Association* 69(2):181–189.

———. 2006. The "taking" of Europe: Globalizing the American ideal of private property? Working paper, Lincoln Institute of Land Policy, Cambridge, MA.

———. 2007. New actions or new arguments over regulatory takings? *Yale Law Journal Pocket* 117:65–70. http://yalelawjournal.org/2007/09/16/jacobs.html.

———. 2008a. The future of the regulatory taking issue in the U.S. and Europe: Divergence or convergence? *Urban Lawyer* 40(1):51–72.

———. 2008b. L'engrenage de la croissance urbaine: La place de la propriété dans la planification urbaine (The machinery of urban growth: The role of property in the planning process). *Études Foncières* 132:12–16.

———. 2009. An alternative perspective on U.S.-European property rights and land use planning: Differences without any substance. *Planning and Environmental Law* 61(3):3–12.

Kayden, Jerold S. 2002. *Tahoe-Sierra Preservation Council v. Tahoe Regional Planning Agency*: About more than moratoria. *Land Use Law and Zoning Digest* 54(10):3–5.

———. 2004. Charting the constitutional course of private property: Learning from the 20th century. In *Private property in the 21st century*, ed. Harvey M. Jacobs, 31–49. Northampton, MA: Edward Elgar.

Locke, John. 1952 (1690). *The second treatise of government*, ed. T. P. Peardon. Indianapolis, IN: Bobbs-Merrill Educational Publishers.

Marzulla, Nancie G. 1996. Property rights movement: How it began and where it is headed. In *A wolf in the garden: The land rights movement and the new environmental debate*, ed. P. D. Brick and R. McGreggor Cawley, 39–58. Lanham, MD: Rowman and Littlefield.

McClaughry, John. 1975. The new feudalism. *Environmental Law* 5(3):675–702.

———. 1976. Farmers, freedom, and feudalism: How to avoid the coming serfdom. *South Dakota Law Review* 21(3):486–541.

Meltz, Robert, Dwight H. Merriam, and Richard M. Frank. 1999. *The takings issue: Constitutional limits on land-use controls and environmental regulation.* Washington, DC: Island Press.

Miniter, Richard. 1994. You just can't take it anymore: America's property rights revolt. *Policy Review* 70:40–46.

Molotch, Harvey. 1976. The city as a growth machine: Toward a political economy of place. *American Journal of Sociology* 82(2):309–322.

Moss, Elaine, ed. 1977. *Land use controls in the United States: A handbook on the legal rights of citizens by the Natural Resources Defense Council, Inc.* New York: Dial Press/James Wade.

Nelson, Arthur C., and Casey J. Dawkins. 2004. *Urban containment in the U.S.: History, models, and techniques for regional and metropolitan growth management.* Planning Advisory Service Report 520. Chicago: Planners Press.

New York Times. 2008. Cuba to allow thousands to own homes. April 12 (national edition):A9.

Pollot, Mark L. 1989. The effect of the federal takings executive order. *Land Use Law and Zoning Digest* 41(5):3–7.

Reid, T. R. 2004. *The United States of Europe: The new superpower and the end of American supremacy.* New York: Penguin.

Ring, Ray. 2006. Taking liberties. *High Country News*, July 24. http://www.hcn.org/servlets/hcn.Article?article_id=16409.

Roddewig, Richard J., and Christopher J. Duerksen. 1989. *Responding to the takings challenge: A guide for officials and planners.* Planning Advisory Service Report 416. Chicago: American Planning Association.

Salkin, Patricia E. 2001. *Trends in land use law from A to Z: Adult uses to zoning.* Chicago: American Bar Association.

Schlatter, Richard. 1951. *Private property: The history of an idea.* New Brunswick, NJ: Rutgers University Press.

Schleuning, Neala. 1997. *To have and to hold: The meaning of ownership in the United States.* Westport, CT: Praeger.

Scott, Mel. 1969. *American city planning since 1890.* Berkeley: University of California Press.

Scott, William B. 1977. *In pursuit of happiness: American conceptions of property from the seventeenth to the twentieth century.* Bloomington: Indiana University Press.

Thallam, Satya. 2008. 2008 report—International property rights index. Washington, DC: Property Rights Alliance. http://www.internationalpropertyrightsindex.org/UserFiles/File/022508ot-report%20(2).pdf.

Treanor, William Michael. 1995. The original understanding of the takings clause and the political process. *Columbia Law Review* 95(4):782–887.

Turner, Frederick Jackson. 1893. The significance of the frontier in American history. *Report of the American Historical Association,* 199–227.

Yandle, Bruce, ed. 1995. *Land rights: The 1990's property rights rebellion.* Lanham, MD: Rowman and Littlefield.

4

China's Land System: Past, Present, and Future

Dwight H. Perkins

Changes in China's land system have been an integral part of the transformation of China from a centrally planned command economy to a decentralized market economy. Going forward, China's land system will play a key role in ongoing structural changes that are changing China from a predominantly rural and agricultural society to one that is urban and industrial. To understand China's market reforms in general and the role of land in particular, it is helpful to describe the system as it existed prior to the reforms.

The only markets that existed in China before 1979 were small markets for secondary farm products such as vegetables and eggs. Everything else was allocated by administrative means governed by the national plan and implemented by China's large government bureaucracy. This was particularly true with respect to the distribution of factors: land, labor, and capital. Even under the prereform system, however, land—at least rural land—was different. There was very little reallocation of land once the agricultural cooperatives and then the rural communes were formed. In effect the communes, or, more accurately, the brigades and teams under the communes, had a kind of property right over the land they tilled. Formally the land was owned "collectively," that is, by the local production unit rather than "by the whole people," meaning effectively the state. Existing villages were not forced to accept immigrants from outside, and land was typically not transferred from one commune or commune subunit to another. The one exception was when a major construction project required taking land by China's version of eminent domain for infrastructure projects, such as a large dam. Urban factories, in contrast, could not ask higher planning authorities to transfer rural land to their use under an eminent domain procedure. Such transfers did occur, of course, but they generally involved elaborate negotiations with the affected rural unit. Vestiges of this system still exist, and they played a particularly important role in the 1980s. The constraints on the acquisition of land (and rural labor), for example, indirectly played an important role in the rapid growth of township and village enterprises (TVEs) that were located in rural areas but often had close ties to urban enterprises.[1]

When market-oriented reforms began after 1978, China found it politically and ideologically easier to introduce allocation through markets for industrial products and farm commodities than for factors of production. Even with industrial products, however, there was considerable political resistance to market reforms, and this led to the dual price system for the allocation of industrial inputs: (1) a lower price for planned allocations to existing state-owned enterprises; and (2) a higher market price for the same input allocated to others and for above-quota allocations to the state-owned enterprises.

Labor was the first factor to be increasingly subject to market allocation. The system of government allocation of all university graduates and many other skilled workers, including sending husbands and wives to different cities, was abolished early on. Similarly, the state-set wage structures gradually gave way to market-determined wages. Capital became subject to market forces more slowly. The government shifted responsibility for large investments to the individual state-owned enterprises, but these enterprises were allowed to go to the state-owned banks for investments they could not fund from their own earnings. Above a certain size, these investments still had to be approved by what was called the State Planning Commission and is now called the State Development and Reform Commission. The decision-making process for bank lending was governed more by politics than by commercial considerations, and this has changed only gradually. Even foreign direct investments (FDI) and private domestic investments above a certain size still require higher-level government approval. Thus, administrative measures still play a major role in the allocation of capital today.

Making land purchases and sales subject to market forces has come last, although, in the case of urban land, one can argue that market forces today are more prevalent than in the allocation of capital. In the rural areas, however, land cannot be legally purchased or sold on an open market, although local authorities do have the right to lease land through negotiations that are anything but transparent and that are closely related to other transactions that can be best described as black market transfers (see, for example, Ho and Lin 2003). This way

---

1. State-owned enterprises in the cities could not ask the city or national planning authorities to allocate land and labor for expansion of factories if that land and labor had to come from outside the city's jurisdiction. In many cases in the 1980s, the state enterprises would instead work out a relationship with a nearby commune, and the commune (or brigade) would set up a collective township or village enterprise that would produce components for the state-owned enterprise in the city.

of transferring land has become a major source of contention in the countryside. Because the urban and rural land systems are so different, they will be taken up in turn, starting with today's urban market for land.

The Urban Land Market

Well before there was a well-established urban land market, urban service and government units and industrial enterprises had acquired a kind of property right to the land they occupied. The local and national government could override this right for public purposes and has done so regularly, but there generally has been a quid pro quo. For example, in preparation for Shanghai Expo scheduled for 2010, many state-owned industrial and port facilities along the Huangpu River are being moved out of the city to a new location on the coast, with the needed infrastructure and subsidies provided by the Shanghai government.

In the early reform years, new housing developments often had to "persuade" existing residents to move to alternative sites. These residents did not own their apartments, and their rents did not reflect market forces. Rent in state housing (virtually all the urban housing in the 1980s) was set at a level that barely covered the cost of utilities, if that. Access to housing depended on an individual's work unit. That unit "owned" housing that was sometimes near the place of work and sometimes not. Allocation was based on status within the work unit together with family size and related criteria. This system lasted into the 1990s, at which time the state decided to privatize housing. When housing was gradually privatized, families typically bought their existing housing at highly subsidized rates.[2]

Moving from these work unit apartments, whether owned by the residents or not, presented a problem even after privatization. Residents typically could not afford comparable apartments elsewhere in the city unless they also were subsidized. The quality of existing housing was poor. In 1978 urban floor space per capita was only 6.7 square meters, or roughly 20 square meters for a family of three (National Bureau of Statistics 2007, 380). Toilet and even cooking arrangements were typically shared. By 2005, in contrast, per capita space was 26.1 square meters or around 80 meters for a family of three, still not luxurious, but a vast improvement over the situation two decades earlier. With this large expansion in housing of higher quality in all the major cities (see table 4.1), it probably became easier to persuade families to move.

The more prosperous families also had time to save to purchase more desirable apartments, and the banks were increasingly willing to finance mortgages. Some individuals still resisted moving, as in the well-publicized case of a woman in Chongqing who refused to move from her house while the foundations for a major apartment complex were being dug around her, but the issue in that

---

2. For a brief but more substantial history of the housing market in China from 1949 on, see Song, Knaap, and Ding (2005).

Table 4.1
Current Levels of Urban Housing Construction

| | Investment in Housing (Billion yuan) | | Housing Floor Space (sold) (Million square meters) | |
	High Grade	Affordable	High Grade	Affordable
1997	15.63	18.55	2.54	12.12
2000	27.01	54.24	6.41	37.60
2003	63.29	62.20	14.50	40.19
2005	104.94	51.92	28.18	32.05

Source: National Bureau of Statistics (2007, 240, 242).

instance was simply how much the developer was willing to pay. In effect, the groundwork had been laid for a true market-based residential housing system with some major caveats as discussed below.

The urban residential land system today, together with much urban commercial real estate, is patterned in a general way—whether deliberately or not—on the Hong Kong system. Land is owned by the state, meaning the local government or some other government agency, and is leased to individuals and developers for a fixed number of years. The longest lease allowed is for 70 years for residential areas, and for less time for land used for commercial buildings (*Finance Asia* 2004). The leases in effect are purchased by the developers, with the funds going to the "owner." Land leasing has thus become a major source of revenue for local governments as well as for many other government units. Typically, the revenue from such leases is received as a lump sum rather than as a monthly or annual payment. However, some localities have been experimenting with a system in which only a portion of the fee is paid up-front, with the remainder amortized in equal installments through the period of the lease.

This system differs from the Hong Kong system in that the Hong Kong government decides which parcels to lease each year, puts the parcels up for public auction, and receives the revenue from the auctions. In China many different units have effective rights to parcels of land, and they "sell" the land to developers in ways that are often far from transparent. The state unit "owners" who are not local governments receive most of the revenue from these "sales." That is, the local governments generally receive revenue only from the land that is not owned by some other state unit. Alternatively, these owners sometimes develop the land themselves. Another common variation is that state-owned enterprises frequently negotiate with foreign direct investment firms to form joint ventures. Typically, the main contribution of the state enterprise is land that it effectively controls, and the value of the land is set in the negotiations between the foreign investor and the state enterprise. This last system existed well before there was a well-developed urban land market. It was not uncommon for the process to be a back-door form of privatization, with many of the benefits going to the senior managers of the state-owned enterprises in the form of high salaries and other perquisites in the new joint venture.

For well-off urban residents, the purchase or rental of housing is a relatively straightforward process.[3] Real estate firms post notices about properties in their windows much as in the United States and other high-income countries. There are 96 publicly traded real estate firms listed on the Shanghai and Shenzhen stock exchanges and more than 20,000 that are not listed.[4] Long-term urban residents who cannot afford purchases at market prices—a large percentage of registered urban residents fall into this category—still can either rent higher-quality public housing or purchase such housing at highly subsidized rates.

Two kinds of urban residents cannot take advantage of this system. The first group is made up of the urban unemployed and other registered urban residents with low incomes, a category that probably includes at least the bottom two-fifths of the registered urban population.[5] They cannot afford to purchase most apartments in cities because they cannot afford the price or the periodic mortgage payments, although some of these lower-income residents can afford to rent public housing and even to purchase it if the price is sufficiently subsidized. In one sample of 52 countries, the average cost of housing relative to household income was 5 to 1, and in high-income countries it was often less than 3 to 1, whereas that ratio would be over 10 to 1 for the bottom fifth of the Chinese population and around 6 to 1 for the next fifth, with the ratio presumably being higher in cities such as Shanghai and Beijing where land prices are particularly high.[6] Thus, even among the registered urban population, there is a need for subsidized public housing, and the government does provide public housing. There have been recent decisions to increase the amount of such housing.

---

3. In the city of Beijing in 2000, nearly 72 percent of the long-term registered urban population lived in either public rental housing or formerly public housing purchased at a highly subsidized rate. Only 3 percent of the population of Beijing lived in housing purchased at market prices, and another 10 percent lived in housing that they built and owned themselves, which in the case of Beijing meant lower-quality housing than the former or present public housing (Logan, Fang, and Zhang 2008, table 3).

4. In 1999 the number of real estate companies reached 25,762 (Zhang 2005, 186).

5. The second fifth from the bottom of the urban population had an average per family income of RMB 24,300 yuan in 2006 (US$3,420), and affordable housing (based on an assumed three persons per family) was six times that figure.

6. The international ratio is referred to in Zhang (2005, 190). The ratios for income in China were calculated from National Bureau of Statistics (2007, 349), and the housing figures were for affordable housing of 80 square meters from the same source as elsewhere in this chapter.

Migrants and the Urban Housing Market ———————————————

Of much greater quantitative importance is the plight of urban residents who are still registered as rural residents. These rural to urban migrants now total at least 200 million and probably more, and they have been subject to the rules of the household registration (*hukou*) system. In effect, unless a person is registered as an urban resident—and becoming registered as such has been difficult to achieve—that person has few rights in the city. Specifically, the person has had no right to public education or public health care. These migrants thus often have to set up their own schools, although the central government has now called for cities to open their public schools to migrant children. In recent years, the national government has taken steps to gradually eliminate the *hukou* system, but many of the system's restrictions have effectively been turned over to local authorities, who continue to expel migrants deemed undesirable and to set high fees for formal registration as an urban resident, among other measures that effectively maintain much of the discrimination present in the *hukou* system.

People not registered as residents of a particular city, however, can buy apartments in another city either legally or by getting someone with a permit to register the property. Current efforts to restrict purchases of residential property by such nonresidents are aimed mainly at well-off individuals buying apartments as investments, not at migrants (Li 2008).[7] But why would a migrant want to buy a home if the children could not attend the government schools or obtain adequate health care?[8]

The real problem for migrants is that their income is too low for them to afford an apartment. An average apartment in China's cities has about 80 square meters, and the cost for an apartment designed for lower-income residents is RMB 1,729 yuan per square meter, for a total of RMB 138,000 yuan (US$19,200 at the 2008 exchange rate).[9] The average migrant makes only RMB 1,200 yuan (US$167) per month, or RMB 14,400 yuan per year (Xie 2008). Even if migrants could obtain mortgages from banks at relatively low interest rates, which is unlikely given their nonresident status, the payments would use up their entire

———————————————

7. For a detailed discussion of how the system now operates, see Wang (2008).

8. As pointed out in Duda and Li (2008, 14–19), there is a lack of data that can be used to estimate whether the *hukou* system directly affects the ability of non-urban residents to obtain housing. The point here is that restrictions on migrant rights not directly related to housing could have a major impact on whether it makes sense to buy housing, although these rights issues are probably less important than the low-income problem discussed in the next paragraph.

9. The square meter cost is for "economically affordable housing" in China and is from National Bureau of Statistics (2007, 243).

income.[10] Thus, a large and rising portion of China's urban population is effectively excluded from the urban real estate market. Instead, these people live on construction sites, in air raid shelters built in the 1970s, on the street, many to a room in rented apartments, and in dormitories supplied by their employers.[11] The people who can participate in the urban housing market are those with high incomes, families that received highly subsidized first apartments from their urban employers, residents of Hong Kong, and people with middling incomes who are registered urban residents and can obtain mortgage financing at a reasonable cost. Under the situation that predominates today, future migrants will have to continue to live in urban slum conditions or will have to rely on urban public housing or some other subsidized living arrangement if the government makes that choice available.

What makes this situation in many ways different from the usual shack communities on the edges of cities of many low-income countries is mostly a matter of scale. China is in the midst of the largest rural to urban migration within a single country in human history. Basically, China's 2008 per capita income and urbanization levels are comparable to those experienced by Japan, South Korea, and Taiwan in the 1950s and 1960s. These economies experienced high GDP growth rates similar to those currently prevailing in China for two to three decades between the 1950s and the 1990s. During that time, their population in agriculture fell from 50 percent or more of total employment to 10 percent or less, and the proportion of population in the countryside fell from over 60 percent to 25 or 30 percent or less. As the data in figure 4.1 indicate, China is following this same path. Today its urban population is officially 43 percent of the nation's total, and over the next two-plus decades that share is likely to rise to over 70 percent, assuming the pattern found elsewhere in East Asia holds.

In other words, China's rural to urban migration is likely to add another 400 million people to the more than 200 million who have arrived in its cities during the past decade and a half, with the urban population increasing from 560 million to roughly 1 billion people. In 20 years, half of that population will be migrants who were born and, in most cases, raised in the countryside.

There are only two ways to reduce this massive migration: (1) by markedly slowing China's growth rate and urban employment opportunities; or (2) by continuing to try to keep the families of a large portion of the migrants in the

---

10. A rate of only 10 percent (interest plus payment of a small portion of the principal) would use all of the average migrant's income. If there were two income earners in the family, the cost would still be prohibitive. They could probably not get a mortgage at this rate in any case.

11. In Shanghai a decade ago, 33.1 percent of migrants lived in dormitories, 33.4 percent rented private, mostly low-quality rooms or apartments, 8.6 percent shared space with urban residents (for example, as servants), 7.2 percent owned or rented low-quality self-built sheds, and only 13.9 percent rented higher-quality public housing (Wu 2002, 216).

Figure 4.1
Share of Agriculture, Forestry, and Fisheries in Total Employment

a. By year

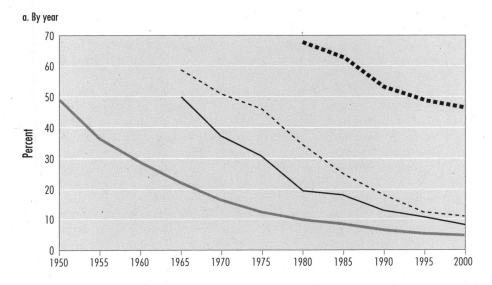

b. By income per capita (purchasing power parity)

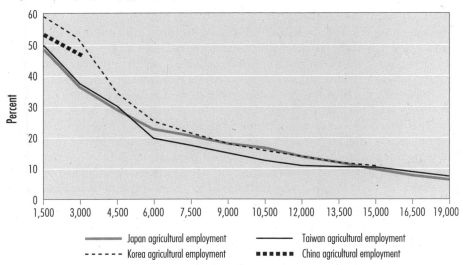

Note: Employment data are often available only in five-year intervals. GDP per capita could change substantially in five years when growth was 8 or 9 percent a year. Simple extrapolations have been used to fill in the gaps in agricultural employment data. Source: Heston, Summers, and Aten (2006); Korean, Taiwan, and Chinese statistical yearbooks.

countryside. Both would have negative consequences for China that are complex and well beyond the scope of this chapter. The main point here is that China, barring a large external shock or domestic political upheaval, is going to make every effort to maintain a high rate of growth, and it is my belief that the Chinese are likely to succeed in doing so.[12] As the *hukou* system is dismantled, its limitations are also likely to largely disappear, but it remains to be seen whether local urban governments will welcome migrants and attempt to ease their transition to urban life or instead will put obstacles in their path.

One way or another, China's urban land system will have to adjust to this new environment. First of all, China faces a challenge in making the current market-based system work better for those in a position to use it. The question of who actually owns various properties will have to be answered. The process of property transfer from one entity to another will have to become more transparent. An urban real estate tax system will have to be markedly improved. (Some of these issues are discussed in greater length later in the next section.) Desirable as resolving these issues are, however, they will be dwarfed by the problem of how to house a half billion migrants who cannot afford real estate of even the low-cost variety as currently defined. The current level of housing construction, large as it is (see table 4.1 above), is far short of what will be required by an influx of 5 to 6 million migrant families a year.

Hong Kong and Singapore are probably appropriate models for what individual families will require. Public housing initiatives in those two economies began at a time when their per capita income (purchasing power parity per capita of US$3,300 and US$4,600 respectively in 1960) was similar to that of China today (Heston, Summers, and Aten 2006). Virtually everyone who required such housing received it, and the shacks on the Hong Kong hillsides disappeared. Singapore and Hong Kong, however, had to provide perhaps 1 million public housing units in total. China will have to provide several times that number each year.

In summary, China has gone a long way toward creating the rules of a modern urban land market, but important as these changes have been, the migration challenge will continue to require a different effort. China basically faces a major market failure brought about by the wide disparity in the incomes of the better-off portion of the registered urban population and the poverty of the new migrants. Registered urban residents in effect received windfall income when ownership of their housing was transferred to them at highly subsidized rates. Something similar will have to be done for the migrants.

Conceivably, the migrants could be given large cash grants to pay for housing, and developers could respond to this newly created demand by building low-cost housing, but that does not seem realistic. More likely, housing will have to be

---

12. For a more complete analysis of why economic elements are not likely to derail rapid economic growth during the next two decades, see Perkins and Rawski (2008).

provided or paid for by local governments or Beijing. Sometime after this public housing is built and occupied, when the incomes of all urban residents rise to a level where even the migrants can get affordable mortgages, all housing, not just housing for the well-off, can be governed mainly by market forces. In Singapore, in particular, citizens in public housing were encouraged to buy their apartments, typically using loans from their provident (compulsory savings) fund, but this did not occur until per capita income in Singapore was far higher than it is in urban China today.

Enforcing Urban Property Rights and Implementing Public Housing: Missing Institutions

The previous discussion has been based on an implicit assumption that a person with an income high enough could readily purchase a secure right in housing, that a business could do much the same with its offices and factories, and that the central and local governments would build the public housing and infrastructure that were not provided by profit-oriented developers responding to market forces. The key assumptions are that property rights are secure or enforceable and that local governments will respond to what to an outsider seems like a clear priority.

In a full market economy with the necessary supporting institutions, property rights are secured, conflicts over these rights are resolved in accordance with law, and law is enforced by a judiciary that is independent of the executive branch of the central and the local governments. In China, however, Mao Zedong abolished all lawyers in the 1960s and 1970s, and law was little more than whatever a person with political power said it was. Even prior to that Cultural Revolution period, the Chinese legal system was never particularly well developed. The basic Confucian view of government was that good government depended on good people, not good laws. Thus, at the beginning of the reform period, China had to build a legal system suitable for a market economy from scratch.

Writing the laws required by the new market system was not particularly difficult. The real problem was how to enforce them and settle disputes in an efficient and equitable way. China's courts were staffed by individuals who lacked formal legal training and, more important, were expected first and foremost to represent the interests of the state and the Communist Party. Furthermore, the courts often had great difficulty enforcing their decisions. Not only did the top leaders of the government overrule the decisions of the courts, but even enterprise managers could often ignore judgments brought against them. Ultimately, the courts had to turn to the government to enforce their decisions, but there was no government tradition of supporting court decisions—even decisions the government agreed with. Put differently, the courts were expected to support the mandates of government and party officials, and the government and party officials had considerable discretion in deciding whether the courts had carried out those mandates. This process turned the courts into one more way of implementing government directives rather than serving as a check on abuse by those in power.

China's legal system, however, is not static. The judiciary is gradually being professionalized, and the power of the courts to decide disputes is increasing. People in urban areas, particularly in the more advanced regions of the country such as on the coast, are increasingly going to court to settle disputes. In many areas, the courts, while far from independent, are now expected to follow the law and not be particularly concerned about the outcome preferred by a senior government official. The real guarantee of urban property rights at present, however, is not the law so much as it is the potential political consequences of ignoring these rights for the government and the party.

Because the ultimate decisions regarding the use of urban land are to a large degree within the discretionary power of the executive branch of the central and local governments, what actually is implemented with respect to land, housing, and infrastructure depends most of all on what the local government wants. What the local government wants, however, is often different from what the central government wants, and the power of the central government to enforce its will on local governments is limited. This is not because the local governments have formal legal rights that override the decisions at the center. It is more because China is a huge country, and central governments today and for centuries past have found it necessary to allow local governments a great deal of leeway in how and even whether to implement directives. Ultimately, if a local government defies the wishes of the center, the center can, and often does, remove the local official. But removal of an official or the top echelons of an entire local government is a blunt instrument that cannot be used to deal with subtle differences between the center and the locality over economic and social issues.

The central government and many urban governments often disagree about priorities. In recent years, the central government has increasingly realized that it has to deal more effectively with a variety of social issues in order to create what is now called a more harmonious society. In 2006 and 2007, this often took the form of calling for measures to improve the situation of urban migrants. Some of these measures have involved little more than ordering local businesses to pay the migrant workers their wages. But it has also led to directives to open up urban public schools to migrant children and a more general relaxation of the household registration rules.

What is far less clear is whether local governments give priority to the issues that the center thinks are most important. The large coastal cities of China, for example, are competing to become modern urban centers by patterning themselves on centers in countries with much higher per capita incomes. Shanghai is trying to catch up with and surpass Hong Kong or eventually even New York, and lesser cities have sister city relationships with comparable urban centers elsewhere. Longtime higher-income urban residents want better apartments and highways on which to drive their new automobiles, and they often see migrants as the source of increasing crime. Urban governments are responsive to this affluent part of their population. They tolerate migrants because migrants are needed by the local economy, but many see little point in spending large sums to provide these migrants with housing, education, and infrastructure.

Local governments and a weak legal system, therefore, are contributing to the creation of what amounts to a dual economy within urban areas. On one side are the long-term urban residents with high levels of education living in a prosperous market economy with respect to land, housing, and much else. The property rights of these residents and the rights of the enterprises where they work are protected in part by law, but mostly because local governments see their main task as serving this part of their population. On the other side are the migrants, who have few secure rights of any kind, including property rights in land. They are harassed by the police; they do not always receive their wages; and most live in facilities that they do not own. Their schools are often self-financed, use facilities that typically involve violation of some regulation, and so can be taken from them. There is no real market for the land and infrastructure used by the migrants, and there are no property rights. Hernando de Soto (2000), among others, has written extensively about people around the world who are in similar situations.

Efficiency and Equity in the Real Estate Market

In many ways, China's current urban land market operates much like that in other market economies. Land prices, with the important exception of eminent domain cases, are determined by market forces, not by the state. The prices vary by city and region in ways that appear plausible for a market economy, with average 2005 land prices ranging from RMB 780 yuan per square meter in the more remote and less developed northwest to RMB 1,309 yuan in the more developed cities of the north that include such well-off areas as Beijing, Tianjin, and Qingdao (*People's Daily Online* 2005).

Real estate more generally is priced at levels that the more prosperous urban residents can afford, especially those who can trade in owned apartments obtained earlier at highly subsidized rates. In 2006 the average price of a high-grade 150-square-meter apartment was just under RMB 1 million yuan (less than US$140,000), although prices in such cities as Shanghai and Beijing could be much higher. Most urban residents do not live in housing of this quality. As noted above, low-cost housing of 80 square meters had an average cost of just under US$20,000. While this cost is too high for rural migrants to the cities, it is affordable for urban residents in the second quintile of the income distribution, whose average family income in 2006 was approximately RMB 30,000 yuan (US$4,200) per year and even for those in the third quintile with average family incomes of RMB 24,000 yuan (US$3,330) (National Bureau of Statistics 2007, 349).

However, there is a danger that market forces could push urban prices out of reach of a larger number of residents than is currently the case. Households in China today have relatively few investment options. They can put money in the bank, where real deposit interest rates are low, or they can buy shares on the stock market, where prices are volatile. Housing has afforded better returns than the banks, at least during the past decade, and has been less volatile than the stock market. Residential housing prices rose by an average of 7.5 percent per year from the end of 2002 to the end of 2006. For well-to-do urban people, who have high savings rates and accumulate funds, housing prices could be driven increasingly by investment demand rather than by the demand for housing to live in. Also, far wealthier people in places such as Hong Kong are now buying large amounts of housing in mainland China as investments, and that speculative demand could drive prices of higher-quality housing out of the range of all but the wealthiest locals. Although this speculative demand from outside probably focuses on a relatively few cities, such as Shanghai, the problem is serious enough for the government to have already discussed policies to limit real estate investments by individuals from outside such cities.

Of equal importance is the question of whether real estate prices are high enough to elicit a rapid increase in supply. The answer to this question is unequivocal. As China has moved to a real estate development system based on the market, the response of developers has been rapid and dramatic. In 1991 China saw urban housing and business real estate sales totaling 30 million square meters of floor space. In 2000, when domestic and foreign developers were becoming increasingly involved, the floor space had increased to 189 million square meters, and in 2006 to 618.6 million square meters (National Bureau of Statistics 2007, 241). This large building boom explains how China could triple the space available per urban household at a time when the urban population was itself doubling and while also rapidly expanding commercial space.

Creating a Reliable Real Estate Tax

A problem that has not been solved is how localities can generate the revenue they need on a steady and substantial basis. The Hong Kong model of selling leases in one up-front sale does not appear to be serving this goal well except perhaps in a few wealthy cities such as Shanghai, and perhaps not even there. There are many dimensions to improving the current system, but they all can be thought of as components of what would be required if China were to implement an effective real estate tax to go along with a revised way of handling leasing fees.[13]

---

13. There has been a debate over whether the leasing fee should be considered a land use tax (see Hong 2003, 66–71). In this chapter, we follow Chinese practice of referring to leasing fees and land taxes as separate sources of revenue.

The biggest single problem with the current land leasing fee and tax system is that the principal source of revenue is a one-time leasing fee at the time the land is leased by the commercial developer. This system worked well in Hong Kong for a long time because the government had a great deal of land and could auction it off on a limited and steady basis over many years. The land chosen for auction could be picked on the basis of a long-term land use plan. Hong Kong, in recent decades at least, also established effective controls over corruption. In China, in contrast, the amount of nonagricultural land is limited, and conversion of agricultural land is strictly controlled. Land in the wealthier urban areas that can be leased by the government is expensive, leading to large one-time payments to the local government or to the government entity that owns the land. These kinds of one-time payments, unlike in Hong Kong, are not sustainable over many decades, so local revenue gets a large windfall boost for a time, but not indefinitely. The current land use tax, in contrast, provides the local government with a steady, if much smaller, stream of income. Furthermore, the local government actually gets the revenue, whereas the leasing fee system generates revenue for whichever government entity happens to control a given piece of land.

Large one-time payments are also tempting targets for corruption, and land transactions have become a major source of corruption ranging from highly publicized cases involving municipal leadership in Shanghai and Beijing to smaller-scale cases in rural townships. It is not as difficult to hide a large payment to an official if it is only, say, 10 percent of the total price. Bribes are also easier to hide when they are one-time transactions rather than ongoing payments. A land tax paid as a small percentage of the value of the land could also lead to side payments to officials to get the tax lowered, though an official's reward would be far lower and the chances of being caught greater.

Corruption in land transfers could be partially dealt with if auctioning off the land, as in Hong Kong, became standard practice. In China in the mid-1990s, only 5 to 10 percent of the total land sold was auctioned off, with the rest, according to the then director of the General Office of State Land Administration, transferred "through unhealthy practices based on personal factors, power-and-money swaps and behind-the-scenes insidious dealings, and thus hindering the realization of a normal market" (Sun 1995, 5). In 2002 the central government mandated that the cities lease land to private developers only through public tender or auction, but there is no evidence of the degree to which this directive has been implemented.

Another land tax system issue involves transparency, which requires an open system of recording ownership of or user rights over the land. According to the land law, all urban land is owned by all the people, meaning the state. The problem, as pointed out above, is that the state can be a local government, or a factory, or a government entity that is neither an enterprise nor a local government. A similar murkiness can apply to who actually owns a lease, although this is probably less of a problem. The murkier the land user rights, the easier it is for individuals administering these rights to divert funds for personal gain. This lack of transparency is a large part of the reason there is large-scale corruption in real estate transactions. And even when corruption is not involved, the distribution of land user rights is inequitable and probably inefficient.

Solving the transparency problem is difficult. Because the state formally owns all the land, the control rights that allow one group or another to reap the benefits of a transaction are difficult to define. In part, it depends on the relative power of those claiming control rights. It also depends on who historically has had control rights over the land. No doubt other considerations enter in as well. The only national land survey during the reform period began in 1984, when land was both owned and controlled by the state and allocated administratively, and took 11 years to complete, ending in 1995, when the market economy was well established and land was mainly leased to users. Planning for the next land survey is currently under way, with a target finishing date of 2010 (*China Economic Review* 2007). In theory, it will cover the ownership of every piece of land in use. Whether that will prove to be a practical goal remains to be seen.

Given the difficulty of establishing who has user rights over pieces of land, an effective land tax system that provides an annual stream of revenue cannot wait until the owners of user rights are properly identified with transparent titles. Fortunately, there is a simpler alternative: local governments can have a fiscal cadastre that need not be related to a legal cadastre based on actual ownership. The fiscal cadastre would identify and value a plot of land and post a notice that that land owed a given amount of tax. If no one stepped forward to pay the tax, the government could seize it. This approach has worked in Indonesia, where identification of the legal owners of land was nearly impossible both politically and technically, in the sense of producing a steady stream of revenue from the land tax. There is every reason to believe it would work in China.[14]

Today's Chinese land tax system also has a variety of, for lack of a better term, administrative problems. The urban real estate tax, for example, was developed in 1951 and is out of date. Some of the taxes are redundant; the land value incremental tax, the enterprise income tax, and the personal income tax are all based in part on the net rental transaction income from property. The tax base is also narrowly defined, with commercial properties paying taxes and residential properties exempt. Foreign direct investment properties often pay less than domestically owned properties. There is also a great deal of local variation from one

---

14. I am indebted to Jay Rosengard for this paragraph. As Rosengard points out, this approach also requires keeping the land tax rate low so that the incentive to evade taxes does not become so great that it is worth the risk of losing the land through nonpayment of taxes or that it pays to bribe the taxpayer. For a further discussion of the current Chinese and Indonesian real estate tax systems, see Rosengard et al. (2007).

city to the next in how the taxes are administered and calculated. There is thus a need for a thorough revision of the taxes that apply at least in part to land.[15]

The Rural Land System

China's rural land system is fundamentally different from its urban land system. The Communist Party came to power in China in 1949 largely on the basis of its ability to mobilize a discontented peasantry. Rural poverty was at the heart of that discontent, and the unequal distribution of agricultural land had much to do with that poverty. In the southern half of the country, half of the land was owned by landlords (mostly absentee) and was leased to tenants in return for rent that amounted to half of the main crop output. In the north, particularly away from the North China Plain, tenancy was less prevalent, but lack of water and mountainous terrain meant widespread poverty of an extreme kind.

A common view of the problem was that private land ownership was highly unequal, and people with less land typically went into debt to a moneylender because of a bad harvest or other crisis, could not repay the debt, lost ownership of the land, and became impoverished tenants. For most members of the Communist Party and others who held this view, a return to private land ownership would simply re-create this situation. Under the commune system, where individuals did not have user rights over particular plots of land, there was no realistic way for land to pass into the hands of rich landlords. With abolition of the commune system and the restoration of household agriculture, however, farmers did have user rights over particular plots of land. If they were also given formal ownership of that land, they could presumably sell or lease it, causing a return to the path to rural inequality. Given the huge population in the countryside during the first decade of the twenty-first century, this was a real, if potential, threat to rural stability.

Another widely held belief of leaders of the Chinese Communist Party in recent decades (and also of past emperors) is that food self-sufficiency is critical in maintaining a stable country. Famine would lead to massive discontent and could bring down a dynasty. The famine of 1959–1961, which led to the premature deaths of as many as 30 million people, was perceived as a real threat to continued rule by the Communist Party. The practical impact of this belief was that China instituted, on paper at least, strict controls on the ability to convert land from agricultural to industrial and other nonagricultural uses. There have also been controls on the ability of farmers to shift out of grain into higher-income-producing cash crops. During Mao Zedong's era, these controls were rigid, but they have been steadily relaxed during the reform decades in order to allow farmers to earn higher incomes from crops more lucrative than grain. The basic belief

---

15. This paragraph is based on Ding (2005).

in the importance of grain for food self-sufficiency remains, however. The concept of food security, where imports and strong foreign exchange earnings can be one way of maintaining that security, is an idea more accepted and understood among technicians than among the politicians who make the critical decisions.

These beliefs and the government directives emanating from them apply to a Chinese countryside that still had 325.6 million farmers employed in agriculture, forestry, and fisheries in 2006. The share in agriculture has been declining as a percentage of the workforce, as figure 4.1a indicates. In absolute numbers, there has also been a decline from 391 million farmers in 1991. In 2006, however, there were still 2.5 workers per hectare (one per acre) on China's 130 million hectares of cultivated land.[16] South Korea, by comparison, had 850,000 farmers cultivating 1,824,000 hectares or 0.47 farmers per hectare in 2005, and the United States had 0.015 farmers per hectare (Council of Economic Advisors 2008, table B-100; Korea National Statistical Office 2006, 221, 263).[17] China thus has far more farmers than can be used effectively on the land, particularly now that Chinese farmers have considerable amounts of capital equipment.[18] The low incomes that go with this low marginal productivity are the main reason so many are migrating to the cities.

The land system created when China reverted back to household agriculture in the early 1980s assumed that farm families would stay on the land. Formally, land was owned collectively, which meant that it was effectively owned by the village as a whole. User rights to the land were distributed to individual households based on family size and similar criteria. At least within the territory of the old commune, brigade, and team units, distribution was egalitarian, although landholdings between communes were far from equal. Gradually, the time households were guaranteed use of their designated plots was lengthened in order to encourage investment in the land. Initially, in fact, because of uncertainty about how long they could farm particular plots, farmers put 85 percent of their investment into housing, where property rights were relatively secure (Huang 1998, 52). At the beginning of the 1980s, farmers typically were told that they were being assigned particular fields for two or three years; this quickly was changed

---

16. Chinese employment figures are notoriously unreliable, but they are usable in terms of the general magnitude of employment, as is the case here. These data are all from National Bureau of Statistics (2007, 130–131). The cultivated land figure is also probably high even though it is the published figure in the 2007 statistical handbook. A senior official in the Ministry of Land and Resources indicated that total arable land in 2007 was only 121.8 million hectares, largely because of alienation of arable land to nonagricultural uses (Li 2007, 1).

17. The U.S. figure is farmers per area of crops harvested, which, where there is more than one crop per year, is a bit higher than total cultivated acreage.

18. There were, for example, 1.4 million large and medium-sized agricultural tractors in China in 2005 and 15.3 million small tractors, or one for every 8 hectares (National Statistical Office 2007, 461).

to fifteen years by 1985 (Parish 1985, 18). In 1993 this number was increased to thirty years, and the rights could be passed on to the farmer's children (Wu 2005, 126–127). Today, rights of this sort are sometimes held for as long as fifty years.

But the rural population began to leave the farms to work in the cities. Those leaving could not sell their land, and many attempted to hold onto it by having close relatives farm it in their absence. This practice was facilitated by the fact that the migrants were typically the young, and many of their parents were still farmers and were "too old" to move. In many cases, however, this meant that the land was not farmed as intensively as it would have been if the original families allocated the land had continued to farm it.

The commune organization had been abolished, but the new township governments took over many of its functions, since the jurisdiction of the commune over land and the jurisdiction of the township (*xiang*) were more or less identical. Similarly, the former commune subunits, the production brigades, were largely synonymous with villages and village governments. The township and village governments often took a negative view of migrants' efforts to hold onto their land. Instead, no doubt with the backing of many people who remained on the land, the land was periodically redistributed. Redistribution could happen because of migration, but also because of changes in family size within the rural population that remained. In one survey, two-thirds of the villages had experienced this kind of land reallocation, and a quarter of them had experienced three or more such redistributions (Rozelle and Li 1998). In general, there was a good deal of variation in redistribution practices among villages, with the variation largely determined by the local authorities. These redistributions may have promoted welfare within a village, but they also undermined a family's sense of having a secure property right.[19]

Renting land was permitted in most villages, according to two large surveys taken seven years apart (Brandt et al. 2002, 80). The percentage of land rented rose between 1988 and 1995 in all but one of the provinces from which data were collected (the exception was Yunnan Province). The average amount of land rented in 1995 was only 2.5 percent of the total, with the highest percentage in a province at 6.9 percent in Zhejiang, a coastal province with a high degree of support for private activity from early in the reform period (Brandt et al. 2002, 80). The small share of rented land suggests that families may have been reluctant to take advantage of the opportunity of renting out their land for fear that it could be used to take the land from them and reallocate it. Also, large-scale rural to urban migration was just getting fully under way in 1995, and most families may

---

19. For an interesting discussion on who benefited from and hence supported redistributions of land and who did not, see Kung (2002).

have had enough labor still in the countryside to farm the land themselves. A later survey, say in 2005, would be needed to test this hypothesis.

The other major issue is a result of the increasing demand to use land for nonagricultural purposes. In principle, the government has set a national target of not allowing arable land to fall below 120 million hectares (Li 2007, 1). But the decision about whether land can be used for nonagricultural purposes rests with village and higher levels of government or with individual families. In principle, farmers whose land is taken from them for nonagricultural purposes are supposed to receive full compensation. But there is no established market for rural land, so the price is set in negotiations between local authorities and the unit desiring the land.

The potential for abuse is enormous. It is not just that local officials often do not pay attention to the national laws and procedures, but that in many cases the transfer of the land involves a corrupt arrangement between the local official, who receives a payment, and the purchasing unit, which gets the land at a favorable price. In some cases, local governments collude with developers to simply expand the boundaries of what is considered urban and thereby convert land from collective to government ownership, thus confiscating rural land without compensation (Wang 2008). China's farm families have increasingly taken to resisting these arrangements, sometimes resorting to violence. The widely reported figure of over 87,000 mass incidents serious enough to require police intervention in 2005 is widely believed to be related to a significant degree to abuses in rural land transactions. This figure is a 50 percent increase over the number of such incidents in 2003 (*Xinhua* 2006).

In early 2007 the inspectors of the Ministry of Land and Resources instituted a hundred-day crackdown on illegal land seizures and investigated 30,000 cases. Some 3,700 officials were designated to receive administrative discipline, and 2,700 were transferred to judicial departments for trial. This compares to a total of 1,221 who faced legal charges in 2000–2006 (*China Daily* 2008, 8; Li 2007, 1). Given that the amount of land transferred since 1996 amounted to 8 million hectares and the crackdown involved a total of only 0.22 million hectares, it is likely that the great majority of abuses were not investigated (Wu 2008, 2).

There is no easy solution. The institution of rural elections that allow villagers to vote abusive local officials out of office probably has helped, but local elections can often be manipulated not just to protect the Communist Party, but sometimes also to protect abusive local bosses. Nor is it feasible to have the central government enforce the law in more than 700,000 villages. Campaigns like the one in 2007 will scare abusive local officials for a time, but the incentives to continue these practices are too strong to be held back for long. Villagers can appeal to higher levels of government and even all the way to Beijing. One book that was available for a time in China before being withdrawn detailed how peasants in Anhui facing serious local abuses over taxes, fees, and other matters did on a number of occasions go all the way to Beijing (Chen and Wu

2006).[20] The farmers received sympathetic hearings from the Beijing officials, and steps were taken to try to rectify the situations. The abusive local officials, however, often ignored the directives from higher up and retaliated against the local farmers when they returned home. Eventually, some of the local officials went too far, to the point of committing murder, and they were caught and put in prison or executed, but incarcerating a few of the most abusive cases will not solve the problem.

The long-term solution is to create a transparent market for the purchase and sale of land and let the market determine the price. Where the concentration of land pushes some rural people into poverty, the solution could be a welfare or retraining program. Where local officials still seize land and do not offer fair prices, the farmers should be able to go to independent and efficient courts to plead their case. But, as pointed out above, courts of this kind do not yet exist, particularly in the rural areas, and the government is only now beginning to spend major resources on rural welfare programs in order to put a floor under how low family income can fall.

Conclusions

China's land system is still in transition. It is clear where this transition started, but it is not entirely clear where it will end. In many respects, it is a dual system. Property rights in land in the rural areas are significantly different from property rights in urban areas. The urban and rural land systems also have important elements in common.

Formally, rural land is collectively owned by the local village or township, and urban land is owned by the state. In both cases, local officials play the primary role in deciding whether a piece of land under their jurisdiction can be leased for commercial uses. The method of transfer is occasionally open auction, but far more often such transfers are arranged in private negotiations between the local government official and the company desiring a lease. The situation is fraught with conflicts of interest, and the result is often corruption, sometimes on a grand scale. Such corruption is common in developing countries—and is often not rare in more advanced economies; in China, as elsewhere, it is a source of considerable instability in the countryside and embarrassing scandals affecting the strength and legitimacy of the government in the cities.

In the urban areas, there is a well-developed market for land, and land prices appear to reflect the relative scarcity and location of particular plots. The average urban resident desiring housing or the urban company desiring commercial

---

20. Most of the cases dealt with excessive illegitimate taxes and fees and corrupt use of government funds rather than with land issues per se, but the sale of land was subject to the same kinds of problems.

property can obtain the land in what is basically a market transaction, if some-times not a transparent one. Where there are disputes resulting from the trans-action, individuals and companies increasingly resort to the courts, although government officials still have a major say in the outcome of disputes and are often parties to the transaction. The courts are not independent of the executive branch of government, and they are not staffed by highly trained jurists, but this situation is gradually changing. True court independence from the executive branch of the government and from the Communist Party, however, is a long way off.

The urban land ownership system also falls far short of an ideal in terms of how land provides revenue to the government. The main source of revenue from land is a one-time payment at the time of the transaction. While this system works well in Hong Kong, in mainland China it is or soon will be an unstable source of urban government revenue. A reformed land tax system would provide less revenue at the moment, but would be a steadier source of government income in the long run.

The biggest challenge for the administration of land (and much else) in both urban and rural areas is that China is in the midst of the largest rural to urban migration within a single country in history. There are 200 million or more mi-grants in the cities, and another 400 million are likely to arrive over the next two decades. This large influx of mostly low-income people presents an enormous problem of how to allocate land for housing and expanded infrastructure. Urban planning issues include questions of where these migrants should live and how they will get to work. In the rural areas, the problem is what to do with the land that these former farm families have left. The current practice of having local of-ficials redistribute it to those who remain may be good for local rural equity, but the resulting insecurity of property rights does little for the migrants who left and does not provide adequate incentives for investment in agricultural land.

China's land system, therefore, is likely to look different a decade or two from now. Whether the differences will be large enough to meet the enormous challenges that China faces remains to be seen.

REFERENCES

Brandt, Loren, Jikun Huang, Guo Li, and Scott Rozelle. 2002. Land rights in rural
    China: Facts, fictions and issues. *China Journal* 47(January):67–97.
Chen, Guidi, and Chuntao Wu. 2006. *Will the boat sink the water? The life of China's
    peasants.* London: Public Affairs.
China Daily. 2008. Editorial: Fighting for our land. January 24:8.
China Economic Review. 2007. China to have second national land survey. May. http://
    China.org.cn.
Council of Economic Advisors. 2008. *Economic report of the president 2008.* Washing-
    ton, DC: U.S. Government Printing Office.

de Soto, Hernando. 2000. *The mystery of capital: Why capitalism triumphs in the West and fails everywhere else.* New York: Basic Books.

Ding, Chengri. 2005. Property tax development in China. *Lincoln Institute of Land Policy, Land Lines* 17(3).

Duda, Mark, and Bingqin Li. 2008. Housing inequality in Chinese cities: How important is hukou? *Lincoln Institute of Land Policy, Land Lines,* January:14–19.

Finance Asia. 2004. China's land law: An overview. August 23. http://www.hic.net.org.

Heston, Allan, Robert Summers, and Betina Aten. 2006. Penn world table version 6.2. Center for International Comparisons of Production, Income, and Prices, University of Pennsylvania.

Ho, Samuel P. S., and George C. S. Lin. 2003. Emerging land markets in rural and urban China: Policies and practices. *China Quarterly* 175:681–707.

Hong, Yu-Hong. 2003. The last straw: Reforming local property tax in the People's Republic of China. Working Paper WPO3YH1, Lincoln Institute of Land Policy, Cambridge, MA.

Huang, Yiping. 1998. *Agricultural reform in China: Getting institutions right.* Cambridge: Cambridge University Press.

Korea National Statistical Office. 2006. *Korea statistical yearbook 2006.* Daejeon: Korea National Statistical Office.

Kung, James. 2002. Choices of land tenure in China: The case of a county with quasi-private property rights. *Economic Development and Cultural Change* 50(4):793–817.

Li, Cao. 2008. Non-residents face ban on property purchases. *China Daily,* January 3:4.

Li, Fangchao. 2007. Illegal land use poses major threat. *China Daily,* September 18:1.

Logan, John R., Yiping Fang, and Zhanxin Zhang. 2008. Residence status and housing—the case of Beijing. In *One country, two societies? Rural-urban inequality in China,* ed. Martin K. Whyte. Cambridge, MA: Harvard University Press.

National Bureau of Statistics. 2007. *China statistical yearbook 2007.* Beijing: China Statistics Press.

Parish, William L., ed. 1985. *Chinese rural development: The great transformation.* Armonk, NY: M. E. Sharpe.

People's Daily Online. 2005. Land price varying trend in China's major cities in first quarter 2005. April 26.

Perkins, Dwight H., and Thomas G. Rawski. 2008. Forecasting China's growth over the next two decades. In *China's great economic transformation,* ed. Loren Brandt and Thomas Rawski. New York: Cambridge University Press.

Rosengard, Jay, Bui Van, Huynh The Du, Vu Pham Tin, Fang Xu, and Mochamad Pasha. 2007. *Paying for urban infrastructure and services: A comparative study of municipal finance in Ho Chi Minh City, Shanghai, and Jakarta.* Hanoi: United Nations Development Program.

Rozelle, Scott, and Guo Li. 1998. Village leaders and land rights formation in China. *American Economic Review* 88(2):433–438.

Song, Yan, Gerrit Knaap, and Chengri Ding. 2005. Housing policy in the People's Republic of China: An historical view. In *Emerging land and housing markets in China,* ed. Chengri Ding and Yan Song. Cambridge, MA: Lincoln Institute of Land Policy.

Sun, Yinh-hui. 1995. China's land market: Current situation, problems and development trends. *Urban Management Programme—Asia Occasional Papers*, June.

Wang, Fei-Ling. 2008. Renovating the great floodgate: Reform of China's hukou system. In *One country, two societies? Rural-urban inequality in China*, ed. Martin K. Whyte. Cambridge, MA: Harvard University Press.

Wu, Jiao. 2008. Illegal land use in cross hairs of new nationwide scheme. *China Daily*, February 2–3:2.

Wu, Jinglian. 2005. *Understanding and interpreting Chinese economic reform*. Mason, OH: Thomson.

Wu, Weiping. 2002. Temporary migrants in Shanghai housing settlement patterns. In *The new Chinese city*, ed. John R. Logan. Oxford: Blackwell.

Xie, Chuanjiao. 2008. Most migrant workers in cities unhappy: Survey. *China Daily*, January 14:3.

Xinhua. 2006. China strives to handle mass incidents. December 9.

Zhang, Xing Quan. 2005. Development of the Chinese housing market. In *Emerging land and housing markets in China*, ed. Chengri Ding and Yan Song. Cambridge, MA: Lincoln Institute of Land Policy.

COMMENTARY
Scott Rozelle

The chapter by Dwight H. Perkins is superbly written and covers an immense amount of ground about one of the most important of all factors of economic production (and beyond): land. If there is a bias in the piece—this is not a criticism—it is that the heart of the work is on the urban land system.

Perkins exhaustively makes two major points. First, he examines the evolution of China's land system and documents the emergence of true land markets. He convincingly writes that as of 2008, there are beginning to be well-developed land markets in urban China. Land prices appear to reflect the relative scarcity and are higher when the plots have desirable characteristics or traits. The average urban resident desiring housing or the urban company desiring commercial property can obtain that property in what is basically a market transaction, if sometimes not a transparent one. Where there are disputes resulting from a transaction, individuals and companies increasingly resort to the courts, although government officials still have a major say in the outcome of those disputes, and government officials are often parties to the transaction. Although no one would call China's urban land markets perfect (in fact, few countries can say this), they certainly are better than they were a decade ago.

The second major point, which is labeled a constraint to future land market development, is the way land provides revenue to the government. The main problem, according to the chapter, is that the main sources of land revenue are one-time payments made at the time of the transaction. Although this system worked well in Hong Kong, in this regard, according to Perkins, China is not equal to Hong Kong. In China land is already—or at least soon will be—an unstable source of urban government revenue. The biggest problem is the de facto ownership of China's urban land by a variety of different units. This fragmentation means that the benefits are dispersed, the rules of sales are not transparently applied, and land does not always get used efficiently. The challenge, according to Perkins, is that China needs to move toward a modern land tax system. Although such a system would provide less current government revenue, it would be a steadier source of revenue in the longer run.

One of the main areas of future inquiry, which the chapter does not now address, is that if economists and land scholars agree that this change is needed, why is it not on the immediate policy agenda? What political economy factors are keeping land tax reform from moving ahead? How close is it to being on the agenda? I hope that scholars can pursue this line of research, since it may uncover some of the constraints that are keeping this needed reform from being realized.

The chapter also has a section on rural land that makes a lot of good points about rural land policy. I believe, however, that there is a more succinct way of looking at the management of rural land resources, which make up a vast majority of China's land. In the rest of this commentary, I examine these issues and hope that these, too, are the focus of research in the coming years.

Cultivated Land in China: A Brief Review of Current Policies, Recent Achievements, and Future Challenges

Secure property rights and well-functioning land markets are considered important catalysts for economic growth, the argument being that investment and resource mobility can flourish only when there is a reasonable chance of reaping the rewards of improvements and when the resource can be transferred to someone who will use it for an activity that produces the highest return. Reduced risk of capital expropriation by the state historically has contributed to higher growth. In the past, poor land rights in China have been blamed for low investment in agriculture, the absence of land rentals, and the unwillingness of some farm households to move out of the village. Blame has often focused on deficiencies in national laws and policies. As China's development accelerates, especially in a world in which international trade agreements have limited the government's ability to provide artificially high returns on land through pricing policies (for example, in the ways that China's neighbors in Japan and Korea did for their farming populations), strong land laws and policies are going to be needed to (1) encourage the expansion of farm size—to help farmers to increase their farming income by increasing the scale of their operations; (2) help provide financial resources through land rents and use of land as collateral for bank loans to aid movements of rural households to the off-farm sector and to make investments in private businesses; and (3) provide secure land rights that will allow land to act as an insurance policy and encourage farmers to take risks and earn higher rewards (since, if they were to fail in their efforts off the farm, the family could rely on the land to earn a minimum standard of living).

In seeking to create a land system that can help raise rural incomes, encourage investment, and facilitate China's development process, the government needs to fully implement the new Rural Land Contracting Law and take additional steps to make it more effective. This innovative and far-reaching law, which greatly improves the security of land tenure for most people in China's rural areas, is well thought out. Among other things, it provides farmers with land for a contract period of 30 years and uses strong, unambiguous language to prohibit local governments and village leaders from reallocating land among households during the contract period. The law also explicitly protects the farm household's right to transfer land to other households without fear of losing the land, allows households to enter into long-term rental contracts, and stipulates that villagers can bequeath their land to their heirs during the contract period. The main weakness of the law is that it depends on local governments for implementation, and in many cases there are incentives to not implement it. Therefore, the central government needs to make a great effort to publicize the law and issue strong directives through both the government and the party hierarchy to convey its importance.

Besides implementing the new law, additional efforts—especially in the area of land registration—are needed to promote well-functioning land rental markets. In an economy like China's (with only small land resources per capita, in which the main new source of income in the future for most farmers will be off-farm employment, and in which the government is unable to use price policy to artificially inflate returns to land), households with opportunities off the farm need to be able to rent their land out, and those that are left in the village need to be able to rent land to be able to raise their incomes from farming. Today, although rental transactions are increasing—especially in well-off areas—most such transactions are informal, occurring between relatives or close friends, only lasting for one year, and subject to considerable uncertainty. Farmers would benefit from having more choices with more formal rental arrangements that could be carried out among individuals in a larger pool over longer periods of time. The decision to shift land among users also should not be carried out, as before, by village officials. Instead, decisions to transfer land among users should be left to the farmers themselves.

In promoting the mobility of land among users and other benefits, it should be recognized that the government still has a role to play. The government should begin to consider promoting the registration of land use rights. According to the experience of other countries in Asia and elsewhere, land registration has played an important role in increasing the confidence of farmers in their tenure security (which should promote investment and lead to higher incomes), has led to increased rental market activity, and has laid a foundation for banks to begin to use land for collateral for loans. If the land leases were extended for 50 more years or indefinitely, land registration would also lay the foundation for the beginning of de facto land sales. This would help rural households that have decided to move to the city finance that move. It would also give them a key asset on which to build a livelihood strategy.

5

Property Rights and Real Estate Privatization in Russia: A Work in Progress

Bertrand Renaud, Joseph K. Eckert, and R. Jerome Anderson

Why Is Russia So Different?

The institutional response in Russia to the collapse of the Soviet order and the development of markets—in particular, of land and real estate markets—has been different from the historical experience of Western countries. It has also been different from the experience of the post-communist societies of Central and Eastern Europe and of the Baltic states over the past two decades. It took Estonia only four years to enact a better and more complete set of laws for land and real estate than exist in Russia today. Why may it take Russia three decades and possibly more to develop its institutions for land and urban real estate markets? How have property rights and real estate privatization developed since the new Russian Federation emerged from the collapse of the Soviet Union in December 1991?

The struggle for legal clarity and consistency, administrative effectiveness, and operational stability in the development of property rights and real estate privatization over the past two decades in Russia appears to result from three immediate factors: (1) an initial level of significant ideological objection to private ownership of land; (2) a weak governance environment, as compared with international standards; and (3) emergence of conflicting economic incentives and sharp day-to-day competition among federal, regional, and local governments over public revenues from land and real estate resulting from the weak governance environment. These conflicts are usually built upon the remaining institutional legacies of the Soviet era. Upon further examination, it is also difficult to ignore the extent to which Russia's history explains the fitful pace of reforms so far.

The following analysis is organized in five parts. First, we examine the path dependence of Russian institutions and governance historically. Second, we contrast Russia with Estonia to highlight the critical impact of the quality of governance on the development of property rights and real estate markets and the importance of institutions to the transition. Third, we review the often conflicted legal development of property rights during the first two decades of the Russian transition. Fourth, we evaluate the current status of property institutions today, especially the land registration system and the urban land use rules that affect the development of real estate markets. We close with the argument that effective land use and real estate market institutions are a major channel of Russian long-term economic growth. Flexible and cost-effective real estate markets will be essential to the diversification of the Russian economy away from its rising dependence on the energy sector and extractive industries generally.

Path Dependence of Russian Institutions

By path dependence of Russian institutions over time, we mean that past and existing institutions shape the development of new institutions.[1] At the start of its transition in 1991, the Russian Federation did not have a tradition, long or short, of well-defined and secure property rights. Property relations have been characterized through virtually all of Russian history by the threat of confiscation by government power and by a lack of any concept of mutual obligations between state and citizen. Thus, the state, in both czarist and Soviet times, was not viewed as an impartial enforcer of private property rights.

Probably the single most important element of path dependence throughout Russian institutional development is the lack of reciprocity of obligation, which is a core element of all sound legal systems and of the modern rule of law.[2] Both Velychenko (1995) and Hedlund (2001) emphasize the lack of reciprocity of obligation in Russian feudalism: the lord commanded, the vassal obeyed, and the vassal did not expect the czar to provide for him in return for his obedience. This lack of reciprocity in obligation, which significantly differentiates Russian feudalism from Western European and East Asian feudalism, has had lasting consequences for property relations in particular. In Hedlund's analysis, it gave rise

---

1. See David (2000) on path dependence in historical economics. For a discussion of path dependence in the context of U.S. common law, see Hathaway (2000).

2. We appreciate Robert Ellickson's private remark at the Lincoln Institute of Land Policy's 2008 land policy conference about the critical role of reciprocity of obligation as a core element of any sound legal system.

to the creation of private networks designed for maximum self-benefit, with the state not viewed as legitimate because it was not a guarantor of private rights.

A brief review of Russian history shows a number of practices and laws that support the conclusion reached above. These historical practices are ingrained in Russian political economy and society, and today the World Bank's World Governance Indicators (WGI) show Russia ranked consistently low on governance criteria. Among those historical laws and practices affecting Russia are the following:

- Pipes notes that Russia was the only country to have established a Chancery of Confiscations. "From the end of the fifteenth century to the end of the eighteenth, Russian rulers appropriated the estates of their subjects at will, without observing any legal procedures because they considered all the land in the realm to be ultimately theirs" (1994, 530).
- The 25 chapters and 967 articles of the *Ulozhenie* (Muscovite Law Code) of 1649 is a landmark in the legal history of Russia. The code relied on fear, obligation, and rewards. Under it, nobles were subject to a variety of punishments, and historians report that punishment was prevalent. The code also formally established hereditary serfdom for peasants. While Weickhardt (1993) has argued that the law in Muscovite Russia gave the nobles rights in land equivalent to that of a fee simple, his is a minority view. Pipes (1994) argues that, by the end of the sixteenth century, the lands held by the nobility were conditioned on service in the feudal sense, and the nobles did not hold the equivalent of freehold estates as maintained by Weickhardt.
- The obligation of service to the state by the nobility did not end until 1762, and confiscation without due process of law was not abolished until the Charter of Nobility of 1785, during the reign of Catherine the Great (Pipes 1994). Thus, feudal land relationships lacking reciprocal obligation continued for a long time in Russia, at least up to the time of American independence.[3]
- The 1906 Stolypin rural land reforms in favor of peasants were based, in large part, on a "growing recognition that the land commune prevented economic growth, and that reform must be focused on the individualization of economic activity" (Skyner 2003, 889). It should be noted that land and property markets existed in the cities of industrializing Russia in

---

3. In his classic book *Empire of the Czar* originally published in 1839, Adolphe de Custine gives a firsthand account of life in Russia in the nineteenth century and illustrates how the lack of reciprocity between ruler and ruled had become deeply embedded in Russian behavior. Custine repeatedly describes how the czar meted out swift, frequent, and severe punishments on the aristocracy that trickled down throughout society. Because of its continued societal relevance, this account was republished in the United States in 1990 with a foreword by Daniel Boorstin and an introduction by George Kennan.

the early twentieth century prior to the revolution of 1917 (World Bank 1995).

- The Bolshevik Revolution of October 1917 imposed its own notions of rule by law, and "the real core of Lenin's program was that of a resurrection of the patrimonial and essentially rights-free system of old Muscovy" (Hedlund 2001, 223).

- The 1922 Land Code of the Russian SFSR (*Zelmeniy kodeks*) was written under the direct supervision of Lenin. Codes for other Soviet republics modeled after it followed between 1922 and 1929. It took until the 2001 Land Code of the Russian Federation, together with modification of the Civil Code, to have an operational recognition of private ownership of land for the first time in Russian history. Legal application of the new code to rural land occurred only the following year.[4]

What is important for understanding the current dynamics of land and real estate privatization processes is that early Bolshevik leaders determined not to establish a rights-based government or society, so the lack of a reciprocal relationship between the ruler and the ruled that originated in czarist times continued through the Soviet period (Hedlund 2001). It even continued after the end of socialism as rights became privately enforced by oligarchs and others (Braguinsky 1999). As Polishchuk and Savvateev (2001) note, public protection of rights discourages plundering. When the gains from plundering exceed the gains from legitimate production, plundering will be encouraged and public protection of rights discouraged. According to Polishchuk and Savvateev's analysis, this is exactly the situation that prevailed in Russia through 1998 as the oligarchs sought to maximize their returns through plunder. Through their influence on the government, they sought to prevent public enforcement of private rights. Braguinsky (1999), approaching the issue from a somewhat different perspective, reaches the same conclusion.

Four challenging initial conditions prevailed in Russia in the late 1980s. They shaped the first decade of transition and the overall emergence of a market economy as well as the emergence of land and real estate markets (Hedlund 2001). First, the transition to market carried the requirement of a total change in the mode of operation of government at all levels from the command economy to the use of incentives relying on tax, subsidies, and regulations. There was a strong official bias to the point of hostility against small and medium enterprises (SMEs). The high transaction costs of dealing with administrative systems remain a barrier to entry to this day. In 2007 Russia had one of the lowest SME output to gross domestic product (GDP) ratios (in the low 10 percent range) of the emerging market economies.

---

4. For a perceptive commentary on this historical moment, see chapter 6, "Land Privatization: The End of the Beginning," in Aron (2007).

Second, there were no Soviet enterprises with legal autonomy and economic accountability to privatize. State-owned enterprises were specialized components of the bureaucracy that focused on physical output, not value creation for the client (Dyker 1976). In fact, the notion of customer did not exist. The level of technology was inferior by international standards, except in some military areas. "Red managers" responded to a totally different set of incentives than did profit-oriented, market-focused managers.

Third, the political agenda of transforming the Soviet-educated population into a nation of stakeholders and even stockholders was unrealistic, at least in the short and medium term. There was a profound and widespread historical distrust of the state and its bureaucracy. The notion of rights was, at best, seriously undeveloped. During 70 years of Soviet control, market behavior was punishable by law as "speculation" (Hedlund 2001). None of the laws and institutions of the market existed, even in rudimentary form.

Finally, for 70 years the implicit goal of using the law had been to build bureaucratic organizations that were the real power base in the Soviet system. Understanding of the dual technical and ethical dimensions of property rights as social norms was uncommon (Hedlund 2001). There was not even a basic market terminology. During the first contacts between Russian officials and international experts in the 1990s, there was a strong demand for developing glossaries of new market-oriented Russian terms such as *loan*.

These four conditions rendered a shock-therapy approach to privatization and market creation unlikely to succeed. The first decade of Russian transition brought about a disastrous economic depression twice as severe as the Great Depression in the United States. Russian per capita income did not return to its 1990 Soviet level until the end of 2007 (International Monetary Fund 2008). This difficult social, political, and economic environment has contributed to the fitful and erratic development of property rights and real estate markets.

Privatization in Estonia and Russia: A Study in Contrast ————

Both Russian and international analysts have noted the difficulties experienced in the development of private property rights in land and real estate resources in the Russian Federation since the official collapse of the Soviet system in December 1991 (Braguinsky 1999; Heller 1998; Lazarevsky, Khakhalin, and Trutnev 2000; Skyner 2003). In countries of Central and Eastern Europe as well as in the Baltic states, privatization of real estate resources has proceeded quickly and relatively smoothly, comparatively speaking (Meyers and Kazlauskiene 1998). These different outcomes raise the question of why.

We begin by comparing the transition experiences of the Baltic Republic of Estonia with those of the Russian Federation to note similarities and differences in the processes by which the two countries approached the issue of privatization of land. While the two countries are obviously different in a number of respects, the comparison may be instructive precisely because of the sharp contrast in the way they have approached land privatization.

LAND REFORM IN ESTONIA'S TRANSITION TO MARKETS

In the early 1990s, at the beginning of the transition from administrative-command systems to market economies, it was often said that some countries, such as Russia, did not have usable pasts upon which to create market economies. Other countries, however, did have usable pasts upon which to build. To understand the land reform process in Estonia following its secession from the Soviet Union, it is necessary to understand Estonia's usable past—the processes of land privatization in Estonia in the latter part of the nineteenth century and in the period between the two world wars.

According to Meyers and Kazlauskiene (1998), by the late nineteenth century many of the large estates that had characterized Estonia had been divided and peasant farming established. Peasants were granted the right to purchase the land they worked. Estonia was independent between the two world wars. It continued land reform by redistributing land to, among others, small landholders. By the time of World War II, there were more than 140,000 family farms in Estonia. The country thus established a tradition, albeit a short-lived one, of individual landholdings and private ownership of land.

Given Estonia's brief, but real, experience with private ownership of land, it is not surprising that land reform was one of the earliest measures taken as the Baltic republics moved toward independence. All three Baltic countries began the process of land reform in 1989, well before their independence from the Soviet Union. The 1989 laws granted the right to establish family farms based on long-term use rights. This set the precedent for non–state methods of farming and paved the way for the introduction of private ownership.[5] Laws establishing private ownership of land in Estonia were adopted in June 1991, two months prior to the recognition of its independence.

After independence Estonia moved rapidly to establish the basis for private ownership of land and a free market in real estate. In October 1991 the Land Reform Act was passed. This comprehensive law, 50 pages long in English translation, sets forth the intention of the Estonian government to establish private property in land as the basis for all land relationships in both rural and urban areas. The law provides the mechanism by which citizens may apply for restitution of lands expropriated from them or their forebears during Soviet times. It also specifies the means whereby land may be privatized. Moving away from the operational problems caused by the vague concept of state ownership of land in

---

5. Lerman (1995) notes that these early laws in the Baltic countries distributed land to members of the collective farms and others who wished to engage in farming. When the restitution laws were passed, distributions of this type ceased.

socialist economies, provisions for state and municipal ownership of land are also included in the law. Estonian officials thus enunciated a clear policy toward land ownership and provided relatively straightforward procedures by which the policy could be implemented. Based on the legislative record, there was no ambiguity or confusion. The goal was private ownership of land, restitution where possible, compensation when restitution was not feasible, and an open market in real property.

In 1993 the Land Reform Act was followed by four new acts clarifying property rights and solidifying the market: the Land Tax Act in May, the Law of Property Act in June, the Land Register Act in September, and the Law of Property Act Implementation Act—clarifications of and amendments to various previously enacted laws—in October. In 1994 the Land Valuation Act was passed, changing the way land is valued for purposes of the land tax and for compensating individuals for illegally expropriated land. The Land Cadastre Act was also passed that year. In 1995 the Land Readjustment Act was passed, and in 1996 a law restricting alienation of land to foreigners, foreign corporations, and Estonian juridical entities was passed. This history is summarized in table 5.1.

Table 5.1
Estonian Laws Related to Real Property Privatization

Date	Law	Description
17 October 1991	Land Reform Act	The purpose of the Land Reform Act is to change the relationship of physical and legal persons to the land from state or socialist ownership to private ownership. The act states rules and procedures governing two major components of changing these land relations. One is restitution, in which land unlawfully expropriated in Soviet times is returned, to the extent possible, to the original owners or their descendants. The second means used to convert land to private ownership is privatization. Lands remaining in state ownership after restitution may be privatized according to the rules for privatization. The act also contains rules for lands in municipal and state ownership.
6 May 1993	Land Tax Act	This act imposes a tax on land. Usual exemptions for land owned/used by foreign embassies, governments, and cemeteries are granted. Land is to be valued in accordance with the Land Valuation Act. Data regarding the land are provided by local authorities; the tax is administered by the Tax and Customs Board and is paid to local government budgets.

Table 5.1
(continued)

Date	Law	Description
9 June 1993	Property Act	The Property Act sets forth a comprehensive framework of property rights and includes provisions for the creation, transfer, and extinguishment of those rights. Because the act covers both movable and immovable property, it is properly called a property act and not a land code. Among the rights covered by the act are the rights of ownership, servitudes, encumbrances (other than mortgages), superficies (important because buildings have been built on land owned by third persons), preemption, and security. The provisions on security cover both movable and immovable property and provide for security interests in intangibles.
15 September 1993	Land Register Act	This is a comprehensive act establishing and regulating the registry to be established in county and city courts. It prescribes the contents of the registry, describes how entries are to be made, details the registration process, provides for appeals, and, importantly, provides for open access to registry records. An electronic register is also authorized.
27 October 1993	Implementation Act for the Property Act	The Implementation Act for the Property Act deals with practical problems arising due to the complexity of the various rights sought to be established and implemented through the privatization and restitution processes. Rights of owners of structures vis-à-vis the owners of the underlying land are defined; rules governing illegal constructions are stated; the right of perpetual use of agricultural land is clarified; and the respective rights of owners of land and owners of utility structures erected on that land are enunciated. Rights of spouses in collective farmlands and farm households are also specified.
9 February 1994	Land Valuation Act	This act sets forth the rules for valuing land for purposes of the land tax and for compensating individuals for unlawfully expropriated land that cannot be returned by restitution. For purposes of the land tax, valuation is to follow international best practice, and is to follow the comparable sales, capitalization of income, or cost approaches to valuation.

(continued)

Table 5.1
(continued)

Date	Law	Description
12 October 1994	Land Cadastre Act	The Land Cadastre Act establishes the land cadastre, a national spatial database containing digital map data at scales of 1:10,000, 1:2,000 and 1:500 covering the entire country. The cadastre is maintained by the Ministry of the Environment, and stores data from the land registry to create a comprehensive description of land parcels and the rights and other attributes associated with them.
25 January 1995	Land Readjustment Act	The Land Readjustment Act complements land privatization and restitution. Its purpose is to allow landowners whose plots are not economically efficient to adjust their boundaries with their neighbors to make more usable land plots. Readjustment may be accomplished by "simple" procedures of agreement by adjoining landowners, or may be effected by more elaborate "reallotment plans." County governments supervise the process. Compensation and dispute resolution procedures are contained in the act.
29 May 1996	Restrictions on Transfer of Immovable Property Act	This act regulates the ownership of land plots (but not apartments) by non-Estonian natural and legal persons as well as Estonian legal entities. The act contains a list of areas in which land may not be owned by any of the three listed categories, unless the government of Estonia grants an exception. Outside of the listed areas, the local governor may permit foreign individuals or legal entities or Estonian legal entities to own land.

Source: Analysis of Estonian laws by the authors.

 While other acts covering particular issues of land reform were passed, the acts enumerated above were the primary laws governing land reform in Estonia. Most were passed within three years of independence, and amendments were few and generally involved technical corrections, not substantive or policy changes. In this short time, Estonia developed a coherent and comprehensive legal framework for property rights and real estate market reforms comparable to most other transition economies.

 This clear legal framework has resulted in the registration of a significant number of parcels in the land cadastre. According to statistics provided by the Estonian Land Board (2008), the number of registered properties in the Estonian Land Cadastre increased from 104,086 in 1997 (no month was given) to 544,841 in July 2007, an increase of 440,755, or 423 percent.

LEGAL FRAMEWORK FOR PRIVATE PROPERTY RIGHTS AND LAND REFORM IN RUSSIA

The process of land reform in Russia could not be more different. The first major difference between the two countries is the history of land relations. The second major difference is in the legislative process for creation of property rights reforms. In Russia the process has been marked by a lack of clarity, coherence, and consistency across laws (*zakoni*) passed by the Duma and executive decrees (*ukazi*) issued by presidents of the Russian Federation. There is also inconsistency among various legal documents over time. The first two decades of transition have been marked by frequent antagonistic relationships across levels of government and across the 89 regions and autonomous ethnic republics as well as between oblasts and municipalities.

As in Estonia, land reform legislation was passed by the Russian Soviet Federal Socialist Republic (RSFSR) in 1990 under then RSFSR President Boris Yeltsin prior to the dissolution of the Soviet Union. Several laws were passed, including the Law on Land Reform and the Law on Property. The Law on Property provided that physical and legal entities could own land parcels (Eagle 2006; Overchuk 2001). However, as Overchuk explains, these laws restricted other rights, such as the right to mortgage and the right to lease. They were restricted because of philosophic differences among members of the Duma regarding property rights; there was no real agreement as to how, or even whether, land privatization should move forward. Decrees of the president of the Russian Federation attempted to remedy some of the more egregious deficiencies in these laws (Overchuk 2001), but the result was a patchwork of legal requirements, not a coherent, unified legal regime. Following the adoption of the Constitution of the Russian Federation in 1993, the Law on Land Reform was repealed because it was not in keeping with the provisions of the new constitution. Thus, these laws did not have a lasting impact on land reform in Russia.

Article 35 of the 1993 Constitution of the Russian Federation guarantees all citizens the right of private property. This right includes the right to possess, use, and dispose of property and to receive compensation in the event of a taking by governmental power. However, these provisions were not self-executing, and Polishchuk and Savvateev conclude that "property rights in Russia [had] no adequate protection from the state" by the end of the first decade of transition (2001, 3). The authors identified many powerful economic actors who could gain more from predation than from state protection of all property rights.

Supporting the conclusion of Polishchuk and Savvateev, only one law tangentially relating to land was passed between 1993 and 1997, that being a law on organizing and operating agricultural cooperatives (Wegren 1998). Several decrees were issued and government resolutions adopted addressing specific issues such as agricultural experimentation in Nizhniy Novgorod Oblast and allowing owners of structures to purchase the land under their structures. However, no comprehensive land reform legislation was enacted. The Russian Civil Code was adopted in 1994, but members of the Duma could not agree on the property provisions contained in its chapter 17, so it was adopted without that chapter. In short, as Polishchuk and Savvateev (2001) note, the first seven years of the transition saw no improvement in the security of property rights in the Russian Federation.

In 1998 the Law on State Registration of Real Estate Rights and Transactions was adopted. It was the first significant land-related legislation to pass the Russian Duma since the adoption of the Russian constitution in 1993. That law originally assigned land registration to the Ministry of Justice, with implementation in the ministry's offices in each administrative region of the Federation. In 2004 the Federal Registration Service was established within the Ministry of Justice, and the land registration function was assigned to that body in 2005 (Rumyantsev 2008). In contrast with Estonia's 1993 Property Act, which reestablished the critical concept of property that recognizes land and improvements as a single integrated legal and functional economic entity, the Russian real estate legal and registration systems still separate land rights from the improvements over that land.

In 2001, three years after the Registration Law passed, the Land Code was finally adopted by a new Duma. This historical milestone recognizes for the first time in Russian history the full private ownership of land in both rural and urban areas (Aron 2007). That same year, chapter 17 of the 1994 Civil Code, which defines the implementation rules for private ownership, was also passed. However, the version of chapter 17 that was passed did not apply to agricultural lands. For political reasons, it was not until 2002 that the third Duma passed legislation applying the provisions of chapter 17 to agricultural lands. The last piece of legislation dealing with land was the 2007 law about a cadastre of real estate objects, which took effect in March 2008.

Symptomatic of the fitful Russian process of land reform, the Federal Real Estate Cadastre Agency, under the Ministry of Economic Development and Trade, had been created four years before the 2007 cadastre legislation was passed (Rumyantsev 2008). Rumyantsev notes confusion and overlapping jurisdiction between the duties of the Federal Real Estate Cadastre Agency and the land registration functions of the Federal Registration Service. Thus, even with land legislation in place, the confusion and uncertainty of the earlier years remains present in Russian land relations. A timeline showing the dates of enactment of various land-related laws in Russia is shown in the Appendix on pages 127–131.[6]

As Russia approaches the end of its second decade of transition, official statistics show a low level of land privatization for residential and industrial land

---

6. A more detailed timeline covering the period from *perestroika* and *glasnost* onward appears in table 5.4. As shown in that table, the passage of land legislation correlates well with the associated political periods as defined by Åslund (2007) in his review of the first two decades of the transition in Russia.

Table 5.2
Russian Residential and Industrial Lands in Private Ownership

	Percentage of All Russian Federation Land	Percentage of This Land Category in Private Ownership
Human Settlement Land	1.08%	18.5%
Industrial Land and Others	1.02%	0.39%

Source: Overchuk (2001).

and stagnation in the privatization of agricultural land. Confusion, uncertainty, and high transaction costs are reflected in the statistics showing the amount of land ownership by physical and legal persons. The relatively small percentage of private ownership of residential and industrial land is shown in table 5.2. These figures reflect privatization activity through the late 1990s.

Overchuk (2001) reports that federal tax and leasing policies appear to be important contributors to the low levels of private land ownership. Under Russian tax and leasing laws, rates for leasing land have often been lower than tax rates applying to owned land. Therefore, citizens and legal entities often choose to rent state-owned properties rather than privatize them because doing so is more economical.

With respect to agricultural lands, significant privatization has occurred. Overchuk (2001) estimates that 97 percent of all privately owned land in Russia is agricultural land, with nearly 12 million owners holding 117.6 million hectares. By the year 2000, there were over 200,000 peasant farmer enterprises in Russia, and more than five million citizens had applied for plots for private housing construction in agricultural areas. However, as Overchuk (2001) notes, the number of applications for land plots decreased substantially from a high of 1,827,600 in 1995 to a low of 336,400 in 1999. He attributes this decrease to the fact that the most valuable agricultural land had been privatized, with little good agricultural land remaining. Furthermore, some privatized land has been returned to the state, presumably because individuals decided to leave farming or found the tax burden excessive.

ESTONIA AND RUSSIA COMPARED

Cultural, political, and economic factors have resulted in stark differences in land and real estate privatization between Russia and Estonia. Table 5.3 compares the dates of passage of core land legislation in the two countries. The Estonian Registration Law was passed five years before the Russian Registration Law, the Land Code eight years prior to the corresponding Russian law, and the cadastre law in Estonia a full 13 years before the Russian cadastre law. Without a clear legislative

Table 5.3
Dates of Passage of Major Land Laws: Estonia and Russia

Type of Act	Year of Enactment	
	Estonia	Russia
Land Reform Act	1991	No equivalent law*
Land Code (or Equivalent)	1993	2001
Registration Law	1993	1998
Cadastre Law	1994	2007

*The Russian Soviet Federal Socialist Republic enacted two laws in 1990: (1) the Law on Land Reform in November; and (2) the Law on Property in December (Overchuk 2001). The Law on Land Reform was repealed following the creation of the Russian Federation, as were other laws (Food and Agriculture Organization 2008). No Russian Federation law passed in the early days of the Federation established comprehensive private property rights similar to the Estonian Land Reform Act.

basis for land reform, it is not surprising that Russia's land privatization has been so hesitant, tentative, and at times bewildering.[7]

Estonia, with its brief but important history of land ownership and private farming, created a land privatization process based on a coherent body of laws. These laws were enacted quickly after independence and implemented consistently. Russia, on the other hand, did not have a tradition of well-defined property rights. Following the demise of socialism, private parties, seeking to benefit from the plunder of state and private assets, helped to delay introduction of any cohesive system of public protection of private property rights.

RULE OF LAW, RULE BY LAW, AND THE QUALITY OF GOVERNANCE DURING THE TRANSITION

The development of the rule of law is the central pillar of the transition to political democracy. Under the rule of law, not only individual citizens but also the government itself is subject to and limited by the law. Specific human rights are protected against infringement by other individuals, organized groups, and the government itself. The concept of rule of law assumes a politically and socially legitimate source of the law. The prevalent view today is that democratic institutions and processes should be the sources of the law for a rule-of-law environment to exist.

It is not because they did not uphold the "rule of law" of market democracies that socialist societies were lawless. Rather the law was used as a tool to communicate and enforce the will of a powerful subset of society over the rest of society, with major implications for the structure and organization of the economy (Kor-

---

7. The only real exception to this consistent Estonian process was that initial privatization of agricultural land across the three Baltic states was to collective farm workers (Lerman 1995). This process was stopped quickly in Estonia once the decision was made to make restitution, wherever possible, to landowners as of 1940 or to their known descendants.

nai 1990, 1993). Alexander Yakovlev, who was one of the key framers of the democratic 1993 Russian constitution passed during the Yeltsin era, characterized the Soviet "rule by law" as "the law as a tool of dominance" (Lloyd 1998, 95).

The view that has emerged from the experience of transition economies as well as from the 1997 Asian financial crisis is that institutions and the quality of governance are critical factors for economic growth and long-term development— much more so than packages of economic policies such as the Washington Consensus or some institution-free, abstract reform proposals advocated by some Western economists for transition economies in the early 1990s. The sharp contrast between the transition in Estonia and in Russia suggests the central role that the quality of governance plays in the diverging experiences of these two countries.

The World Bank's WGI quantify six dimensions of governance:

1. Voice and accountability
2. Political stability and absence of violence
3. Government effectiveness
4. Regulatory quality
5. The rule of law
6. The control of corruption[8]

These perception-based indicators of governance yield informative and sharply contrasting results for Estonia and Russia that correlate well with the development of property rights and real estate markets in each country. Estonia scores in the top 25 percent of countries for each of the six governance categories, and over the 10 years between 1996 and 2006, trends in the quality of governance have been rising (see figure 5.1). In contrast, WGI data place Russia in the bottom 25 percent of all countries, with unstable indicators of governance without clear trends over time. In particular, Russia scores comparatively poorly on rule of law and corruption indicators (see figure 5.2).

In an analysis of Russian land and real estate reforms at the beginning of the transition, Renard (1997) pointed out that both the starting and the end points of the transition to market economies and democracy differ across countries. In the case of Estonia, the end point of the transition was unusually clear and

---

8. The World Governance Indicators (WGI) research project that started at the World Bank in 1999 is the most systematic effort to develop credible indicators of the comparative quality of governance across countries. In 2007 the WGI project covered 212 countries and territories for 1996, 1998, 2000, and annually for the period 2002–2006. The indicators are based on "several hundred individual variables measuring perceptions of governance, drawn from 33 separate data sources constructed from 30 different organizations" (Kaufman, Kraay, and Mastruzzi 2007, 1). For disaggregated comparative indicators of individual countries and individual years between 1996 and 2006, refer to the Web site http://www.govindicators.org.

Figure 5.1
Rising Quality of Governance in Estonia

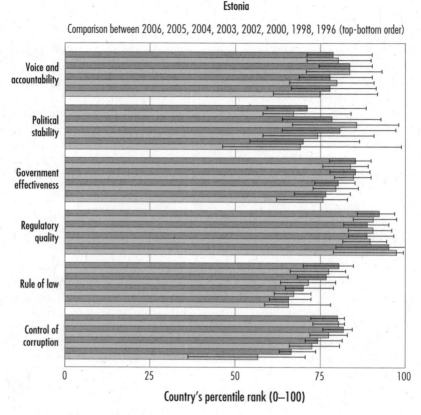

Source: From Kaufman, Kraay, and Mastruzzi (2007).
Note: The information is from the World Bank's WGI for 212 countries based on 33 data sources from 30 organizations.

agreed on by most Estonians even before the collapse of the Soviet Union in December 1991. The key strategic features were full independence from Russia by peaceful means, modernization and reenactment of the Estonian constitution in force prior to the Soviet invasion, move to a full and open market economy, and eventual entry into the European Union with its specific standards for the rule of law (*acquis communautaire*). It must also be noted that, from the beginning of its recovered independence, Estonia pegged its currency to European legal tender, first to the German mark and then to the euro. Privatization of land and real estate markets was an explicit part of the overall Estonian strategy.

Figure 5.2
Low Quality of Governance in Russia

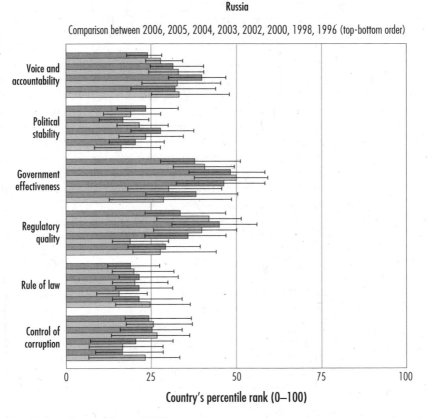

Source: From Kaufman, Kraay, and Mastruzzi (2007).
Note: The information is from the World Bank's WGI for 212 countries based on 33 data sources from 30 different organizations.

Culturally, technically, and in terms of easy access to international information, Estonia has benefited from its close proximity to Finland, the country that holds the highest WGI scores for the quality of its governance. In the case of large, inward-looking Russia, the actual end point of the transition remains unknown. However, one may still ask why Russia scores so poorly on governance and what factors are shaping the institutional transition to private land ownership and open real estate markets across its system of cities.

Development of Property Rights in Russia: The First Two Decades

THE FIRST DECADE OF TRANSITION (1989–1999)

The first decade of transition began before the actual collapse of the Soviet Union. This decade was marked by a genuine push by Boris Yeltsin for what amounts to a democratic revolution in Russia, first in his capacity as president of the RSFSR within the Soviet empire and after December 1991 as president of the Russian Federation. The outcome of the reformers' efforts to move toward democratic institutions and a market-based economy were uneven. Notably, the period was marked by the massive and most problematic privatization of state-owned enterprises whose after-effects are felt to this day (Freeland 2000).

The legislative process to achieve the privatization of land and real estate assets generated a plethora of often inconsistent, contradictory, and/or incomplete laws and executive decrees. Often the reformist presidential administration felt the need to issue decrees to correct the negative effects of laws passed by the Duma. As explained earlier, this state of affairs arose because different parts of the government at the federal, regional, and local levels often aimed to achieve their immediate economic self-interest irrespective of the public's need for a coordinated institutional infrastructure for land and real estate markets.

Politics, economics, and severe infighting within the national government structure combined to create a dynamic that was once described as a "war of laws." Nonetheless, a lasting achievement of the period is Russia's 1993 democratic constitution. This document recognizes the principle of the private ownership of land and allows Russians to buy and sell land. Notwithstanding this pathbreaking constitution, the first two Dumas of the new Russian Federation did not enact laws that would put these rights into effect. Communists and Agrarians, who dominated the Duma in the Russian Federation's early years, strongly opposed land and real estate privatization and blocked all attempts to pass implementing legislation.

The failure to privatize land in Moscow illustrates the erratic nature of the reform process during the first decade of the transformation. Taking advantage of their political access and of the intense institutional debates, city authorities succeeded in having Moscow exempted from the privatization decrees and in giving the city itself ownership of all the land within its boundaries. Under current regulations of the Moscow city government, land in the city may be leased by private businesses for up to 49 years only, which is the length of lease taken from the old Stolypin land reforms of 1906. In practice, this means that land cannot be owned by private businesses in Moscow. In most other cities as well, myriads of conflicting regulations have stymied real estate privatization.

Stressed Russian Urban System During the First Decade of Transition   The real estate privatization process was further hindered by the stresses placed on

Russia's urban economy by the collapse of the inefficient and massive Soviet industrial structure. Urban economic restructuring when GDP growth was sharply negative meant no maintenance of urban real estate assets and infrastructure, as well as severe depreciation of the urban real estate stock. Domestic capital and the limited amount of foreign direct investment (FDI) that took place during the first decade went mostly to Moscow and St. Petersburg. These two cities received over 60 percent of total FDI, and much of the rest went to a few energy-based cities (World Bank 2002). On the urban consumer demand side, the economy was volatile and stressful for the great majority of the Russian population. Income inequalities rose very sharply, even compared with large emerging market economies like Brazil and India.

Two other factors added to the difficult Russian transition compared to the cities of Central and Eastern Europe: the severely distorted spatial structure of Russian cities, and the fragmentation of property rights among multiple owners of the same state property at the start of privatization. Both factors further depressed the potential demand for privatization of urban real estate by residents and businesses.

From the low level of urbanization of 16 percent at the start of the 1917 revolution, Russia reached its full urbanization level of 77.5 percent by the end of the Soviet era. The development of these socialist cities took place in the absence of land markets and without land recycling for over 70 years, resulting in the strikingly inefficient spatial structure of Soviet cities. Because the cities have low densities in the center and high densities at the periphery, they have very low energy and transportation efficiency as well as extremely poor environmental quality (Bertaud and Renaud 1994, 1997). The proportion of land in industrial use was a multiple of that observed in market cities. Moreover, the industrial land was in very central locations and was underutilized. During the transition to markets, the distorted spatial structure in Russian cities generated a majority of losers among urban residents living in the periphery and a minority of winners among those who acquired housing in the city center.

For commercial businesses and offices, privatization created new property rights that conflicted with the processes inherited from Soviet times when federal, oblast, and local governments allocated land and building rights. Use rights, revenue rights, and transfer rights were fragmented among different agencies that were initially unwilling or unable to cooperate, making it impossible to use desirable buildings (see figure 5.3 and Harding 1995). Anticommons property may appear whenever new property rights are defined. In Moscow, for example, multiple owners have been endowed initially with competing rights in each storefront, so no owner holds a bundle of usable rights and the storefront remains empty (Heller 1998). These "anticommons" property use problems were also present in the initial years of transition in other socialist economies, but they were resolved relatively rapidly by the new legal frameworks. This did not happen in Russia because a viable alternative legal framework had not yet developed.

Figure 5.3
Fragmentation of Rights Between Agencies

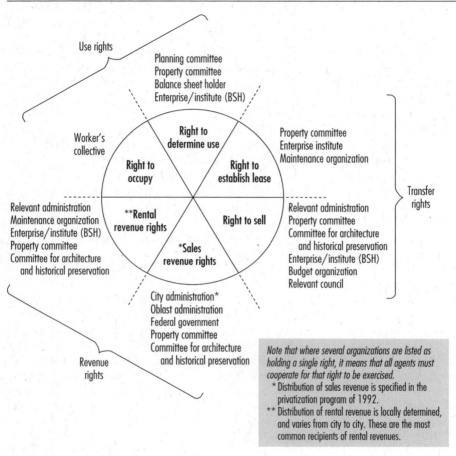

Note that where several organizations are listed as holding a single right, it means that all agents must cooperate for that right to be exercised.
 * Distribution of sales revenue is specified in the privatization program of 1992.
** Distribution of rental revenue is locally determined, and varies from city to city. These are the most common recipients of rental revenues.

Source: Harding (1995, 12). Reprinted by permission.

The End of the First Decade   At the end of the first decade of transition, a review of the status of real estate market privatization by Lazarevsky, Khakhalin, and Trutnev (2000) found that the transition faced a series of major urban land and real estate market problems. Among their findings are the following:

- There is inadequate federal legislation.
- Sale prices of state land privatized by enterprises are excessive.

- Local administrations have generally unfavorable attitudes toward privatization and cause unreasonable bureaucratic delays.
- The procedures for the purchase and registration of land rights from the state are lengthy. For example, it could take two and a half to three years for a sale to be completed, and then another six months to one year for a title certificate to be issued.
- Interpretation of federal legislation by local administrations is arbitrary; prices are arbitrary; and treatment of companies that wish to sell their land is uncertain.
- Targeting of land use is rigid. Even as the owner of a land plot, a company cannot fully dispose of it. The use of a land parcel is strictly and very narrowly regulated, and the landowner cannot change it for a more beneficial use. Commonly, local administrations fail to provide clear procedures for changing land use.
- There is no secondary market for enterprise lands, land mortgages, and other market transactions.
- The procedures for registration of land rights when ownership rights are sold by state or municipal authorities are vague.

THE SECOND DECADE OF TRANSITION (2000–2008)

Significant economic and institutional developments took place from 2000 to 2008 during Vladimir Putin's presidency. The economy entered a period of sustained high economic growth driven by the continuous rise of export prices in the oil and gas sectors. There were major improvements in macroeconomic policy and taxation. This period has also seen a strong trend toward recentralization of government powers. The Kozak reform package submitted to the Duma in 2004 and in force starting in 2006 aims at greater uniformity and control over the "subject governments" of the Federation. The democratic revolution of the Yeltsin era was followed by the Putin restoration of centralized powers.

The central achievement of the decade with respect to land and property rights is the historic passage of the Federal Land Code on 29 October 2001. Almost 74 years to the day of the Bolshevik Revolution, the Federal Land Code overturns a core legacy of the Soviet Union: state ownership of land. The code finally permits private ownership of land with sales and purchase transactions. Together with chapter 17 of the Civil Code (also passed that year), the Land Code now governs transactions in land. Initially, agricultural land was excluded by the Putin administration to accommodate organized opposition in the Duma. The application of the Land Code to agricultural land was enacted in 2002. For the first time in its long history, Russia fully recognizes the private ownership of land. Technically, the 2001 Land Code defines seven "prescribed uses of land":

1. Agricultural land
2. Land for towns and settlements

3. Commercial land for use by industrial enterprises, power companies, communications companies, and other industrial activities
4. Protected areas (land situated beneath an object that is itself specially protected, such as a nature park)
5. Forestry land
6. Waterfront land
7. Reserve land (land that is owned by the state, is not used for commercial purposes, and can be transferred to any of the other six categories)

Looking back at the entire period of Russian transformation from 1985 to 2008, there has been a relationship between the dominant features of political periods and the development of the legal and regulatory framework to create the infrastructure of private real estate markets. Table 5.4 presents a timeline of key laws, decrees, and administrative decisions aimed at creating private land ownership and the institutional infrastructure for real estate markets, to which has been added a column showing Anders Åslund's (2007) characterization of the political periods during which new institutional developments took place.

The development of efficient and free real estate markets did not improve greatly in the second decade of transition. The problems in 2008 are similar to the inventory of real estate privatization problems made by Lazarevsky, Khakhalin, and Trutnev in 2000. At the start of the new Medvedev administration, unresolved problems remain in three critical areas: (1) the absence of an integrated real estate registration system; (2) the lack of market-oriented land use planning regulations; and (3) the very slow emergence of land and real estate markets in every Russian city.

Russia's Property Institutions Today

Russian land registration policy has developed in fits and starts. It has been heavily influenced by a strong vested interest in the inventory system for land and improvements that was in place at the time of the fall of communism. The immature development of a unified titling system is due as well to the lack of the development of a coordinated real estate finance system and unified property tax system. The situation is exacerbated by the lack of demand by developers for urban land that results from the continuation of the Soviet site-specific land use planning process. These factors, when taken together, significantly reduce the demand from both developers and real estate consumers who otherwise would want to develop or own urban land and would require a strong and rational registration system to protect their property rights.

TRANSFORMATION, CONSOLIDATION, AND UTILIZATION OF THE REGISTRATION SYSTEM

A modern national registration system, if designed properly, will lay the foundation for a good real estate information system that is essential for the development

Table 5.4

Timeline of Russian Land Reforms, 1985–2008

Awakening	1985	*Perestroika* Announced
Collapse	1990	Law on Land Reform of the RSFSR
		Law on Peasant Farms
		Law on Property in the RSFSR
		Law on Enterprises and Entrepreneurship in the RSFSR
	1991	Land Code of the RSFSR
		Law of Privatization of the Housing Stock
		Presidential Decree "On Immediate Measures for Implementation of Land Reform"
Revolution	1992	Government Resolution "On the Course and Development of Agrarian Reform"
		Decree 301 "On the Sale of Land Plots to Citizens and Legal Entities Within Privatization of State and Municipal Enterprises"
		Law "On the Right of RF Citizens to Privatize and Sell Land Plots Designated for Subsidiary Farming, Gardening and Individual Residential Construction"
		Decree 631 "On Approval of the Procedure for Land Plot Sales Within Privatization of State and Municipal Enterprises, Extension and Development of the Premises of the Said Enterprises, as Well as Those Allocated to Citizens and Their Associations"
		Government Resolution "On Procedures for Privatization and Reorganization of Enterprises in the Agro-Industrial Complex"
	1993	Presidential Decree "On Regulation of Land Relations and Development of Agrarian Reforms in Russia"
		Decree 2130 of 1993 "On the Registration of Land Rights"
		Constitution of the Russian Federation
Rise/Fall of SOE Managers	1994	Government Resolution "On the Practice of Agrarian Transformation on Nizhniy Novgorod Province"
		Government Resolution "On Agricultural Enterprise Reform Allowing for the Experience in Nizhniy Novgorod"
		Decree 1535 "On Main Provisions of State Program of Privatization of State and Municipal Enterprises in the Russian Federation After 1 July 1994"
		Decree 478 "On Measures for Ensuring Stable Revenues to the Federal Budget from Privatization"
		Civil Code (Without Chapter 17)

(continued)

Table 5.4
(continued)

Rise/Fall of SOE Managers	1995	Government Resolution 96 "On Procedures for Realization of Rights of Owners of Land and Asset Shares" Law on Agricultural Cooperation
Oligarchy	1996	Presidential Decree "On Realization of the Constitutional Rights of Citizens Concerning Land" Decree 1368 "On the Purchase Price of Land"
	1997	Decree 485 "On Guaranteeing Real Property Owners the Acquisition of Ownership in Land Under Their Property" Decree 1263 "On the Sale or Lease of Land Parcels to Citizens or Legal Entities Located in Urban and Rural Settlements for Construction Purposes"
	1998	Law on State Registration of Real Estate Rights and Transactions Resolution No. 2 "On Approval of Procedures for Organizations of Sales (Auctions, Tenders) of Lands in Urban and Rural Settlements, or Lease of Them, to Natural and Legal Entities"
Stabilization	1999	Presidential Decree 632 "On the Right of Local Self-Government to Set Land Privatization Procedures and Terms" Government Resolution No. 1024 "The Concept of Public Property Management and Privatization in the Russian Federation"
	2001	Federal Law No. 45 Implements Chapter 17 of the Civil Code as to Nonagricultural Lands Law on the Delimitation of State-Owned Lands Land Code
	2002	Law on Circulation of Agricultural Lands (Implements Chapter 17 of the Civil Code for Agricultural Lands)
Authoritarian Recentralization	2004	Federal Registration Service Created
	2005	Registration Function Transferred to the Federal Registration Service
	2007	Law "About a Cadastre of Real Estate Objects"

Source: Authors' analysis of Soviet and Russian laws; Åslund (2007).

of the real estate sector and the overall economy. A sound and complete registration system should

- integrate land and improvements as property;
- organize the system around a parcel identifier within a national reference system;

- register the full bundle of property rights;
- limit restrictions to the bundle of rights based on public goods;
- list current and past right holders;
- provide dispute resolution; and
- provide state protection of real property rights.

When matched against these design features, it is clear that the registration system of Russia remains a work in progress. Reforms are needed to bring the current system in line with international best practices.

Overview and Historical Legacies of the Russian System   At the time of the fall of communism, information on land, buildings, and other improvements was managed by two different, independent agencies. The Land Committee (*Roszcomzen*) managed national land information, while the Bureau of Technical Inventory (BTI), which was part of the Ministry of Construction, managed the information on improvements. Each institution used a different numbering system to identify land and improvement units. There was no system for consolidating information on the improvements located on a specific land parcel save for the address information in each inventory. The location of parcel boundaries under existing buildings was often not recorded.

The registration system inherited from the Soviet era remains virtually intact today, overlaid with new legislative requirements and organizations. The first change occurred in 1998, when the Registration of Rights in Real Estate law was passed. This law allowed the property rights provided by the Civil Code of 1991 (amended in 2001) regarding rural and urban land and improvements to be registered and protected in the Unified State Register of Property (EGRP) administered by the Ministry of Justice (see figure 5.4, bottom rectangle). In 1994 the land and improvement registration agencies were administratively consolidated to become the State Cadastre of Real Property under the Ministry of Trade and Economic Development (MTED). The land committee is now called the Unified State Register of Land (EGRZ), and the BTI is renamed the Unified State Register of Capital Construction (EGROKS), as shown in the upper three rectangles of figure 5.4. In 2007 the law about the Cadastre of Real Estate Objects was passed. It became effective in March 2008 and retroactively provided the legal basis for this reorganization.

Complicating matters further, the registration of rights is not mandatory under the 1998 registration law. Furthermore, there is no automatic data transfer of information from MTED to EGRP. Essentially, registration is conducted at two separate levels. At the first level, there are no operational links between the land registration registry (EGRZ) and the parcel improvements registry (EGROKS), or between either of them and the EGRP. Furthermore, because the two first-level registration agencies (EGRZ and EGROKS) do not share common ID numbers, buildings cannot be located on a specific land parcel.

Figure 5.4
Russian Registration System, 2008

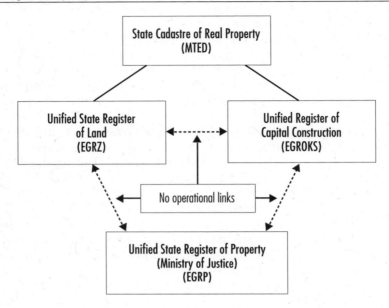

Any registration of property rights in EGRP, and thus the transfer and consolidation of data from EGRZ and EGROKS into EGRP, must be driven by an owner who is intent on having the property registered. Without the active role of the owner, there would be no unified registration system in Russia today because such registration is not mandatory. The system is thus driven by its clients.

In practice, despite the 1998 law that established a unified cadastre, to the extent owners do register their properties, they tend to register buildings and land rights separately rather than in the new consolidated system. This is in part because of the bureaucratic battles to control the fees from registration that occur between the land registry (EGRZ), the improvement registry (EGROKS), and the integrated registry (EGRP). This situation is also a result of the multiple bureaucratic rules and changes in business processes that have been complicating the process since 1991. Both EGRZ and EGROKS have been privatized and operate as state monopolies at the *rayon* and municipal levels and are aggressive in protecting their respective registration businesses. Each registration unit has now developed its own database structure and software. Each also supports a parallel paper structure because the legal framework does not recognize rights registered in electronic form.

Additional factors that favor maintenance of the old system include the mandatory purchase of an expensive improvement passport from EGROKS in order to activate the unified registration system. Also, people must waste considerable time waiting in lines to accomplish each step of the registration process.

Weak Demand for EGRP Registration from Residential Owners   The bifurcated nature of property rights in Russia, stemming from the Marxist view that land has no value, is another reason that owners of residences typically do not register their properties in EGRP. An owner of an apartment (the main form of ownership of residential property in Russian cities) typically has no defined land rights and hence has no reason to register anything in EGRZ. For that reason, and also because existing properties already have a passport in EGROKS, it is much simpler and far less expensive to simply register the sale and purchase transaction in EGROKS. Hence, there is little demand for registration in EGRP by residential owners. The only exception is the ownership of dacha property, which does include land rights.

Weak Demand from Urban Landowners and Developers   Urban landowners are a potential source of demand for the EGRP unified registry. This demand is muted, however, because most urban land available for business development remains in state or municipal ownership. While the public ownership of the land per se is not of particular concern, the problem is that most of this publicly held property has not been registered in any registry (Butler and Khakhalin 2005).

Furthermore, much urban land in Russia is difficult to privatize because there are too many right holders delineated by past laws (see figure 5.3 and the earlier discussion of the anticommons problem) and most city land has never been divided into parcels and linked to the improvements constructed thereon. It is thus common to find many buildings on the same land parcel or one improvement on a parcel that is not economically efficient, in other words, that is much too large. These factors cause uncertainty for urban developers.

OTHER IMPEDIMENTS TO LAND REFORM

The Land Code of 2001 and Local Land Use Regulation   The revenue structure of local government is mainly supported by land rents. Without a clear idea of how this revenue can be replaced, local governments lack motivation to carry out land reforms and instead undertake activities that preserve the current system. For example, the Land Code of 2001 regulates land use at the local level and provides for ownership of land by legal entities and persons for housing, industry, trade, and services. This law authorizes zoning and appears to put in place a reformed system by which developers can move forward with projects based on rights to land provided for in the Civil Code, rather than relying on the previous city-initiated and potentially revocable rights to land. Unfortunately, the 2001 Land Code confuses the issue regarding construction upon and use of land without a rigid use (the zoning approach) and the site-specific approach inherited from the past. Under a zoning approach, the legal status of the land is clear: a developer that buys zoned land can secure financing and begin construction of a permitted use without further government action.[9] If a use subsequently becomes obsolete, it can be changed as long as the new use is permitted by the zoning regulations. Under the site-specific approach, the developer must pick a parcel and then complete construction of a predefined use before the municipality will transfer the ownership of the lease right to the developer. The developer does not choose the use. More importantly, if there is a future change in use, the land parcel must be legally redefined, and a new contract with the city must be made to permit the new use. This scenario carries the risks of financial loss, potential corruption, and lack of construction financing options. Unfortunately, the Land Code provides for both zoning and site-specific planning without resolving the conflict between the two approaches. This lack of clarity has led a few cities to embrace the zoning approach while most other cities, including Moscow, have continued with the site-specific approach.

Real Estate Finance   Real estate finance in Russia is also problematic. In the formal banking sector, there is relatively little lending to developers who wish to develop residential properties. Commercial lending is complicated by low loan-to-value ratios and demands for equity participation by banks. Residential development outside the major cities is usually done via cooperatives organized by the developer. This process requires the ultimate owner of an apartment to contribute to the cost of construction by prepaying for the unit before construction begins, or by contributing periodic payment as construction progresses. The Russian banking sector does not act as an efficient conduit for collecting personal savings to be channeled into productive real estate investments. Furthermore, products such as equity loans that would allow capital to be taken out of real estate and be put to a better use do not yet exist in Russia. Thus, capital is trapped in real estate and unavailable to fund other uses that could accelerate economic development.

The Property Tax System   The current property tax system is also problematic and has a dampening effect on the demand to develop urban land. There are three types of property taxes in Russia today: a tax on land, a tax on business assets, and a tax on personal property (apartments, garages, and cars). When a developer considers construction on a privatized parcel of land, there is uncertainty about the ultimate land tax burden as compared to the current land rent. This is because leases are based on current use and the land tax is based on the current market value of the land put to its highest and best use (cadastre value). If the development is residential, the personal property tax on the apartment house

---

9. Building or other permits may be required, but they do not relate to the use of the property.

would be based on inventory cost or original cost, which in this case is current construction cost. The tax would thus be much higher on a new apartment than on a similar apartment built 20 years ago, even though the market value of the apartments in the new and old complexes may be close to the same. The business asset tax, which is now based on the current value of the real estate of a new enterprise, could be considerably higher than that on a similar but older enterprise because of the new improvement housing the new plant. Disincentives to build new facilities are thus built into the tax structure.

RECOMMENDATIONS TO IMPROVE THE RUSSIAN REGISTRATION SYSTEM

Four reforms are needed to improve the current registration system: (1) land and buildings should be considered as a unit; (2) a single identifier should apply to the parcel and the buildings erected thereon; (3) electronic records should be as valid as paper records for title purposes; and (4) land use regulation should move to a zoning scheme.

The first two reforms are the most important. Currently, the land registry, EGRZ, and the improvement registry, EGROKS, use a classifier of administrative territorial division (KLADR) that identifies land and improvement information down to street level. When records from EGRZ and EGROKS are consolidated in EGRP, a record number is assigned that uses the date of registration and the book and page number of the current registration book. This system severely complicates the title search process that would be needed, for example, to verify title and encumbrances to support a viable mortgage system. A new Russian classifier of municipalities (OKTMO), which has been under development by the Unified State Cadastre Agency since 2004, provides identification to the parcel level. If it were adopted by the EGRZ, EGROKS, and EGRP to identify land and improvement on the land, quick title searches at EGRP by developers, banks, and buyers and sellers of real estate would be possible. Use of this single identifier would also allow for wide public access to the data.[10] Further, integrated registration would facilitate the resolution of disputes and reduce government liability for inaccurate information on property rights in the EGRP registry.

Providing for property rights to be legally recorded electronically rather than just on paper documents would facilitate the automation of EGRP using uniform data formats and a common software platform operating throughout Russia. This could provide the technical basis for federal, regional, and local authorities

---

10. Laws would need to be changed to allow public access to real estate data; currently in Russia only parties interested in a particular land plot or improvement may have access to the data.

to move from a client-based system to a transaction-based system, improving the administration of local revenue generation and intergovernmental revenue sharing.

Finally, by eliminating the urban planning legacy of administrative and site-specific land use decisions that carry high transaction costs and instituting a rules-based zoning system, as well as replacing the existing property tax system with a transparent, predictable, and consolidated tax on real estate, cities would have the motivation to undertake land reforms. They would not be concerned with lost city income and/or the need to protect a large group of special interests who currently may prefer a titling system that lacks clarity.

VELIKY NOVGOROD AS A MODEL FOR REFORM

A model for these recommended reforms was implemented in Veliky Novgorod (Novgorod the Great) as a by-product of a tax experiment that began in 1996. This city now incorporates many of them in its legal and fiscal cadastre.

In July 1997 an enabling law was passed authorizing Tver and Novgorod to establish legal/fiscal cadastres and introduce a consolidated tax based on real estate—that is, on land and improvements together. The weight of the base was to be market value, and the taxpayers were to be physical persons and legal entities possessing the rights of use or ownership of real property. A computerized, parcel-based legal/fiscal cadastre that defined real estate as land and improvements together identified by a unified property record number was implemented to support tax administration. The historical site-specific land use allocation system was replaced by a rules-based market-oriented zoning system, and data on permissible uses were included in the cadastre. Currently, there are more than 260,000 real estate records in the electronic fiscal/legal cadastre. Registration and transfers of property are done at the Novgorod Unified State Register of Property (EGRP), and the records held at EGRZ and EGROKS are linked electronically to the corresponding EGRP records. In part because of the complete listing of properties made possible because of this reform and the use of transparent valuation methods, over 30 percent of Novgorod's municipal revenue now comes from the property tax, as compared to an average of 8 percent for all other municipal governments in Russia.

It is not clear how easily and how quickly this model could be extended to the other 170 cities in Russia. Veliky Novgorod has a long history of local democratic rules that were established well before the start of the communist regime. Elsewhere the current bureaucratic mindset is firmly locked into the site-based planning system of the Soviet era, and there appears to be little desire for change. This is evidenced by the attitude of many central government officials who continue to resist reforms that would encourage a stronger real estate market. Yet in spite of this inertia, and with Veliky Novgorod as a model, the federal government has embarked on a large new initiative that involves the Federal Tax Service, the State Cadastre of Real Property, the Federal Registration Service, municipal governments, and the private sector. The object is to develop a cadastral mass valuation system for the Russian Federation and to test it first in four oblasts: Kaluga, Kemerovo, Samara, and Tver, after which the system will be implemented in 25 of the 77 territorial tax offices. This project is a promising indicator that the Russian government, at least in some branches at the federal level, is recommitted to moving to a market-based property tax system and to the complete registration of all real estate assets.

Conclusions: Known Unknowns for the Third Decade of Transition

Given the specific path dependence of Russian institutions, success in the transition toward a market-oriented real estate economy is dependent on four factors: technology, laws/legal framework, institutions, and the macro economy. Russia's current status, based on the authors' latest 2008 observations in the country, is that, in terms of technology and the macro economy, conditions in Russia have improved significantly and the country is poised to move forward. In working on property registration projects and real estate market development, Russian counterparts are every bit as savvy and up-to-date as experts in the West. Discussions with Russian colleagues indicate that modern real estate information systems could be quickly implemented, given the necessary political support at the federal level. It is clear that information technology is not an impediment to development of a market economy in real estate.

Likewise, until mid-2008 Russia's macro economy was doing well, thanks to high commodity and energy prices. Conditions have changed markedly due to the sudden drop in energy prices in the fourth quarter of 2008, likely resulting in a slowing of growth in 2009. Oil- and gas-producing nations, including Russia, will likely take steps to manage output to keep prices at a level that will provide the liquidity needed for economic growth and expansion. Problems will arise in the future if Russia's economy remains overly dependent on resource extraction, but for now budgets are flush, thus relieving some financial pressure and giving some room for flexibility and experimentation with market methods both at the federal and the local levels.

Conditions are more problematic at the legal and institutional levels. As noted, registration of rights to real estate objects is not mandatory, a situation that should be remedied. In addition, the law should provide for electronic substitutes for paper records. This will facilitate transaction-based legal and fiscal cadastres. A further need in the legal framework is abolition of site-specific land use requirements and their replacement with zoning schemes along the lines developed in the West. This will give developers and owners greater flexibility in using their properties. Concomitantly, computer-assisted mass appraisal (CAMA) systems based on market valuation should be developed to support a modern property tax. These latter two changes will facilitate the highest and best use of land resources in Russian cities, thus raising property tax revenues for local budgets and stimulating the development of efficient land and property markets across cities.

In terms of institutional development, a distinction should be made between the federal government and governments at the local level, which are tellingly called "subject governments." The uncertain registration situation at the federal level described earlier should be resolved so that property owners know where and how they should register their properties. Infighting among registration offices should likewise be curtailed and a more customer-oriented approach developed. At the municipal level, there is evidence that local governments are beginning to see the benefits of following the Novgorod model in order to increase revenues. Diffusion of the Novgorod model to other municipalities should be encouraged. The current registration project sponsored by key federal ministries and agencies suggests that institutional barriers and perverse incentives are on the decline. As the results of the initial four-oblast registration project are evaluated and other cities are invited to replicate those efforts, the diffusion of international best practice in real estate taxation and management will spread across the Russian Federation. This will not be a rapid process at first, but diffusion can be steady and successful with the proper municipal involvement. If these legal and institutional changes are made, significant changes in the development of real estate markets can be expected.

Russia will soon enter its third decade of transition. Dmitry Medvedev, who was inaugurated as president of the Russian Federation in May 2008, is a lawyer by training and has declared that strengthening the rule of law is one of his top priorities. This could lead to a better environment for improving the institutions of real estate markets across the country. However, the outcome will result from the interplay among federal agencies, the demand for registration services, and better land use regulation at the local level. After the period of government recentralization during the two terms of Vladimir Putin, there appears to be strong interest among local governments to improve their fiscal autonomy, which could broaden nationwide support for market-oriented real estate reforms and a better registration system.

The Russian government's current economic objectives are to consolidate the macroeconomic successes of recent years, to maintain stable growth, and to widen, diversify, and internationalize the economy. These goals imply structural changes that are urban based: diversification into new industrial and services activities, expansion of the small and medium enterprise sector, sustained productivity increases, and a broadly based opening to the international economy. This strategy requires a sound real estate sector operating in revitalized cities because real estate costs rank second only to labor costs for service firms and small and medium enterprises (SMEs). The opportunities for growth are there because the SMEs' share of GDP is extremely low by international standards, less than 15 percent in 2007. A faster pace of development of the institutions of urban real estate markets will reduce a major constraint on the diversification of urban economic activities. This urban outcome, however, is not a foregone conclusion, as Russia may continue to depend heavily on its energy and natural resources and fail to develop a more broadly based economy.

APPENDIX

Table 5.5

Timeline of Land- and Property-Related Laws (and Selected Events) in Russia, Eleventh Century to Present

Date/Year	Name of Legal Document	Description
Eleventh century	The Russian Law, short version	"First great codification in Rus" (Weickhardt 1993, 666)
Twelfth century	The Russian Law, expanded version; codification of Russian law	
1280 or earlier	Court Law for the People	Maybe a code of laws or maybe a "set of moral guidelines" (Weickhardt 1993, 667)
Fourteenth and fifteenth centuries	Pskov Judicial Charter	Code of Laws
Fifteenth century	Novgorod Judicial Charter	Code of Laws
1497	Muscovite Code	Code of Laws
1550	Muscovite Code	Code of Laws
1649	*Ulozhenie*	Code of Laws
1729	Chancery of Confiscations	Kept records of lands confiscated by the czar
1785	Nobility Charter of Catherine the Great	"marks the beginning in Russia of private property in the true sense of the word" (Pipes 1994, 530)
1835	Codification under Nicholas I	Code of Laws
3 March 1861	Emancipation Manifesto of Alexander II	Abolished serfdom in Russia
14 December 1893	Legislation	Confirmed that peasant allotments were part of the system of administration of peasant estates; prohibition on alienation of allotment land
1901	Special Conference on the Needs of Agriculture	Conclusion: "Commune was the principal obstacle to agricultural advancement" (Powelson 1989, 117)

(continued)

Table 5.5
(continued)

Date/Year	Name of Legal Document	Description
9 November 1906	Decree "On additional regulations for the implementation of the law on peasant land ownership and land use"	Households taking title to land could not leave their villages
1 January 1907	Law canceling redemption debt	Abolished the obligation of peasants to compensate nobles for the land they acquired upon abolition of serfdom
14 June 1910	Law "On Peasant Ownership"	Reaffirmed that transfer of land held by (peasant) individuals was controlled by 1861 legislation
1911	Land Organization Statute	Codified previous decrees; provided for division and enclosure of communal land among individuals
9 November 1917	Bolshevik government organized	
19 February 1918	Land nationalized	
Spring 1921	New Economic Policy	
30 December 1922	USSR came into being	
27 December 1927	End of New Economic Policy	
1 October 1928– 31 December 1932	First Five-Year Plan	Collectivization begins
1936	Stalin's constitution	
11 March 1985	Gorbachev becomes general secretary	
October 1985	Gorbachev announces *perestroika* reform plan	
23 November 1990	Law on Land Reform of the RSFSR	
November 1990	Law on Peasant Farms	
December 1990	Law on Property in the RSFSR	
December 1990	Law on Enterprises and Entrepreneurship in the RSFSR	
April 1991	Land Code of the RSFSR	
August 1991	Independence of Baltic states recognized by the Soviet Union	
July 1991	Law on the Privatization of Housing Stock	

Table 5.5
(continued)

Date/Year	Name of Legal Document	Description
25 December 1991	Gorbachev resigns; USSR dissolved	
27 December 1991	Presidential decree "On Immediate Measures for Implementation of Land Reform"	
March 1992	Government resolution "On the Course and Development of Agrarian Reform"	
25 March 1992	Decree 301 "On sale of land plots to citizens and legal entities within privatization of state and municipal enterprises"	Permits enterprises to purchase land under their facilities
14 June 1992	Decree 631 "On approval of the procedure for land plots sales within privatization of state and municipal enterprises, extension and development of the premises of the said enterprises, as well as those allocated to citizens and their associations for business activities"	Permits purchase of land under privatized enterprises
23 December 1992	Law "On the Right of RF Citizens to Privatize and Sell Land Plots Designated for Subsidiary Farming, Gardening and Individual Residential Construction"	
September 1992	Government resolution "On Procedures for Privatization and Reorganization of Enterprises in the Agro-Industrial Complex"	
27 October 1993	Presidential decree 1767 "On Regulation of Land Relations and Development of Agrarian Reforms in Russia"	
11 December 1993	Decree 2130 of 1993	Registration of documents affecting rights to land in the RF Committee for Land Resources and Land Management

(continued)

Table 5.5
(continued)

Date/Year	Name of Legal Document	Description
December 1993	Constitution of the Russian Federation	
April 1994	Government resolution "On the Practice of Agrarian Transformation on Nizhniy Novgorod Province"	
July 1994	Government resolution "On Agricultural Enterprise Reform Allowing for the Experience in Nizhniy Novgorod Province"	
22 July 1994	Decree 1535 "On Main Provisions of the State Program of Privatization of State and Municipal Enterprises in the Russian Federation after July 1, 1994"	Permits purchase of land under privatized enterprises; apparently permitted a price of from 20 to 200 times the land tax
1994	Decree 478 "On Measures for Ensuring Stable Revenues to the Federal Budget from Privatization"	Regulates the purchase price of land; uses land tax rate and permits a price of five times the rate, with no ceiling
October 1994	Civil Code	
1 February 1995	Government resolution no. 96 "On Procedures for Realization of Rights of Owners of Land and Asset Shares"	
December 1995	Law on Agricultural Cooperation	
March 1996	Presidential decree "On Realization of the Constitutional Rights of Citizens Concerning Land"	
1996	Decree 1368	Regulates the purchase price of land
16 May 1997	Decree 485 "On Guaranteeing Real Property Owners the Acquisition of Ownership in Land Under Their Property"	Regulates the purchase price of land
26 November 1997	Decree 1263 "On the Sale or Lease of Land Parcels to Citizens or Legal Entities Located in Urban and Rural Settlements for Construction Purposes"	

Table 5.5
(continued)

Date/Year	Name of Legal Document	Description
30 January 1998	Law on State Registration of Real Estate Rights and Transactions	
7 May 1998	Resolution no. 2 "On Approval of Procedures for Organization of Sales (Auctions, Tenders) of Lands in Urban and Rural Settlements, or Lease of Them, to Natural and Legal Entities"	Procedures for sales
1999	Presidential decree no. 632	Right of local self-government to set their own land privatization procedures and terms
1999	Government resolution no. 1024 "The Concept of Public Property Management and Privatization in the Russian Federation"	
16 April 2001	Federal Law no. 45 implements chapter 17 of the Civil Code	
July 2001	Law on Delimitation of State-Owned Land	Marked the start of the process of allocating ownership rights to state land among the federal, regional, and municipal governments
25 October 2001	Land Code signed into law	
25 July 2002	Law "On the Circulation of Agricultural Lands" signed into force	Implements chapter 17 of the Civil Code with respect to agricultural lands
2004	Federal Registration Service created	
2005	Registration function transferred to Federal Registration Service	

Sources: Analysis of Russian laws by the authors and sources cited in the Appendix.

REFERENCES

Aron, Leon. 2007. *Russia's revolution: Essays 1989–2006.* Washington, DC: American Enterprise Institute Press.

Åslund, Anders. 2007. *Russia's capitalist revolution: Why market reform succeeded and democracy failed.* Washington, DC: Peterson Institute for International Economics.

Bertaud, Alain, and Bertrand Renaud. 1994. *Cities without land markets: Lessons from the failed socialist experiment*. World Bank Discussion Paper No. 227, Washington, DC.

————. 1997. Socialist cities without land markets. *Journal of Urban Economics* 41(1):137–152.

Braguinsky, Serguey. 1999. Enforcement of property rights during the Russian transition: Problems and some approaches to a new liberal solution. *Journal of Legal Studies* 28(2):515–544.

Butler, Stephen, and Andrei Khakhalin. 2005. *Final report on business access to land*. Prepared for the Ministry of Economic Development and Trade of the Russian Federation.

Custine, Adolphe de. 1990 (1839). *Empire of the czar, journey through eternal Russia*, trans. Daniel J. Boorstin, intro. by George F. Kennan. New York: Doubleday, Anchor Books.

David, Paul. 2000. Path dependence, its critics and the quest for historical economics. In *Evolution and path dependence in economic ideas: Past and present*, ed. P. Garrouste and S. Ioannides. Cheltenham, U.K.: Edward Elgar.

Dyker, D. 1976. *The Soviet economy*. New York: St. Martin's Press.

Eagle, Steven J. 2006. Private property, development and freedom: On taking our own advice. *Southern Methodist University Law Review* 59(Winter):345–383.

Estonian Land Board. 2008. Statistics on land registration in the land cadastre. http://www.maaamet.ee/index.php?lang_id=2&page_id=202&menu_id=87.

Food and Agriculture Organization (FAO). 2008. Russian Federation: Law No. 374–1 of 1990, On land reform. http://faolex.fao.org/cgibin/faolex.exe?database=faolex&search_type=query&table=result&query=LEXFAOC027852&format_name=@ERALL&lang=eng.

Freeland, Chrystia. 2000. *Sale of the century: Russia's wild ride from communism to capitalism*. New York: Crown Business.

Harding, April. 1995. Commercial real estate development in Russia. World Bank, CFS Discussion Paper Series No. 109, Washington, DC.

Hathaway, Oona A. 2000. The path dependence of the law: The course and pattern of legal change in a common law system. Boston University School of Law, Working Paper Series on Law and Economics, WP00-06.

Hedlund, Stefan. 2001. Property without rights: Dimensions of Russian privatization. *Europe-Asia Studies* 53(2):213–237.

Heller, Michael J. 1998. The tragedy of the anti-commons: Property in the transition from Marx to markets. *Harvard Law Review* 111:621–688.

International Monetary Fund (IMF). 2008. World economic outlook update: Global slowdown and rising inflation. http://www.imf.org/external/ns/cs.aspx?id=29.

Kaufman, Daniel, Aart Kraay, and Massimo Mastruzzi. 2007. Governance matters VI: Aggregate and individual governance indicators 1996–2006. World Bank, Working Paper WPS4280.

Kornai, Janos. 1990. The affinity between ownership forms and coordination mechanisms. *Journal of Economic Perspectives* 4(3):131–147.

————. 1993. *The socialist economy: The political economy of communism*. Princeton, NJ: Princeton University Press.

Lazarevsky, Andrei, Andrei Khakhalin, and Eduard Trutnev. 2000. Development of the real estate market and registration of real estate rights in the Russian Federation. In

Urban management reform in Russia, 1998–2000, ed. Nadezhda B. Kosareva and
    Raymond J. Struyk. Moscow: Urban Economics Institute.
Lerman, Zvi. 1995. Changing land relations and farming structures in former social-
    ist countries. In *Agricultural land ownership in transitional economies*, ed. Gene
    Wunderlich. Lanham, MD: University Press of America Inc.
Lloyd, John. 1998. *Rebirth of a nation: An anatomy of Russia*. London: Penguin
    Group, Michael Joseph.
Meyers, William H., and Natalija Kazlauskiene. 1998. Land reform in Estonia, Latvia
    and Lithuania: A comparative analysis. In *Land reform in the former Soviet Union
    and Eastern Europe*, ed. Stephen Wegren. London and New York: Routledge.
Overchuk, Alexei. 2001. *Development of private landownership in Russia*. Madison:
    Land Tenure Center, University of Wisconsin.
Pipes, Richard. 1994. Was there private property in Muscovite Russia? *Slavic Review*
    53(2):524–530.
Polishchuk, Leonid, and Alexei Savvateev. 2001. Spontaneous (non) emergence of
    property rights. IRIS Center Working Paper No. 241. http://papers.ssrn.com/sol3/
    papers.cfm?abstract_id=260036#PaperDownload.
Powelson, John. 1989. *The story of land: A world history of land tenure and agrarian
    reform*. Cambridge, MA: Lincoln Institute of Land Policy.
Renard, Vincent. 1997. The reform of the real estate system in the Federation of Russia.
    In *The real estate reform process in the post-communist countries*, ed. Jeong-Sik
    Lee. Seoul: Korea Research Institute for Human Settlements Press.
Rumyantsev, Igor. 2008. Personal communication with Jerome Anderson.
Skyner, Louis. 2003. Property as rhetoric: Land ownership and private law in pre-Soviet
    and post-Soviet Russia. *Europe-Asia Studies* 55(6):889–905.
Velychenko, Stephen. 1995. Identities, loyalties and service in imperial Russia: Who
    administered the borderlands? *Russian Review* 54(2):188–208.
Wegren, Stephen K. 1998. The conduct and impact of land reform in Russia. In *Land
    reform in the former Soviet Union and Eastern Europe*, ed Stephen Wegren. Lon-
    don and New York: Routledge.
Weickhardt, George G. 1993. The pre-Petrine law of property. *Slavic Review*
    52(4):663–679.
World Bank. 1995. Russia: Housing reform and privatization: Strategy and transition
    issues. Report No. 14929-RU.
———. 2002. *Russia: Economic report No. 4*. Russia Office, October.

COMMENTARY
Robert M. Buckley

"Property Rights and Real Estate Privatization in Russia" provides an interesting discussion of the evolution of real estate registration issues in Russia. It traces the history of property rights over the past 400 years, suggesting that the lack of reform is deeply affected by the path dependency of this legacy. It then compares the rather tepid reforms that have been implemented in Russia with the more extensive reforms undertaken in nearby Estonia. It goes on to describe the benefits of the extensive reforms that have been achieved in one place in Russia, the city of Veliky Novgorod, and suggests that those reforms could be a model for a broader reform agenda. Finally, it makes a number of recommendations about the sorts of registration system improvements that could promote the efficiency of real estate markets and in so doing contribute to broader economy-wide reforms.

It is a well-written piece that provides a rich history of the evolution of Russian property rights and considerable detail on the operation of effective land and property registration systems. More important, enactment of the proposed reforms would go a long way toward improving the functioning of real estate markets, and these improvements would, in turn, contribute to economic growth and welfare. Hence, the work will be a useful resource for those interested in land and property reforms in Russia.

I think the extensive discussion of policies implemented in Russia for more than 100 years, and sometimes as long ago as the seventeenth century, is interesting. History is certainly important, but so too are other, more current policy issues such as the pricing of utilities. Until such pricing issues are addressed, I have considerable doubts about whether there will be motivation to undertake the sorts of property rights reforms the authors identify as the most important ones.

Considering some of the factors not discussed in the comparison of the reforms in Estonia and Russia will help explain why current and much broader policy issues may be at least as important as the behavior of the czars or the interaction of Catherine the Great with the nobility in the eighteenth century. Two factors in the current comparison could be made more prominent.

First, some features of the structure of the economies, which could hardly be more different, have potentially enormous implications for reform. In particular, Estonia is a tiny, open, resource-constrained economy. Russia is the opposite—large, resource rich, and with not nearly as open an economy. These differences have important implications for the strength of the incentives to undertake resource pricing reforms that have played such a large part in motivating real estate reforms in Estonia and not in Russia.

Second, differences in the credibility of the property rights systems that existed in the two countries are pronounced. In particular, the Estonian property rights system was imposed from abroad after World War II rather than evolving, albeit fitfully, through domestic actions. In Russia the system may have also been imposed, but the imposition was not done by foreigners. Hence, on a basic level, the Estonian reforms can be seen as throwing off the yoke of an invader. Russia did not have a similarly strong rationale for reform. This bit of history would be worth discussing further as a reason for the much stronger motivations for reform in Estonia than in Russia.

The effects of the aforementioned differences in the two countries' economic structures may best be highlighted by a personal anecdote. During a 1997 visit to St. Petersburg, I heard this anecdote from a Russian analyst: Six years earlier, upon learning that oil-dependent Estonia was about to introduce utility price increases, he had looked across the Gulf of Finland to Estonia and conjectured that it was on the brink of social unrest. He went on to say that the unrest had not occurred and that by 1997 Estonia had digested the higher utility prices. Oil-rich Russia, unfortunately, had not yet begun to reform its utility pricing policies, keeping them far below market prices.

Why do utility prices matter for the incentives to create well-functioning property registration systems? Perhaps most fundamentally, they matter because as Hegedus, Mayo, and Tosics (1996) show, Russia began its reforms with an administrative rather than a physical shortage of real estate, as well as a very energy-inefficient real estate capital stock. That is, except by accident, all families and firms held nonoptimal amounts of poorly insulated real estate. One of the main ways to induce the reshuffling and retrofitting of this misallocated and inefficient real estate would be to rely on the prices of utilities to encourage the trade and renovation of assets. Of course, it would be far easier to undertake such trades or to realize the full gains from retrofitting investments with an effective property registration system. Hence the need for reform. However, when energy prices continue to be heavily subsidized as they are in Russia, there is much less incentive to trade or retrofit. That is, when the costs of holding more real estate are not borne by the asset owner, that owner has considerably less interest in trading down or retrofitting a property. In such an environment, the gains to asset owners from improving ownership rights—such as those conferred by improved registration systems—are not obvious and may not be present even if they could yield large social benefits.

On the other hand, in places where these resource costs have been recognized by higher prices, such as Estonia, it is not surprising to find considerably more interest in reform. But that is not the only motivation for more rapid and far-reaching reform in Estonia. Resource scarcity, as well as the size and location of its economy, also matters. For Estonia's small, open economy on the edge of Europe to thrive, it had to welcome foreign investors. This condition, in turn, meant that it had to provide clarity to asset ownership; otherwise, foreigners would not invest. In Russia the many tales of fleecing foreign investors stand in stark contrast to this situation. In a word, it could be argued that Estonia acted on property rights establishment because it had to, and Russia, like many other resource-rich countries, did not have to act to gain access to the resources and, unfortunately, did not.

Trying to establish the role of various factors in determining whether reforms are implemented will always involve conjecture. Rather than deeply constrained utility prices, the path dependency generated by Russia's institutions and legal code may have been the driver of the snail pace of reforms. In the end, we don't know. However, at the very least, certainly before recommending extensive institutional reforms in the way property is registered, it would be useful to determine whether the owners whose assets would be registered are interested in registration. If they are not, such far-reaching reforms will continue to be difficult to implement and even harder to maintain.

REFERENCE

Hegedus, Jozsef, Stephen Mayo, and Ivan Tosics. 1996. Transition of the housing sector in the East Central European countries. *Review of Urban and Regional Development Studies* 8:101–136.

6

Developing Land Markets Within the Constraint of State Ownership in Vietnam

Stephen B. Butler

*I*n 2003 Vietnam adopted its Law on Land (LOL), a comprehensive framework law on allocation and use of land.[1] The law introduced a number of new concepts to land relations that had been developing gradually over the prior 10 to 15 years. It became effective as of 1 January 2004, but implementation continues today. Vietnam is one of a handful of emerging markets that maintains exclusive state ownership of land, and a main objective of the LOL was to approximate the dynamics and efficiency of a true land market within the constraint of state ownership. The idea was to facilitate access to and turnover of land, maximize its use and value, and enhance economic development.[2]

This chapter arises from work performed under a joint project of the Foreign Investment Advisory Service (FIAS), a division of the International Finance Corporation (IFC) and a member of the World Bank Group; the Mekong Private Sector Development Facility (MPDF), a division of the IFC located in Hanoi; and

---

1. Law on Land (2003); see also Decree No. 181/2004/ND-CP (2004) on implementation of the LOL.

2. Prior to the start of the work described in this chapter, the objectives of the LOL were determined by analysis of the law and its legislative history and by interviews with government officials and private sector stakeholders. The law, of course, has multiple objectives, not the least of which was to enhance government revenues from land resources.

the Vietnam Ministry of Natural Resources and the Environment (MoNRE).[3] The work was supported by FIAS and the Australian Agency for International Development (AusAID 2000a, 2000b). Main objectives of the work were to use the techniques of survey research and in-depth interviews to assess the impact of the LOL on business access to land, to determine the extent to which the objectives of the LOL are being achieved, and to recommend possible approaches to addressing any shortcomings in the law and its implementation. The work also assessed the main administrative procedures established in the LOL and accompanying regulations for allocating state-owned land to businesses and registering land rights and transactions. It attempted to elicit the views and perceptions of public officials, small and medium-sized enterprises (SMEs), and land market intermediaries (LMIs) regarding laws and policies on land user rights, land use planning, security of land rights, and other issues relevant to investment in land. A main area of inquiry was the cause and effect of the presumed large number of land transactions in the informal sector.

The major part of the work underlying this chapter, which focused on improvement of public administration and assessment of the efficiency of administrative procedures for allocating and transferring land to businesses, is not discussed here. The focus of this chapter is rather on the experiences and perceptions of SMEs in acquiring and transacting land rights. After briefly describing the research methodology, the chapter provides general background on the legal and regulatory framework for land relations in Vietnam today and an overview of the primary (state) and secondary land markets. The perceptions and experiences of SMEs in the land markets are discussed, with particular attention to issues such as informality, security of land rights, and investment.

Research Methodology

The research was carried out in 12 provinces, ranging from Ho Chi Minh City, with a population of over 6 million and a population density of 2,560 per square kilometer, to Lao Cai province, with a population of 550,000 and a density of

---

3. The underlying research was undertaken with the advice and assistance of many individuals and organizations, including many representatives of the government of Vietnam and private businesses who generously gave their time and the benefit of their expertise. Major contributions were made by Frederique Goy, Ivan Nimac, and Russell Muir of the IFC; the Vietnam Ministry of Natural Resources and the Environment; Trung Tran Nhu of the Joint Stock Company of Consultancy Service and Technology Development for Natural Resources and Environment (TECOS); the staff of the Mekong Private Sector Development Facility, in particular Lan Van Nguyen and Trung Thanh Duong; the "Strengthening Environmental Management and Land Administration" project (SEMLA) funded by the Swedish International Development Agency and the Asian Development Bank; and Professor John Gillespie of Monash University, who shared his work and advice on issues of law and business regulation in Vietnam. Any errors of fact, or opinions, or conclusions expressed in this report are solely those of the author.

Figure 6.1
Interview Regions

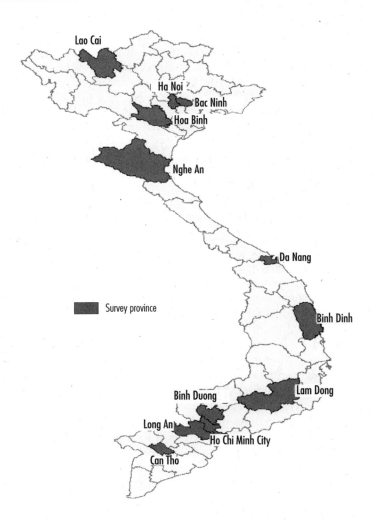

only 88 persons per square kilometer. The selected provinces are shown in figure 6.1. The 665 SMEs interviewed included registered firms, household enterprises, and individual entrepreneurs with recent experience in the land markets, but did not include unregistered or "informal" businesses or large firms and foreign or state-owned enterprises (SOEs), both of which also tend to be large. The fact that most respondents had already registered their businesses demonstrates a willingness to play by the rules and perhaps a perception that registration offers benefits. This may not be true of many unregistered or informal businesses. Accordingly, the study does not draw conclusions about the prevalence of informality in land markets generally. The exclusion of large, foreign, and state-owned enterprises is attributable solely to the fact that this was a project focusing on SMEs. Other work has suggested that large, foreign, and state-owned firms have different experiences in land markets than do small and medium-sized domestic firms, a suggestion that is supported somewhat by some of the findings of this study, such as the finding that firm size is related to location in state-sponsored industrial parks and receipt of investment subsidies.[4]

Almost half of the SMEs characterized themselves as being involved in trade, and a quarter in manufacturing. Sixty-six and a half percent had 20 or fewer employees, and only 6.2 percent had more than 100 employees. Forty-four percent had total annual revenues of less than approximately US$133,000, and only 12 percent had revenues in excess of approximately US$1.3 million.

The sample was selected to assure representation of businesses that held registered land rights and those that did not, and to assure an adequate representation of enterprises that obtained land from the state as well as in the secondary market. In this sense, the sample was not randomly selected or designed to produce statistically robust results. The survey instruments included over 130 questions, many with multiple parts, on topics that included, among others, landholdings and tenure; land use planning; experiences with land transactions, including costs, time, disputes, and interactions with public officials; attitudes toward security and informality; and perceived problems in the market.

Interviews were also conducted with public officials in the 12 provincial Departments of Natural Resources and the Environment (DoNREs) using uniform templates describing the main land transaction procedures. The interviews were open and in-depth, allowing for expression of opinions and recommendations. The survey instrument was designed to isolate and bring into focus those elements of the current administrative procedures that are considered to be most problematic from the point of view of administrators, providing a focus for management action.

The third component of the study consisted of in-depth interviews with 65 land market intermediaries (LMIs), which were defined as individuals or firms that receive compensation for providing advice and assistance to others in the acquisition of land rights and development of properties. Given the relatively recent emergence of business land markets in Vietnam, this definition encompassed a variety of firms and professionals, including land brokers, lawyers, engineers, and construction firms. As in many emerging markets, some had present or former relationships with public agencies, but they did not include government-affiliated "one-stop shops" or state-sponsored industrial/economic zone developers.

---

4. See, for example, Foreign Investment Advisory Service (2001).

The Legal Framework for Land Relations

All land in Vietnam is owned by the state, and much of the LOL can be characterized as an attempt to achieve the benefits of a true land market within the constraint of state ownership. Citizens and legal entities of all stripes have rights only to use the land for either defined or unlimited terms. The land use right is not a civil property right, but rather a unique form of civil right regulated in part by the Civil Code, but mostly by the LOL. The attributes of the land use right may depend on various factors, including the characteristics of the right holder, the nature of the land use, and whether the right was acquired under current or prior law. Not all forms of land rights are available to all persons or types of business organizations.

The first tier of land rights is made up of grants to users directly from the state or its agencies and arises in what is typically referred to as the primary market. Important among these rights are grants in state-sponsored industrial zones (IZs), a major element of Vietnamese land policy, about which more below. For these primary rights, the basic distinction is between a lease and an allocated right of land use (referred to herein as a "right of use"), a form of property right commonly found in current or former socialist countries. The right of use can be either for a defined term or perpetual, the perpetual form being referred to as the right of "long-term and stable use" (LTSU). The LTSU has an unlimited duration and is almost the equivalent of freehold ownership. It may be alienated, and it will retain its characteristics in the hands of the transferee, even if the transferee—for example, a foreign company—could not have obtained the right directly from the state. Although there is no right of private land ownership, a basic distinction in Vietnamese parlance is between purchase and lease, with the term *purchase* frequently used to refer to the LTSU right.

Acquiring land in the primary market in most cases requires payment of a single land use fee to the state. The major exceptions are the small plots of land, now approximately 300 square meters, to which each citizen is entitled for subsistence agriculture, and land granted to social institutions and other types of nonprofit organizations. All other uses, including residential land and amounts of agricultural land exceeding the basic subsistence grant, usually require payment. Leases always entail payment of rent to the state, either by a single payment at commencement of the term or annually. However, while all types of users may lease land from the state, only foreign investors and legal organizations, including the so-called overseas Vietnamese (OVN), may have prepaid leases.

Land rents are based on the normative land values, or prices. The basic land rent is equal to 0.5 percent of the normative value, but this can be lowered in some zones, mostly rural and underdeveloped, and raised in others, particularly urban areas. The maximum rent cannot exceed four times the basic rent, or 2 percent of the normative value. Because they are based on the normative values, the absolute value of rents varies depending on land use designation and other valuation factors.

Land rents are promulgated annually in a schedule by the provincial People's Committee, in the same way as the normative values and land use fees. Rents are fixed for periods of five years, at which time there is an adjustment or "mark to market" based on the then-current land valuations, followed by another five-year fixed period. If a lessee chooses a prepaid lease, the rent sum is calculated on the basis of the current normative land rent multiplied by the number of years in the lease. All first-year costs incurred by the lessee, in particular land recovery compensation and official infrastructure development fees, are deductible from the land rent. In addition, land rent concessions are specifically recognized as allowable incentives to economic development.

The duration of rights of land use for a defined term depends on the use. Agricultural uses may range from 20 to 50 years. Nonagricultural rights are typically limited to 50 years, but can be as long as 70 years in targeted geographic or economic areas characterized by low rates of return on investment. In most respects, a right of land use for a defined term is the same as a lease, and in most respects, a lease in Vietnam resembles a lease in other common and civil law systems. The state is legally obligated to renew leases for certain purposes, primarily agricultural production by individuals and household enterprises, if the lessee has complied with the rules of the LOL and the use still conforms to the current land use plan. However, the state agrees only to consider renewal of all other leases, and the law and regulations offer little guidance on the conditions under which such consideration will be given or the lease renewed, a source of some consternation to business interests. The forms of land tenure and their eligible recipients are described in table 6.1.

A distinctive feature of primary land rights, again common in most socialist systems, is that all new grants are subject to a covenant to actually develop and use the land for the permitted purpose within a specified time period. Purposeless landholdings are not permitted, and speculation is reserved to the state. With respect to citizens and households with small holdings and to SOEs, it appears that the rules on making productive use of the land are not often enforced. However, if a start-up business receives a grant from the state today and fails to meet its development obligation, the land right may be terminated, and this appears to happen with enough frequency to be a consideration.

As in many other emerging socialist systems, Vietnamese law distinguishes between land rights and rights to other real property. There is no legal presumption that the rights to objects attached to the land in a permanent way are accessories and follow the rights to the land. Buildings or portions of buildings (for example, apartments) and other facilities attached to land can be owned as property and are freely alienable, and buildings can be mortgaged or sold apart from the land right. Objects built on the land must be separately registered.

LAND TITLE REGISTRATION
Under the LOL, all current land users must formalize their rights by registering and obtaining land use right certificates (LURCs). Issuance of an LURC is often a legal

Table 6.1
Forms of Land Tenure

Landholder	Form of Tenure
Household and individual subsistence farmers, agricultural cooperatives, community-wide agricultural enterprises, various forms of state and nonprofit institutions and organizations, and religious organizations	Allocated long-term stable land use right, without payment of land use fee
Household and individual citizen	Allocated long-term stable land use right, with payment of land use fee, for residential and business land Allocated land use right for a defined term, with payment of land use fee Prepaid lease (if prior to 2004) Lease with annual rent
Domestic legal organization (including SOEs)	Allocated land use right for a defined term, with payment of land use fee Prepaid lease (if prior to 2004) Lease with annual rent
"Overseas Vietnamese" investors	Allocated land use right with payment of land use fee (conversion from lease upon completion of investment) Prepaid or annual lease
Other foreign investors (legal entities or individuals)	Prepaid or annual lease
All individuals, households, and legal organizations	Allocated long-term stable land use right if acquired from a legal holder of such right in a market transaction, with or without payment of land use fee

entitlement and not a discretionary act of land allocation by the state since the law recognizes many preexisting land rights of individuals, households, and enterprises established under valid prior laws, albeit often upon payment of land fees.

Vietnam has a variation of the Torrens title registration system. Registration is a state function and is mandatory, or constitutive of the right, in the sense that an unregistered property right may be considered to be a legal nullity by the state and also has no legal effect on third parties dealing with the property. The LURC is a physical document that must be amended, delivered, canceled, and reissued from time to time to reflect transactions. The land title is, in theory, dispositive of the right, establishing a very strong legal presumption of accuracy and validity, though the present Vietnamese law does not address that issue in any significant detail. This paper-based certificate of title system is arguably outmoded in the electronic age; a comprehensive system-wide review is under way now, and changes may be forthcoming.

Like all registration systems of its kind, the system distinguishes between first registration, which enters a property object into the system for the first time, and registration of subsequent transactions. First registration results in issuance of the initial LURC, which establishes the chain of title and relies to a significant extent on cadastral assessment of the property. Completing first registration can be a lengthy process, but that is true in many systems. Registration of all secondary transactions is expected to be quicker, and regulations require completion in a period of seven to ten days. By law, mortgages must be registered within five business days, and a simple assignment of land rights must be completed in nine working days. These times are mostly aspirational and are not often met in practice.

The LOL establishes what would be called a unified cadastre, in which all real property objects and rights to them are registered in a single cadastral file by a single agency. However, as has been the experience in many transitional socialist systems, this aspect of the law has not been implemented pending resolution of a bureaucratic battle to control the cash cow of registration. Today buildings and apartments are registered separately from the land by an entirely different government ministry, which issues a separate title certificate for constructed property.[5] In Vietnam, as in other transitional socialist states, divided registration systems are hangovers from the past or arose primarily because of the need to register rights to privatized housing quickly when the more complex land registration systems were not fully functional. In a number of cases, they have proven difficult to dismantle because of vested bureaucratic interests.

SECONDARY MARKET TRANSACTIONS

Most forms of secondary market transactions with land rights are permitted if the holder has an LURC or is entitled to issuance of an LURC, if the land right is not subject to a dispute or to an attachment for execution of judgment, if the term of the right has not expired, and if all land use fees owed to the state are paid currently or legally deferred.

Only fully paid rights may be alienated. A curious rule has been that holders of annual rent leases may not mortgage or alienate their land rights per se, though they are free to alienate any structure on the land. In practice, this limitation has turned out to be of questionable utility and was under review when this chapter was prepared. Not the least of the problems was that domestic enterprises may not hold prepaid leases and few other investors are interested in prepaying a lease, having better things to do with their money.[6] The rule apparently arose in part

---

5. Most developed countries with a legal concept of accessory rights to constructed objects do not register buildings or building rights at all. If they do, it is as a cadastre practice, for purposes of land information or taxation, not to establish property rights.

6. In the case of land rights acquired directly from the state, particularly in economic and industrial zones, many land users are actually prepaying the lease rents regardless of whether

from fear of speculative activity. It is questionable (though perhaps not impossible) whether much speculative value can be built up in a lease that is subject to periodic rent increases calculated under a system in the state's sole control and under the threat of termination for failure to develop the land within a strict time schedule.

Restrictions on alienation have had practical implications in only a few limited cases, one of which is an annual rent leasehold on vacant land. For example, even though a lessee under an annual lease cannot assign or mortgage his land rights per se, he can assign or mortgage his rights to the buildings he constructs on the land. The obvious question has been, what happens to the land rights if the building is sold or mortgaged? The law does not say, but the clear implication is that the land rights will follow the rights to the buildings. Most creditors act accordingly, reporting that they have no problem granting loans on the security of buildings constructed on leaseholds even without a pledge of the lease.

A variation on this theme is that SOEs, often large landholders, may not alienate their land, including through subleasing, if the funds with which the land was acquired came from the public budget. Accordingly, most SOEs are not legally permitted to sublease their land or facilities. Despite this restriction, there is widespread belief that SOEs are one of the primary sources of land and facilities in the secondary market, a point only partially supported by the work underlying this chapter. Nevertheless, the issue of SOE land is high on the government's land policy agenda; as in most transitional socialist countries, SOEs hold some of the most valuable land—well located, well serviced, and frequently underutilized.

COLLATERAL

Land rights and real property may be mortgaged. Some banks have relatively large and growing residential loan portfolios, and they are aggressively staking out positions in the residential mortgage market as a main pillar of their retail loan portfolios.[7] Few personal loans today are unsecured, and real property is the banks' preferred form of security. Many banks are performing their own prop-

---

the lease itself is characterized as prepaid, but are not getting credit for the prepayment. These users are required to pay compensation to recover the land from its present holders as well as substantial infrastructure connection charges. All these payments are made in year one and are deductible from rents payable in the future. In addition, landholders in economic zones may have received extended free rent periods. In effect, rents may not actually be payable in many economic zones for 20 years after incentives and deduction of year one costs.

7. In 2006 there was some concern in the government of Vietnam that some banks were overexposed in residential mortgage lending in light of a dramatic downturn in the residential property market, which some alleged was caused by new rules prohibiting developers from selling off the plan and using proceeds to finance construction. The Central Bank dismissed the possibility of real risk to the financial system from the alleged overexposure, but nevertheless urged housing developers to lower prices and clear the market, and banks to exercise more caution in residential lending. See *Viet Nam News* (2006).

erty valuations using specialized in-house valuation departments, and some are developing sophisticated geographic information system (GIS)–based electronic valuation databases. The positive growth in mortgage lending and a trend toward longer loan maturities, higher loan-to-value ratios, and decreasing interest rates suggest that creditors feel a certain level of security in their rights and are not affected by the complexity of land rights. However, relatively few loan transactions are secured with nonresidential land rights.

The Vietnamese mortgage is a relatively modern legal device, and its main principles are set out in a handful of provisions in the Civil Code.[8] To become legally effective, the mortgage document must be written, notarized, and registered in the land registry. Typical of practice under Torrens title registration systems, secured creditors are required to take physical possession of the borrower's LURC. (Whether actual possession of the LURC or registration of the mortgage is sufficient to perfect the creditor's mortgage lien is unclear.) Creditors' priorities to the mortgaged property are established in accordance with the date and time of registration of the mortgage. With the exception of agricultural loans, a mortgage of a building or other constructed property is presumed to include all additions and fixtures attached to the property. The mortgage encumbers all insurance proceeds paid upon damage or destruction of the property, and the proceeds are payable directly to the creditor. A creditor has the right to expect proper maintenance of the property and to perform occasional inspections.

The law appears to give the creditor the right to sell the property through judicial procedures or in a private-sale transaction if such is agreed in the mortgage contract. Commonly referred to as a "power of sale," the right of private sale is the approach recommended by most legal commentators in emerging markets, but it is not often adopted in emerging socialist markets.[9] Even in Vietnam, there are conflicting views on whether this is the rule. Some creditors contend that enforcement of the mortgage is possible only through court action. In fact, there have been very few mortgage loan enforcement actions by banks, and banks interviewed reported default and delinquency ratios in the range of 0.1 percent of portfolio value, not unusual for emerging markets in which loan underwriting is carefully done and timely repayment of debts is a strong social value.

LAND USE PLANNING

The survey questionnaire included a module on land use planning issues, including perceptions of and participation in planning processes and incidence of illegal construction, most of which is beyond the scope of this chapter. Some commentary on the planning system (Gaston 2005; Sharpe and Quang 2004) reviewed in preparation for the project concluded that it suffers from poorly

---

8. Articles 342 et seq.

9. See, for example, Butler (2003).

defined objectives for planning activity; inadequate resources and training at the local level; poor participatory procedures, both for lower-level officials in preparing higher-level plans and for citizens and landholders; excessive detail, particularly with respect to detailed land use plans; and inflexible planning, leading to local circumventions of planning requirements in the name of expediency and economic development.

The SME Land Market

The primary land market is divided into several distinct segments. Outside of industrial zones, primary rights to land can be directly acquired only from provincial and local governments or through an occasional public auction conducted by state actors. Land rights also may be acquired from intermediaries that are designated to develop and market land in IZs by the national or sub-national governments, and creation of IZs is arguably the major component of state land policy today.

Reflecting the importance of the IZ in national land policy, some IZs are designated directly by the Prime Minister's office, and there is an IZ Management Authority within the Prime Minister's office that exercises oversight nationally. Provincial People's Committees authorize creation of some IZs and must approve any transaction within an IZ. A sub-provincial authority may create a de facto IZ, called an "industrial cluster" or IC, by designating in the local master plan an area for conversion of agricultural land to business or industrial use.

Provincial land development agencies and industrial zone management boards, which are unincorporated public entities, are typically responsible for supervising and implementing IZ projects. However, responsibilities may be delegated by lease or equivalent concession to a wide variety of project management units (PMUs). The job of the land development fund agency or the PMU is to install infrastructure in the designated area and to market land to investors. PMUs may take a number of legal forms, including public corporations, public-private ventures, and wholly private entities. The Asian Development Bank (2005) noted complex interlocking corporate structures engaged in IZ development having various degrees of public and private participation. In a small but growing number of cases, state land may be acquired from private companies that have acquired rights to develop IZs and sublease land to businesses. While playing the same role as a state IZ, these are essentially private operations, in the nature of concessions, and subleases from such an entity are considered to be secondary, not primary, market transactions.

Prior to commencement of this work, research undertaken by the Asian Development Bank (2005) suggested that the primary land market, in particular IZs, serves a very small portion of SMEs. This point was confirmed; few of the SMEs participating in this survey acquired land in an IZ. Small and medium-sized businesses cannot afford the rents, particularly the infrastructure charges, in IZs, which tend to focus on large, custom-built, owner-occupied structures. In addition, provincial governments are authorized by regulation to establish minimum investment ratios to evaluate requests for land in IZs. Even though they are directed by law to assure that the ratios are practical under the circumstances and anticipate different types of projects and the needs of different geographic areas, it is widely conceded that the ratios typically restrict access to IZs to the largest and most capital-intensive businesses.[10] SMEs, therefore, typically turn to the secondary market.

IZs were relevant to the work of this investigation, which primarily focused on the needs of SMEs, mostly because of what they say about state land policy. Emphasizing IZs, the government of Vietnam chose not just a policy that assured greater state control over land allocation and development, but also an emphasis on the needs of larger, often export-oriented businesses, including direct foreign investment. Whether this is the appropriate emphasis can be debated. There is evidence that indigenous small business development is likely to be a powerful engine of employment growth in Vietnam and other emerging markets. At the same time, direct foreign investment and large businesses are as likely to be sources of long-term technical development and export earnings. It is perhaps arguable that emphasis on the needs of larger investors may rightly acknowledge the difficulties of assembling and servicing larger land parcels in transitional economies and the fact that SMEs appear to be getting along well in the secondary market. Larger investors may in fact need more help.

The LOL and its regulations appear to require that land be auctioned in many circumstances.[11] A narrow reading of the law would suggest that practically all land offered by the state for commercial housing production and all land offered to private developers for industrial zone concessions must be offered by auction.[12] Inquiries during project preparation revealed that auctions were occurring in only three cities—Hanoi, Ho Chi Minh City, and Da Nang—and primarily for residential land. Available research suggests that very few business users acquire land through auction, and none of the SMEs interviewed in this survey obtained land by public auction.

---

10. The investment ratio is defined as the amount of the proposed investment divided by the size of land area to be allocated.

11. Exceptions include transactions involving investment incentives or where there is a change of land use; land used for construction of public works for business purposes; land for housing for low-income people; and land that must be cleared of current occupants and compensation made. This last category or exception to the auction requirement, expropriation of occupied land, may apply to a significant portion of the state land that is made available to businesses.

12. By way of comparison, Russian law was amended in 2006 to provide that all land offered for housing production be offered only by auction, a reaction to perceived sweetheart deals between local officials and favored housing developers, in particular state-owned construction companies, that resulted in some developers' monopolizing the market for residential land and driving up housing prices.

Figure 6.2
Size of Most Recently Acquired Plot

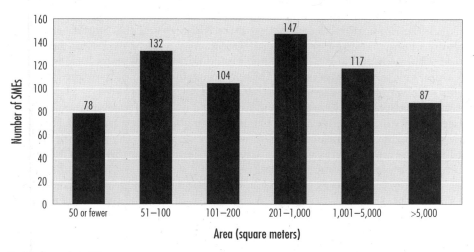

Number of respondents: 665.

LANDHOLDINGS

Landholdings of SMEs are typically small. Slightly more than half of the SMEs interviewed held only one land parcel, and only 6.5 percent held four or more. As shown in figure 6.2, 47 percent of respondents reported that their most recently acquired land plot was 200 square meters or less. More than half of all respondents claimed to hold less than 500 square meters of land (1/20th of a hectare), and only 12.3 percent held a hectare or more. This finding reflects the preponderance of trade establishments in the survey; other types of businesses held larger amounts of land.

The primary market is the main source of large land parcels, which is to be expected as private landholdings are small and assembling a significant parcel could be a difficult task, though some SMEs clearly do manage to acquire and consolidate multiple small parcels. Almost 90 percent of SMEs that acquired land in the secondary market held less than 1,000 square meters, while 73 percent of those that received land directly from the provincial or local governments or in state-sponsored industrial zones held more than 1,000 square meters. Fifty-seven percent of grants in state-sponsored industrial zones exceeded 5,000 square meters, compared to only 4 percent of secondary market acquisitions.

FORMS OF TENURE

There is a choice among various forms of land tenure in the current market, and all forms of tenure except the so-called prepaid leases are found in significant numbers. Three-quarters of the SMEs claimed to have chosen the form of tenure on their most recently acquired land parcel, and many of those that did not exercise choice inherited their land rights. Whether this means they could have obtained a different form of land right from the transferor, or a different land parcel, the implication was clear that there is choice and that purchasers weigh tenure options based on a variety of factors. As would be expected, more than three-fourths of holders of LTSU cited long duration as the main benefit of their form of tenure, and 61 percent of those holding annual rent leases cited the benefits of lower land acquisition costs.

The SMEs held a variety of land rights, and multiple parcel holders held different rights on different parcels. The largest single category was the LTSU, held by 52 percent of the respondents on at least one parcel. The preponderance of LTSU rights among SMEs was to be expected, since so many SMEs hold property zoned for mixed residential-business use, which is typically LTSU, and so many are household enterprises or individual entrepreneurs, the primary recipients of LTSU rights. About 40 percent held some form of lease or sublease. Figure 6.3 shows the distribution of forms of tenure among the sample.

Leases predominate among SMEs receiving land directly from local or provincial governments (77.8 percent) or in industrial zones (94.3 percent). Only 19 percent of SMEs that obtained land in primary market transactions hold an LTSU,

Figure 6.3
Forms of Land Tenure

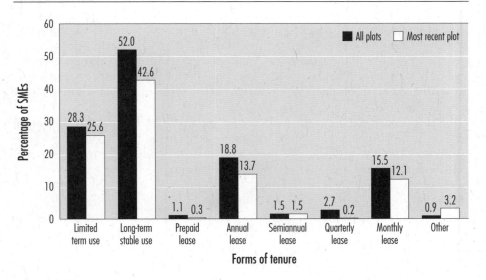

Number of respondents: 665.
Note: The total percentage of "all plots" do not add to 100 because of firms that hold multiple plots in different forms of tenure.

Figure 6.4
Duration of State-IZ Leases

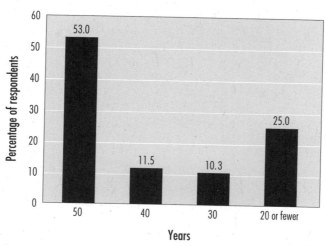

Number of respondents: 156.

and by law these would be household enterprises or individual entrepreneurs. More than 70 percent of the SMEs holding leases were tenants or sublessees of primary right holders.

As shown in figure 6.4, more than half of the leases granted by provincial and local governments and in IZs had durations of 50 years, the legal maximum in most areas. Eleven percent were in the range of 40 years; 10 percent were for 30 years; and 25 percent were for 20 years or less. Not shown in figure 6.4 is that 50-year leases are more common in IZs, in which they were held by 65.7 percent of firms, and that only 11.8 percent of IZ leases were for terms of less than 20 years. The survey did not gather data on duration of secondary market leases and subleases, but similar research carried out by the World Bank (2005) suggests that typical leases average from 19 to 25 years for SMEs.

ACQUIRING LAND RIGHTS

About 70 percent of the SMEs interviewed obtained land in the secondary market, suggesting the emergence of a robust private market in land rights. Though this was not a random distribution, based on the experience of selecting the sample, there were good reasons to believe that the number of SMEs that obtained their land rights in the secondary market would be even higher than 70 percent in a random sampling. Of the remainder, 23 percent obtained land directly from the provincial or local government; 4 percent acquired land from an industrial zone; and about 3 percent of respondents leased land from an SOE.

Of the firms holding an LURC that obtained land in the secondary market, about 16 percent had first unsuccessfully tried to obtain land from the state. Of those, 35 percent said they did not complete the primary market process because of long and complicated procedures; 16 percent had their applications rejected; and others indicated that the government land price was too high (9 percent), no suitable state-owned land parcel was available (7 percent), and land parcels available in the secondary market were more suitable for their needs (7 percent).

Eighty-five percent of those who acquired rights in the primary market requested specific sites, and 98 percent of them received the sites they requested. Of the small number who did not receive the sites they requested, about half were dissatisfied with the sites they were offered. Only 12 percent of the respondents who ultimately obtained land in the primary market had at least one request for land completely denied.

As shown in figure 6.5, the largest segment of the SME sample, 28.9 percent, acquired land rights through outright purchase of an LTSU from another holder in a secondary market transaction, followed by a segment of 21.2 percent that obtained rights by leasing from other individual right holders.

As was expected, only a small portion of SMEs obtained land in an IZ. Many more obtained land outside of IZs directly from provincial and local governments,

Figure 6.5
Sources of Land Rights

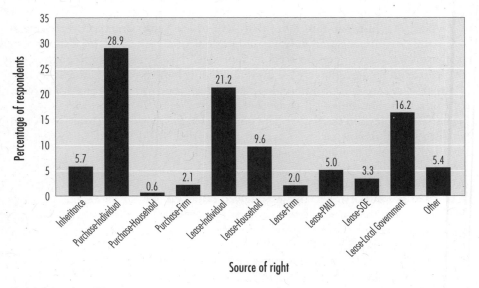

Number of respondents: 665.

which appear to be serving a broader segment of the SME market. Larger SMEs (more than 20 employees) were about six times more likely than smaller ones (fewer than 20 employees) to receive land directly from provincial or local governments, but fifteen times more likely to receive land in an IZ. Thirty-seven percent of the SMEs receiving land directly from provincial and local governments had fewer than 20 employees, compared to only 14.5 percent of firms locating in IZs.

LAND MARKET INTERMEDIARIES

The story of land market intermediaries was interesting for the insights it provides into development of land market infrastructure, but most of that discussion is beyond the scope of this chapter. It was usually difficult to identify LMIs working with business clients. While a large and growing number of real estate brokerages exist in the larger cities, very few firms or individuals can be characterized as LMIs in the more rural provinces.[13] Even in the larger cities, most intermediaries are engaged in residential transactions, and a much smaller number with business property per se. (To the extent that much SME property is mixed residential-business use in the urban areas, there may be some overlap.) Seventy percent of the LMIs interviewed did more than 70 percent of their work with residential property, and only 12 percent were exclusively business land brokers. More than three-quarters of the LMIs operated in only one province, and almost half worked exclusively in urban areas. Only 12 percent worked in smaller towns and villages, and such work was generally a small portion of their business.

Two-thirds of the SMEs that obtained land in the secondary market located the land through word of mouth and family and friends; 12.4 percent did so through advertisements; and only 2.5 percent used the services of LMIs. The highest incidence was in the urban areas, but even in Ho Chi Minh City, only one in five used the services of an LMI. Half the LMIs believed that their clients' most important source of information about available land was word of mouth, and 29 percent said it was direct contacts with government officials.

MARKET EXPERIENCES

SMEs that acquired land in a secondary market transaction were asked to identify the most problematic aspect of the transaction, and half said simply locating the land was the major issue, exceeding other issues such as administrative procedures and obtaining LURCs by a factor of three. There are many reasons, including shortage of serviced land zoned for business in good locations, but it also appears that market mechanisms for locating business land are undeveloped.

---

13. Review of business registrations in preparation of the survey revealed well over 4,000 firms licensed for real estate–related activities.

Figure 6.6
Most Difficult Aspect of Acquiring Land in the Secondary Market

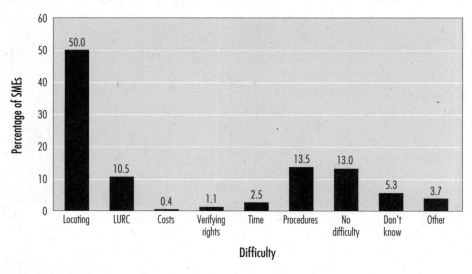

Number of respondents: 449.

Figures 6.6 and 6.7, respectively, summarize the responses of SMEs regarding difficulties experienced in acquiring land and the effects on their businesses.

Fifty-nine percent of respondents who obtained land from provincial and local government obtained it in less than three months, and 22 percent in more than six months. The mean duration for obtaining land from the state was 184 days, and the median was between 80 and 90 days. This is much longer than the average time to complete a transaction in the secondary market, which is typically measured in days or weeks: 72 percent of transactions in the secondary market were completed in one week, and about 28 percent took more than 30 days.

Fifty-one percent of the SMEs believed unavailability of land was an obstacle to growth, with a slightly higher percentage for firms experiencing growth in employment in the past year. As shown in figure 6.7, 51.8 percent of SMEs that believed unavailability of land was an obstacle to growth saw the problem as major or very severe, and that increased to 73.8 percent among the SMEs that experienced growth in the prior year.

Of the SMEs that received land directly from a provincial or local government or in an IZ, only 9 percent obtained an investment incentive that reduced land costs. Of those, about 60 percent received incentives that reduced their land

Figure 6.7
Intensity of Problem Caused by Availability of Land: SMEs

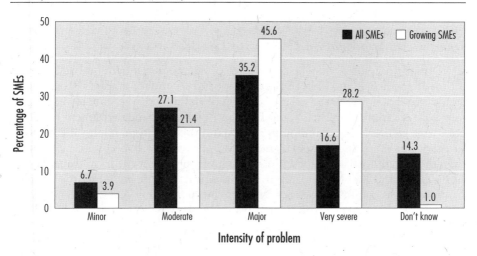

Number of respondents: 665.

costs by 30 percent or less, and one-third received incentives that eliminated their land charges entirely. As would be expected, 35 percent of the firms receiving incentives had 100 or more employees, while only 6 percent of the firms in the entire sample were that large. More than 75 percent of the firms receiving incentives had more than 20 employees, but only 34 percent of the firms in the entire sample were that large.

Of the SMEs that obtained land directly from government, 71 percent believed that land was more expensive in the private sector, and only 6 percent thought that state land was more expensive. Slightly over 10 percent thought prices in the primary and secondary markets were about the same. Fifty-eight percent of these SMEs thought that the primary market land prices were about right, 16.5 percent that they were too high, and 16.5 percent that they were a bargain. The largest proportion, 36.2 percent, believed that the real cost of state land rents would increase in the future. Twenty-seven percent thought that rents would remain the same in real terms, and 17 percent said they would decrease.

SMEs that worked with the state to obtain land sites had different experiences and opinions. Of the 188 that obtained land from the state, 68 percent were offered a choice of sites, and 20 percent were not. Forty-seven percent received assistance from public officials in locating a land parcel, but 30 percent did not. Fifty-eight percent believed that government land officials were helpful and cooperative, but about 19 percent disagreed. Of the SMEs that obtained land from the state, 52 percent had no problem with the land sites offered to them.

The most frequent complaints about the land offered were size (19.7 percent) and location (11.7 percent). Utility services and the need for land recovery were only minor considerations.

Investment Approval and Access to Land

In Vietnam an investor may be required to obtain an investment license as a condition of acquiring land in both the primary and secondary markets.[14] Land allocation in Vietnam is viewed as a process of allocating a scarce state resource, and new land is rationed, in theory, on the basis of how well the investment proposal conforms to economic planning priorities and the investor's financial capability to carry out the plan. The evaluation and approval are done by agencies other than those that deal regularly with land matters, primarily the local Departments of Planning and Investment, but also by political organs, including the People's Committees at commune, district, and provincial levels.

The requirement of investment approval cut across all types and sizes of businesses, and it was required of 96.5 percent of all SMEs interviewed. However, the research for this chapter was completed prior to complete implementation of the new investment law, under which smaller businesses and those of a less sensitive nature may be exempted from business licensing or subjected to simplified licensing requirements. The investment evaluation standards of the new law are very broadly drawn. As indicated in table 6.2, if the investment is not made in an economic sphere deemed conditional by the law, investments of less than approximately US$1 million by domestic investors will not require a license. This covers many SMEs. Somewhat larger investments by domestic investors, up to approximately US$20 million, would be required to register the investment with the provincial investment agency in a simplified procedure in which the agency is required to issue or deny an investment certificate within 15 days of receiving a complete application. A foreign investor is required to obtain an investment license for any unconditional investment below US$20 million, and both domestic and foreign investors are required to obtain licenses for investments over that amount.

Most conditional investments pertain to sectors in which SMEs are unlikely to invest, such as banking, finance, and any real estate business.[15] Investments that are deemed to be conditional, or that are over US$20 million, are subject to

---

14. The procedures for investment licensing are described in the new Law on Investment, which took effect on 1 July 2006.

15. What comprises real estate business is not defined in the law, but the draft regulations suggest that it includes only investment in property for rent or sale, such as development of industrial parks or speculative commercial space. Moreover, any real estate investment in excess of VND 800 billion (approximately US$50 million) must be licensed by the prime minister's office.

Table 6.2
Investment Licensing Procedures

	Unconditional Investment (million)			Conditional Investment (million)	
	<US$1	>US$1 and <US$20	>US$20	<US$20	>US$20
Domestic Investor	Investment certificate not required	Registration, simple form; certificate issued in 15 days	Registration and evaluation	Registration and evaluation	Registration and evaluation
Foreign Investor	Registration Proof of financial ability Submission of joint venture contract (if any) Certificate issued in 15 days		Basic evaluation of financial ability and environmental issues Certificate issued in 30–45 days	Basic evaluation of financial ability and environmental issues Certificate issued in 30–45 days	Enhanced form of evaluation Certificate issued in 30–45 days

licensing and an enhanced form of project evaluation. Even so, the law requires issuing or denying the investment license within 30 days of completion of the application, or 45 days in exceptional circumstances.

In its simplified form, evaluation of the investment application seems to be primarily informational. The more elaborate form of evaluation appears to focus on financial capability, conformity with economic planning objectives, and environmental protection. Assessment of financial capability is not unusual in systems that allocate state-owned land to investors, as there is a concern that once begun, projects should be completed. Incomplete projects tie up valuable land sites and can cloud titles. The enhanced evaluation may also require the investor to prepare detailed environmental assessments, but that work might be required in any significant development project.

A problematic aspect of the current law is that it seems to assume that the land for an investment has already been identified, while at the same time the land allocation regulations assume that the investment license has already been granted when the land allocation application is submitted. In other words, each process requires the other to have been completed. Among the SMEs interviewed, 64.5 percent applied for an investment license before requesting land; 20.4 percent sought the land first; and only 11.8 percent began the processes simultaneously. Clarification of the relationship between these processes was under development as this chapter was prepared.

Conceivably, investment approval could be a cause of delay in land transactions as well as an opportunity for local officials to discriminate against some investors, protect local industry against competition, or engage in unauthorized economic planning. This does not appear to be the case in Vietnam. While investment approval does add time and costs to the process of land acquisition,

Table 6.3

Time to Obtain Investment Approval

Weeks	Number	Percent	Cumulative Percent
1 or less	177	27.5	27.5
1–2	83	12.9	40.4
2–3	154	23.9	64.3
3–4	98	15.2	79.5
4+	131	20.4	100*
Total	643	100*	

*These totals do not add up to 100 because of rounding.

it does not seem to be a major burden on businesses at this time. Asked to rate the difficulty of various steps of the land acquisition process, about 13 percent of the SMEs and 32 percent of the LMIs characterized investment licensing as a difficult process. About 40 percent of all SMEs interviewed reported obtaining the approval within two weeks, and 79.5 percent in a month or less. Table 6.3 shows time for investment approval for the entire sample. At the same time, as discussed further below, the limited amount of information acquired on unofficial payments to public officials suggests that investment approval is the stage at which such payments are likely to be made.

Interestingly, government officials characterized investment approval, along with site selection and evaluating the land request, as the most difficult aspects of the state land allocation process. Local land officials often noted the difficulty of evaluating investments as part of the land allocation process, stating that too many agencies were involved, their activities were not coordinated, financial data prepared by applicants were unreliable and difficult to verify, standards for evaluating investments and for connecting land needs with different types of investments were lacking or inadequate, and staff responsible for evaluating investments was inadequate or poorly trained.

Informality

In Vietnam registration of land rights and land transactions is required by law, and an unregistered right or transaction may be considered informal and even illegal in the sense that, under some circumstances, it may not be recognized by the state.[16] Accordingly, informality is sometimes defined as the failure to register

---

16. While registration is characterized as mandatory, the Civil Code provides that an unregistered right is not really void as a matter of law, but only voidable if it is not registered within two years of demand by a court or other authority. Presumably, this rule would not affect third parties damaged by the landholder's failure to register.

a land right or transaction and obtain or amend the LURC. In fact, as in many other countries that require registration of titles, characterization of an unregistered right as illegal or even informal is questionable, and in the absence of a superior claim from someone damaged by the right holder's failure to register, an unregistered right based on valid legal papers probably would not be disturbed in Vietnam.

In this inquiry, questions on registration were directed only to those that obtained land rights in the secondary market; in preparing the sample of respondents, a deliberate attempt was made to assure representation of SMEs that did and did not hold registered rights. Fifty-eight percent of the SMEs either possessed or were in the process of obtaining an LURC for their land parcel, and of those 32 percent took the initiative to register the land for the first time.[17] Almost all (96.3 percent) of the SMEs that obtained an LTSU right in the secondary market held or were applying for an LURC, but only 5.4 percent of those that leased or subleased land. This was not surprising, since under current law a tenant or sublessee of a primary right holder is not entitled to receive an LURC, regardless of the duration of the lease. The high level of formality among the landowners, however, was somewhat surprising.

As shown in figure 6.8, among the SMEs that held LURCs, the main reasons for registering rights were clearer rules (41.7 percent), security or avoidance of disputes (24.6 percent), and access to credit (16.3 percent). Asked for the main reasons their clients registered rights and transactions, the LMIs whose responses are shown in figure 6.9 cited security and avoidance of disputes (50.8 percent), clearer rules and easier transactions (30.8 percent), and greater access to credit (12.3 percent). Regarding which types of clients would be more likely to obtain LURCs, 20 percent of the LMIs identified those seeking some sort of privilege, such as bank credit, construction permit, or investment license, with an emphasis on obtaining credit and capital infusion from outside investors.

Preliminary research for the project suggested that availability of mortgage finance would be an inducement to register land rights, but among the SMEs interviewed, mortgage finance per se appears to be of only moderate importance at this time. Its significance may be greater in residential property markets. However, when combined with SME responses that suggested that the LURC was important for attracting outside capital investment, presumably including informal credit and equity investment as well as formal bank credit, the general concept of attracting investment may become a more important factor in explaining a preference for formality. It is also possible that the responses of clearer procedural rules and easier transactions get at the issue of credit from another direction.

---

17. The incidence of registered land parcels could have been much higher, as the survey sought to determine only whether the occupant held an LURC. Since many respondents were lessees or sublessees, the primary right holder may have held an LURC while the tenant did not. Tenants mostly did not know whether their landlords held a registered right.

Figure 6.8
Main Reasons for SMEs Obtaining LURC

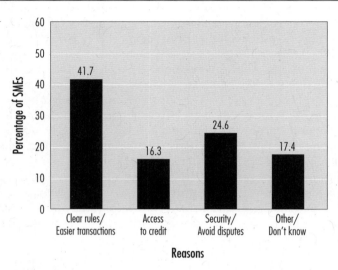

Number of respondents: 388.

Figure 6.9
Main Reasons for LMI's Clients Obtaining LURC

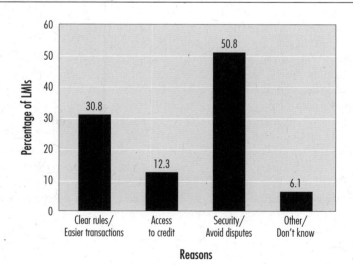

Number of respondents: 65.

Figure 6.10
Perceived Increase in Land Value from LURC: LMIs

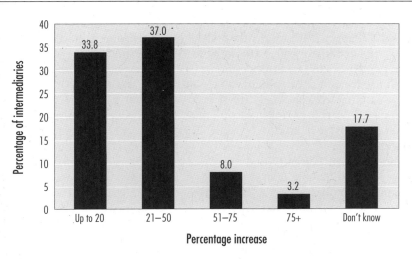

Number of respondents: 65.

Seventy percent of the SMEs said the main reason for failure to register was that they were prohibited from doing so by their landlord. The sense that property rights were secure without registration was the second most frequently cited reason, occurring in about a third of the responses. A significant number of respondents simply believed that registration was not worth the effort. Asked why clients do not register, over 40 percent of the LMIs referred to costs of one sort or another; 18 percent cited marginal security benefits from registration; and 12 percent the complex registration procedures.

About 27 percent of the LMIs suggested that clients seek out unregistered land because it is cheaper, which supports the finding that over 30 percent of secondary market purchasers initiate first registration after acquisition. As shown in figure 6.10, practically all LMIs believed that the LURC increases the value of the land, with 34 percent estimating an increase up to 20 percent, 37 percent up to 50 percent, and 11 percent even greater than 50 percent. Premiums of this size on registration might reflect not only the fact that the land use fee will have been paid to the state, but also the amount of effort and inconvenience experienced by participants in the registration process. Almost one in four LURC holders was dissatisfied with the process. Most of them cited long and complex procedures, and completing registration was cited as the second most difficult administrative procedure facing landholders. However, the perception of price premiums on registered property is directly at odds with the empirical findings of Kim (2004) that in the residential property markets of Ho Chi Minh City, apparently including many apartments, registration of the property had about as much effect on price as an upgraded toilet. It is possible to agree that registration of land rights is not a major consideration in residential markets in major cities and at the same time to distinguish this from markets for business and developable land. Whether there in fact is a difference in the residential and commercial property markets or whether other factors are at work here would have to be determined.

Respondents cited various fees and costs as disincentives to registration, but the land use fee, which usually must be paid at first registration of any property, was not as much of a factor as the 4 percent transfer tax and 1 percent stamp duty imposed on transactions. At this time, legal entities are subject to income taxation on transfer of land rights starting at 28 percent and increasing progressively, but there is no personal income tax on transfer of land rights or on income from land leasing. Presently under consideration is a proposal to impose a significant personal income tax on transfer of land rights and income from leases, which might discourage sale or lease of rights by smallholders as well as registration of sale and lease transactions.

Many transactions still occur with unregistered rights. Most LMIs offered opinions on what types of legal documents were sufficient to complete a transaction in the absence of registration. The leading categories in order of importance were sales agreements, either certified by a local official or uncertified; tax documents and payment receipts; official unregistered land allocation decisions; pre-socialist land papers and documents; inheritance papers; and cadastral registration of the land parcel (as opposed to legal registration of the right).[18] A small number noted that no other document was a good substitute for the LURC, though transactions would proceed nevertheless. Almost 40 percent of the LMIs claimed that a government official—usually a commune-level official—is involved even in informal transactions. The primary role of such officials is certification of the transfer document or the transaction as a substitute for a notary, which is permitted by law, but many such certifications appear also to provide the information that there is no pending dispute with regard to the possession of the land, which is in effect an informal title report.

Tenev et al. (2003) suggest that excessive informality and avoidance of the rules by some businesses in Vietnam place those that obey the rules at a competitive disadvantage, which is plausible, but an issue that the current work did not address. Avoidance of registration may also be causing problems for government, including avoidance of taxes and transfer fees and the hindering of development of cadastral information. The findings of this survey suggest that informality in the real property sector may be a function of several factors, including costs (land use fees, transfer and other taxes, avoidance of higher land prices, and so on)

---

18. In many places, cadastral records also contain a title history, even though that information is not given legal effect, but it is not unusual for property to trade on the basis of these records.

and a sense that land rights are sufficiently protected without formal registration. There are not a great many disadvantages to avoiding registration at this time, as evidenced by the facts that even unregistered rights appear to be well documented and frequently sanctioned or certified by a local official, there are few land-related disputes, and transactions with unregistered land rights remain possible. At the same time, many business land users believe that registration provides greater transparency and enhances security, facilitates transactions, and increases land value. It should be noted that the registered businesses included in this survey had already demonstrated willingness to play by the rules. Results likely would have been different if unregistered businesses were included in the survey.

Security of Property Rights

In Vietnam most landholders consider their rights to be secure. About 75 percent of the SMEs interviewed believed their rights are either secure or completely secure against the government, and 80 to 90 percent felt secure against other parties, including landlords, previous owners, and neighbors.

Supporting this perception, only 21 of 665 respondents (3.2 percent) claimed to have been involved in disputes concerning land. There were too few responses to connect the incidence of disputes to informality or to any particular form of tenure, and the incidence of disputes among different forms of tenure was almost equal. The very small number of land disputes essentially made the remaining questions regarding the nature of land-related disputes and the process of dispute resolution uninteresting, but the most frequent type of dispute was land boundaries, and after that compensation. Less than a quarter of the disputes were settled through court action, and almost half through negotiations or intervention of other, nonjudicial local authorities. Most disputants (66.7 percent) considered nonjudicial approaches to be the most effective way to resolve disputes, with only 19 percent preferring court action.

Though the government is considered to be the most significant threat to land rights, it is not by a wide margin. As shown in figure 6.11, about one in four landholders did not feel secure against the government, but a significant fraction were uncertain. In a large number of cases, respondents did not know where they stood with respect to government claims. This may reflect the fact of government land recovery operations for economic development purposes at compensation levels with which many respondents disagree, as well as inadequate communication of land use planning information.

Perceptions of security differed somewhat depending on the type of land right held. As reflected in figure 6.12, 86 percent of LTSU holders felt secure or completely secure, but only about 70 percent of holders of annual rent leases. Twenty-eight percent of LTSU holders, but only 3.3 percent of annual leaseholders, felt completely secure. These differences probably arise from the perception of the LTSU as a form of land ownership and the perception of lease rights as mere contractual rights. The perception of a lease as an inferior form of property

Figure 6.11
SME Perception of Security of Land Rights Against . . .

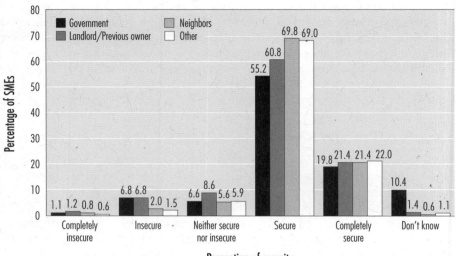

Number of respondents: 665.

Figure 6.12
Forms of Tenure and Perceptions of Security

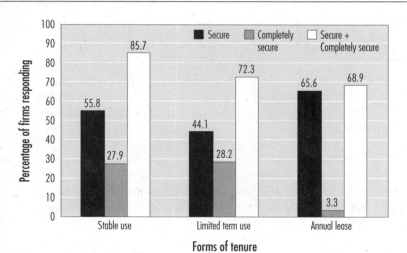

Number of respondents: 663.

right offering less security to the holder is probably accurate. Leases can be terminated for a variety of vague reasons—for example, violation of the land laws; they are rarely registered today; and there have been cases of abuse of leaseholder rights in a number of emerging markets. It would be incorrect to assume that emerging legal systems like Vietnam's have endowed leases with the legal protections of more developed legal systems. Moreover, contractual rights imply courts, which are not held in high esteem as forums for dispute resolution.

The source of the right—private market, government, or PMU—does not appear to have much relation to the perception of security of property rights, though respondents feel slightly more insecure in direct relationships with government than they do with PMUs or private market transactions. About 7 percent of those who acquired their land in private market transactions felt insecure or completely insecure, compared to 11 percent of those who acquired land from provincial or local government. This small difference probably reflects the fact that most grants from government are leases and rights of use, while most grants in the private market are LTSU. Uncertainties regarding state lease rents also may contribute somewhat to feelings of insecurity. Under the current system, rents are administrative normatives set annually and adjusted on existing leases every five years based on then-current normative rental schedules. Thus far, rents appear to have been reasonable; about 75 percent of the SME respondents thought that they were at about the right level or a bargain. It is as likely that the current ambiguities regarding rights to renew state leases are a cause of concern.

Land Recovery

Government frequently takes land in and around urban areas under the rules of land recovery, which is a highly regulated process of moving land from low-value to higher-value uses, or a process of moving land from poor smallholders to investors, depending on one's perspective. The process is complex and time consuming, involving practically every level of government that has some authority over land and land use. Involvement of various actors and agencies at various levels of government appears to be a means of providing some transparency and protection of smallholders, but also arguably a means of spreading the political accountability for a controversial practice.

The actual procedures of land recovery are beyond the scope of this chapter, but one aspect worth noting is the unavoidable government involvement in land pricing. Government sets the prices for confiscated land rights through a normative pricing mechanism that may be compared conceptually, but not yet in practice, to mass appraisal methodologies used in some modern property tax systems. Local governments set the valuations, and while the law requires them to approximate market prices, they often acknowledge that they lack the data or the technical capacity to do so. And, while the Ministry of Finance is responsible for supervising application of the normative pricing system, its representatives sometimes acknowledge that it lacks the resources to do so.

In addition to attracting investment by keeping land prices low, government policy seems to be concerned about the threat of serendipitous windfalls to current landholders if price controls are eliminated. That windfalls would occur in many places may be questionable, all things considered, and current policy seems to result mainly in transferring windfalls to investors. Some research suggests that the benefits that are supposed to be provided to current landholders as additional compensation, including relocation and retraining or job assistance, apparently are often not provided, or, put another way, the price of the land is distorted (Asian Development Bank 2005; Center for Rural Progress 2006; Centre of Land Investigation and Planning 2005). The upshot is a system that is now widely perceived as discriminating against poor smallholders and effecting significant transfers of wealth to wealthier investors, and that is inducing more public protests and refusals to relocate among the smallholders. Most of the government officials and 80 percent of the LMIs interviewed considered land recovery to be the most difficult aspect of the state land allocation process. Arguably, the current approach may also distort land allocation by underpricing and, at the same time, by engendering perceptions of unfairness and protests, reducing the amount of land available for conversion to higher use.

Local officials interviewed remarked that users frequently do not accept the normative prices, that negotiating pricing is the most difficult aspect of the process, and that frequently the prices paid are higher than the normative prices, in violation of the law. Some opined that the present compensation policy was irresponsible, unrealistic, and unpopular. Because the sample included relatively few SME respondents with land recovery experience (46 out of 665, or about 7 percent of the entire sample and 25 percent of those who received land in the primary market), the information obtained may not be reliable, but 25 percent believed recovery prices to be too low or lower than they should be. Of those who answered the question, eight out of ten claimed to have made illegal side payments in excess of normative prices to facilitate transactions, supporting the perception of local officials that such payments are routinely made.

Some experimentation with a flexible policy that emphasizes, in the first instance, the role of investors in seeking out their own deals and negotiating prices with current landholders may be appropriate at this stage of development of the secondary land market. In fact, this is what appears to be happening in some jurisdictions, with local officials looking the other way as side payments are made; more open support for this approach perhaps could lead to better policies. Opinions among professionals and land users are divided on how best to carry out land recovery, with some believing that private negotiations are more efficient and some supporting continued government control. Of the SMEs that were not required to participate directly in the land recovery process, 70 percent believed it was more efficient for the state to carry out the entire process, but only 52 percent of direct participants thought this. Thirty-three percent of those who actually participated in the recovery process believed direct negotiations between investors and landholders were more efficient, compared to only 10 percent of

those who did not participate. Of the 22 LMIs that assisted clients in land recovery procedures, somewhat more than half believed that it was more efficient
to have the state carry out the procedure, and 41 percent believed it was more
efficient for the investor to engage in direct negotiations.

One aspect of land use planning dovetailed to some extent with the issues
of land recovery, and that was the risk taken by small investors when investing
in land that might have been in the path of urban expansion by land recovery.
When preparing the project, other research had suggested that SMEs were being
damaged by poor planning processes (for example, Asian Development Bank
2005). In the survey, of the 40 percent of SMEs that were aware of the land use
plan, about one in five claimed to have been damaged in some way by planning.
Of those, about 6.5 percent were forced to relocate; 11.4 percent experienced the
loss of some land; and about 16.5 percent claimed to have experienced financial
loss, including a decrease in the value of their land.

Undoubtedly, some SMEs were harmed by planning processes, dislocation,
and inadequate compensation. Some of this may be a result of inadequate telegraphing of land use plans. However, as in most other countries, change of the
land use plan in Vietnam does not terminate the land use rights for current holders in the absence of a separate government decision to take the land. A change
in the land use plan may restrict the ability of the holder to expand or modify
the present facility, which can be serious enough if the original investment was
made in the expectation of future expansion. More important, change of plan
can prevent renewal of a lease or right of use beyond the initial term, which
could limit the amount of investment in business facilities to an amount that can
be profitably amortized over the initial term. That risk may be as much related
to inadequate lease durations and poorly defined rights of lease renewal as it is
to the planning process.

The problem may not be planning rules and procedures, but the rapid pace
of urban change and development in Vietnam. Under the circumstances, businesses in Vietnam are well advised to become familiar with land use planning and
think carefully about choosing locations for significant investments. It seemed
clear that government could be doing a better job of telegraphing information on
land use planning and communicating in advance the possible direction of future
urban development.

Investment

The level of investment in land improvements may be somewhat related to the
form of tenure. As shown in figure 6.13, SMEs were asked to describe the nature
of their activity on the land. Fifty-eight percent of those holding LTSUs claimed
to have had constructed new buildings, compared to only 12.7 percent of those
holding other forms of rights, which are of limited duration. Those holding limited duration forms of land rights were more likely to modify buildings than to
construct new ones, and three times more likely to make no improvements to the

Figure 6.13
Tenure and Land Improvements

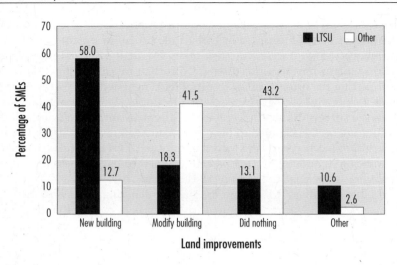

Number of respondents: 659.

land. Overall, over 80 percent of those who owned the land invested in construction or renovation, and of those about 60 percent invested in new construction. In contrast, only about 15 percent of lessees constructed new buildings.

The relationship of new construction to ownership could be expected, as a significant portion of the secondary land market in Vietnam is a market for both land and existing improvements, and 41 percent of lease-holding respondents leased to use existing improvements. But in theory, many leaseholders, in particular primary leaseholders, had the option of investing more, and all other things being equal, owners tend to invest at a higher rate. This relationship may reflect the different durations of LTSU and leases and the different perceptions of security attaching to each form of tenure.

As shown in figure 6.14, 56 percent of annual rent leaseholders said they would invest more if they felt greater security, while only 42.8 percent of LTSU holders would do so, implying that leaseholders may be more likely to underinvest. Similarly, and not surprisingly, 45 percent of annual rent leaseholders said they would invest more if their rights had longer duration.

INVESTMENT AND PERCEPTION OF SECURITY
Perception of security is sometimes associated with investment in land improvements. Asked for factors affecting their level of investment, a greater number of SMEs responded that they would invest more if their land rights were more secure than if they had rights of longer duration, access to more land, or greater

Figure 6.14
Factors Determining Land Investment

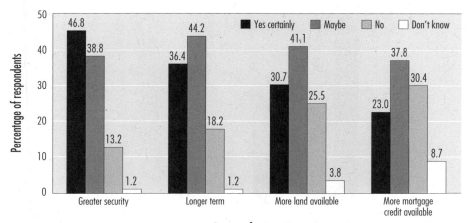

Number of respondents: 665.

access to credit. This was the case despite the relatively high sense of security among the sample as a whole. This anomaly may reflect the speculative nature of the question, but it also may be approaching the issue of lease durations and rights of renewal from a different direction.

In any case, the level of investment in land improvement seems high. Of the 665 SMEs interviewed, fewer than 23 percent did not invest in the land when they acquired it, regardless of how it was acquired or the form of tenure. Over three-fourths of all respondents engaged in some construction or renovation.

INVESTMENT AND REGISTRATION
Possession of an LURC does not seem to greatly affect the intention to invest more in the business, as 45 percent of those holding LURCs said they would certainly invest more if they felt greater security, while 50 percent without LURCs said they would invest more.

There was greater investment in land improvements by those who held LURCs. However, possession of the LURC was highly correlated with possession of an LTSU right, and the long duration and ownership characteristics of the LTSU are the better explanation for the level of investment. In figure 6.15, about 62 percent of the respondents who held LURCs claimed to have constructed new buildings, as opposed to only 28 percent of those who did not hold LURCs. Those without LURCs were more likely to modify buildings, and about three

Figure 6.15
LURC and Land Improvements

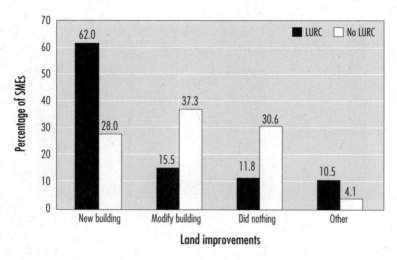

Number of respondents: 687.

times more likely to make no improvements to the land, but many of those were tenants who often could be assumed to prefer tenancy and were looking for usable existing facilities.

Unofficial Payments

State control of an important resource is often seen as an opportunity for official rent seeking. SMEs and LMIs were asked about the amount of unofficial payments to public officials and the instances in which they were most often demanded and made. Among those that chose to respond to the question, unofficial payments were not perceived to be a significant problem, though these questions were not answered by many respondents. Obtaining information on the incidence of unofficial payments to public officials can be difficult, for obvious reasons, and conclusions based on the lack of responses to these questions may be doubtful. For purposes of comparison, similar questions posed to businesses in the equivalent IFC study of land markets in Russia obtained more responses and, in cases of state land allocation, revealed a substantially greater incidence of unofficial payments (Coolidge and Kisunko 2007). Whether this sort of practice is simply more prevalent in Russia, which had many of the same rules and procedures as Vietnam with respect to allocation of state-owned lands, or whether

Table 6.4
Unofficial Payments or Private Relationships to Facilitate Issuance of LURC

Response	Frequency	Percent	Cumulative Percent
Yes to both	13	25.5	25.5
Yes, unofficial fees	17	33.3	58.8
Yes, private relationship	6	11.8	70.6
No	15	29.4	100
Total	51	100	
Did not answer	337		

Russians are simply more willing to talk about such matters is a question that cannot be answered by the present work.

As might be expected, payments were likely made in connection with activities for which discretion was wide and standards were vaguely defined, such as agreeing on the location of the land site or obtaining investment approval. Of the 188 SMEs that obtained land from government or in an IZ and answered the questions, only 21 (11.2 percent) responded that they had made unofficial payments. Activities in which unofficial payments were made by SMEs included obtaining the investment license (16), obtaining the lease or land allocation agreement (14), obtaining the LURC (14), obtaining environmental permits (7), changing land use purpose (5), obtaining cadastre data (5), obtaining a land recovery and compensation plan (4), and obtaining land use fee calculations (3). Thirty-four percent of those who responded said that the total cost of unofficial payments exceeded 10 percent of transaction costs.

SMEs were asked specifically whether they used personal relationships or unofficial payments to facilitate issuance of the LURC. Table 6.4 shows that of the 388 respondents that held LURCs, only 51, or 13 percent, answered the question. Of those, 13 (25 percent) said they used both relationships and unofficial payments; 17 (33.3 percent) used unofficial payments; and 6 relied on personal relationships alone. Fifteen respondents (29.4 percent) said they used neither unofficial payments nor personal relationships.

Summary and Conclusions

According to the current Five-Year Socio-Economic Development Plan of the government of Vietnam, "Socialist-oriented market economic institutions are incomplete and immature. There have been several difficulties in building socialist-oriented market economic institutions. Financial market, real estate market, science and technology market slowly develop and fail to satisfy requirements. State management of each type of markets contains a number of shortcomings" (Vietnam Ministry of Planning and Investment 2006, 5).

The work described in this chapter generally supports that assessment. With regard to creation of an efficient land market within the constraint of state land ownership ("socialist-oriented market economic institutions"), the effort is immature, and the market fails to satisfy all participants, but it appears to be developing at a reasonable pace. Though it may be inefficient and expensive, there is an active secondary market in land rights now, but it may ultimately reach its limits unless there is an effort to put more secure, long-term, alienable, and appropriately zoned land rights into the hands of citizens and businesses. Business land users often characterize land availability and land prices as barriers to their growth. The difficulty of finding land seems to be a primary complaint of business users, who must rely on word of mouth or information from public officials, which is not always forthcoming.

The question may be not whether land markets are developing at an acceptable pace, but whether the markets that ultimately develop will ever fully overcome the inefficiencies inherent in the state land monopoly and the significant state interventions that follow from it. So long as land is viewed primarily as a tool of state economic planning, there is arguably the risk that inefficiencies will be introduced into the market. Practically all former socialist states of the former Soviet Union and Eastern Europe have embraced the concept of privatization, have abandoned exclusive state ownership of land, and have begun to develop private land markets alongside significant state leasing sectors. Vietnam retains the state land monopoly, and whether the benefits of state ownership are now more costly than the risks of gradual development of private ownership markets, particularly among small landholders, is a fair question.

Land allocation procedures in Vietnam, as in many present and former socialist countries, are defined by the fact that the land is rationed on the basis of factors other than ability to pay. Unlike a market economy, in which the land can be acquired in a more or less simple transaction without regard to the nature of the investment, investor, or ultimate land use, in Vietnam all matters regarding use of the land must be resolved prior to an allocation decision, including not only the nature of the proposed investment and the capabilities of the investor, but also the detailed use, plan for construction, and other technical matters. This dynamic applies in both primary and secondary markets. However, there are some indications that the secondary market may gradually approach the free-market model as some provinces eliminate consideration of the investment and investor from the processing of secondary market transactions, at least for the small transactions of SMEs. This seems also to be the intention of the new Law on Investment adopted in 2006.

In Vietnam allocation of state-owned land through the usual procedures has been as much a political process as an administrative process. In most cases, both the local officials and the LMIs interviewed believe that these political aspects of negotiating an investment, granting investment approval, and identifying a specific land site are the most problematic for a variety of reasons, including inadequate staff capabilities and lack of standards and theoretical underpinnings for approving investments and land transactions. Ironically, perhaps because of the officials' discomfort with these procedures, the investment approval process seems to be completed relatively quickly, and SMEs do not note it as a significant problem.

Regarding the task of locating suitable land, a main complaint of SMEs, the problems are most often related to such factors as shortage of serviced and unoccupied land, poor planning documentation, and inadequate market information. Also contributing to the complexity and opacity of some types of land transactions and administrative procedures is the state land recovery process, or the movement of land from lower to higher value uses by confiscation, which has also involved the state directly in land pricing. There is a significant body of opinion that government is not doing this task well, and procedures for land recovery are among the most contentious in Vietnam, earning the distrust of smallholders whose land is taken and only mixed reviews from the investors who benefit.

SMEs already rely preponderantly on the secondary market to obtain land and facilities. To promote SME development, the highest return might therefore be associated with a multifaceted approach to facilitating and increasing the amount of land available through the secondary market, which may entail measures such as increasing the amount of land zoned for business use, encouraging entry of land rights into the market by appropriate pricing and tax policies, resolving issues concerning the alienability of SOE land rights, aggressively resolving existing land titles, encouraging more speculative development of flexible facilities in state-sponsored industrial zones, and enhancing market-making mechanisms to bring buyers and sellers together. Facilitation of secondary market transactions may entail measures such as reducing the state role in investment approvals for small businesses, reducing the time and costs of transaction registration, developing cheap and reliable official title certification capabilities, and improving land use planning documentation so that change of use may be accomplished more expeditiously in appropriate cases.

REFERENCES

Asian Development Bank. 2005. Industrial and commercial land markets and their impact on the poor: Summary report. Manila, Philippines: Asian Development Bank (December).

AusAID. 2000a. Viet Nam: Land administration. Working Paper 4, Canberra, Australia (December).

———. 2000b. Viet Nam: Legal and judicial development. Working Paper 3, Canberra, Australia (April).

Butler, Stephen B. 2003. Enforcement of mortgage rights in housing finance. Paper presented at the World Bank Conference on Housing Finance in Emerging Markets: Policy and Regulatory Challenges, Washington, DC.

Center for Rural Progress. 2006. Industrial and commercial land markets and their impacts on the poor: A study report in Vinh Phuc and Ha Tay provinces prepared for the Asian Development Bank. Hanoi, Vietnam: Center for Rural Progress.

Centre of Land Investigation and Planning (CoLIP), Central Institute for Economic
    Management (CIEM). 2005. Industrial and commercial land markets and their im-
    pact on the poor in the central region of Viet Nam, a report prepared for the Asian
    Development Bank. Hanoi, Vietnam: Centre of Land Investigation and Planning.
Coolidge, Jacqueline, and Gregory Kisunko. 2007. Survey of land and real estate trans-
    actions in the Russian Federation: Statistical analysis of selected hypotheses. World
    Bank Research Working Paper No. 4115, Washington, DC (January).
Decree No. 181. 2004. ND-CP, 29 October.
Foreign Investment Advisory Service. 2001. Administrative barriers to investment in the
    subjects of the Russian Federation. Washington, DC: International Finance Corp.,
    World Bank. http://www.ifc.org/ifcext/fias.nsf/Attachmentsbytitle/fias_resources
    _russia2_chpt1.pdf.
Gaston, Graham. 2005. Land use planning, environmental management and land ad-
    ministration. Report prepared for Strengthening Environmental Management and
    Land Administration (April).
Kim, Annette M. 2004. A market without the "right" property rights: Ho Chi Minh
    City, Vietnam's newly-emerged private real estate market. *Economics of Transition*
    275:12.
Law on Investment. 2005. No. 59-2005-QH11, 29 December (effective 1 July 2006).
Law on Land. 2003. No. 13-2003-QH11, 29 November.
Sharpe, Henry, and Nguyen Quang. 2004. Vietnam urbanization issues. Paper prepared
    for the World Bank, Washington, DC (July).
Tenev, Stoyan, Amanda Carlier, Omar Chaudry, and Quynh-Trang Nguyen. 2003. *In-
    formality and the playing field in Vietnam's business sector*. Washington, DC: IFC,
    World Bank, and the Mekong Private Sector Development Facility.
Vietnam Ministry of Planning and Investment. 2006. *The five-year socio-economic de-
    velopment plan: 2006–2010*. Hanoi: Vietnam Ministry of Planning and Investment.
Viet Nam News. 2006. Property loans not a concern. 29 March: 15.
World Bank. 2005. *Vietnam: Investment climate assessment*. Poverty reduction and eco-
    nomic management unit, East Asia and Pacific Region, Washington, DC (August).

COMMENTARY
Annette M. Kim

Stephen Butler has provided an invaluable resource for establishing and analyzing the details of the latest legal changes around property in Vietnam, about which there has been a dearth of information. In his summary of findings, he displays a nuanced understanding that, despite the state ownership of land and a large secondary market, Vietnam's land market "appears to be developing at a reasonable pace."

What is curious is that this assessment does not have much to do with the main body of the chapter. Doubts about the long-term efficiency of Vietnam's land delivery system are the reasons given for the large national survey—conducted by Butler's colleagues for the World Bank—that tried to show the importance of land tenure and of legally titling property in order to promote investment and economic growth. This disconnect is the focus of my discussion, as it is indicative of a common divergence between the academic interests of development experts in titling and the empirics of rapidly growing property markets. In these comments, I first provide some context for the data presented by Butler: that Vietnam is now considered a development miracle case, but one that defies many conventional development strategies. Then, I outline some of the reasons why legal title has played a limited role in the growth of property markets and investment in Vietnam. I conclude by suggesting directions for expanding the focus of property rights research and policy making to better reconcile empirics to theory.

Although Vietnam is still a recipient of international development assistance, in discussing policy reforms and future development projects it is important to recognize that Vietnam is atypical of developing and transition countries. As World Bank President Robert Zoellick said during one of his first overseas missions in office, "Vietnam has the potential to be one of the great success stories in development. It has already achieved one of the fastest improvements in living standards in the world, with a great reduction in poverty. . . . Decisions on land reform, market liberalization, investing in social sectors and infrastructure, and enabling the private sector have transformed this country in less than a generation" (World Bank 2007).

While Zoellick's comments suggest the importance of property in market reforms, Vietnam has often been viewed as severely lacking in how it has managed its property rights institutions. For example, using the legal protection of private property rights as one of its criteria, the International Monetary Fund ranked Vietnam as one of the most institutionally backward countries among 31 transition countries (IMF 2000). Similarly, the Heritage Foundation ranked Vietnam as 141 out of 155 countries in terms of providing an economic environment conducive to private investment, noting that the country was particularly weak in property rights protection (Heritage Foundation 2004). Focusing specifically on the property sector of the economy, Jones Lang LaSalle's annual transparency index ranked Vietnam dead last among 56 countries in terms of being a market attractive to global real estate investors (Jones Lang LaSalle 2006). In each of these rankings, the assessments were based on the assumption that property rights that promote investment and market growth are established primarily through legal institutions: laws, titling, and court enforcement of contracts. Since these institutions are weak in Vietnam, it is not surprising that Butler's survey should ask questions that presume that Vietnam's lack of legal institutional development is constraining the growth of firms.

However, the fact is that Vietnam has witnessed incredible economic growth, including the rapid expansion of private real estate markets. Furthermore, this growth includes sizable investment by global investors for over two decades, particularly by investors from the more developed Asian nations of Taiwan, Japan, Singapore, and South Korea. Vietnam's growth also includes considerable amounts of domestic private investment and the emergence of a new class of Vietnamese property developers (Kim 2008). Although Vietnam's economic environment may seem opaque and hostile to development experts who are accustomed to Western institutions and norms, many people have been able to make it work profitably. China is another case where the rule of law has been considered weak, but where there has been phenomenal sustained economic growth rates, including the emergence of an enormous private property market.

These cases suggest that we need to reconsider the connection between legal property rights institutions and private real estate markets. However, there has been little impact on the kind of advice and programming provided by mainstream development agencies. This is despite decades of title regularization programs in various places around the world that have resulted in limited sustained or systemic success (Payne 2001). The focus on legal reforms and titling persists, as we see in the selection of papers presented in the international portion of this conference, the popularity of Hernando de Soto, and the major urban development assistance projects such as Peru's recent nationwide investment in titling.

The logic behind the effort to distribute legal title to property is that, with the state enforcement of clearly defined property rights represented by these pieces of paper, property holders will be confident to transact with each other and more importantly invest in their property to realize its highest economic value. Note that the first three assumptions in this chain of logic require a state with considerable bureaucratic capacity, legislation detailed enough to provide guidance in complex property ownership situations, and social recognition for a specific document. In other words, these three points presume the existence of legal institutions that are supported by a legalistic culture. While it is obvious that people have to feel confident and secure enough to make economic transactions and investments, at question is whether this source of stability and security should come exclusively from formal law.

As noted by experts, Vietnam does not have the ideal set of legal institutions, but it has witnessed high rates of both domestic and international investment. This has been possible because property rights security has come less through the formal law and more by the state directly. Vietnam's one-party state has had few challengers for over 30 years and owns all the land in the country outright. Ironically, the elaborate communist bureaucracy with its neighborhood and city ward offices, rather than the understaffed courts, mediated property disputes and sanctioned most private property transactions during Vietnam's transition. Furthermore, for larger investment projects involving foreigners, the city district offices and bureaus essentially assure the rights to developers and protect the projects by guiding them through the bureaucratic maze and browbeating low compensation rates from current landholders. Of course, one of the dangers with rule by the state is that changes could be made on a whim, leaving investors in an untenably risky position. However, in the case of Vietnam and China, local governments have been reliably accommodating to private business.

In fact, the data in Butler's survey seem to corroborate that tenure and legal title issues are not substantial obstacles to private businesses and entrepreneurialism in Vietnam. Most small and medium enterprises were able to find sites for their production in the private real estate market within one week. Larger enterprises secured land from local government within three months. Furthermore, 77 percent of surveyed firms invested in improvements on their sites despite holding varying types of tenure documents.

These surprising statistics make more sense if one considers the source of these firms' capital. It does not come through banks, which would require title papers, but through private contracting with investors who secure their investment through the threat of loss of future investments (Woodruff 1999). In the residential real estate sectors, much of the development capital comes from home buyers who are willing to provide installment payments years before taking possession, which transfers most of the risk to them. One could always argue that even more investment might have occurred if properties had been titled and rights better secured through legal institutions. But, given the rapid rate of Vietnam's transition and growth, this argument is less compelling.

Still, the bilateral and multilateral development aid institutions are focused on the potential power of legal property titles in Vietnam. In addition to Butler's study, which was funded by the World Bank and AusAID, GTZ conducted a similar study last year (Vietnam Chamber of Commerce and Industry 2007), and Sweden International Development Agency (SIDA) spent over a decade in Vietnam focusing on land law and cadastral reform (Dang and Palmkvist 2001). There appears to be an overemphasis on legal reforms and title at the expense of more pressing property rights issues in these transition countries. Given that businesses have been able to invest and grow despite low rates of title distribution, it would make more sense to ask entrepreneurs and the business community to name their biggest property-related constraints.

In my interviews with local property developers in Ho Chi Minh City, one issue eclipsed all others: the increasing social conflict over compensation in land takings for private development now makes consolidating land parcels and proceeding with development projects difficult. This source of property rights instability results in loss of site area and increased project development costs. This dynamic is not unique to Vietnam but is spreading across the globe. The academic and policy community should focus on the complex problem of creating institutions that can better deal with negotiating the transfer of land in ways that increase equity, do not choke the private sector, and do not compromise public health and safety. Given the pressing and growing nature of the major property rights issue of our time, we risk being irrelevant if we retain a sole focus on a minor technical matter.

REFERENCES

Dang, Hung Vo, and Gosta Palmkvist. 2001. *Sweden-Vietnam cooperation on land administration reform in Vietnam*. Stockholm: Sweden International Development Agency.

Heritage Foundation. 2004. *Index of economic freedom*. Washington, DC: Heritage Foundation and *Wall Street Journal*.

IMF. 2000. *Focus on transition economies*. Washington, DC: International Monetary Fund.

Jones Lang LaSalle. 2006. *Real estate transparency index*. Jones Lang LaSalle.

Kim, Annette M. 2008. *Learning to be capitalists: Entrepreneurs in Vietnam's transition economy*. New York: Oxford University Press.

Payne, Geoffrey. 2001. Urban land tenure policy options: Titles or rights? *Habitat International* 25(3):415–429.

Vietnam Chamber of Commerce and Industry. 2007. Access to land: Issues faced by private sector. *Business Issues Bulletin*:1–4.

Woodruff, Christopher. 1999. Dispute prevention without courts in Vietnam. *Journal of Law, Economics, and Organization* 15(3):637–658.

World Bank. 2007. Vietnam striving to become middle-income country, World Bank president says. World Bank Press Release, No. 2008/43/EAP.

PUBLIC COMPENSATIONS
FOR TAKINGS

7

The Use of Eminent Domain in São Paulo, Bogotá, and Mexico City

Antonio Azuela

*L*egal rules on eminent domain are at the same time rules on property rights. They may not contain all aspects of a property regime, but they allow us to see property in its most intense relationship with the state. By looking at the rules on eminent domain, we can see the sense in which the limits of property rights are the limits of government's power to impose a public interest at the expense and without the consent of the rights holder. Of course, the limits are not eternal; in recent years, a new round of debates has developed regarding the status of foreign investors' property rights in the context of free trade agreements and other international instruments. In those debates, we can talk about expropriations at the global end: we use a single legal language to discuss them, and we assume we are dealing with a prototypical property owner (the multinational corporation) as well as with an international state system that makes possible the whole story. This chapter is about expropriations "at the other end"—that is, expropriations at a local level that include urban landowners, local authorities, and judges acting within the framework of national legal systems.

We examine the conditions under which eminent domain is used in São Paulo, Bogotá, and Mexico City. Although we deal with the legal systems at the national level, we focus on those cities in particular not only because they are the largest urban agglomerations in their respective countries (see table 7.1), but also because there is growing concern about the use of eminent domain in all of them.

Claudia Acosta, Lorena Jaramillo, Melinda Lis, Carlos Herrera, and Camilo Saavedra provided extremely valuable assistance in the research leading to this chapter. I also wish to express my warmest thanks to Vicki Been, Yu-Hung Hong, and Gregory Ingram for their comments on an earlier version of this chapter. The usual disclaimers apply. The chapter uses the expressions *eminent domain*, *expropriation*, and *taking* as synonyms.

Table 7.1
Comparison of Mexico City, Bogotá, and São Paulo

	Population (municipality)	Area (km²)	Population (metropolitan area)	GDP (US$ billions)	GDP (as percentage of national)
Mexico City	8,720,916	1,480	19,239,910	315	20.0
Bogotá	6,776,009	1,732	7,881,156	86	23.1
São Paulo	10,435,546	1,522	19,677,506	225	12.3

Source: INEGI (2005). Bogotá: SDP (2007) and http://www.dane.gov.co/files/censo2005. Brazil: http://www.ibge.gov.br/home/ estatistica/populacao/estimativa and http://www.ibge.gov.br/home/estatistica/economia/pibmunicipios.

Without denying the force and relevance of global trends, the case studies demonstrate that national as well as local processes have strong conditioning effects in the way eminent domain power is used. There are more differences than commonalities in the way eminent domain is changing in those cases. At the same time, to understand those conditions, it is necessary to look at three elements. The first element is eminent domain as part of a constitutional order, which includes not only the constitutional definition of property rights, but also the relations between branches and levels of government. This is especially relevant in Latin America because of what are generally known as democratic transitions that have taken place in the last decades. In particular, the new role of the judiciary has created new conditions for (and in some cases, serious limits to) expropriations in the urban context. This has taken place in very different ways in the three countries under consideration.

The second element is the actual use of eminent domain for urban purposes. The information is scarce in this respect, making it necessary to limit analysis to the individual metropolitan areas of São Paulo, Bogotá, and Mexico City. Here, too, the three situations are so different that we can suspect any hypothesis that structural factors have determined the evolution of eminent domain as an institution in Latin American cities.

The third element refers to the legal treatment of eminent domain as expression of a legal culture. Legal doctrines that are invoked by judges, lawyers, and other operators of the legal system say a lot about the way private property and the power to suppress it are defined in a particular social context. In spite of the frequent contention that all three countries embrace the doctrine of the social function of property, such a doctrine is used in many different ways, reflecting the particular features of each historical experience.

São Paulo: The Precatórios Crisis

One of the most salient episodes in São Paulo's recent history is the financial stress on local governments resulting from compensations awarded by judges in eminent domain cases. A *precatório* is a judicial ruling that orders a government agency to budget necessary funds for fulfilling an obligation—in the case of expropriation, the compensation. Exorbitant compensations combined with high interest rates have put local governments in a critical situation. Many observers believe that this has weakened the power of eminent domain in Brazil.

To understand eminent domain in Brazil, it is important to look at the wider institutional landscape, which includes the 1988 constitution with new provisions to protect property rights and a strong urban planning program, as well as the leading role of municipalities in the use of eminent domain. After more than two decades of authoritarian rule, the Brazilian constitution was the result of a complex negotiation process that began in 1986 and ended in October 1988. It is one of the Latin American constitutions that characterized transitions to democracy in the region. A whole chapter in the 1988 constitution (section 182) is devoted to a *politica urbana* (*the* urban policy).[1] It addresses three issues: town planning, property rights in the urban context, and housing rights. An unusual feature is the centrality given to urban issues in the development agenda. The main objective is no less than "the full development of the social functions of the city and the welfare of its inhabitants."[2]

Urban planning in the Brazilian constitution is more than a neutral administrative tool; it is part of the recrafting of state institutions through decentralization, and more precisely as a tool for local democracy (Gomes-de-Mendonca 2001; Saule 2007). According to section 182, the passing of a *plano diretor*, the equivalent to a master plan, is an exclusive power of the Municipal Council (the Câmara Municipal). Municipalities have eminent domain powers, which is rare in other federal republics in the region, such as Mexico and Argentina, where eminent domain procedures are in the hands of state-level authorities.

The most ambitious aspect of the urban chapter in the Brazilian constitution refers to the social function of property (Duguit 1912), a doctrine that can be equated to what is more generally known as the social obligation inherent in property rights (Alexander 2006). One of its corollaries is that the constitution specifically empowers municipal governments to require owners of undeveloped land in the urban context to promote adequate use of the land. Those who do not comply with urban plans are subject to (1) the compulsory development of their land; (2) progressive property taxes; and (3) expropriation with deferred compensation through deeds with terms of up to 10 years. In other words, the power of eminent domain can be used as a sanction against owners who do not use the land according to urban plans.

---

1. We avoid the translation of *politica urbana* as "urban policies" (plural) in order to keep the force of the idea of a single (and coherent) set of goals regarding urban problems.

2. By contrast, see the recent constitutional debates in Bolivia and Ecuador, where the main concern is the rural (and especially the indigenous) component of society.

The third aspect of the urban chapter refers to housing rights. The focus of the constitution here is on providing security of tenure for dwellers in low-income settlements such as favelas; the uninterrupted possession (the use as a dwelling) of up to 250 square meters of urban land is the basis for the acquisition of rights over that piece of land (Saule 1999, 2001).

The Estatuto da Cidade (Statute of the City), a piece of federal legislation passed in July 2001, contains the most ambitious agenda for urban reform in Latin America. It includes a wide array of legal instruments and brings together ideals of local democracy, collective rights, and strong regulatory powers in the hands of local governments. Nevertheless, when it comes to eminent domain, it only refers to the innovation of the 1988 constitution regarding the possibility of using expropriation as a sanction for leaving urban land unused or underdeveloped. This is striking because the main urban conflict during the previous decade was over ordinary takings: the crisis of the *precatórios*, a crisis that did not get an explicit response in the Estatuto da Cidade.

Turning from constitutional texts and statutes to the way eminent domain powers are exercised in practice, the image is completely different from that of the Estatuto da Cidade. Authors and witnesses agree that a crisis of eminent domain power began in the early 1990s (Haddad, Lopes-dos-Santos, and Franco 2007). Its origins are debatable, but the results were clear, and they reached the public under the guise of a national scandal. By the mid-1990s most urban municipalities in the state of São Paulo, especially the city of São Paulo itself, faced growing financial stress due to the accumulation of debts from *precatórios*. Most were compensations awarded by judges for eminent domain cases (Haddad, Lopes-dos-Santos, and Franco 2007; Maricato 2000a).

Things got much worse because compensations based on questionable methods (Haddad 2000) were combined with high interest and inflation rates.[3] Compensations reached up to 30 times the market value of the land, as in the case of Serra do Mar in Ubatuba, a green area of 13 hectares expropriated for the creation of a park (Maricato 2000b). The best indicator of the magnitude of the problem was that these debts came to represent an enormous burden for municipalities. "Often, the value of an inflated indemnification for land expropriation equals the general budget for one or more political mandates [administrations] of a governmental jurisdiction" (Maricato 2000a, 5).

By the end of the decade, it was obvious that expropriations were good business for landowners, and the notion of an "industry of compensations" became common parlance.[4] There are several interpretations of what was happening. For some, it was mainly a financial crisis due to inflationary conditions. For others,

---

3. For a detailed account of the components of compensations, see Lopes-dos-Santos (2007).

4. The 20 January 1999 issue of the popular weekly magazine *Véja* denounced the practices of unscrupulous "super lawyers" and said that the debt in São Paulo could be close to 30 billion reais (circa US$15 billion) (quoted by Haddad 2000).

it was a question of pure and simple corruption.[5] More nuanced opinions point to the incompetence of judges (particularly their inability to penetrate the "black box" of valuations) as well as the professional weakness of legal teams at public agencies (Haddad 2000; Lopes-dos-Santos 2007). An interesting interpretation signals the propensity of judges in a postauthoritarian context to take every opportunity to present themselves as the defenders of citizens against the abuses of government, a kind of judicial activism that seems to be normal during democratic transitions (Ríos-Figueroa and Taylor 2006). All experts agree that this was a crisis for expropriation as an institution.

During the late 1990s, there were at least two attempts to deal with the crisis: a parliamentary commission of inquiry was created in the legislature of the state of São Paulo, and the Ministry for Agrarian Development issued the white paper "Supercompensations: How to Stop That 'Industry'" (Haddad 2000; Maricato 2000a). However, apart from the public awareness these initiatives may have simulated, no decision came from them except for a measure, issued by the president of the republic and the National Congress, reducing the annual interest rates for unpaid compensations from 12 percent to 6 percent (Lopes-dos-Santos 2007, 125).

At a more modest level, an academic institution, the Getúlio Vargas Foundation, prepared a survey on valuation methodologies, and, more interestingly, the Center for the Support of Fiscal Judges (*Cajufa*) drafted guidelines for valuation procedures. These studies seem to have improved the situation in recent years, although on cases that look small compared to the huge figures of the mid-1990s (Lopes-dos-Santos 2007).

Let us now consider how the legal system has dealt with the crisis of *precatórios*. When we look at legislation regarding eminent domain in the urban context, we see the source of a profound dissatisfaction with urban law (Lopes-dos-Santos 2007), a feeling that contrasts with the enthusiasm that surrounded the Estatuto da Cidade when it was passed in 2001. There were attempts in both the National Congress and in the São Paulo state legislature to do something about the problem, but the only effective measure was the establishment of a system to compensate private firms' fiscal debts with public debts (Maricato 2000a, 38). The law of takings as such did not change. As indicated earlier, the Estatuto da Cidade regulates the innovation in the 1988 constitution that allows the use of eminent domain as a sanction for landowners' withholding their land against urban plans, but at the same time it is silent about the most pressing problem that urban administrators were facing in the same years: exorbitant compensations in ordinary expropriations.

---

5. According to Julio Bruna, who acted as director of INURBE, an urban development agency of the city of São Paulo during the 1990s, the crisis of the *precatórios* grew out of judicial corruption and the complexities and long duration of legal procedures (personal communication, March 2008).

The poorest record was (if not still is) at the judiciary: everyone seems to agree that extremely high compensations established by judges imposed an enormous social cost, at least in the urban areas of the state of São Paulo. With the available information, it is difficult to assert whether those compensations derived from corrupt practices in the judiciary or from ideological biases toward property rights. A concurring factor could have been the judiciary's desire to assert its autonomy vis-à-vis the executive after a long period of authoritarian governments. However, the courts are far from using the contributions of jurists who are offering to rethink the complex issue of how to compensate the taking of land and property (see, for example, Rabello 2007).

On its part, the administration, particularly local governments, appears as the victim of the *precatórios*. There does not seem to be a critical account of the way it may have contributed to the crisis.[6] However, there are reasons to think that a learning process is involved here. Most of the experts who were interviewed believe that, as a result of the experience in the 1990s, administrators are now more careful about preparing necessary budgets for land acquisitions. The crucial question—the arrival of an authentic fair compensation system—will surely depend on capacity building and on healthy interaction between judges and administrators. Even recognizing that "fair" will always be a contested notion, there seems to be a great opportunity to reduce the discretionary margins within which decisions are arrived at. The challenge of Brazilian law in relation to eminent domain is enormous. As Edésio Fernandes has put it, "pointing at legal problems and denouncing unconstitutional practices is easy. The difficult part is that of constructing new arguments which prove solid and consistent, not only from the perspective of socio-political legitimacy, but also from a strictly legal point of view" (2002, 11).

Bogotá: Enlightened Judges and Prudent Administrators —————

Seen only through the newspapers, Colombia looks like another case of an eminent domain crisis due to exorbitant compensations. The "polo court" case, a conflict that has been widely publicized by the media, could lead to this conclusion. For almost eight years, the local government of Bogotá has maintained a legal battle against a country club that occupies a huge piece of land in a desirable central location in the city, the members of which are allegedly the political and economic elite of the country. The Bogotá government wishes to expropriate a small part of that land for the continuation of a main road as well as some 15 acres, now conspicuously a polo court, for a public park. In February 2008 the mayor announced that, should the court order an unreasonably high compensation, he would abandon the expropriation procedure. Ten of the twelve experts

---

6. The limited professional competence of legal teams in local government is the only factor that the literature has pointed out (Lopes-dos-Santos 2007).

interviewed as part of this research think that doing so would be a serious defeat for the institution of eminent domain.

However, when one gets deeper into the way eminent domain is used as a tool for urban policies in Bogotá, the image is completely different. Certainly experts, especially planners, complain that judges award compensations that are too high in expropriation cases. But they all think that land is being expropriated for a number of urban projects without anything like the crisis of *precatórios* that São Paulo suffered in the last decade. Projects with high popular support, such as the transport system Transmilenio,[7] expand through expropriations that are never successfully challenged by land or property owners. Three factors seem to combine to produce this relatively pacific environment: (1) a legal framework in which there is a basic coherence between the constitution, urban law, and the prevailing legal culture in the country's high courts; (2) healthy finances that allow the local government to afford the acquisition of land; and (3) wide social support behind the public works for which the land is being taken.

As in Brazil (and unlike in most other Latin American countries), innovations in urban law have been part and parcel of a recent constitutional change in Colombia that enjoys wide legitimacy. That is why, in principle, such innovations could be expected to have the same legitimacy as the constitution as a whole. Unlike the Brazilian case, however, there is a more fluid dialogue among the three branches of Colombia's government. Even if they may collide in expropriation cases, they share a minimum common code to deal with conflict. Whereas Brazilian judges have ignored the new legal ideas about the city set forth in the constitution and the Estatuto da Cidade, judges in Colombia take innovations coming from the legislative branch more seriously.

In 1989 the National Congress passed a piece of legislation generally known as the Urban Reform Act (*Ley 9 de 1989*). However, the most significant development on the legal status of urban property came with the constitution of 1991, which stands as one of the most significant achievements in contemporary Latin American constitutionalism and probably as the most accomplished balance between the principles of liberal democracy and the commitment to third-generation human rights (economic, social, and cultural rights). For the purpose of this chapter, the new Colombian property regime is interesting in three aspects: (1) the definition of property as a social function; (2) the basic conditions for the expropriation of land; and (3) the criteria for determining compensation.

The definition of property in the Colombian constitution does not rest on the idea that property is a right. The constitutional text makes clear that private property is "guaranteed," but at the same time it states that "property is a social function that implies obligations" (article 58). For Colombian jurisprudence, this is a sea change in the status of private property that breaks with the liberal

---

7. A bus rapid transit system that has inspired other Latin American cities (Rodríguez and Mojica 2008).

tradition in which property rights were a major obstacle to progressive urban policies (Maldonado 2003; Pinilla 2003). The new constitutional compromise tries to balance the acceptance of private property with the commitment to use wealth to benefit society as a whole.

As to the rules concerning eminent domain, four points are worth stressing. First, the constitution authorizes eminent domain not only for public uses, but also for responding to a "social interest," which means it can be used to satisfy the needs of specific groups in society—the vulnerable sectors of society—and not necessarily the needs of the public as a whole. Second, in spite of the general thrust toward a more interventionist scheme regarding urban property, the 1991 Colombian constitution states, as a general rule, that expropriations require previous compensation as well as a judicial resolution (*sentencia judicial*). Not the administration but the judiciary, in principle, makes the decision to take land. At the same time, the constitution provides for administrative expropriations: "Legislation may determine cases in which expropriations can be carried out by the administration. They may be challenged before administrative courts, even regarding the compensation."[8] Although Colombian lawyers seem to agree that this administrative expropriation has an exceptional character, it has been used in Bogotá successfully and in a regular way in recent years.

Third, local governments are empowered to undertake eminent domain procedures. This is important because, up the late 1980s, municipal authorities were not elected, but were appointed by the national government. Thus, decentralization came hand in hand with democratization.[9] Local governments did enjoy eminent domain powers before that, but the fact that they were now elected gave this power a new meaning, the more so because expropriations can now be undertaken by the administration.

However, the most interesting innovation in the 1991 constitution refers to the fourth aspect: the way it deals with the issue of compensation. Obviously, as a constitutional text, it cannot go into the complexities of valuation techniques. But at the same time it does not surrender to the only apparently easy solution of market value. Instead, it gives administrators and judges the difficult task of fixing the compensation, "taking into account the interests of the community as well as those of the affected party" (article 58). It is difficult to find a modern constitution that sets forth in such a direct way the basic tension implied in the task of fixing a compensation for the taking of property.

In 1997 Congress approved new legislation amending the 1989 Urban Reform Act. This new legislation (Act 388 or *Ley 388*) developed the principles regarding urban development in the 1991 constitution and established a variety

---

8. This is not a literal translation. The original in Spanish is "*En los casos que determine el legislador, dicha expropiación podrá adelantarse por vía administrativa, sujeta a posterior acción contencioso administrativa, incluso respecto del precio.*"

9. For the place of decentralization in the Colombian constitution, see Trujillo-Muñoz (2007).

of instruments to implement urban policies. Act 388 sets forth the procedure for administrative expropriations with the intention of allowing local governments to acquire land in a more expedited fashion. This does not necessarily mean an arbitrary procedure, as the act also provides for legal remedies before an administrative court and a one-month term during which the administration may negotiate the conditions of the purchase with the owner. Another salient element of Act 388 is that, in order to avoid windfall gains for landowners, the compensation is not to include the increment of land values due to the announcement of the project.

The constitutional and legal framework is clear enough regarding both the substantive and the procedural aspects of eminent domain. What happens in practice is much more difficult to assess. In Colombia, as in most countries, it is not possible to find systematic information about the use of eminent domain. What follows is the result of a series of interviews with a dozen practitioners and academics who are directly involved in eminent domain practices in Bogotá.

The first finding is that eminent domain is widely used in Bogotá. Civil servants who work with expropriation cases believe that judges tend to award compensations that are too high, but they all agree that, almost without exception (the polo court case being one of them), expropriation procedures are brought to an end successfully. In other words, no public project is canceled because of legal obstacles to the use of eminent domain.

Another important fact is that a very high proportion of expropriation procedures end with voluntary agreements. Some 85 percent of the 2,061 properties procured by IDU (the municipal agency responsible for the Transmilenio project) between 2003 and 2007 had such agreements.[10] To some experts, that means that valuation practices within local government are arriving at high land prices. To others it means that most people do not know their rights, tend to accept whatever the government has to offer, and miss the opportunity to obtain higher compensation by going to court. This refers particularly to homeowners in low-income areas.

These interpretations point in opposite directions regarding the level of compensation—a question that should remain open until more systematic empirical research is carried out at the local level. No matter what the reason, the fact remains that an extremely high proportion of eminent domain procedures end up in voluntary acquisitions, which means that procurement of land does not seem to be a major obstacle for urban projects, at least in Bogotá. Even if eminent domain power works only as a threat, it appears to be alive and well in that part of Latin America.

Two elements have contributed to making land acquisitions successful in Bogotá—a good financial situation, largely derived from an aggressive property

10. This information was not available before the survey. It was delivered to us in the context of a right-of-information procedure conducted by Claudia Acosta.

tax policy in the 1990s, combined with the privatization of several public enterprises—which gave local governments resources to undertake ambitious urban
projects, such as the Transmilenio, that are part of an effort to "retrieve" the city.
That is why the expropriation of land for such projects is widely recognized as
legitimate.

Maybe the most important innovation in the last years is the use of administrative expropriation, which was provided for in the 1991 constitution. Since
2003 it has been the main mechanism for procuring land for the Transmilenio.
Affected owners who want to challenge administrative takings have the right to
go to an administrative court rather than a civil court. It is too soon to evaluate
the impact of this new option. An interesting point about the way administrative
takings are working in practice has to do with the negotiation period. There is no
real bargaining regarding the compensation because administrators are reluctant
to modify the established appraisal; they fear being seen as arbitrary or corrupt.[11]
So they simply hand the appraisal down to the affected owner and wait during
the one-month period to see whether the owner accepts it.

Another interesting feature in the practice of eminent domain in Colombia
is the fact that while judges enjoy considerable discretion in the award of compensations, they never question the purpose for which the land is taken. As in
Brazil, a *Kelo v. City of New London* problem is most unlikely to arise. Even if
there is not an explicit prohibition, judges consistently defer to the administration regarding the substantive justification of an expropriation. (Mexico differs
greatly in this respect.)

In the context of a generally successful policy of land procurement, the conflict around the polo court remains an exception. As interesting as it may be as a
contest between local government and the economic elite of the country, it is far
from being an average case. Whether it will have an influence on future cases or
legislative processes remains to be seen.

The most relevant aspect of eminent domain in Bogotá has to do with legal
culture. Unlike almost every other Latin American legal system, the Colombian
system has been able to deal with the different views on the hard subject of eminent domain. This refers particularly to the way the high courts have dealt with
tensions between conflicting interests and their legitimacy (Uprimny, Rodríguez,
and García-Villegas 2003). Through remarkably well-articulated rulings, they
have developed strong arguments for the implementation of the social function
doctrine of property. This goes beyond the mere statement of grand legal concepts, as can be seen in the establishment of criteria to determine compensations.
In a now-famous 1074/02 ruling in 2002, the Constitutional Court established
a distinction between three different functions of payment for takings: repara-

---

11. Anticorruption laws and policies in Latin America have had unintended consequences,
including that civil servants become paralyzed in order to avoid doing "good things that look
as bad ones," as the Spanish adage goes (Pérez-Perdomo 2006).

tion, restitution, and compensation.[12] This distinction recognizes the situation of homeowners when they are being deprived of the only place they have to live. The idea that they have a right to fuller compensation points at a distinction that legal systems rarely make, the distinction between property as an asset and property as the means for satisfying a basic need such as housing. Interestingly, the ruling does not explicitly mention housing rights, thus apparently ignoring international human rights law. But its content contributes to the promotion of housing rights like no other high court ruling on the continent.

An important empirical question remains to be answered in the Colombian case: are land and property owners affected by too-high compensations for expropriations, as many planners contend? Regardless of the answer, Bogotá's local government has been using eminent domain procedures in a successful way during the last decade, in contrast with the cases of São Paulo and Mexico City. It is difficult to attribute this state of affairs to a single factor, whether a socially committed congress, enlightened high courts, or competent local governments. Perhaps the interaction among them has produced the most salient regime on eminent domain in the region.

Mexico: Silence Before the Monument

Eminent domain was a crucial instrument in the formation of the postrevolutionary Mexican state. During the first half of the twentieth century, it was the instrument of agrarian reform and of the nationalization of strategic economic sectors such as the oil industry, processes on which rested much of the legitimacy of the political regime. However, during the last two decades, using eminent domain to procure land for urban projects has become increasingly difficult. As in Brazil, this is related to an unusual judicial activism, but other elements, mainly in the realm of legal culture, produce different results.

Most Mexican jurists proudly declare that the Mexican constitution of 1917, which marked the end of the military phase of the revolution and placed the interests of property owners below the general interests of society, was the first social constitution in history.[13] There were two strong features in the postrevolutionary Mexican model: it was centered on the transformation of property relations in a rural context, and it was carried out in an authoritarian way. Difficulties have arisen in adapting the social function doctrine to the urban agenda, particularly in the context of a postauthoritarian political order.

As a heritage of the postrevolutionary era, article 27 of the constitution grants wide discretionary powers for the expropriation of land to the president of the republic as well as to state governors. First, instead of the explicit

---

12. An explanation of these concepts is beyond the scope of this chapter.

13. It predated the Weimar constitution, which established the principle of a social obligation inherent in property, by two years.

requirement of a previous compensation that one finds in other countries, the Mexican constitution authorizes expropriations "by means of" (*mediante*) compensation, which allows for deferred payments. Second, although the affected party has a legal remedy to challenge the taking—the *amparo* suit—if that remedy is not used, no judicial authority has to intervene in the process: property is transferred to the state by a simple decree by the executive. The constitution even restricts judicial intervention to certain cases of changes in value, a prohibition that the judiciary has ignored systematically. Third, the supreme court has, until recently, maintained the principle that the affected party does not have the right to be heard before the taking is fully effective—the right to prior hearing that is part of the due process doctrine in Mexican constitutionalism.

Takings at the federal level are ruled by the Expropriation Act of 1936. A remarkable legislative silence of more than 70 years is one of the prominent features in the law of eminent domain in Mexico (Díaz-y-Díaz 1988). Only two legislative processes are worth mentioning.[14] The first is the Human Settlements Act (*Ley General de Asentamientos Humanos*) of 1976, an attempt to bring the ideas of constitutional article 27 to urban development. Agrarian reform had ended, and Mexico had become a predominantly urban society, so this act offered a program for urban reform: social justice in cities plus a system of rational government decisions (a planning system). It provided the institutional framework for using eminent domain as part of urban administration, although it did not have new rules on expropriations; it would have been difficult to increase the eminent domain powers of the executive.

The second legislative initiative on eminent domain was an amendment to the Expropriation Act as part of the negotiation of the North American Free Trade Agreement (NAFTA) in 1993 to make clear that compensations should amount to market values.[15] This was in line with international trends; it can even be called a condition that Mexico was forced to accept as part of a negotiation with a world superpower. But it is not as relevant as internal developments that have changed the conditions of eminent domain in the last years. Those developments can be classified into three groups: democratic transition, social resistance, and judicial activism.

Democratic transition has one aspect that, almost by definition, puts limits on the abuse of eminent domain: political pluralism. To the extent that government positions and seats in the parliament are in the hands of different political

---

14. This looks at federal legislation only. Camilo Saavedra's research in progress for the Lincoln Institute of Land Policy is finding considerable changes at the state level.

15. The most important change in the regime of takings was, however, of a procedural character: even if all expropriations must be paid at commercial values, foreign investors obtained a different remedy for their conflicts with the government. This has been important, as witnessed by the famous *Metalclad* case, but in quantitative terms it has meant much less than conflicts over eminent domain with nationals.

parties, preventing abuses of power is easier. However, two specific traits in the Mexican transition are relevant here. First, decentralization initiatives, widely regarded as forms of democratization, did not modify the old scheme regarding takings. Unlike the Brazilian and the Colombian cases, in Mexico the transfer of eminent domain powers to municipalities is out of the question; such powers are still concentrated in state governors and the president of the republic.[16]

The second element that has made takings particularly difficult is social resistance when it comes to taking agrarian communities' land for public purposes.[17] For decades, the federal government expropriated rural lands for infrastructure and urban development, paying low or even no compensation to peasants. After a long process of legal learning and social organization, those communities are now strong enough to resist expropriations. In fact, taking their land often becomes impossible even when government proceeds according to the law. Strange as it may sound in a predominantly urban society, few approve of the expropriation of their land for urban development. One of the biggest fiascos in the administration of President Vicente Fox (the first opposition candidate to win the presidency in seven decades) was the withdrawal of a project to build a new airport for Mexico City as a result of the opposition of peasants to the expropriation of their lands.

The third and most important factor is judicial activism, which has become a concern for many observers of the Mexican political system because it implies the presence of an actor (the supreme court) that had been a discreet player in the constitutional order (Ríos-Figueroa and Taylor 2006). The role of the supreme court had been extremely ambivalent vis-à-vis the executive's use of eminent domain power. The court tended to "follow" (the euphemism *acompañar* is hard to translate) the executive in what seemed crucial cases, but the image of a completely restrained judiciary is misleading, even for the high moments of the postrevolutionary period—something that, by the way, has been clear in sociological research since the 1960s (Elizondo 2001; González-Casanova 1966). It was not unusual for the supreme court to rule against the government in small cases (for example, declaring expropriations null and void) and for the latter to accept the defeat, although it also happened that the government refused to comply and managed to keep the issue out of public scrutiny. The court used to be discreet in those cases as well.

In that context, nobody seemed to notice the many instances in which the court's resolutions implied an unusual lack of judicial deference and sometimes an outright violation of the constitution. Most notably, the court used to question the purpose of an expropriation, something that is not only uncommon in other Latin

---

16. In 1999 the major political parties made nine different proposals for amending the constitution, none of which included eminent domain.

17. More than 60 percent of land in the urban periphery is owned by agrarian communities (*ejidos* and *comunidades*).

American countries (like Brazil and Colombia), but is also explicitly forbidden by the Mexican constitution (article 27). Thus, when the democratic transition allowed the court to explicitly exert its power as an autonomous branch of government, the executive found itself more restrained by the judiciary than most other governments under constitutional regimes.

In some respects, the new situation resembled that of Brazil in the 1990s: judges began granting exorbitant compensations. It is difficult to distinguish when these compensations were a sign of corrupt practices from when the court was unable to get into the black box of the valuators' logic. For the first time, the court has faced serious criticism from the media. There have also been some interesting rulings establishing reasonable conditions for expropriation procedures. For example, in 2006 the court granted affected parties the right to prior hearing.

Thus, changes in the political system, new forms of social resistance, and an emerging judicial activism have made the procurement of land through expropriation increasingly difficult for both federal and state governments. Some of those conditions resemble the *precatórios* crisis in Brazil, but we do not see anything like a generalized crisis of eminent domain in Mexico. Judges have awarded outrageous compensation in some cases, but this has not led to financial stress, but instead to open political confrontation between branches of government.

The case of Paraje San Juan is a good example. In 1989 an expropriation decree was issued to regularize 12 neighborhoods with around 12,000 households that were the product of four decades of irregular ("pirate") urbanization. A man who presented himself as the owner of the land claimed the compensation for the expropriation. At no point did the judge or the authorities try to clarify whether the man had been responsible for the illegal development or was a victim of the invasion of his land.[18] The compensation awarded by the judges was equivalent to the current value of all the houses and the urban infrastructure in the area, some US$130 million. In 2003 the judge ordered its immediate payment, which would have been equivalent to one-third of the whole budget for social assistance in Mexico City.

The compensation in the Paraje San Juan case became the most widely and hotly debated political conflict of the moment. On one hand, the city government openly refused to pay, arguing that it was an obvious case of judicial corruption. On the other hand, many commentators insisted, in the name of the rule of law, that the compensation should be paid. The affair became so embarrassing to the judiciary that the supreme court "attracted" the case and, in open violation of

---

18. Qualified witnesses (civil servants then at high levels) who chose to remain anonymous asserted that the lands were national, not private, property.

the principle of res judicata, reduced the compensation to a tenth of the original figure.

Legislative silence has prevailed on the subject. As in the case of Brazil, the lack of precise legal rules on several aspects of the expropriation process contributes to the tension between the judiciary and the administration. However, the silence seems to be part of a more general syndrome in the Mexican legal culture: the difficulty of developing new concepts and mechanisms to balance private and public interests in expropriations in the urban context, an issue for which the old paradigm of the postrevolutionary regime cannot offer answers. The problem is not the lack of legislation, but rather the prevalence of a legal culture that emphasizes social justice in a rural society and maintains private property rights in cities in an ambiguous place. It is as if the glorious postrevolutionary past bequeathed a legal monument no one dares modify.

In Mexico the use of expropriation for urban purposes has become increasingly difficult due to a combination of factors. Besides an unusual judicial activism, governments face the general political conditions of a democratic transition as well as social resistance for certain projects, all of which make the use of eminent domain more complicated. The main challenge in overcoming the current situation is to develop a new institutional design that reduces administrative discretion, but also that restrains a judiciary that has become an erratic legislator. The international standards of institutional reform are far from providing all the components for the new scheme. A solution will depend on the specific path that the Mexican legal system might follow and its political and cultural dimensions, which are as distinctive as those of any other nation-state.

Final Remarks

The rules for, as well as the use of, eminent domain for urban projects in Brazil, Colombia, and Mexico have changed in the last two decades according to the conditions of what can be generally labeled as a postauthoritarian situation, or democratic transition. Those changes imply, by definition, changes in the content of property rights. They have meant finding new ways of dealing with the tension between private and public interests that arise in every case of eminent domain. This chapter has emphasized developments, as well as their consequences, characteristic of each of those countries. Even some aspects that appear to be common to all three, such as judicial activism, have produced different outcomes.

To fully understand the changes, it is necessary to look at them from three points of view: (1) the place of eminent domain in the constitution and especially in the constitutional life of each country; (2) the actual use of eminent domain (in order to consider financial and other conditions of its use); and (3) the legal culture within which public and private actors give meaning to (and eventually legitimize) their respective practices.

Regarding constitutional changes, two aspects are worth mentioning. The first has to do with local democracy and decentralization. The Local governments in both Brazil and Colombia have the power to start eminent domain procedures, and this is part of their strength in urban affairs, whereas in Mexico that power is in the hands of the federal and state executives.

The second and most important constitutional question is the role of the judiciary. Whereas in Brazil and Mexico the intervention of judges has aggravated (rather than solved) conflicts over eminent domain cases, in Bogotá the courts have been able to arrive at decisions that not only enjoy wide acceptance, but also support the use of eminent domain for urban projects without compromising the basic rights of property owners. This means that the role of the judiciary in postauthoritarian situations can vary enormously.

Leaving aside for the moment the inclusion of administrative takings in the 1991 Colombian constitution, there and in Brazil the rule has been that the administration requests the expropriation and a court makes the final decision. In contrast, an expropriation in Mexico produces immediate effects once it is declared by the executive, which gives the impression of a formidable concentration of power in the president and state governors. But in practice this affects only weak owners who do not have access to legal services. In fact, through *amparo* suits, owners can obtain injunctions to indefinitely stop procedures; often judges modify the compensation and also examine whether the motive of an expropriation is correct. They do so in open violation of the constitution. Colombian and Brazilian judges may exert considerable power in establishing compensation, but they show remarkable deference in relation to the motives of the expropriation compared to judges in Mexico. If two decades ago the problem was how to restrain the executive, today the constitutional debate is around the limits of the supreme court's power.

The system for appointing justices of higher courts is the same in all three countries: the legislative power appoints them from a list provided by the executive. However, in the case of Brazil, *precatórios* were issued by state-level judges, who are appointed without intervention of the legislative branch. Constitutional lawyers and political scientists have a large research agenda to cover in this area before the relationship between institutional design and courts' performance will be clear.[19]

When we look at the way eminent domain works in practice (something we can do for individual cities only, not for whole countries), we find interesting facts. The city of Bogotá seems remarkable compared to São Paulo and Mexico City in that it has been able to use eminent domain successfully. Although many planners complain that compensations are too high—a contention that remains

---

19. For a discussion, see Ríos-Figueroa and Taylor (2006).

to be confirmed—none of the city's important urban projects have been frustrated due to problems in eminent domain procedures. The main factors in that success are the wide popular support that projects such as the Transmilenio enjoy, as well as the healthy local finances of the city due to property tax increases.

In contrast, the use of eminent domain by local governments in São Paulo and Mexico City have faced serious difficulties, mainly due to judicial activism that has, so to speak, taken the institution of eminent domain by surprise. In São Paulo the financial impact of the *precatórios* created a real crisis in the use of eminent domain, although there are signs that the crisis is over. In the case of Mexico, exorbitant compensations have prompted serious political conflicts, but the most important effect of judicial activism is that many projects are not even considered because of the uncertainty created by erratic judicial decisions. In both cases, the explanation of the courts' behavior (ideological or political bias, corruption, and/or professional incompetence) remains an important issue for future research.

The practice of eminent domain in those three cities is so different that it is difficult to suspect that something structural in Latin American urban societies would necessarily produce its demise. No matter how real and strong the factors that make its use difficult in some cases, they do not seem to be of a global nature.

Even if jurists in all three countries proclaim the social function of property as the doctrine that illuminates the rules on eminent domain, there is not a homogeneous use of the doctrine. In Mexico during the long agrarian reform, expropriation was the instrument for the creation of a form of land ownership that enjoys wide legitimacy in the rural world, but that cannot be easily adapted to the urban context, if only because the system, in its classical form, relied on an arbitrary use of eminent domain power. As a result, there is not a widely accepted doctrine within which expropriation for urban projects can be seen as legitimate by significant sectors of society.

In Brazil, as in any other country, some (or most) judges do not share the ideas that legislators have introduced in the Estatuto da Cidade or even in the constitutional text; they did not find convincing arguments for their resolutions in the *precatórios* crisis, which undermined their authority. In contrast, the Colombian courts have taken upon themselves the task of elaborating arguments to deal with the complex problems involved in eminent domain cases. In particular, the distinction between different species of compensations has helped both legislators and administrators find solutions that are coherent with urban legislation and the constitution. The diffusion of new (and old) ideas on property and eminent domain throughout the region should be welcomed. Our argument here is that it is more important to understand diversity than to perpetuate the incorrect idea of a single Latin American legal culture. Any initiative aimed at getting the institutions right (whatever "right" means) will have to deal with that diversity.

REFERENCES

Alexander, Gregory. 2006. *The global debate over constitutional property: Lessons for American takings jurisprudence.* Chicago and London: University of Chicago Press.

Constituição da Republica Federativa do Brasil. 1988.

Constitución Política de la República de Colombia. 1991.

Constitución Política de los Estados Unidos Mexicanos. 1917.

Díaz-y-Díaz, Martín. 1988. Las expropiaciones urbanísticas en México: Aproximaciones a un proceso sin teoría. In *Desarrollo urbano y derecho,* ed. Fernando Serrano. Mexico City: UNAM / Plaza y Valdes.

Duguit, Leon. 1912. *Las transformaciones generales del derecho privado desde el Código de Napoleón.* Madrid: Librería de Francisco Beltrán.

Elizondo, Carlos. 2001. *La importancia de las reglas: Gobierno y empresariado después de la nacionalización bancaria.* Mexico City: Fondo de Cultura Económica.

Estatuto da Cidade (Statute of the City), Brazil. 2001.

Fernandes, Edésio. 2002. Estatuto da Cidade: O grande desario para os juristas brasileiros. In *Il Congresso Brasileiro de direito urbanístico: Avaliando o Estatuto da Cidade,* ed. Betania Alfonsín et al. Porto Alegre: Prefeitura de Porto Alegre / Escola Superior de Direito Municipal.

Gomes-de-Mendonca, Jupira. 2001. Plano diretor, gestao urbana e descentralizacao: Novos caminhos, novos debates. In *Direito urbanístico e politica urbana no Brasil,* ed. Edésio Fernandes. Belo Horizonte: Livraria del Rey.

González-Casanova, Pablo. 1966. *La democracia en México.* Mexico City: Ediciones Era.

Haddad, Emílio. 2000. Comments on the procedures used to establish the amount of compensation for real estate property expropriated by the public authorities. In *Urban land and social policies: Acquisition and expropriation,* ed. Erminia Maricato. Cambridge, MA: Lincoln Institute of Land Policy.

Haddad, Emílio, Cacilda Lopes-dos-Santos, and Reinaldo Silveira Franco, Jr. 2007. Novas perspectivas sobre o instituto da desapropriacao: A protecao ambiental e sua valoracao. Paper presented to the Conference Law and Society in the 21st Century, Berlin, July 2007.

INEGI. 2005. *Il conteo de población y vivienda.* Mexico: Instituto Nacional de Estadística, Geografía e Informática.

Lopes-dos-Santos, Cacilda. 2007. Novas perspectivas do instrumento da desapropiacao: A incorporaczao de princípios urbanísticos e ambientais. Ph.D. thesis, University of São Paulo, Faculty of Architecture and Urbanism.

Maldonado, María-Mercedes, ed. 2003. *Reforma urbana y desarrollo territorial: Experiencias y perspectivas de aplicación de las leyes 9ª de 1989 y 388 de 1997.* Bogotá: Alcaldía Mayor de Bogotá / Lincoln Institute of Land Policy / Uniandes / Fedevivienda.

Maricato, Erminia. 2000a. The price of land expropriations. Limits to public policy in the areas of housing, environment, and transportation in São Paulo. Lincoln Institute of Land Policy Research Paper.

Maricato, Erminia, ed. 2000b. *Urban land and social policies: Acquisition and expropriation.* Cambridge, MA: Lincoln Institute of Land Policy.

Pérez-Perdomo, Rogelio. 2006. Corrupción, instituciones y contexto político: El caso de Venezuela. In *La corrupción en América. Un continente, muchos frentes*, ed. Antonio Azuela. Mexico City: Instituto de Investigaciones Sociales, UNAM.

Pinilla, Juan Felipe. 2003. *Evolución del sistema urbanístico Colombiano. Reflexión pendiente desde el derecho*. Bogotá: Serie Documentos de Investigación "Nuevos Estudios Socio-Jurídicos" / Ediciones Uniandes Facultad de Derecho, Julio.

Rabello, Sonia. 2007. O conceito de justa indenizacao nas expropriacoes imobiliárias urbanas: Justica social ou enriquecimento sem causa? *Revista Forense* 388.

Ríos-Figueroa, J., and M. M. Taylor. 2006. Institutional determinants of the judicialisation of policy in Brazil and Mexico. *Journal of Latin American Studies* 38(4):739–766.

Rodríguez, Daniel, and Carlos Mojica. 2008. Land value impacts of bus rapid transport. *Landlines* 20(2).

Saule, Nelson, Jr. 1999. *Direito a Cidade. Trihlas legais para o direito as cidades sustentáveis*. São Paulo: Polis / Mas Limonad.

———. 2001. Formas de protecao de direito a moradia e de combate aos despejos forcados no Brasil. In *Direito urbanístico e politica urbana no Brasil*, ed. Edésio Fernandes. Belo Horizonte: Livraria del Rey.

———. 2007. *Directo urbanístico. Vias jurídicas das políticas urbanas*. Porto Alegre: Sergio Antonio Fabris Editor.

Trujillo-Muñoz, Augusto. 2007. *Democracia y territorio. El ordenamiento territorial entre el derecho y la política*. Bogotá: Siglo del Hombre Editores / Academia Colombiana de Jurisprudencia.

Uprimny, Rodrigo, César Rodríguez, and Mauricio García-Villegas. 2003. Entre el protagonismo y la rutina: análisis sociojurídico de la justicia en Colombia.

COMMENTARY
Vicki Been

Antonio Azuela has given us a rich and insightful examination of eminent domain practices in three of the leading cities of Latin and South America. Comparative scholarship, at least in legal fields, sometimes can be frustrating for the reader because it often lacks a helpful frame and either compares apples to oranges or simply fails to compare at all. Azuela, however, is self-consciously careful to note differences between the cities and regimes, and he is astute in drawing implications from the comparisons.

Azuela's perceptive analysis suggests several lessons for eminent domain scholars and policy makers here in the United States and around the globe. His work, along with Jerold Kayden's empirical study in chapter 8, also reveals how much empirical work must be done in order for us to understand how to improve the practice and regulation of eminent domain. The two chapters make clear how little we know, other than through anecdotal evidence, about the actual use of eminent domain, or about the potential effects that measures to limit governments' eminent domain powers (such as those now popular in the United States) may have on urban land use and economic development.

There are several useful lessons that those focused on eminent domain and, more broadly on property rights, can draw from Azuela's portrait of São Paulo, Bogotá, and Mexico City. First, he reminds us of the critical, but often overlooked relationship between the legal rules for the use of eminent domain and the institutional context in which those rules apply. The institutional context has at least two critical dimensions: the relationship between the judiciary and the legislative or executive branch, and the distribution of authority over eminent domain among the national, state, and local governments. In the United States the debate over *Kelo v. City of New London*, 545 U.S. 469 (2005), often forgets the key explanation the Supreme Court offered for what some (indeed, many) thought was an erroneous decision: the fact that the legislative and executive branches are elected, democratically accountable, and charged with the responsibility of ensuring livable and thriving cities, while judges are charged not with legislating, but rather with interpreting and enforcing the Constitution and laws of the jurisdiction (*Kelo*, 481–483, 489–490). Azuela's exploration of the role the courts have played in limiting the use of eminent domain, especially in São Paulo, is a fascinating reminder that judges are not necessarily good city planners or experts in real estate valuation; nor are they free from ideology, corruption, and institutional pressures.

Vicki Been gratefully acknowledges the support of the Filomen D'Agostino and Max E. Greenberg Research Fund.

Second, Azuela's work suggests that we need to pay more attention to how institutional structures can be deployed to control judges, administrative officials, and politicians from overcompensating those whose property is taken by the exercise of eminent domain. The charge that politicians have used eminent domain to reward supporters or to disadvantage enemies has been explored extensively over the years (see, for example, Caro 1974, 850–894), but the threat that either the executive or the judicial branch might award compensation far in excess of fair market value, at the taxpayer's expense, has received little attention. Such overcompensation might result from judges' (and administrators') difficulty in understanding what Azuela correctly notes is a "black box" of valuation. But it also may be that eminent domain scholars need to assess whether compensation payments are similar to economic development incentives—difficult to set at the right level, hard for taxpayers to monitor, and even harder for diffuse and unorganized taxpayers to constrain.

Ideally, Azuela will give us an update in about 10 years to enable us to better understand whether the *precatórios* crisis in São Paulo was a short-lived transitional problem or whether judges continue to be overly generous to landowners in response to public opinion, institutional pressures to show independence from the executive or legislative branch, or undue or corrupt influence of the landowners. If continued study shows that overcompensation is more than just a short-term transitional problem, scholars and policy makers must assess alternative strategies for constraining overly generous payments. Azuela's description of how the courts in Colombia have forged a productive and fluid dialogue with the other branches on matters of eminent domain suggests that scholars should focus as well on how the manner in which judges (or administrators offering settlements to landowners) are selected, trained, protected from outside influence, and constrained from overstepping their roles correlates with the accuracy of the compensation they offer.

Third, Azuela highlights the need for scholars to focus more attention on valuation conundrums. In the United States some academics have begun to untangle the theoretical questions underlying valuation methods. A leading recent example is Serkin's (2005) work on how different philosophies about when compensation should be paid for regulatory takings are reflected in valuation mechanisms. But much more needs to be done to address the hard questions about how compensation should be determined and what the judicial role should be in overseeing that process. Azuela's insights about how ill-equipped judges are to assess expert valuations and the effect of such ignorance on a municipality's budget show how critical further research in the area is. Azuela hints that Brazil should have dealt with some of the valuation issues in its constitution or laws, but notes in his description of the Colombian constitution that a constitution cannot be too detailed. The extent to which constitutions or other legal texts should try to define the required compensation with greater specificity than general standards like "just compensation" or even "fair market valuation" is one of the many perplexing problems scholars might address. Similarly, Azuela's insight that property owners seem not to care whether compensation is paid before or after the taking suggests that additional research is necessary about what determines whether landowners believe the compensation they receive is appropriate.

Fourth, Azuela's work reveals the need for further analysis of the ways in which eminent domain practices vary between regimes that limit the use of eminent domain to the national or state level and those that allow local governments to exercise eminent domain. Local governments may be particularly prone to capture by what Fischel (2001) calls the "homevoter block," which may have an interest in public works or economic development projects, even if such projects may involve the aggressive exercise of eminent domain. State or national governments, on the other hand, may be too prone to impose one-size-fits-all policies or too susceptible to capture by, for example, groups ideologically opposed to all but the most traditional uses of eminent domain. A comparison of the frequency and type of condemnations when authority to exercise eminent domain is withheld from local governments, as well as an analysis of how governments or markets get around limits on the exercise of eminent domain, would be extremely useful.

Fifth, one of the most provocative lessons we can draw from Azuela's article lies in his description of provisions in the Colombian constitution and of interpretations of the eminent domain power by the Colombian courts that have the potential to be far more protective of the lower and middle classes than does the Fifth Amendment to the U.S. Constitution. He tells us that the Colombian constitution allows the use of eminent domain for social interest—to satisfy the needs of specific groups in society. Similarly, he notes that the Colombian courts have distinguished between the use of eminent domain that takes fungible assets and the use of eminent domain that takes homes or other property used as a means of satisfying a basic need such as housing. Those hints of more radical views of eminent domain are tantalizing, but they left me thirsty for more information about how, if at all, those provisions are being used. How does eminent domain under such a regime look different from the eminent domain practice in the United States or other, more property rights–oriented countries? Could the more liberal eminent domain provisions paradoxically result in less use of eminent domain than in jurisdictions that supposedly are more protective of private property?

Similarly, Azuela's comparative work would be even more useful if he could tell us more about the purposes for which the exercises of eminent domain that he studies were invoked. Of course, one of the challenges of the debate about *Kelo* is the difficulty of drawing a line between economic development and more traditional uses of eminent domain, but there likely are differences between the exercise of eminent domain for the purposes of building a transport system or a park and the economic development context that *Kelo* addressed. Perhaps the key is, as Azuela suggests, wide community support, but it may be that community support for an economic development project will not legitimate an exercise of eminent domain in the same way that community support of a public works project does. The critical issue may be the support for the use of eminent domain for a particular purpose, not whether the community supports the project at issue.

I hope that we will hear more from Azuela about Brazil's efforts to give local governments the power to ensure that lands are adequately used. Before the current foreclosure crisis in the United States, cities and nonprofits in many areas were struggling to compete in the market for parcels on which to build affordable housing. Now, nonprofits and local governments are struggling to get foreclosed properties back into productive use. Both problems have led to a variety of calls around the United States for more governmental power to encourage dysfunctional owners, financial institutions holding foreclosed properties without maintaining them, and other landowners who seem to be sitting on land that could be used more efficiently to use the land or lose it, or at the very least to pay dearly for the privilege of underusing it. Azuela's account of the use of eminent domain as a sanction is fascinating, and I hope to learn more from him about that practice.

Finally, Azuela's work reminds us once again about how much more empirical scholarship on eminent domain could reveal about optimal eminent domain practice. To help spur additional work of the quality of Azuela's comparative analysis, I suggest below several categories of questions additional research should address to illuminate the use of eminent domain today and its costs and benefits.

Understanding the Use of Eminent Domain Today

We know surprisingly little about the who, what, when, where, and why of eminent domain. Until Kayden's work (see chapter 8), all we knew about the use of eminent domain in the United States was from the Institute for Justice's review of newspaper accounts and blunt categorization of all or virtually all exercises of eminent domain as abusive (Berliner 2003). There were a sprinkling of case studies, such as Nicole Garnett's (2006) work, but no systematic count or classification of condemnations. Similarly, around the globe, there is little empirical evidence about the actual use of eminent domain. The questions scholars should address include the following.

Who is using and paying for eminent domain—the national government, states, or local governments? Agencies with land use and planning oversight, or agencies whose portfolios are either transportation or other infrastructure management or economic development? The agency paying for the condemnation, or an agency able to pass the costs on to the general budget? Big cities or smaller local governments? Suburbs or central cities? Governments subject to free trade agreements' protection of foreign investors, or those that have not entered into a free trade agreement's protection? We know that such differences among governments affect how they respond to compensation requirements, political pressure, and other constraints; but in order to make wise policy about how the law should regulate eminent domain practice, we need to know much more about who is making the condemnation decision, and what constraints influence those decision makers.

What compensation is being paid, and how does that compensation relate to market value, to costs such as relocation expenses, and to subjective values owners attach to their properties? Does the relationship between compensation and fair market value vary according to the purposes for which eminent domain is being exercised, or according to the nature of the eminent domain scheme (such as whether the scheme has a quick-take provision). There has been surprisingly little work on the issue of how close compensation comes to fair market value. The last major study in the United States is decades old (Munch 1976).

How often is eminent domain being used? Are governments using eminent domain more frequently than in the past? Has the outcry over *Kelo* resulted in fewer exercises of eminent domain? Where frequency of use has changed, what is responsible for the change? If there has been an increase or decrease in the use of eminent domain, for example, is that change related to an expansion (or contraction) in the purposes for which eminent domain can be used, an increase in the pressure compensation awards exert on condemnors' budgets, a change in investor protection agreements, or other variations across jurisdictions or over time?

Why is eminent domain being used? What efforts did the condemnor make to buy the property on the open market? We need a richer understanding of the bargaining (or lack thereof, according to Azuela's analysis) that takes place in the shadow of eminent domain.

Conclusions

Our understanding of who benefits from the exercise of eminent domain, who suffers, and how that differs according to the characteristics of the legal regime is limited. Similarly, we know much too little about what adjustments the market makes when the use of eminent domain is constrained. Do constraints distort institutional arrangements by leading to more public-private partnerships, or by making governments unduly cautious about involving potential private developers in planning discussions, for example?

Azuela's wonderful comparative analysis of eminent domain practice in São Paulo, Bogotá, and Mexico City sets a high bar for the quality of future research. It provides a compelling illustration of the contribution a richer understanding of the use of eminent domain around the world can make to current debates about how to regulate exercises of condemnation authority. I hope that Azuela's example will spur much more work on these critical questions.

REFERENCES

Berliner, Dana. 2003. *Public power, private gain.* Institute for Justice. http://www
.castlecoalition.org/index.php?option=com_content&task=view&id=312.

Caro, Robert A. 1974. *The power broker: Robert Moses and the fall of New York.*
New York: Alfred A. Knopf.

Fischel, William A. 2001. *The homevoter hypothesis: How home values influence local government taxation, school finance, and land-use policies.* Cambridge, MA:
Harvard University Press.

Garnett, Nicole. 2006. The neglected political economy of eminent domain. *Michigan
Law Review* 105:101.

Munch, Patricia. 1976. An economic analysis of eminent domain. *Journal of Political
Economy* 84:473.

Serkin, Christopher. 2005. The meaning of value: Assessing just compensation for regulatory takings. *Northwestern University Law Review* 99:677.

8

The Myth and Reality of Eminent Domain for Economic Development

Jerold S. Kayden

*I*n the continuing wake of the U.S. Supreme Court's controversial opinion in *Kelo v. City of New London*, 545 U.S. 469 (2005), this chapter partly addresses a question begging for a nonideologically determined empirical answer: how widely does government actually use the power of eminent domain to advance economic development goals? Although *Kelo* upheld the constitutionality of using eminent domain to take single-family homes for higher and better urban redevelopment uses that, among other things, produce more jobs and tax revenue, the subsequent public outcry revealed that *Kelo* was less a constitutional law, and more a political science, story. Was the reaction fueled in part by extensive, yet relatively underpublicized, government exercise of this power?

This chapter provides part of the answer, reporting the results of a survey of cities with populations of 100,000 or more that asked how many properties were taken in the city for economic development purposes in the five years preceding the *Kelo* case. The answer is a surprisingly low number. To be sure, other data could illuminate the answer further, including how partially exercised takings, announced threats of exercise, or even the mere existence of the power affects property-owning individuals. Nonetheless, the actual data to some degree undercut the claim put forth in some reports of an "abusive" use of the power. Whatever else may influence people's attitudes about eminent domain, the risk of being the object of a completed land taking for economic development purposes is not a factor.

Background

The eminent domain power is the power of government to take property without the consent of the owner as long as the taking satisfies three conditions: it is for a public use; compensation is paid; and a fair process is followed. Federal and state constitutions and statutes draw contours for exercising the power. The just compensation (or takings) clause of the U.S. Constitution implicitly authorizes and explicitly limits the power when it states "nor shall private property be taken for public use, without just compensation." Further elaborated by federal, state, and local statutes, land takings functionally identify themselves as condition precedent and/or condition subsequent takings. Condition precedent takings address problematic existing conditions of land use; the focus is on the before-taking land use. Most famous (some would say notorious) is the legislatively mandated blight condition precedent, the gold standard for land takings pursued under the federal urban renewal program of the 1950s and 1960s. Condition subsequent takings address future conditions of land use without regard to existing conditions; the focus is on the after-taking land use. Statutes nationwide offer laundry lists of such future uses, including roadways, runways, rail rights-of-way, reservoirs, and public facilities.

Urban redevelopment takings that clear blighted conditions and replace them with new development, whether conducted under formal urban renewal laws or not, reside in the Venn diagram intersection of the condition precedent and condition subsequent categories. The land taken is blighted, and subsequent redevelopment is planned from the beginning. The *Kelo* case addressed land takings for urban redevelopment, but without the above-described intersection; there was no condition precedent of blight or other harmful situation preceding the taking.

Let's briefly rehearse the case. The New London Development Corporation, a private not-for-profit entity created in 1978 to help revitalize the city of New London, Connecticut, prepared a development plan for a 90-acre area adjacent to the site of a proposed global research facility developed by pharmaceutical giant Pfizer. The purpose of the development plan was to "create jobs, increase tax and other revenue, encourage public access and use of the city's waterfront," and generally kick-start revitalization. The development corporation sought 115 privately owned individual land parcels that would together be leased to a private developer for 99 years at $1 per year. The developer would build a high-tech research and office project along with parking and a marina. According to an economic development consultant working hard for its money, the project benefits included 518 to 867 construction jobs, 718 to 1,362 direct jobs, 500 to 940 indirect jobs, and $680,544 to $1,249,843 in taxes.

Several of the land parcels contained nonblighted single-family homes, including those of Susette Kelo, who had lived in the area since 1997, and Wilhelmina Dery, who was born in her house in 1918. Dery's husband, Charles, had lived with Wilhelmina since they married some 60 years earlier. Of the fifteen properties contested, ten were occupied by owners or family members, five were investments, and none was blighted or otherwise in bad condition. Nine parties declined to sell their land voluntarily and challenged the development corporation's subsequent exercise of the power of eminent domain. In a five-to-four decision authored by Justice John Paul Stevens, the Court held the exercise constitutional. The just compensation clause's "public use" proviso was interchangeable with the phrase "public purpose," and the comprehensive, carefully considered development plan served such a purpose, said the majority. Justice Sandra Day O'Connor's dissenting opinion memorably warned, "Nothing is to prevent the State from replacing any Motel 6 with a Ritz-Carlton, any home with a shopping mall, or any farm with a factory."

Described as "perhaps the term's most disputed decision" by Linda Greenhouse, the *New York Times* Supreme Court reporter, the case ignited a firestorm of negative media, political, and public responses. Newspapers across the country, after mischaracterizing the decision in their reporting by headlining that the Court had expanded government's authority to take private property, editorialized against it. *Parade* magazine's cover showed a house; father, mother, and three children standing in front; the headline "Will the Government Take Your Home?" and the subhead "A family fights back." Conservative and liberal politicians alike were outraged. Democratic Representative Maxine Waters of California and Republican Senator John Cornyn of Texas decried the decision on the same day, the political equivalent of a "once in a millennium" celestial alignment of planets. The NAACP, conservative think tanks, and other special interest groups that rarely agree on anything found concord.

The response even affected members of the Court's majority. In an address to a bar association meeting in Las Vegas two months after the opinion's release, Justice Stevens, apparently uncomfortable with the public reaction, referred to the outcome in *Kelo* as "unwise," adding "I was convinced that the law compelled a result that I would have opposed if I were a legislator." "[T]he free play of market forces," he said, "is more likely to produce acceptable results in the long run than the best-intentioned plans of public officials." A local gadfly in Weare, New Hampshire, organized a campaign to have the town take a farmhouse owned by Justice David Souter for a hotel to be named the Lost Liberty Hotel. The proposal failed on a ballot initiative.

State legislatures busily considered and enacted laws banning or otherwise limiting the exercise of eminent domain for economic development. Referenda initiatives restricting use were placed on state ballots. The U.S. House of Representatives passed its own limiting bill. The Anchorage, Alaska, city council banned eminent domain for economic development.

The Survey

Why did substantial segments of the media, the public, and the political class react with such hostility to the *Kelo* decision? Were they disturbed solely with what happened to Susette Kelo and fellow homeowners without regard to a broader context? Were they aware of similar cases in their neighborhoods? Were they assuming that this was the tip of the iceberg? Were they concerned that their own properties were at risk of being taken for economic development purposes, a concern fanned by either the reality or the perception that government widely exercises the eminent domain power for economic development?

To partially address these questions, I conducted a nationwide survey of cities with populations greater than 100,000, asking officials whether, how often, and how widely their cities had taken property for economic development purposes during the five-year period of January 2000 through December 2004. Economic development here was defined as condition subsequent, privately owned or leased, privately developed land uses that would generate new jobs and additional tax revenue on site. Takings that included condition precedent land uses of blight or other harmful conditions were not disqualified from the survey count as long as conditions subsequent of economic development were present. Owing to data limitations, filed but uncompleted eminent domain actions were not counted. Oral or written threats of eminent domain actions were similarly not counted.

The survey specified a random sample of 153 cities (see Appendix, Table 8.1) out of the population of 251 cities with 100,000 or more residents, yielding a 95 percent confidence level for reaching conclusions about all 251 cities. Survey researchers contacted local officials by phone, supplemented by e-mail and occasionally surface mail, to determine who would know this information and to secure the data. Respondents mostly worked at city departments charged with economic development, community development, legal issues, and housing and local urban renewal agencies. Contacted on multiple occasions, respondents took several days or weeks to conduct the research necessary to answer the survey question. For reasons of data availability, the survey used the number of properties taken by eminent domain rather than the number of owners affected. Thus, if one owner had 10 properties taken, the survey cited the number ten rather than the number one. The survey also declined to use the number of economic development projects, rather than the number of properties taken, as the data point. Thus, the exercise of eminent domain in *Kelo*'s New London would register as 15 observations rather than one.

The survey found 207 properties taken for economic development purposes in the surveyed cities over the five-year period, suggesting a per city average of 1.3 properties over five years, or 0.26 annual takings. Of the 153 cities, 112 reported no takings for economic development at all.

Importance and Limitations of the Results

The results of the survey show that completed eminent domain exercises for economic development are rare. Reactions to the *Kelo* outcome are unlikely to have evolved from historic experience with or knowledge about such examples.

However, the survey results have limitations. The survey methodology of phone calls, e-mails, and letters, although comprehensive and systematic, left this researcher wondering if the numbers reported to the surveyors by local officials captured every qualified land taking. The survey did not determine the number of eminent domain cases filed against property owners if the properties were never obtained through completed exercise of the power. The survey also did not determine how often local governments threatened use of the power without filing actions. Finally, the survey did not address the role played by the mere existence of the power, a proverbial sword of Damocles hanging over everyone's head.

The Institute for Justice, a Washington-based private property rights organization, published a report in April 2003 entitled *Public Power, Private Gain: A Five-Year, State-by-State Report Examining the Abuse of Eminent Domain* (Berliner 2003). The report sprang from the ideological fount that every exercise of the power of eminent domain for economic development axiomatically constitutes abuse. It compiled its information from "published accounts and court papers." The survey found 3,722 properties subject to filed takings and 6,560 subject to threatened but unfiled takings, for a total of 10,282 properties. The survey classified these results as the "tip of the iceberg" and called them "chilling." A comprehensive evaluation of the results is beyond the purview of this chapter, and a comparison between this chapter's study and the Berliner report is made difficult by different methodologies, populations, and definitions. However, a cursory reading of the report reveals questionable classifications that undermine confidence in the overall results. For example, the eight properties counted in the five years of Alabama results were subject to a filed takings action for a "municipal parking facility." One of the filed takings counted in the Arkansas results was for the Clinton presidential library. This analysis is limited to states starting with the letter *A*. It is probable that the land takings upheld in the Supreme Court's seminal *Berman v. Parker*, 348 U.S. 26 (1954), decision would be deemed abusive by the Institute. The Institute subsequently released a June 2006 report entitled *Opening the Floodgates: Eminent Domain Abuse in the Post-Kelo World* (also authored by Dana Berliner) arguing that the "*Kelo* decision opened the floodgates of abuse, spurring local government to press forward" with more projects involving the use of eminent domain for private parties.

Conclusions

Empirical studies often influence public policy debates. Statutory law is informed by the perception, if not reality, of misuse of a publicly wielded technique. Even constitutional law can turn on the sense that judges have of the extent of the problem. The first Institute report was cited in Justice O'Connor's dissenting opinion in *Kelo*. This study offers a modest contribution in ascertaining the breadth and frequency of use of eminent domain. It is not an argument for or against its use, but it does suggest that Americans can sleep tonight without the anxiety that, by the next morning, they will be out of house and home to accommodate a Motel 6.

APPENDIX

Table 8.1
Surveyed Cities with Populations Over 100,000, by State

Alabama
Birmingham
Huntsville
Mobile

Alaska
Anchorage

Arizona
Chandler
Gilbert
Mesa
Phoenix
Scottsdale

California
Bakersfield
Berkeley
Burbank
Chula Vista
Concord
Corona
Downey
El Monte
Escondido
Fremont
Fresno
Garden Grove
Irvine
Long Beach
Los Angeles
Modesto
Moreno Valley
Oceanside
Ontario
Palmdale
Pomona
Rancho Cucamonga
Richmond
Riverside

Roseville
Sacramento
San Buenaventura
Santa Clara
Stockton
Sunnyvale
Thousand Oaks

Colorado
Arvada
Denver
Lakewood
Pueblo
Thornton

Connecticut
Hartford
New Haven
Stamford

Florida
Cape Coral
Clearwater
Coral Springs
Fort Lauderdale
Gainesville
Hollywood
Miami Gardens
Orlando
Pembroke Pines
St. Petersburg
Tallahassee

Georgia
Augusta-Richmond (County)
Columbus
Savannah

Hawaii
Honolulu

Idaho
Boise City

Illinois
Aurora
Chicago
Joliet
Naperville
Peoria
Rockford

Indiana
Fort Wayne
South Bend

Iowa
Des Moines

Kansas
Kansas City
Olathe
Overland Park
Wichita

Kentucky
Lexington-Fayette

Louisiana
Lafayette
New Orleans
Shreveport

Maryland
Baltimore

Massachusetts
Cambridge
Lowell
Springfield
Worcester

(continued)

Table 8.1
(continued)

Michigan
Detroit
Grand Rapids
Sterling Heights
Warren

Minnesota
Minneapolis

Mississippi
Jackson

Missouri
Independence
Kansas City
St. Louis
Springfield

Nebraska
Lincoln
Omaha

Nevada
Henderson
North Las Vegas
Reno

New Jersey
Elizabeth
Newark

New Mexico
Albuquerque

New York
Buffalo
Rochester
Syracuse
Yonkers

North Carolina
Cary
Charlotte
Durham
Fayetteville
Greensboro
Raleigh
Winston-Salem

Ohio
Akron
Dayton
Toledo

Oklahoma
Oklahoma City
Tulsa

Oregon
Eugene
Salem

Pennsylvania
Allentown
Philadelphia

Rhode Island
Providence

South Dakota
Sioux Falls

Tennessee
Chattanooga
Clarksville
Nashville-Davidson

Texas
Amarillo
Arlington
Carrollton
Garland
Houston
Irving
Lubbock
McAllen
Pasadena
San Antonio
Waco
Wichita Falls

Utah
Salt Lake City
West Valley City

Virginia
Alexandria
Hampton
Norfolk
Richmond
Virginia Beach

Washington
Bellevue
Vancouver

Wisconsin
Green Bay
Madison
Milwaukee

REFERENCES

Berliner, Dana. 2003. *Public power, private gain: A five-year, state-by-state report examining the abuse of eminent domain.* Washington, DC: Institute for Justice.
———. 2006. *Opening the floodgates: Eminent domain abuse in a post-Kelo world.* Washington, DC: Institute for Justice.

COMMENTARY
John D. Echeverria

I have three observations to offer on Jerold Kayden's piece aimed at debunking the myth that the use of eminent domain is widespread in the United States. Kayden points out that the Institute for Justice has published several reports purporting to document widespread use of the eminent domain power for economic development. He further points out that at least one of these studies was cited by Justice Sandra Day O'Connor in her dissenting opinion in *Kelo*. He raises the question whether the strong public reaction to the *Kelo* decision was influenced by the belief that the use of eminent domain has been common and whether citizens voted in favor of state measures curtailing eminent domain power out of fear that they themselves would be subjected to eminent domain.

First, there is no question that Kayden has tried to fill a yawning information gap. As the coauthor of one of the many amicus briefs filed in the *Kelo* case (on behalf of the American Planning Association) and a participant in subsequent policy debates about whether and how the eminent domain power should be reformed, I can testify to the almost complete absence of systematic information about the actual extent of the use of this government authority. There is even a lack of good anecdotal examples of the use of eminent domain for economic development. The lack of good data is arguably an indictment of those who care deeply about land use activities, including those of us who participate in Lincoln Institute proceedings. If the lawyers have any excuse in this regard, it may be that they justifiably believed that the legal legitimacy of this governmental power had been completely resolved by the U.S. Supreme Court, an assumption that was arguably affirmed by *Kelo* itself, but only just barely.

This lack of information has had serious adverse consequences for the quality of the public debate about eminent domain. Lacking any other information, reporters and others have been forced to rely on the Institute for Justice reports, which, as Kayden points out, contain numerous errors and exaggerations that serve to overstate the extent of the use of the eminent domain power. Representatives of local government groups in Washington, DC, were even reluctant to conduct a survey of cities and towns to assist the Government Accountability Office in its study of eminent domain based on their uncertainty about what the survey might reveal.

Second, as Kayden acknowledges, the challenges of gathering good data on this topic inevitably mean that this valuable new study will have to be viewed as a first step rather than as the final word. The survey is obviously incomplete, and therefore undercounts the incidence of eminent domain, because it focuses only on relatively large cities (100,000-plus) and does not include an estimate of instances in which the government's power to use eminent domain was the cause of a property acquisition even if the government did not actually file a condemnation action. One also wonders, especially in the aftermath of the firestorm generated by *Kelo*, whether survey subjects were completely forthcoming about the extent of the use of eminent domain. Finally, ambiguities in the definition of eminent domain for economic development suggest a further possible cause of undercounting.

Looking forward, it may be useful to supplement this type of extensive survey with an intensive examination of the experiences of several individual cities with eminent domain. This approach is further supported by my impression (again, not based on hard evidence) that some cities use eminent domain a great deal (for example, New York City) and some use it little if at all (for example, Santa Fe). An intensive examination within a particular community should start with an effort to identify all the parcels that the government either acquired from private parties for economic development or helped transfer to new private owners for that purpose, to ensure that all transfers attributable to the existence of the eminent domain power are being counted.

Finally, while I strongly believe that this study begins to fill an information gap and that public perception of the incidence of the use of eminent domain is a factor in the debate, we should not overlook the fact that the *Kelo* debate is largely about the fundamental legitimacy—the morality, even—of government forcing the transfer of private property from one owner to another for economic development purposes. In my view, public engagement with that fundamental issue, rather than concerns by individual citizens that they might actually be subject to eminent domain, has been driving the debate. In this sense, the *Kelo* debate is less like popular revolts over high property taxes and more like debates about such issues as whether Elián González should be returned to Cuba or whether murderers should be incarcerated for life or subjected to the death penalty. While property owners who are the objects of the eminent domain power can justifiably assert powerful moral claims, those claims must be weighed against the rights and responsibilities of elected representatives, exercising their authority within a democratic system, to shape a community's physical, social, and economic future. It is ultimately on that battlefield, I suggest, that the debate over eminent domain must be waged.

9

Property Rights Protection and Spatial Planning in European Countries

Vincent Renard

Property Rights in Europe After World War II

The question of the relationship between planning and the protection of property rights has been central to the management of urban growth and urban regeneration in Western Europe since the beginning of planning in, approximately, the second half of the nineteenth century. The key problem raised by the interference between the right of property and the activity of planning and zoning became really sensitive at the beginning of the twentieth century, at least in Great Britain, Germany, and France, and to some extent in Spain and Italy.

The first element of property rights protection is the guarantee of property and the related exception in practically every country: the possibility of expropriation under strictly defined conditions. The legal definition of and the practical process for expropriation are to a large extent similar in several European countries. This topic is treated in chapters 7, 8, and 10.

The other key aspect of property rights protection relies on the impact of planning and zoning on increases or decreases in the value of property, especially the allocation of development rights by local plans. A different tradition with respect to property rights has led to a different type of relationship in northern Europe than in southern Europe. Among the 27 members of the European Union, the history, traditions, legal systems, and economic mechanisms of the Baltic countries, Great Britain, Portugal, Bulgaria, and Austria do not have much in common. This chapter mostly focuses on key features of some of the main countries of continental Europe—France, Germany, Spain, and Italy—with some comments on other countries, notably Sweden and The Netherlands. It also takes into account the recent development of European law with respect to property.

The Origins of Property Rights in Europe

Property rights have different origins in different parts of Europe. The main differences appear in northern European countries, southern Europe, and Germany, which have specific histories of the emergence of property rights (Needham 2006). One such difference results from the definitions of property rights in the constitutions of the countries. In most original constitutions, the definition is close to the strong statement about the guarantee of property in the U.S. Constitution. In the French civil code, property is considered "*un droit inviolable et sacré*," with the possible exception of the right to expropriate when an evident public interest requires it ("*nécessité publique*" in the French Declaration of Human Rights).

In France the Civil Code of 1804 that explicated the right of property freed peasants from the feudal system, in which serfs did not have any property in the sense of "*fructus* and *abusus.*" Unlike the United States, where property has been created to a large extent ex nihilo, in France peasants had a new right to the property they were cultivating through the transformation of so-called possession into property that can be sold and mortgaged, thus becoming a "*droit réel.*"

The balance between the guarantee of property and the possibility that the state can expropriate it for the public interest has evolved very differently in different European countries, especially in light of the evolution of U.S. jurisprudence about takings. Some countries, such as Denmark, have introduced general legislation about takings, stating that "if a regulation goes too far, some compensation is due to the landowner." Such legislation can be compared to the well-known U.S. case of *Pennsylvania Coal v. Mahon*, 260 U.S. 393 (1922), introducing the concept that compensation must be paid if regulation goes too far. The notion has been applied in Denmark in a very restrictive way, thus limiting the amount of compensation. Other countries, such as France or Italy, have not introduced this possibility. Article L 160-5 of the French Code de l'Urbanisme states that "regulations and norms that result from this code, including the prohibition to build anything, do not open a right to compensation" (Renard 2007, 42–43).

There is a paradox: countries such as France and Italy that deny a general right to compensation have practices, both legal and negotiated, that allow the introduction of some form of compensation. Other countries, such as Denmark, that have legislated a general principle of compensation have applied it in a very restrictive way, only when the planning blight is long-lasting and very severe as compared to neighboring landowners. In these countries, the general principle acts as a kind of safety belt in extreme cases and is not at all a common practice.

Roughly speaking, the balance between the guarantee granted to the owner and the social obligation of property owners is probably more in favor of landowners in southern Europe than in northern Europe. Such a broad statement should be refined. Harvey Jacobs (2006) makes an interesting comparison between the European and U.S. systems in that respect.

The Definition and the Contents of the Right of Property on Land —

In most Western European countries, the right of property on land was defined or redefined after World War II. Most countries' constitutions include a solemn definition of the guarantee of the right of property, as is the case in France, Italy, and Spain. The definitions vary from country to country in terms of the balance between the interest vested in the right of the owner and the general interest, and they can also vary to a large extent from one country to another.

For example, in Germany, the basic law about land and planning (the Baugesetzbuch) limits the guarantee of property in two ways, by stating that "the content and limits of the guarantee shall be defined by the laws," and that "property entails obligations, and its use shall also serve the public good." This is clearly more balanced between the general interest and the interest of the landowner than are the French and Italian definitions.

In Sweden, as in most countries, property is guaranteed except when there is an urgent public need. But the very general principle of *allemansrätt* (the right of anybody in the territory of Sweden) makes explicit the fact that the whole territory of Sweden is in a way a public good that everyone is entitled to use freely. A series of conditions guarantees the free and exclusive use of a property by the owner, but there is an expression of the state of mind—visible in patterns of urban development—in which the balance between the public interest and the interests of landowners is differently related. The idea of "private property—no entry" is not an obsession. The notion of sustainable land use policy fits better with such a socio-legal context. It follows from this principle that the capital gains on land are mostly recouped by public authorities.

In most southern and Eastern European countries, the basic principle is that the owner receives the benefits of the valorization of his land. Devices, especially forms of taxation, allow the government to recoup part of the betterment, but the basic principle remains. Some attempts have been made in those countries to change the rules of the game. Examples from Great Britain, France, and Italy are presented in the following section.

Does the Landowner Own the Development Rights Attached to a Piece of Land? ———

The determination of whether the landowner owns development rights evolved during the second half of the twentieth century when strong urban pressure led to soaring land prices. The specification of development rights in local plans led to sharp differentiations in land prices, thus raising the problem of equity among landowners.

According to a concept fairly widespread in northern Europe, ownership of land does not include a right to the development value that results from urban growth in general and the provision of infrastructure in particular. This is, for example, the case in Sweden and The Netherlands, but by means of different mechanisms. In Swedish towns, it is accomplished by means of long-term land reserves for towns; towns have played a key role in the development process in The Netherlands, at least until recently. In both, most of the value added by urban development is collected by the community.

The other concept, which prevails in several countries in southern Europe, allows the original landowner to keep the capital gain, subject to some form of tax collection such as a value-added tax or a tax on capital gains. In such systems, the introduction or amendment of urban development regulations is generally perceived as an additional constraint on previously held rights, the assumption being that ownership at the outset was unconditional and included development rights. There is no pure case, and the reality is not that clear. Nevertheless, zoning restrictions are seen as a loss for the landowner by reducing the value of the property.

One possible legal technique to solve the problem of inequity is the redefinition of the contents of the right of property separating the development rights from the property of land, and thus socializing, totally or partially, the development rights. This occurred in different ways in Great Britain in 1947, France in 1975, and Italy in 1977. None of these attempts have been successful in the long run.

THE 1947 TOWN AND COUNTRY PLANNING ACT IN GREAT BRITAIN

The priority in Great Britain after World War II, given a severe housing crisis, was to "recoup betterment," in the terminology of the "Uthwatt" report of 1942, through the full nationalization of development rights (Expert Committee on Compensation and Betterment 1942). This was a key point of the Town and Country Planning Act (TCPA) of 1947. During a transitory period, until the anticipated monopoly of local governments in the land development process, the developer had to pay a development charge—the difference between the market price of development land and the agricultural value of land—when getting the planning permission. A fund was created to provide one-time compensation to landowners for the loss of the development value of their lands.

Based on an erroneous assumption, the inelasticity of land supply, this drastic legislation first resulted in land hoarding by landowners, who did not accept the drastic reduction of their proceeds from the sale, and then resulted in their selling the land for somewhat higher prices than its agricultural value. As a result, the price of new housing increased until the act was repealed in 1951.

The same idea, to recoup betterment, has been reintroduced twice since. In particular, the 1976 Development Land Tax Act was an attempt to follow the same plan in a more limited way, but it was also soon repealed when a new government took power.

THE 1975 LEGAL DENSITY CEILING IN FRANCE
In France the 1975 Town and Country Planning Act instituted the legal density ceiling (*plafond légal de densité*, or PLD), which set limits to a landowner's development rights independent of other constraints resulting from regulations. That is, when the developer gets a building permit with a floor area ratio greater than the legal density ceiling, he has to buy the excess development rights from the authority. Initially, the PLD for most of the country was fixed at a density of 1.0 square meters of floor area per square meter of land; in Paris it was 1.5 square meters. When regulations allow a higher floor area ratio, the developer may build at a density higher than the PLD after paying a fee equivalent to the market price of the area of extra land that would be needed in order to not exceed the PLD. The purposes are to partially recoup betterment and to finance local authorities.

The PLD was aimed at reducing the increase in land values that benefited high-density, centrally located plots. The idea was to discourage high-density schemes by fiscal means that also brought extra resources to the local councils, thus providing at the same time some recovery of windfall gains that resulted from zoning. The results were not convincing, and the proceeds were limited. The main effect was to limit density to avoid payment, thus increasing urban sprawl. The PLD was repealed in 2000.

THE 1977 CONCESSIONE DI EDIFICARE IN ITALY
A third illustration of this type of policy is the reform of the Concessione di Edificare, which modified the legal and fiscal framework in Italy in 1977. A first legal step resulted from a 22 October 1971 statute stating that the property of land would not include the development right. Theoretically, the development right was vested in the public authority, and that became fact, albeit in a very limited way, with the passage of a 28 January 1977 statute stating that land use is sold by the state (*concessione di edificare*). The developer was supposed to purchase the development right from the public authority granting the permit.

This legal construction was rapidly destroyed by the Constitutional Court, first by a January 1980 decision declaring illegal the separation between the right of property and the right to develop and build on a piece of land, and then canceling, as a consequence, all local plans that had been approved before 1977. To an extent, this chain of decisions weakened the Italian planning system for the next decade.

The principle of equitable redistribution, or betterment recoupment, is generally accepted. However, these three experiences show that the practical implementation of the principle remains a serious challenge.

The Regulatory Taking Issue in Some European Countries ————

Roughly speaking, a majority of countries in Western Europe, particularly in southern Europe, have adopted the principle that constraints on urban development are not liable to compensation. As expressed in the French Urban Development Code, for example, this principle applies "to any constraint affecting the road system or prompted by health, aesthetic or any other considerations and concerned with such matters as land use, heights of buildings . . . or prohibition of development in given zones" (article 160-5). A constraint on the right to make use of a given piece of land is not considered grounds for compensation unless it infringes a vested right (for example, if it involves withdrawal of a building permit already granted) or is a change in the previous state of the site resulting in "direct, material and indisputable damage to property."

This latter comes close to taking and rarely applies, doing so only under restrictive circumstances. So the rigorous application of the principle of no compensation, which makes landowners subject to unequal treatment, has met with considerable opposition and has led to the generation of de facto and de jure loopholes. In France, for example, the introduction in 1976 of procedures for the transfer of development rights falls under this heading and was attacked as a breach of the principle of no compensation.

However, legal systems vary from one country to another. There are very few European comparative studies on this topic, and the recent "Symposium on Regulatory Takings in Land Use Law: A Comparative Perspective on Compensation Right" stresses the difficulty of summarizing such a comparison:

> The differences are significant and often unpredictable. They exist even though nine of the eleven countries under scrutiny belong to the EU. If one imagines a hypothetical scale of degrees of compensation rights, only a few of the countries take one of the two extreme positions along that scale and say either a stark "no" or a broad "yes." Most countries hold some middle-ground position along the scale and have their own matrix of specific policies, and each country's set of laws and policies differs significantly from every other's equivalent set. (Alterman 2006, 476)

This is reflected to some extent at the level of the European Union in the application of the European Convention on Human Rights, and more specifically the First Amendment to Protocol no. 1 of this convention, which states that compensation is due "in cases where the prejudice is exceptional and the servitude is disproportionate in comparison with the purpose of general interest of the servitude." On one hand, this amendment seems to introduce a general principle of compensation; on the other hand, compensation is supposed to remain an exception and, in practice, be left to national courts. This point is detailed later.

Restrictive Zoning Without Direct Compensation

Most European countries apply a series of zoning devices intended to protect natural areas or buildings without direct compensation. Most include a specific zoning category in local plans, usually described as "natural areas to be protected because of the interest of landscapes, historical value, or ecological interest." Urban development is usually prohibited in these areas. In them—for instance, in

Germany, France, and The Netherlands—no direct compensation is implied as a consequence of the classification.

More restrictive and long-lasting protections have been introduced in several countries under the form of listed buildings protected for their architectural and/ or historical interest. These protections do imply restrictive regulations and some form of indirect compensation. In France, for example, the restrictive regulations result from legislation enacted in 1913 and 1930 about *"sites et monuments historiques."* Any transformation or improvement of such buildings must be approved by a specific body, and there is compensation in the form of subsidies that can be as high as 50 percent of the overall cost of the work. In spite of this compensation, the maintenance cost of such buildings is often high. In countries such as France, where there are over 8,000 listed buildings, the cost of losing any right to develop the property can be high, which gave rise to a different method, the transfer of development rights.

An Ambiguous Answer: The Transfer of Development Rights ———

A possible answer to the inequity raised by zoning relies on the separation between transferable development rights (TDRs) distributed evenly in the area on one hand, and on the other hand an effective right to develop obtained by an owner, who is not able to develop the land, by purchasing development rights. Such was the basic rationale behind the introduction of the TDR mechanism, a way to make a restriction on development rights acceptable to landowners.[1]

In comparison with other areas in which tradable permits apply, such as air and water, land has some distinct features, not the least because the many entangled legal instruments that govern it play a large part in determining its price. The TDR method has been applied in an explicit way in some European countries, mainly France and Italy, and a limited number of areas have been protected. However, the concept of tradable rights has come to the fore in recent years, particularly in the context of climate change, the greenhouse effect, and air pollution. An important threshold was crossed with the protocol adopted at the December 1997 Kyoto Conference, which envisaged trading quotas or emission credits.

There is a primary conceptual difference between a tradable permit attached to land and a tradable emission quota. In the case of pollution, the object of the trade is an entitlement to emit an ongoing level of pollution, measured, for example, in tons of nitrogen dioxide discharged into the air per year. What is involved is a continuing process, and the relevant quotas may go on being bought or sold ad infinitum. With tradable land rights, by contrast, the right is sold outright or for a very long period. Although the right is salable only in part or may be bought back at a later date, the purpose of the transaction is not to engage in an ongoing process.

---

1. The information in this section of the chapter is based to an extent on Renard (2007).

This obviously has a major impact on the way the instrument is employed with respect to allotting rights and the conditions for buying them back. The concept, therefore, has to do with property law as applied to geographical space, and it reveals a major difference between legal systems. Those originating in Roman law are based on the indivisibility and absolute nature of land ownership. By contrast, Anglo-Saxon law, in particular North American law, considers land ownership to be a bundle of rights, some components of which—such as development rights, air rights, and mineral rights—can be treated separately.

CREATING A MARKET OR COMPENSATING RESTRICTED LANDOWNERS?

Central to the creation of a market in development rights is the issue of the financial and fiscal implications of land use regulations. In urban and peri-urban areas, the value of a piece of land lies in the rights attached to it, which are conditioned by zoning and other environmental regulations by which the price of land can be strongly affected.

As far as urban and especially peri-urban areas are concerned, the response has differed from country to country. Roughly speaking, most countries in Western Europe have adopted the principle that constraints on urban development are not liable to compensation unless the development infringes a vested right or contradicts investment-backed expectations.

The development of case law over time matches the gradual change that has taken place in property rights law, in which a distinction is made between private property in the strict sense of the term (that may thus be put on the market) and common property. It appears that the TDR can be more a way to compensate restricted landowners to make zoning more acceptable than a way to develop a market in development rights in which buyers meet sellers and prices adjust to supply and demand.

WHAT IS REALLY TRADED?

Postulating the existence of transferable rights assumes that there is something to trade—in other words, that one of the parties is ready to relinquish an attribute of his property (the right to build, for example) to another owner. Whatever the circumstances, no market will operate unless the exercise is worthwhile—that is, unless there is a demand for rights. This raises the issue of initial allotment of rights. Two concepts can be distinguished, depending on the methods used to value land and real estate, which are themselves based on the way property is conceived, as absolute and unitary property or as a bundle of rights, some of them being possibly public (air rights or mineral rights).

Such is the context in which it is possible to conceive of trading a right that is assumed to be in existence but whose actual use has not been authorized. This point is essential to understanding the crucial importance of the original allotment of rights and the conventional nature of that allotment.

SOME EVALUATION CRITERIA

The application of the TDR technique in Western Europe has led to results that are limited in their scope and controversial in their results (Renard 2007). As a whole, trials of the practice have not yet reached a critical mass that allow statistically reliable conclusions to be drawn. Even though there are a fairly large number of examples in the United States, they are in different geographical areas, have different aims, use different operating methods, and show different results. Many of them—generally in built-up areas and generally on an informal level—occur among small groups of owners and operate by consensus without formal legal or institutional frameworks. They have a long history in the form of TDRs in the United States and private law constraints in France. Nevertheless, use of the method in a vast geographical area by means of a universally applicable mechanism formally established in advance is still fairly limited, and most have specific features that make general conclusions difficult.

The aims attributed to most schemes are generally environmental and architectural. The most frequent goal is nature conservancy, preservation of sites of outstanding natural beauty and protection of agricultural land in the vicinity of built-up areas. Success is often measured in terms of surface area preserved for conservation in perpetuity. An area conserved in perpetuity means that all its development rights have been transmitted and that the area is closed to development. However, this particular aim is frequently a backdrop to the prime objective of redistribution—namely, to provide compensation for the constraints society places on the use of the property; in other words, to render acceptable the inequitable distribution of development rights created by zoning laws. The goal of nature conservancy (or the preservation of structures of architectural merit) is the prime objective of the regulatory procedure. The TDR technique is therefore more an intermediate instrument to facilitate implementation of a plan. The technique may also serve as a legal safety net for the planner. Even if the scheme is not in operation, the mere fact that it is in place enables disputes over compensation for constraints to be avoided.

The Legal Nature of TDRs

In all countries that have made use of transferable development rights of one sort or another, the legal status of those rights has been a point of contention and litigation. Are they an integral part of property (even when destined to be used at another site), or are they merely financial instruments to provide compensation for value lost as a result of a constraint? This is an important point both because of its impact on the legal appreciation of the issue (in France and Germany, for example, it is unlawful for planning restrictions to be liable to compensation except in very special circumstances) and because of the way it is applied and the way compensation is assessed.

The concept of property rights itself has never been finally defined. Many commentators see them as a bundle of rights in which ownership of land is a series of autonomous, separable rights—to use, to develop, to fly over, to cross, and so on. This idea does not settle the question of transferable rights in legal terms, namely, which of the rights attached to land are by their nature part of ownership (such as the right to farm the land) and which are rights whose attribution may be determined by the social function of the property (such as the right to build).

In a different context, a similar debate has been going on in France, although from a different starting point because the basic principle there is that constraints are not liable to compensation. When the 1976 act was drafted, voices were heard denouncing the risks involved in introducing rights that could be considered imaginary (Lenôtre-Villecoin 1975). Like the decision in *Suitum v. Tahoe Regional Planning Agency*, 520 U.S. 725 (1997), in the United States, this amounts to an attack on the principle behind the creation of the legal entity of transferable right. According to Lenôtre-Villecoin, "the capacity to transfer an imaginary development right establishes a *jus abutendi*, or a right of disposal, in a case in which the public interest, in the form of regulation of urban development, is against existence of the right to build at all" (1975, 535).

Zoning and Transferable Rights

There is a clear link between zoning and transferable rights. The transferable rights procedure is in itself a zoning instrument in that it implies a division into transmitter and receiver zones. Greater precision may be introduced by stipulating that the zones must be of precisely specified dimensions; if the dimensions differ, the whole scheme will be invalidated. For the scheme to operate properly, owners in both transmitter and receiver zones need to be given the right incentives, which should help balance supply against demand with respect to development rights.

In the case of receiver zones, where conventional planning regulations operate as usual, the purpose of zoning is to ensure a high standard of urban development. The quality of urban development is thus the criterion to be taken into account. As the process proceeds, however, it becomes difficult to provide adequate incentives. Many schemes use a system of bonus zoning; in other words, the authorized density increases if transferable rights are purchased. This makes it tempting for the planner to reduce the ordinary density (where no rights have been purchased) and increase the bonus density. However, such a policy is likely to fall foul of the principle of vested rights and to lead to litigation. Incentive zoning is thus a difficult process.

Another sensitive issue is the eligibility of a zone to be designated a transmitter zone, which opens the way to a grant of transferable rights. The subject is one of endless debate with no evident way of settling it on a systematic basis. Should agricultural land be allocated TDRs and, if so, on whose behalf? Generally speaking, the price of agricultural land could be considered to reflect its productivity, the current net value of its future yield. It is paradoxical to allot development rights to land on which farming is expected to continue, even if the rights are not to be used on that land. Arguments in France and the United States are often based on the natural beauty and biological diversity of the site. However, this takes no account of existing usage and places owners with different relationships with their land on the same footing.

Although no general conclusion on the linkage between zoning and transferable rights can be reached, the risk of distorting zone demarcations and urban planning regulations in order to make the rights market work should be noted. It is important to maintain a proper perspective; the transferable rights procedure is no more than an aid to good urban planning, not an end in itself.

Is the Price of Rights a Market Price?

It would be pleasant to be able to answer the question of whether the price of rights is a market price affirmatively, taking market price to mean the price that would balance supply against demand under conditions of atomicity, transparency, and so on. Even in the most successful cases, the small number of transactions involved and the short time the scheme has been in operation do not allow statistically significant findings to be made. The only firm conclusion—reached in settings as different as Auckland, New Zealand; Turin, Italy; Montgomery County, Maryland; and the commune of Taninges in the French Alps—is that prices rise sharply when the procedure is beginning to be implemented and then level off or even decline.

To be more specific, there has to be a way to make detailed analyses of local markets in order to set the market price of a development right on a residual basis (from the market price of the end product, the building, minus the costs of the operation, deducting the highest likely level of land tax, resulting in the value of the development rights to be purchased). The actual price will probably be nowhere near this market price unless the purchase of tradable rights is mandatory and there is no nearby alternative (a development zone not subject to the transfer system). This comes back to the paradox mentioned earlier, that the system of tradable rights will work properly only when land use is subject to strict planning regulations.

Equity and Efficiency

The concept of equity has to be considered from the point of view of landowners and the inhabitants of the city as a whole. For landowners, tradable rights fulfill an essential function in the absence of a fiscal system capable of recouping added value. The price of land is dependent on the development rights allowed by the zoning regulations, and tradable rights make it possible to correct inequities introduced by zoning. If the concept of equity is extended to all inhabitants, assessment of the method becomes more difficult and depends on the way property rights are conceived and the tax system allows them to be put into operation.

There are two contrasting situations. In some countries, such as the countries of North America and southwestern Europe, there is no universally applicable mechanism for recovering capital gains from urban development and/or payments for development rights. The practice of transferring development rights is thus equivalent to distributing the overall capital gain generated by urban development among the subgroup of landowners only, whereas it might be expected to be returned to the community as a whole, in particular when the public amenities that give rise to added value are funded by the taxpayers. This is a limited view of equity, which may help in particular cases at the cost of a broader notion of equity requiring a general mechanism to recoup betterment by a public authority (unless, which is unusual, land is divided up in a comprehensive and equal way among the inhabitants).

The second type of situation, which is found mainly in northern Europe, is founded on the principle that the capital gain by urban development should return, at least in large part, to the community. Using various methods (described above), the initial procedure that increases the value of land essentially benefits the community rather than the landowner. The equalization made possible by transferable rights therefore serves no purpose.

The Emergence of a European Law of Property

As noted previously, some elements of law about the right of property were introduced in the European Convention on Human Rights in 1950 and completed in March 1952 by a first additional protocol stating that a compensation is due "in cases where the prejudice is exceptional and the servitude is disproportionate in comparison with the purpose of general interest of the servitude." This opened the door to a possible application of takings, but at the same time limited it.

The Convention, as a fundamental text of the European Union, can be applied directly by European courts without an intermediate step of a translation, interpretation, and adaptation in national legislation. Three basic principles thus apply directly at the European level:

1. The guarantee of property
2. The possibility of expropriation in the public interest
3. The possibility of restricting land use without compensation for general interest purposes

Up to now, European courts have followed the principle of subsidiarity, considering this part of the responsibility of national governments, as stated explicitly by a 2004 decision before the European Court of Human Rights (CEDH): "Planning and zoning are fundamentally domains of intervention of national governments, especially through regulation of land use in the general interest. In such policies, where general interest is at stake, the margin of appreciation of national governments must be greater than when only questions related to civil courts arise" (CEDH 2004).

There have been limited exceptions to this general principle in the evolution of case law of the CEDH. A key decision, often referred to and quoted in the last 25 years, is related to the classification of a piece of land as reserved for public use and supposed to be expropriated in the future, but without indication of delay. After 23 years under this threat, the owner went to the European Court, which confirmed the legality of the classification, but also considered that the delay was "unreasonable, and that the balance between the interest of the municipality and the interest of the owner had been disrupted," thus violating article 1, since this was considered as a "special and outrageous" burden (CEDH 1982).

The Challenge of Land Value Assessment in Volatile Markets

The very notion of "windfalls for wipeouts" implicitly refers to some reference price of land, some type of benchmarking, making it possible to define and measure when there is a windfall and when a wipeout. In the context of a slow and steady evolution of land and property prices, this can be considered a reasonable expectation and makes imagining an equitable treatment of gains and losses more or less possible.

Land and property markets are more and more volatile; "irrational exuberance," to quote Alan Greenspan and Robert Shiller (2000), is increasing, as exemplified by the subprime crisis, the effects of which have extended around the world. New instruments to analyze the phenomenon, as well as different tools of public policy, are needed.

Conclusion: Toward a Redefinition of the Right of Property on Land

We thus return to the definition and content of property law, which is the key to the problem. Any treatment of windfall or wipeout problems resulting from planning and zoning relies basically on the assumption of an extensive definition of the right of property, including the right to the capital gain on land, even if the gain is the result of general evolution, urban growth, or the construction of infrastructure by public authorities without any activity by the landowner.

As noted by Donald Krueckeberg:

> Property is not just the object of possession or capital in isolation, but a set of relationships between the owner of a thing and everyone else's claim to the same thing. This understanding of property highlights considerations of distributive justice that are particularly important in light of the issues in the contemporary debate about property rights. Rights to personal use of property are fundamental to individual and social well-being: rights to profit from property, in contrast, have always been subject

to reasonable constraints for the benefits of the entire community and society. Attempts to establish a contrary case by appealing to natural rights, market necessity, liberty, social utility, or just desert all fail to withstand scrutiny. . . . These concepts of use rights and profit rights in property are at the heart of the planning question. (1995, 301–309)

REFERENCES

Alterman, Rachelle. 2006. Introduction: Regulatory takings viewed through cross-national comparative lenses. *Global Studies Law Review* 5(3):469–476.

CEDH. 1982. Sporrong et lonnroth c. Suède. 23 September.

———. 2004. Gorraiz lizarraga et crts c. Espagne. 27 April.

Expert Committee on Compensation and Betterment. 1942. Final report. Cmnd 6386, September.

Jacobs, Harvey D. 2006. The "taking" of Europe: Globalizing the American ideal of private property? Working paper, Lincoln Institute of Land Policy, Cambridge, MA.

Krueckeberg, Donald. 1995. The difficult character of property: To whom do things belong? *Journal of the American Planning Association* 61(3):301–309.

Lenôtre-Villecoin, J. 1975. Urbanisme et propriété du sol: Les propriétaires vont-ils pouvoir monnayer des droits de construire fictifs? *Les Études*, April, 431–440.

Needham, Barrie. 2006. *Planning, law and economics: The rules we make for using land*. Oxford and New York: Routledge.

Renard, Vincent. 2007. Property rights and the "transfer of development rights": Questions of efficiency and equity. *Town Planning Review* 78(1):41–60.

Shiller, Robert J. 2000. *Irrational exuberance*. Princeton, NJ: Princeton University Press.

COMMENTARY
Barrie Needham

Land use planning restricts the exercise of, and reduces the value of, property rights. That is clear, and the contribution by Vincent Renard describes the tensions to which it gives rise. But the same applies to many other forms of government activity. For example, a person may not make so much noise with her radio that she causes a nuisance; nor may someone discharge waste into the river that runs through his land; nor may someone drive her car faster than 50 kilometers per hour in a built-up area. Why do we pay so much attention to the effect on property rights of one type of government regulation (land use planning) and not of other types? Why is the concept of taking not applied, for instance, to the reduction in the value of a person's car caused by the fact that he cannot use it in the way that gives him the most value?

The answer lies partly in the emotional and symbolic value attached to land. This is less now than in feudal times, but some people still derive feelings of security or status from owning land and identify themselves with a particular piece of land (more so than with, for example, a car). But much more important is the fact that the restrictions on car use, noise, and so on apply to everyone everywhere in a particular jurisdiction, whereas the restrictions of land use planning apply selectively; they are "locationally specific" (Needham 2006, 20 et seq). For example, one farmer may use his land for urban development, but another farmer may not because the land use plan has drawn a zoning boundary on a geographical map. One farmer becomes a millionaire; the other has to make do with selling potatoes or grain. The resistance to this sort of selectivity becomes even clearer when we consider another type of restriction on using land, namely, building regulations (ceiling heights, fire resistance, and so on). These are rarely contested, mainly because they apply equally to everybody.

A legal principle addresses this issue, and I find it interesting that Renard does not mention it, because it is a French legal doctrine: *égalité devant les charges publiques*. This means that when a government body takes a measure, no citizen should be more disadvantaged by that measure than other citizens. It is clear that land use planning transgresses this legal principle. Unless a practical solution to this can be found, the tension between land use planning and property rights will continue. If the tension becomes too great, it could result in the scrapping of otherwise desirable land use planning.

Where should we look for a solution? Not, I suggest, in redefining property rights in land, which is what Renard suggests. I reject that because the issue is not that property rights are restricted, but that such restriction is clearly unequal between citizens. It is not a question of more or less protection for property rights, but of more or less protection for the citizen against unequal treatment by the government (Needham 2007).

The only general and effective solution I can think of is to compensate property owners who are disproportionately disadvantaged by land use planning. This can be compensation for the financial disadvantage only; if in addition there is loss because of emotional attachment to land (hypersensitivity), it is generally accepted that it cannot be compensated.

In extreme cases, this principle is already accepted in most countries. Expropriation is the biggest restriction on property rights in land and is clearly very selective. Only when the financial compensation is regarded as unfair is expropriation contested (apart from cases where there is emotional attachment to land). The case is also extreme when land use planning reduces the value of property so much that no more reasonable beneficial use (the term is from English jurisprudence) is possible. This, too, is compensated in most countries (Needham 2006, 47–48). In U.S. terms, it is a taking, and in the member states of the European Union it has to be compensated under the jurisprudence that has arisen around the First Protocol to the European Treaty on Human Rights (and see chapter 9).

In less extreme cases, however, compensation for disproportionate disadvantage by land use planning is rarely paid. TDRs is a solution, but clearly with only limited application. The English got themselves into a terrible mess when trying to tackle this with compensation and betterment in the 1947 Town and Country Planning Act.

Let me close by describing how the pragmatic Dutch have tackled this. Under Dutch law (Dutch Spatial Planning Act 2008, article 6.1–6.7), the owner of a property right is entitled to compensation if a land use plan is changed. The principle is that somebody who owns property knows the restrictions (including those from land use planning) on how he may use that property and that, because living in society always imposes restrictions on individual behavior, the disadvantages must be accepted without compensation. So it is only when the restrictions are changed in ways the owner had not been able to anticipate that he is entitled to compensation. The compensation is restricted to 90 percent of the depreciation (the other 10 percent must be accepted under normal social risk). And there are possibilities for requiring those who benefit from the change in the plan to pay the compensation to those who lose.

REFERENCES

Needham, Barrie. 2006. *Planning, law and economics*. London: Routledge.
———. 2007. Land use planning and the law. *Planning Theory* 6(2):183–189.

10

Should Decreases in Property Value Caused by Regulations Be Compensated?

Abraham Bell

*F*or nearly a century now, land use controls have been the domain of regula-tion rather than private law. Nuisance and other private lawsuits are still available to neighbors quarrelling over land use. But most of their land use questions—from construction materials to building size and shape, and even to the types of use (number of residences, permissibility of commercial activity, and so on) are resolved by the municipal and state regulatory system called land use law.

Since the dawn of the modern land use era, American law has struggled to deal with what came to be known as the regulatory takings question: whether the state would have to recompense landowners whose property values declined as a result of the regulatory scheme. Three legal analogies suggested themselves to courts as the key to resolving the compensation question. First, eminent do-main—or government takings of title to property—is subject to the takings clause of the Fifth Amendment to the U.S. Constitution; consequently, all takings under the power of eminent domain must be accompanied by payment of just compen-sation to the owner (see Epstein 1985). Second, judicial applications of the com-mon law rule of nuisance can eliminate valuable land uses, but are not generally seen as requiring compensation to the party whose use is found to be a nuisance. (For an interesting exception, see *Spur Industries, Inc. v. Del E. Webb Develop-ment Co.*, 494 P.2d 701 [Ariz. 1972].) Third, a number of government powers, ranging from taxation to criminal forfeiture to welfare legislation, are never seen as requiring compensation; indeed, the very purpose of the power is often inimi-cal to compensation (cf. Penalver 2004). Over the years, all three analogies have been used and recycled in the jurisprudence of regulatory takings in service of inconsistent results. (For descriptions of the inconsistencies of the doctrine, see Epstein 1985; Farber 1992a; Kanner 1998; Krier 1997; Rose 1984.)

Whatever one might think of the value of the analogies for legal doctrine, they should have little appeal for consequentialists. Whether a regulation that diminishes property value looks doctrinally more like a tax or like an exercise of eminent domain does not seem to provide any independent reason to favor or oppose compensation. One irrationally drawn line should not command another—or so it would seem.

However, upon closer examination, the doctrinal background is important even for the consequentialist. The consequentialist arguments for and against regulatory takings compensation ultimately cannot be uprooted from their doctrinal backgrounds. Whether and when regulatory takings compensation should be paid is a question that cannot be answered solely by reference to the question of whether payment for regulatory harm is optimal in the abstract; it must be answered in reference to a world that offers certain kinds of compensation for certain kinds of government action and that does not extract charges for many benefits.

This chapter attempts to determine the correct regulatory takings compensation policy given the general doctrinal framework in other bodies of American law. In particular, it addresses the following questions: First, given a compensation requirement for eminent domain, is it sensible to interpret the government's regulatory authority as permitting the elimination of property value without compensation? Second, since regulations often produce benefit as well as harm, how can a regulatory givings be incorporated into a consequentialist analysis of regulatory takings compensation? Should the right of property owners to benefit from capital appreciation caused by regulations without returning the windfalls to the government be interpreted as implying a denial of the right to receive compensation where the regulations produce adverse effects? Third, given the likelihood that overlapping regulations will produce both benefit and harm for property owners over time, should land use regulations remain uncompensated in light of the probability of a future or past beneficial land use regulation? Fourth, in light of the ubiquity of ad valorem property taxes, should regulations that adversely affect property be seen as implicitly accompanied by compensation, given that a reduction in housing values will lead to lower tax payments just as an increase in property prices caused by a public action will increase tax liabilities for property owners?

The findings of the chapter may be summarized as follows: The case for takings compensation is far from perfect, and serious arguments can and have been made against it. However, once compensation is a required accompaniment to eminent domain takings, it is extremely difficult to draft a cogent argument for ruling out compensation for regulatory takings in general. Adding consideration of givings and taxes to the picture further demonstrates the problematic nature of much of the law of takings, but does not make a compelling case against compensating for regulatory takings.

The first part of the chapter explores the concept of takings compensation and briefly sketches the consequentialist case for compensation. The second part asks how regulatory takings may be distinguished from other takings and asks whether they ought to be. The third part introduces the concept of regulatory givings and questions whether a givings analysis ought to change the conclusions of a takings analysis. The fourth part briefly addresses the issues concerning interplay with other doctrinal bodies, especially tax, to determine whether tax capitalization effects are the equivalent of compensation.

Takings Compensation

The Fifth Amendment to the U.S. Constitution guarantees just compensation to property owners whenever "private property [is] taken for public use." The compensation guarantee goes back in Anglo-American legal history to the Magna Carta and, though ambiguous in scope, is thoroughly uncontroversial as a matter of law.

While beyond the scope of this chapter, fairness concerns appear to animate many popular understandings of the compensation requirement. The most familiar formulation of these concerns is found in the U.S. Supreme Court's announcement in *Armstrong v. United States*, 364 U.S. 40 (1960), that, per Justice Blackmun, fairness in the takings context requires that "Government [not force] some people alone to bear public burdens which, in all fairness and justice, should be borne by the public as a whole." Drawing heavily on the work of John Rawls (1958, 1971), Frank Michelman (1967) argued that the fair compensation requirement represents the legal regime that the citizenry would have chosen behind a veil of ignorance. Specifically, Michelman argued that the scope of the just compensation requirement is that which the citizenry would choose if it knew of a governmental power of eminent domain in the abstract but did not know how the burden of exercising that power would be distributed among the general public.

Essentially, Michelman assumed that if people had no knowledge of what their future property holdings would be, they would nevertheless have a shared notion of an acceptable risk of exposure to eminent domain. In this understanding, people would accept some takings only with compensation, to be identified by situations in which the demoralization costs of having one's property taken exceeded the settlement costs of arranging for payment of compensation. More precisely, Michelman suggested that compensation should be paid when settlement costs are low, the gains from the government action are dubious, and "the harm concentrated on one individual is unusually great." On the other hand, compensation may be denied when property owners who are burdened by the government action also benefit from it or when the burden falls on the shoulders of many people.

The Michelman formulation has greatly influenced the development of takings doctrine. It played an important role in the majority opinion in *Penn Central Transportation Co. v. New York City*, 438 U.S. 104 (1978), the Supreme Court's 1978 reentry into the field of regulatory takings. But it is difficult to translate into economic terms. In particular, demoralization costs, the key utilitarian term in

Michelman's analysis, are difficult to translate into workable terms. This chapter focuses instead on economic justifications for takings compensation: (1) fiscal illusion; (2) counteracting the interest group power of property owners; and (3) reducing the ability for profiting from corrupt use of political power.

Before exploring these explanations, I must add an important caveat regarding the dual nature of compensation. Takings compensation, like any other compensation required by law—such as compensation for torts and breaches of contract—creates incentives for both the actor who pays the compensation and the actor who receives it. Often, the rule that properly incentivizes one party creates the wrong incentives for the other. Consider, for example, bilateral accidents—accidents whose likelihood or scope of damages may be limited both by the party that causes the accident and by the accident's likely victims. A tort standard of strict liability, which requires the tortfeasor to pay for all damages caused by the accident irrespective of fault, will properly incentivize the would-be tortfeasor to engage in optimal levels of care to prevent the accident as well as optimal levels of activity in carrying out the accident-prone pursuit. However, the strict liability standard provides complete insurance for all victims irrespective of whether the victim herself might have reduced or eliminated the damage by being more careful or refraining from the activity in which she was harmed. Thus, the strict liability rule may encourage potential victims to engage in supra-optimal levels of activity and suboptimal levels of care (Shavell 1987). Where both the tortfeasor and the victim may take measures to prevent social harm, optimal deterrence may be achieved only by imposing a standard that creates "double responsibility at the margin" (Cooter 1985). Thus, economic analysis dictates that where the victim must be induced to optimize a level of care, either the tortfeasor must be given the opportunity to avail herself of a defense of contributory negligence or the tortfeasor must be subject to a standard of negligence. In this way, both tortfeasor and victim will be induced to take responsibility for reducing the incidence of tort harms (Shavell 1987).

An optimal rule of compensation must not only address incentives to the potential taker (the government). It must also concern itself with the incentive effects created by the compensation rule on property owners. I therefore examine the incentive effects on each party—first the government and then the property owner—and finally attempt to combine the rules into one creating optimal incentives for both parties.

COMPENSATION AND GOVERNMENT BEHAVIOR

Fiscal Illusion   Fiscal illusion is perhaps the most common economic justification of the constitutional mandate of just compensation (Blume, Rubinfeld, and Shapiro 1984; Blume and Shapiro 1984; Fischel 1995). Proponents of this explanation of the utility of compensation argue that government decision makers overlook costs that do not directly affect government revenues and expenditures. When operating under fiscal illusion, decision makers are blind to costs (and benefits) their actions impose (and bestow) on private property owners, save those that appear on the budget. As a consequence of their limited vision, decision makers subject to fiscal illusion take insufficient heed of costs they impose on private property owners and potentially will take too much if unconstrained by a compensation requirement, because uncompensated takings enrich the government by adding property holdings while imposing relatively small costs, such as administrative costs.

The requirement of compensation remedies the problem by forcing the government that takes property to place the costs incurred by the private property owners on the budget. Once the government must pay compensation (and if social benefits are properly accounted for), the cost of takings appears in the decision-making process, and fiscal illusion no longer distorts it.

To be sure, there are some significant gaps between the requirements of the fiscal illusion justification and current compensation doctrine and practice. First, it is at odds with the legally mandated compensation standard of compensation at market value. Taken to its logical conclusion, the fiscal illusion justification calls for a more generous compensation measure than that currently employed, namely compensation at subjective value—at the value the owner attaches to the property rather than the value attached by the marketplace. As Judge Posner wrote in *Coniston Corp. v. Village of Hoffman Estates*, 844 F.2d 461 (7th Cir., 1988), "market value is not the value that every owner of property attaches to his property but merely the value that the marginal owner attaches to *his* property. Many owners are 'inframarginal,' meaning that because of relocation costs, sentimental attachments, or the special suitability of the property for their particular (perhaps idiosyncratic) needs, they value their property at more than its market value." Since the fiscal illusion theory is concerned with full accounting for costs and benefits, the only measure that reflects the full cost of government projects is not payment of market value to the aggrieved owners but rather the payment of compensation at the owners' subjective value, which reflects the true loss as a result of the coercive transfer (Bell and Parchomovsky 2007; Krier and Serkin 2004; Merrill 2002; Serkin 2005). Second, the theory of fiscal illusion implies that decision makers ought to be just as blind to the effect of benefits bestowed on others as to the costs imposed on them. Thus, the fiscal illusion justification calls for assessing charges for givings just as much as it demands compensation for takings. Yet, while a handful of doctrines—such as the doctrine of average reciprocity of advantage and local exactions or levies—account for givings, they generally do so only partially and as offsets, leaving an expected situation of too few givings (Bell and Parchomovsky 2001a).

Additionally, as an empirical matter, the fiscal illusion justification appears to overstate decision makers' adherence to the requirements of government budgets. However, political actors are independent agents whose interests are not entirely identical to the state's (see, for example, Niskanen 1971; Peters 1978; Posner 1974; Stigler 1971; Tullock 1989). They take account of nonbudgetary concerns and clearly do not exclusively maximize budget surplus. For instance, political actors will invariably care about the effect of their actions and decisions on their personal utility functions and, especially, on the probability of being reelected. Hence, decision makers might pay compensation for political reasons without being required to do so.

Property Owners as an Interest Group   A different explanation focuses on property owners' political grievances created by uncompensated takings. This explanation operates on the assumption that government makes benign decisions for the benefit of society, but may be foiled by well-organized compact interest groups. When it comes to takings, this model envisions that an initially efficient proposal to take property for the benefit of society may not be implemented on account of opposition from politically powerful property owners who can and will stop the government initiative by exercising their political clout unless paid enough money to remove their opposition. As a result, efficient takings would be likely blocked absent the payment of compensation (Farber 1992b). The touchstone for this explanation is Mancur Olson's (1965) theory of the superior political power of minority interest groups.

While maintaining some surface appeal, the explanation comes apart upon further examination. In fact, the theory provides no explanation for why it is necessary to mandate compensation by law. If the theory is right, the government will always choose to pay compensation of its own accord in order to carry out efficient projects. At best, the compensation requirement can be seen as a pre-commitment mechanism under which the government concedes the inevitable to the politically powerful. Additionally, there is no need to compensate owners at the full value of their property (whether measured by market price or subjective value). On one hand, politically powerful homeowners have no reason to be appeased at the payment of market value or even the full subjective value they attach to the property. Once they understand their power to hold out and block the project, such owners will require the payment of the largest amount they can extract from the government commensurate with the group's political power; this can range from zero up to the full value of the project to society. On the other hand, if the owners are not sufficiently powerful to block the project, there is no need to offer them any compensation. Indeed, in such cases the payment of compensation is not only unnecessary, but also a waste of resources (Bell and Parchomovsky 2009).

Compensating Against Corruption   A third and final explanation for takings compensation is that it helps reduce the incentives for corruption by limiting the ability of politicians to profit from takings. The touchstone for this theory is rent-seeking accounts of government behavior. In such theories, actors attempt to harness the powers of government to transfer to themselves market power or other benefits in order to earn rents—the socially undesirable extra profit earned by the use of the regulatory powers in a socially suboptimal manner. Government powers, in this view, are auctioned off to the highest bidder and are employed toward that bidder's desired end. Aside from the costs of auctioning, avoiding detection, and the like, government activity divides rents between interested bidders and politicians. Given the rent seeking that attends all public decision-making processes in this model, the best way to improve the quality of public decision making is to reduce the profitability of rent-seeking activity by minimizing available rents. Takings compensation does just that. It reduces the profitability of rent seeking, in this account, by reducing the pool of funds available for extracting rents. If government could take property by eminent domain without paying compensation, the full value of the property would be available for rent-seeking activity. Once compensation is paid, however, the value of rent-seeking activity is reduced to the value of the property less the compensation paid (Bell and Parchomovsky 2009).

This explanation of the purpose of takings compensation avoids many of the difficulties of the fiscal illusion and interest group explanations of takings compensation. However, it relies on a limiting assumption: Specifically, in order to extract funds from owners in exchange for not taking properties, decision makers must have some means of credibly assuring owners that their property will not be at further risk from takings. This means not only that politicians must be able reliably to assure owners that the politician will not threaten a taking a second time after receiving payment; it also means that owners must be reasonably assured that other decision makers will not threaten the same taking.

COMPENSATION AND OWNER BEHAVIOR
The imperfect case for takings compensation becomes more complicated once the effects on owner incentives are included. The problem here is that compensation for property owners grants each a de facto government insurance policy against takings. A reasonable case can be made in favor of the benefits of such social insurance. However, like all cases of insurance, the granting of an insurance policy creates moral hazard in the insured, the risk that the insured will recklessly expose herself to risk given the lack of financial consequences (Arrow 1971).

The social insurance case for takings compensation is straightforward. Property owners, like others, are risk averse. Insurance against the loss of takings improves social utility by partially eliminating disutility engendered by uncertainty. For the risk averse, insurance provides a benefit beyond the actuarial value determined by the magnitude and likelihood of expected loss. That is to say, for the risk averse, even if the premiums paid are worth enough to fully cover the probabilistic likelihood of loss, the insured will come out with greater utility. Of course, in order to justify mandatory takings compensation, it is not enough to point to likely social gains from insurance. One must further explain why—if insurance provides such utility—private markets do not provide such policies and why the government ought to provide that insurance rather than the private market. Rent-seeking accounts of government might explain the lack of private insurance as impossible under a rent-seeking regime or, at the very least, explain why such private insurance might lead to social loss. This is because rent-seeking actors would take advantage of government decision makers' knowledge about future takings decisions by purchasing this information about future takings. Insurance companies could then use the information both to deny coverage to the parties imperiled by future takings and to bribe government decision makers to change their takings decisions and impose takings on the uninsured rather than on insured parties. Given these possible corruptions of the system, the likely losses created by the combined effect of inefficient takings, unnecessary insurance policies, and bribes would outweigh social gains created by private insurance (Bell and Parchomovsky 2009). Additionally, private insurance might be plagued by problems of adverse selection, thin markets due to the rarity of eminent domain takings, and monitoring of moral hazard (Blume, Rubinfeld, and Shapiro 1984).

Yet, even if there are social gains to be realized by public provision of the social insurance of takings compensation in the form of greater security for the risk averse, it is far from clear that takings compensation is socially optimal when all gains and losses are taken into account. After all, irrespective of insurance's positive effects in increasing security, it necessarily creates risk of moral hazard. In the context of takings insurance, as Louis Kaplow (1986), Lawrence Blume, Daniel Rubinfeld, and Perry Shapiro (1984), and others have identified, the risk is that owners will overdevelop their properties. Knowing that takings compensation will insure them for the value of any development that ends up being rendered worthless by a taking, and knowing they will enjoy a full benefit if there is no taking, owners will naturally overspend on developments that should never have been built had the risk of takings been accounted for.

In legal schemes that provide compensation, there are a number of standard remedies for moral hazard. For instance, to prevent moral hazard created by tort compensation in bilateral accidents, the law may impose a contributory negligence defense (Shavell 1987). In contract cases, the law may require victims to mitigate their damages. Insurance companies may privately impose various duties upon insured parties to ensure due care, and they may require the insured to accept a policy with a deductible—an agreement that the insurance company will deduct a fixed amount from any compensation for the loss in order to ensure that insured parties are properly motivated to take care. The takings literature has offered a number of such remedies in order to resolve the moral hazard problem. But while there are elements of such remedies to be found in existing takings compensation law, as a general rule takings compensation does little to discourage overdevelopment (Bell 2003; Miceli and Segerson 1994).

As a consequence of the adverse incentive effects on property owners, a number of scholars have proposed that takings compensation is inefficient altogether if viewed from the perspective of property owners only, and only partially justifiable if the government is considered subject to fiscal illusion or other decision-making frameworks that would be adversely affected by immunity from takings compensation (Blume, Rubinfeld, and Shapiro 1984). This may be correct. Indeed, without a clearer picture of the degree of risk aversion of the general public to takings, it may be unknowable whether the losses created by moral hazard exceed the gains produced by social insurance and discouragement of inefficient takings or bribe extraction. Unfortunately, as there is no market for private takings insurance, the value of this service is difficult to determine.

In summary, various economic cases may be made for takings compensation, but none is free from controversy.

Regulatory Takings Compensation

In contrast to the difficulty of making a case for general takings compensation, making a case for regulatory takings compensation is easy once the appropriateness of takings compensation in general is conceded. This is not to say that the law of regulatory takings has found it easy to determine when compensation ought to be paid. On the contrary, finding the line between regulations that are considered constitutional takings (which must therefore be paid for by just compensation) and those that are not (which may remain uncompensated) has proved one of the most difficult tasks in modern law (see Kanner 1998). Regulatory takings questions have remained on the Supreme Court's docket for several decades now, and the numerous cases have created as much confusion as they have resolved.

The formalist case law for differentiating between regulatory takings and ordinary takings is both textual and functional. Traditionally, the state has been required to pay compensation to property owners only when it has used its power of eminent domain, but not when it has used the other regulatory powers encompassed within its police powers. This reflects the fact that the Constitution extends its guarantee of compensation for takings only to the use of the eminent domain power and not to the use of any other government power.

However, this formalistic treatment does not resolve very much. In the seminal *Pennsylvania Coal v. Mahon*, 260 U.S. 393 (1922), the Supreme Court acknowledged that regulations may sometimes go too far in reducing property value such that they must be considered takings, although not formally acts of eminent domain. Thus, ruled Justice Holmes in the name of the Court, a Pennsylvania regulation forbidding mining that would cause subsidence damage to buildings on the surface above the mine was a taking because it unduly diminished the value of the subsurface owned by the mining company.

Unfortunately, Justice Holmes refrained from clearly explaining when and how a regulation was to be identified as a taking, and in the four decades since regulatory takings returned to the Supreme Court docket in *Penn Central Transportation Co. v. New York City*, the judiciary has failed to craft a coherent doctrinal approach. In *Penn Central*, the Court established an ad hoc inquiry comprising three factors for identifying takings in actions that purport to be exercises of the police power: the owner's reasonable investment-backed expectations, the nature of the government action, and the degree of diminution in property value. At the same time, the Court refused to let go of traditional identification schemes characteristic of the pre–New Deal era. Notwithstanding the *Penn Central* test, permanent physical invasions alone are takings (*Loretto v. Teleprompter Manhattan CATV Corp.*, 458 U.S. 419 [1982]); prevention of noxious uses may block the finding of a taking (*Hadacheck v. Sebastian*, 239 U.S. 394 [1915]), and a complete wipeout of property value not ascribable to nuisance prevention is a per se taking (*Lucas v. South Carolina Coastal Council*, 505 U.S. 1003 [1992]).

From an economic perspective, all this is meaningless. Indeed, in the view of property rights economists, the takings versus regulatory takings distinction is even more meaningless than might at first appear. To economists like Yoram Barzel (1997), valuable entitlements are property rights, whether so defined by law or not. They may be defined as property rights by law, or as administrative or contract rights. They may be *in rem* or *in personam*. They may even be illegal. For the property rights economists, these distinctions are little more than curiosities.

For property rights economists, then, there is no difference between a government action that takes away all value in extracting rights from a mine by means of eminent domain and one that takes away the same value extracting rights by means of what the law calls a regulation. For the property rights economists, in both cases, the rights taken are property rights, and there is no reason to treat any of them as different in kind than the other.

This is not to say that economists have nothing to say about the regulatory takings debate. Several economic explanations have been offered for why some regulatory takings remain outside the realm of compensation. In the main, these explanations have focused on a parallel between mandated takings compensation and other mandated compensation. For example, Saul Levmore (1991) suggested that the kind of acts that would be considered noncompensable under private tort law ought not to be compensable under takings compensation law. Similarly, William Fischel (1995) suggested that regulatory takings lines should track the local development norms and that compensation should be paid only where government compels the use of land in a more restrictive manner than local norms would indicate.

Ultimately, however, these explanations appear to do little more than describe a set of cases where takings compensation of any kind would be inefficient, because, properly understood, the property right claimed to be taken by the owner never, in fact, existed. These explanations do not describe an approach that justifies treating regulations generally as distinct from eminent domain in compensation policy.

And, indeed, on the other side of the regulatory takings divide, one can find an economic argument that regulatory takings present a better candidate for compensation than other kinds of takings. Again, this is not due to a difference in the nature of the power or property rights involved. Rather, argue Thomas Miceli and Kathleen Segerson (1996), because regulatory takings are more frequent than eminent domain takings, they may present better candidates for efficient compensation under an unusual theory involving preemptive development. According to their theory, where governments make efficient decisions regarding takings and owners properly anticipate takings and the government's reluctance to destroy valuable developments by takings, uncompensated owners will attempt to reduce the likelihood of their property being taken by overdeveloping it. This is particularly true when takings involve a number of candidate properties and owners need only slightly overdevelop to make it efficient to seize another slightly less-developed property. Miceli and Segerson (1996) conclude that takings compensation eliminates this risk by eliminating the incentive to invest inefficiently to alter the takings risk.

Finally, the practice of requiring compensation for some kinds of takings of property rights (by eminent domain) and not requiring compensation for other kinds of takings of property rights (by regulation) can create its own set of distortions. Since the government may, in many cases, accomplish the same result of taking and transferring property rights by either regulation or eminent domain, requiring compensation in one of these cases but not the other would push the government toward using the regulatory tool, even where it would be less efficient. Whether the government was subject to fiscal illusion or corruption (as in standard rent-seeking models), it would be ready to use a less-efficient regulatory tool in order to avoid the mandated budgetary expenditure on compensation.

Thus, from an economic perspective, it is difficult to justify a broader rule against compensation for regulatory takings than against compensation for ordinary takings. For the economist, property rights are property rights, whether described as title or as regulatory permissions.

Regulatory Givings and Compensation

There is one readily observable difference between regulatory powers of the state and naked eminent domain. In an act of eminent domain, the state appropriates title to a property. Generally, that property will subsequently be put to some use that benefits at least one person, but the act of eminent domain itself involves only the taking, not the subsequent benefit. Regulations, by contrast, generally combine both giving a benefit and taking property value. Land use regulations, in particular, almost invariably involve some losses and some gains for a number of property owners.

Bell and Parchomovsky (2001a) labeled the distribution of such benefits "givings" in an attempt to tie the rules of conferring benefits more explicitly to the law of takings. (An earlier work, Hagman and Misczynski [1978], referred to such benefits as "windfalls.") The issue of givings is not unique to regulation; it is merely highlighted by the combination of givings and takings in the same act. Givings are ubiquitous. They exist not only when government grants licenses or regulatory favors, but also when government directly grants money and properties to private actors. In a sense, granting givings is the major business of government, and takings or taxes are simply means to the end of givings.

How should takings compensation policy deal with the fact that regulations generally involve both givings and takings? One possibility might be to exempt regulations altogether from the general obligation to pay takings compensation, on the assumption that the givings and takings in regulations will generally cancel one another out. Second, one might urge dealing with the combination of givings and takings that is usually found in regulations in the same way as the law deals with ordinary takings that are not directly accompanied by givings. Today, this means paying compensation for takings while neglecting to assess charges for givings. In this part, I endeavor to show that the optimal means of dealing with givings, in both regulatory and ordinary takings, is to assess charges for them. I also argue that even in the absence of givings charges, it is preferable to pay compensation for regulatory takings on the same terms as ordinary takings than to exclude regulatory takings from compensation altogether.

Since the dawn of modern regulatory takings jurisprudence, regulatory takings law has included a doctrine called the average reciprocity of advantage. This doctrine was first introduced in *Pennsylvania Coal v. Mahon*. As Justice Holmes explained it, it excluded some regulations that would otherwise be thought to be regulatory takings from the compensation requirement. The specific case to which Justice Holmes was referring was a regulation requiring mining companies to leave pillars of coal in place along adjoining mines. These pillars were necessary to prevent flooding mine collapses, but, naturally, they also required mining companies to leave substantial amounts of coal in the ground. Justice Holmes insinuated that without average reciprocity of advantage, a regulation requiring that coal companies leave as much as one-third of their coal behind in pillars in the mine would constitute a taking. However, Justice Holmes argued that the pillars rescued the mining companies' own miners. Thus, while on one hand, the regulation destroyed valuable property rights by preventing the company from taking up large portions of coal, on the other hand, the regulation also rescued another valuable resource of the company, namely, the health and safety of its workers. The reciprocity was to be found in examining the whole scheme: while the pillars in X's mine might be more valuable than the safety benefit to X's workers from the pillars, X's workers also benefited from Y's pillars, and, together, X's and Y's workers benefited more from leaving the pillars in place than X and Y would earn together had they mined the pillars.

Unfortunately, neither *Pennsylvania Coal v. Mahon* nor any subsequent decision spelled out precisely what is meant by average reciprocity of advantage. One possible meaning is that where those affected by the regulation as a whole are benefited more than they are harmed, the regulatory action is not a taking. The important contribution of the doctrine is that the harm and benefit need not be measured at the same time, but rather over the entire effects of the regulatory scheme. In one period of time, a mining company may lose more as a result of leaving coal in place than it saves as a result of better worker safety. In other periods, the reverse may be true. Over time, however, for all affected parties, the regulation should produce benefits.

Yet, this is not the only possible meaning of the doctrine. While applying the term in his dissent in *Penn Central Transportation Co. v. New York City*,

Justice Rehnquist asserted that average reciprocity of advantage could only be utilized to save a regulation from mandatory compensation where the regulation's effects were widely felt, rather than applied to a small number of singled-out properties. This condition was apparently meant to supplement rather than replace the requirement that all ultimately benefit. Others have highlighted what appears to be an ironic aside in Justice Brandeis's dissent in *Pennsylvania Coal v. Mahon*, arguing that where a regulation produces more good than harm overall, it meets the conditions of average reciprocity of advantage because it is part of the larger web of regulations that affect businesses in society (Coletta 1990). Some scholars have suggested that average reciprocity of advantage presents the best explanation of why the government need not compensate landowners for permitting airplanes to fly over their land, notwithstanding the traditional *ad coelum* role, which grants landowners title to all air space up to the heavens (Epstein 1985). In this instance, it is unlikely that all affected parties will benefit as much as they are harmed, and vice versa. Some landowners doubtless fly little while residing close to airports and therefore suffering greatly from overflights. Other landowners suffer trivial losses from overflights while benefiting greatly from air travel. This concept of average reciprocity of advantage appears to refer to balance of benefits and harms not for individual parties, but rather over the entire affected populace. This latter concept of average reciprocity of advantage is difficult to justify from an economic standpoint.

To see why universal offsetting takings might not be the best approach, consider a regulation limiting or forbidding building within wetlands. In preserving the wetlands, the regulation doubtless alleviates drainage problems and therefore flooding of many properties. However, the benefits and harms are almost certainly not evenly distributed. To take the most extreme example, those who own properties within the wetlands that must remain undeveloped lose a huge portion—perhaps all—of the value of their lands. By contrast, those whose properties are upland of the wetlands, at the edge of where the floodwaters would reach were the wetlands developed, almost exclusively enjoy benefits from the regulation. They earn the entire value of the reduction in flooding risk to their property. When aggregating these costs and benefits over the entire society, it may well be that the benefits outstrip the harms. But this is true of any taking. Depending upon one's understanding of the reason for takings compensation, compensation should still be mandated for the regulation.

Consider first a corruption-blocking explanation of takings compensation. Because a regulation of this kind predictably helps certain types of owners and harms others, it represents an excellent opportunity for decision makers to extract payment from potentially aggrieved owners in order to sidetrack the regulation, or to extract payment from beneficiary owners in order to push it forward. Mandatory takings compensation for aggrieved owners reduces the pool of valuable regulatory favors that can be sold off by those decision makers. To be sure, the absence of mandatory givings charges still leaves decision makers with the ability to benefit from the sale of regulatory favors. They may still withhold beneficial regulation until adequately paid, and they may support socially harmful legislation because owners who benefit are willing to offer payment for the favor. This might seem to indicate that symmetry in not paying compensation and not assessing charges would lead to auctions for regulatory favors clearing the market at efficient prices. However, somewhat ironically, the imperfections of the corrupt market for political favors block this happy outcome. Specifically, because the benefits and harms are not symmetrically distributed, harmed owners will not be able to act collectively at the same cost as benefited owners. While this will not be true of every potential regulation, would-be beneficiaries will naturally seek out regulations where harmed owners cannot respond adequately, leading to adverse selection and the likelihood of inefficient regulations alongside efficient ones.

Next, consider a fiscal illusion explanation of takings compensation. If one assumes that a regulation is social welfare enhancing, there is no need to require payment as compensation for the taking; after all, the government has independently arrived at the decision to which takings compensation was to have led it. However, it is not clear why the overall utility of the regulation may not be assumed. This seizure of land by eminent domain and its subsequent transfer to a private developer may well enhance social utility. However, the fiscal illusion explanation of takings compensation is based on the idea that the best way to ensure that, in fact, such takings are social welfare enhancing is to mandate compensation. The same is true of a regulation. Indeed, if we were to assume that government always mandates welfare-enhancing regulations and is unaffected by fiscal illusion, there is little reason to worry about compensation. Compensation, in this view, would have no effect on the social welfare calculation other than administrative costs of compensating and social gains in reduction of uncertainty for the risk averse. Thus, absent extreme effects in one direction or the other due to administrative costs and insurance gains, regulatory decisions should be unchanged by compensation requirements for a benevolent government.

It is doubtless true that a fiscal illusion explanation would expect too few beneficial wetlands regulations, because decision makers would not take full account of the benefits to properties within the floodplain and outside the wetlands. However, this would be just as true of any taking carried out by eminent domain. The giving problem is ubiquitous and not restricted to regulatory takings. If it does not justify eliminating compensation for eminent domain, it cannot justify eliminating compensation for regulatory takings.

Finally, the interest group explanation would strongly indicate the value of compensation to wetlands property owners, lest there be too little wetlands regulation. Politically powerful owners of wetlands properties would use their concentrated political power to block beneficial wetlands regulation unless paid off. Guaranteed compensation sidelines them and permits the beneficial regulation to go forward.

It is worth noting that a handful of methods are used at the local level to recapture givings. These include transferable development rights, in-kind or monetary exactions, and betterment levies (see Bell and Parchomovsky 2001b; Hagman and Misczynski 1978). While none of these techniques is comprehensive—and none generally aims at recapturing the full value of the giving—each partially ameliorates the givings problem. To the extent that such techniques exist, they undermine the argument that givings can be seen as implicit compensation for regulatory takings. In any event, givings require separate analysis.

Regulatory Takings and Taxation

Taxation is the central means by which government raises revenues and naturally greatly affects property values. Surprisingly, however, few models have attempted to deal with taxation and takings in an integrated fashion. This is particularly surprising for believers in fiscal illusion explanations of takings compensation. If the government truly suffered from fiscal illusion, it would doubtless tax too much. Yet, there is no legal requirement of compensation for tax, and, indeed, such a requirement would be impossible, as it would involve returning the same revenue sought to be raised.

If we accept that taxation must remain uncompensated and that takings should remain compensated, the existence of taxation remains important for takings compensation analysis when the taxation is assessed on the basis of ownership of an asset. For land use, this type of taxation is an important part of the analysis, as ad valorem taxation is used almost universally throughout the United States as a means of raising local revenues. The use of ad valorem taxation thus opens up two possible amendments to the takings compensation analysis thus far. First, taxation and land use regulation might be viewed as explicitly linked in a manner that allows Tiebout competition. In other words, we might view the decision to live in a given municipality as essentially a question of accepting a given package of local property taxes and land use regulations, with the result that land use regulations could be viewed as accurately reflecting the preference of residents who have chosen to take up residence in the municipality. Second, the changes in tax revenues resulting from regulatory givings and takings could be seen as partial takings compensation and givings charges that might alter compensation policy.

Charles Tiebout created an entire branch of economic analysis of municipal competition in a pathbreaking article in which he challenged the traditional view (see Musgrave 1939; Samuelson 1954) that the absence of an effective preference revelation mechanism prevents efficient provision of public goods. Tiebout observed that at the local level, however, multiple localities with different revenue and expenditure patterns compete to attract residents, and residents choose among them by "voting with their feet"—by moving to the locality that best fits their preferences (Tiebout 1956). The greater the number of communities and the larger the variance among them, the closer individuals will come to satisfying their preferences. This analysis led Tiebout to conclude that, under certain conditions, it is possible to achieve efficient provision of local public goods. At least to some extent, the Tiebout hypothesis has found support in empirical studies that appear to suggest that migration patterns between city and suburbs are significantly affected by tax levels and investment in education (see Poindexter 1997).

If Tiebout is right and municipalities compete among one another for residents on the basis of property tax and land use policies, there is no need to mandate compensation for any land use regulation. This is because a municipality that takes too much property by land use regulation will find itself losing residents. The municipality will therefore reach the optimal amount of regulatory takings and taxation to fit the preference of the market niche of residents to which it caters. Indeed, William Fischel has argued in his homevoter hypothesis that homeowners dominate local politics because, as a group, homeowners' most valuable asset is generally their homes, and that asset's value is dramatically affected by local political decisions (Fischel 2001). However, Fischel also noted that the dominant local good that determines homevoter sorting is local school expenditures, rather than land use law. At the same time, local property controls enhance local property owners' voice at the expense of other interest groups that might compete for control of local property law. The result, Fischel argues, is that land use controls are more likely to resemble monopoly production and pricing by the local political controllers of land use law than efficient competitive results (Fischel 1985). Thus, a Tiebout analysis provides no reason to assume efficient regulation and therefore provides no reason to eliminate the compensation requirement.

I turn to viewing taxation as partial takings compensation and givings charge. Any reduction of property value reduces tax revenues that may be realized from that property, and vice versa. Even without a requirement of takings compensation or givings charge, government will already be partially incentivized not to take too much or give too little.

Tax policies also interact explicitly with regulatory takings and givings. First, tax policy is often explicitly tied to regulatory favors or restrictions. Extra taxes may be levied against areas that have received zoning benefits (betterment levies), and development areas may receive favorable tax treatment as part of a plan to encourage the full exploitation of regulatory benefits (Bell and Parchomovsky 2001b). Second, expected tax burdens are known to the marketplace and are therefore capitalized into the price of realty. Specifically, the price of a piece of real estate in a given area reflects the tax-adjusted stream of benefits and costs that would be realized by anticipated owners (Fischel 2001).

However, once again, this does not provide good reason for treating regulatory takings differently. Since property taxes are generally assessed at a very small percentage of the value of the asset, taxation changes will reflect only a small percentage of the value of the taking or giving. Blume, Rubinfeld, and Shapiro (1984) have made a case that partial compensation is the best result that may be obtained given the restraints of fiscal illusion and moral hazard, and one might anticipate that relying on property taxation would be appealing in their model. However, the model offers no reason to treat regulation differently than any other taking of properties subject to ad valorem taxation. Indeed, if it is optimal to rely upon the partial compensation effect created by property taxation to produce the correct amount of land use regulation, it is optimal to rely upon the same to produce the correct amount of eminent domain takings of land. Thus, if the small changes in tax burden resulting from regulatory changes constitute adequate compensation for regulatory takings, the elimination of taxes that result from having property taken by eminent domain should be sufficient compensation for the ordinary taking. Of course, that is not an argument that holds sway under current law.

Conclusions

In this chapter, I have explored the economic understandings of takings compensation in order to determine the proper regulatory takings compensation policy. The case for takings compensation is far from perfect, and serious arguments can and have been made against it. In addition, a case can be made that property regulation and takings are made inefficient by the failure to properly account for givings and the incentives created by the interaction of ad valorem taxation and takings compensation. However, once compensation is a required accompaniment to eminent domain takings, it is extremely difficult to draft a cogent argument for ruling out regulatory takings in general.

REFERENCES

Arrow, Kenneth. 1971. *Essays in the theory of risk-bearing.* Chicago: Markham Publishing.
Barzel, Yoram. 1997. *Economic analysis of property rights.* New York: Cambridge University Press.
Bell, Abraham. 2003. Not just compensation. *Journal of Contemporary Legal Issues* 13(1):29ff.
Bell, Abraham, and Gideon Parchomovsky. 2001a. Givings. *Yale Law Journal* 111: 547–618.
———. 2001b. Takings reassessed. *Virginia Law Review* 87(2):277–318.
———. 2007. Taking compensation private. *Stanford Law Review* 59:871–906.
———. 2009. Compensating against corruption. Unpublished manuscript.
Blume, Lawrence E., Daniel L. Rubinfeld, and Perry Shapiro. 1984. The taking of land: When should compensation be paid? *Quarterly Journal of Economics* 99(1):71–92.
Blume, Lawrence E., and Perry Shapiro. 1984. Compensation for takings: An economic analysis. *California Law Review* 72:569–628.
Coletta, Raymond R. 1990. Reciprocity of advantage and regulatory takings: Toward a new theory of takings jurisprudence. *American University Law Review* 40:297ff.
Cooter, Robert. 1985. Unity in tort, contract, and property: The model of precaution. *California Law Review* 73:1–51.
Epstein, Richard A. 1985. *Takings: Private property and the power of eminent domain.* Cambridge, MA: Harvard University Press.
Farber, Daniel A. 1992a. Public choice and just compensation. *Constitutional Commentary* 9:279–308.

————. 1992b. Economic analysis and just compensation. *International Review of Law and Economics* 12:125–138.

Fischel, William A. 1985. *The economics of zoning laws.* Baltimore: Johns Hopkins University Press.

————. 1995. *Regulatory takings: Law, economics, and politics.* Cambridge, MA: Harvard University Press.

————. 2001. *The homevoter hypothesis: How home values influence local government taxation, school finance, and land-use policies.* Cambridge, MA: Harvard University Press.

Hagman, Donald, and Dean Misczynski, eds. 1978. *Windfalls for wipeouts: Land value recapture and compensation.* Washington, DC: Planning Press, American Planning Association.

Kanner, Gideon. 1998. Hunting the snark, not the quark: Has the Supreme Court been competent in its effort to formulate coherent regulatory takings law? *Urban Lawyer* 30:307–308.

Kaplow, Louis. 1986. An economic analysis of legal transitions. *Harvard Law Review* 99:509–617.

Krier, James. 1997. The takings-puzzle puzzle. *William and Mary Law Review* 38(1): 1143ff.

Krier, James E., and Christopher Serkin. 2004. Public ruses. *Michigan State Law Review* 2004:859–875.

Levmore, Saul. 1991. Takings, torts, and special interests. *Virginia Law Review* 77:1333–1368.

Merrill, Thomas W. 2002. Incomplete compensation for takings. *New York University Environmental Law Journal* 11:110–135.

Miceli, Thomas J., and Kathleen Segerson. 1994. Regulatory takings: When should compensation be paid? *Journal of Legal Studies* 23(2):749–776.

————. 1996. *Compensation for regulatory takings: An economic analysis with applications.* Stamford, CT: JAI Press.

Michelman, Frank I. 1967. Property, utility, and fairness: Comments on the ethical foundations of "just compensation" law. *Harvard Law Review* 80:1165ff.

Musgrave, Richard A. 1939. The voluntary exchange theory of public economy. *Quarterly Journal of Economics* 53:213–237.

Niskanen, William A. 1971. *Bureaucracy and representative government.* Chicago: Aldine, Atherton.

Olson, Mancur, Jr. 1965. *The logic of collective action: Public goods and the theory of groups.* Cambridge, MA: Harvard University Press.

Penalver, Eduardo. 2004. Regulatory taxings. *Columbia Law Review* 105:2182–2254.

Peters, Guy. 1978. *Politics of bureaucracy: A comparative perspective.* Essex, UK: Longman Group.

Poindexter, Georgette C. 1997. Collective individualism: Deconstructing the legal city. *University of Pennsylvania Law Review* 145:607ff.

Posner, Richard A. 1974. Theories of regulation. *Bell Journal of Economics and Management Science* 5(2):335–358.

Rawls, John. 1958. Justice as fairness. *Philosophical Review* 67:164–194.

————. 1971. *A theory of justice.* Cambridge, MA: Harvard University Press.

Rose, Carol M. 1984. Mahon reconstructed: Why the takings issue is still a muddle. *Southern California Law Review* 57:561ff.

Samuelson, Paul A. 1954. The pure theory of public expenditure. *Review of Economic Statistics* 36:387–389.

Serkin, Christopher. 2005. The meaning of value: Assessing just compensation for regulatory takings. *Northwestern University Law Review* 99(2):677–742.

Shavell, Steven. 1987. *Economic analysis of accident law*. Cambridge, MA: Harvard University Press.

Stigler, George J. 1971. The theory of economic regulation. *Bell Journal of Economics and Management Science* 2(1):3–21.

Tiebout, Charles M. 1956. A pure theory of legal expenditures. *Journal of Political Economy* 64:416–424.

Tullock, Gordon. 1989. *The economics of special privilege and rent seeking*. Norwell, MA: Kluwer Academic Publishers.

COMMENTARY
Perry Shapiro

Abraham Bell's excellent work is both cogent and wide ranging. It starts with a review and critique of the existing work on compensation for takings and extends that to compensation for damage from regulation. Its theme is that the desirability and degree of compensation, whether for physical or regulatory taking, depends on the motivation of both the landowners and the government. Therefore I choose to do variations on Bell's theme.

No Compensation for Physical Taking

In the early 1980s Larry Blume, Dan Rubinfeld, and I published a paper that challenged the prevailing view, namely that the government must pay prices for its actions or else its rapacious appetite would not be satisfied until it condemned much too much private property (Blume, Rubinfeld, and Shapiro 1984). We showed that compensation incentives can cut both ways: while they may direct the government toward more efficient choices, they may also encourage landowners to engage in inefficient rent seeking.

Later, Bill Fischel and I demonstrated that, if efficiency is the sole criterion by which compensation rules are judged, the answer to what is efficient depends on what the true model of government is. In two papers, admirably summarized in Bill's important book *Regulatory Takings*, we employed the veil of ignorance (the constitutional perspective) to examine the relationship between governmental objectives and efficient compensation (Fischel 1995). From the ex ante perspective of the veil of ignorance, no compensation for taking is efficient in two polar cases: The first is when the government is both omniscient and social welfare-maximizing. The second is when the government's course is undeterred by any costs. For governments at neither of the two extremes, some compensation, but not at full market value, is necessary for efficiency.

Fairness remained open in the quest for (two-sided) efficient compensation rules. It can be argued that ex ante fairness of the constitutional approach is a reasonable moral objective. While this is good in principle, it does not translate well into public policy. Maybe it is equitable to find ultimate winners and losers in a voluntary participation lottery, but it is not the same when the government is involved. When a person loses the family home in a roll of the Las Vegas dice, that is viewed as fair. When a person's home is taken by the government for a public purpose, it is grossly unfair.[1]

---

1. On fairness, according to *Armstrong v. United States*, 364 U.S. 40 (1960): "Government [should not] forc[e] some people alone to bear public burdens which, in all fairness and justice, should be borne by the public as a whole."

Whatever the conclusion about efficient and fair compensation, how can the use of eminent domain be justified when public policy appears to have the loosest connection to the public welfare? Isn't it suspicious when a public agency acquires condemned property at current market value and then hands it to a developer at hugely favorable terms? The eminent domain practice is ripe for abuse and corruption. Nonetheless, there are reasonable justifications for it, but our models of government behavior and choice are too narrow to highlight its benefits.

In the standard model, landowners returns are concave functions of the amount invested in capital that is lost in the event of a taking. Government is motivated in different ways, depending on the view of the modeler. The objective of government is always certain returns from its input of condemned land. The developer, if he appears in the models, is the passive recipient of land that is turned into his profit. It is as if redevelopment projects grow instantaneously and without risk from the land (enjoyed on a 99-year land lease for $1 a year). In point of fact, at their inceptions large redevelopment projects are risky undertakings. The parties involved, government and developers, contribute different things to them. The expertise to successfully accomplish a redevelopment is likely not available in the government. Successful developers know a considerable amount about that business, and it makes good sense for the development to be done by private agents. Nonetheless, the large risks involved may deter developers unless the possible profits are extraordinary. The assemblage of land put at the disposal of the developer may be nothing more than a way for the private and public sectors to share the development risk.

Taking and Giving

The U.S. Constitution is clear that compensation for physical taking is compensable, and the standard for compensability is strict—but perhaps is in the process of changing. Proposition 98 on California's June 2008 ballot, had it been successful, would seemingly have required government to compensate individuals whose land value was diminished by the government's actions (most specifically, by changes in zoning). But it did not require those whose land values were enhanced by regulation to surrender the increment to the public treasury. This, by the way, was the proposal explored by Hagman and Misczynski (1978). Such a proposal might find some support among the disciples of Henry George.

The "windfall for wipeout" proposal, if not likely to find much political support, is at least implementable if all public benefits are reflected in land values. Georgian disciples will quickly understand that a properly assessed ad valorem tax (one that fully covers the cost of the public project) can be used to satisfy the cost of the taking by collecting some of the giving. Things are more difficult when the benefits are diffuse and not fully reflected in land values.

Concerns about fairness may motivate the desire to compensate the losers from a regulatory change. Nonetheless, even if it would be possible to compute the size of the losses, the costs of doing so are potentially very large. If claims of loss require litigation, without other ways to measure loss, the costs can be very high. If it is true that governments are deterred by the potential high costs, the end result is looser regulation than is efficient.

It seems to me that a more serious criticism of the proposal to compensate landowners for regulation-induced capital losses is that it selects but one segment of the population—namely, the landowning class—for special treatment. Almost all actions of government can be construed as regulation. Is it righteous for landowners to be compensated for a downzone loss while workers are not compensated for lost jobs and stockholders for capital losses resulting from eliminating a tariff?[2]

A Modest Proposal

A general prescription for compensation is not possible. Potential taking situations are numerous, and a type of compensation that can work in one situation has problems when applied to another. The notion of taxing the beneficiaries of a public taking to recompense the taking is appealing. The prescription works only if the beneficiaries are identifiable. When all benefits accrue to untaken land (as, for instance, a road that makes some land more accessible), a fully efficient and equitable compensation scheme is possible. The market can supply the data to fully implement it.

Assembling land to build a public road is the least controversial use of eminent domain. The condemned receive the pre-road market value, and the survivors enjoy a capital gain because the drive to the city takes less time. Compensation of speculative market value creates the moral hazard problem highlighted by Blume, Rubinfeld, and Shapiro (1984). Suppose that compensation is the road-enhanced value as reflected by the market for surviving land (Niemans and Shapiro, in press). In this case, the pre-project market value of the condemned land will be the same as that of the land that is not condemned. The practical advantage is that the information for correct compensation is supplied by the market. The compensation scheme promotes efficient landowner decisions and is equitable. Efficiency is achieved because there is no advantage for landowners to engage in wasteful rent-seeking investments. It is equitable because the owners of condemned land participate in the benefits of the public projects to the same extent as do their uncondemned neighbors.

---

2. This, of course, is not fully correct. Unemployment insurance can be thought of as public compensation for canceled government contracts. But it is financed in part by ongoing contributions from employers to a public unemployment fund. Perhaps unemployment compensation could be a model for landowner compensation, namely, that all landowners are offered the chance to enter a mutual insurance scheme that reimburses them for capital losses resulting from changes in regulations.

Conclusions

Rather than a critique, my comments are a variation on a theme. The rules for a variation require a return to the theme at the end. The examples support Abraham Bell by highlighting that the efficient amount of compensation for a physical taking or a regulation-induced capital loss depends on the motivation of both landowners and government.

REFERENCES

Blume, Larry, Daniel Rubinfeld, and Perry Shapiro. 1984. The taking of land: When should compensation be paid? *Quarterly Journal of Economics* 99:71–92.

Fischel, William A. 1995. *Regulatory takings: Law, economics, and politics.* Cambridge, MA: Harvard University Press.

Hagman, Donald G., and Dean J. Misczynski, eds. 1978. *Windfalls for wipeouts: Land value capture and compensation.* Washington, DC: Planner Press, American Planning Association.

Niemans, Paul, and Perry Shapiro. In press. Efficiency and fairness: Compensation for takings. *International Review of Law and Economics.*

PROPERTY RIGHTS APPROACHES TO ACHIEVING LAND POLICY GOALS

11

Land Registration, Economic Development, and Poverty Reduction

Klaus Deininger and Gershon Feder

While early theories of development focused on accumulation of capital, macroeconomic policies, and natural endowments as key determinants of performance in terms of growth and poverty reduction, an influential strand of literature has postulated a central role of institutions as a precondition of economic growth. A growing body of evidence based on cross-country data (Acemoglu and Johnson 2005; Acemoglu, Johnson, and Robinson 2001), country-level studies (Acemoglu, Johnson, and Robinson 2004; Banerjee and Iyer 2004; Nugent and Robinson 2002), and firm-level analysis (Johnson, McMillan, and Woodruff 2002) emphasized the overarching importance of good institutions for economic development.[1] Specifically, institutions guaranteeing property rights were found to be far more important for growth than were contracting institutions (Acemoglu and Johnson 2005).

In developing as well as developed economies, land and real estate are a key part of households' wealth. The extent to which such assets are used to leverage credit that can be used for investment and other economic pursuits varies widely. For example, in 2002 the ratio of mortgage debt to GDP in the United States was 58 percent as compared to at most 14 percent in any Latin American country, 11 percent in any Middle Eastern country (with the exception of Israel),

---

1. An influential paper defines good institutions as follows: "There must be enforcement of property rights for a broad cross-section of society so that all individuals have an incentive to invest. There must also be some degree of equality of opportunity in society, including such things as equality before the law, so that those with good investment opportunities can take advantage of them" (Acemoglu, Johnson, and Robinson 2004, 12).

and 22 percent in any South or East Asian country except Japan, Taiwan, Singapore, and Hong Kong (Besley and Ghatak 2008). This striking difference has led influential thinkers to suggest that a main reason for low growth in developing countries is their relatively undeveloped system of property rights and, in particular, the extent to which land and real estate are registered, restricting the ability to transform "dead assets" into "live capital" (de Soto 2000).

Attention to property rights institutions is hardly a recent phenomenon. Throughout history the social and economic benefits from secure and well-defined land rights and from public recording and notice of transactions have led many societies to develop customs and pass laws to define the nature of such rights; to establish public institutions, such as courts and police, to enforce the laws; and to establish registries to record land rights or transactions, often with the goal of obtaining tax revenue. A key element in the enforcement of land rights that evolved over history is a system of land records that provides evidence of individuals' or groups' property rights. As early as 2350 B.C. evidence from Egypt indicates that "ownership of land would be transferred by a 'house document' drawn up on papyrus by sellers, signed by three witnesses, and stamped by an official seal which indicated the end of the document so that nothing could be added. . . . All lands were accounted for centrally, being registered in the office of the visier, the Pharaoh's prime minister. Wills were recorded, and new titles issued there" (Powelson 1988, 17). Similar systems are reported for the Assyrian Empire centered in Mesopotamia (c. 1200–750 B.C.) and its successor Babylonian and Sassanian empires (500 B.C.–A.D. 651) (Powelson 1988).

In modern times demarcation and survey of land boundaries, registration and record keeping, adjudication of rights, resolution of conflicts, and land management are normally referred to as "land administration" (UNECE 1996). In many developing countries the absence of such institutions and the supporting legal framework have prompted bilateral and multilateral institutions to support interventions to establish them or improve their functioning, with the expectation that they will enhance the security of property rights. Such programs, often referred to as land titling projects, normally include elements of legal and institutional reform, upgrading of land registries, and large-scale adjudication of individual land rights together with publicity campaigns and mechanisms (such as mobile tribunals) to resolve disputes quickly and at low cost. This is normally followed by issuance and registration of individual and in some cases group rights to land (not always in the form of titles).

The objective of this piece is to review existing evidence on the effectiveness of arrangements for land administration and related interventions in improving economic outcomes. In cases where evidence is weak or controversial, we sketch ways in which research to evaluate the impact of ongoing programs, possibly with minor additions or changes in their design, could help to provide insights to guide policy. To set the stage, the following section reviews the justification for public involvement in adjudication of property rights and the main possible channels through which well-defined property rights will affect economic and social outcomes under ideal conditions. This is followed by a discussion of obstacles that may undermine the effectiveness or sustainability of such interventions or may even result in undesirable outcomes: specifically, highly unequal preexisting power relationships and poor governance, imperfections in markets for credit and insurance, high transaction costs, and low land values due to relative land abundance. The next section presents available evidence on the impact of land policy interventions in terms of improving administrative efficiency, reducing the need for households to engage in costly property rights protection, fostering land-related investment, increasing land values and land market participation, and improving credit access. The chapter concludes by highlighting implications for development practitioners as well as researchers.

Conceptual Framework

JUSTIFICATION FOR GOVERNMENT INTERVENTION TO IMPROVE TENURE SECURITY

Property rights are social conventions backed by the enforcement power of the state (at various levels) or the community that allow individuals or groups to lay "a claim to a benefit or income stream that the state will agree to protect through the assignment of duty to others who may covet, or somehow interfere with, the benefit stream" (Sjaastad and Bromley 2000). By defining who is entitled to reap the benefit streams that flow from a resource, the way in which land rights are distributed is a key element of the power structure and social fabric of society. Moreover, by establishing a correspondence between the effort expended in increasing resource values and the rewards from such activity, land rights are also a key determinant of investment, the scope for efficiency-enhancing land transfers, and economic growth. In this section we first discuss the reasons underlying public provision and enforcement of property rights to land, the ways in which this is normally accomplished, and the economic implications expected to arise from doing so in an ideal setting. Real-world circumstances differ, of course, from the ideal world assumed in the conceptual discussion, an issue that is taken up in subsequent sections.

The justification for public interventions to secure property rights is threefold: (1) the public good nature of property rights enforcement; (2) the cost savings from having reliable information on land ownership available publicly; and (3) the scope for providing other public goods and infrastructure at least cost. The broad distribution of the benefits associated with providing information about the assignment of property rights to land and the enforcement of such rights provide a strong rationale for government involvement. Well-defined property rights reduce the need to expend economically valuable resources in defending claims and allow the resources to be used for productive investment instead (Grossman and Mendoza 2001). If property rights are incomplete or ill-defined, the entrepreneurs and households who hold property rights to land will need to spend resources to maintain their rights. Investments such as guards and fences to defend rights against possible intruders and challengers often have little direct social or productive value, lead to dissipation of rents, and divert resources from more productive uses (Allen and Lueck 1992). The privately optimal amount of spending on protection will often be excessive from a social point of view (De Meza and Gould 1992; Feder and Feeny 1991; Malik and Schwab 1991), while economies of scale in protection add another argument for public sector involvement. The poor may not be able to afford the associated costs at all and, without the ability to enlist the power of the state to protect their property rights, may end up in otherwise avoidable poverty traps. Public enforcement of property rights to land clearly has benefits that extend beyond individual landowners and that are to a large extent nonrival, that is, one person's enjoyment will not reduce others' ability to benefit from them, although some of them allow exclusion of others, characteristics generally associated with a club good, arguing for public provision (Lueck and Miceli 2006; Shavell 2003).

Having reliable information on land rights available publicly, such as in a deeds registry or a title registration system, will also reduce the need for individual agents to conduct costly searches to verify the true owner of a tract of land and at the same time reduce the risk of illegitimate challenges to an owner's right. This can encourage temporary land transfers to more efficient producers through land rental arrangements and reduce inefficiencies from the presence of asymmetric information. Such informational asymmetries are less of an issue as long as potential transactions are limited to members of the same community who have good and symmetric information on the identity of the possessors of rights and the legitimacy of their claims, even if no formal titles or officially sanctioned deeds exist. In such cases public conduct of land transactions in front of witnesses is often sufficient to prevent fraudulent outcomes.[2] In more complex settings where greater mobility of agents implies opportunities for land transactions among individuals and groups beyond the community, the scope for asymmetric information is much higher; the would-be buyer cannot be certain that the seller is indeed the legitimate possessor of the rights and is entitled to convey them further.

Finally, availability of land information also provides an opportunity to effectively reduce externalities and supply public goods, in particular infrastructure, in a cost-effective way. Even in the most individualistic system, the rights enjoyed by individuals are never unrestricted, but are instead limited by the need to have rights holders contribute to broader public goods. Individuals can come together in user groups and other formal or informal associations to establish voluntarily norms and restrictions on owners' ability to exercise their rights. Such rules can set limits on externalities and provide public goods such as en-

---

2. An early example of such a practice is reported in Genesis, where a land purchase by Abraham took place in public in front of notables and elders who served as witnesses.

vironmental amenities and green spaces. Authorities can also use land information to restrict land use decisions by individuals to avoid socially and environmentally harmful outcomes and internalize externalities, such as by using zoning regulations to prevent undesirable externalities or by passing planning laws to ensure minimum standards based on consensus reflecting their social value (Ellickson 1993).

CHANNELS FOR IMPACTS

If property rights are secure and well-defined and public institutions can be relied upon for enforcement, the risk of expropriation is low (Clark 2003). There will be less need for individuals to exert effort—for example, by spending time or resources to physically guard land or to secure or clarify land rights, often in the context of conflicts. To the extent that the time freed up this way can be used more productively, land registration programs provide net social gains. The magnitude of these gains depends on the extent to which the land registration system induces higher levels of tenure security and the nature, magnitude, and opportunity cost of the resources thus freed up as compared to the cost of the land administration apparatus.

The ability to verify boundaries at low cost and the legal measures to remove reasons for conflicts or allow dealing with conflicts in a more expeditious manner can reduce the incidence of conflict. Programs to establish land administration systems often include low-cost means for expedited conflict resolution. These not only reduce the amount of time and resources spent in unproductive activities, but they can also increase peace and social stability and allow land that had been "frozen" due to conflict to be developed and brought to more productive uses. To the extent that land-related conflicts in many developing countries clog up the courts and reduce the effectiveness of the judicial system, avoiding such conflicts can also enhance the overall effectiveness of the judicial system.

While most of the literature implicitly relies on a unitary household model, women's ability to own land is often severely constrained. Even in countries where the constitution outlaws gender discrimination, females can often access land only through male relatives, and their ability to inherit land or hold on to it in case of divorce is severely limited.[3] This affects their bargaining power within the household, the allocation of household spending among alternative uses, the efficiency with which land is used (Udry 1996), and participation in

---

3. In many monogamous African countries, land rights at death remain in the husband's lineage. Even though such arrangements are under pressure to change from a number of directions, including high levels of mortality in the context of HIV/AIDS, they still expose a woman to the risk of losing access to assets, in addition to family labor, in case of the death of her spouse and, in a number of cases, have led to female land being registered in the name of male relatives. Also, in Uganda land conflict has been shown to affect women disproportionately (Deininger and Castagnini 2006).

nonfarm opportunities (Quisumbing and Maluccio 2003). Legal changes as well as interventions to register land can provide a basis for better enforcement of existing provisions in favor of gender equality or enhance women's awareness of their rights and their ability to demand compliance, such as by issuing joint certificates. Land registration that takes into account local realities and enforcement capacity can contribute to women's social and economic empowerment (Joireman 2008).

In addition, programs that increase tenure security or reduce the threat of expropriation, such as titling programs under appropriate circumstances, encourage land-related investment unless such factors as a severely depressed economic environment prevent these impacts from materializing. If institutions to enforce them are effective, secure property rights provide land users with assurance that they will be able to enjoy the fruits of their labor, encouraging them to make long-term investments and manage land sustainably (Besley 1995).

Adding the right to transfer land to others, through either rental or sale, encourages investment by making it easier to liquidate and recoup the full value in case of exogenous shocks (Ayalew, Dercon, and Gautam 2005; Deininger and Jin 2006). Transferability is also necessary to allow land to move toward more efficient users, thereby maximizing allocative efficiency and output. Furthermore, the ability to rent land allows labor to move from agricultural to nonagricultural work in the context of economic development by enabling landowners to participate in the rural nonfarm economy without closing off the possibility of returning to farming, while enabling those remaining in farming to increase their income by cultivating larger areas (Carter and Yao 2002; Deininger 2003; Kung 2002). However, unless land rights are sufficiently secure, landowners may not want to rent land out because the land may be taken away from them (Holden and Yohannes 2002; Yang 1997) or out of fear that renters will claim land ownership and refuse to return the land upon expiry of the contract, possibly leading to large efficiency losses (Benjamin and Brandt 2002). Land registration can do much to remove the perceived risk of land rental transactions by strengthening property rights and providing documentation that will allow enforcement at lower cost. Such a reduction of perceived risk will allow more rental transactions, possibly at lower rental prices. The magnitude and economic impact will depend on the extent to which productivity-enhancing land rentals were inhibited by lack of security without land registration and the size of the productivity differential between the parties involved. In rural settings the latter will be higher in a more-developed nonagricultural economy. For example, land rental in China has been shown to contribute to the diversification of the rural economy (Deininger and Jin 2008b).

Low-cost access to reliable information on land ownership will also reduce the transaction cost of exchanging land in sales markets by eliminating uncertainty as would-be buyers reflect the risk to their future ability to enjoy the benefits from the land by offering lower prices than in situations where no uncertainty exists. The would-be seller, when comparing the proceeds from a sale transaction to the revenues that can be generated by operating the land, will be less inclined to sell even though there may be no uncertainty about the property rights and no real reason for a lower price for the land. There is thus asymmetry in the information available to the buyer and to the seller. If it is assumed that transactions in a well-functioning economy normally take place when the would-be buyer has a higher stream of benefits from the land than the would-be seller, and is therefore able to offer a price that reflects those higher benefits, it can be intuitively concluded that economic efficiency is lost when some transactions do not take place due to asymmetric information. The possession of land rights documented by a state-sanctioned document can eliminate the asymmetry of information and facilitate more efficiency-enhancing transactions in which land rights are transferred through sale from individuals or groups with lower benefit streams to those who can obtain higher benefits from the same land.

Finally, a formal and low-cost way to unambiguously identify land ownership without physical inspection, inquiry of neighbors, or interaction with an extensive bureaucracy will allow the use of land as collateral, thereby reducing the transaction cost of access to credit. In the absence of other obstacles to the operation of financial markets and the effective exercise of land rights, formalizing land tenure and establishment of registries can encourage development of financial markets and the associated sophisticated financial instruments that draw on the abstract representation of property rights provided by formal titles (de Soto 2000). Even where there is limited activity in land sales markets, the ability to sell land has important implications through the scope of using land as a collateral for credit (Besley and Ghatak 2008). As a large literature discusses, lending entails the provision of resources at present against a promise of repayment with interest in the future. Lenders face risk due to the uncertain nature of the borrower's future ability or willingness to repay. The borrower has better information than the lender about his own prospects of being able to repay, and it is intuitively apparent that this leads to the delivery of a lower volume of credit, in particular since interest cannot be adjusted fully to reflect the risk, necessitating credit rationing (Stiglitz and Weiss 1981). With less credit than in a world with symmetric information, efficiency is lost; at the margin, some investments that would be remunerative even after accounting for the current opportunity costs of loanable funds are not undertaken.

To reduce the presence of asymmetric information, credit markets developed the procedure of collateral, with land as a universally common form of collateral due to its immobility and relative indestructibility (Binswanger and Rosenzweig 1986). The usefulness of land as a collateral depends on the absence of uncertainty and asymmetric information regarding the ability of the borrower who offers the collateral to convey the rights over land to the lender in the case of default on the loan (Feder and Feeny 1991). Thus, in the same way in which titles can facilitate a larger volume of land transactions, they can contribute to a larger volume of credit transactions. This can increase the efficiency of credit markets by facilitating loans whose true risk is less than that perceived by lenders in the absence of collateral. To the extent that this allows more investments that are worthwhile, there will be an improvement in overall economic efficiency.

The formal work on the impact of risk and uncertainty provides much of the theoretical underpinnings of the discussion on the hypothesized impacts of titling that were outlined rather heuristically above. But some specific formal models address the role of titled land rights (Feder et al. 1988). Within a farming context, the models perceived two types of land—titled and untitled—and three types of credit: institutional short- and long-term credit available only with titled land as a collateral, and short-term informal credit that depends on the value of land regardless of whether it is or is not titled. Owners of untitled land face a risk of loss of land, with a given probability. Maximizing a utility function of terminal wealth (exhibiting risk aversion) by choosing the amount of land and capital to acquire and variable inputs to use in farming provides the characterization of optimal decisions by farmers, while land price determination is driven by a condition that the optimal value of the farmer's utility be equal on titled or untitled land. The model yields results that are compatible with the intuitive propositions suggested. In particular, in equilibrium the price of titled land will be higher than the price of untitled land, and capital as well as output per unit of land will be higher on titled land. Furthermore, the equilibrium price of untitled land is negatively related to the probability of land loss. The policy implication is that, at the margin, moving untitled land to titled status increases investment and output and thus improves social welfare. An important insight from the model is a proof that the difference between the prices of titled and untitled land can provide a measure of the social welfare gains of titling hitherto untitled land, if appropriate adjustments are made for the distorting effects of risk and imperfections in capital markets. A variant of this model demonstrates that individual willingness to pay for titling is higher than the true social benefits of titles (Feder and Feeny 1991).

Realities That Can Prevent Beneficial Effects from Materializing ——

The above discussion suggests that the magnitude of the impact of systems of land registration will vary with circumstances and will be negatively affected by market imperfections. This section discusses situations in which one would not expect the successful introduction and operation of land registration systems, in particular: (1) unequal distribution of power, bad or ineffective governance, and absence of the necessary checks and balances that will undermine the impartiality or credibility of the registration system; (2) limitations of credit markets that can limit the supply of or demand for credit and the scope for use of land as collateral; (3) low efficiency of land administration systems that prevents them from delivering value-added services in a cost-effective manner; and (4) relative land abundance that can reduce the scarcity value of land and lead to adoption of alternative arrangements to secure rights. In each case, we aim to draw conclusions regarding the design and implementation of effective registration systems.

POWER RELATIONS AND DEFICIENCIES IN GOVERNANCE

Land has historically been a key source of social and economic power. While the tendency to monopolize land access was particularly strong in colonial contexts (Binswanger, Deininger, and Feder 1995; Conning and Robinson 2007), it did not disappear thereafter in situations with highly unequal land access (Baland and Robinson 2003) or in African countries, which often established state monopolies over land, resulting in high levels of mismanagement and corruption (Durand-Lasserve and Royston 2002; Mabogunje 1992). This implies that considerable efficiency gains may be achieved from better management or privatization of state land (Kaganova and McKelar 2006). At the same time, it is evident that the assumption underpinning our conceptual discussion—of an honest, efficient, and effective government and a social system in which checks and balances preclude abuse of power—may not always hold. The state's monopoly on the exercise of legitimate power, which is a precondition for the functioning of advanced societies and secure property rights, can be abused to appropriate property or to assist unfair acquisition of land by elites, thus undermining the security of property rights. Increased land values and demand for land by outside investors increase the potential rent-seeking gains from bureaucratic interference. The politically motivated award of state land to political cronies has been a concern in Kenya, Cambodia, and Nicaragua.[4] In such situations, land registration programs risk becoming a way of ex post formalizing land grabs. Even if abuse of power is not widespread, weak and ineffective government can render a land registration system (and other public services) ineffective and not worth the cost of setting up.

An unbalanced power structure within society exacerbates the inadequacies of a titling system under ineffective governments, as the combination of these deficiencies provides opportunities for abuses and utilization of the titling system to provide advantages to the powerful (Feder and Nishio 1999; Jansen and Roquas 1998). If corruption is endemic, individuals and groups cannot rely on state-issued documents, which could have been altered fraudulently with the assistance of corrupt officials and legal personnel to benefit challengers who

---

4. The Ndungu commission in Kenya notes that land grabbing by public officials that had reached systemic proportions during 1980–2005 was "one of the most pronounced manifestations of corruption and moral decadence in our society" (Government of Kenya 2004, 192). In Cambodia, concessions were often of a speculative nature as indicated by the fact that fewer than half had even demarcated their boundaries and few started production. As they were often established without following proper processes such as community consultation and investigation in the field, protests or encroachment on concession land by local people was reported in two-thirds of the cases. However, the cadastral commission and courts were often unable to rectify problems against physical violence and intimidation by concession holders (Kato 1998; Leuprecht 2004). The economic impact was limited by the fact that fewer than one-third of concessionaires paid the required deposit, very few made the rather low rent payments, and tax payment was virtually nonexistent (McKenny and Tola 2002).

can pay higher bribes. This creates uncertainty and risks, the elimination of which paradoxically was a key reason for introducing land registration in the first place. Not surprisingly, the weaker and poorer segments of society suffer the negative consequences of land titling in situations of ineffective or dishonest government. Without effective enforcement, including impartial courts and police forces, the rights presumably protected by titles may exist on paper but not be enforceable. For titling programs to have the desired effects, good governance is thus essential.

When titling of land is introduced in replacement of customary or less formal systems of land rights allocation and verification, information regarding the procedures to be undertaken may not be easily available to all affected. In fact, in Uganda, where the law was changed but little implementation occurred, legal knowledge, as ascertained by an "objective" test, had a significant impact on productivity of land use, but cannot be assumed as given (Deininger, Ali, and Yamano 2008), suggesting that the potential for systematic dissemination and awareness campaigns may have been underestimated. Wealthier segments of society often have better access to information and, if they are able to influence or bribe officials, may utilize the opportunities opened by the new system to acquire and document rights that did not fully belong to them. A less nefarious, yet still unfair, form of taking advantage of access to information is the ability to buy up untitled land before it becomes eligible for titling. Since the price of untitled land can be significantly lower than the price of the same land once it is titled, the possession of information on lands that will be served by titling and the knowledge of how to obtain title provide opportunities for capital gains for the better informed. There are, of course, measures to reduce opportunities for abuses and for taking advantage at the expense of the weaker segments. The effectiveness of such measures depends on the efficiency and quality of governance. Thus, while it is important for land administration institutions to provide high-quality service in a cost-effective way, an appropriate and broader policy, legal, and institutional environment needs to exist as well.

LIMITATIONS OF CREDIT MARKETS

The discussion thus far has abstracted from imperfections in markets for credit and insurance that are widespread in most developing countries. The existence of such imperfections and their interactions with other markets affects the potential benefits from land market interventions. The credit market effects of formally documented land rights may differ in rural and urban areas; within urban areas they may differ for residential land and commercial land. Rural credit markets in developing countries are typically less developed in that their dependence on weather and other natural phenomena (for example, pest attacks) introduce risks that are correlated across large numbers of would-be borrowers, limiting the ability of lenders to diversify and increasing the risk of rural lending. Consequently, the utility of collateral is lessened in rural areas; a bad outcome will imply default by many borrowers at once, flooding the land market with foreclosed properties whose value may be much diminished. While long-term credit markets in rural areas of developing countries are limited and tend to be dominated by state entities, short-term credit markets are more prevalent, and there is a significant presence of informal lenders. The transaction costs of collateral registration may often exceed the benefit it generates for the relatively small loans undertaken for seasonal (short-term) purposes. However, informal, and even formal, lenders sometimes invoke a procedure that is not fully formal, whereby they demand physical possession of the title document. This does not entail formal recording of collateral encumbrances, but it prevents the borrower from selling the land under favorable (formal) terms to others without respecting first the obligations to the creditor (Siamwalla 1990).

Urban credit markets have different characteristics. They are typically more developed than credit markets in rural areas and entail greater participation of private (nonstate) lending institutions. Residential credit often relies on collateralized long-term loans to finance housing acquisition, and documented land ownership is important in facilitating such transactions. The use of residential property to finance business investments is less common. Commercial land property is often used as collateral for business-oriented investments. There is said to be a high potential of credit expansion to informal (undocumented) landowners in urban areas (many of them illegal squatters in poor slums) once their possession is formalized and legitimized (de Soto 2000). This has been disputed based on banks' difficulty in repossessing or liquidating low-quality dwellings in poor neighborhoods (Benjaminsen 2002; de Soto 2002; Mathieu 2002). Credit market effects will also be less than expected if there is "risk rationing," that is, if potential borrowers who would be creditworthy are unwilling to use titles for fear of losing them in a risky environment (Boucher, Carter, and Guirkinger 2008).

AFFORDABILITY AND COST-EFFECTIVENESS

An often-neglected issue with important consequences for cost-effectiveness and sustainability of land registration relates to the way in which liability for defects in registry information is assigned. This differs markedly between systems for registration of deeds and title registration systems, the two most common forms of land registration. A deeds registration system is a public repository in which documents to provide evidence of land transactions are lodged, numbered, dated, indexed, and archived. Recording gives public notice of a transaction, serves as evidence for it, and may assign priority to the right claimed in the document in the sense that, in most contexts, registered deeds take priority over unregistered ones or deeds registered subsequently. However, registration of a deed does not imply an inference about the legal validity of the transaction. By contrast, in registration of titles, the register itself serves as the primary evidence of ownership as commonly identified by three attributes: (1) the mirror principle, indicating that the situation in the registry is an exact reflection of reality; (2) the curtain principle, implying that anybody interested in inquiring about the title status of a given property will not have to engage in a lengthy search of documents, but can rely on the evidence from the title registry as definitive; and (3) the assurance principle, according to which the government will indemnify parties for damages incurred as a consequence of errors in the registry.[5]

Put simply, a deeds system is cheaper to operate but provides a less-comprehensive service because the residual risk of verifying ownership information remains with the transacting parties, who incur the cost of due diligence. By contrast, to be able to assume responsibility for the accuracy of information in the registry, the state will have to assume responsibility, which implies higher setup as well as operating costs.[6] As landowners fail to register transactions if the cost of doing so is too high compared to the benefit (the reduction in residual risk), a title registration system will be socially optimal if land values are high, whereas for lower land values a deeds system is more appropriate (Arrunada 2003). While most land registration projects funded by multilateral agencies recommend adoption of a title registration system—and in some cases even the conversion from a system based on deeds toward one based on title—this has rarely been substantiated by rigorous analysis of the associated costs and benefits and, possibly as a result, has not always led to the desired outcome.[7] This is

---

5. To illustrate, if, under title registration, person A fraudulently sells land (which actually belongs to C) to B, who purchases it in good faith, B becomes the rightful owner, and any claims by C are extinguished as soon as the sale is registered. The only recourse open to C is to demand compensation, but not restitution of the property, from the state, which in turn has the option to sue A. The need to ensure that the responsibility taken up by the state can be met is one of the reasons that title registration systems are normally associated with a guarantee fund to facilitate payment of such compensation. By contrast, under a deeds system, it is B's responsibility to investigate the veracity of A's ownership claims, and C will be able to demand restitution of the property from B, implying that B will incur the loss.

6. The specific historical circumstances of the United States, which operates under a deeds system, have given rise to a system of title insurance in which private companies, rather than the state, have developed a comprehensive record of all land transactions that enables them to examine the legal validity of transactions and insure against defects. Given the long time it took to assemble the required information, this is not an option for developing countries (Arrunada and Garoupa 2005).

7. While a number of well-functioning systems with high land values (Hong Kong, Britain, Scotland, various Canadian provinces) have successfully made the transition from a deeds to a titling system, though often over a long period of time, attempts to shift from a deeds system to one of title registration in developing countries do not have a good record. A project in Sri Lanka failed to put in place the legal, regulatory, and institutional framework for systematic adjudication of land parcels and instead accomplished only very limited survey and titling of parcels, with limited economic benefits (World Bank 2007). In St. Lucia households received provisional documents that were supposed to be replaced by full titles after 12 years, but 75 percent of titles were never collected by their owners (Griffith-Charles 2004). In Ghana, where a new title registration system has been introduced, fewer than 1,000 titles were issued per year, and the rate at which titles entered the system was below that of new transactions to be registered, implying a widening gap between the registry and reality and increasing levels of informality (Nettle 2006).

particularly relevant as measures that include standardization of deeds, parcel-based indexing, compulsory registration, and a requirement for registrars to perform basic checks on deeds and the persons presenting them before accepting them for registration all offer opportunities to strengthen deeds systems. With access to computerized information about the chain of deeds and other instruments pertaining to a given parcel, differences between the deeds and title registration systems have narrowed significantly. From an applied perspective, deeds systems are also more robust, and good systems, as in The Netherlands and South Africa, offer most if not all of the features of well-run titling systems. Even in titling systems, a regulatory framework that fails to disclose relevant rights or encumbrances in the registry can put the integrity and usefulness of a land registration system in question. Where the failure to register potentially long-standing rights allows them to be ignored in practice, there have been very negative social impacts.[8] This suggests that, in addition to the type of recording, close scrutiny of the information actually captured by the land registration system is warranted.

While establishment of land registries is an important investment in infrastructure, the resources required for first-time registration can be increased by the fact that the cost of mapping increases exponentially with precision. A widespread confusion between tenure security and precision of measurement, together with lobbying by survey professionals, has often led countries to impose survey standards that exceed local implementation capacity and impose costs with no reasonable relationship to land values. As a consequence, in many of the early projects financed by bilateral or multilateral institutions, the cost of first-time registration was high, possibly in excess of land values, with costs ranging on average from between US$20 to US$60 per parcel, and in some cases significantly above US$100 (Burns 2007). Not surprisingly, this has often limited the speed with which such programs could be implemented and the coverage they were able to achieve. Where first-time registration was heavily subsidized by the state, landowners often failed to register subsequent transactions.

As most of the benefits from land registries accrue to users, observers generally agree that it is desirable for registries to recover their cost through user fees, although in most countries fees from urban areas with higher frequency and value of transactions are used to cross-subsidize rural areas. In addition to

---

8. The case of tenants on *mailo* land in Uganda is a particularly striking example. Although many of the tenants had been on the land for more than a generation, their presence was not indicated on landlords' titles. Banks that lent against such titles discovered that liquidation was impossible because of the presence of tenants with far-reaching rights on the land they had accepted as collateral, making it difficult even for owners of unencumbered land to use it as collateral, thereby undermining the value of existing titles and making the state guarantee (which extends to ownership only) worthless from their point of view (Deininger and Ali 2008).

operational inefficiencies, costs are normally increased by three factors: (1) unreasonably high precision requirements for surveys; (2) a need to involve lawyers in transactions; and (3) stamp duties levied on land transfers. To the extent that the costs exceed the benefits (in terms of increased security) that users obtain from registering, high cost can lead to reemergence of informal practices up to a point where "de-formalization" undermines the sustainability of a land registry system that was established at high cost (Barnes and Griffith-Charles 2007). In practice, the costs associated with registering property are by no means trivial. Despite reforms to reduce costs significantly, the mean in 173 countries included in the World Bank's "Doing Business 2008" amounts to 6.6 percent of the property values and 81 days of waiting time.[9] Informal fees can further increase these costs, with possibly far-reaching consequences for users' ability to access information and their confidence in the land registry. For example, in India the costs of registering even inheritances is exorbitant, and a recent study estimated bribes paid annually on land administration to amount to US$700 million (Transparency International India 2005), three-quarters of India's total public spending on science, technology, and environment. The dramatic improvements achieved in Eastern Europe by making registries financially independent and their information publicly available on the Internet, involving private surveyors, reducing staff, and increasing salaries highlight the scope for improving efficiency and governance of land registries (Dabrundashvili 2006).

As it will be critical for both the feasibility and continued viability of property rights institutions, the cost of establishing and running the land registry system requires more attention to the system's design, especially in the African context, where resources are limited. Failure to take into account the cost of the institutional infrastructure that was to be established is one of the reasons that implementation of the 1998 Land Act in Uganda stalled (Hunt 2004); almost a decade after its passage, not a single certificate of customary ownership has been issued. By contrast, in Ethiopia a low-cost method of certification with

---

9. The World Bank's "Doing Business" survey has rightly identified the cost of registering property as a key impediment to private sector activity by including it as one of the indicator variables in its global survey. Because these figures are based on expert opinion for an unencumbered property in the capital city, they should be used with care (Arrunada 2007) and are likely to constitute a lower boundary for the cost of registration faced by the average landholder. For example, a field-based study in St. Lucia found the transaction cost for what was considered a typical transaction by the local population to be almost three times the 7 percent given in the "Doing Business" survey (Griffith-Charles 2004). Also, the cost of registering property is highly bimodal; while it is 2 percent or less of property value in 32 cases, it amounts to 5 percent or 10 percent and more of property values in 92 (53 percent) and 41 (24 percent) of the cases, respectively (World Bank 2007). To make such figures more representative and bring them closer to the cost of service provision, the World Bank is undertaking efforts to link this to administrative data. Doing so is likely to provide a more precise measure that could be used to track changes over time.

high levels of community participation that involved field measurement, but not creation of a graphical record, managed to register more than 20 million plots at a cost of less than US$1 per parcel in less than three years. While a system for updating has not yet been implemented, a modest fee of US$0.65, in line with users' willingness to pay, would be enough to finance a partly computerized system that could be self-financing. Options for adding at least a cadastral index map at a cost that is sustainable are being explored as well (Deininger et al. 2008).[10]

VARIATION IN LAND SCARCITY

It has often been argued that, in situations where land is relatively abundant, households will undertake investments and expenditures designed chiefly to enhance their tenure security over the land being used. The direction of causality in such circumstances is therefore from investments to more secure tenure, rather than from improved tenure security to more investment. This implies (according to this line of argument) that even if interventions to improve tenure security were feasible, they may have little impact in terms of bringing forth new investment (Brasselle, Gaspart, and Platteau 2002; Sjaastad and Bromley 1997). In particular, land-abundant areas in West Africa such as the Ivory Coast have a long tradition of migrants' planting trees to establish property rights over all or part of the land (Colin and Ayouz 2006). The literature notes that, in such contexts, efforts at land registration need to confront four issues. First, especially in situations where traditional institutions still work relatively well, introducing a system to register land may lead to speculative land acquisition on a large scale and set off a "race for the prize" that can polarize the land ownership structure (Benjaminsen and Sjaastad 2002; Peters 2004) as powerful individuals use their informational and other advantages to grab land. Second, by introducing an additional institution that is intended to replace traditional actors—though an institution with limited state presence is often not capable of doing so—such interventions may create a parallel system. Instead of complementing each other, traditional and modern systems may compete with each other, as was the case in Kenya (Atwood 1990), thereby increasing transaction costs, giving those who are better off or better informed an opportunity to resort to "institutional shopping" by, for example, pursuing conflicts in parallel through a variety of channels (Firmin-Sellers 2000), and increasing conflict (Berry 1997; Fred-Mensah 1999). Third, traditional registration programs have often paid little attention to secondary or communal land rights, such as the right of temporary use of arable land after the crop harvest for grazing pastoralists'

---

10. In Ethiopia 95 percent of households that do not have certificates would like to get them, and 99 percent of those with certificates would be willing to pay an average of B12 (US$1.50) to replace a lost certificate, while 90 percent of those willing to pay would like to add a sketch map (Deininger et al. 2008).

animals or for firewood collection by the poor. Unless measures are taken to recognize, and if necessary record, such rights, they may intentionally or unintentionally be curtailed, with negative consequences for those who benefited from them (Meinzen-Dick and Mwangi 2009). Also, if land is not the scarcest factor, land registration will be effective only if it is combined with establishment of secure rights to other resources (for example, water) that may limit the ability to make productive use of the land. Fourth, especially but not only in high-risk environments, individualization of communal land rights that neglects the important safety-net function of such arrangements may entail loss of the flexibility essential for risk management and insurance, thus leaving everybody worse off (Baland and Francois 2005). This is consistent with the importance of open fields in Europe for long periods of time (Bekar and Reed 2003; Fenoaltea 1976; McCloskey 1975).

These issues will have to be taken seriously in the design of any intervention on land registration, but they also need to be put in perspective. While their specific manifestations will depend on the conditions at hand, secular trends such as population growth, urbanization, and increased land demand for nonagricultural purposes, including by outsiders, are unlikely to be reversed. Increasing land scarcity can reinforce preexisting inequalities along lines of gender, ethnicity, and wealth and set in motion a spiral of conflict, resource degradation, and social strife that can spread beyond the narrow realm of land and have negative social and economic consequences. For example, if, as in much of West Africa, the descendants of migrants can be easily identified as outsiders, increased land values provide a strong incentive for locals to renege on earlier sales contracts. In the case of the Ivory Coast, land access is interlinked with questions of nationality and the fact that only nationals may own land, which can give rise to conflicts that extend far beyond the land (Lavigne-Delville et al. 2002). In Rwanda, where extreme land scarcity coincided with accumulation of land by individuals with access to nonagricultural incomes, land conflict was one of the principal causes of the civil war in 1994 (Andre and Platteau 1998).

Traditional land institutions may offer considerable flexibility, but they may also have limitations and be eroded through a trickle of transactions (Chimhowu and Woodhouse 2006). For example, especially with weak governance, land sales by chiefs who reinterpret their trusteeship role as ownership and pocket the receipts are common, and they risk undermining traditional social safety nets (Lavigne-Delville 2000). Also, customary systems are well suited to resolving conflicts within a community, but they face much greater difficulty in reducing conflicts across groups, ethnicities, and type of land use, such as between pastoralists and sedentary agriculturalists (Van den Brink, Bromley, and Chavas 1995). Finally, under traditional systems, women are often severely disadvantaged, and access to institutions for land administration are biased by gender and wealth (Henrysson and Joireman 2007). It will thus be important that analyses of the impacts of changes in land administration systems construct a proper counterfactual and do not mistakenly attribute positive or negative developments that would have happened even without changes in the land system.

Given its spatial extension, defining property rights to land or writing contracts regarding their exchange is costly. Therefore, in traditionally settled areas at low levels of population density, boundaries may be defined only loosely; transfers will normally involve only usufruct rather than ownership and will often be confined to community members. This allows much of the content of land rights and associated transactions to be defined informally by unwritten custom. Changing economic and social conditions that make land more valuable and increase the benefits to be obtained from land transfers imply that the value of attributes that have previously been left undelineated may increase sufficiently to offset the transaction costs associated with more precise delineation of land rights. Thus, even in land-abundant settings, appropriate ways of registering individual and communal land can have significant benefits, provided that adequate mechanisms for accountability and good governance are in place, that there is a menu of options from which communities can choose to suit their requirements, and that registry information is maintained in a coherent format so as to prevent the emergence of parallel and potentially contradictory systems and to allow flexibility to facilitate individualization if the need arises.

A large number of jurisdictions now include provisions for registration of communal land (Alden-Wily 2003) that provide opportunities to delimit community boundaries while leaving registration and management of individual plots to community institutions.[11] This is not only more cost-effective than individual titling, but it also allows covering much larger areas very quickly. Doing so can avert threats of large-scale land alienation to outside investors who neglect community rights (Alden-Wily 2008). Moreover, if it is combined with a mechanism, and possibly training, for communities to directly negotiate with investors, possibly establishing joint ventures, this may reduce bureaucratic bottlenecks and corrupt dealings that often slow such investment. While transparent mechanisms for allocation and transfer of land rights within the community will have to be established, rules that regulate land alienation to outsiders can help to reduce undesirable social effects and keep them from driving some people into destitution (Andolfatto 2002) and can also reduce the potential benefits of land grabs. As long as such rules are the product of a conscious choice by the group and the group has clear and transparent mechanisms for changing the land tenure regime, they are less likely to be harmful. As traditional social ties loosen or the efficiency loss from the sales restriction becomes too high, groups are likely to move toward a gradual individualization and sales to outsiders. The recent

---

11. For a discussion of institutional options, see Fitzpatrick (2005), and for a detailed example of legislative arrangements to put this in practice, see Government of Mexico (2000).

constitutional reform of the land rights system in Mexico is an example, with the fact that the transition toward individual rights can only be made by a 75 percent majority of the whole group, providing a safeguard against land grabs. The fact that less than 15 percent of *ejidos*—mostly those in peri-urban areas where land had already been de facto individualized—made use of this opportunity suggests that, even at relatively high levels of per capita income, the spatial reach of insurance mechanisms to replace the safety net function of communal land ownership remains more limited than is often thought (Zepeda 2000).

Evidence on Impacts

The above implies that well-implemented land registration programs can help improve governance and administrative efficiency, reduce the need to expend resources to enforce land rights and enhance gender equality, increase land-related investment, and enhance operation of land markets as well as credit access. However, these effects are by no means automatic, and in many instances they cannot materialize. A review of empirical evidence suggests that, while there is strong evidence that land registration systems have reduced the need to expend effort in enforcing rights and have enhanced land-related investment, this experience is not uniform. Furthermore, evidence that interventions have improved credit access is less strong and in general suggests that a direct positive impact on the poor has been limited.

IMPROVED GOVERNANCE AND ADMINISTRATIVE EFFICIENCY

The earlier discussion suggests that land registration interventions and associated legal reforms will be more effective in a context of good governance, although legal and policy changes can also contribute to improvements. The case of land rights reform in China, where property rights to land have traditionally been insecure and where increased pressure on land in peri-urban areas has given rise to well-publicized conflicts, provides a basis for understanding these interactions. Officials' ability to apply eminent domain principles with little public scrutiny and to rely on readjustment (land reallocation) to acquire large tracts of land without cash outlays further implies extensive use of land taking not only as a source of income by local government but reportedly also for individual enrichment and corruption.

The 2003 Rural Land Contracting Law includes a number of measures that aim to significantly change the cost of acquiring land. It does so by increasing the security of individual land use rights and enhancing individuals' ability to lodge appeals against violation of such rights. Data from a representative nationwide survey suggest that legal reform had a significant and quantitatively important impact on increasing the security of property rights in terms of reducing the probability of illegal land reallocation and increasing the amount of compensation received by those who were affected by legitimate land takings. The impact was significant only in villages where the leadership was elected, suggesting that, for legal reform to be effective, means to hold the state accountable are needed, an interpretation supported by the fact that village leaders' knowledge of the law had an independent impact on reducing the probability of illegal reallocation. Availability of land use certificates did not significantly reduce the risk of unauthorized land reallocation, suggesting that such certificates will be useful only within an appropriate institutional framework (Deininger and Jin 2008b).

A natural experiment in Buenos Aires allows assessment of the impact of land registration not only on economic outcomes but also on attitudes and beliefs. Title was given to some but not to other urban squatters, all of whom had started out in exactly the same conditions. Some 14 years later, those who, by chance, had benefited had significantly more individualistic and materialistic attitudes, a result that is very robust.[12] The effect was equivalent to an additional 4.4 years of education by the household head. Despite their much inferior socioeconomic situation, beneficiaries' beliefs are virtually indistinguishable from the population average. By comparison, attitudes by those who did not get regularized are consistent with what one would expect based on their socioeconomic characteristics (Di Tella, Galiani, and Schargrodsky 2007).

Land registration can also have a major impact on local government's ability to generate resources, governance, and efficient service provision. In the Indian state of Karnataka, computerization of textual records is estimated to have saved users US$16 million in bribes annually (Lobo and Balakrishnan 2002). By using this figure as a basis to automate registration and the associated valuation, stamp duty could be cut from 14 percent to 8 percent and tax revenue quadrupled from US$120 million to US$480 million, thus illustrating the scope for land registries to be self-financing.[13] In Mexico before reforms were initiated in 1992, the *ejido* sector was subject to numerous restrictions on land rights; the rural economy was characterized by clientelism, inefficient land use, and low levels of investment; and peri-urban areas were subject to chaotic informal settlement (Gordillo, de Janvry, and Sadoulet 1998). In qualitative interviews, beneficiaries of a program to establish more secure and better administered land rights indicated that the most important aspects of the reforms were their impact on reducing conflicts and on increasing transparency, with an associated reduction of political influence in the *ejido* sector (World Bank 2002). Based on promising results from earlier pilot programs, Ethiopia embarked on a large-scale and highly participatory registration of landholdings by 6 million

---

12. Among other attitudes, they were more likely to believe that people can succeed economically on their own, that having money is important to be happy, and that others can be trusted. No significant differences emerged regarding the belief that those who put in effort will do better economically.

13. In Thailand a program of land titling provided the basis for a substantial increase in the total amount of land revenue collected, from US$300 million in 1984 to US$1.2 billion in 1995 (Burns 2007).

households in 2003–2005. Although land remains state-owned and many restrictions on land transfers continue to exist, more than 80 percent of respondents in a nationwide survey indicated that certification increased the chance of getting compensation when land was acquired for nonagricultural uses, helped to reduce conflicts, and improved bargaining power by females, especially in regions where women's pictures were included on the land certificate (Deininger et al. 2008).

REDUCED ENFORCEMENT EFFORT AND INCREASED GENDER EQUALITY

In Peru a significant land titling effort was carried out in rural and urban areas. Estimates indicate that, in urban areas, having received a title resulted in a significantly increased perception of tenure security. Recipients of titles increased their participation in the formal labor market when they were no longer required to invest in a multitude of informal activities to maintain tenure security (Field 2007). The magnitude of these effects is large. Initially labor supply is estimated to have increased by about 13.5 hours per week, rising about 50 percent to 45 hours after four years. This is in marked contrast to other welfare programs, which generally reduced labor force participation. Since adults have an advantage over children in protective activity, a reduction in the need for home protection could also reduce the demand for child labor. To the extent that changes in tenure security can bring about an independent reduction in the productive value of children (for example, as a result of better old-age insurance, better credit access, or increased bargaining power of females), they could also prompt a reduction in childbearing.

The program's requirement that titles be issued jointly in the names of husband and wife provides an opportunity to test for gender-specific effects. If the titling program led to a redistribution of household assets in favor of females that shifted intra-household bargaining power, one would expect other outcomes more favorable to the women.[14] This is consistent with a 22 percent reduction of fertility for squatters who received property titles and twice the reduction in the probability of having a child among females who received joint titles compared to those where the title was in the husband's name only (Field 2003).

A study in Nepal found not only a positive association between higher levels of women's land rights and their socioeconomic empowerment and the health of their children, but also an impact comparable in magnitude to the effect of increased education and employment, two areas that have received much more attention in the policy debate (Allendorf 2007). This is in line with evidence

---

14. A positive nutritional effect on children's weight, but not height, was found in another study using the same data (Vogl 2007).

from India, where access to land allows women to escape significant gender discrimination by choosing self-employment on their land instead (Deininger, Jin, and Nagarajan 2006), and in line with earlier qualitative evidence on the importance of land for women's social status (Panda and Agarwal 2005). In the Indian state of Punjab, joint titling made women significantly more assertive of their rights, increased attachment to their homes, and enabled them to use formal means (courts) rather than informal ones to counter (hypothetical) sales of land by their husbands (Datta 2006). In Gujarat land ownership was found to be a key determinant of women's empowerment that increased self-stated propensity to invest in land (Baruah 2007). All of these studies point to potentially important gendered impacts of land titling.

In the long term, land registration could affect household size by allowing members of the extended family to separate their inheritance, move out, and start independent enterprises. In Buenos Aires a study found reduced family size—via less presence of extended family members—and lower fertility, as well as improved educational outcomes of children among titled squatters as compared to untitled squatters (Galiani and Schargrodsky 2005). While there were no differences in the number of children born before titling, untitled households were much larger than the titled households due to the presence of extended family members and larger numbers of children born after the time of titling. If household resources for education are fixed, the decreased number of children provides opportunities for investment in human capital. Children of titled squatters attended school 0.4 days per week more than did children of the control group, and their level of school achievement was higher by 0.42 years. This is roughly equivalent to the estimated impact of a program (Progresan Mexico) that provides cash transfers to households with school-age children conditional on these children attending school, suggesting that land registration can have potentially large effects. Also, teenage pregnancy rates and children's short-term nutritional indicators (weight for height, but not height for age) are better on titled than on untitled parcels, suggesting that titling allows families to improve investment in human capital (Galiani and Schargrodsky 2004).

LAND-RELATED INVESTMENT AND LAND VALUES
The hypothesis of positive tenure security effects on economic incentives is hardly controversial and has been quantitatively demonstrated by numerous recent studies, such as in China (Jacoby, Li, and Rozelle 2002), Latin America (Bandiera 2007; Kazianga and Masters 2006), Africa (Deininger and Jin 2006; Goldstein and Udry 2006), and Eastern Europe (Rozelle and Swinnen 2004). What is still debated is whether and under what circumstances land registration programs are an effective way to enhance tenure security, especially in relatively land-abundant settings, and how to design them to be most effective.

Evidence about the potential gains from titles is not uniform. A study in a rice-growing area in Madagascar suggests that formal titles had no effect on

plot-specific investment and little impact on productivity. Land values are estimated to have increased by 6 percentage points at most due to titling, implying
that the cost of land titling would have to be very low to be justified economically
(Jacoby and Minten 2007). By contrast, within-household analysis of new investments on owned as compared to merely occupied *(mailo)* plots by owner-cum-
occupants in Uganda points to significant and quantitatively large investment
effects of full ownership: the shift from *mailo* occupancy to ownership is predicted
to double the likelihood of soil conservation and increase tree investment fivefold.
Tenant registration is estimated to have no investment effect, while measures to
strengthen occupancy rights attenuate, but fail to fully eliminate, investment disincentives originating in overlapping rights (Deininger and Ali 2008). In Ghana
tenure insecurity is shown to lead to reduced investment in the form of fallowing,
reducing output by about one-third and leading to very large aggregate efficiency
losses, according to estimates (Pande and Udry 2005). While this supports the
importance of secure land tenure as a precondition for growth, it suggests that
the magnitude of possible impacts can vary widely and that interventions aiming
to increase tenure security need to be context-specific to be effective.

In urban settings a first indicator of the effectiveness of titling programs
would be housing investment. In Buenos Aires regularized squatters have a 40
percent higher probability of having good walls and a similar increase in the
probability of having good overall housing quality. Apparently, the shift from
use to ownership increased the incentive to invest, but failed to make households
richer or increase the transferability of their assets (Galiani and Schargrodsky
2005). In Peru evidence on improvements in housing between 1994–1995 and
1999–2000 suggests that, for titled households, rates of house renovation increased more than two-thirds above baseline levels, though most of the increase
was financed out of pocket rather than through credit (Field 2005).

The same methodology was applied to analyze the impact of a program
that provided duly registered titles to rural households in Peru. The analysis distinguished between households with pre-program high levels of tenure security
(due to possession of an agrarian reform title, a notarized sales contract, or a
judicial resolution) and households that lacked such documents and thus had
low levels of security before the program was implemented. Levels of investment
were found to have increased significantly due to the program, particularly for
the latter, whose propensity to invest in land almost quadrupled due to the increment in tenure security. This is consistent with findings for a smaller region in
Peru, where registration was found to increase the probability of terrace investment by 6.6 percent (Antle et al. 2003). Since 97 percent of such investments
were financed out of pocket, a big credit impact is improbable (Fort 2007). Externalities are suggested by the fact that the titling density within a district has a
significant effect on infrastructure investment. Use of a linear probability model
of export crop adoption suggests that receipt of title had a highly significant and
positive effect on its own and that it appeared to make households more responsive to price changes, leading the authors to conclude that market liberalization

helps only when conducted in an appropriate institutional environment (Field, Field, and Torero 2006).

In Nicaragua full registration of a plot after the 1990 revolution resulted in an increased propensity to invest of between 8 and 9 percent. By contrast, award of agrarian reform title without registration had insignificant investment impacts. At about 29 percent, marginal returns to land-attached investment are much higher than those from investment in mobile capital, pointing toward scope for gains in overall economic efficiency by shifting resources from the latter to the former. This suggests that, in addition to enhancing overall levels of investment, the higher level of tenure security brought about by land titling in Nicaragua can lead to a more appropriate balance in the investment mix between movable and fixed capital. Land values for plots with registered title are higher by 30 percent (Deininger and Chamorro 2004). Reduced form regressions from Nicaragua lead to similar conclusions regarding the superiority of full as compared to reform title in terms of enhanced land values, investment in perennials, and higher crop yields (Broegaard 2005).

The presence of an investment incentive effect independent from credit is also highlighted by evidence from a land settlement program in Guatemala that started in 1986. A 1993 survey suggests that, while all the sample households had benefited from credit provided under the program, those that had exogenously received titles to their property took greater care of their parcels and, most likely as a result of past and recurrent investment, had higher yields than did those that had not received titles (Schweigert 2007).

In Vietnam, in addition to awarding about 11 million land use certificates (LUCs) through land registration efforts between 1993 and 2000, legal changes expanded users' rights to include transfer, inheritance, exchange, lease, and mortgage (Do and Iyer 2008). While the magnitude of new registration was comparable to the Ethiopian case, it was much larger and more rapid than that achieved by other interventions, including the 8.7 million titles distributed in Thailand since the 1980s, the 1.8 million titles in Indonesia from 1996, and the 1.2 million urban and 1.5 million rural titles in Peru between 1992 and 2005. A difference in the district-level estimation strategy in Vietnam suggests that provinces in which certification made more progress have devoted more of their land to perennials and have expanded nonfarm activities. In any given province, introducing complete coverage of the farming population by LUCs is estimated to induce an increase of 7.5 percentage points in the proportion of land under perennials as compared to a situation of no coverage at all. Since restrictions on crop choice that require households to keep land in rice remained in effect, this is likely to be a lower bound estimate of the true effect. Of equal interest, the supply of labor to nonagricultural employment is estimated to increase by 11 to 12 weeks compared to the situation without the LUCs, an outcome that is more pronounced for the poor than for the rich. Much of this effect comes through diversification of income portfolios within households rather than specialization in different types of activities by households. There is, however, no evidence of either a credit effect or a measurable impact on income or expenditure, which is consistent with the notion that without complementary changes in banking and rules for land transactions, titling alone is unlikely to set off big changes in economic structure.

In Ethiopia's nationwide program, which is too recent to have had a longer-term effect, plots in villages where land certificates were distributed were 5 percent more likely to receive new investment than were controls (Deininger et al. 2008). This is consistent with evidence on the impact of the predecessor to the national program in the Tigray region, which had led to significantly higher levels of investment (Holden, Deininger, and Ghebru 2008a).

In Thailand land ownership titles induced greater investment in farming capital (attached investments and other capital), and titled land had significantly higher market values and higher productivity per unit. Output was 14 to 25 percent higher on titled land than on untitled land of equal quality (Feder et al. 1988). Housing prices in the nonsquatter formal residential areas of the city of Davao in the Philippines were 58 percent higher than in the informal areas, and rents were 18 percent higher (Friedman, Jimenez, and Mayo 1988). In Jakarta registered land was up to 73 percent more valuable than similar land held by weak claims (Dowall and Leaf 1992).

Self-assessed land values provide an upper boundary on the gain in utility from property registration. In Ecuadorian slums title increases the expected market value of a plot by 23 percent (based on responses by the same household for hypothetical changes), an effect that increases to more than 50 percent in situations where, because the settlement was recently invaded and has no organizer to provide political protection, tenure security is very low. Comparing the hypothetical benefits to the cost of such a program suggests a positive return, even taking into account the tendency for people to overvalue the possible gains from title. Particularly large benefits to women-only households are interpreted as indicating a need for interventions to incorporate gender concerns (Lanjouw and Levy 2002).

OPERATION OF LAND MARKETS
In the Dominican Republic insecure property rights not only reduce the level of activity on the land rental market, but also induce market segmentation. Landlords who have reasons to fear losing their land restrict renting to narrow local circles of confidence. This segmentation further reduces rental activity by limiting opportunities to find suitable tenants. Simulations show that improved security of property rights through title registration can lead to efficiency and equity gains; improving tenure security would increase total area rented by the poor by 63 percent (Macours, de Janvry, and Sadoulet 2004). Similarly, in Nicaragua producers who have title are significantly more likely to rent out their land, providing an opportunity for more effective producers to increase their cultivated area (Deininger, Zegarra, and Lavadenz 2003). In contrast, descriptive statistics from Peru suggest that perceived rights to rent, sell, or exclude others

(in contrast with rights to use, invest, and inherit) are not significantly different between titled and nontitled households (Fort 2007).

In Vietnam within-household regressions as well as cross-sectional estimates suggest that having long-term use rights secured through registration will increase the tendency to rent out to nonrelatives, but does not affect the propensity to rent out to relatives, consistent with the notion that land registration can substitute for informal enforcement through social capital. Moreover, and in line with the expectation that, in the case of informal transactions with friends and relatives, the smaller number of potential partners reduces the scope for efficiency-enhancing transactions, rental transactions among nonrelatives—but not among relatives—contribute to a significant increase in efficiency (Deininger and Jin 2008a). In Tigray land certification contributed to higher levels of land rental market participation, especially by female-headed households (Holden, Deininger, and Ghebru 2008b) and considerably enhanced opportunities for women to benefit from land rental (Bezabih and Holden 2006). Drawing out tenure-induced increases in land rental market activity and their impact on diversification of economic activity, especially in rural areas, is an important topic for future research.

Evidence on potential impacts of land registration on sales markets mostly compares before and after situations in a descriptive way. In Eastern Europe recent interventions to register land rights were generally followed by considerable and often rapid growth in land market transactions and, in the case of urban land and real estate, in mortgages, but construction of a counterfactual is difficult, so the evidence is suggestive only. In St. Lucia sales market activity and the number of registered mortgages increased immediately after introducing the title system (and remained high in peri-urban areas). However, the marginal increase in formal land market activity after introduction of the system was not sustained over time (Barnes and Griffith-Charles 2007), suggesting limited impacts. Descriptive evidence suggests that titling of frontier land in Guatemala, while helping to reduce conflict and the perceived danger of land invasion, has little effect on investment and credit access and fails to prevent informal sales, implying that the registry is becoming outdated (Gould 2006).

CREDIT ACCESS

Early study of the impact of titling in Thailand, where informal credit markets had already operated and land markets functioned relatively well before the intervention, points to significant impacts on credit access (Feder et al. 1988). In Paraguay a significant credit supply effect was demonstrated, but accrued only to medium and large landowners, whereas producers with less than 20 hectares remained rationed out of the credit market, something that could set in motion worrisome longer-term dynamics in terms of equity (Carter and Olinto 2003), similar to what was found in Guatemala (Mushinski 1999).

However, if land markets are illiquid or nonexistent, or if the cost of registering mortgages or foreclosing on them is very high, one would not expect land registration to have an immediate impact on credit access. For example, in Peru land registration increased the likelihood of obtaining a loan (by between 9 and 10 percentage points) only for credit through a state bank, but not through the private sector. One explanation is that, due to the political nature of the application process, the likelihood of foreclosure is actually lower (or the transaction costs higher) for those with titles. There is reason to believe that the politicized nature of the titling process may have reduced rather than increased banks' ability to foreclose. This is in line with evidence suggesting that, even after land registration, more than one-third of households remained completely rationed out of formal credit markets (Field and Torero 2006). While interest rates charged by the private sector are lower (by about 9 points) for titled than for untitled households, this appears to be due to signaling rather than the ability to collateralize debt. This is similar to what was found in Indonesia, where land registration was contingent on demand, and significant payment by owners and possession of a title could be used as a proxy for entrepreneurial drive (Dower and Potamites 2005). Evidence from rural areas in Peru points in the same direction (Field, Field, and Torero 2006; Fort 2007). Similarly, in Buenos Aires, despite significant effects on house-related investment and other variables, no credit effect was found, implying that even with titles, households will be unable to fully ensure their consumption or use their talents more efficiently in entrepreneurial activity, and suggesting that growth implications of titling programs may be overstated (Galiani and Schargrodsky 2005). This is consistent with what was found by a recent comprehensive descriptive review of urban titling (Payne, Durand-Lasserve, and Rakodi 2008).

Implications for Policy and Research

The main objective of this chapter is to assess whether the assertion of a positive impact of land registration on a range of economic and social outcomes is supported by empirical evidence. Where it is or is not, we are interested in the underlying reasons, the magnitude of estimated effects, and the implications for policy. Where existing evidence is weak, we are also interested in areas and scope for research to answer open questions.

Our review allows a number of conclusions. First, there is ample but not uniform evidence of positive tenure security effects of land registration in a variety of circumstances. These manifest themselves in higher levels of investment, less need for activities to protect land rights, and—especially if female rights are enhanced or made more visible—gender empowerment. Second, while there is some evidence that land registration has helped to activate land rental markets, its impact on off-farm labor market participation is underresearched, especially in rural areas of developing countries, where occupational diversification is likely to be one of the key drivers of growth. Third, even though land registration has helped to improve credit access in a number of situations, the effect is contingent on a number of other factors, not all of which can be taken for granted in developing countries. Even if there are credit effects, direct benefits to the poor are often limited. Fourth, few quantitative studies have explored the interaction of land registration with other initiatives or with the broader social and economic environment, even though these might be relevant to the nature and magnitude of expected effects. Few studies assessed the cost-effectiveness, long-term sustainability, and longer-term impact of land administration interventions. Fifth, even though one would expect impacts of systematic land registration to be more pronounced in urban environs, quantitative studies tended to focus more on interventions in rural areas and understood land regularization almost exclusively in terms of allocation of individual rights, neglecting both group rights and state land management. Related to this, key governance aspects did not receive the attention they deserve in this context.

In view of the above, there would be merit in using the large number of recent and ongoing interventions introducing or upscaling land registration to derive relevant conclusions on the magnitude and incidence of benefits, circumstances of unintended negative outcomes, and ways to increase benefits, target them more effectively to the poor, and enhance sustainability and cost-effectiveness. The scope for retrospective analysis to yield forward-looking and operationally relevant insights will often be limited by data quality and designs that may not have incorporated recent thinking. Using the significant number of projects under implementation or preparation could help provide more specific insights on key research questions with respect to both the economic and governance aspects of land registration.

Concerning economic effects, it will be important to complement evidence from rural areas with insights from urban interventions where, at least in such settings as middle-income residential neighborhoods that remain informal, credit effects can more reasonably be expected. This would also require accounting for the interaction of land-related interventions with other interventions and for characteristics of the environment such as access to the banking system, beneficiaries' interest in acquiring credit, their ability to make productive use of such credit, and the extent to which credit access can be enhanced. In this context, interaction between land regularization and infrastructure upgrading would be of particular interest so as to compare the effects of land rights with and without upgrading to the effects of upgrading itself. Individuals' demand and willingness to pay for a continuum of land certificates could provide a first descriptive approach with clear implications for ways for local governments to finance the upfront cost of such programs and recover the cost thereafter, such as through land taxation. With much of the population ignorant about applicable legal provisions, exploring how these and other issues may be affected by information campaigns or legal assistance could be appropriate. While the effect on establishment and expansion of microenterprises in urban areas will be of great interest, investment impacts in rural areas should be complemented by assessing the impact of land registration on productivity and diversification of the occupational structure, including the extent to which it facilitates rural to urban migration.

With respect to governance, important issues include the need for a more detailed explanation of the impacts and cost-effectiveness of registering group rights, including the extent to which such intervention improves access to and productive use of land by outside investors. This would include whether such interventions trigger land grabbing and the extent to which there is scope for replacing traditional safeguards (land sales restrictions) with more effective ones, such as a requirement of systematic community-level registration on demand. This is linked to the need for evidence on the most effective institutional and decision-making arrangements to manage land at the local level in an equitable and flexible way and the impact of land use planning and its possible interaction with, or substitution for, land registration. Finally, two areas that have not been much researched are the establishment or reconstitution of land records in postconflict and postdisaster environments and the impact of legal and institutional reforms on management of state land.

Many of these issues lend themselves to an experimental setting that could be included in ongoing interventions. If combined with regular and standardized administrative information that can be compared over time and, with proper precautions, across countries, this research could help to better appreciate the potential positive effects and risks of land registration, the adequacy of different actions in specific circumstances, and the links to other policies. Given the complexity of the issues, these will be of great relevance not only to depoliticize the issue, but also to guard against potential negative effects.

REFERENCES

Acemoglu, Daron, and Simn Johnson. 2005. Unbundling institutions. *Journal of Political Economy* 113(5):949–995.

Acemoglu, Daron, Simn Johnson, and James A. Robinson. 2001. The colonial origins of comparative development: An empirical investigation. *American Economic Review* 91(5):1369–1401.

———. 2004. Institutions as the fundamental cause of long-run growth. NBER Working Paper 10481, National Bureau of Economic Research, Cambridge, MA.

Alden-Wily, Liz. 2003. Governance and land relations. A review of decentralization of land administration and management in Africa. IIED Issues Paper 120, International Institute for Environment and Development, London.

———. 2008. Custom and commonage in Africa: Rethinking the orthodoxies. *Land Use Policy* 25(1):43–52.

Allen, Douglas, and Dean Lueck. 1992. Contract choice in modern agriculture: Cash rent versus cropshare. *Journal of Law and Economics* 35(2):397–426.

Allendorf, Keera. 2007. Do women's land rights promote empowerment and child health in Nepal? *World Development* 35(11):1975–1988.

Andolfatto, David. 2002. A theory of inalienable property rights. *Journal of Political Economy* 110(2):382–393.

Andre, Catherine, and Jean Philippe Platteau. 1998. Land relations under unbearable stress: Rwanda caught in the Malthusian trap. *Journal of Economic Behavior and Organization* 34(1):1–47.

Antle, John M., David Yanggen, Roberto Valdivia, and Charles Crissman. 2003. Endogeneity of land titling and farm investments: Evidence from the Peruvian Andes. Working paper, Montana State University, Bozeman, MT.

Arrunada, Benito. 2003. Property enforcement as organized consent. *Journal of Law, Economics, and Organization* 19(2):401–444.

————. 2007. Pitfalls to avoid when measuring institutions: Is doing business damaging business? *Journal of Comparative Economics* 35(4):729–747.

Arrunada, Benito, and Nuno Garoupà. 2005. The choice of titling system in land. *Journal of Law and Economics* 48(2):709–727.

Atwood, David A. 1990. Land registration in Africa: The impact on agricultural production. *World Development* 18(5):659–671.

Ayalew, Daniel, Stefan Dercon, and Madhur Gautam. 2005. Property rights in a very poor country: Tenure insecurity and investment in Ethiopia. Global Poverty Research Group Working Paper Series, GPRG-WPS-021, Oxford University, Oxford, England.

Baland, Jean M., and Patrick Francois. 2005. Commons as insurance and the welfare impact of privatization. *Journal of Public Economics* 89(2–3):211–231.

Baland, Jean M., and James A. Robinson. 2003. Land and power. Discussion Paper 3800, Centre for Economic Policy Research, London, England.

Bandiera, Oriana. 2007. Land tenure, investment incentives, and the choice of techniques: Evidence from Nicaragua. *World Bank Economic Review* 21(3):487–508.

Banerjee, Abhiji V., and Lakshmi Iyer. 2004. History, institutions, and economic performance: The legacy of colonial land tenure systems in India. MIT Working Paper 02-27, Cambridge, MA.

Barnes, Grenville, and Charise Griffith-Charles. 2007. Assessing the formal land market and deformalization of property in St. Lucia. *Land Use Policy* 24(2):494–501.

Baruah, Bipasa. 2007. Gendered realities: Exploring property ownership and tenancy relationships in urban India. *World Development* 35(12):2096–2109.

Bekar, Cliff T., and Clyde G. Reed. 2003. Open fields, risk, and land divisibility. *Explorations in Economic History* 40(3):308–325.

Benjamin, Dwayne, and Loren Brandt. 2002. Property rights, labour markets, and efficiency in a transition economy: The case of rural China. *Canadian Journal of Economics* 35(4):689–716.

Benjaminsen, Tor A. 2002. Formalising land tenure in rural Africa. *Forum for Development Studies* 29(2):362–366.

Benjaminsen, Tor A., and Espen Sjaastad. 2002. Race for the prize: Land transactions and rent appropriation in the Malian cotton zone. *European Journal of Development Research* 14(2):129–152.

Berry, Sara. 1997. Tomatoes, land and hearsay: Property and history in Asante in the time of structural adjustment. *World Development* 25(8):1225–1241.

Besley, Tim. 1995. Property rights and investment incentives: Theory and evidence from Ghana. *Journal of Political Economy* 103(5):903–937.

Besley, Tim, and Maitreesh Ghatak. 2008. Creating collateral: The de Soto effect and the political economy of legal reform. Working paper, London School of Economics, London, England.

Bezabih, Mintewab, and Stein Holden. 2006. Tenure insecurity, transaction costs in the land lease market and their implications for gendered productivity differentials, mimeo. Norwegian University of Life Sciences, Aas, Norway.

Binswanger, Hans P., Klaus Deininger, and Gershon Feder. 1995. Power, distortions, revolt and reform in agricultural land relations. *Handbook of Development Economics* 3B:2659–2772.

Binswanger, Hans P., and Mark R. Rosenzweig. 1986. Behavioural and material determinants of production relations in agriculture. *Journal of Development Studies* 22(3):503–539.

Boucher, Steven, Michael R. Carter, and Catherine Guirkinger. 2008. Risk rationing and wealth effects in credit markets: Theory and implications for agricultural development. *American Journal of Agricultural Economics* 90(2):409–423.

Brasselle, Anne S., Frederick Gaspart, and Jean Philippe Platteau. 2002. Land tenure security and investment incentives: Puzzling evidence from Burkina Faso. *Journal of Development Economics* 67(2):373–418.

Brink, van den, Rogier, Daniel W. Bromley, and J. P. Chavas. 1995. The economics of Cain and Abel: Agro-pastoral property rights in the Sahel. *Journal of Development Studies* 31(3):373–399.

Broegaard, Riike J. 2005. Land tenure insecurity and inequality in Nicaragua. *Development and Change* 36(5):845–864.

Burns, Tony A. 2007. Land administration: Indicators of success and future challenges. Washington, DC: World Bank Agriculture and Rural Development Department.

Carter, Michael R., and Pedro Olinto. 2003. Getting institutions "right" for whom? Credit constraints and the impact of property rights on the quantity and composition of investment. *American Journal of Agricultural Economics* 85(1):173–186.

Carter, Michael R., and Yang Yao. 2002. Local versus global separability in agricultural household models: The factor price equalization effect of land transfer rights. *American Journal of Agricultural Economics* 84(3):702–715.

Chimhowu, Admos, and Philip Woodhouse. 2006. Customary vs. private property rights? Dynamics and trajectories of vernacular land markets in sub-Saharan Africa. *Journal of Agrarian Change* 6(3):346–371.

Clark, Ephraim. 2003. Pricing the cost of expropriation risk. *Review of International Economics* 11(2):412–422.

Colin, Jean Philippe, and Mourad Ayouz. 2006. The development of a land market? Insights from Côte d'Ivoire. *Land Economics* 82(3):404–423.

Conning, Jonathan H., and James A. Robinson. 2007. Property rights and the political organization of agriculture. *Journal of Development Economics* 82(2):416–447.

Dabrundashvili, Tea. 2006. Rights registration system reform in Georgia. Paper presented at the Expert Meeting on Good Governance in Land Tenure and Administration. Rome: Food and Agriculture Organization of the United Nations.

Datta, Namita. 2006. Joint titling—A win-win policy? Gender and property rights in urban informal settlements in Chandigarh, India. *Feminist Economics*:271–298.

Deininger, Klaus. 2003. *Land policies for growth and poverty reduction*. Oxford and New York: World Bank and Oxford University Press.

Deininger, Klaus, and Daniel A. Ali. 2008. Do overlapping property rights reduce agricultural investment? Evidence from Uganda. *American Journal of Agricultural Economics* 90(4):869–884.

Deininger, Klaus, Daniel A. Ali, Stein Holden, and Jaap Zevenbergen. 2008. Rural land certification in Ethiopia: Process, initial impact, and implications for other African countries. *World Development* 36(10):1786–1812.

Deininger, Klaus, Daniel A. Ali, and Takashi Yamano. 2008. Legal knowledge and economic development: The case of land rights in Uganda. *Land Economics* 84(4):593–619.

Deininger, Klaus, and Raffaella Castagnini. 2006. Incidence and impact of land conflict in Uganda. *Journal of Economic Behavior and Organization* 60(3):321–345.

Deininger, Klaus, and Juan Sebastian Chamorro. 2004. Investment and income effects of land regularization: The case of Nicaragua. *Agricultural Economics* 30(2):101–116.

Deininger, Klaus, and Songqing Jin. 2006. Tenure security and land-related investment: Evidence from Ethiopia. *European Economic Review* 50(5):1245–1277.

———. 2008a. Land sales and rental markets in transition: Evidence from rural Vietnam. *Oxford Bulletin of Economics and Statistics* 70(1):67–101.

———. 2008b. Securing property rights in transition: Lessons from implementation of China's rural land contracting law. *Journal of Economic Behavior and Organization*, forthcoming.

Deininger, Klaus, Songqing Jin, and Hari K. Nagarajan. 2006. Gender discrimination and the returns to self employment: Evidence from rural India. World Bank Policy Research Working Paper, Washington, DC.

Deininger, Klaus, Eduardo Zegarra, and Isabel Lavadenz. 2003. Determinants and impacts of rural land market activity: Evidence from Nicaragua. *World Development* 31(8):1385–1404.

De Meza, David, and John P. Gould. 1992. The social efficiency of private decisions to enforce property rights. *Journal of Political Economy* 100(3):561–580.

de Soto, Hernando. 2000. *The mystery of capital: Why capitalism triumphs in the West and fails everywhere else.* New York: Basic Books.

———. 2002. Rejoinder to Mathieu. *Forum for Development Studies* 29(2):376–388.

Di Tella, Rafael, Sebastián Galiani, and Ernesto Schargrodsky. 2007. The formation of beliefs: Evidence from the allocation of land titles to squatters. *Quarterly Journal of Economics* 122(1):209–241.

Do, Quy Toan, and Lakshmi Iyer. 2008. Land titling and rural transition in Vietnam. *Economic Development and Cultural Change* 56(3):531–579.

Dowall, David E., and Michael Leaf. 1992. The price of land for housing in Jakarta. In *Spatial development in Indonesia, review and prospects*, ed. K. A. Kim. Avebury, England: Aldershot.

Dower, Paul, and Elizabeth Potamites. 2005. Signaling credit-worthiness: Land titles, banking practices and access to formal credit in Indonesia, mimeo.

Durand-Lasserve, Alain, and Lauren Royston. 2002. *Holding their ground: Secure land tenure for the urban poor in developing countries.* London: Earthscan Publications.

Ellickson, Robert C. 1993. Property in land. *Yale Law Journal* 102(6):1315–1400.

Feder, Gershon, Yongladaron Chalamwong, Tongroj Onchan, and Chiwa Hongladarom. 1988. *Land policies and farm productivity in Thailand.* Baltimore and London: Johns Hopkins University Press.

Feder, Gershon, and David Feeny. 1991. Land tenure and property rights: Theory and implications for development policy. *World Bank Economic Review* 5(1):135–153.

Feder, Gershon, and Akihiko Nishio. 1999. The benefits of land registration and titling: Economic and social perspectives. *Land Use Policy* 15(1):143–169.

Fenoaltea, Stefano. 1976. Risk, transaction costs, and the organization of medieval agriculture. *Explorations in Economic History* 13(2):129–151.

Field, A. J., Erica Field, and Maximo Torero. 2006. Property rights and crop choice in rural Peru, 1994–2004. MTID Discussion Paper 100, International Food Policy Research Institute, Washington, DC.

Field, Erica M. 2003. Fertility responses to land titling: The roles of ownership security and the distribution of household assets, mimeo. Cambridge, MA: Harvard University.

———. 2005. Property rights and investment in urban slums. *Journal of the European Economic Association* 3(2–3):279–290.

———. 2007. Entitled to work: Urban property rights and labor supply in Peru. *Quarterly Journal of Economics* 122(4):1561–1602.

Field, Erica, and Maximo Torero. 2006. Do property titles increase credit access among the urban poor? Evidence from a nationwide titling program, mimeo. Cambridge, MA: Harvard University.

Firmin-Sellers, Kathryn. 2000. Custom, capitalism, and the state: The origins of insecure land tenure in West Africa. *Journal of Institutional and Theoretical Economics* 156(3):513–530.

Fitzpatrick, Daniel. 2005. "Best practice" options for the recognition of customary tenure. *Development and Change* 36(3):449–475.

Fort, Ricardo. 2007. *Property rights after market liberalization reforms: Land titling and investments in rural Peru.* Wageningen, NL: University of Wageningen.

Fred-Mensah, Ben K. 1999. Capturing ambiguities: Communal conflict management alternative in Ghana. *World Development* 27(6):951–965.

Friedman, Joseph, Emmanuel Jimenez, and Stephen K. Mayo. 1988. The demand for tenure security in developing countries. *Journal of Development Economics* 29(2):185–198.

Galiani, Sebastian, and Ernesto Schargrodsky. 2004. Effects of land titling on child health. *Economics and Human Biology* 2(3):353–372.

———. 2005. Property rights for the poor: Effects of land titling. Documento de Trabajo 06/2005, Universidad Torcuato Di Tella, Centro de Investigación en Finanzas, Buenos Aires, Argentina.

Goldstein, Markus, and Christopher Udry. 2006. The profits of power: Land rights and agricultural investment in Ghana. Economic Growth Center Working Paper 929, Yale University, New Haven, CT.

Gordillo, Gustavo de Anda, Alain de Janvry, and Elisabeth Sadoulet. 1998. Between political control and efficiency gains: The evolution of agrarian property rights in Mexico. *CEPAL Review* 66:151–169.

Gould, Kevin. 2006. Land regularization on agricultural frontiers: The case of Northwestern Peten, Guatemala. *Land Use Policy* 23(2):395–407.

Government of Kenya. 2004. *Report of the Commission of Inquiry into the Illegal/Irregular Allocation of Public Land.* Nairobi: Government Printer.

Government of Mexico. 2000. *Marco legal agrario. Edición commemorativa—reforma agraria 1915–2000.* Mexico, D.F.: Procuraduria Agraria.

Griffith-Charles, Charise. 2004. The impact of land titling on land transaction activity and registration system sustainability: A case study of St. Lucia. Ph.D. diss., University of Florida.

Grossman, Herschel I., and Juan Mendoza. 2001. Butter and guns: Complementarity between economic and military competition. *Economics of Governance* 2(1):25–33.

Henrysson, Elin, and Sandra F. Joireman. 2007. On the edge of the law: The cost of informal property rights adjudication in Kisii, Kenya. Working paper, Wheaton College, Wheaton, IL.

Holden, Stein, Klaus Deininger, and Hosaena Ghebru. 2008a. Land certification, land related investment, and productivity in Tigray, Ethiopia. Working paper, Norwegian University of Life Sciences, Aas, Norway.

———. 2008b. Low-cost land certification and land rental market participation in Tigray, Ethiopia. Working paper, Norwegian University of Life Sciences, Aas, Norway.

Holden, Stein, and Hailu Yohannes. 2002. Land redistribution, tenure insecurity, and intensity of production: A study of farm households in southern Ethiopia. *Land Economics* 78(4):573–590.

Hunt, Diana. 2004. Unintended consequences of land rights reform: The case of the 1998 Uganda Land Act. *Development Policy Review* 22(2):173–191.

Jacoby, Hanan, Guo G. Li, and Scott Rozelle. 2002. Hazards of expropriation: Tenure insecurity and investment in rural China. *American Economic Review* 92(5):1420–1447.

Jacoby, Hanan, and Bart Minten. 2007. Is land titling in sub-Saharan Africa cost effective? Evidence from Madagascar. *World Bank Economic Review* 21(3):461–485.

Jansen, Kees, and Esther Roquas. 1998. Modernizing insecurity: The land titling project in Honduras. *Development and Change* 29(1):81–106.

Johnson, Simon, John McMillan, and Christopher Woodruff. 2002. Property rights and finance. *American Economic Review* 92(5):1335–1356.

Joireman, Sandra F. 2008. The mystery of capital formation in sub-Saharan Africa: Women, property rights and customary law. *World Development* 36(7):1233–1246.

Kaganova, Olga, and James McKelar. 2006. *Managing government property assets: International experiences.* Washington, DC: Urban Institute Press.

Kato, Elisabeth 1998. *We have rights, they have power. A case study of land expropriation in northwest Cambodia.* Phnom Penh: Oxfam Land Study Project.

Kazianga, Haroun, and William A. Masters. 2006. Property rights, production technology, and deforestation: Cocoa in Cameroon. *Agricultural Economics* 35(1):19–26.

Kung, James Kai-Sing. 2002. Off-farm labor markets and the emergence of land rental markets in rural China. *Journal of Comparative Economics* 30(2):395–414.

Lanjouw, Jean O., and Philip I. Levy. 2002. Untitled: A study of formal and informal property rights in urban Ecuador. *Economic Journal* 112(482):986–1019.

Lavigne-Delville, Philippe. 2000. Harmonising formal law and customary land rights in French-speaking West Africa. In *Evolving land rights, policy and tenure in Africa,* ed. C. Toulmin and J. Quan. London: DFID/IIED/NRI.

Lavigne-Delville, P., Camilla Toulmin, Jean-Philippe Colin, and Jean-Paul Chauveau. 2002. *Negotiating access to land in West Africa: A synthesis of findings from research on derived rights to land.* London: IIED/GRET.

Leuprecht, Peter. 2004. Land concessions for economic purposes in Cambodia: A human rights perspective. Report by the Special Representative of the Secretary General for Human Rights in Cambodia. Phnom Penh: United Nations, Cambodia Office of the High Commissioner for Human Rights.

Lobo, Albert, and Surseh Balakrishnan. 2002. Report card on service of bhoomi kiosks: An assessment of benefits by users of the computerized land records system in Karnataka. Working paper, Public Affairs Centre, Bangalore.

Lueck, Dean, and Thomas Miceli. 2006. Property law. Discussion Paper 06-19, Arizona Legal Studies, University of Arizona, Tucson.

Mabogunje, Akin L. 1992. Perspective on urban land and urban management policies in sub-Saharan Africa. World Bank Technical Paper No. 196, Africa Technical Department Series, Washington, DC.

Macours, Karen, Alain de Janvry, and Elisabeth Sadoulet. 2004. Insecurity of property rights and matching in the tenancy market. Working Paper 992, Berkeley: Department of Agricultural and Resource Economics, University of California, Berkeley.

Malik, Arun, and Robert M. Schwab. 1991. Optimal investments to establish property rights in land. *Journal of Urban Economics* 29(295):309.

Mathieu, Paul. 2002. Security of land tenure papers and unleashing grass-root investment for rural development in Africa: Some comments. *Forum for Development Studies* 29(2):367–372.

McCloskey, David N. 1975. *The persistence of English common fields*. Princeton, NJ: Princeton University Press.

McKenny, Bruce, and Prom Tola. 2002. Natural resources and rural livelihoods in Cambodia: A baseline assessment. Working Paper 23, Cambodia Development Resource Institute, Phnom Penh.

Meinzen-Dick, Ruth, and Ester Mwangi. 2009. Cutting the web of interests: Pitfalls of formalizing property rights. *Land Use Policy* 26(1):36–43.

Mushinski, David W. 1999. An analysis of offer functions of banks and credit unions in Guatemala. *Journal of Development Studies* 36(2):88–112.

Nettle, Kevin. 2006. Titles vs. deeds: International experience and implications for India. Paper presented at the MoRD/World Bank Workshop on Land Policies for Accelerated Growth and Poverty Reduction in India, New Delhi.

Nugent, Jeffrey B., and James A. Robinson. 2002. Are endowments fate? CEPR Working Paper 3206, London.

Panda, Pradeep, and Bina Agarwal. 2005. Marital violence, human development and women's property status in India. *World Development* 33(5):823–850.

Pande, Rohini, and Christopher Udry. 2005. Institutions and development: A view from below. Working Paper 928, Yale University, Economic Growth Center, New Haven, CT.

Payne, Geoffrey, Alain Durand-Lasserve, and Carol Rakodi. 2008. *Social and economic impacts of land titling programmes in urban and peri-urban areas: International experience and case studies of Senegal and South Africa*. Oslo and Stockholm: SIDA and Norwegian Ministry of Foreign Affairs.

Peters, Pauline. 2004. Inequality and social conflict over land in Africa. *Journal of Agrarian Change* 4(3):269–314.

Powelson, John P. 1988. *The story of land: A world history of land tenure and agrarian reform*. Cambridge, MA: Lincoln Institute of Land Policy.

Quisumbing, Aagnes R., and John A. Maluccio. 2003. Resources at marriage and intra-household allocation: Evidence from Bangladesh, Ethiopia, Indonesia, and South Africa. *Oxford Bulletin of Economics and Statistics* 65(3):283–327.

Rozelle, Scott, and Johan F. M. Swinnen. 2004. Success and failure of reform: Insights from the transition of agriculture. *Journal of Economic Literature* 42(2):404–456.

Schweigert, Thomas E. 2007. Land title, tenure security, investment and farm output: Evidence from Guatemala. *Journal of Developing Areas* 40(1):115–126.

Shavell, Steven. 2003. Economic analysis of property law. NBER Working Paper 9695, National Bureau of Economic Research.

Siamwalla, Ammar. 1990. The Thai rural credit system: Public subsidies, private information, and segmented markets. *World Bank Economic Review* 4(3):271–295.

Sjaastad, Espen, and Daniel W. Bromley. 1997. Indigenous land rights in sub-Saharan Africa: Appropriation, security and investment demand. *World Development* 25(4):549–562.

———. 2000. The prejudices of property rights: On individualism, specificity, and security in property regimes. *Development Policy Review* 18(4):365–389.

Stiglitz, Joseph E., and Andrew Weiss. 1981. Credit rationing in markets with imperfect information. *American Economic Review* 71(3):393–410.

Transparency International India. 2005. India corruption study 2005. New Delhi: Transparency International.

Udry, Christopher. 1996. Gender, agricultural production, and the theory of the household. *Journal of Political Economy* 104(5):1010–1046.

UNECE. 1996. *Land administration guidelines, with special references to countries in transition*. ECE/HBP/96. New York and Geneva: United Nations Economic Commission for Europe.

Vogl, Tom S. 2007. Urban land rights and child nutritional status in Peru, 2004. *Economics and Human Biology* 5(2):302–321.

World Bank. 2002. *Mexico—land policy: A decade after the ejido reforms*. Washington, DC: The World Bank, Rural Development and Natural Resources Sector Unit.

———. 2007. *Doing business 2008*. Washington, DC: World Bank, International Finance Corporation, and Oxford University Press.

Yang, Dennis T. 1997. China's land arrangements and rural labor mobility. *China Economic Review* 8(2):101–115.

Zepeda, Guillermo. 2000. *Transformación agraria. Los derechos de propriedad en el campo Mexicano bajo el Nuevo Marco Institucional*. CIOAC, Mexico, Mexico City.

COMMENTARY
Alain Durand-Lasserve

Interestingly, the chapter by Klaus Deininger and Gershon Feder shifts progressively from what should be an ideal world (that can be seen as a highly ideological approach about how human society should organize) to a very prudent and nuanced appreciation of the limits of development policies based on the allocation of property rights. Based on recent studies, it provides an excellent review of existing evidence on the effectiveness of land registration in improving economic growth.

This ideal world, which is described in the presentation of the conceptual framework, is a conflicts-free society in which public intervention is expected to enforce property rights, save costs, and provide goods and infrastructure at least cost. The main stated objective is to encourage land transfers to more efficient users. The hypothesized impacts of land titling are to increase security of tenure, reduce the costs of protecting property, encourage investment, stimulate rental transactions, and reduce transaction costs. The possession of registered land rights is supposed to improve economic efficiency and encourage the development of financial markets, with titled land being used as collateral for credit.

The chapter goes far beyond this conventional thinking and proposes an argued inventory and analysis of what works and what does not. It provides useful benchmarks for understanding complex interactions and dynamics. The shift from an ideal world to realities reflects the current international debate about land registration and land titling, from a rather simplistic approach (which is reflected in Hernando de Soto's [2000] statements about the relationship between property rights and economic development) to a much more pragmatic approach incorporating cultural and economic differentiation between and within societies.

However, given the bibliographical sources on which the authors rely, the first section of the chapter, which reviews the justification for public involvement in adjudication of property rights, might generate misunderstandings or misinterpretations. The emphasis is mainly on economic efficiency. The conflicting nature of tenure relations tends to be underestimated, and the conflict resolution and administrative capacity of public authorities to implement land registration programs tends to be overestimated. Societies are presented as politics-free and potentially consensual (with illusory win-win policies). The social dimension of tenure and the effectiveness of social regulation mechanisms of potential land conflicts are minimized (yet tenure is a social relation). A short comment would be welcomed to inform readers that the authors are aware of the limits of their sources, which all rely on the same sets of hypothesis and assumptions.

Methodology and Approach ────────────────────────────

The beginning of the chapter defines good institutions for economic development as those institutions guaranteeing property rights, such rights being "far more important for growth than contracting institutions." I am skeptical of the use of normative appreciations (and especially the overuse of the term *good*) as well as about universal values and paradigms/models.

The relationship between security of tenure and land registration/land titling should be clarified at the beginning of the chapter. There is an implicit assumption among the studies to which the chapter refers that there is a tight correlation between property rights, economic development, and poverty reduction. Yet, the wealth redistribution mechanisms that would ensure poverty reduction tend to be taken for granted.

A clear definition of some of the key terms used in the chapter and by authors quoted is needed: *land administration, land registration, land titling* (various types of land titling), *property rights, tenure regularization, tenure formalization*, and the relationship between security of tenure and property.

A short inventory or typology of the main types of tenure rights (possibly in an appendix) would avoid some misinterpretations in the debate (individual property rights, real rights, other types of individual or collective titles, administrative permits, certificates). The objective is not to give any right or consensual definition of key terms and concepts used (many definitions are debatable) but to agree on a common language.

There is sometimes a lack of clarity in the review about two different and sometimes contradictory objectives: (1) securing investment and stimulating economic development; and (2) providing security of tenure and ensuring social stability. Securing tenure does not equate securing property.

Policy and Research Implications ────────────────────

RESEARCH-RELATED ISSUES

Research-related issues include difficulties associated with the exploration of interactions among land registration, economic development, and poverty reduction because of few quantitative studies. Large-scale land registration and land titling programs have been implemented too recently to be correctly assessed. As in most socioeconomic impact assessments, the biggest methodological challenge is to separate the effects of land registration and titling intervention from other factors that are likely to produce similar impacts. Political factors that determined eligibility of settlements or neighborhoods for land registration and tenure formalization can still have an impact on the neighborhood after land registration (political protection and its consequence on access to credit, provision of services, and so on). Possible selection bias is likely to be magnified where land registration was sporadic rather than systematic. Sporadic allocation of property rights is not random, but is likely to be influenced by wealth, family characteristics, political clientelism, and other selection mechanisms. Longitudinal or before-and-after study could overcome such biases. It would suit situations where baseline data on the variables under investigation exist for the period prior to land registration. Actually, due to lack of reliable data, very few quantitative studies are comparing a group that had benefited from land tenure regularization/registration with a control group that did not benefit (Galiani and Schargrodsky 2005).

RESEARCH TOPICS
Future research topics include an assessment of land registration impacts on various segments of land markets, including informal land markets. Analysis of interactions between land markets would require a systemic approach. A better understanding of market-driven displacements following land registration is also needed. Regarding governance in land administration, particular attention should be given to the analysis of the interactions between land registration and corruption. There is a need to evaluate the benefits of land registration for those receiving land titles in relation to the public or private costs involved. Overall costs and benefits, cost-effectiveness, and the cost and outcomes of titling need to be considered in comparison to alternative options improving security of tenure and poverty-reducing interventions. Better understanding of the land registration effects on tenants of urban land and dwellings is necessary. There is a need for better understanding of social regulation institutions of land management and land-related conflict resolution.

POLICY PRIORITIES
Some policy priorities follow:

- Correct the asymmetry in access to information. Particular attention should be given to land information systems that are accessible and development of a land administration system that can support all forms of land rights, social tenure relations, and overlapping claims to land, taking into account continuum of land rights.
- Develop a variety of tools that can be used within a range of technical, social, and legal processes to enable people, especially the poor, to assert their land rights.
- Emphasize incremental processes (from de facto protection against evictions to de jure tenure regularization). To what extent are the weaknesses or negative effects of land registration projects related to their implementation pace (gap between the time required to set up a land administration system and the time frame of land registration programs).

REFERENCES

de Soto, Hernando. 2000. *The mystery of capital: Why capitalism triumphs in the West and fails everywhere else*. New York: Basic Books.

Galiani, Sebastian, and Ernesto Schargrodsky. 2005. Property rights for the poor: Effects of land titling. Documento de Trabajo 06/2005, Universidad Torcuato Di Tella, Centro de Investigacion en Finanzas, Buenos Aires, Brazil.

12

Looking Beyond Land Titling and Credit Accessibility for the Urban Poor

Edésio Fernandes

T he gigantic scale of informal urban land development has been repeatedly
confirmed by recent data from various sources (Davis 2006). However, the
structural nature of the process is still to be fully recognized by policy
makers and public administrators at all levels. This chapter presents and critically
discusses, from a socio-legal perspective, some of the main findings resulting from
international research and academic literature on urban land regularization—not a
rosy picture—and aims to contribute to improving future policies and programs.

I also draw from my more than 20 years of experience of regularly working
with informal development and regularization programs, mainly in Brazil, but also
in several Latin American countries, South Africa, Albania, Kosovo, and Syria. As
director of land affairs at the Ministry of Cities in Brazil in 2003, I coordinated the
formulation of the National Programme to Support Sustainable Land Regularisation in Urban Areas (Fernandes 2006). This chapter argues that the widespread
adoption of large-scale titling programs by many countries and cities reflects an
international tendency to reduce urban land regularization to its legal dimension,
thus provoking a simplistic juridification of the more complex discussion of informal development. Such programs have been largely based on the assumption
that land titling structurally impacts several processes, especially the conditions of
access to formal credit, poverty eradication, security of tenure, and socio-spatial
integration. However, these titling programs need to be reassessed from a broader
and more qualified legal perspective. Far from resolving problems resulting from
informal development, they have created several new urban and legal challenges.
Instead of questioning the legal order that produced informal development in the
first place, large-scale titling programs have repeatedly confirmed it.

Following a brief critique of the assumptions underlying large-scale titling
programs, the chapter discusses the main causes of the informal development

296

process, as well as the broad context in which regularization programs have been formulated. The matter of land legalization is then reexamined within a more critical socio-legal framework, thus supporting the argument that land titling is indeed of utmost importance, but not for the reasons generally claimed. The chapter concludes that consistent progress in the complex field of land regularization will ultimately require the combination of new legal concepts and technical criteria, making possible the adoption of a broader concept of regularization as well as requiring suitable options for the legalization of informal settlements. The legal causes of informal development need to be directly confronted for successful regularization of existing situations, as well as for prevention of future informal development.

The process of informal access to urban land and housing is by no means new. Several cities have informal settlements constituted over a hundred years ago that still have not been regularized. In Latin America, where some 75 percent of the people live in urban areas, at least 25 percent of urban people—a conservative estimate—live in informal settlements. However, the process of informal development is clearly getting worse—increases in the number of informal settlements and the deterioration of living conditions in these areas—at the global level, especially in the current context of rapid urbanization in Asia, Africa, the Middle East, and Eastern Europe. UN-HABITAT numbers suggest that more than 1 billion people currently live in informal settlements. Globally, since 2007 the urban population exceeds the rural population. Whereas informal land development used to mostly take place in large cities, more recently it has also been verified in middle-size and small cities.

New processes of informal development, as well as new variations of old processes, have occurred in both public and private areas. Current processes of informal development in Latin America include the occupation of public and private land, the illegal subdivision of private and public land followed by the sale of individual plots, the development of rural areas for urban purposes, the illegal subdivision of previously existing legal plots, and the widespread occupation of water reservoirs and other environmentally protected areas, among others (Abramo 2003; Cravino 2006). Comparable processes have occurred in such countries as India, South Africa, and Turkey (Durand-Lasserve and Royston 2002; Huchzermeyer and Karam 2006; Neuwirth 2005).

The serious social, environmental, political, economic, cultural, and legal implications of this growing phenomenon have been widely discussed, but the centrality of the issue has not been properly recognized by governments, international development agencies, and financial institutions.[1] More than ever

---

1. Although the existing data are imprecise, several Latin American municipalities such as Salvador and Fortaleza, Brazil, and Caracas, Venezuela, admit to the existence of over 50 percent of informal urban development. About 50 percent of urban land development in Tirana, Albania, and Damascus, Syria, has been promoted informally. The list goes on.

before, informal land development has become the rule of access to urban land and housing, rather than the exception. It is not merely a symptom or a dysfunctional, isolated aspect of a territorial and socioeconomic development model, but rather has increasingly become the development model itself. Successfully confronting this phenomenon through both preventive and curative policies and programs to democratize access to serviced land in urban areas, as well as to promote better conditions of sustainable development, is a major challenge for policy makers globally.

Although from an immediatist perspective, the informal processes of access to land offer concrete and necessary housing alternatives to the urban poor, from a broader, more articulated perspective, the combined effects of the phenomenon have been fundamentally harmful to the cities increasingly produced this way; to the overall urban population; and to the residents of the informal settlements. For these reasons, the processes should not be condoned or left unquestioned. Above all, despite the commonly held belief, urban informality is not a cheap option. It generates expensive, fragmented cities; requires highly costly regularization programs; and results in increasingly higher land prices and services for people living in precarious conditions in the informal settlements (Abramo 2003). All parties lose.

Especially in countries such as those in Latin America where the urbanization process has already been consolidated, informal land development involves not only the urban poor, but also more privileged social segments. Moreover, the growth rates of informal development in these countries have been higher than the growth rates of poverty, thus indicating that other significant factors are at play. These factors need to be identified and understood to explain the phenomenon, beyond the traditional recourse to poverty growth as the sole cause of urban informality. In some cases, several agents have financially and politically benefited from the phenomenon, and an informal development industry has been identified (Fernandes and Smolka 2004).

Several financial institutions, international development agencies, and national and local governments have unreservedly proposed and/or supported large-scale titling programs aimed at legalizing consolidated informal areas in Peru, El Salvador, Albania, Vietnam, Cambodia, and many other countries. This approach has significantly reduced the scope of the complex debate over informal settlement and the nature and possibilities of state intervention in the process. Property rights are intrinsically and inevitably ideological, but the current uncritical fetishist treatment of titling programs can no longer be left unquestioned. Their negative effects have considerably outweighed the positive ones.[2]

---

2. Far-fetched studies have tried to link recent land titling programs to significant social transformations, such as the number of children attending school and an increase in levels of caloric intake.

The Limits of Large-Scale Titling Programs

There is an international dispute on conceptual paradigms about how to confront consolidated informal settlements. Whereas some governmental programs have proposed upgrading the informal areas, others have focused on the legalization—also referred to as titling and formalization—of the areas and of individual plots.[3] Legalization has been the dominant approach for the last decade, due to a large extent to the influential ideas of Peruvian economist Hernando de Soto (Fernandes 2002a).

There are at least three different types of regularization programs:

1. Programs in both private and public areas where subjective rights have been created through time and/or have been recognized by legislation
2. Programs in areas of social interest that are expressions of the discretional power of the public authorities
3. The discretionary regularization of informal development in areas that are not legally considered to be of social interest, such as those occupied by socioeconomic groups other than the urban poor

These are different legal situations that require different legal treatment. The specifics of each situation need to be taken into consideration by policy makers in charge of the formulation of regularization programs.

Large-scale titling programs have often been justified by policy makers on the grounds that land titling impacts access to formal credit for the urban poor, significantly contributes toward poverty eradication, promotes security of tenure, and guarantees socio-spatial integration. In particular, much has been made of the assertion that large-scale titling programs enable access to formal credit, increase the participation of residential and commercial mortgages in the gross national products of developing and transitional countries, and revive the gigantic amount of "dead capital" accumulated through informal development processes. Several countries, including Peru and El Salvador, have already implemented titling programs in different ways and to different extents, while other countries, such as Albania, are currently in the process of doing so. As a result, millions of individual freehold titles have been given to the residents of informal urban settlements (Calderón 2006; Zeledón 2006).

Now that considerable time has passed since the implementation of the pioneering Peruvian program and the first comprehensive analyses of it and other programs have been produced, this unqualified assumption can be criticized. Detailed research in the paradigmatic case of Peru has clearly shown that the

---

3. A good example is the paradigmatic case of the long-standing Favela-Bairro program in Rio de Janeiro sponsored by the Inter-American Development Bank, which only recently introduced, in a very timid way, a discussion of the legalization of the occupied areas.

level of access to formal credit by the urban poor over the years has not been significant. In the traditional banking and financial system, commercial banks do not readily lend to the poor and do not automatically accept the newly titled properties as collateral, especially in peripheral areas where properties have no significant market value (Calderón 2006). The financial and technical criteria used by the commercial banks, the bureaucracy involved, the required documentation and proof of income, and the banks' lack of confidence in the repossession process in the event of default have precluded access to official credit for most people living in informal settlements. This differs from unsecured microcredit transactions, where a main assumption is not people's lack of capacity to pay back loans, but rather their incapacity to prove that they can pay according to the traditional formalistic requirements.

In the Peruvian case the available data have shown that employed workers who do not have property titles have had easier access to formal credit than have unemployed people who have titles (Calderón 2006). Moreover, as has long been the case in several countries such as Brazil, several governmental programs have regularly offered credit, mostly through public banks, for the acquisition of building materials, usually without requiring proof of property titles.[4]

Another factor identified by recent research—for example, in Colombia—is that many, if not most, people living in informal settlements do not want access to official credit through the commercial banking system; they have informal, more flexible, means of getting limited credit through their social and capital networks (Gilbert 2002). Furthermore, they fear the financial risks involved in offering their sole properties—usually their family homes—as collateral in exchange for the limited financing offered by the commercial banks. High interest rates, lack of flexibility, and ever-changing financial regulations add to their fear. Their trepidation seems to be justified, especially in light of the widespread credit crisis currently affecting the housing sector, with record numbers of repossessions in countries such as the United States and the United Kingdom. The credit crunch seems to indicate that the inclusion of mortgages in the calculation of the GNPs of several countries was highly artificial.

It is also clear that titles are not necessarily needed for people to invest systematically in their informal houses and businesses. The perception of security is sufficient to generate this effect (Payne 2002).

The catchy, albeit misleading, notion of dead capital requires critical understanding. In most developing countries, indirect taxation paid through services and consumption has long played a significant role in overall tax revenues, often

---

4. In Brazil, Caixa Economica Federal, the largest public bank, has long had a Building Materials Bank line of credit.

being more relevant than direct taxation of property and capital. For example, recent official dàta from Brazil, where most of the taxation is indirect, indicate that the poor pay 44.5 percent more tax than the rich. Most citizens, including those living in informal areas, decisively contribute to the national economy. Countries such as Greece and Italy have even started to systematically include the data from the informal economy in the calculation of their GNPs. This seems to support the argument that the categories of formal and informal, legal and illegal, and regular and irregular are limited conceptual and/or pedagogical attempts at describing complex processes. Rather than being static or monolithic, these processes are fluid, multidimensional, intertwined, and overlapping (Fernandes and Varley 1998).

The widely accepted assumption that titling contributes to poverty eradication also needs to be revisited in a more critical way. Upgrading programs bring concrete benefits to the residents' daily lives, but legalization programs per se do not fully include people in the market economy and thus have no structural impact on social poverty. Again, the paradigmatic case of Peru is revealing. While the country is South America's fastest-growing economy, fresh data indicate that poverty has fallen only slowly despite highly expensive investments in large-scale titling programs for over a decade. As a result, there is a growing sense of social dissatisfaction (Economist 2008, 10). In Peru as in other countries, effective poverty eradication requires consistent significant investments in infrastructure, education, and social policy as well as solid job- and income-generation strategies.

Policy makers have also commonly referred to the promotion of security of tenure and socio-spatial integration as effects of titling programs, as if they were the same thing, or as if one objective necessarily and automatically follows the other. Land titling does provide individual security of tenure and protection against forced eviction. However, as examples in several countries such as Vietnam and Cambodia have clearly demonstrated, the recognition of individual security of tenure, if considered in isolation, can lead to so-called expulsion by the market (or by land barons, property speculators, drug dealers, or other forces) and thus aggravate socio-spatial segregation. By the same token, as proved by the Brazilian case, it is possible to promote significant socio-spatial integration without distributing land titles (Fernandes 2002b).

The challenge is to conceive a legal-political formula to reconcile individual interests and rights with public interests and obligations so that individual security can be assured and the collective interests of maintaining communities in the upgraded and legalized areas affirmed. Doing so will guarantee that the urban poor will be the main beneficiaries of the public intervention. As discussed below, the Brazilian Special Zones of Social Interest formula might be a way to address all such concerns.

Large-scale titling programs have generated many positive effects, although in many cases failure to register the new titles in the official registration system still undermines their legal validity.[5] However, research has clearly indicated many negative effects resulting from large-scale titling programs conceived and implemented in isolation. Density has increased in legalized areas as more people have come to live in them, thus provoking further saturation of the precarious infrastructure. The mere announcement that titling programs will be implemented automatically leads to increases in land and property prices in the internal informal markets. Titling programs have also generated more informal development and further distortions in the broader land and property markets.[6]

Even in strictly legal terms, more problems have been created by unidimensional titling programs. As a result of the excessive emphasis on individual titling to the detriment of other dimensions of the process of land regularization, totally inadequate areas and constructions have been legalized, and many unsustainable situations have been worsened. Titles have been given in areas with disputed ownership, to people who have other properties, and to occupiers whose possession is contested by informal landlords, family members, or other parties. They have been given to occupiers of areas needed for the implementation of infrastructure and public equipment. The broader discussion of social housing rights has been reduced to a limited discussion of property rights, leading, among other factors, to the excessive privatization of public land and the failure to recognize the possible configuration of adverse possession rights in private areas (Fernandes 2002b).

Titling is indeed important, but not for the reasons usually claimed. Policy makers need to fully understand and address the causes of informal development so that they can properly confront it.

Causes of the Informal Development Process and the Context of Regularization Programs

The growing process of informal access to urban land and housing results from a combination of still little-understood reasons, and is itself an underlying reason for many other serious problems. Considered together with other factors, it can go a long way toward explaining what has been called the "structural inability" of local public administrations in many developing and transitional countries to guarantee sufficient access to serviced, central, accessible, and affordable land in urban areas.

---

5. Given the incapacity to effectively confront and modernize the anachronistic national registration system, a parallel system was created within the ambit of the land titling program in Peru, and consistent efforts to reconcile the two systems have only recently been made. Albania has the same problem.

6. There are several, still scattered, studies on Latin American cities sponsored by the Lincoln Institute of Land Policy that discuss a range of negative implications of land regularization programs.

The main causes of the phenomenon of informal development range from global macroeconomic factors to local variables. Five intertwined causes deserve special mention:

1. Lack of formal access to serviced urban land resulting from the nature of governmental land, urban, housing, and fiscal policies
2. The exclusionary dynamics of formal land and housing markets that do not cater to the needs of the urban poor
3. Long-standing political manipulation of the people living in informal settlements through renewed clientelistic practices
4. Elitist and technocratic planning systems of local administrations that often fail to account for both the socioeconomic realities determining the conditions of access to urban land and housing and the capacity of local administrations to implement the urban legislation
5. Fundamentally obsolete legal and judicial systems in many developing and transitional countries

The importance of the global and macroeconomic factors should not be underestimated, but a great deal can be done at the national and, especially, local levels to reverse the process of informal development. In particular, innovative and inclusive land, urban, and housing policies can be formulated. Unfortunately, this has not occurred in the vast majority of cases.

In particular, policy makers have not properly identified or addressed the legal problems at the root of the informal development process. Informal development involves one or more intrinsic violations of private and/or public ownership rights; of urban, environmental, and/or building regulations and standards; of registration requirements; and/or of taxation provisions. Although informal settlements often have the same physical expressions, their specific legal problems are distinct. A Brazilian favela, for example, cannot be treated with the same legal criteria used to confront a clandestine land subdivision; occupation of privately owned land in South Africa should not be treated with the same legal criteria used for occupation of public land.

The urban legal order has been one of the main factors in the increase of socio-spatial segregation in at least three main ways:

1. The limited, if not distorted, materialization of the notion of the social function of property through urban and environmental regulations
2. The bureaucratic and technocratic dynamics of the urban management process
3. The contradictory and confused workings of the overall legal and judicial system

These factors have combined to determine the formation of land and property prices in both the formal and informal markets, thus generating the exclusionary pattern of urban development in developing and transitional countries. They have also determined the space reserved for the poor in urban areas, making it necessary for them to increasingly live outside of formally regulated areas, on public land, or in environmentally sensitive, unsuitable, or risky areas.

The tradition of unqualified individual ownership rights is still dominant in many countries, and people still believe that informal development is the result of the lack of urban planning. Most countries have at least an incipient planning tradition. However, planning systems have often involved unrealistic technical standards and elitist rules that do not take into account the socioeconomic realities determining access to land and housing (Verma 2002). In most cases, urban planning has expressed an alleged objective rationality. Failing to understand the dynamics of formal markets and the impact of urban and environmental regulations on those markets, the plans have been thoroughly appropriated by market forces and immediately translated into growing land and property values.

The plans include little flexibility to promote the gradual upgrading of new residential areas. They lack adequate legal instruments to allow for the full materialization of social and environmental rights. They do not oblige owners to develop and build, or to refrain from doing so. Serviced urban land is not earmarked for social housing. There is no consistent policy for the use of public land and property.[7] As discussed below, local administrations could adopt several types of intervention in the land structure to promote a more inclusive urban order. Public authorities rarely try to recapture for the community some of the enormous surplus value generated by the implementation of public infrastructure, provision of services, and changes in land use and development regulations. In Latin America, Colombia has clearly led the way in discussion of the possibilities of recapturing surplus resulting from urban legislation (Maldonado 2006).

Existing urban planning schemes and territorial organization policies have not been properly integrated with housing, environmental, transportation, taxation, and budgetary policies at all governmental levels. As a result, while old land conflicts have gained new momentum, new forms of land conflicts have emerged. Despite the difficulty, attempts need to be made to overcome the tradition of conceptual, legal, and institutional fragmentation, as has happened in a promising way in Medellin, Colombia.

The cumbersome conditions of urban management have also played an important role in informal development. Excessive bureaucracy, long licensing procedures, the imposition of strict obligations and inflexible guarantees, the lack of institutional integration and of one-stop shops have together entailed high

---

7. Addressing South African local administrations in 2007, President Thabo Mbeki criticized them for having failed to promote spatially inclusive planning policies and for instead confirming apartheid practices through developer-oriented strategies and ignoring the need to earmark land for the development of social and/or affordable housing.

costs that have been systematically transferred to land and property prices. In many Latin American cities, the fragmented institutional procedures and excessive requirements cause the licensing of development applications to take up to five years.

Moreover, urban management tends to be technocratic, if not authoritarian. It fails to involve popular participation or to take into account the capacity of public administrations to act, especially at the local level. This has generated widespread tolerance of law violations and of impunity, thus fomenting the long-standing process and corresponding culture of informality.

This complicated picture has been aggravated further by the confused and contradictory workings of the legal and judicial systems in most developing and transitional countries. Some of the factors affecting urban management that are possible reasons for the reproduction of urban informality include the approval of legal institutions that are not adequate for the declared objectives, the lack of legal treatment of existing processes, ill-defined and imprecise legal concepts, conflicts between laws, excessive formalism and irrational requirements, obscure legal language, presumption of bad faith, lack of publicity and transparency, and lack of efficiency and accountability.

Costly and lengthy land and property registration practices, which have excluded an increasingly larger number of people from the legal security of tenure generated by the registration, are an important factor.[8] Adequate mechanisms and processes for extrajudicial conflict resolution are lacking, and court actions have been characterized by long and costly procedures, unreasonable formal requirements, excessive numbers of appeals, ill-prepared judges and lawyers, conservative and anachronistic jurisprudence, lack of collective procedures, and all sorts of inconsistencies.

In sum, the combination of unrealistic technical criteria, heavy financial obligations, inflexible financial guarantees, tight schedules, undetermined licensing procedures, formalistic contractual rules, obsolete registration practices, and inefficient conflict resolution mechanisms produces a highly prohibitive legal formula. The role of law in the production of exclusionary urban development—and of informal development—must no longer be ignored, as attested by the existing data on housing deficits, vacant serviced land, abandoned or underutilized properties, environmental degradation, spatial segregation, and high rates of property speculation in urban areas.[9]

---

8. The importance of registration is even greater in countries such as Brazil, where the registration of the transaction at the registry office is all that constitutes ownership.

9. Brazil's housing deficit is currently estimated at 7,900,000 units, with 93 percent of it affecting families earning less than three minimum wages. The same census indicates a stock of abandoned and/or underutilized properties, both private and public, of over 5,500,000 units. In many Latin American countries, between 25 and 35 percent of the total serviced urban area is kept vacant for speculation reasons.

A process of so-called legal pluralism has been increasingly identified in many countries: given the crisis of the legal order generated by the growing gap between legality and legitimacy, several informal social processes and complex codes have been formed to promote the distribution of justice according to the claims of organized social groups, many of which are not legal. There is nothing unregulated in informal development processes.[10]

In many contexts, this process has corresponded to the growing social claim for the legal empowerment of local administrations in matters of urban regulation and territorial organization. Several tensions between representative and participatory democracy, as well as between local and national governmental levels, have been identified. They have been aggravated further, within the context of the globalization of land and property markets, by the adoption of unqualified privatization policies and by the pressure for deregulation and flexibility of the urban regulations in force (World Bank 2004). It is becoming increasingly clear that urban reform requires the reform of the legal order as well. This involves redefining ownership rights, integrating urban law and management, broadening the scope for popular participation in the decision-making process, and, above all, creating the basis of a process of land governance to support the democratization of access to land and housing.

Democratizing access to urban land and housing is no easy task. It requires the combination of several public policies:

- Inclusive urban policies and more realistic urban and environmental regulations and standards
- More housing policies and construction of new housing units by the public and the private sectors and by organized communities, for example, through housing cooperatives
- New mechanisms and strategies of urban management, especially through the recapture of land value increments
- The earmarking of serviced land for social housing
- Giving a social function to public land and property
- Compulsory development and/or utilization of vacant land and abandoned or underutilized properties
- Regeneration of central areas
- Regularization of consolidated informal settlements

It is in this broad and utterly complex context that the matter of land regularization should be discussed.

---

10. The codes of behavior in several Brazilian favelas, for example, have become increasingly complex, regulating civil, commercial, urban planning, and criminal matters. Building authorizations are paid for and recorded through informal mechanisms.

Rather than insisting on a perverse series of policies that favor unqualified deregulation, unsustainable housing subsidies, and questionable regularization programs, the public administrations need urgently to intervene directly in the land structure so as to break the vicious cycle that has long produced informal development.[11] Regularization policies are merely palliative and remedial. They need to be articulated with inclusive land development, housing construction, and innovative financing programs. Preventing informal development is cheaper, faster, and easier than regularizing informal settlements.[12]

Guaranteeing the permanence of existing communities in the consolidated settlements is of utmost importance. There is not enough serviced land to make adequate relocation possible. Sufficient financial resources for that purpose are also lacking. The environmental footprint of such a policy would be enormous. Consolidated communities do not want to be relocated, given the social and capital networks they have formed over the years. In many cases, communities have a legal right to stay where they live. The challenge is to reconcile the recognition of individual security of tenure with the socio-spatial integration of informal settlements and communities. This requires a broad approach to regularization, combining legalization, upgrading, and several other social programs, with the clear determination of a gender dimension. As stressed above, the legal specifics of each situation must be taken into consideration by the policy makers in charge of the formulation of regularization programs.

The Matter of Legalization

Given the lack of proper acknowledgement of the phenomenon of informal development and its implications, most institutional responses have so far proved wanting. If anything, a dangerous tolerance of the process of informal urban land development seems to be growing. Institutional responses at all levels generally have fundamental problems of scale and contents and have not been adequate. Important as they are, UN-HABITAT campaigns and the Millennium Development Goals, as well as existing national, regional, and local programs, have covered only a small drop of the ocean of informal land development. On the whole, governmental policies and programs have tended to be isolated, fragmented, sectoral, marginal, and seriously underfunded.

---

11. Although they are both impressive in terms of the scale and high numbers involved, the housing subsidy programs in Chile and South Africa have been increasingly criticized for having failed to confront the process of socio-spatial segregation and generating instead social, urban, and environmental problems as well as further informal development.

12. Many Latin American studies sponsored by the Lincoln Institute of Land Policy suggest this approach, although deeper, more organized and comprehensive research is still due.

Adequate responses are urgently necessary; policy makers and public administrators can no longer afford to keep reinventing the wheel. They should all learn from the experiences of more than 40 years of regularization programs, which provide enough elements at least to indicate what should not be done. In particular, African, Asian, and transitional Eastern European and Middle Eastern countries should look closely at Latin America, where the process of urban development has been consolidating for a while.

Even within the same financial institutions and development agencies, there is no organized knowledge of how to confront the phenomenon, and contradictory responses often result. All institutions and agencies need to take stock so as not to keep repeating the same old mistakes.

The main problem affecting the vast majority of regularization programs is that they have failed to directly confront the nature and above-mentioned causes of the phenomenon and, as a result, have often generated further distortions in urban land and property markets. They have not intervened in the land structure in a significant way, especially in that they have borne little relation to other public policies concerning vacant land, underutilized properties, and public land. Large-scale titling programs have not been properly reconciled with the broader set of policies on public land, urban areas, housing, and fiscal matters, and they have failed to reverse the long-standing unequal spatial concentration of equipment and services. Generally speaking, they have failed to reconcile their declared objectives with the necessary processes, mechanisms, resources, and instruments. Very often, they have been the object of political manipulation.

Moreover, large-scale titling programs have failed to address the abovementioned problems of urban management and the legal, registration, and judicial systems. If anything, they have made them worse. In Albania, for example, besides being reduced to its titling dimension, the land regularization program currently being implemented does not fully interact with property restitution policies, the land registration system, and the urban land regulation framework, thus generating further legal, financial, and urban problems (World Bank 2007).

After decades of public investment through regularization programs, there are no adequate assessments of their efficacy; there are no clear indicators to be observed for that purpose. There appears to have been a significant waste of limited resources, and the beneficiaries of the programs have not always been the urban poor living in the regularized informal settlements. Among the many inevitable lessons is that regularization programs take time, are complex—skipping stages is not an option—and are intrinsically costly. It is easier and cheaper to prevent the process of informal land development from happening. Given the diversity of existing situations, there are no automatic, magic, simplistic, or one-size-fits-all solutions.

Given the scale of the problem, not regularizing informal settlements is no longer an acceptable policy. Given the lack of proper governmental action over the years, new international and national laws and judicial decisions have consistently affirmed that traditional discretionary policies are not sufficient. There has been increasing recognition that the communities living in informal settlements have a right to have them regularized, often against the will of the public authorities. Land regularization has become a fundamental element of the widely recognized social right to adequate housing. In a growing number of judicial cases, eviction orders have been conditioned to offers, by public authorities or by private landowners, of acceptable relocation alternatives.[13]

The question is how to regularize. The conceptual format and institutional design of regularization programs should reflect the answers given by policy makers to three fundamental, interrelated questions: why informal settlements should be regularized, what regularization is, and what the objectives of the regularization programs are. In this process, policy makers should take into account the need to reconcile the scale of intervention with the proposed technical criteria, the existing institutional capacity for action, the available financial resources, and the nature of the rights to be recognized.

Ideally, regularization programs should combine several dimensions so as to guarantee the sustainability of the public intervention: (1) physical upgrading of the areas; (2) legalization of land, plots, and constructions; (3) socioeconomic programs aiming at generating income and jobs; and (4) cultural programs to overcome the stigma attached to the residents and to the informal areas. When discussing why they need to formulate regularization programs, policy makers should determine the terms for the distribution of rights and responsibilities, and duties and obligations, among all stakeholders, including the residents, who should participate in all stages of the process. A crucial aspect concerns the responsibility for financing the regularization programs; mechanisms such as planning gains and microcredit instruments should be considered. Involving the residents in financing the regularization programs is a difficult discussion in most Latin American countries, where the political understanding is that such programs are part of the social debt to be paid by the public authorities and society.

In this context, the question of the legalization of informal settlements becomes even more relevant and complex. The existence of titles is not a requirement for the occupiers to invest in their informal houses and businesses; as several studies have clearly shown, the existence of a solid perception of security resulting from a sociopolitical pact is sufficient for that purpose. There is no automatic access to credit resulting from legalization programs either; banks usually do not lend to the poor and do not easily accept their new titles as collateral. Above all, although regularization programs have certainly improved the residents' living conditions, they have had no structural impact on social poverty.

---

13. For example, several judicial decisions by the South African and the Colombian constitutional courts have clearly determined the materialization by the public administrations of the nominally recognized social right to housing.

However, legalization programs should be promoted as the main means to provide protection against forced eviction, to minimize family and other civil law conflicts, to promote some degree of economic realization of rights as well as of sociopolitical stability, to allow for increased taxation, and to clarify legal (land) regimes and facilitate investments. The sociopolitical pacts that generate the perception of security of tenure can, and often do, change, as attested by the worrying numbers of forced evictions recently identified in several Latin American cities (COHRE 2006). Land titling is and will remain the main way to promote full legal security of tenure, and the importance of tenure security cannot be underestimated.

The question, then, is how to legalize. Policy makers should take the three above-mentioned questions into account. They should think not only of the individual interests of the residents in informal settlements, but also of general interests of the broader urban population. There is a wide range of legal-political options to be considered, including individual or collective freehold or leasehold; permits, licenses, or authorizations; social rentals; and more. The choice will depend on the realities of each situation.[14] This is not to say that there is a continuum of rights. Some rights are not intrinsically better than others; they are the best options only in a given context. There is no automatic, incremental process leading from a more precarious form of occupation toward a freehold title.

Moreover, there are important urban planning tools to consider. The Brazilian Special Zones of Social Interest corresponding to the demarcation of the areas occupied by informal settlements have kept land and property values low, thus allowing the original communities to stay on the legalized land. Above all, the demarcation creates a legal order of social interest, which allows for the establishment of specific regulations to express the specific characteristics of each zone. Settlements are upgraded and public spaces created with popular participation in the decision-making process. Land titling is considered in this broad, articulated context. Rather than creating urban ghettoes, this approach recognizes the processes of socio-spatial segregation and offers a sort of legal protection to the communities, which hopefully will be dispensed with once the overall conditions of wealth distribution—so clearly imprinted on the territory—have improved in the country (Fernandes 2002b).

Policy makers should never forget the main role and obligation of the state, as recognized in international documents and national laws: to provide adequate social housing. This is by no means the same as exclusively recognizing ownership titles, let alone individual titles. Especially as regards settlements on public land, individual ownership may not always be the best option. There is

---

14. A particular fallacy of de Soto's argument is that the development of capitalism in Western countries was due to their having clearly adopted property policies, when in fact all industrialized and wealthy European countries have a range of public policies, including significant social housing and rental programs.

no absolute need to promote the privatization of public land for the social right to housing to be recognized. On the contrary, maintaining the public ownership of the land might be the best way to guarantee the permanence of the communities in the areas where they have lived. Confronted with new quotas of social housing units established by the national government, some local administrations in London, for example, have recently been trying to buy back some of the housing stock that has been privatized, paying for the surplus value generated by their own actions.[15] Given the scale of informal land development, there is no way it can be tackled through the attribution of individual ownership titles only. Collective legal solutions need to be considered.

In that context, Brazil and Peru offer two distinctly different legal paradigms regarding regularization of informal settlements. In particular, the Brazilian legislation clearly expresses the understanding that settlements in public areas cannot be treated the same way as those in private areas. As a result, individual and collective forms of leasehold are proposed for the legalization of settlements on public land (Fernandes 2002b).

Conclusions

The main lesson for policy makers and public administrators is that there is an urgent need for integrated and articulated responses by the public administrations, with regularization programs being fully and directly reconciled with other land, urban, housing, environmental, and fiscal policies. Traditional bottlenecks need to be overcome, especially the lack of proper information and cadastres; the lack of institutional capacity to act, especially at the local level; the difficulties with anachronistic registration systems; and the many problems created by the conservative judiciary. In most cases there has been no proper follow-up of existing programs, nor a continued state presence in the regularized areas. Most newly titled properties have not been fully incorporated into taxation systems.

The ultimate lesson is that broad and solid sociopolitical pacts are needed to guarantee the success of future regularization programs. Solutions cannot be left to market forces alone or to the state alone. Proper responses will require national, truly public policies in which all sectors and stakeholders are involved, with renewed, but qualified, support from international development agencies and financial institutions. Permanent intergovernmental articulation is fundamental, as is partnership of the private, community, and voluntary sectors. This should be promoted within the context of a clearly defined, comprehensive, and articulated policy. Strong leadership is of utmost importance.

---

15. It can be argued that there is a growing general process of reevaluation of the nature and efficacy of many of the privatization strategies adopted since the 1990s in the U.K., since prices have gone up considerably in many areas and the quality of service provision has significantly decreased.

The promotion of consistent progress in this complex field will require new legal concepts and technical criteria allowing the adoption of a broader concept of land regularization and the establishment of options for the legalization of informal settlements. The legal causes of informal development need to be confronted as one of the main conditions for a successful regularization of de facto situations as well as for the prevention of future informal development.

REFERENCES

Abramo, Pedro, ed. 2003. *A cidade da informalidade—O desafio das cidades latino-americanas*. Rio de Janeiro, Brazil: Sette Letras.

Calderón, Julio. 2006. *Mercado de tierras urbanas, propiedad y pobreza*. Lima, Peru: Lincoln Institute of Land Policy/SINCO Editores.

COHRE. 2006. *Desalojos en America Latina*. Geneva, Switzerland: COHRE.

Cravino, Maria Cristina. 2006. *Las villas de la ciudad—Mercado e informalidad urbana*. Los Polvorines, Argentina: Universidad Nacional de General Sarmiento.

Davis, Mike. 2006. *Planet of slums*. London and New York: Verso.

Durand-Lasserve, Alain, and Lauren Royston, eds. 2002. *Holding their ground: Secure land tenure for the urban poor in developing countries*. London: Earthscan.

Economist. 2008. Poverty amid progress. *The Economist*, May 10:69.

Fernandes, Edésio. 2002a. The influence of de Soto's *The mystery of capital*. *Land Lines* 14:5–8.

———. 2002b. Combining tenure policies, urban planning and city management in Brazil. In *Land, rights and innovation: Improving tenure security for the urban poor*, ed. Geoffrey Payne. London: ITDG.

———. 2006. Principles, bases and challenges of the National Programme to Support Sustainable Urban Land Regularisation in Brazil. In *Informal settlements: A perpetual challenge?* ed. Marie Huchzermeyer and Aly Karam. Cape Town, South Africa: UCT Press/Cordaid.

Fernandes, Edésio, and Martim Smolka. 2004. Land regularization and upgrading programs revisited. *Land Lines* 16:12–16.

Fernandes, Edésio, and Ann Varley, eds. 1998. *Illegal cities: Law and urban change in developing countries*. London: Zed Books.

Gilbert, Alan. 2002. On the mystery of capital and the myths of Hernando de Soto: What difference does legal title make? *International Development Planning Review* 24:1–19.

Huchzermeyer, Marie, and Aly Karam, eds. 2006. *Informal settlements: A perpetual challenge?* Cape Town, South Africa: UCT Press/Cordaid.

Maldonado, Copello Maria Mercedes. 2006. El proceso de construcción del sistema urbanístico colombiano: Entre reforma urbana y ordenamiento territorial. In *Direito Urbanístico—Estudos Brasileiros e Internacionais*, ed. Edésio Fernandes and Betania Alfonsin. Belo Horizonte, Brazil: Del Rey.

Neuwirth, Robert. 2005. *Shadow cities*. New York: Routledge.

Payne, Geoffrey, ed. 2002. *Land, rights and innovation: Improving tenure security for the urban poor*. London: ITDG.

Verma, Gita Dewan. 2002. *Slumming India*. New Delhi, India: Penguin.

World Bank. 2004. *Urban land markets and urban land development: An examination of three Brazilian cities*. Washington, DC: World Bank.

———. 2007. *Albanian urban sector review*. Washington, DC: World Bank.

Zeledón, Aída. 2006. Reflexiones en torno al marco juridico de El Salvador. In *Direito Urbanístico—Estudos Brasileiros e Internacionais*, ed. Edésio Fernandes and Betania Alfonsin. Belo Horizonte, Brazil: Del Rey.

COMMENTARY

Ernesto Schargrodsky

In his chapter, Edésio Fernandes criticizes the adoption of large-scale land titling programs in the developing world. He states that implementation of these
programs has been based on the assumption that land titling improves access
to formal credit and contributes to poverty eradication. He then argues that
the available evidence does not support the claim that titling improves access
to credit, and he also casts doubts on the findings of "far-fetched studies [that]
have tried to link recent land titling programs to significant social transformations, such as the number of children attending school and an increase in levels
of caloric intake." According to Fernandes, land titling programs have had no
structural impact on social poverty. He proposes replacing them with a more
comprehensive approach that, rather than reducing the notion of urban land
regularization to its legal dimension, combines legalization with infrastructure
upgrading, integrative social programs, housing policies, and other urban management interventions.

I fully agree with Fernandes that land titling has not delivered the promised impact on access to credit. Large-scale legalization programs launched in
recent years under the influence of de Soto (2000) were presented as a powerful shortcut to economic development. The main assumption was that land
titling rapidly improves access to credit, which could be invested as capital to
increase labor productivity and, hence, the income of the poor. The available
empirical evidence does not support this hypothesis. Titles do not significantly
improve the level of access to credit (see, for example, Carter and Olinto
2003; Field and Torero 2003; Galiani and Schargrodsky 2008). Formal institutions do not easily lend money to agents with informal sources of income.
They may not accept as collateral titles from peripheral areas in which eviction costs may be higher than the market value of the land parcels. Moreover,
people may not want to jeopardize their houses in risky entrepreneurial activities. Without improved credit access, there is little effect on current labor market
performance.

I also agree with Fernandes on the need for a more comprehensive approach
that considers not only land titling, but also infrastructure upgrading, social programs, and housing interventions. A difficult problem that policy makers face,
however, is the high cost of these more complete interventions, which highlights
the need for careful cost-benefit analysis. I also agree with Fernandes on the need
to implement prevention policies to avoid informal land development. I know
less about how to put these attractive prevention policies into practice and how
costly they are. Finally, I share with Fernandes the concern over the endless
nature of regularization. The "day after" a legalization program, titled parcels
start to get irregular again as people move, die, marry, and divorce, creating the
need for chronic interventions.

I disagree with Fernandes, however, in his statement that titling programs have no structural impact on social poverty. My own research experience provides an example. In a set of studies, Galiani and Schargrodsky (2004, 2008) and Di Tella, Galiani, and Schargrodsky (2007) exploited a natural experiment in the outskirts of Buenos Aires, Argentina, to analyze the causal effect of titling on several variables. The studies found that entitled families build much better houses than untitled families. The households with usufructuary rights invest, but titled households invest significantly more. Moreover, households in the titled parcels are smaller as a result of lower fertility and a weaker presence of extended family members. These smaller families invest more in the education and health of their children. The children from titled households have superior school performance, lower absenteeism, better anthropometrics scores, and inferior teenage pregnancy rates. New results confirm that they are more likely to complete high school than children from untitled families. Moreover, the beliefs declared by squatters with property rights are significantly different from those of untitled squatters in a direction that may help their inclusion in a market economy. Besley (1995), Lanjouw and Levy (2002), Do and Iyer (2008), Field (2005), and Field (2007) have documented concurrent positive effects of land titling on investment, household structure, and labor supply. Thus, the transmission mechanism and speed may be very different from those hypothesized by de Soto, but entitling the poor seems to enhance their investment both in physical capital and in the human capital of the children, which will help to reduce the poverty of the next generations.

REFERENCES

Besley, Tim. 1995. Property rights and investments incentives: Theory and evidence from Ghana. *Journal of Political Economy* 103:903–937.

Carter, Michael, and Pedro Olinto. 2003. Getting institutions right for whom? Credit constraints and the impact of property rights on the quantity and composition of investment. *American Journal of Agricultural Economics* 85:173–186.

de Soto, Hernando. 2000. *The mystery of capital: Why capitalism triumphs in the West and fails everywhere else.* New York: Basic Books.

Di Tella, Rafael, Sebastián Galiani, and Ernesto Schargrodsky. 2007. The formation of beliefs: Evidence from the allocation of land titles to squatters. *Quarterly Journal of Economics* 122(1):209–241.

Do, Quy Toan, and Lakshmi Iyer. 2008. Land titling and rural transition in Vietnam. *Economic Development and Cultural Change* 56(3):531–579.

Field, Erica. 2005. Property rights and investment in urban slums. *Journal of the European Economic Association* 3(2–3):279–290.

———. 2007. Entitled to work: Urban property rights and labor supply in Peru. *Quarterly Journal of Economics* 122(4):1561–1602.

Field, Erica, and Maximo Torero. 2003. Do property titles increase credit access among the urban poor? Evidence from a nationwide titling program in Peru. Mimeo, Princeton University.

Galiani, Sebastián, and Ernesto Schargrodsky. 2004. Effects of land titling on child
    health. *Economics and Human Biology* 2(3):353–372.
———. 2008. Property rights for the poor: Effects of land titling. Mimeo, Universidad
    Torcuato Di Tella.
Lanjouw, Jean, and Philip Levy. 2002. Untitled: A study of formal and informal prop-
    erty rights in urban Ecuador. *Economic Journal* 112:986–1019.

13

Property Rights Created Under a Federalist Approach to Tradable Emissions Policy

Dallas Burtraw and Richard Sweeney

ederal and state policies aimed at slowing the heating of the planet will impose potentially significant costs on the economy. To reduce such costs, economists have promoted the use of incentive-based approaches such as emission fees and cap and trade to complement other regulations for reducing greenhouse gases (GHGs). These approaches are particularly well suited for reducing GHG emissions because the emissions are uniformly mixing in the atmosphere and their damage is not related significantly to location or timing. Consequently, the administration of incentive-based programs is much simpler for GHGs than for a pollutant that has an important spatial or temporal dimension. Furthermore, there is tremendous variation in the cost of emissions reductions among agents in the economy, and indeed among nations; therefore, an incentive-based approach leads to much lower overall compliance costs than do

The authors are indebted to David Evans, Bill Shobe, and Margaret Walls for contributing to the development of ideas presented here. This research was supported in part by Mistra's Climate Policy Research Forum (Clipore). This chapter also draws on work funded by the United States Environmental Protection Agency under contract EP-D-04-006 to Industrial Economics and Resources for the Future, which has not been subject to the agency's review and therefore does not necessarily reflect the views of the agency, and no official endorsement should be inferred. The authors appreciate the collaboration of Jim Neumann, Jason Price, and Nadav Tanners at Industrial Economics. Anthony Paul and Erica Myers provided technical assistance. All errors and opinions are the responsibility of the authors. Please send comments to burtraw@rff.org or sweeney@rff.org.

traditional pollution control methods. Incentive-based approaches provide a financial signal to agents in the economy about the social opportunity cost of their actions, just as prices in a market provide a signal about the resource costs of goods and services. In each case, the signals help ensure that resource capabilities are allocated to their highest valued use.

Most experience with incentive-based regulation is with emissions cap and trade programs, which is the primary approach for comprehensive climate policy aimed especially at reducing carbon dioxide (CO_2), the most ubiquitous GHG. The United States has substantial experience with cap and trade policies, and the European Union launched the world's largest cap and trade program for CO_2 in 2005. As the name implies, a cap and trade approach has two elements. The emissions cap represents the maximum allowable emissions (for example, tons of CO_2) that can occur in the aggregate over all regulated emissions sources. The second element is the use of tradable emissions allowances, which introduces an intangible property right that can be bought and sold and, if banking is allowed, saved for use in the future. Every regulated source is required to surrender an emissions allowance for every ton it emits. While both the regulator and the regulated sources view the surrender of allowances as a requirement, an allowance also presents the regulated sources with a valuable and scarce right to emit.

One criterion that plays an important role in designing a regulatory program is the extent to which the policy disproportionately burdens any one segment of the population. This chapter provides evidence for how a cap and trade policy may affect different types of households and guidance for how to modify those effects. Because a cap and trade approach puts a price on CO_2, it can have a severe distributional effect. This effect depends on how the price on CO_2 changes expenditures and ultimately consumer surplus throughout the economy. Equally important, its distributional effect depends on how the policy distributes the value created by the imposition of a price on CO_2, such as the allocation of emissions allowances (Boyce and Riddle 2007; Dinan and Rogers 2002; Parry 2004).[1]

This chapter also examines the notion that state government may be better situated to address local issues and especially to ameliorate the distributional burden of policy on particular groups, and the possibility that states continue to play a leading role within the context of a federal cap and trade program. For example, states may be given the responsibility of allocating some portion of emissions allowances. Climate change is a global problem, and its solution will require international cooperation, which seemingly places the federal government in a central role. However, in the United States and some other nations, including Australia, state and local governments have been active in developing policy,

---

1. Another way climate policy will affect households is by affecting opportunities for employment, and some of the economic impacts may be concentrated in severely affected communities, which is not part of this analysis.

including regional cap and trade programs.[2] One hears at least two justifications for climate policy initiatives at the state and local levels. Local political bodies sense that they have to do something to address the problem. For over a century, state and local governments have had the primary role in enforcing environmental regulations and in land use planning, building codes, and so on. Second, state policy makers undoubtedly recognize the importance of broader efforts and view their own actions not as ultimate policy solutions, but rather as providing models and impetus for federal and even international action. Nonetheless, state policies will likely be designed to maximize the states' own net benefits, which raises the possibility for strategic behavior.

The example we consider is for states to be given latitude to determine some portion of the allocation of emissions allowances under a federal carbon dioxide emissions allowance cap and trade program. As we describe below, the common architecture of most previous cap and trade programs has held states to allocating emissions allowances, which is an element of the current leading federal proposals. One question is whether the action of one state affects the costs in another state. Will the combination of local interests and conditions result in a pattern of regulatory development that leads to higher costs of compliance overall?

In the United States the allocation of emissions allowances under a CO_2 program would constitute the largest creation and distribution of new property rights in more than a century. Depending on how the program is designed, the value of emissions allowances for an economy-wide CO_2 program could be $130–$370 billion annually by 2015 (Paltsev et al. 2007). This value would grow as the stringency of the program grows over time, at least over the first decades. Although the level of the emissions cap is the most visible decision facing policy makers, the assignment of the value of these rights is the most important aspect of the design of the policy. The allocation decision affects both the efficiency and the distributional consequences of the program. If allocation is not treated carefully, it could undermine the efficiency virtues of cap and trade and could lead to unexpected distributional outcomes. How allocation will occur, and the role of state governments within federalist climate policy, could lead to a range of possible outcomes.

The first part of this chapter provides background on the historic relationship between federal and state authority with respect to environmental policy. The second part briefly describes the emerging design of U.S. federal legislation and its plausible alternative, implementation of regulations by the U.S. Environmental Protection Agency (EPA) under the authority of the Clean Air Act. Then we provide an overview of the distribution of costs from climate policy across

---

2. Ten northeastern states are participating in a regional CO_2 trading program that took effect in January 2009, and California is considering whether to use cap and trade to implement its own climate policy. Regional coalitions of states in the West and Midwest are also considering cap and trade programs.

income groups and across regions. This distribution can be quite uneven, posing a challenge for federal policy. Subsequently, we look at federalist aspects of the design of the program when some portion of the allocation decision is delegated to the states. States will inevitably try to address their own regional issues. We search for strategic elements in state-level decisions and how they may affect the overall performance of the program.

Federal and State Conflict Over a Vast, Newly Created Intangible Property Right

The use of air and water for disposal of waste has always had substantial economic value, but in prior approaches to regulation the value has been implicit because there was no formal market for these resources. The ownership of common-pool resources such as air and water is generally seen as vested in the public, held in "public trust" for the benefit of the public. Historic conflicts over air and water pollution have been about what share of these public resources should be allocated to waste disposal services and what share should be reserved to protect public consumption of air and water. For as long as environmental policy was viewed primarily as an issue of what regulations to apply to the use of the air and water, the value of environmental resources remained implicit; the issue of ownership did not arise; and the discussion of environmental federalism was in terms of what level of government had the power to establish and enforce regulatory standards. The introduction of formal markets for tradable emissions allowances makes the value explicit, portending a dramatic shift in the level of authority for resource management (Burtraw and Shobe 2007).

Emissions allowance trading took a long time to come to fruition in public policy. Pigou (1920) was the first economist to suggest that incentive-based policies for environmental policy, specifically an emissions fee, would be a way to internalize the environmental costs of pollution into private decisions. Emissions trading was identified as an alternative far later when Crocker (1966) proposed that the government set a cap on aggregate emissions and let the market determine the degree of abatement at individual facilities and the price of emissions, rather than having the government set the price through an emissions fee.

The earliest application of trading emissions rights introduced flexibility to the traditional way of implementing environmental regulation. In the late 1970s, the U.S. government began to impose sanctions such as restrictions on highway funds on areas of the country that were in "nonattainment" with local ambient air quality standards.[3] It was also recognized that these standards and sanctions might restrict economic growth in regions in violation. To enable localities violating the air quality standards to continue to enjoy economic development without

---

3. Standards for local air quality are set by the federal government.

further increasing emissions, the EPA designed a system whereby new emitting sources could pay existing sources to reduce their emissions sufficiently to offset any increase in emissions. Related programs included the "bubble" policy that allowed a facility to comply with a standard defined over multiple sources, rather than having to comply with individual restrictions for each source. In the 1977 Clean Air Act amendments, Congress recognized the offset policy in law and also made it possible for existing sources to bank emissions reductions for later use. While an improvement from the status quo, these programs constituted an informal market in which property rights were not well defined. Trades had to be preapproved by the environmental regulator. There was limited ability to bank reductions; some unused emissions reduction credits were lost; and the transaction costs for each trade approached 50 percent of the value of the trade.

Title IV of the 1990 Clean Air Act amendments provided for the advent of emissions allowance trading within a formal market in the sulfur dioxide (SO_2) emissions allowance trading program. The introduction of a formal market transformed the disposal services of atmospheric resources into an asset with a stream of valuable monetary returns. The power to regulate in a formal cap and trade program implies the power to determine the disposition of the stream of valuable returns on the regulated activity. Although no one seemed to remark on it at the time, by transferring the right to allocate the economic value of SO_2 emissions from sources covered by the law, the program transferred a valuable ownership interest from the states to the federal government. For all intents and purposes, an asset that had been held in trust by state governments became the property of the federal government. The law created an asset with substantial market value and gave the asset to the regulated firms free of charge. The current annual market value of SO_2 allowances is approximately $5 billion, just under 1 percent of all state expenditures in 2006.

Although there have been subsequent trading programs, the SO_2 program is unique as the only example of appropriation of the common-pool resource value of the atmosphere by the federal government. The second large federal experiment in cap and trade, the nitrogen oxide (NOx) budget program, is comparable in terms of the value of emissions allowances and followed a different pattern. The program was the result of negotiations among the participating states to establish state budgets for allowable emissions of NOx. Implemented with the oversight, monitoring, and enforcement of the federal EPA, this program gave the states control over how the allowances were allocated to firms. A variety of approaches were used, including various forms of free allocation for the majority of allowances and some portion of direct sale (Kentucky) and auction (Virginia).

The two existing mandatory programs for cap and trade of CO_2 also follow the precedent of the NOx budget program rather than the SO_2 program. The European Union (EU) Emissions Trading Scheme leaves the allocation of emissions allowances to member states. In the first two phases of the program (2005–2012), the EU provided guidelines on allocation and approved allocation plans, but this was mostly because the member states had the authority to determine which sources would be included in the program. The important constraint was the requirement that the vast majority of allowances had to be given away for free. Beginning with the third phase (2013–2020), the EU will require the member states to auction over two-thirds of allowances, including 100 percent to the electricity sector, but the member states will retain broad discretion about the disposition of funds from the auction. The second mandatory program is the Regional Greenhouse Gas Initiative, which leaves the allocation decision to the 10 participating northeast states. At least 25 percent of the allowances are required to be auctioned, with revenues dedicated to complementary program goals. In practice, nearly 90 percent of the allowances will be distributed by the states through auction. It is noteworthy that these states are, in fact, claiming ownership of assets that various legislative proposals for a U.S. federal cap and trade program would claim for the U.S. Treasury or for federally determined free allocation to other interests.

A Fork in the Road for U.S. Climate Policy

In the years leading up to 2006, the lack of momentum for climate policy in Washington, DC, set the stage for the emergence of initiatives at the state and regional levels. Inaction in Washington also helped precipitate a recent Supreme Court ruling (discussed below) requiring the EPA to initiate regulatory activities pertaining to climate change, under the auspices of the Clean Air Act, that must go forward in the absence of new legislative direction. However, a growing flurry of legislative activity since the election of 2006 could preempt both state and regional actions and other federal regulatory developments.

POTENTIAL FEDERAL LEGISLATION
It is difficult to follow the plot in federal legislative proposals. At least 12 major bills are being considered by Congress. The leading vehicle in 2008 was the Lieberman-Warner proposal (SB 2191), which would implement an economy-wide approach based on a mix of upstream and midstream compliance responsibilities.[4]

The allowance distribution plan for SB 2191 reflects a variety of goals and interests, but about 22 percent of the allowances in the year 2012 would be allocated to states in one fashion or another.[5] One major portion is directed to electricity load-serving entities (9 percent) and natural gas distribution companies (2 percent), the retail entities that interact directly with customers. These allocations are intended to address a variety of purposes, including promotion of

---

4. This legislation is the reincarnation of the previous McCain-Lieberman proposal (SB 280). Over time, the evolution of SB 280 to SB 2191 included a growing role for auctioning allowances and adoption of the compliance architecture of Bingaman-Specter (SB 1766).

5. The remainder is allocated using a mix of free allocation to industry and an auction.

investment in end-use efficiency and direct rate relief for customers. Discretion in large part is left to state regulators. The states also receive a general allocation (4.5 percent) for unrestricted use of allowance value. A portion (1 percent) goes to states to promote mass transit. Another portion (5 percent) provides incentives for a variety of specific programs, including decoupling of electricity revenues from sales, rewards for early reductions, land use planning, and efficiency investments. A final portion (0.5 percent) is directed to tribal governments.

EPA RESPONSIBILITY UNDER THE CLEAN AIR ACT

In the absence of new federal legislation, responsibility appears to fall to the EPA. Although the Clean Air Act provides broad applicability to different pollutants and sources, the EPA had declined to regulate CO_2 based on the claim that it does not fit the act's definition of an air pollutant. In April 2007 the U.S. Supreme Court found in *Massachusetts v. EPA*, 549 US 497 (2007), that "greenhouse gases fit well within the Act's capacious definition of 'air pollutant'" and therefore may be regulated under the Clean Air Act.[6] The practical implication is that the EPA is required to take steps, beginning with a determination of the danger of CO_2, and subsequently to develop and promulgate regulations to mitigate the harm.

A second recent decision addressed the EPA's ability to adopt cap and trade as a strategy for regulating pollutants under the Clean Air Act. In *New Jersey v. EPA*, 517 F.3d 574 (D.C. Cir. 2008), the Washington, DC, Circuit Court invalidated the EPA's Clean Air mercury rule, which would have implemented a cap and trade program for mercury. The trading program was premised on the EPA's decision that mercury should not have been classified as a hazardous air pollutant, which would preclude the use of trading in compliance. It is notable that the decision did not address the legality of cap and trade per se, leaving open the possibility that the EPA could itself administer a cap and trade program for CO_2.

The third decision led to the demise of the Clean Air Interstate Rule, which was an important regulatory measure to tighten emissions of SO_2 and NOx from electricity generating units and major industrial sources. In *North Carolina v. EPA* et al., No. 05-1244 (D.C. Cir.) (2008), the Washington, DC, Circuit Court ruled that the cap and trade approach failed to follow the mandates of the Clean Air Act in part because it could not ensure that pollution sources in one state did not cause significant pollution loads in other states. The reason is that emission

---

6. Massachusetts and other states, along with some environmental groups, sued the EPA after the EPA denied the states' petition to regulate CO_2 from vehicles. The court found that the "EPA can avoid promulgating regulations only if it determines that greenhouse gases do not contribute to climate change or if it provides some reasonable explanation as to why it cannot or will not exercise its discretion to determine whether they do." While the ruling of the court focused narrowly on vehicle emissions, it is generally believed that, in the absence of new legislation, the ruling would also affect the regulation of CO_2 emissions from fixed sources through a finding of endangerment from CO_2.

reductions in one state might lead to the transfer of emissions allowances to an upwind state. CO_2 emissions do not have geographically specific consequences, so this leaves open the possibility that the EPA could administer a cap and trade program for CO_2, but a variety of other regulatory outcomes are also possible.

One plausible approach would be for the EPA to adopt a national cap on CO_2 covering point sources and to delegate responsibility and limited authority to the states to achieve those goals. As under the existing NOx trading programs, the states could be apportioned CO_2 emissions budgets as a share of a national cap and could allow their sources to participate in a federally managed trading program. The states would retain the value of the emissions allowances and could allocate the rights as they wished. They could even choose to opt out of the trading program if sources in the state do not emit more than allowed under the state's share of the cap.

Given the structure of the Clean Air Act, there might be multiple caps on CO_2, each being specific to a sector. This would reduce the efficiency of the program. If sources were separated by their sector, each sector would face a different price for CO_2 emissions, and trading opportunities that reduced overall resource costs would be unrealized. Furthermore, the EPA might revert to the familiar paradigm of prescriptive regulations, for example, by promulgating prescriptive emissions standards for some or all sectors and treating new sources differently from existing ones. The most likely outcome is that the EPA would have to borrow from each of these possible strategies to regulate many source categories. This mix of potential outcomes, along with the heterogeneous allocation of allowance value that could emerge under federal legislation, motivates interest in the possible distributional consequences across regions of the country.

Regional Impacts from National Climate Policy

Climate policy implemented in a uniform way at the national level will have non-uniform effects on regions of the country. This section of the chapter presents an analysis of how different approaches affect different income groups by region of the country under a national cap and trade program.[7] Results are illustrated for each of 11 regions in the country and for households sorted into annual income deciles. Effects are calibrated to roughly correspond to effects that would occur in 2015 from policies enacted in 2008. Most of the previous literature focuses on income distributions at the national level and the impact of the policy on each income category. We extend this literature by focusing on regional differences that we and some other analyses (such as Batz, Pizer, and Sanchirico 2007) find to be important.

---

7. This analysis is updated and developed fully in Burtraw, Sweeney, and Walls (2008).

One way to measure the distributional impact is to look at the absolute measure of cost born by different types of households. However, an absolute measure does not take into account relative ability to pay. The term *vertical equity* is used to suggest that households with a greater ability to pay should be asked to pay more. From the perspective of vertical equity, a policy that affects households in a neutral way is usually thought to impose costs as an equal percentage of household income. A regressive policy imposes the greatest costs, as a percentage of household ability to pay, on lower-income households. Conversely a progressive policy imposes the greatest costs, as a percentage of ability to pay, on relatively wealthier households.

We measure ability to pay on the basis of imputed income, net of taxes and transfers, for households as reported in the Consumer Expenditure (CEX) survey for 2004–2006 (Bureau of Labor Statistics 2008). Substantial literature suggests that annual income may underestimate ability to pay for households at the lower and upper ranges of the scale. One reason is that lower-income households may have unreported income. In addition, younger and older persons may have low current income that does not reflect lifetime earnings or savings.[8] Most taxes look more regressive using annual income instead of lifetime income (Fullerton and Rogers 1993), and this caveat should be kept in mind when viewing our results.

There are several paths through which different mechanisms to control CO_2 emissions affect low-income households. We account for the following:

- Changes in prices of fossil fuels, which impose a direct cost on household expenditures and increase the cost of production of other goods consumed by households, which poses an indirect expense on households.
- Changes in quantities consumed that result from higher prices. We use a partial equilibrium approach employing elasticity estimates from a variety of sources and new calculations from a detailed electricity market model to estimate and account for these changes.
- Changes in producer behavior in the electricity sector (only).

---

8. Some authors have constructed proxies for lifetime income based on information on age, education, and other factors (Casperson and Metcalf 1994; Hassett, Mathur, and Metcalf 2009; Rogers 1993; Walls and Hanson 1999). Others have relied on annual consumption expenditures as a proxy for lifetime income, based on the permanent income hypothesis that annual consumption is a relatively constant proportion of lifetime income (Poterba 1989; West 2004). Some experts have argued that there is merit in using annual income. It may in fact underestimate the ability to pay at the upper-income levels, because these families may have substantial wealth that provides much greater ability to pay than is revealed by annual income, and thereby offset the potential bias among low-income families. Barthold (1993) argues that it is politically impractical to talk about lifetime income because of the inherent uncertainty in measuring it and because of the shorter time horizons of elected officials and the voting public. Moreover, empirical evidence on the permanent, or lifetime, income hypothesis is mixed (Shapiro and Slemrod 1994).

- Changes in consumer surplus resulting from the change in expenditures and the quantities of goods and services consumed.
- Changes in government taxes and transfers, including the allocation of CO_2 emissions allowance value created under an emissions trading program. For example, a cap and trade policy that freely distributes emissions allowances to emitters directs their value to owners of shareholder equity in these firms, at least in competitive industries. Households that own shares of these firms receive this value as a form of nonlabor income. When allowances are auctioned, the value is transferred to the government, which could potentially use the revenue to offset the cost of the program on the economy in general or on specific types of households in particular.

It may be equally helpful to understand what we do not account for:

- Ancillary effects from changes in employment and income that may result from a shift in economic activity away from relatively more-energy-intensive sectors of the economy to less-energy-intensive sectors
- The relative competitiveness of industries that are regulated by the policy, especially in an international context where they may face competition from unregulated competitors
- Changes in factor (labor and capital) markets that may have preexisting distortions away from economic efficiency (Goulder et al., 1999; Parry, Williams, and Goulder 1999)

ESTIMATING CONSUMER EXPENDITURES IN 2015

A variety of technological, economic, and demographic changes can be expected by 2015. We account only for changes in transportation-related emissions resulting from corporate average fuel efficiency (CAFE) standards that are likely to take effect based on recent legislation and proposed regulations. We also implicitly account for equilibrium changes in electricity markets, including incremental but important changes in investment in supply and demand technologies that occur under both the baseline and the climate policy by 2015. Otherwise, we assume that expenditure and income patterns in 2004–2006 are a proxy for the patterns that would be in effect in 2015 without climate policy.

The population sampled in the CEX survey includes 110,301 observations for 40,843 households (one observation equals one household in one quarter), as summarized in table 13.1. The Bureau of Labor Statistics (BLS) builds a national sample and a regional sample in four census divisions, with corrections to achieve a statistically reliable sample at these geographic scales. We are interested in a finer level of geographic detail than is apparent in the four census divisions, so we examined the data with state-level indicators, ignoring observations in Alaska and Hawaii. Where confidentiality cannot be protected because of a small sample in any category, the BLS masks information at the finer geographic level, thereby

Table 13.1
Observations by Region and Income Group

Region[a]	States	1 Less than $11,000	2 $11–19,999	3 $20–27,999	4 $28–37,999	5 $38–45,999	6 $46–59,999	7 $60–73,999	8 $74–93,999	9 $94–117,999	10 More than $118,000	Total
1 AEV	AL, AR, DC, GA, LA, MS, NC, SC, TN, VA	1,461	1,923	1,573	1,847	1,268	1,577	1,157	1,293	995	1,371	14,465
2 CNV	CA, NV	724	1,169	1,040	1,334	934	1,509	1,145	1,321	974	1,734	11,884
3 ERCOT	TX	493	677	675	804	551	799	611	579	424	644	6,257
4 FRCC	FL	473	766	615	839	512	746	560	565	341	439	5,856
5 MKIO	IL, IN, KY, MI, MS, OH, WV, WI	1,350	2,041	1,925	2,174	1,468	2,220	1,795	2,052	1,264	1,844	18,133
6 MPM	DE, MD, NJ, PA	666	1,131	1,115	1,290	829	1,289	1,094	1,152	785	1,452	10,803
7 NE	CT, ME, MA, NH, RI	310	416	440	412	357	600	450	529	421	673	4,608
8 NWP	ID, MT, OR, UT, WA	464	584	574	739	513	820	677	662	404	648	6,085
9 NY	NY	468	523	410	534	379	598	471	502	427	687	4,999
10 PPPP	KS, MN, NE, OK, SD	237	335	335	430	328	538	440	427	237	412	3,719
11 RA	AZ, CO	330	481	400	555	388	504	375	367	278	394	4,072
National		10,557[b]	12,803	10,883	12,844	8,786	12,861	9,906	10,525	7,193	10,952	107,310

[a] The region names are not acronyms. They are from the North American Electricity Reliability Council, the U.S. Department of Energy, and the authors.
Source: Bureau of Labor Statistics. 2008. *Consumer Expenditure Survey Public Use Microdata,* http://www.bls.gov/cex/csxmicro.htm.
[b] Numbers in this row are not column totals.

blocking responses from five states. Consequently we have 90,881 observations for 33,315 households in 43 states plus the District of Columbia, aggregated into 11 regions.[9]

We construct income groups based on national-level household-level after-tax income deciles. We then distribute observations based on the CEX survey data into these income groups. It is important to keep in mind that the income "buckets" do not represent regional income deciles; rather, they are constructed as deciles at the national level, based on 2006 BLS estimates.

The transportation sector is given special consideration because of the new CAFE standards proposed by the Department of Transportation's National Highway Traffic Safety Administration in April 2008. These standards would bring the fuel economy standard for cars to 35.7 miles per gallon (mpg) and for trucks to 28.6 mpg by the 2015 model year.

The new regulations affect our baseline 2015 expenditure calculations in two ways. First, new vehicles are more costly than they would otherwise be and more costly than what is reflected in the 2006 CEX survey data, all else equal. According to data from the Bureau of Transportation Statistics (BTS), the percentage of new car sales out of total registered cars in a given year is 5.7 percent and the percentage of new trucks is 7.6 percent.[10] We use these figures to gradually increase the proportion of vehicles on the road that meet the new standards, and we rely on estimates in Fischer, Harrington, and Parry (2007) to obtain the higher vehicle price for those new vehicle purchases.[11] A new car in 2015 that meets the 35.7 mpg standard will cost $149 more than it would in 2006, all else equal; a new truck will cost $246 more. To account for these cost increases, we have increased new vehicle costs by this amount in the base case.

Second, gasoline expenditures, all else equal, are lower than they would be without the new standards (and lower than in 2006) because the gradual vehicle turnover leads to improvements in on-road fleet-wide average fuel efficiency. We estimate that the average fuel efficiency of cars on the road will be 26.3 mpg in 2015, while the average for trucks will be 21.9 mpg. These are improvements of 17

---

9. BLS refers to observations as "consumer units," which we loosely interpret as households. The five missing states are Iowa, New Mexico, North Dakota, Vermont, and Wyoming. Observations with missing state identifiers are used in our calculations at the national level. Further documentation of the methods used here can be found in Burtraw, Sweeney, and Walls (2008).

10. These are the figures for 2005, the most recently available data. See http://www.bts.gov/publications/national_transportation_statistics/. The rate of replacement for new car and truck sales could also be affected by CAFE standards and the rising price of fuel that is not the result of carbon policy.

11. Fischer, Harrington, and Parry (2007) rely on the National Academy of Sciences (2002) study of fuel economy technologies for their estimates of the costs of meeting higher CAFE requirements.

percent and 22 percent, respectively, over the fleet-wide average in 2006.[12] When fuel economy increases, the cost per mile of driving falls, and people drive more. The net change in gasoline consumption thus equals fuel savings on current mileage from a unit reduction in mpg, less the extra fuel consumption from the increase in vehicle miles traveled. Based on recent estimates, we assume this rebound effect is 10 percent—a 1 percent decrease in the cost per mile of driving leads to a 10 percent increase in gasoline consumption (Small and Van Dender 2007; U.S. Department of Transportation 2008). As a result, assuming the new CAFE standards, gradual turnover in the vehicle stock, and the 10 percent rebound effect, baseline average gasoline expenditures per household in 2015 are estimated to be 15 percent lower than the 2006 levels.

Figure 13.1 illustrates the direct expenditure categories as a percentage of reported income at the national level. The 10 vertical bars represent income deciles, and the amount of expenditure in various categories is displayed for the average household within each decile. The categories that are reported include four categories representing direct purchase by the average household of electricity, gasoline, natural gas, and heating oil. These are relevant because their consumption leads directly to CO_2 emissions, and climate policy would directly increase their cost. At the national level, direct expenditure on energy represents 30.6 percent of annual income among the households in the lowest income category, which is the greatest percentage of any group. For the highest income households it is 3.2 percent. On average across all income groups, the share of expenditure on energy is 6.3 percent of annual income.

The nation is divided into 11 regions in our analysis. Figure 13.2 displays the regions with overlays representing the percentage of household expenditure dedicated to direct energy use in each income bracket. To understand the graph, imagine you live in Nebraska with a family income of $41,854. Your household would fall into the fifth income bucket for states in the region, which also includes Minnesota, North Dakota, South Dakota, Nebraska, Iowa, Kansas, and Oklahoma. Figure 13.2 indicates that your family spends $3,072 annually on direct energy expenditures, equal to 7.3 percent of your household's income. Of this, 2.2 percent goes to electricity, 3.2 percent to gasoline, and 1.9 percent to natural gas and fuel oil.

In all regions of the country, lower-income households have the highest direct energy use as a percentage of income. Moreover, there is a large difference in the magnitude of expenditure as a percentage of income for lower-income households across regions. For the two lowest income brackets, the highest values are observed in New England, the mid-Atlantic, the South from Texas to Florida, and the Midwest, where expenditures exceed 30 percent of income.

---

12. On-road average fuel efficiency is available from BTS. See http://www.bts.gov/publications/national_transportation_statistics/.

Figure 13.1
Household Direct Energy Expenditures as a Fraction of Income, by Energy Types

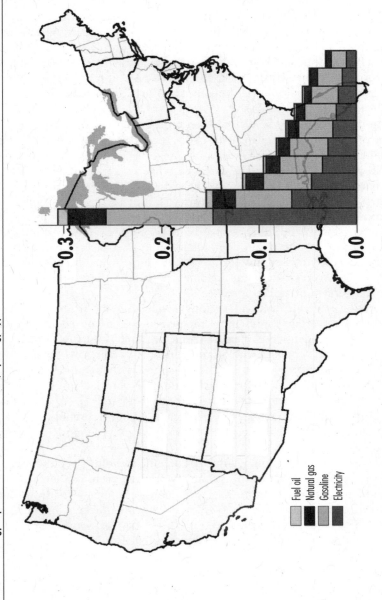

Fuel oil
Natural gas
Gasoline
Electricity

Note: The vertical axis of the bar chart is share of income, and the horizontal axis is income decile.
Source: Bureau of Labor Statistics (2008). *Consumer Expenditure Survey Public Use Microdata*, http://www.bls.gov/cex/csxmicro.htm.

Figure 13.2
Household Direct Energy Expenditures as a Fraction of Income, by Region

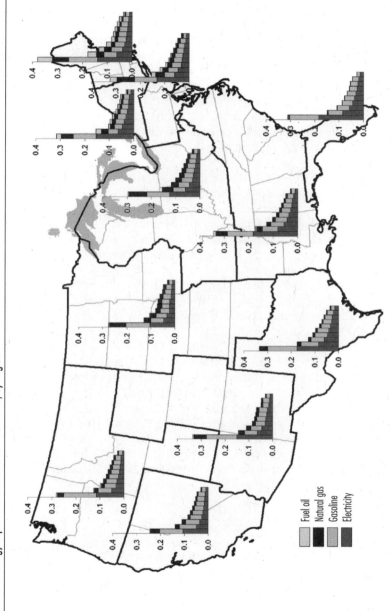

Note: The vertical axis of the bar chart is share of income, and the horizontal axis is income decile.
Source: Bureau of Labor Statistics (2008). *Consumer Expenditure Survey Public Use Microdata*, http://www.bls.gov/cex/csxmicro.htm.

Fuel oil
Natural gas
Gasoline
Electricity

Consequently, concerns about the distributional effects of the policy may be more acute in some regions than others.

Moreover, the categories of expenditure vary considerably among the low-income group. In New England and the mid-Atlantic states, home heating contributes significantly to expenditures, but not so in the South, where electricity and gasoline expenditures are greater. The Midwest represents a sort of transition, with intermediate levels of expenditures in all categories among the eastern regions. New York's levels would be as high as the other regions except for lower gasoline expenditures. Overall expenditure in the West tends to be lower, but gasoline expenditure is relatively high, especially compared to the Northeast. As a consequence, the ways to provide relief to low-income households from the cost of climate policy may vary considerably by region.

ESTIMATING THE CO_2 CONTENT OF EXPENDITURES

The first step in understanding how household expenditures would be affected by climate policy is to calculate the CO_2 emissions of the average household in each income group. Taking expenditures from BLS, we use fuel-specific, state-specific energy prices from the Energy Information Administration (EIA) to calculate the quantities of fuels purchased by households in each group. The carbon content of natural gas, fuel oil, and gasoline is well established. For electricity, the CO_2 content varies across regions depending on the fuel used for generation over seasonal and diurnal periods. This pattern is identified from the Haiku electricity market model built and maintained by Resources for the Future (Paul, Burtraw, and Palmer 2008).[13]

Expenditures are also affected by changes in the cost of energy embodied indirectly in other goods and services, especially food, durable goods, and services. Calculations of CO_2 emissions resulting from indirect energy consumption are based on data in Hassett, Mathur, and Metcalf (2009), who provide information on the emission intensity of goods aggregated into 38 indirect expenditure categories, updating methods developed in Metcalf (1999).[14] Although the estimates of direct fuel use and the implied CO_2 emissions based on the CEX survey data correspond well to data collected by EIA (Energy Information Administration 2007), the total emissions calculated fall short of economy-wide EIA estimates, and we

---

13. Haiku models regions with either regulated (cost-of-service) or market-based prices. Haiku finds the emission reductions that can be achieved by a given price of CO_2 to be slightly greater than the EIA model.

14. Hassett, Mathur, and Metcalf provide information on the change in product price assuming no behavioral adjustments in response to a tax of \$15 per metric ton of CO_2. Dividing these price changes by 15 yields the implied CO_2 content in each category. Metcalf (1999) has been the basis for similar calculations elsewhere in the literature (Boyce and Riddle 2007; Dinan and Rogers 2002).

Figure 13.3
Emissions (mtCO$_2$) per Capita by Income Decile for the Nation

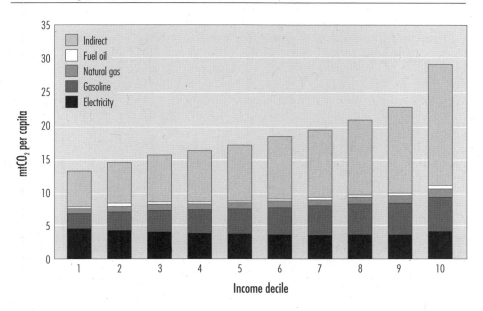

scale up our indirect emissions estimates so that the total corresponds with EIA estimates.[15]

The EIA estimate of metric tons CO$_2$ (mtCO$_2$) per capita is 20.2 (Energy Information Administration 2007a). After scaling the indirect expenditure category in the CEX survey data and before the CAFE adjustment, we find that personal transportation accounts for 21 percent, home heating for 7 percent, residential electricity use for 20 percent, and indirect expenditures for 52 percent. After adjusting for CAFE, the emissions per capita fall from 20.2 to 19.3 mtCO$_2$. Figure 13.3 illustrates the CO$_2$ content of expenditures for the average household in

---

15. Prior to scaling, our analysis of the CEX survey data accounts for per capita emissions of 16.4 metric tons of CO$_2$ (mtCO$_2$), where information from EIA indicates per capita emissions of 20.2 mtCO$_2$, based on U.S. population in 2006. We scale the emission intensity of the indirect expenditure category, increasing it by 54 percent (3.65 mtCO$_2$ per capita) to achieve overall EIA emission levels. The literature reveals a variety of approaches to deal with the inconsistency. Batz, Pizer, and Sanchirico (2007) correct for oversampling in their demographic model. Dinan and Rogers (2002) scale the CEX survey data so that they align with expenditures reported in the National Income Product Accounts, which implicitly scales emissions from fossil-fuel use at the national level. Boyce and Riddle (2007) do not scale and appear to account for only 13.46 mtCO$_2$ per capita in their data. On the other hand, Hassett, Mathur, and Metcalf (2009) appear to account for emissions of 24.4 mtCO$_2$ per capita, well above the EIA estimate.

each income group at the national level. We interpret this as a proxy for baseline (no climate policy) emissions per capita in 2015.

ESTIMATING THE EFFECT OF PLACING A PRICE ON CO_2

Cap and trade incorporates not only the cost of investments and changes in processes into product prices, but also the value of emissions allowances. For the next couple of decades at least, the value of emissions allowances under a cap and trade program can be expected to be substantially larger than the value of resources actually used to achieve emissions reductions. Hence, the allocation of emissions allowances plays the key role in determining the regressivity of climate policy under incentive-based policy.

We benchmark the stringency of climate policy to an emissions reduction of 3.17 $mtCO_2$ per capita, including the CAFE adjustment, resulting from a price of $41.50 per ton of CO_2 (2006 dollars) in a cap and trade program.[16] The 2015 time frame allows for some technological evolution in transportation and electricity; otherwise, expenditure patterns of households are assumed to match those in the CEX data. In evaluating alternative policies, we scale the CO_2 price in order to hold per capita emissions constant so that the alternatives can be compared to the benchmark climate policy in an emissions-neutral manner.

The change in product prices is expected to lead to a change in consumer expenditures, which we calculate using short-run elasticity estimates specific to each fuel.[17] The policy-case emissions of 16.9 $mtCO_2$ per capita, a 16 percent reduction from baseline, are distributed across categories, with 21 percent for transportation, 8 percent for home heating, 11 percent for residential electricity use, and 60 percent for indirect goods and services. This approach implicitly assumes that all cost changes are fully passed through to consumers in every industry except electricity, due to the long-lived nature of in-place capital in that sector.

Figure 13.4 illustrates the distribution of costs over income groups at the regional level after accounting for changes in expenditures but before accounting

---

16. This price reflects a marginal cost approximately three times greater than what would have been expected from the McCain-Lieberman proposal (SB 280) and is roughly equal to the price of emissions allowances in the EU Emission Trading Scheme for the second trading period (2008–2012), which are currently trading at about US$40 $mtCO_2$. The irregular price number results from converting units and the dollar-year for which data are reported.

17. We use a short-run elasticity (ε) for gasoline of -0.1 taken from Hughes, Knittel, and Sperling (2008). For indirect expenditures, we use several short-run elasticities taken from Boyce and Riddle (2007) and ranging from -0.25 to -1.3. For natural gas, we use -0.2 taken from Dahl (1993); we also use this elasticity for fuel oil. To model the change in residential electricity demand, we use the Haiku model, which solves for equilibria including changes in investment in generation capacity, electricity price, and demand at the regional level. The change in carbon emissions ($mtCO_2$) for residential customers in the electricity sector for a $1 change in the carbon price is $\Theta = -0.13$.

Figure 13.4
Cost of Pricing Carbon as a Fraction of Income

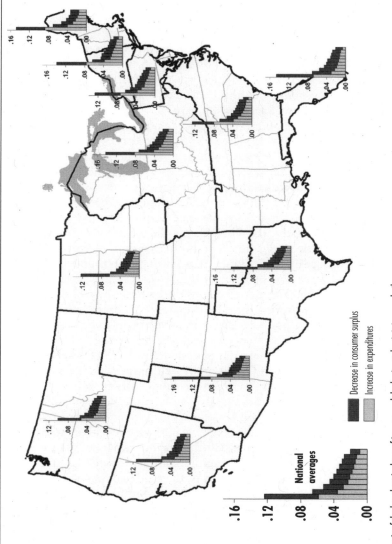

Note: The vertical axis of the bar chart is share of income, and the horizontal axis is income decile.
Source: Bureau of Labor Statistics (2008). *Consumer Expenditure Survey Public Use Microdata,* http://www.bls.gov/cex/csxmicro.htm.

for the CO_2 revenues. The insert at the lower left presents the effect at the national level. Consider an average family in the fifth decile. Ignoring the change in consumption that would be expected, as has been done in much of the previous literature, the introduction of the CO_2 price would cause expenditures for direct energy use to increase by $807 (1.9 percent) and total expenditures to increase by $1,711 (4.1 percent). However, after accounting for changes in consumption behavior in response to the higher prices, this family would experience an increase in total expenditures of $868 (2.1 percent). The smaller bar in the figure indicates this change.

The change in expenditure does not account for the change in consumer surplus. To see how misleading this could be, imagine an expenditure category with own-price elasticity of demand equal to –1. An increase in price would lead to a reduction in quantity, but there would be no change in expenditure. Simply equating expenditure change with well-being, therefore, would underestimate the cost of constraining CO_2. To measure the impact on households, we calculate the change in consumer surplus associated with the change in consumption by measuring the change in area under the Marshalian demand curve corresponding to elasticity estimates provided in the previous footnote. The larger quantity in the bar graphs indicates the change in consumer surplus as a percentage of income. Positive values indicate the absolute value of the magnitude of the loss, which is always larger than the change in expenditure. Again, the greatest losses in consumer surplus as a percentage of income occur for low-income households.[18]

One way to represent the distribution of costs in a quantitative manner is the Suits Index, which is the tax analog to the better-known Gini coefficient that serves as an index measuring income inequality. A Lorenz curve is constructed by plotting the relationship between cumulative tax paid and cumulative income earned.[19] The area under this curve is compared with the area under a proportional line in order to calculate the Suits Index. If all tax collections are nonnegative, the index is bounded by –1 and 1, with values less than zero connoting regressivity and values greater than zero connoting progressivity. A proportional tax has a Suits Index of zero (Suits 1977). We modify the standard interpretation to measure the incidence on households according to their loss in consumer surplus rather than taxes paid. Second, we allow for negative tax payments and other forms of subsidies, so our modified Suits Index (MSI) is not bounded by –1 and 1. At the national level, not accounting for the revenue that may be collected or the allocation of emissions allowances, the modified Suits Index value for the CO_2 price of $41.50 is –0.19. This does not account for the revenue; it is simply an illustration of the distribution of the change in expenditures and consumer

---

18. West (2004) showed that, when demand elasticities vary by income group, using consumer surplus rather than expenditures can lead to different distributional findings.

19. A Lorenz curve graphically represents a cumulative distribution function showing the proportion of the distribution that is assumed by a given percent of values.

surplus. The figure illustrates that the changes as a percentage of income appear to be greatest for low-income households because they have proportionately higher energy-related expenditures.

In contrast to our findings, Hassett, Mathur, and Metcalf (2009) conduct a comparison of the incidence of a carbon tax across regions, finding it "quite remarkable how small" the differences are across regions. However, Batz, Pizer, and Sanchirico (2007) reach a different conclusion. Although they look at direct energy use only, they do so with much greater geographic detail than did previous efforts by looking at data at the county level and at differences in the emissions intensity of electricity generation across the country. They find "substantial variation in the incidence of a carbon emissions tax" (12) across regions, which they explain as due to variation in energy use as well as differences in the carbon intensity of electricity generation. Our analysis does not have the detail at the county level, but it does have more detailed estimates of electricity generation, and it includes indirect expenditures.

The Regional Effects of Policy Alternatives

The price on CO_2 emissions creates significant revenue that must be accounted for in some manner. We assume that the first claimant is government, which is subject to budget constraints (at the federal and state levels combined). Throughout the following analysis, we assume that 35 percent of the revenue collected is immediately directed to the government, leaving 65 percent for other purposes.[20] In some cases the climate policy could lead to additional sources of government revenue such as taxes collected on extra dividends that result if free allocation of allowances is given to emitters. In such a case we net out this effect so that the government retains a constant 35 percent share of revenue in each scenario. We examine three policies in detail.

CAP AND DIVIDEND (LUMP SUM TRANSFERS)
One straightforward policy to alleviate the regressivity of the carbon policy would be to return the CO_2 revenue to households on a per capita basis. This approach recently has been called "cap and dividend" (Boyce and Riddle 2007) and previously was known as "sky trust" (Barnes 2001; Kopp et al. 1999). Using information from the CEX survey, we identify the number of persons per household in each income group in each region and calculate the net change in expenditures given a per capita dividend payment.

---

20. Dinan and Rogers (2002) estimate that the government would need about 23 percent of the allowance value to offset higher costs stemming from its own consumption of allowances, adjustments to higher energy prices, and higher transfer income payments due to indexing to cost of living and lower revenues. We round the figure up to 35 percent to provide for increased government expenditure on research and development and other measures to address climate change.

The results are presented at the regional level in Figure 13.5, with vertical bars representing the effect on households in each income group. The bar with darker shading and the greatest vertical height represents the incidence of the CO_2 price, measured as the loss in consumer surplus as a share of after-tax income. (This value repeats information that was illustrated in Figure 13.4.) For example, a family in Nebraska with an income of $41,854 would fall into the fifth income bucket. Before considering the dividend, the climate policy would cause this family to increase its expenditures by $816. This amounts to a loss of consumer surplus of $1,597, which is equal to 3.8 percent of its household income.

The bar with the lighter shading represents the incidence of the policy after allocating the value of allowances as a per capita dividend. The family in Nebraska receives a post-tax payment of $973, and the incidence of the policy (measured as lost consumer surplus) falls from 3.8 percent to 1.5 percent of income.[21] The magnitude of the dividend varies across regions because of differences in persons per household. According to the CEX survey data, the national average number of persons per household is 2.57. The California/Nevada region has the greatest number of persons per household (2.9), and Florida has the smallest number (2.43). There is also a difference across income groups. The lowest income group has 1.6 persons per household, and the highest income group has 3.3 persons. These differences affect the size of the dividend received by households when it is paid on a per capita basis.

The inset bar graph in the lower left of Figure 13.5 represents the effects at the national level. Households in the lowest group realize gains from the dividend equal to 15 percent of their income. The coefficient reported in the inset is the Suits Index after accounting for the dividend. The value increases from −0.19 before accounting for the revenue to 0.10 after. The dividend has the biggest effects on low-income households when measured as a portion of income, making the dividend policy appear progressive. The lowest income groups in many regions and at the national level realize a net benefit under this policy.[22]

EXCLUSION OF TRANSPORTATION SECTOR FROM THE CO_2 PRICE
The transportation sector is responsible for 32.3 percent of emissions nationally, and the CEX survey data indicate that personal automobile emissions from use of gasoline account for about 21 percent of per capita emissions. Gasoline use

---

21. Since our results are derived in a partial equilibrium setting, we do not consider any effects that this lump sum payment would have on household expenditures. However, recent behavioral economics literature suggests that consumers are unlikely to factor the expectation of such payments into their short-run energy consumption decisions (Sunstein and Thaler 2008).

22. If no revenue were retained by the government to offset its increase in costs, the dividend would be positive for the bottom five income groups nationwide. However, this would mask the need for increased revenues from other sources, which would also affect family budgets.

Figure 13.5
Cap and Dividend

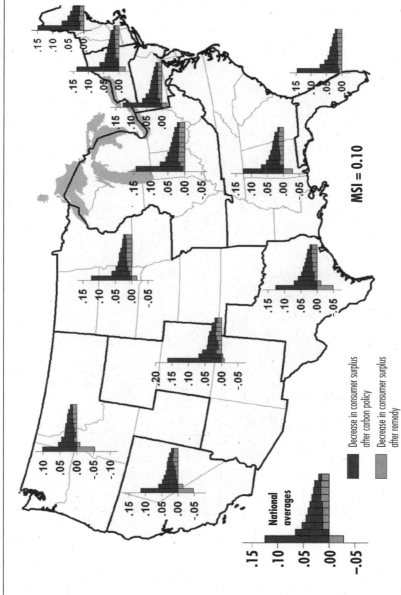

Note: The vertical axis of the bar chart is the loss in consumer surplus as a share of after-tax income, and the horizontal axis is income decile.
Source: Bureau of Labor Statistics (2008). *Consumer Expenditure Survey Public Use Microdata*, http://www.bls.gov/cex/csxmicro.htm.

is not spread equally around the nation. Table 13.2 illustrates that gasoline use in the West and Southwest is considerably higher than in the Northeast. Furthermore, as illustrated in figures 13.1 and 13.2, transportation expense is not distributed evenly across income groups. The largest expense as a share of income belongs to the lowest income group, and the share decreases as households move up the income ladder.

Transportation-related emissions ultimately depend on where people live and work. Land use patterns in general are expected to change as a result of climate policy, and they probably will need to change in order to attain long-run emission reduction goals. However, they are unlikely to change by 2015. The demand for gasoline is inelastic in the short run, and the expected reduction in emissions associated with personal transportation would fall by only 2.2 percent in 2015 due to the CO_2 price. Many authors have suggested that important changes in the performance of automobiles as well as changes in personal transportation will depend on other kinds of policy. Therefore, one way to lessen the incidence of the CO_2 price without undermining environmental goals might be to exclude the transportation sector from coverage. This approach would resemble the design of the EU Emissions Trading Scheme, which covers major point source emissions

Table 13.2
Mean Direct Energy Consumption by Region

	Region[a]	States	Electricity (kWh)	Gasoline (gallons)	Natural Gas (tcf)	Heating Oil (gallons)
1	AEV	AL, AR, DC, GA, LA, MS, NC, SC, TN, VA	17,455	970	36	47
2	CNV	CA, NV	8,516	1,049	37	23
3	ERCOT	TX	16,032	1,125	27	16
4	FRCC	FL	15,897	921	3	13
5	MKIO	IL, IN, KY, MI, MS, OH, WV, WI	13,858	973	73	45
6	MPM	DE, MD, NJ, PA	13,101	863	54	133
7	NE	CT, ME, MA, NH, RI	8,676	932	36	353
8	NWP	ID, MT, OR, UT, WA	13,845	932	45	41
9	NY	NY	8,965	802	39	219
10	PPPP	KS, MN, NE, OK, SD	12,562	976	74	27
11	RA	AZ, CO	13,606	905	48	21
	National[b]		13,289	930	42	76

[a] The region names are not acronyms. They are from the North American Electricity Reliability Council, the U.S. Department of Energy, and the authors.
[b] Numbers in this row are not the column averages.
Source: Bureau of Labor Statistics (2008). *Consumer Expenditure Survey Public Use Microdata*, http://www.bls.gov/cex/csxmicro.htm.

totaling roughly 50 percent of total CO_2 emissions in the EU, but which excludes the transportation sector as well as direct fuel use for home heating or cooling.

Figure 13.6 illustrates the impact at the regional and national levels of excluding transportation. The revised CAFE standards are assumed to be in place, helping to achieve important emissions reductions compared to 2006 emissions per capita. Nonetheless, exclusion of the transportation sector erodes the emission reductions that otherwise would be expected to occur in the sector. To meet the aggregate emissions goal, more reductions have to be achieved in other sectors, thereby raising the costs in those sectors. Nationally, we estimate that the allowance price has to rise from $41.50 mtCO$_2$ under an economy-wide approach to $42.83 when the transportation sector is not included, which in turn has implications for the incidence of costs incurred in other sectors. The price of CO_2 allowances goes up to reach the same CO_2 emissions target because this policy does not take advantage of the possibility of achieving emission reductions in the transportation sector. The darker bars in the figure indicate the incidence of the policy before accounting for revenue, measured as the lost consumer surplus as a percentage of income. (As noted previously, the change in consumer surplus is greater than the change in expenditures.) Before accounting for the revenue, the initial incidence of the policy is lower across all income groups, especially across lower-income groups, when transportation is excluded.

The lighter bar indicates the incidence after returning CO_2 revenue to households as dividends on a per capita basis. Although the CO_2 price is greater, the amount of revenue is less than under the economy-wide policy. As before, the government withholds 35 percent of the revenue before returning the rest to households. The figure indicates that the two lowest income groups in every region realize a net gain, or break even, under the policy. At the national level, the modified Suits Index is 0.02, roughly neutral, when the transportation sector is excluded.

Overall, this approach has a large distributional effect. It appears to reduce the regressivity of the climate policy compared to an economy-wide approach, although this depends on what is done with the revenue. This approach may be compelling, since few emission reductions are expected to result from the application of the CO_2 price on gasoline in the short run. However, policy makers should keep in mind the possible hidden costs of the free pass for transportation. Compared to costs of CO_2 emissions elsewhere in the economy, the exclusion of the transportation sector is effectively a subsidy to gasoline use. This may cause people to be less likely to consider the effects of climate change in their personal transportation and land use choices. Furthermore, the subsidy may be sticky; removing it in the future may be even more difficult politically than including transportation in the program from the outset.[23] Finally, our analysis takes place

---

23. California's Market Advisory Committee (2007) for implementation of the state's greenhouse gas legislation reached a similar conclusion: "If the state chooses to embrace the

Figure 13.6

Excluding Personal Transportation from the CO$_2$ Price

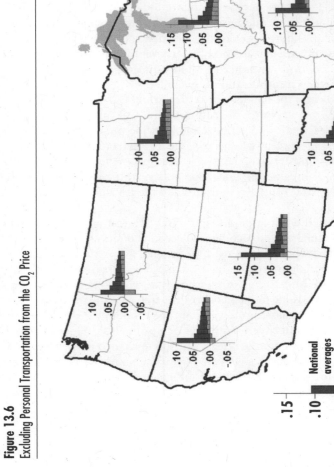

MSI = 0.02

■ Decrease in consumer surplus
   after carbon policy

■ Decrease in consumer surplus
   after remedy

Note: The vertical axis of the bar charts is the loss in consumer surplus as a share of after-tax income, and the horizontal axis is income decile.

Source: Bureau of Labor Statistics (2008). *Consumer Expenditure Survey Public Use Microdata*, http://www.bls.gov/cex/csxmicro.htm.

prior to the recent substantial increase in gasoline prices and subsequent collapse. The volatility of oil prices may have led consumers and industry to make investments to reduce exposure to price fluctuations and especially sharp increases in the future, but this is not considered in our analysis. To the extent that price increases have already caused people to reduce their gasoline consumption, our estimates might overstate the initial impact of capping CO_2. At the same time, increased prices have probably made excluding the transportation sector more politically popular.

FREE ALLOCATION TO ELECTRICITY CONSUMERS

Free allocation to electricity consumers can be accomplished by allocation to load-serving entities (retail utilities), which would act as trustees on behalf of retail electricity customers. An important question is the basis on which allocation would be made to the load-serving entities. The many options include allocation on the basis of consumption, population, and emissions (or emission intensity of generation). Allocation on the basis of consumption is used to illustrate the policy.

Figure 13.7 illustrates the benefits to electricity consumers. Results are presented only at the national level because there is little variation across regions. The greatest changes occur for the lowest income groups under this policy. Over most of the income range, this approach is fairly neutral, and the Suits Index is reported as –0.08 in the figure.

Despite its advantages, free allocation to consumers has a deleterious effect on the efficiency of the program. The electricity sector uses more of the overall emission target because the lower electricity price leads to greater emissions. When electricity prices do not rise, consumers invest less in improving end-use efficiency. In effect, allocation to consumers is a subsidy to electricity consumption that raises the overall cost of the program. The Haiku electricity model accounts for this with endogenous price formation and price responsive demand functions. Because consumers do not see higher prices, the reductions necessary elsewhere in the economy increase. Compared to the central policy case (cap and dividend), total emissions in the electricity sector rise by 6 percent under load-based allocation. Consequently, the allowance price increases above that in the central policy case to $46.56, and this is reflected in the overall incidence of the policy. Government is assigned 35 percent of the CO_2 revenue, and the portion outside the electricity sector is returned as a per capita dividend.

Allocation to load-serving entities on the basis of consumption is just one of at least three plausible approaches. Alternatives include allocation on a per capita basis, which would be identical to cap and dividend, and allocation on the basis

---

fundamental principle of comprehensive coverage, it should strive to incorporate that principle from the outset, when the cost of doing so is relatively low. This would reduce uncertainties about whether this sector will ever be included, and establish an efficient architecture for the cap-and-trade program to grow in stringency over time."

Figure 13.7
Free Allocation to Consumers (Load-Serving Entities) in the Electricity Sector

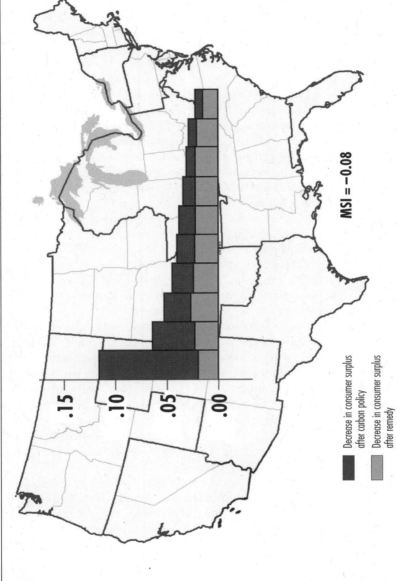

.15

.10

.05

.00

MSI = −0.08

Decrease in consumer surplus
after carbon policy

Decrease in consumer surplus
after remedy

Note: The vertical axis of the bar chart is the loss in consumer surplus as a share of after-tax income, and the horizontal axis is income decile.
Source: Bureau of Labor Statistics (2008). *Consumer Expenditure Survey Public Use Microdata*, http://www.bls.gov/cex/csxmicro.htm.

of emissions. The alternatives could double or halve the allocation to electricity consumers on a regional basis.

Figure 13.8 illustrates these three approaches with two comparisons for the 20 regions represented in the Haiku electricity model that are mapped into the 11 regions in this analysis. One approach compares allocation on the basis of consumption to allocation on the basis of population; the second approach compares allocation on the basis of emissions relative to allocation on the basis of population. California and Nevada at the far right of the figure provide an interesting example. Allocation on the basis of consumption reduces the allowances going to load-serving entities by nearly half compared to allocation on the basis of population. This reflects the relatively low electricity consumption per capita in the region, the result of three decades of conservation programs. Allocation on the basis of emissions would be even more dramatic, reducing the allowance value going to electricity consumers by 80 percent compared to allocation on a per capita basis because of the relatively low emitting mix of generation technology in the region. On the other hand, coal-intensive regions would benefit tremendously from allocation on the basis of emissions.

ADDITIONAL OPTIONS WITH VARIED EFFECTS
We also investigate other options, including free allocation to emitters, reduction in income taxes, and investment in end-use efficiency (Burtraw, Sweeney, and

Figure 13.8
Apportioning Allowances to Load-Serving Electricity Companies

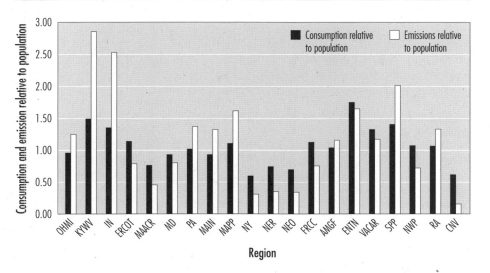

Note: The region names are not acronyms. They are from the North American Electricity Reliability Council, the U.S. Department of Energy, and the authors.

Walls 2008). These alternatives lead to a wider array of values for the modified Suits Index, indicating that they have significant effects on the distribution of costs across income groups at the national level. These effects are most concisely illustrated through the calculation of a modified Suits Index, which is shown in table 13.3. The greater the value of the index, the more progressive the policy.

The three policies examined in detail in this chapter are relatively neutral from a distributional standpoint. By contrast, the two most regressive policies are free allocation to emitters, which has a modified Suits Index of –0.39, and the use of revenue to reduce income taxes, which has a modified Suits Index of –1.32. The latter value results because we assume a proportional reduction in taxes paid across all income groups. However, tax reform is not necessarily regressive. Burtraw, Sweeney, and Walls (2008) explore other approaches, including a reduction in the payroll tax and expansion of the earned income tax credit.

The policy scenarios also have significantly different effects across regions of the country. For example, cap and dividend, which has a Suits Index that is slightly progressive, yields more progressive outcomes in the western states than in the Midwest, Florida, and the Northeast. Excluding the transportation sector from the program is moderately progressive at the national level, but there is considerable variation in the impact across regions. This policy benefits lower-income households in the West, but remains moderately regressive in parts of the Northeast and Southeast.

While the case for equity across income groups is straightforward, inter-regional equity is somewhat complicated. To the extent that some regions have enacted policies to reduce their carbon footprint, one can make the case that their citizens deserve the relative benefits that incentive-based policies would bring them. On the other hand, there is considerable resource and lifestyle heterogeneity across regions, and some states do not have the resources to reduce their carbon consumption quite as easily. Despite the ambiguity of the merits of inter-regional equity, the relative burden of climate policy across regions will shape political considerations as such policies come to fruition.

Table 13.3
Modified Suits Index

Scenario	Modified Suits Index		Equilibrium Allowance Price (2006$/mtCO$_2$)
	After CO$_2$ Price	Including Revenue	
Cap and Dividend	–0.19	0.10	$41.52
Exclude Transportation Sector	–0.19	0.02	$42.83
Load-Based Allocation	–0.18	–0.08	$46.56
Reduce Income Taxes	–0.19	–1.32	$41.52
Free Allocation to Emitters	–0.19	–0.39	$44.85
Invest in Efficiency	–0.19	0.05	$36.87

An additional trade-off faced by policy makers is the design of policy that is more efficient versus one that achieves desirable distributional outcomes. This analysis indicates that using revenues to reduce preexisting taxes, which public finance economists suggest is the most efficient approach, can have deleterious distributional consequences. On the other hand, some approaches that would ease the burden on specific economic activities, such as personal transportation and electricity use, have negative efficiency consequences. Table 13.3 illustrates the range of allowance prices required to meet the same climate goal under these various approaches. All other things being equal, a higher permit price will correspond to a greater marginal burden of compliance in the covered sectors.

We examine a fairly stringent climate policy with a CO_2 price of $41.50 in 2015, which can range from $36.87 to $46.56 over the policies we consider. The lowest-cost options for reducing carbon emissions lie in the electricity sector; thus, the highest allowance price across the policy cases occurs with free allocation to electricity consumers because it removes the CO_2 price from the electricity price, leading to higher electricity consumption and emissions from this sector. A similar outcome occurs with free allocation to emitters in regions of the country with regulated electricity prices, but not in regions with market-based prices. In both cases, the higher allowance price relative to cap and dividend indicates that more reductions and greater costs are realized in other sectors of the economy. In contrast, direct investments in energy efficiency in the electricity sector yield the lowest overall allowance price. In each case where allowance value is dedicated to meet specific distributional goals within one sector, it constitutes a subsidy to that sector or the exclusion of another sector. This implies a violation of the law of one price in climate policy, which is a fundamental tenet of economic efficiency. When a resource, good, or service attracts a different price in different parts of the economy, efficiency is undermined because resources are not consistently allocated to their highest-valued use. The violation of the law of one price raises the overall social cost of achieving climate goals, even if it addresses distributional concerns.

How Might State-Level Interests Shape Climate Policy?

Although climate change is a long-run problem, climate policy takes shape with a more immediate political dynamic. Delivering compensation or finding ways to alleviate disproportional burdens of the policy seems especially important in the early years of climate policy. If all politics are local, then the local and regional effects of policy may be fundamentally important to building the political coalition necessary to enact climate policy.[24] Just as at the national level, policies on

---

24. There are regional differences in the pattern of benefits as well as costs. Deschênes and Greenstone (2007) estimate interstate differences that are striking, with California agriculture losing around $1 billion annually and Pennsylvania gaining about half that much due to a changing climate.

climate change at the local level will be driven in part by interests not necessarily related to climate change.

STATE-LEVEL STRATEGIC INTERESTS

Responsiveness to local and regional interests arguably may improve the policy outcome in general or may be essential to achieving any policy outcome, but it seems unlikely to enhance the efficiency of the policy. For a firm with a scope of operations that spans multiple jurisdictions, regulatory standards that vary substantially among regions would impose larger compliance costs than would regulations with relatively cross-regional uniformity. Given that, variations in greenhouse gas policies at the state level may result in higher compliance costs than would policies implemented on the national or even international level. Standards not only may be different, but they may also be inconsistent with requirements in other states. A regulatory standard in one state may encourage the use of a particular energy source, while another state's standard may specifically prohibit it. A power company selling into both markets would face significant managerial and technological costs in satisfying the joint but inconsistent requirements. Navigating this regulatory maze can place a substantial burden on commerce between jurisdictions, imposing hidden costs on consumers.

For example, several states took steps to promote the use of in-state coal (usually high-sulfur coal) to comply with Title IV of the 1990 Clean Air Act amendments. The promotion of in-state coal inevitably raised costs, but it was consistent with policies that promoted economic development in the state. In-state economic development historically has been a common focus of state public utility commissions and is sometimes even part of their charter in state constitutions (Arimura 2002; Bohi 1994; Burtraw 1996; Rose 1997; Sotkiewicz 2002).

Another example is the geographic limitation of existing renewable energy programs, which raises the cost of achieving specific penetration rates for renewables. Palmer and Burtraw (2005) found that state-level renewable energy portfolio standards aimed at achieving fairly stringent goals appear virtually impossible to achieve in many areas of the nation without incurring large costs for new capabilities in biomass or solar technologies. According to the authors, other areas could achieve less expensive generation from renewables and export renewable energy credits. Nonetheless, all the states that have pursued renewable policies have limited geographic tradability of renewable credits in order to attempt to promote local economic development.

The architecture of a national cap and trade program could take a variety of forms. As described above, sectors could be regulated in different ways and in fact could function under separate regulations. A possibility that mirrors the development of the NOx budget program, for example, might give states the latitude to choose whether various sectors would be in or out of a national CO_2 trading program. A state's decision to exclude a sector from the national trading program may not only benefit local interests but also harm other states. This illustrates a strategic dynamic to the decisions that might be left to states, and that characterize interests that will influence the design of a national trading program.

We construct a reduced-form model of idiosyncratic state and regional interests built on the CEX survey data by modeling a representative agent who might be thought of as an average voter—not necessarily the median voter—in each region. We hold the emission target discussed above constant and calculate the CO_2 price that would be necessary under various scenarios. This exercise is simplified compared to that described above; here we calculate CO_2 expenditures for each agent by multiplying the price times the emissions embodied in consumption at the price necessary to achieve the emissions target; we use linear estimates of the change in emissions that occurs in response to a change in the price; and we do not calculate consumer surplus changes.[25] We focus exclusively on the first-order estimate of the change in expenditures associated with the introduction of the CO_2 price, and the disposition of revenues after accounting for 35 percent of revenues that is always siphoned off to maintain a balanced government budget.

FREE ALLOCATION TO ELECTRICITY CONSUMERS

One possible outcome would be for states to retain authority to allocate some portion of emissions allowances. The natural way for this to occur is for emissions allowances to be apportioned originally to states, perhaps for only some sectors, as occurred under previous emissions trading programs. As noted earlier, the Lieberman-Warner proposal delegates 22 percent of allowances to states, with 9 percent to the electricity sector, specifically designated as allocation to load-serving entities on behalf of consumers, and other value potentially available to the electricity sector at the state's discretion. The 2002 Jeffords bill would have allocated two-thirds of emissions allowances to the states for determination of allocation by trustees. It would be plausible for the decision to be left to the state public utility commissions, which would act as trustees on behalf of consumers.

We model apportionment of emissions allowances for the electricity sector, which effectively directs that portion of value of the CO_2 revenue to the state, which in turn decides how to direct it further. We assume that an auction with per capita dividends is implemented at the federal level for other parts of the economy. The payoffs for individual states consider two options: (1) auction to the electricity sector with value returned as a per capita dividend; and (2) allocation for free to load-serving entities on behalf of consumers, thereby effectively subsidizing electricity consumption.

We define payoffs for the representative agent in each state or region as net CO_2 expenditures equal to payments for CO_2 emissions allowances minus the dividend received. Under allocation to load-serving entities, the electricity price does not increase to reflect the value of CO_2 emissions. There are still significant

---

25. We also do not account for the different number of persons per household, which is relevant when accounting for revenue returned on a per capita basis.

emission reductions in the electricity sector, but they are less than would occur under an auction. In effect, the allowance value is used to subsidize the electricity price, and the dividends are reduced accordingly. Another effect is that more emissions reductions have to occur in other sectors, which pushes up the CO_2 price and associated costs in other sectors. States and regions have different levels of emissions associated with economic activity in various sectors, so the decision will have dissimilar effects across states.

Table 13.4 reports the estimated net expenditures for each region under five different scenarios. Column 1 describes the emissions cap with a nationwide auction for all sectors and with dividends returned on a per capita basis. The scenario in the second column gives special consideration to the electricity sector, where allowances for the sector are apportioned to the states, all states separately auction the allowances, and households receive 65 percent of the allowance value as dividends. Compared to an auction at the national level, this federalist approach for the electricity sector preserves the value of the emissions allowances for each region, providing a sort of compensation for emission-intensive regions.

For example, AEV in the first row includes a large portion of the Southeast and has a relatively large amount of coal-fired generation. The representative

Table 13.4
Net CO_2 Expenditures by Region (2006 Dollars)

Region[a]	Economy-wide Nationwide	Apportionment to States for Electricity Sector	Load-Based Allocation in AEV	Load-Based Allocation in AEV, MKIO, MPM, PPPP	Load-Based Allocation Nationwide
AEV	387	269	162	176	206
CNV	147	225	229	250	282
ERCOT	192	199	207	219	207
FRCC	197	202	207	222	209
MKIO	503	354	353	248	282
MPM	417	320	319	247	281
NE	294	343	334	377	400
NWP	160	241	245	263	301
NY	158	211	214	233	249
PPPP	281	338	324	357	396
RA	185	233	221	251	269
CO_2 Price (2006$/ $mtCO_2$)	41	41	42	46	48

[a] The region names are not acronyms. They are from the North American Electricity Reliability Council, the U.S. Department of Energy, and the authors.

agent in this region receives a larger share of the allowance value when all the value from the electricity sector associated with emissions in the region is kept in the region through apportionment. Compared to a nationwide auction, net expenditures in AEV fall from $387 to $269 per capita. On the other hand, the second row illustrates the California/Nevada region, which has relatively low CO_2 emissions associated with electricity consumption. Here, net expenditures increase from $147 to $225 per capita. The bottom row of the table indicates that there is no change in the CO_2 price; that is, we do not identify an efficiency consequence.[26] Rather, the shift in expenditures among regions is a zero-sum game associated with the assignment of value.

Apportionment to states gives them the discretion to decide differently about how to allocate allowances. The third column illustrates the incentives for the AEV region to use allocation to load-serving entities instead of an auction. Net expenditures in the region fall significantly to $162 per capita. Net expenditures fall in some other regions because they achieve more value from the change in per capita dividend than they pay due to the higher allowance price. However, as the bottom row indicates, the allowance price increases to $42, indicating an overall efficiency consequence from AEV's decision to subsidize electricity consumption.

Column 4 illustrates the outcome when MKIO (much of the Midwest), MPM (the mid-Atlantic), and PPPP (the Great Plains) also decide to allocate to electricity consumers. The movement of these regions as a group erodes AEV's gains. It also further increases the electricity price to $46, imposing costs on other regions and the nation as a whole.

Each region individually has an incentive to move to free allocation to electricity consumers. Column 5 indicates that when all regions do this, the electricity price rises to $48, with efficiency consequences for the nation as a whole. The strategic relationship takes the form of a multiplayer prisoner's dilemma. The individually rational choice of each state or region leads to a collective outcome that is less advantageous from the perspective of efficiency than is a coordinated allocation using an auction at the federal level. Nonetheless, because the distributional consequence of a nationwide auction is severe for regions with emission-intensive electricity use, political considerations may lead to a less-efficient outcome.

Conclusions

Emissions trading is an important policy innovation that promises to dramatically reduce the overall cost of climate policy. The formation of a formal emissions allowance market for CO_2 would create a new asset of enormous value. How that value is distributed in the economy will be important to the long-term

---

26. The allowance price in this simulation differs slightly from that achieved earlier with a more complete model.

impact of efforts to address climate change. Even if the benefits of climate policy dramatically outweigh the costs, the distributional impact of a market for CO_2 could have much bigger economic effects on many households than will the environmental consequences of a changing climate.

State governments are often thought to be better able to address distributional considerations than is the national government because decision makers are more proximate to affected constituencies. This might suggest that states should play a central role in the architecture of climate policy as it is conceived at the federal level. The precedent in most previous environmental regulation places state governments in the primary role of implementing policy. The introduction of national markets for CO_2 emissions allowances by the federal government would represent a significant appropriation of authority and significant economic value from what has previously been the domain of states.

The wide variety of consumption patterns across the nation lead to differences in the incidence of climate policy across regions and across income groups. As a consequence, states not only have concerns about distributional impacts, but also have strategic interests in the design of national climate policy. These interests may be an important influence on the architecture of national policy. If authority for important decisions such as allocation of emissions allowances is delegated to the states, these interests could play a prominent role because of strategic relationships among the states. As is often observed, the devolution of authority is a two-edged sword. States may be better suited to address idiosyncratic distributional concerns, but state-level decisions can also unleash a dilemma that causes overall costs for the nation as a whole to increase.

REFERENCES

Arimura, Toshi. 2002. An empirical study of the SO_2 allowance market: Effects of PUC regulations. *Journal of Environmental Economics and Management* 442:271–289.

Barnes, Peter. 2001. *Who owns the sky? Our common assets and the future of capitalism*. Washington, DC: Island Press.

Barthold, Thomas. 1993. How should we measure distribution? *National Tax Journal* XLVI(3):291–299.

Batz, Michael, William Pizer, and James N. Sanchirico. 2007. Regional patterns of U.S. household carbon emissions: Resources for the future. Unpublished manuscript.

Bohi, Douglas R. 1994. Utilities and state regulators are failing to take advantage of emission allowance trading. *Electricity Journal* 72:20–27.

Boyce, James K., and Matthew Riddle. 2007. Cap and dividend: How to curb global warming while protecting the incomes of American families. Working Paper No. 150. University of Massachusetts, Political Economy Research Institute, Amherst, MA.

Bureau of Labor Statistics. 2008. *Consumer expenditure survey public use microdata*. http://www.bls.gov/cex/csxmicro.htm.

Burtraw, Dallas. 1996. The SO_2 emissions trading program: Cost savings without allowance trades. *Contemporary Economic Policy* XIV (April):79–94.

Burtraw, Dallas, and William Shobe. 2007. Local options on global stocks: How the states are affecting the U.S. debate on climate policy. *States and Climate Change*, Policy Research Institute for the Region at Princeton University, Conference Proceedings.

Burtraw, Dallas, Rich Sweeney, and Margaret Walls. 2008. The incidence of U.S. climate policy: Where you stand depends on where you sit. Resources for the Future Discussion Paper 08-28 September.

California Market Advisory Committee. 2007. Recommendations for designing a greenhouse gas cap-and-trade system for California. http://www.climatechange .ca.gov/policies/market_advisory.html.

Casperson, Erik, and Gilbert Metcalf. 1994. Is a value added tax regressive? Annual versus lifetime incidence measures. *National Tax Journal* XLVII(4):731–747.

Crocker, Thomas D. 1966. The structuring of atmospheric pollution control system. In *Economics of air pollution*, ed. H. Wolozin, 61–86. New York: Norton.

Dahl, Carol. 1993. A survey of energy demand elasticities in support of the development of the NEMS. Contract No. DE-AP01-93EI23499. U.S. Department of Energy, National Energy Modeling System (NEMS).

Deschênes, Olivier, and Michael Greenstone. 2007. The economic impacts of climate change: Evidence from agricultural output and random fluctuations in weather. *American Economic Review* 971:354–385.

Dinan, Terry, and Diane Rogers. 2002. Distributional effects of carbon allowance trading: How government decisions determine winners and losers. *National Tax Journal* LV(2):199–221.

Energy Information Administration. 2007. Emissions of greenhouse gases in the United States 2006. DOE/EIA-05732006.

Fischer, Carolyn, Winston Harrington, and Ian W. H. Parry. 2007. Should automobile fuel efficiency standards be tightened? *Energy Journal* 28(4):1–30.

Fullerton, Don, and Diane Lim Rogers. 1993. *Who bears the lifetime tax burden?* Washington, DC: Brookings Institution.

Goulder, Lawrence H., Ian W. H. Parry, Roberton C. Williams III, and Dallas Burtraw. 1999. The cost-effectiveness of alternative instruments for environmental protection in a second-best setting. *Journal of Public Economics* 723:329–360.

Hassett, Kevin A., Aparna Mathur, and Gilbert E. Metcalf. Forthcoming. The incidence of a U.S. carbon tax: A lifetime and regional analysis. *Energy Journal*.

Hughes, Jonathan E., Christopher R. Knittel, and Daniel Sperling. 2008. Evidence of a shift in the short-run price elasticity of gasoline demand. *Energy Journal* 29(1):113–134.

Kopp, Raymond, Richard Morgenstern, William Pizer, and Michael Toman. 1999. *A proposal for credible early action in U.S. climate policy*. Washington, DC: Resources for the Future.

Metcalf, Gilbert E. 1999. A distributional analysis of green tax reforms. *National Tax Journal* 52(4):655–682.

Palmer, Karen, and Dallas Burtraw. 2005. Cost-effectiveness of renewable electricity policies. *Energy Economics* 27:873–894.

Paltsev, Sergey, John M. Reilly, Henry D. Jacoby, Angelo C. Gurgel, Gilbert E. Metcalf, Andrei P. Sokolov, and Jennifer F. Holak. 2007. Assessment of U.S. cap-and-trade proposals. Report No. 146. MIT Joint Program on the Science and Policy of Global Change.

Parry, Ian W. H. 2004. Are emissions permits regressive? *Journal of Environmental Economics and Management* 47:364–387.

Parry, Ian W. H., Roberton C. Williams III, and Lawrence H. Goulder. 1999. When can carbon abatement policies increase welfare? The fundamental role of distorted factor markets. *Journal of Environmental Economics and Management* 371:52–84.

Paul, Anthony, Dallas Burtraw, and Karen Palmer. 2008. *The Haiku electricity model*. Washington, DC: Resources for the Future Report.

Pigou, Arthur Cecil. 1920. *The economics of welfare*. London: Macmillan.

Poterba, James M. 1989. Lifetime incidence and the distributional burden of excise taxes. *American Economic Review* 79(2):325–330.

Rogers, Diane Lim. 1993. Measuring the distributional effects of corrective taxation. Paper presented at a National Tax Association Session of the Allied Social Science Association Meetings, Boston, MA.

Rose, Ken. 1997. Implementing an emissions trading program in an economically regulated industry: Lessons from the SO_2 trading program. In *Market-based approaches to environmental policy: Regulatory innovations to the fore*, ed. R. Kosobud and J. Zimmerman. New York: Van Nostrand Reinhold.

Shapiro, Matthew, and Joel Slemrod. 1994. Consumer response to the timing of income: Evidence from a change in tax withholding. *American Economic Review* 851:274–283.

Small, Kenneth A., and Kurt Van Dender. 2007. Fuel efficiency and motor vehicle travel: The declining rebound effect. *Energy Journal* 28:25–52.

Sotkiewicz, Paul M. 2002. The impact of state-level PUC regulation on compliance costs associated with the market for SO_2 allowances. University of Florida Public Utility Research Center.

Suits, Daniel B. 1977. Measurement of tax progressivity. *American Economic Review* 67(4):747–752.

Sunstein, Cass, and Richard Thaler. 2008. *Nudge*. New Haven: Yale University Press.

U.S. Department of Transportation – National Highway Traffic Safety Administration. 2008. Average fuel economy standards: Model years 2011–2015. Docket No. NHTSA-2008-0089.

Walls, Margaret, and Jean Hanson. 1999. Distributional aspects of an environmental tax shift: The case of motor vehicle emissions taxes. *National Tax Journal* 521: 53–66.

West, Sarah. 2004. Distributional effects of alternative vehicle pollution control policies. *Journal of Public Economics* 88(3–4):735–757.

COMMENTARY
Wallace E. Oates

The Burtraw and Sweeney chapter is a major contribution to the debate on the design and implications of a national cap and trade system to address the problem of greenhouse gas (GHG) emissions. In the absence of federal legislation in the United States, the initiative for the introduction of such measures has been undertaken by the states. It seems likely that some kind of national cap and trade system will come into existence reasonably soon under the new administration; the U.S. Congress is already considering some measures. In view of the major role that the states have already played on this issue, we can expect national legislation to retain an extensive role for the states. Issues of so-called environmental federalism are thus central to the design of such legislation. I focus my comments on this issue.

At the outset, I want to underline Burtraw and Sweeney's observation about the enormous magnitude of the allowances that would be created by such a program. They note that estimates of the value of the emissions allowances under a national GHG program are in the range of $130–$370 billion annually by 2015. The way these allowances are allocated could have major distributional effects throughout the country. The enormity of the allowances reflects the high cost of reducing GHG emissions, a cost that will ultimately be passed along to consumers in the form of higher prices for energy and energy-intensive goods and services. The bottom line on the distributional impact of these price increases is that they will clearly be regressive in their incidence: low-income households will pay a higher proportion of their income than will households with higher incomes. Burtraw and Sweeney provide a valuable analysis of the extent to which some of this regressive incidence could be offset by a program that returns the revenues from an auction of the permits to households on a per capita basis, by an exclusion of the transportation sector from the program, and by a free allocation to electricity consumers. While such measures may mitigate the regressiveness of the overall program to some extent, they have adverse implications for its efficiency.

What role might the states play in a national program to control GHG emissions? As Burtraw and Sweeney discuss, the intergovernmental architecture of a national program could be configured in a variety of ways. Under the first phase of the European Union program, for example, the individual member countries were granted the authority (and responsibility) first for dividing their country's total cap on GHG emissions between the trading and the nontrading sectors, and second for allocating the trading sector share in the form of tradable permits among individual sources (Kruger, Oates, and Pizer 2007). Sources outside the trading sectors are regulated by more traditional command and control techniques.

The basic problem with this design is that the central EU authority lost control over the supply of permits. The total number of permits in the system was equal to the sum of the shares that the member countries decided to allocate to their sources in the trading sectors. Although the EU had defined which sectors (sources) would constitute the trading sector, the individual countries decided how much of their caps to allocate to these sources in the form of tradable permits. In retrospect it appears that many member countries were overly generous in their allocations to the trading sectors, resulting in a large supply of permits in the EU trading system and a consequent low price for these permits.[1] Had they been required to meet their national caps in the initial phase (as will be required in subsequent phases), member countries would have had to introduce very stringent controls on sources in the nontrading sectors. This would imply some serious inefficiencies, inasmuch as sources in the nontrading sectors would have much higher marginal abatement costs than those in the trading sectors that could purchase permits at a relatively low price.

The early EU experience suggests that it is important for the central environmental authority to retain some control over the aggregate number of tradable permits. In the U.S. context, there is surely some scope for the states to allocate their allotment of permits to individual sources, but it makes sense, I think, for the central authority (perhaps the EPA) to retain some control over the total number of tradable permits.

As the literature has made clear, there is a strong case for auctioning permits rather than distributing them free of charge (for example, Parry, Williams, and Goulder 1999). The so-called recycling effect resulting from the revenues collected under the auctioning of permits can result in substantial efficiency gains. There is thus a strong case for a national program to require (or at least encourage) the states to allocate a large portion of their permits through a sensible auction mechanism. It is interesting in this regard that the Regional Greenhouse Gas Initiative (RGGI) requires the participating states to allocate at least 25 percent of their allowances by auction. As Burtraw and Sweeney point out, these states plan to employ auctions to distribute nearly 90 percent of their allowances.

There are a number of other intriguing and challenging issues in the intergovernmental design of cap and trade systems. For example, some states may wish to introduce banking measures that allow sources effectively to save unused credits for use in future periods. Certain states may want to establish a safety valve in the form of a price ceiling on permits that, when reached, will allow additional emissions upon payment of a trigger price. Just how such provisions are to be embedded in the architecture of a national cap and trade system are interesting and important issues (see, for example, Kruger, Oates, and Pizer 2007).

---

1. Near the end of the first phase, the price of permits fell to nearly zero! This presumably occurred because sources were not allowed to bank their unused allowances for use in later phases of the EU program.

REFERENCES

Kruger, Joseph, Wallace E. Oates, and William A. Pizer. 2007. Decentralization in the EU Emissions Trading Scheme and lessons for global policy. *Review of Environmental Economics and Policy* 1(1):112–133.

Parry, Ian W. H., Roberton C. Williams III, and Lawrence H. Goulder. 1999. When can carbon abatement policies increase welfare? The fundamental role of distorted factor markets. *Journal of Environmental Economics and Management* 37(1): 52–84.

14

Private Conservation Easements: Balancing Private Initiative and the Public Interest

Gerald Korngold

The last quarter of the twentieth century was marked by a historic social movement embracing environmental protection and the preservation of natural habitats and species. While environmentalism in America has roots extending to at least the nineteenth century, it exploded as a popular phenomenon beginning with Earth Day in 1969. Today it is a pervasive ethos. To name a few examples, environmental values are reflected in legislation, regulation, and enforcement on the federal, state, and local levels; in the business models of corporations, both global and local, where they are typically expressed as "sustainability"; in the products marketed and consumed by Americans; in the education programs of our schools; and in many religious institutions, reflecting an ethical and moral orientation.

While government has played a vital role in defining and implementing environmental policy, the nonprofit sector has developed and executed significant and innovative environmental protection programs. These accomplishments go beyond the important role of nonprofits in education and advocacy for natural protection. Rather, nonprofits have acquired, managed, and otherwise utilized private property rights to achieve conservation goals.

The development and implementation of private conservation easements is a prime example of nonprofits' use of private property rights for environmental purposes. A conservation easement gives the nonprofit a perpetual property right that prevents the owner of the land subject to the easement from altering its current natural condition, thus protecting the present state of the land forever. The conservation easement is private, or privately held, because a nonprofit, rather than a governmental entity, owns it.[1]

By using conservation easements, nonprofits can use market forces and the legal protections of property rights to achieve environmental goals. These private initiatives have some key public policy and legal advantages over governmental programs. They help to achieve conservation of the natural environment, which has become an important national value. They bring the efficiency of free market transactions without the costs of government coercion. They represent the free choice of the landowners, which should be respected absent a compelling governmental interest.

This chapter shows that private conservation easements provide a valuable property rights approach to land preservation and that they deserve continued recognition and validation. However, private conservation easements raise public policy and legal concerns relating to the significant tax subsidies accompanying them; the threat to democratic principles and quality decision making of having nonaccountable, nonrepresentative private organizations control local land use decisions; the absence of coordinated planning and public process as well as class issues in the creation of conservation easements; stewardship lapses by some nonprofits; and a potential lack of flexibility by nonprofits in dealing with emerging needs of the community (such as affordable housing and economic development) that might conflict with the conservation easement. The chapter examines these issues and shows how these concerns can be addressed so that private conservation easements can be an even more effective tool for achieving environmental protection through private property rights.

The chapter first describes conservation easements, their attributes, and existing data. It then examines the various life stages of a conservation easement—creation, stewardship, and potential modification and termination—to develop the competing public policy and legal perspectives as well as suggested solutions.

Conservation Easements: Attributes and Data

William H. Whyte (1959) popularized, if not coined, the phrase "conservation easement" in the late 1950s. Generally, conservation easements prevent the owner of the land burdened by the easement from changing the natural, ecological, open, or scenic attributes of the property.[2] Conservation easement documents

---

1. Government also can hold conservation easements. See DePalma (2008); *Sabine River Authority v. U.S.*, 745 F. Supp. 388 (E.D. Tex. 1990), affirmed, 951 F.2d 669 (5th Cir. 1993) (federal Department of the Interior, Fish and Wildlife Service); *Mira Mar Mobile Community v. City of Oceanside*, 119 Cal. App. 4th 477 (2004) (city); Ohm (2000).

2. For a definition of a conservation easement, see Uniform Conservation Easement Act § 1(1).

often contain a general statement of such conservation goals and the agreement of the subject owner to not engage in actions that would violate this purpose (*Glass v. Commissioner*, 471 F.3d 698 [6th Cir. 2006]). Sophisticated conservation easement documents also include a list of specific proscribed activities, such as cutting timber, constructing additional buildings or roadways, disturbing the surface of the land, and displaying signs, among others (Anella and Wright 2004, 61–67). The instruments also may describe retained rights specifically negotiated by the burdened owner, such as the right to erect an additional residence (see *Southbury Land Trust, Inc. v. Andricovich*, 59 Conn. App. 785, 757 A.2d 1263 [2000]). Typically, conservation easements protecting scenic views and natural features do not give the public access to the subject property. Rather, the public benefit is said to be gained through the support of wildlife or the visual access that the public has from outside the property (26 *Code of Federal Regulations* section 1.1701-14[d][3][iii]).

Whyte and other early proponents of conservation easements extolled their benefits.[3] The problem was that the common law in virtually all American jurisdictions barred the creation of these interests. There were various legal impediments. For example, the law permitted nearby neighbors to own veto powers only over the development of a parcel of land (the common law prohibition of "in gross" restrictions), while supporters of conservation easements felt that the nonprofits should not have to own land close to the easement property and could be out-of-state organizations. There were questions at common law about the transferability of easements in gross, making it difficult for one nonprofit to assign a conservation easement to another. Additionally, the common law bias against perpetual restrictions on land ran counter to the prescribed model of unlimited duration for conservation easements.

Statutory validation—required as a separate enactment within each of the 50 states, as real property law is a state, not a federal, matter—was therefore necessary to implement the conservation easement vehicle. This legislative process culminated with the development of the Uniform Conservation Easement Act in 1981 and its subsequent adoption in over 20 states. The Uniform Act recognized perpetual conservation easements as valid property interests and specifically removed common law hurdles. The remaining states passed similar legislation over the last decades of the twentieth century. The result is that conservation easements are now recognized as valid, enforceable property interests.

Data on the number and acreage of conservation easements are limited. (This in and of itself raises a public policy concern, as discussed below.) Only fragmentary data can be teased out, but they reveal both significant absolute numbers of conservation easements and percentage growth. In 2005 the Land Trust Alliance reported that American local and state land trusts held conservation easements

---

3. For other early boosters, see Brenneman (1967) and Cunningham (1968). For a history of the land trust movement and its work on conservation easements, see Brewer (2003).

on over 6.2 million acres, a 148 percent increase from the 2000 figure of 2.5 million (Land Trust Alliance 2005a). The Nature Conservancy held over 2 million acres under conservation easement (in addition to acreage held by land trusts) in 2008 (Nature Conservancy 2008). Combined, these holdings approach the 9 million acre range, and they do not include the many conservation easements held by other nonprofits. Joan Youngman (2006) has provided a useful comparison to provide a sense of the magnitude of this land area: 9 million acres is roughly equivalent to the aggregated size of Rhode Island, Delaware, Connecticut, and Hawaii. Table 14.1 shows the not insignificant percentages of total land in a random sampling of states subject to conservation easement held by land trusts only, as of 2005.

The following sections examine conservation easements from a public policy and legal perspective, presenting the benefits and disadvantages of these interests and offering legislative and judicial proposals to address the public policy shortcomings. The chapter follows these issues over the various stages in the evolution of a conservation easement, from creation to the operational phase to the challenges of possible modification or termination. Conservation easements uniquely serve important public policy goals and deserve continued validation and enforcement by legislatures and courts. At the same time, however, some changes in the structure and process of conservation easements would better ensure a role for the public, a more efficient use of public resources, enhanced conservation results, and the injection of flexibility to respond to changing social, economic,

Table 14.1
Conservation Easement Acreage Held by Land Trusts in Sample States, 2005

State	Total Conservation Easement Acreage	Total Land Acreage Within State	Percentage of State Land Under Conservation Easement
Maine	1,492,279	22,646,400	6.58
Vermont	399,861	6,152,960	6.49
Maryland	191,330	7,940,480	2.40
New Hampshire	133,836	5,984,000	2.23
Virginia	365,335	27,375,360	1.33
Colorado	849,825	66,620,160	1.27
Massachusetts	61,569	6,755,200	0.91
New York	191,095	34,915,840	0.54
Arizona	35,645	72,958,720	0.04
Iowa	6,000	36,014,080	0.01

Source: Land Trust Alliance (2005a, chart 5); U.S. Census Bureau (2006, table E-1) (using a factor of 640 acres per square mile to convert area figures).

and technological needs. This can ensure that these important property rights will continue to serve both current and future generations.

Acquisition of Conservation Easements

Many of the benefits of conservation easements are manifest in the acquisition stage. First, their creation serves the growing conservation value in the United States. Over the past four decades, Americans' attitudes toward our lands and environment have undergone a major evolution. Land is now prized for its natural and historical features, not only for its full-development potential (Kuzmiak 1991). Conservation easements are an important preservation vehicle, useful in balancing development and conservation considerations.

Moreover, private conservation easements are nongovernmental initiatives. Direct acquisition costs of conservation easements are borne by nonprofits, rather than by local, state, or federal government, although there may be tax subsidies, as discussed below (Byers and Ponte 2005, 9–10; Raymond 2007, 16–20). This relieves government from the burden of spending limited resources on conservation activities. Given other pressing needs, the pressures of special interests in the development sector, and the need to preserve the tax base, government may not be as willing to purchase and safeguard conservation easements as is a nonprofit that is free from such forces.

Third, the law's validation of private conservation easements creates efficiency advantages in land markets. The law has typically allowed parties to sell partial interests in land, such as leases, since those free market exchanges achieve an efficient allocation of limited (and nonrenewable) land resources. By allowing conservation easements, the nonprofit can purchase only the restriction and need not buy the right to occupy the property, which the burdened land owner is glad to retain. If we did not allow conservation easements, conservation organizations would have to purchase fee interests in land in order to conserve it, spending far more money than the cost of the easement, decreasing the reach of its conservation purchasing power, and needlessly forcing the landowner to sell complete (possessory) rights in the property. The cost of an easement in a property is far less than a fee (Coughlin and Plaut 1978). Given the cost-effectiveness of easements, it is not surprising that easement acquisition by nonprofits has increased at a far greater rate than fees, as seen in figure 14.1.

Additionally, state and local governments obtain fiscal benefits when a nonprofit acquires an easement rather than a fee. When a nonprofit holds a fee for conservation purposes, the entire fee value is exempt from property taxation. With an easement, the value for property taxation is reduced, but a taxable value remains, so the municipality still collects some tax revenue.[4]

---

4. For an example of a statute requiring reduced real property assessment because of the presence of a conservation easement, see Indiana Code § 32-23-5-8.

Figure 14.1
Increase in Acquisitions by Land Trusts, 2000–2005

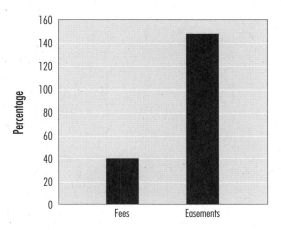

Source: Land Trust Alliance (2005a, chart 5).

Fifth, while public land use regulation (zoning) provides an opportunity for more comprehensive conservation programs within a community and region, such regulation may come with significant costs. Zoning proposals often lead to bitter and divisive battles among landowners, winners, and losers and to expensive, and perhaps winning, challenges by disgruntled owners.[5] A consensual vehicle like a conservation easement avoids the ill will and legal challenges of a coerced regulation.

Finally, freedom of choice is an important part of ownership (Ely 1998, 17). If a landowner wishes to donate or sell a conservation easement, the law should uphold this preference, overriding it only in truly rare situations with compelling reasons.

CONCERNS
Despite the benefits of conservation easements, there are concerns. Although direct acquisition consideration is paid by the nonprofit, there may be a significant tax subsidy on the federal, state, and local levels. Section 170(h) of the Internal Revenue Code permits federal income tax deductions for conservation easements donated to qualified nonprofit organizations. These tax benefits do not apply if the easement is sold for fair market value consideration. The availability of tax benefits are referenced (some may say advertised or promoted) by nonprofits extolling or seeking conservation easement donations (see Nature Conservancy

5. On the topic of zoning in general, see Fischel (2001).

2008). In what has become a key driver for setting the duration of conservation easements, the Internal Revenue Code permits a deduction only if the easement is created in perpetuity. Without such a requirement, one might expect to see easements for a term of years or leases of conservation rights that prevent development for a limited term.

The federal tax subsidy is significant. In tax year 2003, federal income tax deductions for conservation and historic easements equaled $1.49 billion. Assuming that high-income taxpayers made the donations, the revenue loss to the Treasury would be roughly in the $600 million range. As shown in table 14.2, conservation easements were a much larger percentage of the total amount of deductions for noncash property donations in 2003 (4 percent) than of the number of donations (0.01 percent).

The average amount of a conservation easement donation is three times higher than the average amount of the next highest donation, as set out in table 14.3. This supports the inference that conservation easements provide tax benefits primarily for those in higher income brackets and with higher net worth.

Abuses in conservation easement deductions have also led to Treasury losses. Common areas of abuse are dubious appraisals and insider deals.[6] According to recent reports, the IRS has found that deductions on 96 of 108 Colorado conservation easements are sufficiently defective for back taxes to be owed by donors.[7] A conservation easement also lowers the valuation of the burdened property for estate tax purposes, reducing the estate and thus the tax liability (26 Code of Federal Regulations 25.2703-1[a][4]). This creates an additional federal Treasury loss.

Some states grant state income tax deductions for conservation easements, either by special provisions or by paralleling the federal structure. Colorado, for example, has gone even further, providing for a tax credit of 50 percent of the

Table 14.2
Individual Noncash Charitable Contributions for Easements, 2003

Type	Number of Donations	Percentage of Total Donations	Amount to Schedule A	Percentage of Total Deductions
All	14,273,171	100	$36,902,794,000	100
Easements	2,407	0.01	$1,491,924,000	4.0

Source: Wilson and Strudler (2006, figure A).

6. See U.S. Senate Finance Committee (2005) (on abuses) and Pension Protection Act of 2006, 29 U.S.C.A. § 1219 (recent regulation attempting to address appraisal problems).

7. See Migoya (2007) (182 cases still under investigation).

Table 14.3
Individual Noncash Charitable Contributions, 2003

Type of Contribution	Average Amount Per Donation
Easements	$619,727
Real estate	$201,112
Other investments	$158,903
Mutual funds	$43,889
Corporate stock	$34,279
Art and collectibles	$6,282
Clothing	$878
Household items	$808
Average amount, all donations (including those not shown)	$2,585

Not all types of noncash charitable contributions are shown.
Source: Wilson and Strudler (2006, figure A).

easement's value up to a maximum of $375,000. The Colorado credit is transferable for consideration to other taxpayers or tradable to the state for a refund if the state treasury has a surplus (see Colorado Statutes Annotated § 39-22-522). This has yielded an $85.1 million revenue loss in 2005, up from a modest $2.3 million in 2001 (*State Tax Notes* 2007). Widespread abuses have been cited in the Colorado program (Smith and Hubbard 2008).

Local and state property tax revenues are decreased by placing a conservation easement on a property. Assessments for property tax purposes must account for restrictions on the land. So when a conservation easement prevents development, the land's value is lowered and tax revenues are thus decreased.[8] This raises an important public policy concern, since the municipality is now faced with the choice of cutting services or increasing taxes on other residents (Anderson and King 2004). An individual's decision to place a conservation easement and maximize personal welfare can have a negative effect on the town's civic agenda and on other citizens.

In addition, the acquisition stage of conservation easements may not always further true conservation goals and may also frustrate the public land use process. Nonprofits have virtually unconstrained discretion in accepting donations

---

8. See *Gibson v. Gleason*, 20 A.D.3d 623, 798 N.Y.S.2d 541 9 (2005), upholding the decrease of valuation due to conservation easement. There are no good data supporting the suggestion that the conservation easement will increase the value of neighboring properties, offsetting the tax loss (Youngman 2006, 753).

of conservation easements and in purchasing them. Some conservation organizations may simply take any easements that come their way, often initiated by taxpayers seeking tax benefits, even though the easements do not advance a meaningful conservation agenda. Some national organizations have promulgated well-conceived best practices for nonprofit easement acquisition, but they are nonbinding.[9] Section 170(h) of the Internal Revenue Code does not clearly require a significant benefit in exchange for the deduction. For example, a deduction for an open space easement is given if the public has no more than a view of part of the property. The code and regulations fail to specify the extent of what the public must be able to see (for example, is a view of one of one hundred acres sufficient?) and how the view actually will benefit the public (26 Code of Federal Regulations § 1.170A-14[d][3], [4][ii][B]). Moreover, public access is not required, and is rarely granted, for the donor to receive a deduction for a conservation easement to protect habitat or preserve open space.

Nonprofits do not acquire conservation easements pursuant to a public land use plan. This conflicts with several important public policy goals. Without an overall plan, the result can be a checkerboard of easements that do not yield an effective, community-wide preservation plan. The whole might be less than the sum of the parts. This atomized approach conflicts with modern planning theory and practice, which favors broader community, regional, and cross-border solutions to land issues. At least one study reports that "local trusts specializing in providing open space do not consider the impact of their decisions on regional conservation benefits" (Albers and Ando 2003, 312).

Even high-functioning nonprofits with good acquisition practices are operating as private entities. They are not subject to the accountability of the electoral and regulatory processes that motivate and constrain public officials. Outsourcing local land use decisions—separating them from public, democratic governmental processes—raises serious concerns that will multiply as more conservation easements are acquired by private groups. The situation is exacerbated by the ability of geographically distant nonprofits, with less stake in the local community than the people living there, to hold conservation easements in gross and possibly hold key decision-making powers.

A recently reported controversy illustrates how a conservation easement might be acquired by a distant nonprofit in a manner that frustrates local concerns. The *San Francisco Chronicle* reported that the secretive Bohemian Club, comprising leaders in industry, government, and entertainment, sought to engage in logging on its 2,600-acre redwood grove in Northern California. To reduce its redwood holdings below 2,500 acres, which would allow the club to use a streamlined permit process for logging, the club offered to donate a conservation easement on 160 acres to the Rocky Mountain Elk Foundation of Missoula,

---

9. See Byers and Ponte (2005, 26–42) for an example of best practices.

Montana. Local protest was strong, with one local owner calling the proposed donation "at best . . . a cynical use of a conservation easement" (Kay 2008).

Spinning off conservation decisions to private organizations through private conservation easements may serve the goals of local public decision makers. If officials fear negative reactions about conservation decisions they make or fail to make from segments of the electorate or interest groups, delegation seems to be an attractive opportunity. The citizens deserve better.

The unrepresentative, undemocratic nature of private conservation acquisitions is heightened by the potential for class issues and elitism in conservation nonprofits. William H. Whyte (1959, 37), the so-called progenitor of conservation easements, warned of the "muted class and economic conflicts" inherent in these interests:

> Characteristically, the gentry have a strong bias for the "natural" countryside, and it is the preservation of this that the easement device promises. When they think of open space, they usually don't think of parks, or lakes for recreation, or the landscaping along superhighways; they think of farmland, streams and meadows, white fences, and barns.
>
> Conservation easements, which typically limit large tracts of land to a single private home, have the effect of private large-lot zoning that excludes denser, moderate-income housing.

These potential class inclinations are exacerbated if the board of directors making acquisition and other decisions is unrepresentative, parochial, homogenous, and self-perpetuating. This is too often the case with the composition and the governance pattern of nonprofits (Korngold 2005, 138–142), though increased diversity has been urged (Land Trust Alliance 2005b, standard 3B). People's rights to freely associate should be protected. That does not mean, though, that control over public land use policy should be delegated to the private associations.

A final problem arising in the acquisition stage of private conservation easements has been referred to earlier: the data on conservation easements are limited and difficult to extract. In all but a few states, no separate index or set of recording books for conservation easements exists. Thus, while a title searcher can and will find a conservation easement recorded against a specific property, there is no way to see and thus aggregate the total number of conservation easements that have been recorded throughout the county and state.

The absence of data is a significant public policy concern. Elected officials, planners, and citizens have no clear idea of the number of conservation easements, the total acreage, the identity of the nonprofit holders, the scope of the restrictions, and the pattern of easements created on and across the ground of the political subdivision and neighboring communities. It is difficult for government to assess environmental needs and to develop a public land use and conservation policy and plan without knowing even basic information about private conservation easements in the community. Any possibility of leveraging public and private conservation assets requires transparency about the extent of holdings. Moreover, potential market players cannot get an overall view of existing conservation easements in the area.

SOLUTIONS

Adjustments to the legal rules related to the acquisition of private conservation easements can help to address the concerns that have been raised and, at the same time, make private conservation easements an even more effective vehicle. These adjustments will ensure better conservation results in return for the tax subsidies provided through the federal income tax deduction; help to encourage a greater role for the public land use process in the acquisition of private easements by adjusting the current incentive structure, with the additional benefit of mitigating potential class issues to an extent; and provide data for public decision makers and the market.

The key to achieving these advances is altering the tax subsidy of Internal Revenue Code section 170(h). Property owners should be free to do whatever they want with their property, including donating conservation easements to nonprofit organizations. This chapter does not propose infringing on this important freedom. The public, however, should not have to pay for the donations—indeed, encourage them—via tax incentives unless they provide significant and desired public benefits. Currently section 170(h) does not clearly require adequate public benefits from donors of open space and natural habitat easements in exchange for deductions, and it also frustrates public planning.

The code and regulations provide much detail on deductible open space and natural habitat easement, but the requirements do not clearly set a high enough bar for public benefit. An open space easement must only provide for "the scenic enjoyment of the general public." No specific amount of property must be viewable, and the regulations' definition of "scenic enjoyment" uses vague, pliable language (26 Code of Federal Regulations § 1.170A-14[d][4][ii]). Habitat easements are similarly defined in broad terms, and cases indicate that taxpayers sometimes have different views about what is ecologically significant than do the IRS and wildlife experts (*Glass v. Commissioner*). Whether the public is getting what it is paying for via the deductions for open space and habitat easements remains unclear.

In contrast, a deduction for the donation of an easement preserving historically important land areas or structures is available only if there is prior governmental process and approval of the easement (§ 170[h][4][A][iv]). Claimed historic land must be listed in the National Register, and a building must either be listed in the National Register or be part of a registered historic district and certified by the secretary of the interior as having historic significance (26 Code of Federal Regulations §§ 60.4, 67.4). The National Register process involves standards, administrative action, and public voice, and the Secretary of the Interior has promulgated standards for historic districts. Governmental decision makers, the process, and articulated standards help to ensure that deductions are granted for historically significant properties only. The public gets a benefit in exchange for the tax subsidy, and the taxpayer is not making a unilateral decision about the scenic or ecological benefit of the conservation easement.

Therefore, the code should be amended to permit a federal tax deduction for an open space or habitat conservation easement only if there is prior local, state, or federal governmental certification that the easement provides a significant public conservation benefit. The certification would have to be consistent with a specific governmental conservation plan, and the governmental agency would have to approve the particular easement on the specific parcel. Although state and local government funds would not be paying for the federal tax deduction, state and local agencies would be expected to act responsibly in approving easements because an easement would mean a reduction in state and local property tax revenues and because of concern for local land policy. Currently preapprovals are not required for federal deductions, so it is hard to see how the federal tax subsidy would increase if there were an approval system.

There are clear benefits to this proposal. First, because only conservation easements bringing significant public benefit will be subsidized, public funds via federal deductions will be much better spent. The public will be getting value for its dollars. Second, by conditioning the deduction on governmental approval, donors will have an incentive to engage with the public land use process. Government involvement can bring the advantages of planning, process, coordination, and leverage of conservation activities.

While government involvement can bring great benefits, there will be some disadvantages. Transaction costs for donors (and government) may make some donors hesitate about embarking on the process, but the large benefits of the tax deductions are hoped to alleviate this concern. The potentially long delays could discourage potential contributors. This could be addressed by the passage of a statutory presumption of governmental approval within a certain period of time after submission of an application. The experience of Massachusetts, which requires state and local governmental approval for the validity (not just deductibility) of all conservation easements, is encouraging (Mass. Gen. Laws Ann. ch. 184, §§ 31–32). As shown in table 14.1, a significant percentage of Massachusetts land is under conservation easement despite the added requirement of governmental approval.

Property owners will continue to be free to donate conservation easements that do not meet the standards of a revised section 170(h). Though such conservation easements will raise concerns about public land use control, this may be a moot point. Given the past emphasis on tax deductions in acquisition of donations, it remains to be seen whether there will be many donations if there is no tax benefit.

The second major public policy concern—the lack of meaningful data about conservation easements—can be addressed if all states required and enforced the establishment of separate recording books for conservation easements within county recorders offices.[10] These records could be maintained, along with other land records, in the offices of the recorders of deeds in the various counties in the state. The availability of the records would provide policy makers with the necessary information to develop a comprehensive conservation plan. It would also enhance the operations of conservation and the general market by providing information about ownership and the nature of restrictions. The costs of establishing separate recording books for future conservation easements should be minimal: recorders are already absorbing the cost of entering conservation easements into existing indexes and record books, and they would only have to instead enter the documents into separate registers (just as many recorders have separate registers for mortgage instruments). The minimal additional costs should be well worth it.

The Operational Phase

Strong stewardship of a conservation easement is essential to ensure that its value to the public is maintained and tax subsidies are not dissipated. Meaningful stewardship requires periodic inspections and monitoring of the burdened property, conversations with the property owner over present or incipient infringements on the easement, and legal action to enforce easement violations.

During the operational phase of conservation easements, nongovernmental ownership has benefits. The nonprofits, not the government, bear the expense of stewarding the easements. An adequately resourced, well-functioning, and effective nonprofit can do an excellent job, especially if the board and staff members and the volunteers are strongly committed to the conservation mission. Moreover, a dedicated nonprofit has the advantage of being free from political interest group pressures and able to raise philanthropic dollars to fund necessary stewardship.

CONCERNS
There are concerns with easement stewardship by some nonprofits. While many do a fine job, others fail to inspect, enforce, or even keep track of the easements they own (see Pidot 2005, 18–19; U.S. Senate Finance Committee 2005, part two, 2–4). Poorly funded, inadequately governed nonprofits often lack the financial and organizational capital to get the job done.

SOLUTIONS
Some steps may help to enhance nonprofit stewardship, but their effectiveness will have to be tested with longitudinal studies. The Land Trust Alliance has developed a voluntary program of accreditation for land trusts and detailed stan-

---

10. Only a few states have adopted such requirements. One that has is California. See Cal. Govt. Code Ann. § 27255(2).

dards and practices. It remains to be seen whether low-functioning nonprofits will enroll and succeed in this process and whether the standards are adequately drafted to get at the elusive governance issues that prove daunting for nonprofits. Moreover, this is a voluntary program; nonprofits can hold easements without certification. It is unclear whether donors substantially motivated by tax benefits will pay attention to certification.

The most effective answer may be through the power of the attorneys general of the various states to represent the public in the matter of charitable gifts, trusts, and organizations. An attorney general could bring an action to enforce a conservation easement when a nonprofit fails to do so. She could challenge the nonprofit's right to continue to hold the easement if the public interest is not being served.[11] She could also bring, or merely threaten, breach of fiduciary duty actions against board members of nonprofits that have not performed up to standards—a powerful incentive for board members to take notice and exercise their legal authority over operations.

Limited resources are a significant impediment to increased attorney general activity. Attorneys general are sworn to enforce a myriad of laws, many with more immediate impact on a large number of people than the enforcement of conservation easements. Conservation easement enforcement might go to the end of the line. One possible solution is the imposition of a special recording fee for conservation easements. The fees could be placed in a sequestered fund for employing and supporting state attorney general personnel in enforcing conservation easements.

Change and Flexibility

Change is inevitable. Over time there will be new advances and emerging challenges in economic and social circumstances, technology, politics, and the environment. In rare situations, some changes may raise questions about whether a specific conservation easement should be modified or even terminated to serve a greater public interest. For example, due to environmental changes or development in surrounding properties, an open space or habitat easement may no longer bring significant conservation benefits. Conservation biologists and ecologists are wondering how currently preserved lands will change with the climate. In the words of Healy Hamilton, director of the California Academy of Sciences, "[w]e have over a 100-year investment nationally in a large suite of protected areas that may no longer protect the ecosystems for which they were formed" (Dean 2008). Other public concerns, such as the need to build affordable housing or to spur economic development in a severely depressed area, may override conservation in rare circumstances in the future. How will privately held conservation easements stand up to these conflicting forces?

---

11. On the topic of attorneys general power, see Brody (1998).

BENEFITS

Recognizing conservation easement as a protected perpetual property right brings certain benefits when the environment is under pressure. Often development pressures have run roughshod over public land use regulation, compromising conservation goals, perhaps without thoughtful consideration of alternative development plans that would have been more environmentally friendly. Once an area has been developed, it is hard, if not impossible, to "unring the bell" and restore the land to its natural condition. A conservation easement in the hands of a nonprofit is a powerful, property-based restriction on development, free from the vagaries of the political process.

CONCERNS

The lack of flexibility in perpetual easements can present serious concerns in rare circumstances in which countervailing public needs require an adjustment to or perhaps even termination of a conservation easement. The law of conservation easements has decreased flexibility for several reasons.

First, conservation easements are not really easements; they are covenants in that they place negative restrictions on the burdened land (preventing changes in the natural features). This is not a matter of semantics. Easements are generally enforced by the courts without question and are viewed as valuable and valid property rights. Covenants, on the other hand, are traditionally viewed with distrust by the law. The courts have been concerned that restrictions on land reduce marketability by creating multiple ties that increase transaction costs when a sale or financing is sought. More important, the courts have questioned certain attempts in past generations to use covenants to impose their wishes on the autonomy of current owners of property. The policy lessons of covenant law apply to conservation easements, and calling them easements does not make the policy issue disappear.[12]

The perpetual nature of conservation easements presents a threat if an easement is rigidly enforced in the rare circumstances in which unusual public requirements call for flexibility. At a future time, land subject to a conservation easement may be the only viable locus for economic development in a depressed area, for the construction of low-income housing, or for some other pressing social need that we cannot imagine today. Because the conservation easement is privately held, the decision on its modification or termination will be made by the nonprofit, perhaps from a distance. Local citizens will not be able to work out the balance between conservation and other public necessities in a democratic, public, local land use process. Rather, a nonaccountable private organization will be making the decision.

Market forces will unlikely be sufficient to motivate nonprofits to be flexible. Conservation organizations are driven by conservation values and rarely, if ever, enter into market exchanges to sell or release their conservation easements. They

---

12. On the issue of covenants versus easements, see Korngold (2004).

may doubt their power to engage in such transactions under their governing documents, fear losing their nonprofit status if they do so, and need to assure potential donors that the organization can be trusted to adequately preserve property.

Inflexibility and nonprofit control over modification and termination decisions have serious public policy ramifications. Key local land decisions have been moved from the public arena to the private sector, violating essential principles of local democratic control. Class differences and elitist notions may influence the nonprofit's decision about the necessity of additional employment opportunities or affordable housing, not necessarily because of ill will but rather because of a limited worldview. Moreover, perpetual conservation easements, no matter how well meaning and how beneficial they are in the vast majority of cases, can in rare situations violate the autonomy of future generations. Land has played an essential role in American economic, social, and political life. It is a limited and nonrenewable resource. Future citizens should be grateful to today's nonprofits and owners for their conservation efforts, but the price must not be surrendering the ability of future generations to make important land use decisions based on future values, requirements, and trade-offs. The current generation must allow for adequate flexibility and not require perpetual fealty to conservation in all cases. Intergenerational responsibility requires a balance between conservation values, current citizens, and the autonomy of future generations.

SOLUTIONS

A number of steps can be taken to inject flexibility into conservation easements to help to achieve public policy goals. First, the holder of a conservation easement has the power to agree to consensual modifications and even termination of the interest.[13] Nonprofit board members may hesitate to modify or terminate conservation easements out of fear of breaching their fiduciary duty of obedience to the nonprofit's mission or of infringing on its tax-exempt status. Senator Charles Grassley is quoted as saying that "modifying these [conservation] easements is a huge no-no" (Black and Flynn 2005); such statements can chill the willingness of volunteer trustees to act. Nonprofit law needs to be clarified to provide that fealty to an overall mission of conservation in the public interest is not violated by compromises with respect to one parcel. Good directors insurance and opinion letters from lawyers would also embolden boards to accomplish the public interest.

Second, courts can be more aggressive in applying traditional covenant modification and termination doctrines to conservation easements. For example, they could use the rule prohibiting the enforcement of covenants violating public policy to strike the very rare conservation easement that interferes with overriding public values and goals. This doctrine has been applied in the past, for example, to permit the establishment of group homes for the disabled despite restrictions limiting occupancy to single families (Korngold 2004, § 10.02). A disadvantage

---

13. For advice to land trusts on this issue, see Land Trust Alliance (2007).

of using this rule is that when a covenant is struck for public policy, no compensation is paid to the covenant owner. Thus, a conservation organization would not receive funds to buy a replacement conservation easement. Unless the courts were creative and invented a theory that justified the rewarding of compensation, striking covenants for violations of public policy would not adequately accommodate important conservation values.

The doctrine of relative hardship allows courts to enforce a covenant by imposing monetary damages rather than the typical injunction (Korngold 2004, § 11.08). The doctrine is applied when the costs to the parties and the public from an injunction will be too great compared to the benefits that the injunction will bring. When a court applies the relative hardship doctrine, it is, in essence, requiring a forced buyout of the covenant, giving the covenant owner money but not enforcing the covenant as a property right. This doctrine, which is employed judiciously because it rearranges the agreement of the parties, could be applied in the rare case in which public needs are great and the conservation value of enforcement is comparatively low. The conservation organization would receive monetary damages and could reinvest in conservation easements on other properties. There is little case law setting out the measure of damages in relative hardship cases (see *Restatement of the Law of Property* 2000, § 8.3[1]; Korngold 2004, § 11.08). Governmental takings may serve as a model. As discussed below, courts have focused on the increase of value to the formerly burdened parcel when a gross servitude is terminated.

The Third Restatement of Property, a key reform agent in the field of servitudes, has recommended that the court should adjust the particular conservation purpose to allow continuance of an overall conservation purpose when conditions have changed so that the particular purpose of a conservation easement can no longer be accomplished (*Restatement of the Law of Property* 2000, § 7.11). This modification will take place pursuant to the doctrine of *cy pres*, which requires a judicial hearing and approval. Since the public is the true beneficiary of a charitable gift, the *cy pres* process ensures that the nonprofit is truly representing the public's interest in the modification proceeding.[14]

Cy pres provides procedural protections by requiring the state attorney general to represent the public's interest and substantive benefits by preventing valuable conservation easements from disappearing. The requirement of a *cy pres* proceeding for modifications may deter a nonprofit board from making the usual discretionary decisions that do not require formal modifications out of fear of liability or criticism.[15] This will likely decrease flexibility in conservation easement stewardship, something that is necessary for a viable relationship of easement and

---

14. On *cy pres* in conservation easements, see McLaughlin (2005).

15. Statutes, such as Maine's, that require prior judicial approval and participation of the attorney general before amendment of a conservation easement have similar positive effects and costs. 33 Maine Rev. Stat. Ann. § 477-A.

nonprofit with burdened owner over the perpetual term of the easement. The costs of legal representation in *cy pres* judicial proceedings will tax the limited resources of nonprofits, making them unwilling to engage in modifications necessary for the public interest and diverting key funds when they are forced to do so.

Third, the legislative power of eminent domain can provide a key way to eliminate conservation easements in the future when the public interest requires. Eminent domain has long been the tool by which government appropriates land from an individual, for compensation, to serve communal needs. It is an essential tool given the efficiency of communal infrastructure, changing land use needs over time, and the challenge of the monopoly-type power that holdouts wield. The U.S. Supreme Court in *Kelo v. City of New London*, 546 U.S. 469 (2005), held that eminent domain can be exercised under the Constitution for the purposes of economic development pursuant to a clearly conceived municipal plan. The plan in *Kelo* was necessary to revitalize the city's battered economy and involved some 90 acres. Pursuant to the redevelopment, offices, hotels, recreation areas, and public spaces were to be built. The Court held that this was a legitimate public use under the Constitution even though some of the property would end up in the hands of private developers. Under the Court's conceptualization, it would be possible to take a conservation easement by eminent domain as part of a necessary economic redevelopment. Compensation would be paid to the nonprofit, presumably to be reinvested (pursuant to the board's fiduciary obligation) in other conservation easements. *Kelo*'s lesson would allow flexibility for future generations with respect to easements while maintaining conservation values.

When a servitude in gross is taken by government, compensation must be determined. If commercial easements are taken, such as easements granting the right to erect and maintain billboards, income streams can be projected and discounted so the court can arrive at their value (see *State ex rel. Missouri Highways and Transportation Commission v. Muslet*, 213 S.W.3d 96 [Mo. App.] [2006]). With a conservation easement, the calculation is different because a negative rather than an affirmative interest is involved; value is harder to calculate because of the lack of a commercial income stream. When an appurtenant servitude is taken, the damages can be seen as the decrease of the value of the benefited parcel by comparing the value of that parcel with and without the servitude. With a negative in gross restrictions such as a conservation easement, the court may have to use a damages measure based on the difference in the value of the burdened property with and without the servitude (Korngold 2004, 475). As applied to conservation easements, that measure would capture the gain to the burdened owner by the release of easement. It would not measure the subjective value that the conservation organization attributed to the conservation easement that was lost by the taking. As the law prefers objective to subjective measures, this may be where matters are left.

Kelo ignited a storm of protest from commentators, state legislatures, and state courts. Many legislatures have passed laws barring takings for economic development. Courts have found that while such takings are permissible under the federal Constitution, state constitutional provisions bar eminent domain for economic development. These judicial and legislative pronouncements are ill advised as a general matter, condemning future generations to the land use arrangements of the past. With respect to conservation easements, they prevent the flexibility needed to balance conservation values and future needs.

Conclusions

Private conservation easements serve important public policy values, achieving conservation of the natural environment through the use of property rights. The law should continue to recognize and validate these important interests. Private conservation easements, however, come with costs. They are created without overall land use planning and public participation. Stewardship may be inadequate. The easements and the nonprofits holding them may be insufficiently flexible to balance competing public needs. By addressing these concerns, we can create even more effective and valuable private conservation easements that will benefit future generations while respecting their autonomy in an ever-changing world.

REFERENCES

Albers, Heidi J., and Amy W. Ando. 2003. Could state-level variation in the number of land trusts make economic sense? *Land Economics* 79(August):311–327.

Anderson, Christopher M., and Jonathan R. King. 2004. Equilibrium behavior in the conservation easement game. *Land Economics* 80(August):355–374.

Anella, Anthony, and John B. Wright. 2004. *Saving the ranch: Conservation easement designs in the American West*. Washington, DC: Island Press.

Black, Lisa, and Courtney Flynn. 2005. Couple sue neighbor over use of conservation land. *Chicago Tribune*, 1 December.

Brenneman, Russell L. 1967. *Private approaches to the preservation of open land*. New London, CT: Conservation and Research Foundation.

Brewer, Richard. 2003. *Conservancy: The land trust movement in America*. Lebanon, NH: University Press of New England.

Brody, Evelyn. 1998. The limits of charity fiduciary law. *Maryland Law Review* 57(4):1400–1451.

Byers, Elizabeth, and Karin M. Ponte. 2005. *The conservation easement handbook*, 2nd ed. Washington, DC: Land Trust Alliance and The Trust for Public Land.

Coughlin, R. E., and T. Plaut. 1978. Less-than-fee acquisition for the preservation of open space: Does it work? *Journal of the American Institute of Planners* 44(4):452–462.

Cunningham, Roger. 1968. Scenic easements in the highway beautification program. *Denver Law Journal* 45(Spring):168–266.

Dean, Cornelia. 2008. The preservation predicament. *New York Times*, 29 January, sec. B, 1ff.

DePalma, Anthony. 2008. State to preserve heart of Adirondacks. *New York Times*, 15 February.

Ely, James W., Jr. 1998. *The guardian of every other right: A constitutional history of property rights*, 2nd ed. Oxford: Oxford University Press.

Fischel, William A. 2001. *The homevoter hypothesis: How home values influence local government taxation, school finance and land-use policies*. Cambridge, MA: Harvard University Press.

Kay, Jane. 2008. A new logging tactic. *San Francisco Chronicle*, 28 March.

Korngold, Alice. 2005. *Leveraging good will: Strengthening nonprofits by engaging businesses*. San Francisco: Jossey Bass.

Korngold, Gerald. 2004. *Private land use arrangements: Easements, real covenants and equitable servitudes*, 2nd ed. Huntington, NY: Juris Publishing.

Kuzmiak, D. T. 1991. The American environmental movement. *The Geographical Journal* 157(November):265–278.

Land Trust Alliance. 2005a. *National land trust census report*. www.lta.org/census.

———. 2005b. *Standards and practices*. www.lta.org/sp/land_trust_standards_and_practices.pdf.

———. 2007. *Amending conservation easements: Evolving practices and legal principles*. Research report.

McLaughlin, Nancy. 2005. Rethinking the perpetual nature of conservation easements. *Harvard Environmental Law Review* 29(2):421–521.

Migoya, David. 2007. IRS finds a third of easements in probe are faulty. *Denver Post*, 29 November.

Nature Conservancy. 2008. Web site. http://www.nature.org/aboutus/howwework/conservationmethods/privatelands/conservationeasements/about/tncandeasements.html.

Ohm, B. 2000. The purchase of scenic easements and Wisconsin's Great River Road: A progress report on perpetuity. *Journal of the American Planning Association* 66(June):177–188.

Pidot, Jeffrey. 2005. *Reinventing conservation easements: A critical examination and ideas for reform*. Cambridge, MA: Lincoln Institute of Land Policy.

Raymond, Susan. 2007. *Partnerships for the built and natural environment: A briefing on trends in philanthropy and infrastructure*. New York: Changing Our World, Inc.

Restatement of the law of property (third)—servitudes. 2000. St. Paul, MN: American Law Institute Publishers.

Smith, Jerd, and Burt Hubbard. 2008. Abuses taint land deals. *Rocky Mountain News*, 9 February.

State Tax Notes. 2007. Colorado lawmakers want tighter controls on credit for donated land. 13 April.

U.S. Census Bureau. 2006. *State and metropolitan data book*. Table E-1, State ranking—area and population. http://www.census.gov/compendia/smadb/TableE-01.pdf.

U.S. Senate Finance Committee. 2005. *Report on the Nature Conservancy*.

Whyte, William H., Jr. 1959. *Securing open space for urban America: Conservation easements*. Technical bulletin. Washington, DC: Urban Land Institute.

Wilson, Janette, and Michael Strudler. 2006. Individual noncash charitable contributions, 2003. *Internal Revenue Service, SOI Bulletin* (Spring). www.irs.gov/pub/irs-soi/03inccart.pdf.

Youngman, Joan M. 2006. Taxing and untaxing land: Open space and conservation easements. *State Tax Notes*, 11 September.

COMMENTARY
Nancy A. McLaughlin

Gerald Korngold suggests a variety of reforms intended to make conservation easements a more effective land protection tool. While the use of conservation easements has not been free of inefficiencies and abuses, and appropriate reforms could make conservation easements a more effective tool, Korngold's suggested reforms could have a significant adverse impact on what has heretofore been a largely successful voluntary land protection program and a uniquely American form of conservation philanthropy. Given space constraints, the following comments focus on four threshold issues that deserve clarification, as well as the appropriate legal framework within which conservation easements should be modified or terminated to respond to changing conditions.

Four Threshold Issues

Korngold describes conservation easements as private or privately held because they are held by nonprofits rather than government entities. The use of the term *private* in this context is both inaccurate and confusing. Hundreds of local, state, and federal government entities hold thousands of conservation easements. Indeed, in some states, such as Maryland and Virginia, government entities acquire the majority of conservation easements conveyed in the state. Moreover, even conservation easements conveyed to nonprofit land trusts cannot be accurately described as private. A private servitude is a private contract between private parties created for private benefit, such as a traditional right-of-way easement between neighbors. Conservation easements are fundamentally different. They are validated under state law only if they are (1) created for certain conservation or historic purposes intended to benefit the public; and (2) conveyed to a government entity or charitable organization, both of which are organized and operated to provide benefits to the public. The public subsidizes the acquisition of conservation easements through appropriations to easement-purchase programs, and the provision of federal and state tax benefits to landowners who donate conservation easements as charitable gifts. And the administration and enforcement of conservation easements is supervised by regulatory authorities (including state attorneys general and the Internal Revenue Service) on behalf of the public. In sum, conservation easements are public assets. They are created, acquired, and enforced for the benefit of the public, and the public is the beneficiary and beneficial owner of such easements.

It also is not accurate to describe the more than 1,700 land trusts operating in the United States as "non-accountable, non-representative private organizations." While not government entities, land trusts are publicly supported charities and, as such, they depend on the approval and generosity of the public for their very survival. In fact, one could argue that land trusts are more accountable to the public than government entities because land trusts depend directly on the public for their ongoing support, while the accountability of government entities is far less immediate or direct. The activities of land trusts are also regulated on behalf of the public by both state attorneys general and the Internal Revenue Service, both of which have stepped up their oversight role in recent years. Furthermore, it is important to understand that traditional government-controlled land use planning mechanisms have been singularly ineffective in achieving a socially desirable level of land protection. As a result, our democratically elected representatives at the federal and state level have overwhelmingly determined that delegating a certain amount of land protection activity to charitable organizations in the form of voluntary conservation easement acquisitions is in the public interest.

The use of conservation easements as a land protection tool also does not constitute a crisis that requires dramatic and draconian changes to existing law. As of 2005 land trusts reportedly held conservation easements encumbering over 9 million acres of land, but 9 million acres is less than one-half of 1 percent of the total land area of the contiguous 48 states. Moreover, 9 million acres represents the cumulative amount of land protected by land trusts through the use of conservation easements over the last century. In just the five years between 1992 and 1997, more than 11 million acres were converted to development. In addition, the rate of development has since been accelerating, and despite the public land use planning process, much of this development is wasteful. Larger homes are being built on larger lots farther from central cities, and this has significant negative impacts on remaining open space and agricultural lands.

Furthermore, it is the development of land, rather than the conveyance of conservation easements, that is significantly reducing the choices available to future generations. Development generally destroys the natural and ecological values of land, and that destruction is substantially irreversible. The protection of land through the use of conservation easements holds far more options open for future generations because conservation easements do not involve physical changes to the land and they can be terminated to respond to changing conditions either in court proceedings or by condemnation. Put into perspective, the relatively modest conservation gains achieved by land trusts through the use of conservation easements do not constitute a crisis that needs addressing with draconian reforms. Rather, it is the failure of the public land use planning process to prevent or at least reduce the continued rapid pace of wasteful development that should be the subject of immediate and potentially draconian action.

Korngold also suggests that the current use of conservation easements is ill-advised because it results in checkerboard protection and such protection is not consistent with "modern planning theory and practice[, which] favors broader community, regional, and cross-border solutions to land issues." Many, if not most people would agree that effective local, state, and regional land use planning would be preferable to the necessarily incremental and somewhat haphazard system of land protection accomplished through voluntary measures.

Unfortunately, however, many jurisdictions lack effective land use planning. Indeed, the lack of effective land use planning is precisely what led to the popularity of conservation easements as a land protection tool. There also is no indication that the land use planning process has become more effective in the 25 or so years during which conservation easements have become popular. Accordingly, conservation easements should not be compared to an effective land use planning process that is, at this point, largely theoretical. Rather, the use of conservation easements should be understood for what it is—an imperfect but nonetheless effective response to the well-recognized inadequacies of the traditional land use planning process.

Change and Flexibility

Perpetual conservation easements are very special, very powerful land protection tools. They are intended to insulate the land and the conservation and historic values they protect from market forces that do not adequately take into account either the negative externalities that flow from development or the positive externalities that flow from conservation. For this reason, significant hurdles are imposed with regard to the termination of conservation easements, or their modification in manners contrary to their conservation purposes, such as to permit subdivision and development of the land (hereinafter "substantial modification").

Contrary to Korngold's assertion, government entities and land trusts do not have the power to simply agree to substantially modify or terminate the conservation easements they hold. Most conservation easements are donated in whole or in part to a government entity or land trust to be used, not for that entity's general purposes, but for a specific charitable purpose—the protection of the particular land encumbered by the easement for the conservation purposes specified in the deed of conveyance, generally in perpetuity. As explained in the *Restatement of the Law of Trusts* (2003, § 28 cmt.), that type of conveyance creates a charitable trust:

> An outright devise or donation to a . . . charitable institution, expressly
> or impliedly to be used for its general purposes, is charitable but does not
> create a trust. . . . A disposition to such an institution for a specific purpose, however, such as to support medical research, perhaps on a particular disease, or to establish a scholarship fund in a certain field of study,
> creates a charitable trust of which the institution is the trustee.

Accordingly, as with any gift conveyed to a government entity or charitable organization to be used for a specific charitable purpose, the holder of a conservation easement should not be permitted to terminate the easement, or otherwise modify it in a manner contrary to its stated charitable purpose, without receiving court approval in a *cy pres* proceeding. And in such a proceeding, the court would authorize the termination or substantial modification of the easement only if it could be shown that the charitable purpose of the easement had become impossible or impractical due to changed conditions.

Applying such equitable principles to conservation easements is consistent with (1) the position adopted by the National Conference of Commissioners (NCCUSL) in the comments to the Uniform Conservation Easement Act and the Uniform Trust Code; (2) the position adopted by the American Law Institute in the *Restatement of the Law of Property: Servitudes*; and (3) the federal tax law requirements applicable to tax-deductible conservation easements.

The Uniform Conservation Easement Act was adopted by NCCUSL in 1981 and served as the model for easement-enabling legislation in 24 states and the District of Columbia. According to the comments to the act, "because conservation easements are conveyed to governmental bodies and charitable organizations to be held and enforced for a specific public or charitable purpose . . . the existing case and statute law of adopting states as it relates to the enforcement of charitable trusts should apply to conservation easements." The comments to the Uniform Trust Code, which was adopted by NCCUSL in 2000 and has since been adopted by 20 states and the District of Columbia, similarly provide:

> Even though not accompanied by the usual trappings of a trust, the creation and transfer of an easement for conservation or preservation will frequently create a charitable trust. The organization to whom the easement was conveyed will be deemed to be acting as trustee of what will ostensibly appear to be a contractual or property arrangement. Because of the fiduciary obligation imposed, the termination or substantial modification of the easement by the "trustee" could constitute a breach of trust.

The *Restatement of the Law of Property: Servitudes*, published by the American Law Institute in 2000, provides that the modification and termination of conservation easements is governed, not by the real property law doctrine of changed conditions, but by a special set of rules based on the charitable trust doctrine of *cy pres*. In their commentary, the drafters of the restatement explain that, "because of the public interests involved, these servitudes are afforded more stringent protection than privately held conservation servitudes."

Federal tax law also contemplates the application of charitable principles to conservation easements. To be eligible for federal tax incentives, a conservation easement must, among other things, be (1) granted in perpetuity; (2) transferable by its holder only to another government entity or charitable organization that agrees to continue to enforce the easement; and (3) extinguishable by its holder only in what essentially is a judicial *cy pres* proceeding. The interest in the property retained by the easement donor must be subject to legally enforceable restrictions that will prevent any uses of the property that are inconsistent with the conservation purposes of the easement. And the possibility that the easement will be defeated by the performance of some act or the happening of some event must be "so remote as to be negligible."[1]

State attorneys general are also increasingly acknowledging their right and obligation, as supervisors of charitable trusts, to enforce conservation easements on behalf of the public. And various controversies to date confirm that government entities and land trusts do not have the power to simply agree to substantially modify or terminate the conservation easements they hold.[2]

Contrary to Korngold's assertion, requiring the holder to obtain court approval to terminate or substantially modify a perpetual conservation easement also does not mean that the holder's ability to make the "usual discretionary decisions" would be impaired. To the contrary, many conservation easement deeds contain an amendment provision that expressly grants the holder the power to agree with the owner of the encumbered land to amendments that are consistent with or further the purpose of the easement. Indeed, the Land Trust Alliance has discussed the wisdom of including such a provision in conservation easement deeds since the publication of the first *Conservation Easement Handbook* in 1988. In addition, even in the absence of an amendment provision, holders may have the implied power to agree to certain amendments that are consistent with the purpose of a conservation easement, or they can seek court approval for such amendments in more flexible administrative deviation proceedings. It is only the outright termination of a conservation easement, or the modification of an easement in a manner contrary to its conservation purpose (such as to permit subdivision and development of the land), that should require court approval in a *cy pres* proceeding.

Court approval of the outright termination or substantial modification of a conservation easement is appropriate given (1) the significant public investment in conservation easements and the conservation and historic values they protect; (2) the enormous economic value inherent in the development and use rights restricted by conservation easements; (3) the political, financial, and other pressures that will inevitably be brought to bear on both governmental and nonprofit holders to substantially modify, release, or terminate conservation easements; (4) the increasing scarcity of undeveloped land; and (5) the necessity of according a certain amount of deference to the intent of conservation easement donors so as not to chill future conservation easement donations. With regard to this last point, it is well-settled that government entities and charitable organizations cannot "receive a gift made for one purpose and use it for another, unless the court applying the *cy pres* doctrine so commands."[3] The reason for this is simple: it has

---

1. Internal Revenue Code § 170(h); Treasury Regulations § 1.170A-14. See also Private Letter Ruling 200836014.

2. See, for example, *Bjork v. Draper*, 381 Ill. App. 3d 528 (2008); McLaughlin (2006, 2007); and McLaughlin and Weeks (2009).

3. See *St. Joseph's Hospital v. Bennett*, 22 N.E.2d 305, 308 (N.Y. 1939).

long been recognized that failing to honor the wishes of charitable donors would result in fewer charitable donations, and that would be contrary to the public interest.

Finally, one might worry that projects of great importance to the public (such as the construction of highways or electric transmission towers and lines) could be precluded or hindered by the existence of conservation easements and the protection afforded to them under the doctrine of *cy pres*. But those concerns are unfounded. If a community decides that the best place to locate a public works project is on land protected by a conservation easement because it has significant conservation or historic values, the community can simply condemn the easement. None of the conservation easement-enabling statutes preclude the condemnation of easements, and half of them expressly provide that easements are subject to condemnation. The real danger is not that conservation easements will endure in the face of more important public needs. Rather, the danger is that, absent even minimal statutory or judicial safeguards, land protected by conservation easements will become the path of least resistance for condemning authorities.

REFERENCES

Bjork v. Draper, 381 Ill. App. 3d 528 (2008).
Internal Revenue Code § 170(h).
McLaughlin, Nancy A. 2006. Could coalbed methane be the death of conservation easements? *Wyoming Lawyer* 29:18.
———. 2007. Conservation easements: Perpetuity and beyond. *Ecology Law Quarterly* 34:101.
McLaughlin, Nancy A., and William W. Weeks. 2009. In defense of conservation easements: A response to "The End of Perpetuity." *Wyoming Law Review* 9:1ff.
Private Letter Ruling 200836014.
Restatement of the law of property (third)—servitudes. 2000. St. Paul, MN: American Law Institute Publishers.
Restatement of the law of trusts (third). 2003. St. Paul, MN: American Law Institute Publishers.
Treasury Regulations § 1.170A-14.
Uniform Conservation Easement Act. § 3 cmt. 2007. Nat'l Conf. of Comm'rs on Uniform State Laws, http://www.law.upenn.edu/bll/ulc/ucea/2007_final.htm.
Uniform Trust Code § 414 cmt. 2005. Nat'l Conf. of Comm'rs on Uniform State Laws, http://www.law.upenn.edu/bll/ulc/uta/2005final.htm.

15

The Role of Private-Sector Developers in Challenges to Local Land Use Regulations

Keri-Nicole Dillman and Lynn M. Fisher

Within the last 40 years, a diverse set of state judicial and legislative strategies has been employed to confront exclusionary land use at the local level. These state efforts include, for example, requirements that localities develop written land use plans, that they consider affordable housing needs, and that zoning be consistent. A noteworthy element of some state strategies is the heavy reliance on residential developers, who are empowered to challenge local land use regimes deemed out of compliance with state goals. While nearly half of the states have some form of antiexclusionary land use program, a small but growing subset enlists developers in this way for various and multiple goals (referred to here as "housing appeals regimes"): California, Connecticut, Massachusetts, New Jersey, Pennsylvania, Rhode Island, and most recently Illinois in 2004 and New Hampshire in 2008.

This decades-long and increasing state action is often motivated by the negatively perceived impacts of local land use regulations on housing supply.[1] The early empirical work on the interrelationship of local growth management programs and housing markets was mixed. However, increasingly sophisticated methodologies demonstrate its negative supply effects (Quigley and Raphael

---

1. Just as local land use regulations have been seen as imposing constraints on housing supply, they can also afford public benefits. As Fischel argues, such ordinances may "accommodate development at a reasonable pace and, by better planning, [improve] the delivery of public services" (1991, 66).

2005; reviewed in Lewis 2005; Nelson et al. 2002; Quigley 2007). Therefore, there is reason to be concerned that local land use regulations limit the development of all housing, both low-income and market-rate units, resulting in high house prices and exacerbating affordability problems.

We know little about the effectiveness of state antiexclusionary zoning efforts.[2] Lewis (2005) reviews the limited literature on state efforts to induce housing production, which he notes as dominated by descriptions of the mandates and their evolution. He concludes that, overall, rigorous evaluation of the effects of state mandates on residential production and affordability is lacking amid a body of descriptive work (Gale 1992; Weitz 1999).

The evolution and implementation of specific housing appeals regimes has been considered in the literature (for example, Krefetz 2001; see Cowan 2006 for a review). However, rigorous estimates of their effects on housing supply are rare. For example, Meck, Retzlaff, and Schwab (2003) review the limited research and provide secondary data on production outcomes associated with these regimes in various states. Whether these developer-driven strategies actually result in greater production than would have occurred otherwise, or as compared to other state antiexclusionary strategies, is unclear.

Only recently has empirical investigation been brought to bear on state antiexclusionary zoning efforts employing developers, and the findings are positive. Cowan (2006) takes advantage of a natural experiment among New England states (Connecticut, Massachusetts, New Hampshire, and Rhode Island) and finds significant impacts from the adoption of state "antisnob zoning" laws on the rate of production of affordable housing in suburban and urban communities. While suggesting that antisnob zoning laws promote the development of affordable housing, this study does not speak to policy impacts on overall housing production or establish causal mechanisms, particularly the role of developers.

Mitchell (2004) considers housing appeals regimes in the neighboring states of Pennsylvania and New Jersey, specifically considering the role of developers. Both states address municipal exclusionary zoning by empowering residential developers to challenge municipalities, but the definitions of eligible projects differ. New Jersey provides developers with relief from zoning restrictions if they agree to include housing for low- and moderate-income families. By contrast, Pennsylvania empowers developers to challenge municipalities when seeking permits for market-rate developments of all housing types. Comparing housing production outcomes in the two states between 1970 and 1990, Mitchell finds that a significantly higher percentage of townhouses and mobile homes was produced in Pennsylvania, while only a slightly larger percentage of

---

2. Systematically assessing the available knowledge, albeit limited, is further complicated by the inconsistency in nomenclature and focus by scholars examining these state growth management strategies (Weitz 1999).

apartments was produced in New Jersey. The probability that a newly constructed housing unit would be a townhouse, apartment, or mobile home rather than a single-family detached home was significantly higher in Pennsylvania than in New Jersey.

Mitchell's findings are encouraging to those seeking to employ developers in state antiexclusionary zoning efforts. He observes contrasting diversity and density of housing under these regimes. Moreover, while interpreting his findings, he highlights the distinct roles of both developers and municipalities. However, the causal mechanisms are underspecified and unexplored. The research design does not permit direct comparison of contrasting housing outcomes as a result of that state's different program features. The study period, while spanning 20 years, includes only a short period of time when the New Jersey Fair Housing Act was in full operation (as a result of the regime's evolution from the courts to the legislature in the late 1980s). Therefore, while the developer incentives in Pennsylvania may explain the increased density in housing production, that remains to be demonstrated. The observed increases in housing diversity may result from changes to local planning and zoning or may be the result of developer challenges to local zoning on a project-by-project basis.

A more precise framework is necessary in order to get inside the "black box" of these housing appeals regimes: to systematically anticipate the behavior of both developers and municipalities. Recognizing that this is not a one-size-fits-all strategy, we hope to support states' needs to customize policies to their particular housing needs and local governance structures. By clearly articulating the mechanisms (also referred to as "program theory") behind these strategies, we can empower future assessments of their success. Therefore, in this chapter, we develop a conceptual framework that allows us to untangle some of the possible explanations for the observed outcomes in state programs that use developers as agents.

Developer-based programs are particularly worthy of exploration because they highlight the critical role of implementation in intergovernmental efforts. For example, in states requiring local planning for affordable housing, such as Florida and Oregon, there is neither a local obligation to do more than plan nor a mechanism to ensure that affordable housing gets built. Similarly, critical discussions of state efforts to overcome local parochialism have demonstrated that implementation is essential to success (Bengston, Fletcher, and Nelson 2004; Goetz, Chapple, and Luckerman 2003). In their review of lessons learned, Bengston, Fletcher, and Nelson (2004) decide not only that implementation is critical, but that it is difficult. Therefore, these strategies may represent a unique opportunity for administrative efficiency in state growth management programs. Finally, Cowan (2006) observes that the affordable housing production gains through developer-driven strategies often require minimal or no state or federal subsidies, suggesting possible cost savings through developer-driven strategies.

Presenting State Housing Appeals Systems

We are focusing on a set of statutes and judicial standards that provide for state review of local land use decisions.[3] Falling within a broader set of state-sponsored growth management programs, these statutes enlist developers to voluntarily challenge noncompliant localities.[4]

While the enlistment of developers is universal among housing appeals regimes, there is considerable variation in their judicial and legislative features in addition to their intended goals (for example, increased housing production overall or particularly for low-income households). Fully accounting for this programmatic variation falls well outside the scope of this project. However, noting some of the dimensions of variation further motivates our systematic exploration of the one universal feature—the enlistment of developers. A better understanding of this core mechanism will enable systematic evaluation and comparison of this strategy across diverse regimes.

Possibly echoing the diversity of goals within these appeals regimes, the definition of local compliance (or exceptions at law) is an important point of distinction. Compliance is largely defined by the number or level of affordable units that each municipality must provide. Municipal failure to meet these standards renders them susceptible to developer challenge under the appeals regime. The state expectation for municipal planning in order to achieve these standards is also not consistent. More recently, however, municipal protection from the threat of developer challenge is often afforded through planning. The source of the developer right can come from either a state administrative body or the state court system. The schedule of affordable housing requirements for eligible projects (including the proportion of project units that must be set aside as affordable, the income groups intended to be served, and the terms of affordability) varies. Finally, these regimes also include a diverse set of cost offsets to encourage developer participation, such as density bonuses, impact fee waivers or deferrals,

---

3. Among policy and planning scholars, such statutes are variously referred to as state housing appeals systems (Meck, Retzlaff, and Schwab 2003), appeals statutes (*Harvard Law Review* 1995), and antisnob land use laws (Cowan 2006).

4. Following a typology of state growth management policies developed by Weitz (1999), growth management programs are defined by three essential elements: strong state inducement for local planning, provision for state or regional review of comprehensive plans, and other measures to control or manage growth. The third element does not exist in all growth management states. Therefore, as these state housing appeals regimes exemplify this third element (and a planning focus is not consistent among them), this analogy may be imperfect. Still, Howell-Moroney (2007), building on Weitz, argues that New Jersey represents a weak growth management state, suggesting the usefulness of placing the statutes within the broader growth management context. Reflecting the inconsistency in the literature, these housing appeals regimes have also been categorized as inclusionary zoning programs and fair-share programs (Lewis 2005).

fast-track permitting, and reduced parking requirements. While further examples of diversity exist, the extent of variation is unmistakable.

Our exploration of these regimes focuses on Massachusetts and New Jersey. While something of a convenience sample, these regimes represent the variation. For example, Massachusetts requires that 10 percent of the housing units in all municipalities be affordable, while New Jersey's regime defines distinct affordability requirements (or fair share) for each municipality. Since both were among the earliest states employing this technique, their time and experience afford more and higher-quality data on the programs as well as some outcomes.

THE MASSACHUSETTS COMPREHENSIVE PERMIT LAW

The Massachusetts Comprehensive Permit Law of 1969 establishes an affordable housing goal of a minimum of 10 percent state or federally assisted housing for all Commonwealth municipalities (Massachusetts General Laws, chapter 40B, sections 20–23). Towns are deemed compliant with the goal by demonstrating recent progress toward the 10 percent minimum or (since 2002) by having had a state-certified affordable housing plan (760 CMR 31.07[1][i]). Where towns have failed to achieve this goal, affordable housing developers have the right to appeal local project-specific zoning decisions that effectively bar development. The state's three-member Housing Appeals Committee (HAC) can vacate the local decision and order issuance of a permit. Public agencies, nonprofit developers, and for-profit developers have the right of appeal if they agree to limit their returns and set aside 25 percent of the project's units as affordable to moderate income households.[5]

THE NEW JERSEY FAIR HOUSING ACT

Following the New Jersey Supreme Court decision in *Southern Burlington County N.A.A.C.P. v. Township of Mount Laurel*, 92 N.J. 158, 238 (1983), known as *Mount Laurel II*, the New Jersey Fair Housing Act was passed in 1985 (New Jersey Statutes Annotated, section 52:27D-301 et seq. [1986 and Supplement 1999]). It states that municipalities are obliged to provide the opportunity for the development of affordable housing in the state. Currently, a municipality's fair share is determined by the New Jersey Council on Affordable Housing (COAH), a 12-member administrative body appointed by the governor. To address the requirement, a municipality may complete housing elements and fair-share plans, including amendments to zoning. If the housing elements and fair-share plan makes achievement of fair-share goals "realistically possible," COAH provides the petitioning municipality with "substantive certification" of its compliance.

---

5. Moderate income in this case is effectively between 70 and 80 percent of Area Median Income. An alternate but less observed condition is to reserve 20 percent of a project's units for even lower income households (with incomes near 50 percent of Area Median Income) and with correspondingly lower affordable rents or sale prices.

By defining the state's housing goals and local obligations, the New Jersey Fair Housing Act establishes that any local zoning ordinance that denies reasonable opportunity for affordable housing development fails to meet the state's constitutional requirements. Developers are empowered to petition the state courts to declare noncompliant zoning unconstitutional and to receive permission to proceed with affordable housing development. The successful developer-plaintiff is entitled to develop the proposed project as long as at least 20 percent of the units are affordable. Regulation specifies a presumed density of six units to the acre with some exceptions (although this is expected to change in the next round of regulation). This builder's remedy provides developers with an incentive to challenge local exclusionary zoning. Having met their obligations (or demonstrated commitment to do so), substantively certified municipalities are not subject to developer appeals; COAH provides a statutorily created presumption of validity against any claim in an exclusionary zoning lawsuit.

The Bargaining Game of Housing Appeals Regimes

The theory at the foundation of these housing appeals regimes is that private developers and local municipalities are the central actors. That is, policy makers expect developer and municipal behaviors to result in the desired local housing and/or planning outcomes. Although the regimes vary considerably, the program theory appears universal. Game theory, with its focus on rational players' strategic interactions and preferences that produce outcomes, is directly amenable to investigating developer and municipal behaviors. Our investigation of state housing appeals regimes employs a bargaining framework in a stylized bargaining game that results from state housing appeals systems' employing private-sector developers to instigate new development at the local level.

Figures 15.1 and 15.2 present the assumed bargaining game that is central to these regimes. Together they define three possible outcomes: (1) developer nonparticipation and municipal noncompliance; (2) developer challenge without municipal compliance; and (3) developer challenge with municipal compliance. Figure 15.1 presents the game regarding individual residential development projects. It first captures the decision by developers to challenge local zoning. An essential but not exclusive feature of this decision, which we theorize in the following section, is the developer's expectation about success in litigation. The figure also represents the decision by municipalities to pursue either out-of-court negotiations (settlement) or litigation. We assume that litigation is a more costly process to resolve a particular developer challenge. Figure 15.2 represents a municipality's decision to comply with the state goals based on expectations about its aggregate payoffs from developer challenges as compared to compliance. We assess the model's insights by employing empirical analyses of when developers have the appropriate incentives to pursue density bonuses and under what conditions municipalities choose to comply with state goals. A detailed discussion of our methods and findings are presented in the Appendix.

Figure 15.1
Developer Challenge Decision with Municipal Noncompliance (Developer Payoffs)

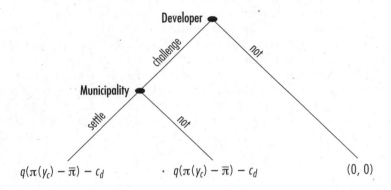

DEVELOPER DECISION MAKING

In this section, we are interested in establishing the mechanism by which state housing appeals systems provide developers with the necessary incentives to challenge local land use regulations (see figure 15.1). Our contribution is to emphasize the voluntary nature of developer participation and how regime features influence developer-expected payoffs from private litigation, thereby motivating their participation.

According to urban economic theory, land value largely depends on the use of land and the intensity of that use. In competitive markets, prospective developers expect to earn competitive returns for undertaking development projects. Developers pay excess expected returns from their current or future development of land toward its purchase. If they pay the landowner less than this full residual, a competing developer could potentially bid the land away by offering the landowner a higher price. Therefore, theory predicts that the developer who proposes the land use and intensity (or density) producing the highest residual value captures the land.

Figure 15.2
Municipality Compliance Decision (Municipal Payoffs)

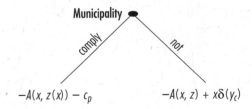

Consider a scenario in which land use is restricted to be residential, but where the density of development is not restricted. Our model uses the following notation:

> y: density, the total housing units per unit of land
> $p(y)$: market price per housing unit as a function of density
> $c(y)$: total cost function for improvements as a function of density[6]

Let π be the residual value per unit of land from a permitted and irreversible residential development with a density of y units per acre where

(1) $\pi = p(y)y - c(y).$

We assume that the price per unit that the market[7] will bear declines with density,[8] and that the marginal total project costs are first decreasing and then increasing with the density of the project.[9]

Under these conditions, competition should result in the successful buyer proposing a density y^* that maximizes π (land value). The first order condition sets marginal benefits of additional density equal to marginal costs of greater density, and y^* solves

(2) $p(y^*) = c'(y^*) - p'(y^*)y^*,$

subject to $\pi(y^*) \geq 0$ and $\pi''(y^*) < 0$.

---

6. We assume fixed factor prices for improvements and thus write the cost function as just a function of output.

7. Rubin and Seneca (1991) point out that single-family, owner-occupied townhomes and multifamily apartments are likely to be sold in separate markets. Here, we focus on multifamily dwellings and assume that the household's utility from a unit of housing is identical across housing types except with respect to the density of the housing type. We expect different types of multifamily housing to have different average project densities; therefore, density loosely corresponds to building type.

8. We motivate this assumption by considering a unit of housing that is of constant quality except for the number of other units contained within the project. It is commonly believed that fewer attached units provide greater privacy and that occupants may incur fewer congestion costs within smaller multifamily housing developments. Hence, the price of units that otherwise provide the same level of housing services will be lower in more densely built housing. For example, townhouse developments typically have lower density than multifamily high-rise condominiums or apartments, and therefore we expect market prices to be higher for a similar unit in the townhouse project, all else equal.

9. Substantial fixed costs of development suggest that, over some range, economies of scale are likely to decrease the cost of housing per unit. As the site is used more intensely, greater costs are incurred in the design of the project, in the structural features (for example, steel versus wood), and in the provision of parking, so that higher-density projects (absent the acquisition

Land Use Regulations and Density Bonuses   As just explicated, where density is unregulated, landowners (and, by extension, developers) favor development densities that maximize the residual value per unit of land. In practice, the maximum density of development is often limited by local land use regulations.

If we let Y be the locally zoned maximum density, the constrained maximum land value is defined as

$$(3) \qquad \overline{\pi} = min(\pi(y^*), \pi(Y)).$$

When the regulated density of land is binding, additional value can be gained by exceeding the density ceiling, if such permission can be acquired. If this value is not as-of-right, the additional value may be distributed between the landowner and developer through a bargaining process. Therefore, when local zoning is restricted, developers as well as landowners may have an interest in achieving higher density.

Developers must request permission from municipalities in order to proceed with development.[10] Authority to regulate land in the United States is granted to local jurisdictions by state legislation or directly by the state constitution. The resulting density-limiting regulations likely reflect local preferences. While these regulations may be beneficial on one hand, they are suspected of overly constraining development on the other hand (see Glaeser 2007 for a recent review of this evidence). Fischel (2008) argues that in metropolitan areas with smaller jurisdictions, municipal governments are dominated by homeowners, making these excesses more likely.[11] Together, the contrasting developer and locality preferences amid local permitting requirements define the heart of the conflict that state housing appeals regimes seek to address.

As just demonstrated, developers may have an interest in challenging local zoning. Traditionally, the courts have recognized the legislatively granted land use authority of localities and have deferred to local decision making. Given this presumption for the municipality, the likelihood of override is essentially nil.

---

of more land) eventually result in increasing costs per unit despite economies of scale. Evidence from apartment construction across six markets confirms that construction costs per square foot are falling with total project square footage, but increasing with building height (Wheaton and Simonton 2007).

10. Therefore, an alternative to state housing appeals systems might include states' rescinding this authority and directly granting permits to developers. However, there are several obstacles to such an approach. First, the implementation and enforcement costs would be exorbitant. Second, state actors, as contrasted with local governments, lack local information critical to land use decisions. Perhaps most prohibitive is the political infeasibility of wresting control from local governments.

11. The two states primarily investigated in this chapter, Massachusetts and New Jersey, are examples of metropolitan areas with highly fragmented government and high regulatory stringency.

Housing appeals regimes redefine the established permitting authority of localities in a manner that uniquely enables developer challenges. Housing appeals regimes define, for the courts, circumstances in which developer challenges have merit and may warrant override of local zoning. The necessary conditions for this dramatic departure from presumption of local authority hinge variously on local adherence to state-defined housing or land use goals. In this manner, housing appeals regimes attempt to capitalize on developer interest in increased density.

The dramatic redefinition of local authority provides several incentives for developers to act on their presumed interest in challenging local zoning. First, and perhaps most important, it increases the likelihood of their success in court. All else equal, knowing they have a chance to win in court should make developers more likely to challenge. Second, the appeals regimes may minimize the costs of litigation, including the costs of filing a lawsuit and hiring attorneys, by clarifying the evidence necessary to convince the court. Third, these statutes typically include override provisions for higher-density permits (such provisions are part of the builder's remedy, as first articulated in *Mount Laurel II*). Such density bonuses, as we define them for this exposition, are development rights for additional housing units per unit of land beyond the amount currently allowed by local regulation. As demonstrated above, this increased density gives developers the opportunity to increase returns to development. Together, the chance of success, the cost savings, and the court awards likely encourage developer challenges.

Following this reasoning and continuing with this bargaining model, we theorize developer willingness to legally challenge localities in the context of housing appeals regimes. The expected outcome in court (the developer's payoff) is assumed to drive developer willingness, and that payoff is a function of, at a minimum, the likelihood of success and the density of development permitted.

Let $0 \leq q \leq 1$ be the probability that the developer is successful; c_d the developer's cost of litigation (appeal), y_c the density that the court will award, and $\bar{\pi}$, as previously defined, the value of the developer's land in its next best use. We make two further assumptions to define a developer's expected payoff from litigation. First, we assume that the developer does not actually acquire the land until (and unless) she successfully obtains the density bonus. Second, we assume that the developer keeps the entire increased value that results from a change in density relative to the value of land as currently regulated.[12] The developer's expected payoff from litigation, P_L, is

$$(4) \qquad P_L = q(\pi(y_c) - \bar{\pi}) - c_d.$$

Notice that $q < 1$ reflects the probability that the court renders a decision in favor of the developer, effectively granting an increase in density. Given the sunk

---

12. Of course, the extent to which the developer may keep this increased value depends on developer competition for the site. Some return is probably due to the developer who pursues the challenge, which results in greater potential land value.

costs in proposing the project and pursuing litigation, combined with the prospect of losing, this process is risky for developers.

Litigation is by no means assured; settlement may be reached prior to a court decision. Recognizing the ultimate local control of permitting and the expected payoff from costly litigation, a developer will accept a municipality's settlement offer for a permit with density y_z if[13]

$$(5) \qquad \pi(y_z) - \overline{\pi} \geq P_L.$$

That is, we assume that the developer accepts a settlement offer if she is made better off or at least indifferent. Since the municipality has the opportunity to make a take-it-or-leave-it offer to the developer (by virtue of a public vote on a particular permit that effectively ends the bargaining), the municipality will never make an offer of value greater than the value that makes the developer indifferent. In other words, when both parties have full information about the relevant payoffs, probabilities, and structure of the game, the developer's expected payoff is the same whether the town issues a permit or the developer proceeds to court.[14]

When Will Developers Use the Bonus?   The necessary condition for developers to voluntarily pursue local challenges is for their expected payoff from litigation to be equal to (if not greater than) the gains from developing the same parcel within local density limits (as-of-right development). This requires that the market would indeed support higher density, $y^* \geq Y$, and that

$$(6) \qquad P_L \geq 0.$$

In order to enlist developers, regulated density must be low relative to market-driven density, and the housing appeals regimes must ensure a sufficiently high success rate with density bonuses able to cover the expected costs of litigation and other program requirements. The history of the Mount Laurel doctrine in New

---

13. In this case, we are assuming that developers are still able to keep the full surplus generated by the density bonus. Also, we assume that developers cannot bribe the town to take more density than the expected court-ordered density.

14. In practice, the game may not be a one-shot game with symmetric information as portrayed here. Rather, bargaining may involve a series of offers and counteroffers that reveal information. However, the fact that municipalities move last is an important feature of the game that our simple setup stresses. The right to approve and modify the permit is what grants municipalities bargaining power. It also plays a role in the extent to which developers will be willing to reveal information about their projects. Sobel (1989) shows that if the revelation of information is costly and the uninformed party (in our case, the municipality) moves last, the informed party (the developer) will not have incentives to reveal private information. Fisher (2007b) shows that when developers hold private information, the qualitative outcomes shown here still hold. However, there may be litigation in equilibrium, and sometimes municipalities will make settlement offers greater than those that make developers indifferent between accepting and appealing, as derived here.

Jersey nicely demonstrates some of these issues. In particular, the *Mount Laurel II* case suggests that clearly defining the conditions in which developer challenges have merit impacts litigation costs and thereby developer willingness to litigate. The 1983 case assessed the original doctrine up until that time and found that developer and municipality costs from litigation were too high to encourage developer challenges. Chief Justice Robert Wilentz delivered the opinion, stating that "The waste of judicial energy involved at every level is substantial and is matched only by the often needless expenditure of talent on the part of lawyers and experts. The length and complexity of trials is often outrageous, and the expense of litigation is so high that a real question develops whether the municipality can afford to defend or the plaintiffs can afford to sue." Addressing these weaknesses, the *Mount Laurel II* decision directed the determination of each municipality's fair-share number of housing units to determine when municipalities were in compliance with the Mount Laurel doctrine. It also firmly established the builder's remedy. Following this decision, as Mount Laurel scholar Payne observes, "it was so easy [for developers] to prove the number and the fact that it wasn't being met that defendant municipalities almost invariably conceded the violation and concentrated on disputing the form of remedy" (Payne 2000, note 18).

Subsequent regulation also defined y_c, the level of density that developers could hope to achieve if they won. While this determination refined the clarity of the regulations, as we suggest below, the presumed density to which developers are entitled may be too low in areas where land values or other development costs are high. Under those circumstances, the necessary condition in equation (6) will fail to hold because y_c is too low, and developers will not challenge municipalities.

The case of Massachusetts provides an additional example and provides a rare opportunity to directly examine the impact of litigation theorized above. Under the Massachusetts Comprehensive Permit Law (or Chapter 40B, as it is known), developers must file all challenges to local zoning using a comprehensive permit process. If litigation results from the challenge, filings must be made with the relevant state administrative body, the Housing Appeals Committee (HAC). Therefore, all the challenges afforded under Chapter 40B and any developer-initiated litigation can be observed. Exploiting this opportunity, Fisher (2007a) assembled a sample of development projects specifically seeking zoning overrides in Massachusetts between 1999 and 2005. Statistics from this sample support the observation that, during the recent housing cycle, developers were well known as challenging local zoning. Over 90 percent of developer challenges resulted in comprehensive permits. Of the challenges in the sample, only 6 percent resulted in litigation outcomes that favored local towns.

However, as argued above, favorable decisions are not enough. The court decision must allow for sufficient density for developers to want to pursue litigation and to be able to finance and build the project when a favorable verdict is received. Under Chapter 40B, locally administered comprehensive permits resulting from developer challenges cannot render the development "uneconomic" (including consideration for other demands placed on the resulting project by state law, like the delivery of price- or rent-restricted units). That is, there is no presumed density, and density awards may vary. In fact, a majority of the court-decided permits resulted in the commencement of construction,[15] suggesting that the courts enforced the legislative intent in Massachusetts and that their awards resulted in feasible projects much of the time. We interpret Massachusetts developers' willingness to instigate litigation given the long track record of this law (established in 1969) as a reflection of their expectations that court-ordered permits will also cover the costs associated with litigation.

Affordability Requirements   Many of the housing appeals regimes that enable developer overrides of local zoning (as well as of other land use regulations) require a quid pro quo from developers in the form of price or rent restrictions on some portion of the resulting housing units. Consider a development proposal that provides a proportion of the housing units at rents below current market value in the absence of restrictions on total density. The residual land value produced by this proposed development is

$$(7) \qquad \pi = \gamma p(y)y - c(y),$$

where $\gamma \in [0, 1]$ is the percent of market price that a blend of market and affordable units will produce, on average, per unit.[16]

It is then straightforward to show that the density, y^A, that maximizes π with the provision of below-market-rate units is strictly less than y^* for $\gamma > 0$ since y^A satisfies the first order condition,

$$(8) \qquad \gamma p(y^A) = c'(y^A) - \gamma p'(y)y^A.$$

In other words, with unregulated density, the developer who proposes to use land for a fully market-rate project will always outbid a developer who proposes a project with affordable or below-market-rate units, all else equal. In this sense, projects with affordable units will not be developed in the private sector without assistance. As argued by Ellickson (1981) and Fischel (1995), if projects are required to provide affordable units, as found in inclusionary zoning ordinances, the rules will serve as a tax on development and will dampen development activity by inducing lower project densities.

When the development of affordable units is voluntary but a density bonus is made available, we replace d^* with d^A, and a necessary condition for developer use of the bonus is that $Y \leq y^A < y^*$. That is, inclusionary requirements reduce the

---

15. For appeals in the Massachusetts sample that were decided between 2000 and 2004, 21 of 33 (64 percent) projects were confirmed to have pulled building permits, indicating that construction had commenced by late 2006 or early 2007.

16. For example, under Chapter 40B the developer can expect to sell or rent a fraction $\beta < 1$ of the units at market rates and the other fraction $(1 - \beta)$ of the units at a rate set by the regulation. By representing the regulated affordable rent or price as a fraction α of the market price, we obtain $(\beta + (1 - \beta)\alpha)p$ as a blended price per unit and $\gamma = \beta + (1 - \beta)\alpha$.

likelihood, all else equal, that developers will voluntarily challenge municipalities relative to when no affordable production is required.

MUNICIPAL DECISION MAKING

Before considering how the threat of developer challenge, in the aggregate, shapes municipal behaviors, we should point out a few features of the municipality's decision-making process in the event of a particular developer challenge, as shown in figure 15.1. In some instances, the prospect of avoiding a particular development proposal altogether (by defeating the developer in court) may outweigh the costs of litigation and other forgone value resulting from failure to settle out of court (Fisher 2007b). Therefore, municipalities may choose to deny a developer's proposed project and proceed to court upon the developer's challenge. In other circumstances, the municipality may choose to settle with the developer because it can exploit the cost savings (alternatively, "extract surplus") generated by sparing developers from trial. This value can be exchanged between developer and municipality as reductions in the proposed density of the project, changes to project design, inclusion of development of public amenities (such as parks), or even direct cash payments, for example.

In Massachusetts over 80 percent of all developer challenges in a sample from 1999 to 2005 resulted in municipality offers to settle—that is, municipalities issued permits without litigation (Fisher 2007a). In these settlements, municipalities obtained reductions in project density of just over 10 percent on average, as compared to the density initially proposed by the developers. If the likelihood of developer success in court (q in our model) is close to 100 percent, then settling a challenge out of court is always in the municipality's interest from a cost-saving perspective because settling affords the municipality these extractions and spares both parties the deadweight costs of litigation.

The Compliance Decision   In the preceding section, we established the conditions under which a developer will challenge a municipality's zoning and under which a municipality will attempt to settle a particular challenge out of court. The discussion now turns to figure 15.2, considering when a municipality will choose to comply with the requirements of housing appeals regimes. In this setup, we presume that municipalities understand developers' incentives as defined above in equation (6). We also assume that compliance is gained through the development of local plans or zoning to achieve state standards (often including zoning consistent with those plans). Therefore, the possible outcomes resulting from municipal decision making under housing appeals statutes are either the investment in a planning effort or in the absence of a plan bargaining with developers who are empowered to challenge existing zoning ordinances.[17]

---

17. For simplicity, we assume that q is close to 1 in this section and that municipalities will settle with developers from whom they expect successful challenges to their local zoning.

Consider the trade-offs to planning. One possible benefit of planning is the mitigation of municipality-wide costs achieved by assigning (and perhaps segregating) locations for new development (Baumol and Bradford 1972; Crone 1982; Fischel 1994).[18] In the event of developer challenges to local zoning, this opportunity is forfeited. Let x be the total number of new housing developments the municipality expects developers to bring through challenges. The number of expected projects is a function of market conditions and the process by which challenges are brought, as defined by the state housing appeals regime and the courts. If developers are expected to bring challenges, then $x > 0$, and there may be a benefit to planning. We assume that, if the municipality chooses to plan for these new projects, it does so at the same density a court would award in the successful developer challenge. Let $z(x)$ be the cost-minimizing location choice with respect to development-related externalities from x projects. In the context of municipal planning, $z(x)$ is a choice variable for the municipality; otherwise, we assume the location of development is given by the developer's choice of site and not influenced by the locality.

By contrast, planning also presents costs to municipalities. First, we assume that compliance with the state's request results in high direct costs for planning (including data collection and analysis, technical expertise, and transaction costs). Second, planning may reduce or eliminate the opportunity to extract surpluses from new developments. Recall the municipality's ability to exchange with developers over the value of avoiding litigation described above. When litigation is risky, as in the case of a developer's challenge to local zoning, the municipality can gain considerably through bargaining out of court.[19] Therefore, a state-mandated planning process establishing higher density development by-right reduces this municipal ability to extract surplus from developers.

Therefore, a main difference between planning and not planning may be municipalities' ability to extract surpluses through bargaining. In the absence of a state-compliant plan, developers likely lack the right to build to desired (higher) densities, and they must credibly threaten to sue the municipality for the desired permit. Therefore, for the same ultimate density, municipalities can extract more in the absence of planning, because developers likely face higher costs to win the necessary permits. Subtracting the right side from the left side

---

18. Here we assume that, in the event of either compliance or noncompliance, communities will receive new development. In this case, depending on the community, the control afforded by planning may be valuable. To the extent that a housing appeals regime allows a municipality to avoid new development through compliance, for example, by allowing payments in lieu of development or by rewarding planning without requiring production, compliance may provide other sorts of benefits and thereby provide different incentives to comply.

19. While even by-right development may require developers to enforce their rights through the courts, we assume here that they prevail with certainty in such cases and at lower costs.

in equation (5) and letting $y_z = y_c$, we see that for a project of density y_c the municipality can extract concessions of up to value

$$(9) \qquad \delta(y_c) = (1 - q)(\pi(y_c) - \bar{\pi}) + c_d.$$

We define the municipality's costs from the development of x new projects in terms of a cost function, $A(x, z(x))$. Recall that $z(x)$ represents the cost-minimizing choice of location for x projects. If a municipality chooses to meet state goals and plan, then $z(x)$ is a choice variable. If the local government is not compliant, we assume that z is given by developers' choices of sites and is not influenced by the locality. Then it is straightforward that $A(x, z(x)) \leq A(x, z)$. If x is equal to zero, we assume that municipal costs are zero and there is no benefit to planning.

The expected municipal payoff to noncompliance, therefore, is $A(x, z) - x\delta(y_c)$. If a municipality chooses to plan at a cost c_p, its payoff will be $A(x, z(x)) + c_p$, for the same amount of new development. Again, seeking to minimize its costs, a municipality will choose to become compliant when the payoff from planning exceeds the payoff from noncompliance,

$$(10) \qquad A(x, z) - A(x, z(x)) > x\delta + c_p.$$

The extent to which municipalities believe that they can lower the costs of new development by controlling site location or availing themselves of other aspects of the state program is, therefore, central to their decision making. The costs likely vary considerably across localities. The expected number of projects (x) may also be a key determinant of municipality behavior. On one hand, in places with low market demand, perhaps due to location or the housing market cycle, there may be little worry about new market-driven development and therefore little incentive to plan. On the other hand, if a locale is attractive for new development, perhaps the payoffs from planning are greater. Finally, the costs of litigation and the costs of planning impact this decision in the same direction: away from compliance. Because municipalities can extract some of the costs of litigation through settlement bargaining, the higher the costs of litigation, the more likely the municipalities may be to engage developers rather than comply with state mandates. Because state compliance is costly, it may also be a potential deterrent to planning.[20]

Put most simply, our modeling stresses the interplay of developer and municipality, in the context of program features and market realities, for housing appeals regimes to function as intended. Therefore, it should afford some insight into real-world outcomes. Consider New Jersey and the municipal behavior under its Fair Housing Act. As of 2003 fewer than half of New Jersey municipalities (41

---

20. We further expect that the ability to bear the direct costs of planning varies across localities as a function of the available resources (including technical expertise and resources for the necessary data collection, analysis, and decision making in support of a comprehensive plan consistent with local zoning).

Figure 15.3
New Jersey Municipality Compliance, 1994–2003

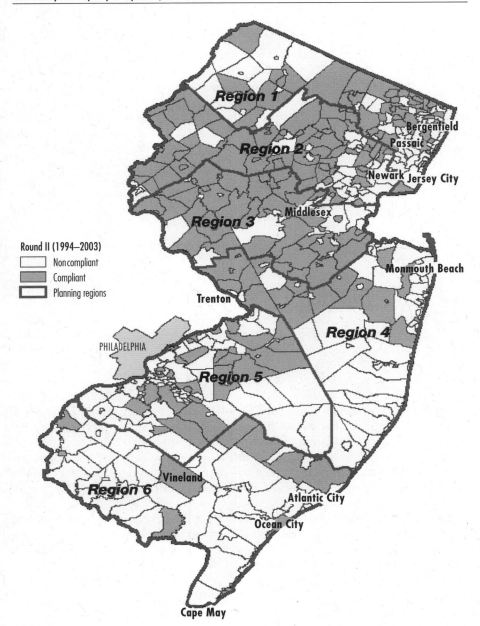

percent) were in compliance. Even in the northern regions of the state where developer challenges were likely during the 1990s (given growing housing demand), a good number of municipalities remained noncompliant (see figure 15.3).

At first glance, this noncompliance would seem puzzling (and perhaps upsetting to policy makers). Therefore, we empirically examined the likelihood of municipal compliance in New Jersey based on a series of municipal-level characteristics relevant to our model. Table 15.1 presents our results, and our methods

Table 15.1

Likelihood of New Jersey Municipal Substantive Certification

Dependent Variable: Certified Round II	All Municipalities		North		South	
	Coefficient	Marginal Effect	Coefficient	Marginal Effect	Coefficient	Marginal Effect
Vacant Land in Growth Areas (1000 acres)	0.0425*** −0.0125	0.02	0.0812 −0.0522	0.03	0.0455*** −0.0019	0.01
COAH Northern Regions+	0.6260*** −0.1689	0.23				
Median Household Income/1000	0.0104*** −0.0032	0.0039	0.0097*** −0.0028	0.0039	0.0123 −0.0127	0.0034
Percent White	0.0930** −0.0373	0.04	0.0979 −0.0608	0.04	0.1268*** −0.0285	0.04
Percent White Squared	−0.0006** −0.0002	−0.0002	−0.0005 −0.0004	−0.0002	−0.0009*** −0.0002	−0.0002
Calculated Need/ Stock × 100	−0.0733** −0.0295	−0.03	−0.0398 −0.035	−0.02	−0.0984*** −0.0276	−0.03
Certified Round I+	0.9195*** −0.1331	0.35	0.7327*** −0.0491	0.28	1.1532*** −0.2669	0.39
Substandard Housing/ Acre × 100	−0.0453* −0.0237	−0.02	−0.0498* −0.0259	−0.02	0.0305 −0.082	0.01
Constant	−4.7960*** −1.3769		−5.3683*** −2.0226		−5.5924*** −1.0209	
Observations	566		298		268	
Pseudo R-squared	0.23		0.17		0.21	
Log Likelihood	−296.2		−169.46		−118.27	

* Significant at 10%; ** significant at 5%; *** significant at 1%
+ Marginal effects for discrete change of dummy variable from 0 to 1; otherwise, marginal effects evaluated at the means of variables
Notes: Probit estimations. Certified municipalities designated as those petitioning for certification in round II prior to 2003. Marginal effects shown next to coefficients. Robust standard errors beneath coefficients (adjusted for clustering by planning region).

and data are explained in the Appendix. As our modeling suggests, municipalities may choose not to comply for several reasons, and those reasons are the result of various regime features (often expressed through developer participation).

For example, municipalities may not comply because they do not face a credible developer threat (*outcome 1*). The market may fail to provide the necessary incentives for developer challenge. In New Jersey's southern regions, which experienced relatively less growth pressure during the 1990s, municipalities were over 20 percent less likely to plan than their northern counterparts, even after controlling for other relevant municipal variation. The interaction between the market and features of the appeal regime itself may also fail to compel developers. For example, we expect that the likelihood of developer challenge in New Jersey's dense, physically distressed cities is mitigated by COAH's presumptive density of about six units per acre. This density fails to provide developers with a sufficient payoff from challenge. City governments may be willing to bargain with developers in these places in order to share in the gains from development. Their bargaining positions are worsened by planning for higher-density development by-right. Therefore, even as the northern communities consistently faced growth pressure, developers were assumed less likely to litigate and cities less likely to plan within the region's dense cities. In fact, we do see a reduced likelihood of planning in the north amid places with increased density and distressed housing (as proxied by the amount of substandard housing per acre). This does not mean that new development was not forthcoming in these mainly older cities, but that it occurred outside the preferred process set forth by the state (Mallach 2008).

Alternatively, municipalities may perceive that the benefits of planning may not outweigh the costs, even in the face of developer challenges (*outcome 2*). In New Jersey's northern communities (where significant developer threats are assumed), compliance is only 55 percent. If the extent of expected development is not great, the incentives to plan may be reduced. To this end, municipalities with less vacant land available for development were less likely to achieve certification. Poorer and relatively minority-rich communities were the least likely to plan.[21] This is consistent with our expectation about the perceived benefits of planning across communities (that is, wealthier and white communities will be particularly interested in controlling development patterns in their municipalities). In addition, the more affordable housing the state requires for compliance (a tally called "calculated need" by COAH), the less likely a municipality is to plan. We expect

---

21. Perhaps, however, we are incorrect in assuming that developer challenges exist in these communities, explaining their lack of compliance. We are unable to directly test this proposition. However, we considered the possibility that these municipalities are under less developer threat than the rest of the north in order to bolster our confidence in this interpretation. We examined the bivariate relationship between compliance and distance from the closest city center among northern municipalities, with the expectation that greater distances experience less development pressure. We found that, on average, the likelihood of compliance increases at greater distances. Therefore, we have greater confidence in believing that noncompliance among the poorer and minority-rich northern communities is likely in the face of developer threats.

that a higher calculated need increases the direct costs of planning and the costs of municipality-supplied subsidy or sponsored programs for affordable housing development. Finally, municipalities that were certified in the previous round were more likely to become certified in the second round. While these are likely to be places facing developer challenges, the costs of compliance may have also been lower due to the experience of undertaking the process previously.

We would be remiss should we not point out that there are 230 New Jersey municipalities in compliance with the Fair Housing Act as of 2003, possibly suggesting that the housing appeals regime is functioning as intended. That is, when developers challenge local land uses, municipalities change their behavior (*outcome 3*). The northern municipalities, which are assumed to be under the highest developer pressure in the state, are more than 20 percent more likely to plan than the southern communities, all else equal. Perhaps most interesting to advocates of housing appeals regimes for "opening up" the suburbs, communities with relatively high incomes and high proportions of white residents are more likely to plan, as predicted in our model. This at least suggests that the communities motivating this state antiexclusionary zoning effort appear particularly motivated to change their behavior as a result.

Before leaving the real world entirely, let us also quickly return to Massachusetts to see what insights our modeling can provide. Municipality compliance is much less frequent in Massachusetts (51 of 351 towns and cities, or 15 percent). Figure 15.4 depicts towns and cities that have reached the threshold of compliance with 10 percent of their 2000 housing stock qualifying as subsidized housing under the rules of the Department of Housing and Community Development (DHCD) charged with administering Chapter 40B. The test for compliance is strict in Massachusetts because it is based on actual production, not plans for anticipated production. In the context of our model, therefore, a change in behavior provides little payoff to municipalities. For the greater part of the 40-year history of the law, neither planning nor zoning afforded any protection from developer challenges. Therefore, it may be easier and less costly to face developer challenges. Given that compliance in Massachusetts is a function of the actual subsidized housing produced, letting developers bear those costs through this challenge mechanism seems logical. In 2002 DHCD adopted regulations facilitating a planning process, not unlike the COAH process in New Jersey, whereby towns and cities could also demonstrate compliance. It is unsurprising, then, that relatively suburban, high-income towns in the Boston metropolitan area have taken the first steps toward achieving certification through this planning process.[22] Still, as depicted in figure 15.4, only 8 have reached that goal to date.

---

22. Of 131 towns near Boston, 56 have entered the planning process as of the first quarter of 2008. The places seeking approval are far less proximate to jobs and have weakly higher income in a simple probit model (pseudo R squared equal to 9 percent).

Figure 15.4
Massachusetts Municipality Compliance, 2008

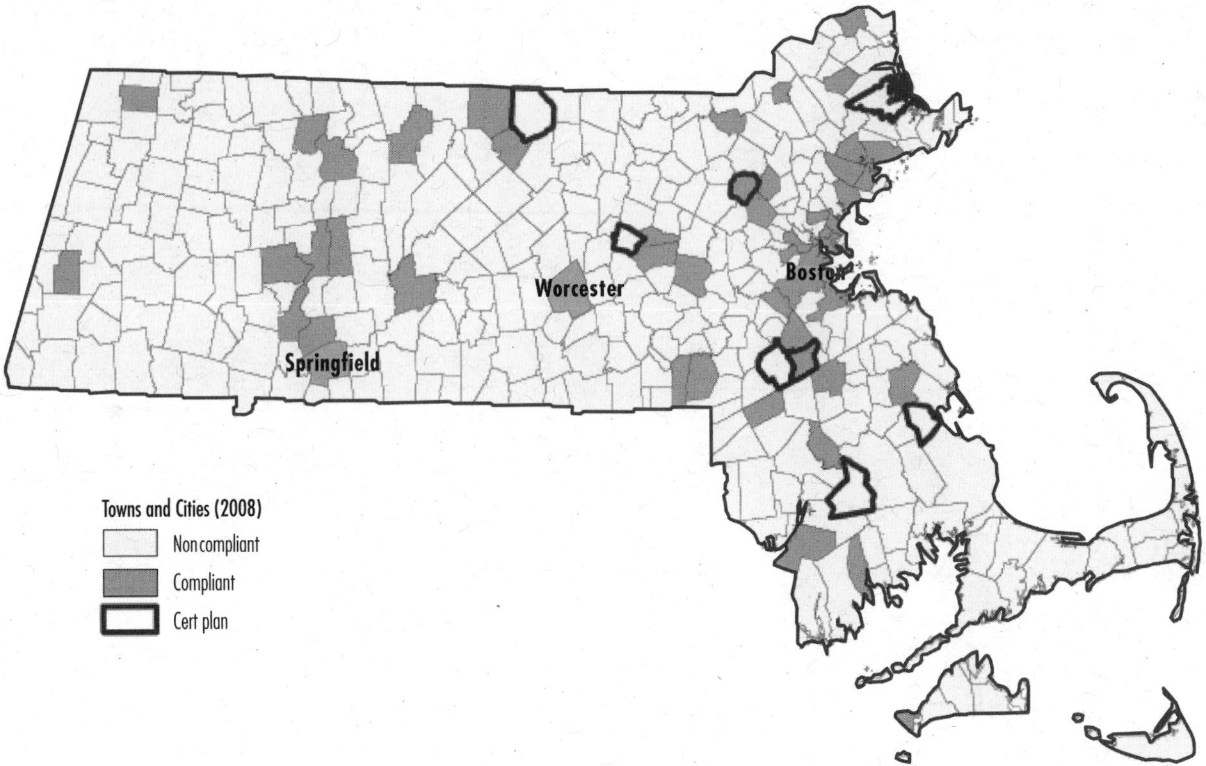

Towns and Cities (2008)

Non compliant

Compliant

Cert plan

Boston

Worcester

Springfield

Conclusions

We have developed a framework to incorporate strategic behavior by and among developers and municipalities in the context of state housing appeals regimes. Our goal has been to open the black box of this strategy to understand the role that developers play in facilitating state goals with respect to land use and housing development at the local level. Understanding the developer role is particularly important as a growing set of states are enlisting developers in state antiexclusionary zoning efforts.

As the model and empirical evidence offered here suggest, outcomes from housing appeals regimes may vary widely, even in the same state.[23] When developers have sufficient incentives to challenge local land use regulations, they may ultimately play one of two different roles (corresponding to alternate outcomes). On one hand, developers may create a credible challenge threat that results in municipal compliance with state-established goals. In this role they can be seen as the enforcers of state policy. That is, any change to land use or housing production is the result of a change in municipal behavior (changes, of course, may not occur). On the other hand, when municipalities fail to proactively strive toward the fulfillment of state goals, developers may be the direct implementers of state policy, pursuing housing production in spite of local municipal behavior.

We expect that this more fully articulated understanding of the interplay between municipalities, developers, state policy, and market conditions in state housing appeals regimes will be useful for more clearly identifying the intent of such policies and creating mechanisms to achieve their expected goals.

APPENDIX: EMPIRICAL EXPLORATION OF
MUNICIPAL COMPLIANCE

As an initial exploration of the propositions of our model, this appendix presents our empirical exploration of variation in municipal compliance with the New Jersey Fair Housing Act. We consider New Jersey municipalities from 1994 to 2003. New Jersey has one of the longest histories with state antiexclusionary zoning efforts and is often looked upon as a model by other states, making it a particularly interesting laboratory for analysis. Despite being one of the smaller states, New Jersey includes a relatively large number of municipalities (more than 500), including dense older cities, suburbs, and rural and farming communities. Unlike regimes where state goals are less clearly articulated, New Jersey's Council on Affordable Housing (COAH) explicitly identifies localities as complying or not complying with requirements.

---

23. Here we are referring to the outcomes of the bargaining game; that is, developer decisions to participate and the municipal compliance decisions. We are not referring to the policy outcomes more broadly, which might include increased housing production, for example.

Therefore, the outcome of interest is the municipal decision to comply, demonstrated by the preparation and substantive certification of a local plan with COAH.[24] We define compliance as the presence of substantive certification during round II gained through petitions filed between 1994 and 2003. Second-round certification provides the most valid measure of voluntary municipal compliance under the New Jersey appeals regime. Defining compliance based on certification in other rounds fails to consistently capture the voluntary nature of municipal planning that is of interest here. Both the earliest years and the most recent were periods of relative upheaval in the regime's implementation.[25] Narrowing our focus to round II petitions prior to 2003 bolsters the consistency of this measure over our full study period. Municipal decision making after 2003, with the proposal of new rules under round III certification in 2003, likely differs from that during the remainder of round II, complicating our understanding of municipal decisions to comply.

Data on municipal certification were assembled from COAH's Web site. Of New Jersey's 566 municipalities, 245 have round II certification. Fifteen of these certifications resulted from petitions filed as of 2003. Therefore, according to our measure, 230 municipalities (41 percent) are compliant.

With this municipal compliance measure, we can document some empirical facts about the spatial variation in compliance across the state. Figure 15.3 maps compliance in New Jersey and within the state's six planning regions. A clear north-south divide exists, with a greater proportion of northern cities in compliance (55 percent as compared to 25 percent of southern cities).[26] This distinction may be a result of contrasting development pressure, which also likely contributes to the extent of developer challenges. The late 1990s were generally a period of growth for the northern municipalities of New Jersey. Mallach (2008) describes strong upward trends in house prices, transactions, and building permits through 2006, especially for urban areas. By comparison, cities in the southern part of the state, such as Trenton and Camden, experienced markedly less growth. The greater compliance in the north may, therefore, be explained by the economic realities there. Nevertheless, variation in compliance also exists

---

24. A further complication exists in understanding municipality choice in New Jersey. Essentially, localities also have the option to petition the courts directly and obtain a judgment of repose for presenting the court with a plan deemed to be in compliance with the Mount Laurel doctrine and COAH guidelines. Without further data, it is unclear which judgments result from voluntary petitions and which from developer litigation. Therefore, we do not consider municipalities under court protection or those that through our understanding of the COAH data have come under COAH's protection from the courts.

25. We could also argue that considerable uncertainty existed from 1999 until the legislature effectively extended the round in 2000 (Kinsey 2008). We recalculate our results below using certifications that resulted from petitions made to COAH prior to the year 2000, and our results remain qualitatively the same.

26. These means are significantly different at better than the 1 percent significance level.

within the north, where, despite consistent development pressure and, presumably, threat of developer challenge, few of the denser older cities in the northeast chose to comply. We turn to our model of municipal decision making with some data on New Jersey municipalities to suggest possible explanations.

Empirical Approach

To begin to relate the likelihood of compliance with observable characteristics of these municipalities, we return to our model. Rearranging equation (10), we expect municipalities to comply with state mandates when

$$(11) \quad [A(x,z) - A(x,z(x))] - x\delta - c_p > 0.$$

Simply put, municipalities compare the benefits and costs of planning in the decision to comply. Our inquiry lends itself to probit estimation of the likelihood of municipal round II certification.

The first term in our model of compliance is the municipality's perceived benefits of planning resulting from the level of anticipated development and the value that control over the location of future developments affords the municipality. We first seek to account for the different market and economic pressures in the northern and southern parts of New Jersey. COAH divides New Jersey into six planning regions with housing needs first determined at the regional level and then allocated among municipalities within those regions. We exploit this fact to divide New Jersey into north and south according to planning regions 1 through 3 and 4 through 6 (planning regions outlined in bold in figure 15.3). Faced with the prospect of more new development, there is even more benefit from controlling where it all occurs. We further proxy for this expectation at the municipal level with a measure of a municipality's vacant land in state-identified growth areas. In growth areas, land is more vulnerable to development because there are fewer environmental and other regional or state-enforced regulatory restrictions. For example, growth areas have fewer restrictions on impervious surfaces and less emphasis on agricultural land preservation, making development more feasible. Finally, we expect the perceived benefits from planning to be positively related to municipality household income and the percentage of the population that is white.[27]

Our model of municipal compliance next considers the costs of planning. All else equal, the number of low- and moderate-income housing units for which

---

27. Alternate means of accommodating fair share are available in New Jersey through the planning and certification process may reinforce this relationship. For example, regional contribution agreements (RCAs) allow certified municipalities to transfer a portion of their obligation to a receiving community in exchange for a per-unit payment. Therefore, wealthier communities willing to pay to avoid some of their obligation may find compliance valuable.

the municipality is responsible (hereafter referred to as calculated need) may influence the perceived benefits of planning.[28] However, greater calculated need may imply greater direct costs of preparing a plan and applying for certification. To the extent that compliance will require a municipality to provide a subsidy for affordable housing development, costs of compliance may be increasing in calculated need. As an additional control, we also employ a categorical variable indicating whether a municipality was certified in round I of the COAH process. Presumably, the process of compliance in the first round may make the decision to comply in the second round less costly. In any of these cases, greater costs are likely to reduce the probability of municipal compliance.

All these influences on municipal compliance are contingent on a realistic threat of developer challenges. Growing municipalities that are attractive to developers likely expect developer challenges and may choose to plan accordingly (such as the north-south difference in compliance rates observed earlier). Consider the density bonus within the Fair Housing Act, which is set at about six units per acre.[29] This density is probably considerably higher than is permitted under by-right zoning in most suburban communities. However, it may provide insufficient incentive for developer challenge in high-density municipalities and those with large proportions of substandard stock. Here, the development costs and surrounding land values would demand a far greater density for a developer to cover construction costs, not to mention the costs and risks of litigation. At the same time, city government may welcome development in these places and hope to participate in the surplus that it may generate. In the absence of a plan that allows higher-density development as-of-right, and in the absence of developer incentives to pursue a builder's remedy that is inadequate, a municipality may exploit its regulatory powers in bargaining with developers. Therefore, both developers and cities may prefer to bargain outside the housing appeals process, and cities will not comply with state mandates. Rather than indicating a weakness in our municipal modeling, this case should be seen as clearly demonstrating that both developers and municipalities are the central actors in these state efforts. Therefore, we recognize the important and complicated influence of development pressure on the likelihood of municipal compliance and include a measure of the percentage of substandard stock per acre in our estimation to control for high-density areas with opportunities for redevelopment.

This joint consideration of developers and municipalities brings us full circle to our original conception of the bargaining game at the heart of these housing

---

28. COAH publishes the calculated need or number of low- and moderate-income housing units for which each municipality is responsible. In general, there may be greater benefits to planning in the face of greater opportunity for new development. COAH intentionally places a greater burden on wealthier communities; therefore, these two assumed benefits of planning likely reinforce one another.

29. See New Jersey Administrative Code 5:93-5.6.

appeals regimes. We identified three possible outcomes: (1) developer nonparticipation (no challenge) and municipal noncompliance; (2) developer challenge without municipal compliance; and (3) developer challenge and municipal compliance. Our empirical exploration attempts to account for these interrelationships in the context of our prior theorizing.

Data

In addition to data on certification, we used COAH data to capture several other municipal-level characteristics relevant to this exploration of municipal planning decisions. These include COAH's round II determination of calculated need. We also assembled information on COAH's round II designation of municipalities as Urban Aid Cities, which are designated by the state legislature as especially deserving of resources.[30] Finally, we assembled COAH's 1993 determination of the percentage of substandard housing and the amount of vacant land in growth areas by municipality. In the first instance, we divided this number by the total municipal acreage to provide a relative measure of the amount of substandard housing per municipality. To these data we add several additional municipality-wide descriptors taken and manipulated from the 1990 census. The census data include the total housing stock per acre, median household incomes, housing density, and the percentage of the population that is white.

Summary statistics for the 566 New Jersey municipalities, shown in table 15.2, nicely demonstrate wide variation among the cities and towns in the state. These statistics first demonstrate that planning is hardly universal. Forty-one percent of the state's municipalities are compliant (had certified plans as of 1993). The fair share that each municipality faced during the study period also differed across the state. The calculated need, in terms of new or rehabilitated housing units, ranged from zero to nearly 3,000 units. As a percentage of 1990 housing stock, the calculated need ranged from 0 percent to 23 percent, with a mean of 3.5 percent. Finally, median household incomes varied fairly dramatically across locations, and the racial composition of municipalities covered the spectrum from completely nonwhite to entirely white.

Calculating these mean values by planning region further demonstrates the north-south divide observed earlier (see table 15.2). The compliance rates differed dramatically (as observed in figure 15.3). The rate of certification in the first three planning regions was 55 percent, while it was 25 percent in the last three regions.[31] The northern regions were also significantly richer than the three southern planning regions. These statistics are generally consistent with greater

---

30. For the purposes of substantive certification, a municipality has to meet additional tests as specified by COAH-specific rules to be designated an Urban Aid City.

31. These means are significantly different at better than the 1 percent significance level.

Table 15.2
Summary Statistics for New Jersey Municipalities

Municipality Characteristics by Region (Means)					
Planning Region	N	Certified Round II	Certified Round I	Calculated Need (87–99)	Calculated Need/Stock
Northeast (1)	122	0.43	0.22	151	3.00
Northwest (2)	104	0.62	0.35	102	1.99
West Central (3)	72	0.67	0.57	121	3.26
East Central (4)	99	0.20	0.17	209	4.54
Southwest (5)	101	0.33	0.29	129	4.19
South Southwest (6)	68	0.19	0.16	175	4.85
The State	566	0.41	0.28	147	3.55
Planning Region	Median Household Income (×1000)	Percent White (×100)	Urban Aid City	Housing Density	Percentage Substandard Stock (×100)
Northeast (1)	51.39	90.30	0.09	3.23	5.88
Northwest (2)	53.79	88.79	0.11	1.98	2.98
West Central (3)	51.36	92.02	0.04	1.23	2.02
East Central (4)	43.86	91.87	0.06	2.06	1.90
Southwest (5)	40.30	86.86	0.12	1.49	1.81
South Southwest (6)	33.18	85.61	0.10	1.14	1.17
The State	46.34	89.34	0.09	1.98	2.87

development pressure, and thereby greater likelihood of developer challenge, in the north.

In an attempt to disentangle the complex interrelationships among developers and municipalities, we estimated probit models of the likelihood of municipal round II certification based on a series of municipal-level administrative and demographic characteristics. In all the analysis below, we controlled for whether a municipality was certified in round I.

In table 15.1 we report the estimated coefficients and the marginal effects of the independent variables on the probability of municipal compliance. Taken together, we think that these findings from New Jersey are supportive of our model as they are consistent with the three outcomes from housing appeals games that we identified. Moreover, they suggest that, just as developers' willingness to participate is important to municipal compliance, developers' threats also vary across municipalities with the features of the housing appeals regime and economic realities.

REFERENCES

Baumol, William J., and David F. Bradford. 1972. Detrimental externalities and non-convexity of the production set. *Economica* 39(154):160–176.

Bengston, David N., Jennifer O. Fletcher, and Kristin C. Nelson. 2004. Public policies for managing urban growth and protecting open space: Policy instruments and lessons learned in the United States. *Landscape and Urban Planning* 69:271–286.

Cowan, Spencer M. 2006. Anti-snob land use laws, suburban exclusion, and housing opportunity. *Journal of Urban Affairs* 28(3):295.

Crone, Theodore M. 1982. Elements of an economic justification for municipal zoning. *Journal of Urban Economics* 14:168–183.

Ellickson, Robert C. 1981. The irony of "inclusionary" zoning. *Southern California Law Review* 54:1167–1216.

Fischel, William A. 1991. Exclusionary zoning and growth controls: A comment on the APA's endorsement of the Mount Laurel doctrine. *Journal of Urban and Contemporary Law* 40:65–73.

———. 1994. Zoning, non-convexities, and T. Jack Foster's city. *Journal of Urban Economics* 35:175–181.

———. 1995. *Regulatory takings: Law, economics, and politics.* Cambridge, MA: Harvard University Press.

———. 2008. Political structure and exclusionary zoning: Are small suburbs the big problem? In *Fiscal decentralization and land policies*, ed. Gregory K. Ingram and Yu-Hung Hong, 111–136. Cambridge, MA: Lincoln Institute of Land Policy.

Fisher, Lynn. 2007a. Chapter 40B permitting and litigation. Report prepared for MIT/CRE Housing Affordability Initiative, Cambridge, MA.

———. 2007b. The selection of developer permit applications for litigation: Asymmetric information and entitlements. Working paper, MIT/CRE Housing Affordability Initiative, Cambridge, MA.

Gale, Dennis E. 1992. Eight state-sponsored growth management programs: A comparative analysis. *Journal of the American Planning Association* 58:4.

Glaeser, Edward. 2007. Restricting residential construction. In *Land policies and their outcomes*, ed. Gregory K. Ingram and Yu-Hung Hong, 21–45. Cambridge, MA: Lincoln Institute of Land Policy.

Goetz, Edward G., Karen Chapple, and Barbara Luckerman. 2003. Enabling exclusion: The retreat from regional fair share housing in the implementation of the Minnesota Land Use Planning Act. *Journal of Planning Education and Research* 22(3):213–225.

Harvard Law Review. 1995. State-sponsored growth management as a remedy for exclusionary zoning. *Harvard Law Review* 108(5):1128.

Howell-Moroney, Michael. 2007. Studying the effects of the intensity of US state growth management approaches on land development outcomes. *Urban Studies* 44(11):2163–2178.

Kinsey, David N. 2008. Smart growth, housing needs, and the future of the Mount
    Laurel doctrine. In *Mount Laurel II* at 25: The Unfinished Agenda of Fair Share
    Housing, published by the Policy Research Institute for the Region, Woodrow
    Wilson School of Public Affairs, Princeton University.
Krefetz, Sharon P. 2001. Symposium: The impact and evolution of the Massachusetts
    Comprehensive Permit and Zoning Appeals Act: Thirty years of experience with
    state legislative effort to overcome exclusionary zoning. *Western New England
    Law Review* 22:381.
Lewis, Paul G. 2005. Can state review of local planning increase housing production?
    Housing Policy Debate 16(2):173–200.
Mallach, Alan. 2008. Challenging the new geography of exclusion: The Mount Laurel
    doctrine and the changing climate of growth and redevelopment in New Jersey.
    Paper presented at *Mount Laurel II*: The Unfinished Agenda of Fair Share Hous-
    ing, sponsored by the Policy Research Institute for the Region, Woodrow Wilson
    School of Public Affairs, Princeton University.
Meck, Stuart, Rebecca Retzlaff, and James Schwab. 2003. *Regional approaches to af-
    fordable housing PAS 513/514*. Chicago: American Planning Advisory Service.
Mitchell, James L. 2004. Will empowering developers to challenge exclusionary zoning
    increase suburban housing choice? *Journal of Policy Analysis and Management*
    3(1):119–134.
Nelson, Arthur C., Rolf Pendall, Casey J. Dawkins, and Gerrit J. Knaap. 2002. *The link
    between growth management and housing affordability: The academic evidence*.
    Washington, DC: Brookings Institution.
Payne, John M. 2000. Reconstructing the constitutional theory of *Mount Laurel*. Spe-
    cial issue, *Washington University Journal of Law and Policy* 3:555–582.
Quigley, John M. 2007. Regulation and property values in the United States: The high
    cost of monopoly. In *Land policies and their outcomes*, ed. Gregory K. Ingram and
    Yu-Hung Hong, 46–65. Cambridge, MA: Lincoln Institute of Land Policy.
Quigley, John M., and Steven Raphael. 2005. Regulation and the high cost of housing
    in California. *American Economic Review* 95(2):323–328.
Rubin, Jeffrey I., and Joseph J. Seneca. 1991. Density bonuses, exactions, and the
    supply of affordable housing. *Journal of Urban Economics* 30:206–223.
Sobel, Joel. 1989. An analysis of discovery rules. *Law and Contemporary Problems*
    52(1):133–159.
Weitz, Jerry. 1999. From quiet revolution to smart growth: State growth management
    programs, 1960 to 1999. *Journal of Planning Literature* 14:266.
Wheaton, William C., and William E. Simonton. 2007. The secular and cyclic behavior
    of "true" construction costs. *Journal of Real Estate Research* 29(1):1–25.

COMMENTARY
Alexander von Hoffman

Keri-Nicole Dillman and Lynn M. Fisher thoughtfully explore the policy of using real estate developers to produce subsidized housing for low- and moderate-
income households in the suburbs. Employing a bargaining analysis derived from
game theory, the authors constructed a model of behavior by the principal figures
in antiexclusionary land use programs created by the Anti-Snob Zoning Act, or
40B, in Massachusetts and the mechanism growing out of the *Mount Laurel*
court decisions in New Jersey. The authors shed light on these housing appeals
systems to help states adjust their policies to be more effective and judge the
programs' success—a laudable goal as the 40B and Mount Laurel programs have
produced paltry numbers of low-cost residences in the decades since they were
first enacted.[1]

As in many states, government bodies in Massachusetts and New Jersey set
quotas of affordable housing for all municipalities. If a town that has not met
its affordable housing quota rejects a proposal for a residential project that includes a certain proportion of affordable housing units, the developer is allowed
to appeal the town's decision to a state housing appeals agency. To compensate
the developer for subsidizing some dwellings, the law offers incentives, such as
density bonuses or waiver of impact fee and/or other costs. In the authors' bargaining game, the chief players are developers and municipalities, while the state
authorities—particularly the housing appeals boards and the judiciary—act as
arbitrators and setters of rules.

This framework provides valuable insights about decision making in builders' remedy programs, but as yet it captures neither the complexity of the interactions involved in local land use decisions nor, more important, the essential
political dynamics at play. Understanding these is essential to understanding and
judging the policy as well as to building a model of its operation.

Developers' Decisions

For the most part, the authors argue that the developers and municipalities decide
what actions to take on land use issues based on their assessment of costs. This
assumption applies best to developers, who need to balance costs with income to
stay in business. Still, the realities builders confront are more complex than an
elementary model can capture. Builders must assess the demand for a given type

---

1. In Massachusetts the principal advocacy group reports that the Anti-Snob Zoning Act has
produced 26,000 dwellings for low-income households since it was enacted in 1969 (Citizens'
Housing and Planning Association 2007). New Jersey has done somewhat better, recording
more than 30,000 units for low- and moderate-income households since the *Mount Laurel II*
compliance measure took effect in 1986 (Payne 2006).

of dwelling—a moving target, as the current housing slump demonstrates; gauge the land use regulations in the town; figure the land, construction, and other costs; calculate interest rates; and decide what is profitable.

Dillman and Fisher assume that the density of dwelling units plays a large part in the decisions of developers to build or to challenge zoning, which no doubt is true in many instances. In practice, however, factors such as type of construction and site layout may influence costs more than density. It is more economical, for example, to build a four-story wood frame building with fewer units than a six-story steel frame structure with more units. It will cost developers less to build required infrastructure such as roads for a single mid-rise building than for a dispersed group of townhouses or detached houses (Rhuda 2008).

As the authors note, restrictive land use regulations can lead the developer to consider building affordable units. The overall balance sheet, however, is crucial. A Boston-area home builder reckons that in Massachusetts a 30-unit condominium project with no affordable units brings the same profit as a 40-unit condominium project in which 10 units (25 percent) are affordable. In New Jersey 32 market-rate condominiums provide the same return as 40 condominiums including eight (20 percent) affordable residences (Rhuda 2008). Hence, only when a density bonus—or a reduction in development costs—is great enough will it entice developers to build low-income homes.

The authors argue that the states' housing appeals systems encourage developers to challenge local zoning codes and rulings. Yet a developer will weigh many factors before going up against the town. Among these is the risk of alienating local officials with whom small-scale home builders may hope to do business at a later date. Then there is the expense of an appeal. Builders in Massachusetts can spend up to $10,000 per unit to produce the documentation (engineers' reports, soil tests, traffic mitigation studies, and so on) required for a permit application, and the appeal before the state court can cost between $50,000 and $200,000 (Rhuda 2008). With all this money at stake, the developer will weigh the risks of an appeal carefully. While a developer of a large project may amortize the costs over many units, a small builder may not think appealing is worth the expense.

Finally, the builder will ponder the likely outcome of a challenge. The developer must consider the specific grounds upon which the local zoning board of appeals denied or placed costly conditions—such as a large percentage of subsidized units or demanding road standards—on the project and whether the court has established clear legal precedents in similar cases. As their high success rate in Massachusetts cases indicates, builders will appeal only if they believe they will likely prevail.

Municipalities' Decisions

However complicated the developer's decision process may be, it is simple compared to that of the municipality. Unlike the one or two decision makers in a small home building firm, many people participate in a municipality's land use decisions. Several town officials, including the town planner, will render opinions on building applications; in towns of a certain size and complexity, a raft of officials and departments—including the building inspector, head of the board of health, town engineer, the zoning board of appeals, and the conservation and historical commissions—have approval power in the matter of special permits, which almost all towns require for multifamily or clustered housing projects.[2] Public hearings or even entire town meetings may be required, and, as Fisher noted recently in an excellent report on chapter 40B in Massachusetts, "private individuals" also play the game (Fisher 2007, 17) by suing and otherwise agitating against developers' applications for comprehensive permits.

With so many people influencing a decision to approve or reject a development proposal, one should not assume that cost is the only or even the major consideration. True, towns may decide to settle out of court to avoid paying for litigation, but many municipalities will delay settling as long as possible in the hope of forcing the developer—who must pay interest charges on mortgage and construction loans—to conclude that the approval process has become too expensive to prolong. As the authors note in their chapter, in some cases the desire of town officials to prevent a project is so strong that they ignore the costs of litigation—even if their actions invite a lawsuit.

Although the authors suggest that a municipality's adoption of planning marks progress toward affordable housing goals, one must be careful about interpreting the meaning of a town's adoption of a land use plan for housing. Since zoning arrived on these shores a century ago, local political interests have exploited land use planning regulations to control the character, amount, scale, and location of new development and frequently to hinder it or stop it altogether.

In this context, it is striking to note that at least 43 percent of eastern Massachusetts towns with inclusionary zoning have generated no affordable housing units, and in scores of other communities the mechanism has produced only a few such dwellings (Dain 2005, 62–64).[3] Clearly the incentives to developers are not great enough, but just as clearly the municipalities have been in no hurry to increase them.

---

2. Asked "Is cluster development, planned unit development, open space residential design, or another type of flexible zoning allowed by right?" only four of the 187 Massachusetts municipalities surveyed by the Pioneer Institute could answer in the affirmative (Pioneer Institute for Public Policy Research and Harvard's Rappaport Institute for Greater Boston 2006).

3. This is a minimum figure. Twenty-five percent of the towns with inclusionary provisions surveyed by the Pioneer Institute did not reply or gave vague answers, and undoubtedly some of these also did not produce affordable units (Pioneer Institute for Public Policy Research and Harvard's Rappaport Institute for Greater Boston 2006).

A Political Game

Although the authors point out that the housing appeals systems has changed behavior in Massachusetts and New Jersey, they ignore the persistent and multifaceted local resistance to housing quotas. This may take the form of sluggish compliance with state standards, foot-dragging, or placing obstacles in front of developers. Or it may take the form of changing the rules of the game. In both states, the municipalities have attempted—with some success—to weaken the standards for compliance with affordable housing goals, thus tilting the playing field in their favor.[4]

At the same time, others are pressing the government for more homes affordable to low-income people. State and metropolitan-area interest groups lobby and sue to strengthen state affordable housing policies. Less recognized but potentially just as important as the advocacy organizations are the local citizens groups that support affordable housing in their home communities. Developers, often working through the state's home builders association, also lobby the state and fund research to expand their opportunities to create more dwellings, both market and affordable.

In short, the conflict over affordable housing in the suburbs is primarily political, even if it is entwined with economic considerations. As such, we policy researchers might do well to put aside our model building kits for the moment and gather the requisite information about the political forces at play. We need to identify all the players, learn their motives, understand their stratagems and the conditions under which they operate, follow their actions in both local and state arenas, and measure the effects of their conduct on the production of homes for low-income families. Then we will know how this game is actually played.

REFERENCES

Citizens' Housing and Planning Association (CHAPA). 2007. Fact sheet on chapter 40B, the state's affordable housing zoning law. http://www.chapa.org/pdf/40BFactSheetOctober2007.pdf.

Council on Affordable Housing (COAH). 2008. COAH adopts revised third round rules and proposes amendments. Press release, 6 May. http://www.nj.gov/dca/coah/june08rules.shtml.

4. In Massachusetts the most important regulatory changes made to chapter 40B between 2001 and 2003 strengthened the ability of the town to limit the number of affordable units it had to build, created steps to slow or impede the progress of proposals, and placed stricter requirements on developers (CHAPA 2007). In New Jersey in 2003, widespread popular resentment led the affordable housing board to propose a growth share formula that would have cut in half the town's requirements for affordable housing (Payne 2006, 142; Retzlaff 2003). A court decision forced the board to retreat, but rules released in May 2008 included a variety of bonuses and exemptions for municipalities (Council on Affordable Housing 2008), which still did not satisfy critics (Lynott 2008).

Dain, Amy. 2005. *Residential land-use regulation in eastern Massachusetts: A study of 187 communities.* Boston: Pioneer Institute for Public Policy Research and Rappaport Institute for Greater Boston, Harvard University.

Fisher, Lynn. 2007. *Chapter 40B permitting and litigation: A report by the Housing Affordability Initiative.* Cambridge, MA: MIT.

Lynott, William P. 2008. COAH regulations discriminate. *Times of Trenton,* 17 April.

Payne, John M. 2006. The paradox of progress: Three decades for the Mount Laurel doctrine. *Journal of Planning History* 5:2(May):126–147.

Pioneer Institute for Public Policy Research and Rappaport Institute for Greater Boston. 2006. Housing regulation database. http://www.masshousingregulations.com/index.asp.

Retzlaff, Rebecca. 2003. Changes to New Jersey affordable housing law. *Zoning News,* October. http://www.planning.org/affordablereader/znzp/znoct03c.htm.

Rhuda, Jeff. 2008. Electronic communication to author, 5 May.

16

The Mediocrity of Government Subsidies to Mixed-Income Housing Projects

Robert C. Ellickson

Since the 1970s a new vehicle for the provision of housing assistance—the mixed-income, or inclusionary, project—has flowered in the United States. In a community of this sort, the developer and its government benefactors designate a fraction of the dwelling units, typically between 10 and 25 percent, as targets for the delivery of aid. Eligible households that successively occupy these particular units pay below-market rents, while the occupants of the other units do not.[1] In this chapter, I situate this innovation within the broader history of U.S. housing assistance policy and evaluate its merits. My central conclusion is that the mixed-income project approach, while superior to the traditional public housing model, is in almost all contexts distinctly inferior to the provision of portable housing vouchers to needy tenants. Although prior commentators have also touted the voucher approach, I enrich their analyses by addressing more fully the social consequences of various housing policies that might be used to economically integrate neighborhoods and buildings. It has traditionally been thought that enhancing socioeconomic diversity within a neighborhood has unalloyed social benefits. Many recent social-scientific studies present a more complex picture and weaken the case for government support of mixed-income projects.

The Basic Policy Choice: Projects or Vouchers

At the outset it is appropriate to articulate the fundamental issues of shelter assistance policy. All developed nations have adopted programs to enhance the

---

1. To simplify, all aided units are assumed to be rentals. In reality, many inclusionary programs also involve the sale of dwellings at below-market prices, subject to resale controls.

housing opportunities of at least some of their less prosperous renters. These programs take either of two basic forms. Historically, most have involved project-based subsidies that reduce rents in specific dwelling units that eligible households apply to occupy. Once admitted, a tenant's benefits typically are conditioned on continued residence in the assigned dwelling. A tenant who leaves a dwelling usually forfeits the subsidy benefits attached to it, and these benefits are transferred to a replacement tenant admitted from a waiting list. Prominent examples of such supply-side programs include HLM developments in France and Council Housing in Great Britain, which house about 17 percent and 20 percent, respectively, of the national population. In the United States, about 1 percent of households live in subsidized government-managed projects (public housing), and another 2 percent in subsidized projects that are privately owned.

The other basic policy alternative is tenant-based assistance, which operates on the demand side of the market for shelter. Demand-side aid typically takes the form of government grants of housing vouchers to eligible householders.[2] If and when a voucher recipient strikes a deal with a private landlord who owns a unit that is not overly luxurious and who is willing to participate in the program, the tenant pays under the chief U.S. program 30 percent of the household's monthly cash income toward the monthly rent, and the government pays the balance directly to the landlord. Housing vouchers typically are portable; a tenant who moves elsewhere can use the voucher to defray a portion of the rental obligation at the ensuing dwelling. Currently, about 2 percent of U.S. households hold housing vouchers.

In a given year, the number of newly built dwellings rarely exceeds 2 percent of the existing residential stock. However, because most new dwellings are higher in quality than the average existing dwelling and because Americans invest large sums to improve existing dwellings, the quality of U.S. housing stock has improved markedly over the course of the twentieth century (Schwartz 2006, 16–23). In France 8 percent of two-person households live in less than 50 square meters of floor space, and in Ireland 17 percent. The comparable figure for the United States is 2 percent (UN Economic Commission 2006, table A4). Most housing experts agree that the chief challenge today is not how to improve the quality of American dwellings, but how to make available dwellings more affordable to households on tight budgets (Currie 2006, 96–97).

A nation's decisions on the mixing of project-based and tenant-based housing aid profoundly affect the form of its metropolitan areas, the mobility of its households, and the welfare of its renters. Vouchers assist recipients in their shopping for dwellings in the mammoth stock of used housing. Project subsidies, by

---

2. A government may prefer to distribute housing vouchers instead of unrestricted cash for a variety of reasons, including concerns about the welfare of children. See Olsen (2003, 368–370). For purposes of analysis, I assume that the provision of in-kind housing benefits is justified and that it does not excessively foster dependency.

contrast, attempt to influence the design and distribution of units in the relatively tiny flow of newly constructed and substantially rehabilitated buildings.

A Short History of the Evolution of U.S. Housing Assistance Policy

A century ago the poor immigrants who flooded into cities such as New York and Chicago typically entered into leases with private landlords who owned tenements. Because these tenements commonly were crowded and unhealthful, many municipalities enacted fire, health, and building codes to regulate conditions within them. In that era, however, U.S. governments rarely appropriated funds for the provision of housing assistance of any kind. The meager aid that was provided typically was municipally financed. A city, for example, might do no more than open shelters for vagrants in police stations and work with local charitable organizations to establish almshouses and asylums for a few of its neediest residents.

Prior to 1937 the federal government seldom provided housing assistance in any form. A notable exception during World War I was the federal creation and funding of corporations charged to help house the workforces of shipbuilders involved in the war effort. The most renowned of these corporations' projects was Yorkship Village in Camden, New Jersey, a community of about 1,000 rental houses. This precedent was effectively repudiated in the early 1920s when the federal corporations auctioned off their developments.

By contrast, during the 1920s many European nations, with Denmark, The Netherlands, and Great Britain in the vanguard, warmly embraced the building of subsidized projects in numbers large enough to supplant much of the private supply of new rental housing. Leading American housing reformers of the period, such as Edith Wood (1923, 1931) and Catherine Bauer (1934), visited these developments, wrote glowingly about them, and chastised U.S. policy makers for continuing to rely so extensively on private enterprise to provide shelter for the masses. Because Wood and Bauer lacked confidence in market forces, they gave no thought to government provision of demand-side assistance to enable the same households to shop more successfully for existing dwellings.

THE RISE AND FALL OF PUBLIC HOUSING

The shock of the Great Depression transformed American politics and eventually prompted lawmakers to emulate the European approach. By the mid-1930s both the state of New York and various New Deal agencies had begun to dabble in the development of subsidized housing estates. Continuing massive unemployment in the construction industry fueled political support for a far more ambitious effort. In 1937 Congress passed the Wagner-Steagall Act, launching a national program to provide what came to be called public housing.[3] Under this program, the federal government provided large subsidies to induce local governments to establish housing authorities to build projects to house working-class families at deeply reduced rents.

By 1959 local housing authorities had completed 420,000 public housing units nationwide (Schwartz 2006, 102). Even at this early stage, however, urban commentators such as Jane Jacobs (1961, 321–337, 392–402) had begun to assail the program. The critics were especially scathing about the largest high-rise projects, such as the 4,500-unit Robert Taylor Homes in Chicago, which were concentrating poor families in a socially destructive environment.[4] As public housing for family households fell into disrepute, policy makers began searching for alternative ways to provide housing assistance to low-income renters.[5] One eventual reform, the HOPE VI program initiated in 1993, was itself designed to help housing authorities raze and redevelop distressed projects such as the Robert Taylor Homes.

PRIVATELY DEVELOPED SUBSIDIZED PROJECTS

Beginning in the late 1950s, federal housing assistance policy splintered into an ever-changing panoply of programs (soon supplemented by state and local initiatives) whose specifics are obscure to all but an intrepid band of specialists.[6] Most of these programs, in contrast to the public housing model, have sought to place assisted tenants in buildings owned and managed by private landlords, some of them nonprofit organizations. While the details of the programs have varied, all have been designed to funnel subsidy benefits to targeted low- and moderate-income households and to prevent project developers and owners from reaping undue profits. Housing wonks signal their mastery of their field by dropping the names of these programs (for example, 221(d)(3), Mitchell-Lama) into their conversations.

By 1999, 1.5 million units of housing had been produced under the various private owner, project-based subsidy programs that the federal government enacted between 1959 and 1984 (Bipartisan Millennial Housing Commission 2002, 87).[7] These programs generally were plagued by troublesome levels of inefficiency

---

3. See generally Oberlander and Newbrun (1999, 130–156).

4. For an overview, see Schill (1993). Many commentators have lauded the New York City Housing Authority's efforts to prevent these sorts of concentrations.

5. Production of public housing continued, but with an increasing portion of units designed for the elderly. The national stock of public housing peaked in 1993 at 1.4 million units, and by 2004 it had declined to 1.2 million units as a result of the razing of some of the most troubled projects (Schwartz 2006, 102).

6. For a detailed overview of the various programs, see Schwartz (2006). Olsen (2003, 370–386) and Weicher (1997, 3–8) provide brief and accessible introductions.

7. This figure excludes rural housing assistance.

and corruption. When stung with embarrassing news about a program, Congress typically would repeal it and enact a new variation. Beginning in the 1980s, in an important structural change, Congress shifted responsibility for the approval of developer applications for the funding of private subsidized projects from the federal department of Housing and Urban Development (HUD) to state housing finance agencies. Today these state entities are largely responsible for meting out low-interest mortgage loans and low-income housing tax credits (LIHTC), both of which are made possible, but also capped, by federal income tax statutes.

THE RISE, AND FLEETING TRIUMPH, OF HOUSING VOUCHERS

Disillusionment with traditional public housing also helped spur support for a far more radical policy innovation: the provision to low-income households of demand-side subsidies in the form of portable housing vouchers. During the New Deal debates, skeptics of public housing had commended vouchers as an alternative (Winnick 1995, 101–102). The idea resurfaced in 1968 when the Kaiser Committee, a blue-ribbon presidential panel, urged Congress to fund an expensive voucher experiment, primarily to investigate the extent to which the introduction of vouchers would inflate rents. Congress concurred, and the experiment was launched.[8] The early findings were auspicious, and in 1974 Congress enacted Section 8, the federal housing voucher program that, with minor amendment, has been in place ever since.[9] The federal government delegated responsibility for administering the vouchers largely to local housing authorities, the agencies initially established to build public housing projects. The number of households receiving Section 8 vouchers grew rapidly. The total had climbed to 0.6 million by 1980 and to 2.0 million by 2005 (Dawkins 2007, 74; Schwartz 2006, 153), making it the largest single branch of federal housing aid.

For a brief period, proponents of vouchers envisioned a more thorough-going triumph, namely the vouchering out of existing subsidized projects and the shifting of all prospective housing aid to vouchers. Between December 1994 (just after the Republicans unexpectedly won control of both houses of Congress) and 1996, prominent figures such as HUD Secretary Henry Cisneros and presidential candidate Robert Dole explored these possibilities (Weicher 1997, 1). Writing during this period, Louis Winnick, one of the deans of American housing policy, stated:

> It is beyond doubt, and has been for some years, that the battle has gone substantially and seemingly permanently in favor of a household-targeted strategy. A paradigmatic shift has occurred. Supply-siders, who reigned supreme during the life of government-assisted housing, are now relegated to the sidelines. (1995, 95)

---

8. Olsen (2003, 424–427) summarizes the many studies that emanated from this Experimental Housing Allowance Program.

9. In 1998 portable Section 8 benefits were formally denominated Housing Choice Vouchers.

But the tide toward vouchering out soon ebbed (Weicher 1997, 32–35). Since 1990, largely because of the influence of the Low-Income Housing Tax Credit (described below), the main increments in federal housing aid have been project-based (Olsen 2003, 375).

The Emergence of Mixed-Income Projects

My thesis, to reiterate, is that demand-side housing aid is superior to project-based assistance in almost all settings. Mixed-income affordable housing developments, the special focus of this chapter, share most of the shortcomings of other forms of project-based aid.

Mixed-income undertakings appear in a wide variety of forms.[10] For a development project to fall within the definition, government subsidies must be tied to only a fraction of the project's dwelling units, and these units must be made available only to households whose incomes fall below a certain ceiling. The emergence of the mixed-income model can be traced to a diverse set of legal and political developments that date from the 1960s, a decade in which the goal of greater social integration came to be central. In rough chronological order, these events included the following:

- The 1965 enactment of the short-lived federal leased housing program (Section 23) that authorized local housing authorities to lease specific units in private rental buildings.
- Adoption in the 1970s by a handful of wealthy suburbs of the first inclusionary zoning ordinances requiring a housing developer to sell or rent, at the developer's expense, 10 to 20 percent of a project's units to targeted households at reduced prices (Ellickson 1981).
- The 1983 New Jersey Supreme Court holding, in the nationally conspicuous *Mount Laurel II* litigation (*Southern Burlington County NAACP v. Township of Mount Laurel*, 456 A.2d 390, 445–450 [N.J. 1983]), that a developer's inclusion of 20 percent affordable units in a development would help satisfy a municipality's state constitutional obligations to poor New Jerseyans.
- Congressional authorization of the Low-Income Housing Tax Credit (LIHTC) program in 1986. As this program has matured, it has become private developers' chief source of project-based subsidies. By 2003 the LIHTC had generated a total of 1.2 million subsidized units, roughly equivalent to the entire existing stock of public housing (Schwartz 2006, 83).[11] To receive the hefty tax credits that the program provides, a

10. Valuable overviews of inclusionary programs include Porter (2004) and Schuetz, Meltzer, and Been (2007).

11. On the LIHTC generally, see Schwartz (2006, 83–100) and Weisbach (2006).

developer is required to set aside, currently for 30 years or more, at least 20 percent of project units as low-rent dwellings for qualifying households. Although the rules that govern LIHTCs allow for developments that are genuinely mixed-income, in practice more than 80 percent of LIHTC projects are entirely low-income (Schwartz 2006, 92).

- In 1991 congressional enactment of the previously mentioned HOPE VI, a program aimed at inducing local housing authorities to replace failed public housing projects with mixed-income developments (see Schwartz 2006, 117–123).
- The federal Quality Housing and Work Responsibility Act of 1998, which, in order to deconcentrate poverty, required local housing authorities to rent more public housing units to households whose incomes were not extremely low.

The concept of the mixed-income project has attracted much support. Many urban policy specialists, aware of the social pathologies associated with the early public housing projects, warm to the prospect of developments in which lower-class households mingle with middle-class role models. Developers of assisted projects understandably anticipate that a local government is more likely to grant approval when a proposed project is mixed-income rather than completely subsidized, partly because neighbors are less likely to object.

Several events of the past decade illustrate both the ebbing of interest in vouchers and also the rising popularity of the mixed-income project. In 1999 Congress established a Bipartisan Millennial Housing Commission. Ranking Republican and Democratic members of key congressional subcommittees were authorized to appoint all 22 commissioners. They selected mostly individuals who had been significantly involved, from either the private or public side, in the production of subsidized projects. The commission's final report, issued in 2002, generally supports the preservation of existing subsidized projects of all types and the construction of many more. The commission repeatedly endorses the mixing of income groups in both projects and neighborhoods. While the report also backs the expansion of voucher programs, it stresses the limitations of this approach. In a section entitled the "Shrinking Rental Supply," the commission estimates that the annual production of an additional 250,000 "affordable units" over the next two decades would be necessary to "close the gap" between the number of extremely low-income households and the number of rental housing units they could afford (Bipartisan Millennial Housing Commission 2002, 16–17). The commission proposes a new program of 100 percent capital subsidies to generate new projects in which extremely low-income households would be roughly 20 percent of the tenants (35–36).

The commission's proposal has helped inspire the introduction of bills to establish a national affordable housing trust fund to accomplish this aim. In October 2007 the *New York Times* editorialized in favor of federal legislation to finance the construction, rehabilitation, and preservation of 1.5 million units of affordable housing, all of it mixed-income, over the next 10 years (*New York Times* 2007). Less than a year later, Congress had taken a small step in this direction. The Housing and Economic Recovery Act of 2008 (Public Law 110–289, § 1338, 30 July 2008), enacted largely in response to the sharp jump in the rate of home foreclosures, includes a provision creating a housing trust fund, albeit one much smaller and more targeted toward aiding the very poor than the version that the *New York Times* had supported.

New York Mayor Michael Bloomberg's 10-year plan for the production of affordable housing in New York City between 2004 and 2013 further demonstrates the continuing political viability of project-based assistance (City of New York no date).[12] The plan contemplates both production of 92,000 new affordable housing units in the city and preservation efforts targeted at 73,000 of the city's 250,000 subsidized units presently in private projects. Mayor Bloomberg calls this "the largest municipal affordable housing effort in the nation's history." Some long-standing New York City programs, such as 421-a property tax abatements, have been specifically aimed at fostering mixed-income developments.

The Case for the Superiority of Housing Vouchers

Like Mayor Bloomberg and the members of the Millennial Commission, many urban experts view project-based subsidies as an essential component of housing assistance. By contrast, most housing economists who have addressed the issue assert that, as a general matter, portable tenant-based subsidies are markedly more efficient and fair than project-based subsidies.[13] Some of them have urged governments to refrain from authorizing the construction of more assisted projects and to voucher out existing ones. Of the economists who have argued in this vein, Edgar Olsen (2003, 427–437; 2006) and John Weicher (1990; 1997, 12–31) are particularly notable for their lucidity and persistence.[14] Compared to vouchers, project-based subsidies have a variety of shortcomings, some well-ventilated in the literature, others not.

---

12. The state and city of New York have long had a distinctive and unusually ambitious array of housing assistance programs (Ellen and O'Flaherty 2003).

13. Despite the general superiority of vouchers, project subsidies may be advisable in a narrow set of circumstances, such as to provide supportive-care facilities for the homeless (Currie 2006, 108–109) and to house workers at a remote and secret military facility.

14. Other pro-voucher economists include, in rough chronological order of their contributions, Ira Lowry, Louis Winnick, Stephen Mayo, Stephen Malpezzi, and Janet Currie (2006, 90–112). Legal scholars who have touted the superiority of vouchers include Stephen Kinnaird (1994), Michael Schill (1993), and David Weisbach (2006).

THE INEFFICIENCIES OF PROJECT-BASED AID

Consider a hypothetical mixed-income project, Evergreen Woods, that a developer proposes to build at a suburban site. The development will consist of several multifamily structures comprising a total of 50 uniformly sized and equipped two-bedroom units.[15] The developer anticipates being able to rent the market-rate units at $1,500 per month. As a condition for obtaining the suburban government's approval, the developer has agreed to rent 10 specific units (out of the total of 50) to tenants with incomes below a certain ceiling. These tenants will pay 30 percent of their income toward rent. The average monthly income of these subsidized tenants is expected to be $2,000 (well below the incomes of most of the actual beneficiaries of inclusionary units). The developer thus will collect, per inclusionary unit, an average of $600 of rent per month. To the developer, this is the rough equivalent of a tax of $900 per month per affordable unit. The public benefits of the program, however, are likely to be far smaller.

Increased Production Costs   Most studies of supply costs have focused on projects in which all units are subsidized, not just some as at Evergreen Woods. Housing economists have consistently found that, all else equal, provision of housing units in subsidized projects, whether publicly or privately sponsored, costs significantly more than provision of unsubsidized units.[16] Developers and funding governments typically spend an average of about $1.60 (although perhaps as little as $1.20) to produce $1.00 of rental value (which, as we shall soon see, is itself likely to exceed the value to the occupying tenant). By contrast, a government need spend only about $1.10 to transfer $1.00 in voucher aid to a tenant.

The development of a subsidized project inherently requires extra time and effort from both the developer and public officials. In most cases, the developer seeks government subsidies and must apply to one or more government agencies to get them. Especially since the advent of the LIHTC in 1986, developers commonly stack different project-based subsidies on top of one another, adding more complexity to application processes. The LIHTC, currently the core project-subsidy financing mechanism, is itself fraught with transaction costs. A developer who is awarded LIHTCs usually sells the tax credits at a discount to a syndica-

---

15. Many governments with inclusionary programs authorize developers to downgrade, perhaps even drastically, the interior amenities of inclusionary units. To simplify the exposition, the developer of Evergreen Woods is assumed to not have this option.

16. See Mayo (1986) and Olsen (2003, 394–399) for summarizing studies. A number of professional housers and planners have challenged the economists' consensus. For a review of the works of these dissenters, see Deng (2005, 472–477). Applying her own methodology, Deng concludes that vouchers indeed are cheaper than LIHTC projects in most metropolitan areas, but perhaps not in all. Her methodology does not take into account the lock-in effects of project-based housing subsidies, one of the basic sources of their inefficiency.

tor, who then sells interests in a pool of credits to third-party investors. Syndicators charge developers about 6 to 10 percent for this service (Schwartz 2006, 85–87). In addition, news that a developer is proposing a subsidized project, even a partial one, is likely to spark an unusual amount of concern on the part of homeowners located near the proposed site. As a result, a developer typically must spend extra time and effort to obtain land use permits from the local government. It is plausible (although the issue appears not to have been investigated) that these various pursuits for permits are associated with efficiencies of scale. If so, when a subsidized project resembles Evergreen Woods, where only 20 percent of the dwellings are to be set aside as affordable, the incremental private and public processing costs per subsidized unit can be expected to be unusually high. If government housing aid were provided solely through vouchers, many of these extra costs of securing permits would be avoided.

Waste from rent-seeking also tends to be greater under project-subsidy programs. For example, state housing finance agencies receive about three times more applications for LIHTCs than they can grant (Olsen 2003, 397). To improve their prospects for obtaining approvals, developers may invest in political connections, a practice that dissipates some of the rents being sought and also corrupts the electoral process.

Slack Arising from the Absence of Market Discipline   The developer's incentive to efficiently produce and maintain the 10 subsidized units at Evergreen Woods would plummet as soon as those units had been earmarked as sites for aid. Because of the generosity of the rent discounts, the developer knows that the queue will be long and that finding tenants for the inclusionary units will be a snap. During construction, the developer's executives therefore may be tempted to cut corners—for example, to tell their superintendents to only casually supervise the work of the subcontractor hired to paint the interiors of those units. Similarly, once tenants have moved into the subsidized dwellings, the developer/owner has less incentive to be attentive to their complaints, say about the crankiness of the heating system. Given the bargain rent, a subsidized tenant cannot credibly threaten to vacate to protest the owner's failure to make cost-justified repairs. Even if the tenant did vacate, the developer could readily find a replacement from the queue. As John Weicher (1997, 6) elegantly puts it, the principal party that the developer of a subsidized project must please is not the tenant but the government agency that supervises the program.

When housing aid takes the form of vouchers, these perverse incentives are much reduced, if not eliminated altogether. Suppose a tenant with a portable $900 per month housing voucher had rented an ordinary $1,500 per month unit at Evergreen Woods. Because this tenant could credibly threaten to leave and might be hard to replace, the developer would have reason to worry about the quality of the initial interior paint job and about the building manager's attentiveness to the tenant's complaints about the heating system. Vouchers, unlike project-based subsidies, thus impose a market discipline that helps pressure building owners to implement maintenance measures that are cost-justified.

Mismatches Between Assisted Households and Housing Units   A project-based subsidy program is likely to be far inferior to a voucher program in placing assisted tenants in dwelling units whose locations and designs are suited to their preferences.[17] Recall the initial assumption that each of the households that applies for one of the 10 subsidized two-bedroom units in Evergreen Woods earns a fixed income of $2,000 per month and thus would pay rent of $600 per month if selected by lottery or queue. Further assume that half of the applicants are high-valuing tenants who value occupancy of one of these dwellings at $1,400 per month, while the other half are low-valuing tenants who regard them as worth only $700 per month. (Given their budget constraints, it is unlikely that any of the applicants would bid $1,500 to live at Evergreen Woods.)[18] A tenant might be low-valuing because of reservations, for example, about the location of Evergreen Woods, the layout of its units, or the suitability of a two-bedroom unit for the tenant's household as the tenant expects it to evolve. If selected, a high-valuing tenant who moved into the development would garner $800 per month in consumer surplus, whereas a low-valuing tenant would garner $100 per month. If a tenant were empowered to transfer occupancy rights in a subsidized unit to another eligible household, one would expect a low-valuing tenant who had been awarded a unit to transfer it to a high-valuing tenant, with the two parties somehow divvying up the $700 per month in increased surplus. The regulations that govern project-subsidy programs, however, almost invariably forbid a tenant from transferring occupancy rights. This is necessary to prevent a recipient household from converting the discounted value of the housing subsidy to a lump sum of cash, an act that would frustrate the program designers' paternalistic aim of inducing program beneficiaries to consume more housing rather than other goods and services.

This stylized example points up the mismatches between tenants and housing units that are likely to occur under any sort of project-subsidy program. Given the assumptions, if the households selected to live in inclusionary units at Evergreen Woods were to be randomly chosen, as many as half of them might be low-valuing tenants. Although low-valuing tenants might be less likely to move in if accepted, they still would have an incentive to do so, especially if there were many names on the application lists for projects. Whenever a low-valuing

---

17. The housing economists who criticize project-based subsidies seldom stress this shortcoming. But compare Glaeser and Luttmer (2003), who identify the mismatch problem as an additional and underacknowledged inefficiency of rent controls.

18. These valuations of alternative locations are those that tenants would hypothetically assign after they had been designated beneficiaries of $600 per month rents at Evergreen Woods.

rather than a high-valuing tenant moves in, there is a deadweight loss of $700 per month in consumer surplus.[19]

In addition, as the years pass, aggregate deadweight losses are likely to increase. Although some households increasingly value a dwelling as they put down roots in it, the passage of time more typically has the opposite effect.[20] In a given year, about one-third of U.S. tenant households move to new quarters, primarily to accommodate changes in either their employment situation or the composition of their household (U.S. Department of Commerce 2003, table 4-11).[21] Suppose that one of the long-term subsidized tenants at Evergreen Woods is a divorcee who originally moved in when her child was an infant. Recently, she has taken a new job that requires a lengthy commute. She also would like to invite her infirm and lonely father to move in with her, but she doesn't think a two-bedroom unit is big enough to accommodate that arrangement. Once a high-valuing tenant at Evergreen Woods, she has become a low-valuing one. If she were to have had the benefit of a $900 per month housing voucher, she would have moved long ago to another dwelling more suited to her altered life circumstances. In sum, project-based housing subsidies tend to have lock-in effects that are likely to worsen as a project ages. These impair the functioning of labor markets and also hamper tenants' abilities to exploit new social opportunities.[22]

The Effects of Alternative Housing Assistance Strategies on Neighborhoods
Most tenants understandably prefer to be free of arrangements that lock them into particular housing units. For example, in a survey of New Orleans public

---

19. Between 1965 and 1979, the headiest era for empirical research on housing assistance policy, a number of economists published studies, mostly of public housing, that attempted to measure the equivalent variation. This is the ratio between the assisted tenants' actual mean benefits (in the example used in the text, $800 per month for a high-valuing tenant and $100 per month for a low-valuing one), and the mean nominal subsidy ($900/month in the example). The reported ratios ranged from 0.61 to 0.92. See Olsen (2003, 416–417).

20. See Glaeser and Luttmer 2003, 1042–1043, who found that the apartments of long-term rent-controlled tenants are especially misallocated.

21. Perhaps partly because of differences in the housing policies of the two nations, Americans move at twice the annual rate of the British (Long, Turner, and Urton 1988, 635).

22. There is much evidence that these sorts of lock-ins exist. In 2004, 52 percent of public housing tenants had been in their present units for five years or more, compared to 36 percent of Section 8 tenants (Schwartz 2006, 107, 159; see also McGough 1997, 10–11). Because the rents of 70 percent of New York City tenants are regulated by either rent control or project-subsidy regulations, tenants there are relatively immobile. From 1990 to 2000, 35 percent of the city's tenants remained in the same dwellings, compared to 17 percent of Chicago's (Ellen and O'Flaherty 2003, tables 7.1, 7.11). Ellen and O'Flaherty speculate that the New York City policies that lock in tenants might be motivated to augment social capital and generate positive production externalities (34–43). Hardman and Ioannides (1999) provide a theoretical discussion of the dynamics of lock-ins.

housing tenants displaced by Hurricane Katrina, respondents were almost twice as likely to state that they would prefer to receive a housing voucher than to return to their former project (*Housing and Community Development Reporter* 2008, 201). Viewed from a broader social perspective, however, a housing lock-in is less unambiguously bad because lock-ins may generate beneficial social externalities. A locked-in tenant has valuable property rights in a particular dwelling and therefore, like one of William Fischel's "homevoters" (2001), has a greater incentive to be active in local politics. This can be presumed to be a socially desirable result (Ellen and O'Flaherty 2003, 40). A locked-in tenant also can more credibly commit to an employer that she is not a fly-by-night worker, which may induce the employer, for example, to invest more in training her (cf. Munch, Rosholm, and Svarer 2008). Adolescents tend to suffer from repeated changes of residence (Adam and Chase-Lansdale 2002), an effect some parents may inadequately weigh. More generally, in a neighborhood where tenants move less often, they possibly may amass more neighborhood social capital and thereby become more trustworthy in their dealings with one another.[23]

The issue is complex, however, because housing lock-ins undoubtedly also generate some offsetting negative social externalities, particularly by worsening landlord-tenant relations (Ellickson 2008, 123–127). When the threat of unilateral exit by either party hangs over a residential landlord-tenant relationship, both sides have a strong incentive to cooperate with one another. Under these circumstances, even arm's-length landlord-tenant relations tend to be comfortable, at least during the midgame of the lease. However, when tenants and landlords are locked in because of either project-based aid or rent controls, the dynamic changes. Landlords then tend to be relatively unresponsive to tenant complaints, and tenants have less reason to act civilly toward landlords. In New York City, where both project subsidies and rent controls have led to an extraordinary level of lock-ins, there is a special housing court that averages 300,000 new cases per year (New York State Unified Court no date), and the media periodically describe multiyear wars between particular landlords and tenants (see, for example, Stodghill 2006). In sum, tenant lock-ins give rise to both social costs and social benefits, but little is presently known about their magnitude.

Some commentators also anticipate that the construction of a subsidized housing project will generate positive externalities that will foster neighborhood rejuvenation. While the effects of housing vouchers on a cityscape are diffuse, a new mixed-income housing project might be deliberately placed at a site where it would function as a spark that inspires private investment in nearby real estate. At least in some contexts, the advent of a subsidized project does generate positive externalities that boost the value of neighboring properties (Ellen et al. 2007; Schwartz et al. 2006). For several reasons, however, this fact does not by itself

---

23. Compare Margaret Radin's (1986) defense of rent control as a means of protecting social ties within a community.

justify government subsidies to housing projects. First, neighborhood renewal commonly is a zero-sum game; that is, the benefits of inserting a project at a given location are entirely offset by the costs of less housing investment, caused by crowding-out effects, elsewhere. Second, a city has many other tools for promoting neighborhood renewal, including the enhancement of streetscapes and other physical infrastructure, grants for facade improvements, concentrated code enforcement, and the building of schools, libraries, and other public edifices. In light of the availability of these other instruments of neighborhood revitalization, why should policy makers select the blunt instrument of the subsidized housing project, given its other inherent flaws?

THE RELATIVE UNFAIRNESS OF PROJECT-BASED AID

Those who favor jettisoning project-based aid in favor of portable vouchers also marshal a potent array of fairness arguments. They assert that tenant-based aid can be more easily delivered in a fashion that treats like persons alike (the goal of horizontal equity) and that funnels benefits to the most impoverished households (the goal of vertical equity).

Horizontal Equity   In the United States a housing subsidy is the only major form of means-tested aid that is not made available as an entitlement to a household that satisfies the stated criteria for eligibility. Only about 30 percent of renters with incomes below the poverty line benefit from federal housing aid (Olsen 2003, 394). By contrast, no person who is eligible, for example, for food stamps or disability benefits is denied aid on the ground that Congress has not appropriated sufficient funds. The high cost of housing subsidies compared to most other forms of means-tested aid is a primary reason that housing subsidies are not entitlements. The federal government incurs costs of roughly $500 per month for each tenant household that it assists.[24]

The heads of households who benefit from housing assistance are the ones who have been relatively adroit or lucky in navigating the queues and lotteries that housing agencies and developers employ to mete out aid among the surfeit of applicants. The Section 8 voucher program generates some of the longest queues. In 1999 the Los Angeles Housing Authority, which provides portable vouchers to around 50,000 households, had 342,000 households on its waiting list (Olsen 2003, 394n). Many project-subsidy programs also attract far more people than can be served. When news spreads that a private project in a prime location will include some affordable units, the list of applicants may exceed the number of available units by a multiple of 100 (Toy 2008). And little wonder: a *New York Times* article reported that a 32-year-old aspiring novelist won a lottery that entitled him to pay $14,000 in cash (and a monthly maintenance payment of $295) to purchase a studio co-op apartment in a neighborhood of Manhattan

---

24. Computed from U.S. General Accounting Office (2001, 1).

where a like unit would sell on the market for perhaps 20 times that sale price (Dominus 2008).[25] The fact that all other major welfare programs are designed to avoid these sorts of haphazard outcomes points up the gravity of the horizontal inequity of all branches of housing assistance.

Janet Currie (2006, 94) pinpoints the lottery aspect of housing assistance as its principal defect. To address this problem, and that of vertical equity as well, Edgar Olsen has recommended converting all current federal spending on project assistance to housing vouchers to which every eligible needy household would be entitled without having to wait in a queue (Olsen 2003, 428–429; 2006, 109–112). In the absence of an increase in total federal appropriations, this reform would require a substantial reduction in the amount of housing aid per recipient from the current level of about $500 per month.

Vertical Equity   Most analysts urge that means-tested transfers be directed primarily to the poorest of poor, the group most likely to be living in substandard housing and to be burdened by rent obligations. Many means-tested benefits are so targeted. To qualify for food stamps, for example, a household's income must be less than 130 percent of the federal poverty line (Currie 2006, 64). Much federal housing assistance, by contrast, is conferred on households with considerably higher incomes (Olsen 2003, 393).

Judged by the criterion of vertical equity, vouchers are by far the best of the current federal housing aids, partly because they are the easiest to target. In 1998, Congress required local housing authorities to award at least 75 percent of vouchers to households whose incomes were below 30 percent of the median income in the metropolitan area, a ceiling roughly equal to the official poverty line (Olsen 2003, 379n).[26] Partly to avoid concentrations of poverty in public housing projects, the same statute specifies that only 40 percent of the units in subsidized projects have to be directed toward these households. In 2005, 78 percent of housing voucher holders did have incomes below 30 percent of the area median (Dawkins 2007, 76).

When measured by the vertical equity yardstick, most mixed-income affordable housing programs come out particularly poorly. The law governing LIHTC projects makes all tenants with incomes under 50 percent of the area median eligible for aid, and many LIHTC projects are aimed even higher (Muralidhara 2006).[27] Scholars who have evaluated inclusionary efforts in New Jersey, which were mostly prompted by the *Mount Laurel* decisions and the state's Fair Housing Act, have found less social integration than proponents of these efforts had

---

25. The co-op apartment was located in a building on 88th Street near Third Avenue. See generally Toy (2008).

26. Quality Housing and Work Responsibility Act of 1998, Pub. L. No. 105-276.

27. By stacking other subsidies on top of the tax credits, however, the developer of an LIHTC project may be able to serve households with incomes near the poverty line.

hoped for. Most of the beneficiaries of the suburban New Jersey projects were themselves suburbanites, principally elderly white women. Notably few were African American (Wish and Eisdorfer 1997, 1302–1305).[28]

In other jurisdictions, the distributive effects of inclusionary zoning programs are similarly suspect. A large majority of the local governments in the San Francisco Bay Area have adopted inclusionary programs, and so have many in the Boston and Washington, DC, areas (Scheutz, Meltzer, and Been 2007, 20). Most agencies that administer these programs release little or no information about the characteristics of the households that occupy their subsidized inclusionary units. It is nonetheless plain that the vast majority of the beneficiaries have incomes far above the average incomes of Section 8 voucher holders (most of whom, again, take in less than 30 percent of area median income). According to Schuetz, Meltzer, and Been (2007), many suburban programs make at least some inclusionary units available to households with incomes up to 120 percent of the area median, and almost all programs, to those with incomes up to 80 percent of that amount.[29]

Montgomery County, Maryland, has by far the largest and one of the most transparent of the nation's local inclusionary programs.[30] Between the program's start in 1973 and 2007, the county exacted over 12,000 inclusionary housing units from developers. Thirty percent of the exacted units were rentals, and the balance were for-sale units. During the first three decades of its program, Montgomery County controlled the prices of its inclusionary units only for a short period, sometimes as little as five or ten years. By 2002 at least one-third of the exacted units had already been freed from price controls and were no longer providing subsidized accommodations (Trombka et al. 2004, 6–1, 7–1).[31]

Montgomery County's inclusionary program is structured to deliver inclusionary units to households whose incomes are well above the poverty line when

---

28. See also Porter (2004, 244–245), who states that inclusionary programs do little to relocate poor and minority households from inner cities to suburbs.

29. Housing regulations typically define households in these respective groups as "moderate-income" and "low-income."

30. Information about the Montgomery County program can be obtained at http://www .montgomerycountymd.gov/dhctmpl.asp?url=/content/DHCA/housing/housing_P/mpdu.asp. Rubin and Trombka (2007) provide an overview.

31. Most of the county's for-sale inclusionary units remain in its affordable stock (Porter 2004, 238). Since 1989, even after the expiration of the control period, the county has exacted half of an owner's excess proceeds from a sale, a policy that discourages sales. In addition, the county has a right of first refusal at the time of sale. The county's public housing agency has purchased 1,600 of the for-sale units over the years and has then rented them to households with incomes below 50 percent of area median income. Because the county could empower its public housing agency to purchase scattered-site units in noninclusionary developments, I credit this tilt toward greater vertical equity to the public housing agency's purchasing program, not to the county's inclusionary zoning program as such.

they first move in. In 2008, for example, a household of three with annual income of up to $58,000 was eligible to occupy a subsidized rental unit. The county establishes a fixed rent (or sale price) for each inclusionary unit rather than requiring, for example, that a household pay 30 percent of its income toward housing costs. The formulas used by the county to determine the reduced rents and sale prices assure that subsidies are not deep enough to make the units affordable by the truly needy. For example, in 2008 the developer of an inclusionary two-bedroom unit in a garden apartment might be entitled to charge a household of three a rent of $1,200 per month (not including utilities).[32] A Montgomery County report issued in 2007 confirms that its inclusionary program primarily serves households whose incomes at time of entry are between 60 and 70 percent of the area median (Rubin and Trombka 2007, 5), that is, just below the 70 percent income ceiling for eligibility. New beneficiaries in 2008 thus would mostly have annual incomes in the $60,000 to $70,000 range.[33] Moreover, the county does not ask a benefited household to report changes in income after it moves into an inclusionary unit. The rents that the developer/owner is permitted to charge in subsequent years are set according to a formula that is entirely based on other variables. Some long-term occupants of Montgomery County inclusionary units are therefore virtually certain to have annual incomes in excess of $100,000. Indeed, between 2005 and 2007, because of quirks in the design of the county's program, a handful of developers were entitled to sell inclusionary units at the controlled price to purchasers of any income (Rubin and Trombka 2007, 48–49).

According to one Montgomery County report, 95 percent of the recipients of its inclusionary units already lived in the county, and all but one of the remaining recipients worked there (Porter 2004, 243). The county periodically releases data on the racial distribution of the latest beneficiaries of its inclusionary program. Most units have gone to members of the county's racial minority groups. In the years for which data are available, Asian Americans, who make up 11 percent of the county's population, have received an average of 40 percent of the units (Porter 2004, 243; Roisman 2001, 79 n81).

Many of the relevant interest groups want an inclusionary zoning program to have the middle-class tilt that characterizes Montgomery County's. Developers who are forced to accept tenants prefer having those who are likely to be both steady in their rent payments and socially acceptable to the households occupying unsubsidized units in the development. Middle-income people who own homes near a proposed inclusionary project also are less likely to object. In a prosperous suburb such as Montgomery County, taxpayers and members of municipal labor unions may warm to a developer-financed program that confers

---

32. Calculated according to formulas in Montgomery County Code § 25A.00.02.02 & .05.

33. In 2008 HUD's official estimate of the median annual income of a family in the Washington, DC, PMSA was $99,000 (http://www.huduser.org/datasets/il/FY2008index_mfi.html).

inclusionary units on its schoolteachers, librarians, and other college-educated professionals who, except for their modest incomes, are solidly middle class.

Methods of Promoting the Economic Integration of Neighborhoods

By definition, mixed-income housing programs are designed to enhance residential integration among households of varying incomes. Given the relative poverty of many African Americans and Hispanic Americans, efforts to promote economic integration can also be expected to contribute to greater racial integration.[34] Because the United States is a highly diverse nation, Americans unquestionably have reason to encourage bridging across social groups that might otherwise be overly isolated from one another. The analysis in this section accepts the premise that economic integration of neighborhoods is a goal of transcendent importance, but concludes that, from what we now know, the mixed-income project model is a mediocre instrument for pursuing that goal. The next section addresses the more fundamental question of whether, in the design of housing assistance policies, the greater economic integration of neighborhoods should be regarded as the summum bonum.

ARE PROJECTS PROMISING MICROCOSMS FOR ECONOMIC INTEGRATION?

A mixed-income affordable project, such as the hypothetical Evergreen Woods, is designed to promote greater economic (and perhaps racial) integration at the level of the residential block. It is not evident that a geographic space this small is a promising arena for the pursuit of this goal. In *Bowling Alone* (2000, 22–24), Robert Putnam famously distinguishes between two types of valuable social capital. Bonding social capital promotes trust and cooperation among the members of a social subgroup, while bridging social capital strengthens ties between members of different social subgroups. Over the course of a day, most individuals rotate through a variety of different (but commonly overlapping) social milieus in which both bonding and bridging may be achievable. For a child, the residential block is likely to be a less important social microcosm than the household and the school. For an adult, workmates, family, and friends are likely to be more important than neighbors. Nonetheless, blocks unquestionably can be sites for the nurturing of both bonding and bridging social ties.

There is evidence that in some social contexts the enhancement of opportunities for bridging among members of different social groups simultaneously diminishes internal bonding among members of an individual group (Putnam

---

34. Partly because of statutory and constitutional constraints, all housing assistance programs are officially race-blind. My analysis assumes that they indeed are administered in race-blind fashion.

2007). If so, those who want to strengthen social capital in the aggregate face a dilemma. Bonding social capital unquestionably is valuable at the block level because it helps enable neighbors, for example, to provide mutual aid and to informally police against nuisance behavior. Enhanced economic integration at the block level, although it might enhance bridging social capital, possibly might impair this sort of inter-neighbor cooperation.[35]

The choice of an optimal social milieu for the pursuit of economic integration therefore is a difficult one. The Supreme Court of New Jersey, in its two famous *Mount Laurel* decisions, flip-flopped on this exact question. The author of *Mount Laurel I* (*Southern Burlington County NAACP v. Township of Mount Laurel*, 336 A.2d 713 [N.J. 1975]) was Justice Frederick Hall, an archfoe of exclusionary zoning. Justice Hall's opinion, however, only required municipalities to allow for an appropriate variety of housing at some locations within their boundaries and explicitly blessed the use of zoning to set aside some neighborhoods as exclusive. To oversimplify, Justice Hall's opinion sought to promote economic integration at the geographic level of the local public high school, not that of the block. Eight years later, in *Mount Laurel II*, a revamped Supreme Court of New Jersey reversed course and prodded municipalities to promote the provision of inclusionary housing units within each new housing development.

Much remains to be learned about the trade-offs between bonding and bridging social capital in different social milieus. From what is now known, there are grounds for skepticism about the capacity of a mixed-income housing project to enhance the aggregate stock of social capital. The authors of the most-cited empirical study on the subject conclude that "the level of interaction between the income groups in the [mixed-income] projects appears to be insignificant" (Brophy and Smith 1997, 25). Other housing experts have cautioned that the mixed-income model rests on sociological assumptions that may not be valid.[36] In addition, sociological theory suggests that lower-income households themselves might dislike the social environment of an inclusionary development. Individuals tend to care a lot about their relative status in a given social setting (Frank 1987). Whatever the other benefits of living in Evergreen Woods, the adults and children in the 10 affordable units (assuming they would socialize with their neighbors)

---

35. In theory, positive and negative social consequences should be at least partially capitalized into housing prices. To my knowledge, there have been no published studies of whether inclusionary units in a mixed-income development affect the market values of the same development's unsubsidized units. Numerous researchers, however, have striven to measure the effects of the construction of a subsidized housing project or the entry of Section 8 tenants on property values in a neighborhood. See Galster (2004) for a review, and Ellen et al. (2007).

36. Hendrickson (2002, 70–81), after reviewing the evidence, urges HUD to concentrate on integrating neighborhoods, not particular projects. Schwartz (2006, 261–267) concludes (at 266) that "the limited research to date on mixed-income housing has yet to show that the presence of higher income neighbors by itself improves the economic or social condition of low-income families (e.g., by providing role models, job leads)."

might be frustrated by their difficulty in keeping up with the Joneses who occupy the other 40 units.

THE POTENTIAL OF VOUCHERS AS AN INSTRUMENT OF NEIGHBORHOOD ECONOMIC INTEGRATION

Assuming that the greater economic integration of neighborhoods is indeed an overriding policy objective, what housing assistance policies would best promote this end? For many observers (such as DeFilippis and Wyly 2008; Schwartz 2006, 175), the main shortcoming of Section 8 vouchers is that they do not do enough to enhance the racial integration of neighborhoods. Many users of housing vouchers live in areas where people like themselves predominate. For example, a poor black tenant who holds a housing voucher commonly ends up renting in a largely poor, largely black neighborhood. Nonetheless, numerous researchers have found that, as a general matter, housing vouchers have done more than project-based subsidies to enhance the economic integration of neighborhoods. A voucher holder is far less likely than a resident of public housing and somewhat less likely than a resident of a privately owned subsidized project to live in a neighborhood with a high rate of poverty (Deng 2007; Kling, Liebman, and Katz 2007, 87–88; Newman and Schnare 1997; Olsen 2003, 393, 407–411; Schwartz 2006, 160–166; but compare DeFilippis and Wyly 2008).[37] When subsidized tenants are asked whether their current neighborhood is better or worse than their previous one, 45 percent of voucher holders answer better and 12 percent answer worse, whereas, in both public and private subsidized projects, the number of tenants answering worse exceeds the number answering better (McGough 1997, 30). In most metropolitan areas, vouchers appear also to have done more than LIHTC projects to promote neighborhood racial integration (Deng 2007, 27–28).

The studies just cited, however, mainly examined the integrative effects of projects in which all units, not just some, were subsidized. Mixed-income projects conceivably could foster economic integration better than housing vouchers can, especially at the block level. The available evidence on this important question, however, is less favorable to the mixed-income project than one might expect. As noted, the recipients of many inclusionary housing units are themselves middle-class suburbanites. And in instances where there is actual economic integration, an advantage of vouchers is that they are not as likely as projects, even mixed-income projects, to stigmatize subsidized tenants in a manner that impairs the development of bridging relationships between members of different income groups. Neighbors commonly know when a new development encompasses inclusionary units, and the residents of a mixed-income development may learn

---

37. Federal law entitles a voucher holder to lease a rental unit outside the boundaries of the jurisdiction that granted the voucher. This portability rule gives rise to complications and, in some instances, resistance on the part of suburban jurisdictions (Feins et al. 1996).

which units have subsidies tied to them. Vouchers are potentially more discreet. If both the landlord and the tenant avoid spilling the beans, the holder of a housing voucher can move into a more prosperous neighborhood incognito. The relative invisibility of a voucher promises to help normalize a voucher holder's future relationships with neighbors.

If the economic integration of neighborhoods is the paramount social objective, lawmakers could shape the rules governing existing forms of housing assistance with this goal in mind. Congress no doubt would hear howls of protest if it were to consider mandating that all new public housing or LIHTC projects be scattered in other than poor neighborhoods. Because vouchers are relatively invisible, however, Section 8 is the more potent instrument for the affirmative promotion of economic integration. Many local housing authorities already provide counseling services to help voucher holders find apartments. Some states forbid a landlord from discriminating against a tenant on the basis of the tenant's sources of income. More pointedly, to encourage a poor voucher holder to choose to live in a more prosperous neighborhood, Congress could adjust the formulas for calculating voucher benefits so as to sweeten the financial rewards of both the landlord and the voucher holder whose combined efforts had brought about this sort of outcome.

The Waning of Confidence in the Social Benefits of Neighborhood Economic Integration

Urban commentators have widely assumed that, all else equal, it is highly disadvantageous for poor adults and children to reside in a poor neighborhood. This premise underpins many of the integrationist visions that flowered in the 1960s and eventually inspired, among many other by-products, the mixed-income housing model.[38] Prominent sociologists closely associated with this traditional view include William Julius Wilson (1987) and, more recently, Robert Sampson.[39] A variety of causal mechanisms are thought to be at work (see generally Ellen and Turner 2003). For example, an adult who resides in a poor neighborhood may be less likely to hear of job opportunities through informal social networks. A child might suffer from a relative paucity of both adult role models and helpful peers at local public schools. The traditional view has inspired support for policies to "dismantle the ghetto" (Massey and Denton 1993, 15, 218) and to economically integrate subsidized housing projects previously occupied only by

---

38. For an overview of issues of neighborhood integration, see Goetz (2003).

39. See, for example, Sampson, Sharkey, and Raudenbush (2008). This study, unlike Moving to Opportunity studies, does not control for the possibility that households that move out of a neighborhood with concentrated poverty differ from households that remain.

the very poor.[40] Initial studies of the effects of the Gautreaux program in Chicago appeared to confirm that moving to a more prosperous neighborhood significantly improves a child's schooling and employment outcomes (Rubinowitz and Rosenbaum 2000).[41]

Most housing policy specialists (for example, Schill 1993) understandably seek to end the ghettoization of poor households in large subsidized projects.[42] The case for dismantling an entire poor neighborhood, however, is hardly so clear. Recently published studies have begun to destabilize the former consensus that a poor adult or child is significantly disadvantaged by residing among other poor people. These studies suggest that the net social benefits of the economic and racial integration of neighborhoods, while probably still positive, are not as large as previously thought.

The Moving to Opportunity (MTO) studies (summarized in Kling, Liebman, and Katz 2007) have been the most influential, largely because of the magnitude of the MTO experiment and the high quality of the research design.[43] The households participating in MTO were volunteers who at the outset had resided in public housing projects in five large cities. Most were both poor and minority. These households were randomly divided into three groups: a control group whose members remained in the projects; a constrained housing voucher group who could use the vouchers only in a low-poverty neighborhood; and an unconstrained housing voucher group who were not limited by neighborhood. Most households in the last group ended up living in mostly poor, mostly minority neighborhoods. Those in the constrained voucher group, the primary focus of the experiment, mostly chose to move to relatively prosperous neighborhoods that also were predominantly minority. Four to seven years later, researchers assessed the outcomes for teenagers and adults. According to the traditional view, the outcomes of children in the constrained voucher group—the beneficiaries of neighborhood economic integration—should have been significantly superior to the outcomes for the children in the other two groups. This proved to be

---

40. The pertinent literature primarily focuses on the integration of entire neighborhoods, not of individual blocks (what a mixed-income project seeks to integrate). Obviously, the social dynamics of neighborhoods and blocks may differ.

41. For concerns about the methodologies used in the Gautreaux studies, see Currie (2006, 103–104) and Schwartz (2006, 169–170).

42. But compare Jacob (2004), who found that living in a high-rise public housing project does not by itself impair the educational outcomes of children.

43. The first-published MTO studies reported greater positive benefits from economic integration (Goering and Feins 2003). In particular, Ludwig, Duncan, and Ladd (2003) found that poor children aged five to twelve in Baltimore had better educational outcomes when their parents moved them to higher-income neighborhoods. Sanbonmatsu, Kling, and Duncan (2006), by contrast, conclude that MTO data indicate that neighborhood effects on educational outcomes are small.

true for teenage girls. For teenage boys, however, living in a more prosperous neighborhood generally turned out to be disadvantageous to roughly the same degree. Perhaps because their parents had moved them to what they regarded to be a "wrong pond," these boys were significantly more likely than the boys in the other two groups to use drugs and alcohol and to be arrested for a property crime. The adults in the MTO experiment who moved to low-poverty neighborhoods showed gains in mental health, but not in physical health, freedom from welfare dependence, or employment.[44]

Also pertinent is a recent and controversial article by Robert Putnam (2007), the most prominent analyst of social capital. After reviewing the vast literature on the consequences of the integration of neighborhoods, particularly by race and ethnicity, Putnam comes to sobering conclusions. He asserts that residents of diverse neighborhoods have less social capital than do residents of more homogeneous neighborhoods. Moreover, the members of a distinct ethnic group who live in a relatively integrated neighborhood are likely to have weaker ties to other members of their group than they would if they lived in an ethnic enclave. Putnam affirms his support for integration, but he is compelled by his findings to shift his emphasis to the long-term benefits of neighborhood diversity.

Other less-publicized studies similarly cast doubt on traditional estimates of the high magnitude of the benefits of economic integration. Contrary to Sampson, Oreopoulos (2003) finds that growing up in a poor neighborhood does not by itself lead to worse outcomes for children. His results indicate that a child's household environment has a far greater effect on the child's welfare than does the child's neighborhood environment.

Various studies on residential preferences suggest that most poor minority households do not warm to the prospect of moving to wealthier white neighborhoods. In surveys most African Americans, for example, state that they prefer to live in a neighborhood that is mostly African American (Farley et al. 1993; see generally Cashin 2001). To some extent, this may stem from a concern that non-black neighbors would discriminate against them. There is recent econometric evidence, however, that many African Americans are positively attracted to living in a mostly black neighborhood (Bayer, Fang, and McMillan 2005). An affirmative taste for stratifying by social class also seems to prevail, even among lower-status groups. Individuals who have not graduated from college, for example, are willing to pay a premium to live in a neighborhood that is not mostly inhabited by college graduates (Bayer, Ferreira, and McMillan 2007, 626).[45]

The revisionist thesis that poor people garner no more than modest benefits from living in a neighborhood that is not poor is consistent with the resi-

---

44. Compare Cutler, Glaeser, and Vigdor (2008), who find that although ghettoization on average helps immigrants to U.S. cities, it is detrimental to poor immigrants.

45. For anecdotal support, see Patillo's account (2007, 297–299) of how a poor woman resented how a wealthier neighbor "looked down on" her.

dential choices that poor people tend to make. As noted, most poor minority voucher holders end up renting in mostly poor, mostly minority neighborhoods. This would be less common, no doubt, if more landlords in prosperous neighborhoods were willing to participate in Section 8 and if voucher holders were unconcerned about how warmly they would be received by their new neighbors. The revisionist works just cited suggest, however, that the unconstrained preferences of voucher holders have much to do with this pattern (see also Goetz 2003, 241). Longtime residents of poor minority neighborhoods, such as those near U Street in Washington, DC, and 125th Street in Manhattan, commonly oppose gentrification (see generally Powell and Spencer 2003). Poor tenants in these neighborhoods seem to anticipate that an influx of more prosperous households will not confer social benefits on them sufficient to offset their risks of having to pay higher rents.

The studies just cited are hardly the final word on these complex social issues. Like most commentators, I welcome the prospect of increased residential integration by race and income, especially within a territory the size of a high school district, a social milieu suitable for fostering bridging social capital. Mixed-income housing projects attempt, however, to promote integration at the fine-grained level of the block, a venue in which the nurturing of bonding social capital plausibly should be given higher priority (Ellickson 2006). Taken as a whole, the recent social scientific findings cast doubt on whether the mixed-income feature of these projects can be expected to generate social benefits large enough to offset the inherent inefficiencies and unfairness of the project-subsidy approach.[46]

Why Support for Project Subsidies Persists

Financial interest and ideology spur much of the support for the construction of mixed-income housing projects. A government program that annually dispenses billions of dollars—whether for the production of ethanol, submarines, or affordable housing—brings into existence constituencies whose members are likely to provide continuing political support for the program. For example, many housing advocates are connected to organizations whose revenues depend on involvement in the development of affordable projects. The Local Initiatives Support Corporation (LISC), one of the nation's largest syndicators of LIHTCs, lobbied fervently to make the LIHTC program permanent. The unions that represent the construction trades tend to favor project subsidies not only because construction projects employ their members, but also because a legislature may be amenable to imposing prevailing-wage requirements. In suburbs where the supply of housing is inelastic, the imposition of inclusionary housing exactions on developers may

---

46. See also Schwartz (2006, 261–266), who concludes that the case for fostering greater income integration is not yet proven.

boost the value of homevoters' houses.[47] Federal, state, and local politicians all have learned that having the power to influence project approvals can provide leverage to raise campaign contributions. It is hardly news that HUD's project programs have frequently been rocked by scandal (Welfeld 1992).

Ideology has primarily motivated some housing advocates who have enthusiastically supported the building of subsidized projects. Edith Wood, the most prominent early proponent of U.S. projects, had scorn for the forces of supply and demand (see, for example, Wood 1931, 43–47). Chester Hartman, for decades one of the most prominent critics of housing vouchers, favors scrapping the market system of housing supply and replacing it with a new system in which non-profit entities, supported with large government grants covering all capital costs, would provide housing at one-third of current market rents (Hartman 2002, 248). These advocates of bricks-and-mortar solutions to the affordable housing problem tend to underappreciate the subtleties of housing markets. An infusion of portable vouchers into a city soon boosts its supply of housing because the rise in demand induces landlords to upgrade their buildings (Currie 2006, 107–108). Conversely, an infusion of subsidized projects adds less than might be expected to the total housing stock because it tends to displace private production that might otherwise occur (Malpezzi and Vandell 2002; Murray 1999). Those who rank project subsidies above vouchers tend to ignore these secondary effects.

The 2002 report of the Bipartisan Millennial Housing Commission evinces a similar lack of confidence in housing markets. Perceiving a "shrinking rental supply," the commission advocates massive government aid to add millions of designated affordable units to the housing stock. In the process of pressing for this solution, the commission's report (2002, 16) provides figures that show that there were 3.2 million more rental housing units than renting households in the United States in 1999. The report claims that "vouchers alone will not be enough in housing markets where the supply is inadequate or to provide housing opportunities in areas with fast-growing employment" (17). The commission, however, failed to name any specific metropolitan area where it deemed these conditions to prevail. In the year of the commission's report, the vacancy rate for rental units in the 75 largest metropolitan areas was 8.8 percent, and it exceeded 14 percent in the fast-growing metropolitan areas of Atlanta, Phoenix, and San Antonio.[48] In virtually all metropolitan areas, providing rent-burdened households with additional funds to help them choose among existing dwellings would be far more efficient than ramping up construction of designated subsidized units (Weicher 1997, 27–28).

---

47. See Schuetz, Meltzer, and Been (2007), who find this result in the greater Boston area, but not in the San Francisco Bay area; see also Knaap, Bento, and Lowe (2008), who find that, from 1988 to 2005, housing prices rose 2 to 3 percent faster in California cities that had adopted inclusionary zoning policies than in those that had not. See generally Ellickson (1981).

48. Data from http://www.census.gov/hhes/www/housing/hvs/annual02/ann02t5.html. Rental vacancy rates tend to be relatively high in the fast-growing metropolitan areas of the Sunbelt.

Nevertheless, the political prospects of a shift to an all-voucher strategy are dim (Olsen 2006, 112–124; Weicher 1997, 43–44). Critics of vouchers marshal a predictable litany of objections. Those on the left assert that vouchers mostly inflate rents and that a large fraction of voucher holders will end up not being able to find housing. Those on the right claim that vouchers overly destabilize neighborhoods (Husock 2000). On balance, the wealth of evidence on all these issues indicates that the concerns are overblown.[49] The staunchest supporters of project-based subsidies, while not numerous, are sophisticated and well organized. The millions of poor households who would be the primary beneficiaries of an expanded voucher program are diffuse and not mobilized. Enough said.

The Mediocrity of Moving from a Ninth-Best to a Seventh-Best Policy

Mixed-income affordable housing projects are unquestionably superior to the large ghettoized public housing projects that until recently blighted many American cities. While the process of developing a mixed-income project is likely to give rise to more red tape per subsidized unit, such private projects are likely to endure longer than public housing and to be better managed and less socially troubled.

Nonetheless, building mixed-income subsidized projects is a mediocre policy approach. In most contexts, using tax revenues to enhance spending on housing vouchers would be far more efficient and fair than devoting those same revenues to providing inclusionary units. To put the point casually, vouchers, which themselves are hardly problem-free, might be ranked as the third-best policy option.[50] The mixed-income affordable project approach, however, ranks far worse, say as the seventh-best option. That the traditional public housing model would rank even lower hardly establishes an affirmative case for the mixed-income model.

Localities in states where housing is exceptionally expensive, such as California, Massachusetts, New Jersey, and New York, have been particularly eager to embrace the mixed-income model. Many local governments in these states have inclusionary zoning requirements that require developers to provide either affordable housing units or in-lieu fees. By 2003 these programs together had generated on the order of 90,000 new subsidized housing units (Porter 2004, 241),

---

49. See Currie (2006, 106–108) and Weicher (1997, 43). Most studies conclude that vouchers do not significantly inflate rents; see Olsen (2003, 421–422), for a summary. Nationally, over two-thirds of Section 8 awardees are able to benefit from their vouchers, with the lowest success rates in New York City, Los Angeles, and other rent-control jurisdictions in which vacant apartments are relatively scarce (Finkel and Buron 2001, ii, iv).

50. Potential shortcomings of vouchers include administrative incompetence, bribe-taking on the part of employees who allocate them (Loose 1994), the fostering of dependency among recipients (as asserted by Husock 2004), and, in comparison with a program of cash transfers, an arguably unjustified level of paternalism.

less than 0.1 percent of the nation's total housing stock. These same states and their municipalities are renowned for the relative severity of their constraints on housing supply.[51] Their restrictions include exclusionary zoning practices, strict growth controls, and complex environmental reporting requirements that enable opponents to delay (and sometimes halt) any major proposed housing development. Many housing advocates in these states have been preoccupied with teasing more affordable units out of developers and preserving subsidized rents in projects built long ago. Advocates who genuinely desire to help poor families would be wiser to devote their energies to documenting and publicizing their states' unjustified constraints on housing supply and to supporting legislation to lower those barriers. These reforms, coupled with more-extensive use of housing vouchers, would do far more to help the low-income households who live in these artificially high-priced jurisdictions.

REFERENCES

Adam, Emma K., and P. Lindsay Chase-Lansdale. 2002. Home sweet home(s): Parental separations, residential moves, and adjustment problems in low-income adolescent girls. *Developmental Psychology* 38(5):792–805.

Bauer, Catherine. 1934. *Modern housing*. Boston: Houghton Mifflin.

Bayer, Patrick, Hamming Fang, and Robert McMillan. 2005. Separate when equal? Racial inequality and residential segregation. Yale Working Papers on Economic Applications and Policy, Discussion Paper No. 09. October.

Bayer, Patrick, Fernando Ferreira, and Robert McMillan. 2007. A unified framework for measuring preferences for schools and neighborhoods. *Journal of Political Economy* 115(4):588–638.

Bipartisan Millennial Housing Commission. 2002. *Meeting our nation's housing challenges*. Washington, DC.

Brophy, Paul C., and Rhonda N. Smith. 1997. Mixed-income housing: Factors for success. *Cityscape* 3(2):3–31.

Cashin, Sheryll D. 2001. Middle-class black suburbs and the state of integration: A post-integrationist vision for metropolitan areas. *Cornell Law Review* 86:729–776.

City of New York. No date. *The new housing marketplace: Creating housing for the next generation*. Department of Housing Preservation and Development. http://www.ny.gov/html/hpd/downloads/pdf/10yearHMplan.pdf.

Currie, Janet M. 2006. *The invisible safety net: Protecting the nation's poor children and families*. Princeton, NJ: Princeton University Press.

Cutler, David M., Edward L. Glaeser, and Jacob L. Vigdor. 2008. When are ghettos bad? Lessons from immigrant segregation in the United States. *Journal of Urban Economics* 63(3):759–774.

Dawkins, Casey J. 2007. Income targeting of housing vouchers: What happened after the Quality Housing and Work Responsibility Act? *Cityscape* 9(3):69–93.

51. On California see Quigley and Raphael (2005); on New York see Glaeser, Gyourko, and Saks (2005).

Deng, Lan. 2005. The cost-effectiveness of the low-income housing tax credit relative to vouchers: Evidence from six metropolitan areas. *Housing Policy Debate* 16(3–4):469–511.

———. 2007. Comparing the effects of housing vouchers and low-income housing tax credits on neighborhood integration and school quality. *Journal of Planning Education and Research* 27:20–35.

DeFilippis, James, and Elvin Wyly. 2008. Running to stand still: Through the looking glass with federally subsidized housing in New York City. *Urban Affairs Review* 43:777–816.

Dominus, Susan. 2008. A co-op for $14,000? It's no fiction. *New York Times*, 15 February, B1.

Ellen, Ingrid Gould, and Brendan O'Flaherty. 2003. How New York housing policies are different—and maybe why. Working paper, 20 November.

Ellen, Ingrid Gould, Amy Ellen Schwartz, Ioan Voicu, and Michael H. Schill. 2007. Does federally subsidized rental housing depress neighborhood property values? *Journal of Policy Analysis and Management* 26(2):257–280.

Ellen, Ingrid Gould, and Margery Austin Turner. 2003. Do neighborhoods matter and why? In *Choosing a better life? Evaluating the Moving to Opportunity social experiment*, ed. John Goering and Judith D. Feins. Washington, DC: Urban Institute Press.

Ellickson, Robert C. 1981. The irony of "inclusionary zoning." *Southern California Law Review* 54:1167–1216.

———. 2006. The puzzle of the optimal social composition of neighborhoods. In *The Tiebout model at fifty*, ed. William A. Fischel, 199–209. Cambridge, MA: Lincoln Institute of Land Policy.

———. 2008. *The household: Informal order around the hearth*. Princeton, NJ: Princeton University Press.

Farley, Reynolds, Charlotte Steeh, Tara Jackson, Maria Krysan, and Keith Reeves. 1993. Continued residential segregation in Detroit: "Chocolate city, vanilla suburbs" revisited. *Journal of Housing Research* 4:1–38.

Feins, Judith D., Paul Elwood, Linda Noel, and W. Eugene Rizor. 1996. *State and metropolitan administration of Section 8: Current models and potential resources.* Report prepared by Abt Associates, Inc., for U.S. Department of Housing and Urban Development. July.

Finkel, Meryl, and Larry Buron. 2001. *Study on Section 8 voucher success rates.* Report prepared by Abt Associates, Inc., for U.S. Department of Housing and Urban Development. November.

Fischel, William A. 2001. *The homevoter hypothesis*. Cambridge, MA: Harvard University Press.

Frank, Robert H. 1987. *Choosing the right pond: Human behavior and the quest for status*. New York: Oxford University Press.

Galster, George C. 2004. The effects of affordable and multifamily housing on market values of nearby homes. In *Growth management and affordable housing: Do they conflict?* ed. Anthony Downs, 176–211. Washington, DC: Brookings Institution Press.

Glaeser, Edward L., Joseph Gyourko, and Raven Saks. 2005. Why is Manhattan so expensive? Regulation and the rise in house prices. *Journal of Law and Economics* 48(2):331–370.

Glaeser, Edward L., and Erzo F. P. Luttmer. 2003. The misallocation of housing under rent control. *American Economics Review* 93(4):1027–1046.

Goering, John, and Judith D. Feins, eds. 2003. *Choosing a better life? Evaluating the Moving to Opportunity social experiment.* Washington, DC: Urban Institute Press.

Goetz, Edward G. 2003. *Clearing the way: Deconcentrating the poor in urban America.* Washington, DC: Urban Institute Press.

Hardman, Anna M., and Yannis M. Ioannides. 1999. Residential mobility and the housing market in a two-sector neoclassical growth model. *Scandinavian Journal of Economics* 101(2):315–335.

Hartman, Chester. 2002. *Between eminence and notoriety: Four decades of radical urban planning.* New Brunswick, NJ: Center for Urban Policy Research.

Hendrickson, Cara. 2002. Racial desegregation and income deconcentration in public housing. *Georgetown Journal on Poverty Law and Policy* 9:35–88.

Housing and Community Development Reporter. 2008. 31 March, 36:201.

Husock, Howard. 2000. Let's end housing vouchers. *City Journal* 10(4):84–91.

———. 2004. The housing reform that backfired. *City Journal* 14(3):81–87.

Jacob, Brian A. 2004. Public housing, housing vouchers and student achievement: Evidence from public housing demolitions in Chicago. *American Economic Review* 94(1):233–258.

Jacobs, Jane. 1961. *The death and life of great American cities.* New York: Random House.

Kinnaird, Stephen B. 1994. Public housing: Abandon HOPE, but not privatization. *Yale Law Journal* 103:961–995.

Kling, Jeffrey R., Jeffrey B. Liebman, and Lawrence F. Katz. 2007. Experimental analysis of neighborhood effects. *Econometrica* 75(1):83–119.

Knaap, Gerrit-Jan, Antonio Bento, and Scott Lowe. 2008. *Housing market impacts of inclusionary zoning.* National Center for Smart Growth Research and Education. February.

Long, Larry, C. Jack Turner, and William L. Urton. 1988. Migration distances: An international comparison. *Demography* 25(4):633–640.

Loose, Cindy. 1994. Five D.C. housing employees charged; only 10 of 400 new rent vouchers issued since 1990 didn't involve bribery, probe finds. *Washington Post,* 13 April, A1.

Ludwig, Jens, Greg J. Duncan, and Helen F. Ladd. 2003. The effects of MTO on children and parents in Baltimore. In *Choosing a better life? Evaluating the Moving to Opportunity social experiment,* ed. John Goering and Judith D. Feins, 153–175. Washington, DC: Urban Institute Press.

Malpezzi, Stephen, and Kerry Vandell. 2002. Does the low-income housing tax credit increase the supply of housing? *Journal of Housing Economics* 11:360–380.

Massey, Douglas S., and Nancy A. Denton. 1993. *American apartheid: Segregation and the making of the underclass.* Cambridge, MA: Harvard University Press.

Mayo, Stephen K. 1986. Sources of inefficiency in subsidized housing programs. *Journal of Urban Economics* 20:229–249.

McGough, Duane T. 1997. Characteristics of HUD-assisted renters and their units in 1993. Report prepared by HUD's Office of Policy Analysis and Research. May.

Munch, Jakob Roland, Michael Rosholm, and Michael Svarer. 2008. Home ownership, job duration, and wages. *Journal of Urban Economics* 63:130–145.

Muralidhara, Shilesh. 2006. Deficiencies of the Low-Income Housing Tax Credit in targeting the lowest-income households and in promoting concentrated poverty and segregation. *Law and Inequality* 24:353–374.

Murray, Michael P. 1999. Subsidized and unsubsidized housing stocks 1935 to 1987: Crowding out and cointegration. *Journal of Real Estate Finance and Economics* 18(1):107–124.

Newman, Sandra J., and Ann B. Schnare. 1997. ". . . And a suitable living environment": The failure of housing programs to deliver on neighborhood quality. *Housing Policy Debate* 8(4):703–741.

New York State Unified Court System. No date. New York City Civil Court Housing Part. http://www.nycourts.gov/courts/nyc/housing/index.shtml.

New York Times. 2007. A new approach to housing. Editorial, 15 October, A20.

Oberlander, H. Peter, and Eva Newbrun. 1999. *The life and work of Catherine Bauer*. Vancouver, BC: UBC Press.

Olsen, Edgar O. 2003. Housing programs for low-income households. In *Means-tested transfer programs in the United States*, ed. Robert A. Moffitt, 365–441. Chicago: University of Chicago Press.

———. 2006. Achieving fundamental housing policy reform. In *Promoting the general welfare: New perspectives on government performance*, ed. Alan S. Gerber and Eric M. Patashnik, 100–127. Washington, DC: Brookings Institution Press.

Oreopoulos, Philip. 2003. The long-run consequences of living in a poor neighborhood. *Quarterly Journal of Economics* 118(4):1533–1575.

Patillo, Mary. 2007. *Black on the block: The politics of race and class in the city*. Chicago: University of Chicago Press.

Porter, Douglas R. 2004. The promise and practice of inclusionary zoning. In *Growth management and affordable housing: Do they conflict?* ed. Anthony Downs, 212–248. Washington, DC: Brookings Institution Press.

Powell, John A., and Marguerite L. Spencer. 2003. Giving them the old "one-two": Gentrification and the K.O. of impoverished urban dwellers of color. *Howard Law Journal* 46:433–490.

Putnam, Robert D. 2000. *Bowling alone: The collapse and revival of American community*. New York: Simon & Schuster.

———. 2007. E *pluribus unum*: Diversity and community in the twenty-first century. *Scandinavian Political Studies* 30:137–174.

Quigley, John M., and Steven Raphael. 2005. Regulation and the high cost of housing in California. *American Economic Review* 95(2):323–328.

Radin, Margaret Jane. 1986. Residential rent control. *Philosophy and Public Affairs* 15(4):350–380.

Roisman, Florence Wagman. 2001. Opening the suburbs to racial integration: Lessons for the 21st century. *Western New England Law Review* 23:65–113.

Rubin, Leslie, and Aron Trombka. 2007. A study of moderately priced dwelling unit program implementation. Montgomery County, Maryland, Office of Legislative Oversight, Report No. 2007-9. 19 July.

Rubinowitz, Leonard S., and James E. Rosenbaum. 2000. *Crossing the class and color lines*. Chicago: University of Chicago Press.

Sampson, Robert J., Patrick Sharkey, and Stephen W. Raudenbush. 2008. Durable effects of concentrated disadvantage on verbal ability among African-American children. *Proceedings of the National Academy of Sciences* 105:845–852.

Sanbonmatsu, Lisa, Jeffrey R. Kling, and Greg J. Duncan. 2006. Neighborhoods and academic achievement: Results from the Moving to Opportunity experiment. *Journal of Human Resources* 41(4):649–691.

Schill, Michael H. 1993. Distressed public housing: Where do we go from here? *University of Chicago Law Review* 60:497–554.

Schuetz, Jenny, Rachel Meltzer, and Vicki Been. 2007. The effects of inclusionary zoning on local housing markets: Lessons from the San Francisco, Washington DC, and suburban Boston areas. Working paper, New York University, Furman Center for Real Estate and Urban Policy. 19 November.

Schwartz, Alex F. 2006. *Housing policy in the United States: An introduction*. New York: Routledge.

Schwartz, Amy Ellen, Ingrid Gould Ellen, Ioan Voicu, and Michael H. Schill. 2006. The external effects of place-based subsidized housing. *Regional Science and Urban Economics* 36(2):679–707.

Stodghill, Ron. 2006. A house divided: Uncivil war on E. 73rd. *New York Times*, 10 December, § 3-1.

Toy, Vivian S. 2008. Winning that one in a million, *New York Times*, 2 March, Real Estate, 1.

Trombka, Aron, Michael Faden, Sonya Healy, Marlene Michaelson, Ralph Wilson, and Sally Roman. 2004. Strengthening the moderately priced dwelling unit program: A 30-year review. Report to the Montgomery County Council. February.

UN Economic Commission for Europe. 2006. Bulletin of housing statistics for Europe and North America. http://www.unece.org/hlm/prgm/hsstat/Bulletin_06.htm.

U.S. Department of Commerce. 2003. American housing survey for the United States: 1999. Washington, DC: Bureau of the Census. March.

U.S. General Accounting Office. 2001. Costs and characteristics of federal housing assistance. GAO-01-901R, 18 July.

Weicher, John. 1990. The voucher/production debate. In *Building foundations: Housing and federal policy*, ed. Denise DiPasquale and Langley C. Keyes. Philadelphia: University of Pennsylvania Press.

———. 1997. *Privatizing subsidized housing*. Washington, DC: AEI Press.

Weisbach, David A. 2006. Tax expenditures, principal-agent problems, and redundancy. *Washington University Law Review* 84:1823–1860.

Welfeld, Irving H. 1992. *HUD scandals: Howling headlines and silent fiascoes*. New Brunswick, NJ: Transaction Publishers.

Wilson, William Julius. 1987. *The truly disadvantaged: The inner city, the underclass, and public policy*. Chicago: University of Chicago Press.

Winnick, Louis. 1995. The triumph of housing allowance programs: How a fundamental policy conflict was resolved. *Cityscape* 1(3):95–121.

Wish, Naomi Bailin, and Stephen Eisdorfer. 1997. The impact of *Mount Laurel* initiatives: An analysis of the characteristics of applicants and occupants. *Seton Hall Law Review* 27:1268–1337.

Wood, Edith Elmer. 1923. *Housing progress in Western Europe*. New York: Dutton.

———. 1931. *Recent trends in American housing*. New York: Macmillan.

COMMENTARY
Ingrid Gould Ellen

In the past two decades, we have witnessed a quiet resurgence of place-based housing subsidies in the United States, a resurgence that ironically began just when most experts and scholars had come to agree that such place-based subsidies were less efficient and effective than tenant-based vouchers.[1] The key driver has been the low-income housing tax credit (LIHTC) program. Operating outside of HUD, the LIHTC has come through the back door of tax expenditure programs to allocate funds for close to 1.6 million units. To put this number in context, the national stock of public housing now amounts to some 1.2 million units. There is also newly found excitement among localities and advocates about the potential of mixed-income housing.

Thus, Robert Ellickson has clearly chosen an apt time to revisit the voucher versus production debate and to explore how mixed-income housing in particular fits into the debate. Ellickson does so in an engaging and persuasive manner. He synthesizes theoretical arguments and empirical evidence extremely effectively. He ultimately concludes that although mixed-income housing overcomes some shortcomings of past production programs, it does not overcome them all, and it introduces a few new troubling features. He comes down strongly for vouchers. The piece offers a serious challenge to mixed-income housing advocates and to production subsidies more generally. The burden of proof is clearly on the production advocates to prove their case.

Ultimately, while I agree with Ellickson that vouchers should be the central feature of our federal housing program, I am not willing to concede that vouchers are always preferable to the production of mixed-income housing. I believe that mixed-income housing is an important tool as well, especially for local governments.

Most fundamentally, I think Ellickson overlooks a series of market failures that may be present in housing markets, especially in distressed neighborhoods. Owners may underinvest in housing in these areas because they fail to take into account the benefits that such investment might deliver to neighbors. The presence of these spillovers may mean that place-based subsidies targeted to distressed areas are in fact economically efficient. Specifically, place-based housing programs may generate positive externalities and help to revitalize the surrounding community. Colleagues at New York University's Furman Center and I have found that New York City's investments in subsidized housing in distressed neighborhoods during the late 1980s and the 1990s helped to increase the value of surrounding properties (Ellen et al. 2002; Schwartz et al. 2006).

---

1. A panel of experts convened by the Urban Institute in 1988 concluded that the voucher production debate had "largely subsided" and essentially declared demand-side subsidies the winner (see, for example, Orlebeke 2000; Turner and Reed 1990).

While we are unsure of the mechanism, it is possible that housing investments may remove disamenities like abandoned housing and vacant lots and may produce nice, new attractive housing that is valued by neighbors. They may also breathe new life into certain communities by bringing in new residents. Finally, these investments may help to overcome information failures. Private developers may be uncertain about the market potential in distressed urban areas and therefore wary of investing. Publicly subsidized mixed-income housing in particular may spur market-rate development by demonstrating to the private sector that a neighborhood is viable. These community development benefits may be particularly valuable to local governments, which will gain property tax revenues from redeveloped areas.

I am also somewhat more sanguine than Ellickson that investments in mixed-income housing overcome the major shortcomings of traditional, place-based housing subsidies. Mixed-income housing developments do not produce the extreme isolation of the poor that has too often been a feature of traditional public housing. Moreover, the discipline of the marketplace is still present in the case of mixed-income housing. The presence of market-rate tenants will provide developers with an incentive to deliver high-quality maintenance.

I am also less sure that the voucher program is a model of unfettered choice and opportunity as often described in academic papers. In 2001 one-third of voucher holders had to return their vouchers because they did not find suitable apartments in the allotted time period (Finkel and Buron 2001). In some tight markets, this proportion was considerably higher. Moreover, voucher holders who successfully lease up tend to do so in the same high-poverty areas they start in. In fact, they are less likely than LIHTC tenants to reach low-poverty census tracts (Ellen and O'Regan 2008). This constrained mobility is due to some combination of limited information, the paucity of apartments available at allowable rent levels in many areas, barriers to using vouchers in new jurisdictions, and landlord discrimination. Of course, the answer to these concerns should be stepped-up efforts to reform and improve the voucher program rather than to dismiss it.

Finally, Ellickson questions how concerned we should be about where voucher holders end up living, given recent evidence from the Moving to Opportunity (MTO) program. I don't think we should read the MTO experiment as proof that integration is not valuable. While the results of the demonstration were not as definitive as many advocates expected and hoped, the treatment group did see significant improvements along several dimensions despite experiencing very minor shifts in neighborhood environment on average (Quigley and Raphael 2007). Given how minor these shifts were—and given that participants had generally lived in distressed neighborhoods throughout their lives—MTO only tests whether a move to a slightly less poor neighborhood can overcome previously accumulated deficits (see Sampson 2008).

In conclusion, Ellickson has provided us with a provocative work that should become required reading in housing policy classes. Reasonable people can disagree on the ultimate merits of mixed-income housing, but the piece raises many important challenges that are worthy of serious consideration and debate.

REFERENCES

Ellen, Ingrid Gould, and Katherine O'Regan. 2009. Siting, spillovers, and segregation: A re-examination of the low income housing tax credit program. In *Housing markets and the economy: Risk, regulation, policy; essays in honor of Karl Case*, ed. Edward Glaeser and John Quigley. Cambridge, MA: Lincoln Institute for Land Policy.

Ellen, Ingrid Gould, Michael Schill, Amy Ellen Schwartz, and Ioan Voicu. 2002. Revitalizing inner-city neighborhoods: New York City's ten-year plan for housing. *Housing Policy Debate* 13(3):529–566.

Finkel, Meryl, and Larry Buron. 2001. Study on Section 8 voucher success rates: Volume I. Report prepared for the U.S. Department of Housing and Urban Development.

Orlebeke, Charles. 2000. The evolution of low-income housing policy: 1949–1999. *Housing Policy Debate* 11(2):489–520.

Quigley, John, and Steven Raphael. 2007. Neighborhoods, economic self-sufficiency, and the MTO. Paper prepared for the Brookings-Wharton Conference on Urban Affairs, November.

Sampson, Robert. 2008. Moving to inequality: Neighborhood effects and experiments meet structure. *American Journal of Sociology* 114(1):189–231.

Schwartz, Amy Ellen, Ingrid Gould Ellen, Ioan Voicu, and Michael H. Shill. 2006. The external effects of place-based subsidized housing. *Regional Science and Urban Economics* 36(2):679–707.

Turner, Margery Austin, and Veronica Reed. 1990. *Housing America*. Washington, DC: Urban Institute.

CONTRIBUTORS

Editors

GREGORY K. INGRAM
President and CEO
Lincoln Institute of Land Policy

YU-HUNG HONG
Fellow
Interdepartmental Programs
Lincoln Institute of Land Policy

Visiting Assistant Professor
Department of Urban Studies and
    Planning
Massachusetts Institute of Technology

Authors

R. JEROME ANDERSON
Attorney and Consultant
Montgomery Village, Maryland

Academic Guest
Global Urban Research Unit
School of Architecture, Planning and
    Landscape
Newcastle University

ANTONIO AZUELA
Professor
Social Research Institute
National Autonomous University
    of Mexico

ABRAHAM BELL
Professor of Law
Bar-Ilan University

DALLAS BURTRAW
Senior Fellow
Resources for the Future

STEPHEN B. BUTLER
Senior Associate
National Opinion Research Center
University of Chicago

KLAUS DEININGER
Lead Economist
Development Research Group
The World Bank

KERI-NICOLE DILLMAN
Associate
Low-Wage Workers and Communities
    Policy Area
MDRC

JOSEPH K. ECKERT
Senior Economist and Land Policy
    Expert
AECOM International Development
    Corporation

ROBERT C. ELLICKSON
Walter E. Meyer Professor of
    Property and Urban Law
Yale Law School

GERSHON FEDER
Consultant
International Food Policy Research
    Institute

EDÉSIO FERNANDES
Jurist and Urban Planner
Development Planning Unit
University College London

Institute for Housing and Urban
    Development Studies

LYNN M. FISHER
Associate Professor of Real Estate
Center for Real Estate
Massachusetts Institute of Technology

HARVEY M. JACOBS
Professor
Department of Urban and Regional
    Planning
Gaylord Nelson Institute for
    Environmental Studies
University of Wisconsin–Madison

JEROLD S. KAYDEN
Frank Backus Williams Professor of
    Urban Planning and Design
Cochair, Department of Urban
    Planning and Design
Director, Master in Urban Planning
    Degree Program
Harvard University Graduate School
    of Design

GERALD KORNGOLD
Visiting Fellow
Department of Valuation and
    Taxation
Lincoln Institute of Land Policy

Professor of Law
New York Law School

ELINOR OSTROM
Arthur F. Bentley Professor of
    Political Science
Codirector, Workshop in Political
    Theory and Policy Analysis
Indiana University Bloomington

Founding Director
Center for the Study of Institutional
    Diversity
Arizona State University

DWIGHT H. PERKINS
Harold Hitchings Burbank Research
Professor of Political Economy
Harvard University

VINCENT RENARD
Senior Researcher
Laboratory of Econometrics
École Polytechnique

BERTRAND RENAUD
International Consultant
Renaud Associates

RICHARD SWEENEY
Research Assistant
Resources for the Future

Commentators
VICKI BEEN
Elihu Root Professor of Law
Director, Furman Center for Real
    Estate and Urban Policy
New York University School of Law

ROBERT M. BUCKLEY
Managing Director
Rockefeller Foundation

ALAIN DURAND-LASSERVE
Director of Research
Centre National de la Recherche
    Scientifique

JOHN D. ECHEVERRIA
Executive Director
Georgetown Environmental Law and
    Policy Institute
Georgetown University Law Center

INGRID GOULD ELLEN
Associate Professor of Urban
  Planning and Public Policy
Robert F. Wagner Graduate School
  of Public Service
New York University

ANNETTE M. KIM
Ford International Career
Development Associate Professor of
  Urban Planning
Massachusetts Institute of Technology

NANCY A. MCLAUGHLIN
Professor of Law
S. J. Quinney College of Law
University of Utah

BARRIE NEEDHAM
Professor Emeritus
University of Nijmegen

WALLACE E. OATES
Professor of Economics
University of Maryland

University Fellow
Resources for the Future

SCOTT ROZELLE
Helen Farnsworth Endowed
  Professor
Stanford University

Senior Fellow and Professor
Shorenstein Asia-Pacific Research
  Center
Freeman Spogli Institute (FSI) for
  International Studies

ERNESTO SCHARGRODSKY
Dean
Business School
Universidad Torcuato Di Tella

PERRY SHAPIRO
Professor of Economics
University of California, Santa
  Barbara

ALEXANDER VON HOFFMAN
Senior Research Fellow
Joint Center for Housing Studies
Harvard University

INDEX

Abramo, Pedro, 298
Abreau, Dilip, 30
accessory rights, 144*n*5
access rights, 28
access to land, in Vietnam, 156–158
Acemoglu, Daron, 257, 257*n*1
acequias (irrigation systems), 36
Acheson, James M., 26
Acosta, Claudia, 181*n*, 189*n*10
Act 388 (*Ley* 388), Colombia, 188–189
Adam, Emma K., 430
Adams, John, 54, 55
administrative expropriations, in Colombia, 188, 190
adolescents: housing effects on, 430; neighborhood effects on, 440
ad valorem property taxes, 233
affordable housing: antisnob zoning laws and, 385; density bonuses and, 18, 19; developer-driven strategies for, 385–386; development costs, 396; housing appeal regimes and, 387–388, 413, 416; lock-in effects, 19–20; Massachusetts Comprehensive Permit Law and, 388; mixed-income housing, 423, 424–425; New Jersey Fair Housing Act and, 388–389; property rights approaches to, 18–20; strategies for, 419; zoning and, 389
Africa: resource boundaries, 39; women's property rights in, 261*n*3
African Americans: neighborhood race composition and, 440; subsidized housing and, 435, 437
Agarwal, Bina, 277
Agrawal, Arun, 38, 39
agricultural cooperatives: in Russia, 105
agricultural employment: in China, 77, 86, 86*n*16
agricultural land: in China, 83, 94–95; conservation easements and, 379; distribution of, in China, 85; land prices, 225–226; nonagricultural demand for, in China, 88; peri-urban, 64; in Russia, 106, 107; transferable development rights and, 225–226; in Vietnam, 141, 142
agriculture: in China, 85–87; credit access, 15; land registration and, 277–279
Ahn, Toh-Kyeong, 31
air pollution, 320, 323
airports, 244
air quality standards, 320–321
Alabama, 210
Albania, 65; informal urban land development in, 297*n*1; land registration in, 302*n*5;

private property rights in, 66; regularization program, 308
Albers, Heidi J., 366
Alchian, Armen A., 30
Alden-Wily, Liz, 273
Alexander, Gregory, 53, 183
Ali, Daniel A., 266, 269*n*8, 271*n*10, 278
alienation rights: defined, 27, 28; value of, 29; in Vietnam, 144–145
Allen, Douglas, 260
Allendorf, Keera, 276
Alston, Lee J., 6
Alterman, Rachelle, 221
American Law Institute, 381
American Planning Association, 214
amparo suits, 192, 196
Anchorage, Alaska, 208
Anderies, J. Marty, 31
Anderson, Christopher M., 365
Anderson, R. Jerome, 8–9, 96
Anderson, Terry L., 5
Andersson, Krister, 30
Ando, Amy W., 366
Andolfatto, David, 273
Andre, Catherine, 272
Anella, Anthony, 360
Anhui, China, 88–89
anticommons property, 113
antiexclusionary (antisnob) zoning, 384, 385, 413; residential developers and, 385–386
Antle, John M., 278
apartments: cost of, in China, 75–76; ownership of, in Russia, 121; ownership of, in Vietnam, 142; work unit, in China, 72
appropriation rules, for common-property institutions, 40
Argentina, 14
Arimura, Toshi, 348
Arkansas, 210
Armitage, Derek, 43
Armstrong v. United States, 234
Aron, Leon, 99*n*4, 106
Arrow, Kenneth, 238
Arrunada, Benito, 268, 268*n*6, 270*n*9
Asian Americans, 434
Asian Development Bank, 138*n*3, 147, 166, 167
Asian fiscal crisis, 109
Aslund, Anders, 106*n*6, 116, 118
Aten, Betina, 78
Atlanta, 442
Atwood, David A., 271
auctions, of land: in China, 83; in Russia, 148*n*12; in Vietnam, 148, 148*n*11
AusAID, 138

ABOUT THE LINCOLN INSTITUTE
OF LAND POLICY

The Lincoln Institute of Land Policy is a private operating foundation whose mission is to improve the quality of public debate and decisions in the areas of land policy and land-related taxation in the United States and around the world. The Institute's goals are to integrate theory and practice to better shape land policy and to provide a nonpartisan forum for discussion of the multidisciplinary forces that influence public policy. This focus on land derives from the Institute's founding objective—to address the links between land policy and social and economic progress—that was identified and analyzed by political economist and author Henry George.

The work of the Institute is organized in four departments: Valuation and Taxation, Planning and Urban Form, Economic and Community Development, and International Studies. We seek to inform decision making through education, research, demonstration projects, and the dissemination of information through publications, our Web site, and other media. Our programs bring together scholars, practitioners, public officials, policy advisers, and involved citizens in a collegial learning environment. The Institute does not take a particular point of view, but rather serves as a catalyst to facilitate analysis and discussion of land use and taxation issues—to make a difference today and to help policy makers plan for tomorrow.

The Lincoln Institute of Land Policy is an equal opportunity institution.

LINCOLN INSTITUTE
OF LAND POLICY

113 Brattle Street
Cambridge, MA 02138-3400 USA

Phone: 1-617-661-3016 x127 or 1-800-LAND-USE (800-526-3873)
Fax: 1-617-661-7235 or 1-800-LAND-944 (800-526-3944)
E-mail: help@lincolninst.edu
Web: www.lincolninst.edu